Oxford Chemistry Series

Oxford Chemistry Series

1972
1. K. A. McLauchlan: *Magnetic resonance*
2. J. Robbins: *Ions in solution* (2): *an introduction to electrochemistry*
3. R. J. Puddephatt: *The periodic table of the elements*
4. R. A. Jackson: *Mechanism*: *an introduction to the study of organic reactions*

1973
5. D. Whittaker: *Stereochemistry and mechanism*
6. G. Hughes: *Radiation chemistry*
7. G. Pass: *Ions in solution* (3): *inorganic properties*
8. E. B. Smith: *Basic chemical thermodynamics*
9. C. A. Coulson: *The shape and structure of molecules*
10. J. Wormald: *Diffraction methods*
11. J. Shorter: *Correlation analysis in organic chemistry*: *an introduction to linear free-energy relationships*
12. E. S. Stern (ed): *The chemist in industry* (1): *fine chemicals for polymers*
13. A. Earnshaw and T. J. Harrington: *The chemistry of the transition elements*

1974
14. W. J. Albery: *Electrode kinetics*
16. W. S. Fyfe: *Geochemistry*
17. E. S. Stern (ed): *The chemist in industry* (2): *human health and plant protection*
18. G. C. Bond: *Heterogeneous catalysis*: *principles and applications*
19. R. P. H. Gasser and W. G. Richards: *Entropy and energy levels*
20. D. J. Spedding: *Air pollution*
21. P. W. Atkins: *Quanta*: *a handbook of concepts*
22. M. J. Pilling: *Reaction kinetics*

P. W. ATKINS
FELLOW OF LINCOLN COLLEGE, OXFORD

Quanta

a handbook of concepts

Clarendon Press · Oxford · 1974

Oxford University Press, Ely House, London W. 1
GLASGOW NEW YORK TORONTO MELBOURNE WELLINGTON
CAPE TOWN IBADAN NAIROBI DAR ES SALAAM LUSAKA ADDIS ABABA
DELHI BOMBAY CALCUTTA MADRAS KARACHI LAHORE DACCA
KUALA LUMPUR SINGAPORE HONG KONG TOKYO

CASEBOUND ISBN 0 19 855493 1
PAPERBACK ISBN 0 19 855494 X

PRINTED IN GREAT BRITAIN
BY FLETCHER & SON LTD., NORWICH

TEC
R

Preface

HERE is a book that attempts to explain the quantum theory without mathematics.

Of course, I agree that quantum theory has an inescapable mathematical structure; I agree that the full precision of the theory, and its richness, can be conveyed only in the language of mathematics; I also agree that to make substantial contributions to quantum theory one needs a firm grasp of its mathematical basis. Nevertheless, I also believe that mathematical precision is not what everyone is after—not everyone has that kind of interest, nor indeed that amount of time.

Most of us have our pictures of the concepts of quantum theory—we have some way of visualizing orbitals, transitions, etc.—and those of us who do research are more often than not guided in broad outline by some visualizable model of the system we are trying to describe. This book contains my ways of thinking about the concepts of quantum theory. The pictures, like all analogies and models, are only a partial representation of the true situation; but I hope they contain the heart of the matter, and enable the reader to understand each idea at a physical, rather than mathematical, level.

I hope that a broad selection of people will find the book useful. I have had in mind both the student of chemistry who at all levels of his studies encounters unfamiliar, little-understood, or half-forgotten concepts, and his teacher who is pressed for an explanation. I hope that by reference to this book all will be provided with just enough information to make the concept clear and perhaps even to be stimulated to find our more. If my explanation is inadequate, my bibliography will direct the dissatisfied along a trail of others' explanations.

Each entry is intended to explain, in plain language, the physical content of its topic. Most are illustrated by examples, and, where appropriate, counter examples. Where the entry draws on information contained elsewhere in the book, or where further development of a topic is desirable, or where the reader might be felt to require more background, I have labelled a word with an unobtrusive ° to signify that it is in the book. For a good reason I cannot now remember, the label precedes the indicated word; the labelled word does not always correspond to an exact entry, but its sense should be sufficient to indicate the appropriate entry without ambiguity. Unlike most dictionaries this has an index: some concepts are buried inside others.

Where I feel it desirable that some mathematics be introduced (for example when it seems helpful to have a collection of formulae to hand, e.g. in °perturbation theory), I have used a system of Boxes and Tables. A Box is part of the text, and contains handy formulae: these are confined to Boxes in order that they be present but held away from the description in the text. A Table contains more detailed information (sometimes of mathematical expressions not required for a reading of the text) which I judge it helpful to have in a volume of this kind (so that it can be used at more than just its principal level of qualitative description), and which I judge would have intruded too vigorously into the main text. These Tables, which are collected at the end of the volume, also contain a selection of experimental data. I think it important that one has an idea of the size of physical quantities, and their trends, and so these numbers are included to sketch out the range of experimental data. The Tables are by no means exhaustive: they simply peg out the terrain.

Nearly every entry is followed by Questions. These are set with a double purpose and are graded from the trivial to the slightly tough. The early parts of each are intended to focus the reader's mind on key points made in the preceding entry. Most of these simple questions can be answered by referring to the entry. The second purpose is to bring a tiny amount of mathematics into the book in an unobtrusive way: the harder parts of the questions (which when they occur are often labelled 2) invite the reader to make his own mathematical exposition of the entry, and contain hints and guidance to that end. The answers to the questions are mostly in the text, in a Box, or on a Table; if that is not so, Further information points the way.

Each entry contains a section headed *Further information.* This is a guide to the literature, and in it will be found references to books and articles where the reader can turn for more information, the development of the topic, and the absent mathematics. This section is not exhaustive (it contains works I have found helpful) but once a trail is indicated the literature is more easily penetrated. In this section I have attempted to list the books in order of complexity so that the reader can make a progression through difficulty. There are however, two important exceptions to this organization. The first is the reference to *MQM*. This is my *Molecular quantum mechanics* (Clarendon Press, 1970); many of the topics are treated in more detail in that book, and a reference to the appropriate section is included at the head of each *Further information*. The second exception reflects the fact that this book is a part of the *Oxford Chemistry Series*—although its size makes it a sport—and I have made a point of directing the reader to the other books in the series where the topics are developed: these are denoted OCS*n* and listed together at the start of the bibliography. OPS*n* books are the first few of the analogous *Oxford Physics Series*, and are listed likewise.

In a few places I have aimed at a higher level of exposition than the rest, especially when I have been unable to give what I consider to be a satisfactory explanation at the low, qualitative level at which in general I have aimed. Let me stress, however, that I do not use the word 'low' pejoratively: it is, I believe, as important for a chemist to have a physical intuition about the behaviour of submicroscopic phenomena as it is for him to be able to manipulate the mathematics of the description. In my 'low' level descriptions I am attempting to train this intuition. I shall not draw attention to the entries I consider to be at this higher level: if they are not noticed, so much the better. If they are noticed, and found bewildering, the ◦ on keywords will guide the reader to quieter waters. In this connexion, however, I must draw attention to one distressing feature of Nature. As in a conventional dictionary, where the unlikely concepts of aardvark, aasvogel, and ablet bring confusion and difficulty in unnatural proportion into A, so by the same quirk does Nature concentrate difficulty into the A of *Quanta*. I find the entries of A more difficult than the entries of B; perhaps you will too. (My message is that reading A—as a browser might feel inclined—gives, I think, a false impression of the overall level of the entries.)

Two other points are worth making. The first is an excuse. In an attempt to keep the price of the book low (at least by the standards we are being trained to expect) all the diagrams are my own sketches. All were done on a balcony in Italy one summer, and each jolt, smudge, or splash tells its story of inquisitive mosquito, local ant, or homing wasp. Please forgive their generally amateur appearance. The second point concerns those to whom notes (such as these entries) are anathema, those who want material for more books, or those who seek an essay. Each should notice that the approximately 200 entries can be permuted in some 10^{300} different ways: surely out of these *some* decent books can be wrought?

The real purpose of writing a preface is to come to the part that gives most pleasure: the thanking of all those who have contributed to the production of the book and easing its grim labour. A quite outstanding contribution—beyond the call of duty and reasonable expectation—has been made by the Clarendon Press and its anonymous officers. Their assistance ranged from advice and help from the drawing office, through detailed and lengthy discussion of presentation, to careful and ingenious production. Two of my research students deserve my thanks: Michael Clugston bent his perceptive eye on the proofs and saved me from much shame, and John Roberts spent time coaxing contours out of computers; to both am I most grateful. To the others I express my thanks for accepting neglect without overt complaint. The typing of the whole obscure manuscript (as my own typed original is better regarded) was done briskly and efficiently by Mrs. E. Price and Mrs. M. Long, both of whom deserve at least what immortality this page can provide.

P.W.A.

A

ab initio. Not the whole of quantum chemistry is conducted in Latin; the small portion to which it has by convention been confined, as an ironic meeting of cultures, belongs to those whose business is computers. *Ab initio,* roughly translated, means *from scratch*, and is applied to the molecular-structure computations that abhor the inclusion of empirical data and attempt to calculate from first principles, which for our purpose are the °Schrödinger equation and the method of °self-consistent fields.

Further information. Richards and Horsley (1970) have prepared a short, simple guide to *ab initio* calculations, and work through a number of examples. They also discuss the relation of such calculations to the *semi-empirical methods* in which approximations and empirical data are introduced into °self-consistent field calculations.

adiabatic process. The term adiabatic is used in both thermodynamics and quantum mechanics, and the uses are analogous. In the former it signifies that the process is occurring without exchange of heat with the environment (as this implies that there is no change of entropy, the process is often called *isentropic*). In the latter it signifies that a change is occurring so that the system makes no transition to other states.

Consider, for example, a hypothetical °hydrogen atom with a variable nuclear charge. If the atom is initially in its ground state, and the nuclear charge is increased extremely slowly, the electron will be sucked in closer to the nucleus; but the atom remains in its ground state, and by the time that $Z = 2$ the system is a ground state He^+ ion: this is therefore an adiabatic process. Conversely, if the nuclear charge of an atom is changed suddenly (for example, by the emission of an electron in β-decay), the bound electron finds itself in a different nuclear potential but with its *original* spatial distribution: this distribution can be expressed as a mixture of °wavefunctions of the new atom, and so in this *impulsive* or *nonadiabatic transition* the system is knocked into a range of states of the final system. The slow compression of a °particle confined in a square well is another example of an adiabatic transition, for if the system is in the nth level of the original box it will be in the nth level of the new, smaller box if the compression is infinitely slow.

Further information. See *MQM* Chapter 7. An account of adiabatic transitions in terms of °perturbation theory will be found in §76 of Davydov (1965), who derives the condition that a motion is adiabatic if the perturbation $V(t)$ changes so slowly that $\mathrm{d}V/\mathrm{d}t$ is much smaller that the energy separations in the vicinity of the initially occupied state: $|\mathrm{d}V/\mathrm{d}t| \ll (\Delta E)^2/\hbar$. See also §50 of Bohm (1951) for a pleasing discussion with straightforward mathematics. Recent review articles on adiabatic and nonadiabatic processes in molecules have been published by Kołos (1970) and Nikitin (1970) respectively. See °non-crossing rule. Thermodynamic adiabaticity is discussed by Smith in his *Basic chemical thermodynamics* (OCS 8) and entropy is related to the distribution of particles among energy levels in Gasser and Richards' *Entropy and energy levels* (OCS 19). This is the key connexion between the thermodynamic and quantum-mechanical uses of the term adiabatic: an unchanged distribution of particles among states is an isentropic situation.

alternant hydrocarbon. A chain of carbon atoms in a hydrocarbon that can be labelled alternately by a star, no star, a star, and so on, such that no two stars are neighbours nor two unstarred atoms are neighbours when the labelling is complete, is an alternant hydrocarbon. An example is propene, which could be labelled C*—C—C*, or C—C*—C; another example is benzene (1), and an example of a non-alternant hydrocarbon is azulene

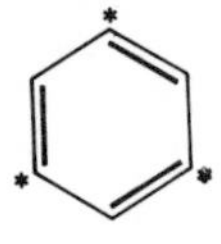

(1)

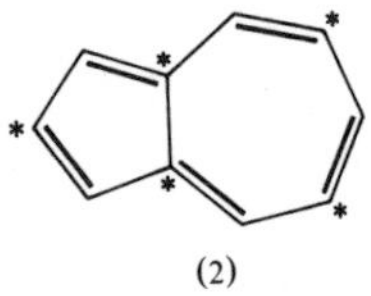

(2)

(2). Alternants are distinguished by several electronic characteristics:

(a) To every bonding orbital of energy $-E$ there is a complementary °antibonding orbital of energy $+E$: the bonding and antibonding orbitals are arranged symmetrically about zero energy (Fig. A1).

(b) In an *even-alternant* the number N of carbon atoms is even, and usually the number n^* of starred atoms is equal to the number n of unstarred. In this case there are $\frac{1}{2}N$ bonding orbitals and $\frac{1}{2}N$ antibonding orbitals. If n^* and n are unequal there are $|n^*-n|$ nonbonding orbitals inserted between a symmetrical array of n bonding and n antibonding orbitals (for $n<n^*$). In an *odd-alternant* the number of carbon atoms is odd, and usually there is one more starred atom than unstarred ($n^*=n+1$), and one nonbonding orbital is inserted between the symmetrical array of n bonding and n antibonding orbitals ($n+n^*=N$).

(c) The distribution of electrons is more uniform in alternant hydrocarbons than in non-alternants. This property is expressed quantitatively by the *Coulson-Rushbrooke theorem* which states that the π-electron °charge density on every atom in the ground state of an alternant hydrocarbon is unity (each carbon has just one π-electron associated with it).

(d) In odd-alternants the electron density of the corresponding cation or anion may be deduced very simply by considering the form of the nonbonding orbital, for it is this orbital from which an electron is taken to form the cation, or to which one is added to give the anion, and in the neutral hydrocarbon the charge distribution is uniform. The form of the nonbonding orbital may also be deduced, virtually by inspection, by relying on the following device. Star the atoms in such a way as to get the maximum number of non-neighbour stars, then the amplitude of the orbital on each unstarred atom is zero. Furthermore, the sum of the coefficients of orbitals on starred atoms attached to a given unstarred atom is zero. This gives the relative size of all the coefficients; to get their absolute size the orbital is °normalized. The charge density on each atom is obtained by squaring the coefficients.

The stability of even-alternants (such as °benzene) can be understood in terms of the preceding properties. In particular, in an N-atom even-alternant each atom provides one π-electron; each of the $\frac{1}{2}N$ bonding orbitals may accommodate two electrons (°Pauli principle), and so only the bonding orbitals are occupied. This structural stability is further protected from reactive attack by the uniformity of the charge distribution, which provides no centres of attraction for potential reagents.

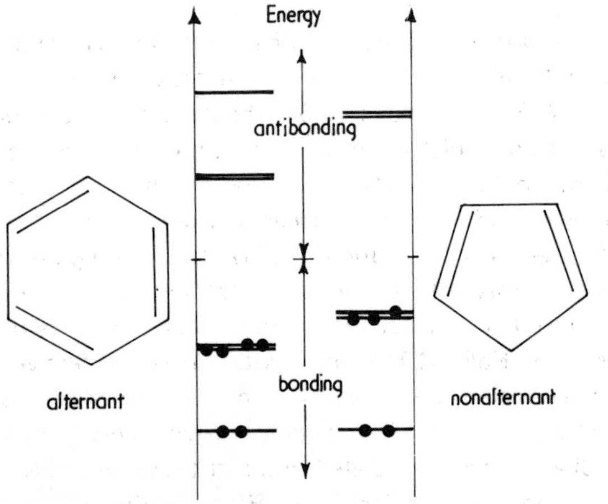

FIG. A1. Energy levels of a typical alternant (benzene) and a typical non-alternant (cyclopentadienyl). Note the symmetric disposition of the levels in the former.

Questions. How is an alternant hydrocarbon distinguished from a non-alternant? Which of the following hydrocarbons are alternant: ethylene (ethene), butadiene (buta-1, 3-diene), cyclobutadiene, benzene, naphthalene, anthracene, azulene, cyclo-octatetraene, phenylmethyl (the benzyl radical), cyclopentadienyl? What properties can you predict for the alternant hydrocarbons of this list? State the Coulson-Rushbrooke theorem. Use the form of the °benzene molecular orbitals (p. 20) to confirm that the charge density in benzene is uniform and in accord with the theorem. Evaluate the form of the nonbonding molecular orbital in the phenylmethyl radical by the method described in note (d). (You should find the coefficients $2/\sqrt{7}$ on CH_2, and a collection of $\pm 1/\sqrt{7}$ and 0 elsewhere.) Deduce from this the charge distribution in the cation ϕCH_2^+ and the anion ϕCH_2^-. Can you deduce anything about the chemical reactivity of phenylmethyl?

Further information. See Coulson's *The shape and structure of molecules* (OCS 9). A helpful account of alternant molecules will be found in Chapter 9 of Roberts (1961*b*), in §2·6 of Streitweiser (1961), in Pilar (1968), and in Salem (1966). A book devoted to them is that of Pauncz (1967). The spectroscopic properties are described by Murrell (1971) and reviewed by Hall and Amos (1969), who furnish further directions to the literature. The calculation of the electronic structure of alternants has been described by Parr (1963), whose book includes reprints of some of the original papers, by Dewar (1969), Pople and Beveridge (1970), and Murrell and Harget (1972). Tables of molecular-orbital coefficients and energies have been prepared by Coulson and Streitweiser (1965). For a proof of the Coulson-Rushbrooke theorem see Coulson and Rushbrooke (1940) and a review article by Coulson (1970).

angular momentum. The angular momentum of an object in classical mechanics is $I\omega$, where I is its moment of inertia and ω its angular velocity (in radians per second): a big object (with a big moment of inertia) need rotate only slowly (have small angular velocity) in order to achieve the same angular momentum as a small object rotating rapidly. In classical mechanics an object may rotate with any angular momentum; but in quantum theory the magnitude of the angular momentum of any body is °quantized and limited to the values $[j(j+1)]^{1/2}\hbar$, where j is a non-negative (zero or positive) integer or half-integer ($0, \frac{1}{2}, 1, \ldots$). Only one component of this angular momentum may be specified (that is, we may state the angular momentum of a body about only one axis), and its values are limited to $m\hbar$, where $m = j, j-1, \ldots -j$. This implies that, contrary to the classical situation, a rotating body may take up only a discrete sequence of orientations with respect to any one selected axis: the quantization of orientation is called *space quantization.*

A convenient representation of the angular momentum is as a vector of length $[j(j+1)]^{1/2}$, see Fig. A2, which may take up a discrete series of orientations as depicted in Fig. A3 for a body with $j=2$; this is the basis of the °vector model of the atom.

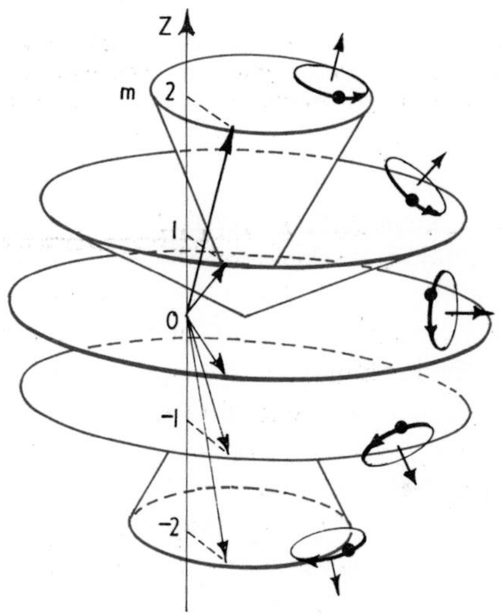

FIG. A2. The classical angular momentum and its representation by a vector of specified projection on the *z*-axis.

Since only one component of this vector can be specified (and conventionally this is taken to be the *z*-component) the azimuth of the vector (its orientation in the *xy*-plane) is indeterminate; the cone of possible orientations represents the property of °precession.

The value of the quantum number for °orbital angular momenta (the momenta arising from the spatial distribution of the particle) is confined to integers; it is convention to use the letter ℓ to denote the *orbital angular momentum quantum number,* and so perforce ℓ is confined to non-negative *integral* values. The intrinsic angular momentum of a particle, its °spin,

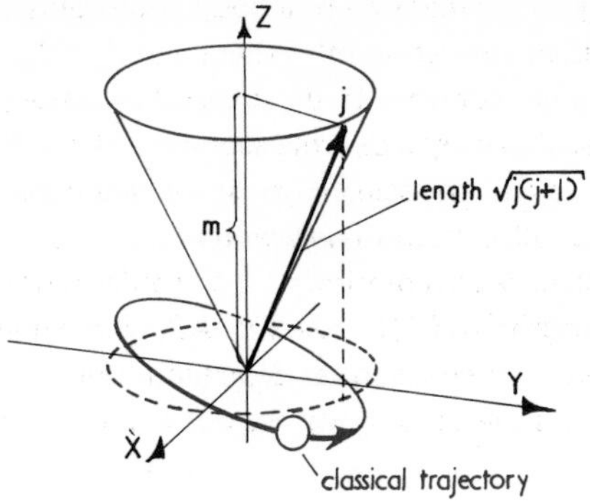

FIG. A3. An angular momentum with j = 2 can take only five $(2j + 1)$ orientations in space according to quantum mechanics, but all orientations according to classical mechanics. The discrete orientations are illustrated.

is described by a quantum number that may have either integral or half-integral values, and which is normally denoted s (or I for nuclei).

If a system contains two sources of angular momentum its total angular momentum is also quantized and restricted to magnitudes $[j(j+1)]^{1/2}\hbar$, with j confined to the values j_1+j_2, $j_1+j_2-1, \ldots |j_1-j_2|$, where j_1 and j_2 are the quantum numbers of the component momenta. This sequence of numbers is known as the *Clebsch-Gordon series.* As an example, an electron with spin $s = \frac{1}{2}$ and in an orbital with $\ell = 1$ constitutes a system with two sources of angular momentum. The total angular momentum of the electron may take on the values given by $j = 1+\frac{1}{2}$, $1+\frac{1}{2}-1$, or $\frac{3}{2}$ and $\frac{1}{2}$, depending on the relative orientation of the two momenta: if the individual momenta are parallel the total momentum is high ($j=\frac{3}{2}$), if they are opposed it is low ($j=\frac{1}{2}$). When the system contains several sources of momentum the overall angular momentum is quantized and constructed by coupling j_1 and j_2, then j_3 to their resultants, and so on, each step being in accord with the Clebsch-Gordon series.

In quantum mechanics an angular momentum can be defined in terms of a set of °commutation rules of the appropriate °operators; any set of operators that satisfies the commutation rule $[j_x, j_y] = i\hbar j_z$ is called an angular momentum, and the properties outlined above are common to all such creatures. In this way the theory of angular momentum expands to embrace intrinsic properties of systems, such as their °spin and their charge.

Questions. What are the features of quantized angular momentum? What magnitudes of angular momentum correspond to quantum numbers equal to $\frac{1}{2}$, 1, 2, 10^{34}? Draw a vector representation of an angular momentum and take $\ell = 1$, $m = 1$, 0, -1; also draw the classical motion of a particle corresponding to the three values of m. Consider the vector representation of the angular momentum of a bicycle wheel: is it possible to ride a bicycle strictly perpendicular to the road? At what velocities would this quantum wobble be intolerable? The spin of a °photon is 1: what is the magnitude of its intrinsic angular momentum? What angular momenta can arise from coupling the spin of an electron with its °orbital momentum in a d-orbital ($\ell = 2$)? What states of total orbital momentum can be obtained by coupling the momenta of two p-electrons, two d-electrons, a p- and a d-electron, three p-electrons?

Further information. See *MQM* Chapter 6 for a detailed discussion of angular momentum. An interesting account which emphasizes the connexion between classical and quantal angular momenta is given by Kauzmann (1957). Books dealing specifically with the quantum theory of angular momentum, and ranging from the moderately accessible to the very difficult, include those by Brink and Satchler (1968), Rose (1957), Edmonds (1957), Judd (1963), and Beidenharn and van Dam (1965); the last contains a number of important original papers. The relation of angular momentum to the way a system changes as it is rotated is described in *MQM* Chapter 6, in Tinkham (1964), which is a good introduction to the connexion between the symmetry of a system and its angular momentum, and in angular momentum books. The wavefunction for a state of coupled angular momentum may be expressed as a combination of the wavefunctions of the contributing uncoupled states; the coefficients of the combination are the °Wigner coefficients. The formal relation of angular momentum to other properties of a system, such as its charge, is described qualitatively by Lipkin (1965) and in more, but not excessive, detail by Lichtenberg (1970).

anharmonicity. There are two types of anharmonicity: mechanical and electrical. *Mechanical anharmonicity* (commonly referred to simply as *anharmonicity*) occurs when an oscillator is in a potential that is not purely parabolic, so that the restoring force is not strictly proportional to the displacement. The energy levels in such a case are no longer strictly those of a °harmonic oscillator, and if the nature of the anharmonicity is to lower the potential at large displacements the levels converge at high quantum numbers, as shown in Fig. A4. The lines in a °vibrational spectrum in the presence of anharmonicity are therefore no longer evenly spaced. Another effect of mechanical anharmonicity is to ruin the °selection rules for a harmonic oscillator: if the molecular vibration is anharmonic it is unreasonable to expect rules developed for a harmonic oscillator to be applicable. Therefore some forbidden transitions become allowed, and *harmonics* of the fundamental transitions are observed (corresponding to changes in the oscillator quantum number by +2, +3, etc.). These transitions increase in intensity with the extent of anharmonicity in the potential.

The intensity of transitions, and the failure of the harmonic oscillator selection rules, are also affected by the *electrical anharmonicity*, which is the name applied when the dipole moment of the molecule depends non-linearly on the displacement. The selection rules are normally calculated on the basis of the assumption that as the molecule is stretched the dipole moment changes linearly with the displacement (that is, the change in dipole moment is directly proportional to the displacement): if this is not so it is possible for the non-linear term in its true dependence, and in particular the term quadratic in the displacement, to induce transitions by $\Delta v = \pm 2$. Thus electrical anharmonicity can cause *intensity* changes in the vibrational spectrum of a molecule similar to those caused by the mechanical anharmonicity; but in contrast to the latter it does not affect the energy levels themselves.

A further effect of anharmonicity on the intensities in a °vibrational (infrared) spectrum of a molecule arises from its ability to mix together vibrations of various symmetries. In the harmonic approximation one encounters the °normal modes of vibration: these constitute a set of independent vibrational motions of the molecule. When anharmonicity is present the normal modes are no longer independent, and vibrational energy in one may leak into others. Interpreted quantum-mechanically, we say that the wavefunction for a normal mode mixes with, and therefore acquires some of the characteristics of, some of the other normal modes. An important case in which normal modes mix as a result of anharmonicity is *Fermi resonance*, which is a mechanism whereby the simultaneous excitation of two vibrational modes (which appears in the spectrum as a *combination band*) is permitted because nearby (in energy) there is a fundamental excitation frequency of another, allowed vibrational mode. The anharmonicity in the molecular motion endows the mixture of vibrational modes with some of the characteristics of the allowed fundamental, and so the transition to the combination becomes allowed. The extent to which it becomes allowed depends on the amount of anharmonicity and the

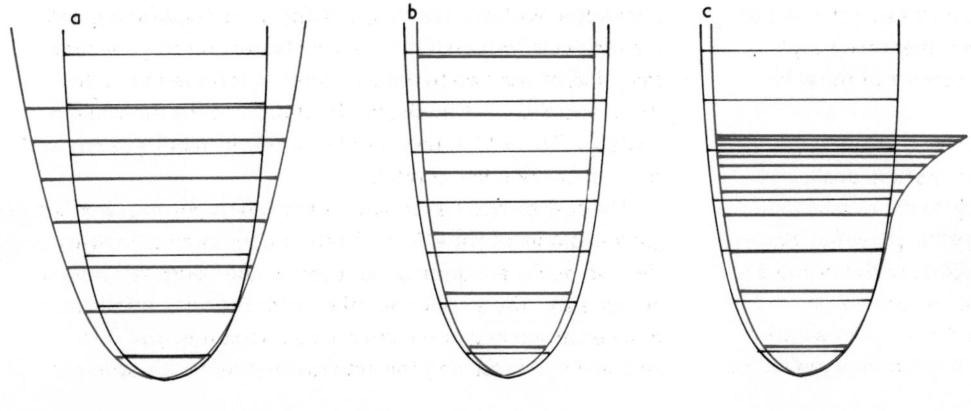

FIG. A4. Anharmonic potentials (shown in colour) distort the even spacing of the levels in a harmonic potential (black). In (a) a broader potential reduces the separation by different amounts; in (b) a narrow potential separates the levels further; and in (c) the complicated anharmonicity typical of a chemical bond is illustrated.

closeness in frequency of the combination and fundamental energies, and is greatest when they are in °resonance.

Yet another manifestation of anharmonicity is through its effect on the moment of inertia of a molecule, and through that on the molecule's °rotational motion and spectrum. A harmonically vibrating molecule has the same mean size whatever its vibrational state; but an anharmonic molecule would tend to swell slightly, and to change its moment of inertia, as it is excited to higher vibrational states (see Fig. A4c). The dependence of the moment of inertia on the vibrational state affects the structure of the °branches in the vibration-rotation spectrum.

Questions. 1. What types of anharmonicity exist, and what do they affect? Discuss the effect of replacing a harmonic oscillator potential by one that is almost parabolic, but (a) gets broader, (b) gets narrower as the displacement increases. What is expected to be the form of the anharmonicity for a typical bond stretch? Discuss the vibrational potential for the out-of-plane vibration of a planar molecule, with special reference to the anharmonicity. What previously forbidden transitions become allowed in the presence of anharmonicity? What transitions does electrical anharmonicity permit? What effect does electrical anharmonicity have on the energy of an oscillator? What effect does the presence of anharmonicity have on the symmetry selection rules? What is the group-theoretical interpretation of this? What is a combination band, and why does Fermi resonance endow it with intensity? What effect is there on the intensity of the allowed fundamental when it takes part in Fermi resonance? What happens to the latter's energy? What group-theoretical reason accounts for our stressing the role of a combination band in Fermi resonance rather than simply another fundamental? (Consider the symmetry of the anharmonic part of the molecular energy.)
2. Consider a potential of the form $\frac{1}{2}kx^2 + ax$. Sketch the form of the potential on the assumption that a is small, and apply second-order °perturbation theory to the calculation of the effect of the linear anharmonicity on the potential. Show that the electric dipole moment may depend both linearly and quadratically on the displacement of the molecule from equilibrium (use a Taylor expansion) and that the quadratic term can induce transitions disallowed in a harmonic oscillator. Use the properties of the °harmonic oscillator in Table 11 on p. 273.

Further information. See *MQM* Chapter 10 for a discussion of anharmonicity, and a discussion of the role of symmetry in governing what vibrations Fermi resonance may mix together. Woodward (1972) has a helpful qualitative discussion in §18·5 and §22·10; so too do Brand and Speakman (1960) in §6·7 and King (1964) in §5·5. See also Barrow (1962), Whiffen (1972), Gans (1971), and Wilson, Decius, and Cross (1955). Extreme anharmonicity leads to dissociation: the extrapolation of anharmonicity to this limit is discussed in Chapter 5 of Gaydon (1968).

antibonding. An antibonding orbital is one that, when occupied, tends to induce dissociation. Imagine the 1s-atomic orbitals on two °hydrogen atoms which are being brought together, and suppose that the signs of the amplitudes of the two wavefunctions are opposite. The effect of bringing the atoms towards each other is to slide the region of positive amplitude of one wave into the region of negative amplitude of the other, and, just as in the case of conventional wave phenomena, the waves interfere destructively and the total wave amplitude in the region of overlap is diminished. The square of this amplitude determines the probability of finding the electrons in a particular region, and so the effect of bringing the orbitals together with opposite phases (signs) is to diminish the electron density in the internuclear region. This has an adverse effect on the energy of the molecule (because the internuclear region is the best place to put the electrons, for then their interaction with the two nuclei is the most favourable), and the molecule formed in this way will have an energy greater than that of the two hydrogen atoms at infinite separation: this is therefore a dissociative situation, and the molecule is unstable. The orbital responsible for this instability is referred to as an antibonding orbital.

The case of two helium atoms being brought together is a good example of the effect of antibonding character. When the two nuclei are quite close together the 1s-orbitals overlap appreciably: the amplitudes taken with the same phase interfere constructively in the internuclear region to give one °molecular orbital, and the amplitudes taken with opposite sign interfere destructively to give another, antibonding, molecular orbital. Four electrons have to be added to these two composite molecular orbitals: two enter the lower-energy orbital and tend to cause the nuclei to stick together; the next electron enters the antibonding orbital and so lowers the strength of the bond. The fourth °pairs with the third in the antibonding orbital, and the combined effect of this pair is sufficient to overcome the bonding of the first pair and to disrupt the molecule. Consequently He_2 is an unstable molecular species (even though He_2^+ is weakly stable in the gas phase). This description enables one to see why two helium atoms collide without sticking together: as the atoms approach the bond and antibond are formed, but both are occupied simultaneously and the rise in energy as the atoms approach appears as a repulsive force. It is quite easy to extend this description to more complicated atoms and molecules and to understand why bulk matter is impenetrable.

Questions. 1. What effect does the occupation of an antibonding molecular orbital have on the energy of a molecule? Why does the overlap of atomic orbitals with opposite sign lead to an antibonding orbital? Why is He_2^+ less stable than He_2^{2+}, and He_2 unstable? Why, then, is the world not littered with He_2^{2+}? Why do not two neon atoms stick together when they collide in a gas, and how may this argument be adapted to account for the same property of methane and N_2? Why is bulk matter impenetrable?
2. Take a 1s-orbital on each of two protons at a separation R, and use the mathematical form for the orbitals given on p. 275 to plot the amplitude of the molecular orbitals that result when they are combined first with the same sign and then with opposite sign. Plot the electron density corresponding to two electrons in the bonding orbital and then to two in the antibonding orbital, and then plot the *difference density* (obtained by ignoring interference effects, calculating the electron density when each electron is confined to its own nucleus, and subtracting this density from the density calculated for the bonding and antibonding cases). Do this calculation for about three judiciously chosen nuclear separations, and reflect on the connexion of these results with the discussion in the text. A proper calculation should use °normalized orbitals, but a simple one is sufficient for illustration. What effect does normalization have on the difference densities?

Further information. Antibonding effects are of considerable importance in determining molecular structure: see Coulson's *The shape and structure of molecules* (OCS 9) and Coulson (1961). A long essay on the importance of antibonding orbitals has been written by Orchin and Jaffé (1967). Further details will be found in *MQM* Chapter 9, and helpful advice on the calculation of overlap integrals is given by McGlynn, Vanquickenborne, Kinoshita, and Carroll (1972) Chapter 2 and Appendix C. A compilation of molecular energies has been published by Richards, Walker, and Hinkley (1971). Difference density maps are given by Coulson (OCS 9) and by Deb (1973), and the latter gives references to many other sources.

antisymmetry. A function f(x) is antisymmetrical (or antisymmetric) if $f(-x)$ is equal to $-f(x)$. A wavefunction of a system containing N indistinguishable particles is *antisymmetrical under particle interchange* if it changes sign when the coordinates of any pair of particles are interchanged; that is, if $\psi(\mathbf{r}_1,\mathbf{r}_2) = -\psi(\mathbf{r}_2,\mathbf{r}_1)$. Do not confuse the word with *asymmetrical*, which means the absence of symmetry. An example of the first type of antisymmetry is the function x, because $(-x) = -(x)$; another example is the function sin x, because $\sin(-x) = -\sin x$. An example of an antisymmetrical wavefunction is $\psi_a(\mathbf{r}_1)\psi_b(\mathbf{r}_2) - \psi_a(\mathbf{r}_2)\psi_b(\mathbf{r}_1)$ because interchanging the coordinates $\mathbf{r}_1$ and $\mathbf{r}_2$, which by reference to Fig. A5 is seen to be equivalent to interchanging the particles, changes the sign of the function.

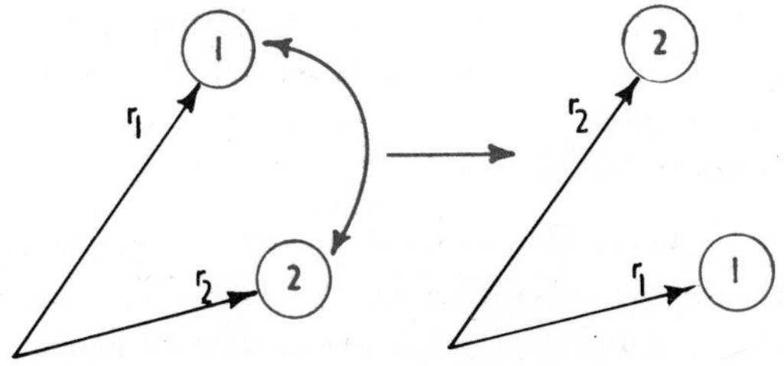

FIG. A5 Interchanging particles 1 and 2 is equivalent to interchanging the vectors $\mathbf{r}_1$ and $\mathbf{r}_2$.

The importance of antisymmetrical wavefunctions stems from the °Pauli principle, which demands that the total wavefunction of any collection of electrons must be antisymmetrical. The formation of a °Slater determinant is one way of constructing a fully antisymmetrized function out of a collection of functions. The imposition of the requirement of antisymmetry on a wavefunction introduces important modifications to the energy: see °exchange energy.

Questions. State the condition on $f(x)$ for it to be an antisymmetrical function of x. Which of the following functions are antisymmetrical: x^2, x^3, $3x^2-2x^3$, $\cos x$, $\tan x$, $\exp x$, $\exp x^2$, $\operatorname{cosec} x$? Show that any asymmetric function $F(x)$ can be expressed as the sum of an antisymmetrical function and a symmetrical function. What is meant by an antisymmetrical wavefunction? Which of the following wavefunctions are antisymmetrical: $\psi_a(\mathbf{r}_1)\psi_b(\mathbf{r}_2)$, $\sin[k(r_1-r_2)]$, $\psi_a(\mathbf{r}_1)\psi_b(\mathbf{r}_2)\psi_c(\mathbf{r}_3) - \psi_a(\mathbf{r}_2)\psi_b(\mathbf{r}_1)\psi_c(\mathbf{r}_3) + \psi_a(\mathbf{r}_2)\psi_b(\mathbf{r}_3)\psi_c(\mathbf{r}_1) - \ldots$? Show that the last can be written as a 3×3 determinant. What is the importance of antisymmetry in quantum mechanics?

Further information. See *MQM* Chapter 8 for the reasons lying behind the use of antisymmetric wavefunctions. Helpful discussions of the reasons and the consequences will be found in §29 of Pauling and Wilson (1935), in §3·1 of Slater (1963), and §1·2 and succeeding chapters of Richards and Horsley (1970). The symmetry and antisymmetry of functions can be envisaged, and treated, as a problem for °group theory; therefore see *MQM* Chapter 5, Cotton (1963), Tinkham (1964), Bishop (1973), and Altmann (1962). The antisymmetrization of wavefunctions is a problem in statistics: see Pauling and Wilson (1935), Condon and Shortley (1963), Hamermesh (1962), and Judd (1963). This reading sequence will illustrate how a simple requirement may have consequences of unbounded complexity.

aromaticity. An aromatic molecule is cyclic, planar, and conjugated (possessing alternating single and double bonds) but with a stability greater than would be expected for a molecule with so many double bonds. The extra stabilization is due to °resonance (in °valence-bond language) or delocalization (in °molecular-orbital language), and the extra stabilization energy is called the °resonance energy or delocalization energy. °Benzene is the archetype of such molecules. It has been found that aromatic molecules possess $4n+2$ electrons (the *Hückel $4n+2$ rule*), where n is an integer. Thus benzene has $n = 1$, and the simplest aromatic molecule of all, which was first prepared not long ago, is the cyclopropene cation ($n = 0$). The large molecule [18]-annulene, consisting of 18 conjugated carbon atoms in a planar ring, is also aromatic ($n = 4$).

The basis of the $4n+2$ rule may be understood by considering the energy levels of cyclic hydrocarbons. From N atoms N molecular orbitals may be formed. The lowest energy (most strongly binding) orbital has no °nodes, all the others have nodes, and, except perhaps the uppermost, are doubly °degenerate. See, for instance, Fig. A1 on p. 2. (This two-fold degeneracy may be viewed as a consequence of the fact that an electron may run round the ring in either direction.) In the case of N being an even number the uppermost level is non-degenerate. Into the lowest energy level one may insert two electrons, and into each doubly degenerate pair one may insert four electrons. Closed-shell molecules therefore contain $4n+2$ electrons, where n is the number of fully occupied doubly degenerate levels. Achieving a closed shell is an energetically favourable situation, especially as one is normally obtained by adding no more electrons than are needed to complete the bonding molecular orbitals, and so leaving empty the energetically unfavourable °antibonding orbitals.

It has also been found that some molecules of a conjugated double-bond nature show an enhanced instability: they contain $4n$ electrons, and include the cyclopropene anion ($n = 1$). This great instability gives rise to the name *antiaromatic.*

Further information. See *MQM* Chapter 10, Coulson's *The shape and structure of molecules* (OCS 9), Coulson (1961), Streitweiser (1961), Salem (1966), and Pilar (1968). A simple account of the preparation and properties of a variety of aromatic and antiaromatic molecules has been given by Breslow (1972). The analysis of the $4n+2$ rule may be carried further by referring to Streitweiser (1961), Chapter 10; there will be found described the concept of *pseudoaromaticity* and *Craig's rules.* See Bergmann and Pullman (1971) for the proceedings of a conference on aromaticity, pseudoaromaticity, and antiaromaticity.

atomic orbital. An atomic orbital describes the distribution of an electron in an atom: it is the °wavefunction for an electron in an atom. The classical Rutherford and °Bohr theory of the hydrogen atom sought a model of its structure in terms of a trajectory of the electron about the nucleus, and so the atom was viewed as a central nucleus with an electron in one of a variety of orbits. The introduction of quantum mechanics, and in particular the impact of the °uncertainty principle, showed that the concept of trajectory was untenable on an atomic scale, and so an orbit could not be specified. Quantum mechanics replaced the precise trajectory, the *orbit,* of the electron by a distribution, an *orbital*. An atomic orbital is a function $\psi(\mathbf{r})$ of the coordinates of the electron, and, in accord with the Born interpretation of the °wavefunction, the probability that the electron may be found in an infinitesimal volume element $d\tau$ surrounding the point $\mathbf{r}$ is $\psi^*(\mathbf{r})\psi(\mathbf{r})d\tau$. It follows that, if the form of the atomic orbital is known, we are able to predict the electron density at any point in the atom.

As an example, the electron in the ground state of the hydrogen atom is distributed in an atomic orbital (an *s-orbital*) of the form exp $(-r/a_0)$, where a_0 is a constant, the Bohr radius ($5{\cdot}29 \times 10^{-11}$ m): this implies that the orbital is spherical (the function depends on r but not on θ or ϕ), and the electron density at any point depends on exp $(-2r/a_0)$. Therefore the density is greatest at the nucleus, and then declines exponentially with distance. Such an atomic orbital can be represented by a spherical *boundary surface* within which there is some probability, let us say 90 per cent, of discovering the electron. In this boundary-surface representation, which is depicted in Fig. A6, the s-orbital is drawn as a sphere of an appropriate radius; but it must not be forgotten that there is some slight probability of discovering the electron at points well outside the boundary surface.

It is normally sufficient in the discussion of atoms to confine attention to the s-, p-, d-, and occasionally the f-orbitals. Of these only the s-orbital is spherically symmetrical; the others have an increasingly pronounced angular dependence corresponding to the electron being concentrated in particular directions in space. The form of these atomic orbitals will be found in the discussion of the °hydrogen atom.

The amplitude of an atomic orbital depends on the distance from the nucleus. It is reasonable to expect the amplitude to diminish to zero at large distances from the parent nucleus, and this is found to be so: when r is very large all orbitals decay exponentially. The decay is not in general exponential at all distances from the nucleus, for in most some incipient undulations occur at small radii. This behaviour is examined in detail in the case of the °hydrogen atom, and only one point need be emphasized here: only for s-orbitals does the amplitude not drop to zero at the nucleus itself (see Fig. A6).

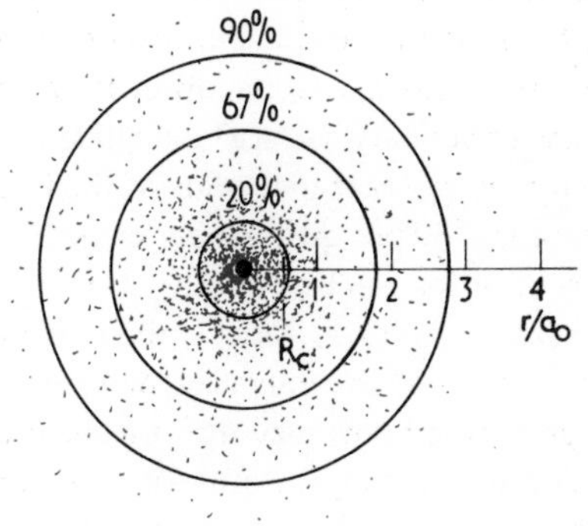

FIG. A6. Boundary surface capturing different proportions of the electron in the ground state of the hydrogen atom (in a 1s-orbital). R_c denotes the covalent radius (30 pm).

The *number of lobes* possessed by an atomic orbital (actually the number of angular °nodes) determines the °orbital angular momentum of an electron in the orbital. The *mean curvature* of the orbital, which is determined by the number of radial and angular nodes (because the more often the wave must pass through zero, the more sharply is it curved), determines the °kinetic energy of an electron that occupies it, and the *mean inverse distance* from the nucleus determines the potential energy in hydrogen and the attractive part of the potential energy in many-electron atoms. In many-electron atoms the energy is also influenced by the interelectronic repulsions, and these have the further effect of distorting the electron distributions from those in hydrogen-like atoms; these effects are calculated by °self-consistent field methods. Although true orbitals of many-electron atoms are complicated functions, it is possible to make a fair approximation to them by orbitals that have the same angular dependence as those of hydrogen, but whose radial dependence is determined by a set of simple rules: these are the °Slater orbitals.

When atomic orbitals are represented by boundary surfaces it must be borne in mind that in many-electron atoms these are only a crude representation of the actual electron distribution, and in fact do little more than designate regions of space where the orbital has appreciable amplitude and where the electron has a high probability of being found.

Questions. What is an atomic orbital? What information does it contain about the distribution and properties of an electron that occupies it? How does an orbital differ from an orbit? What is meant by a boundary surface? Calculate from the wavefunction given in the text the radius of the boundary sphere which captures 50 per cent, 80 per cent, 90 per cent, and 99·99 per cent of the electron density in the 1s-orbital of hydrogen ($a_0 = 53$ pm, 0·53 Å). What is the effect on the shape of atomic orbitals of the interelectronic repulsions in many electron atoms, and how may they be taken into account? Sketch the boundary surfaces for p-, d-, and f-orbitals by referring to the pictures in the article on the °hydrogen atom. What is the evidence that electrons are distributed in atoms in the manner we have described?

Further information. See *MQM* Chapter 8. The shape and significance of atomic orbitals are discussed in detail in Coulson (1961), Herzberg (1944), White (1934), Pauling and Wilson (1935), and Kauzmann (1957). Information about self-consistent field and Slater orbitals will be found under the appropriate headings. The electronic occupation of atomic orbitals is determined by the °*aufbau* process and the °Pauli principle. As well as determining the structure of atoms the atomic orbitals are the basis of descriptions of molecular structure: see °molecular orbitals and °linear combination of atomic orbitals. See also °wavefunction and °radial-distribution function. Read the section on the hydrogen atom for a detailed discussion of its orbitals.

atomic spectra: a synopsis. An atomic absorption or emission spectrum arises when an atom makes a transition between two states (which are often called °terms): the *combination principle* states that all lines in a spectrum can be represented as the difference between two terms (for the word 'term' is also used to denote the energy of a term). The transitions observed can normally be ascribed to °electric dipole transitions, and the lines that may appear in the spectrum are governed by the °selection rules. Their intensity is determined by the magnitude of the transition dipole moment. The appearance of the spectrum may be modified by the application of a strong magnetic field (the °Zeeman effect) or a strong electric field (the °Stark effect), because both fields can cause small shifts in the energy levels of the atom. On the gross structure of the spectrum is seen a °fine structure, which is interpreted in terms of spin-orbit coupling, and an even finer °hyperfine structure which is due to the interaction of the electrons with the °magnetic dipole and electric °quadrupole moments of the nucleus.

The information of chemical interest that can be obtained, or has been obtained, from the spectrum of an atom is as follows:

1. *Identification of species*. Since every element has a characteristic spectrum, atomic spectroscopy may be used in analysis: the spectrum is used as a fingerprint for elements.

2. *Evidence for quantization*. The study of the spectrum of atomic °hydrogen was of profound significance for developing the ideas of °quantum theory and quantization. Out of the study emerged the idea of °atomic orbitals, and all the other paraphernalia of quantum chemistry.

3. *The Pauli principle.* From a study of the spectrum of helium emerged the puzzling result that not all the states of the atom are allowed. The °Pauli principle was the rationalization of these data, and its discovery was the key that enabled the periodic system to be explained.

4. *Atomic energy levels.* The study of atomic spectra yields information on the energy levels of atoms: we are able to say how deeply electrons are buried in inner shells and which electrons and states of the atom are likely to be important in

governing the bonding properties of atoms (their valence, and the strength of the °bonds they form). We need to know the energy of atomic energy levels in order to assess the energy of the °valence state and the role of °hybridization. Photochemistry depends on a knowledge of the energy levels of excited atoms.

5. *Ionization potentials.* The energy required to ionize an atom (its °ionization potential) can be determined from atomic spectroscopy; so too, with more difficulty, can some °electron affinities. Both these properties are central to an understanding of the structure and reactions of atoms and molecules. See, for example, °electronegativity.

6. *Spin-orbit coupling.* From the °fine structure we may determine the spin-orbit coupling constant. This is of use in the discussion of the role of triplet states in photochemistry (for example, the heavy atom effect in quenching °phosphorescence) because it determines the rate of °singlet-triplet inter-system crossing. We also need to know spin-orbit coupling constants to evaluate °*g*-values in °electron spin resonance and to discuss the structure of molecules—see, for example, the °Hund coupling cases.

7. *Hyperfine coupling constants.* From the °hyperfine structure of spectra can be determined the strength of the magnetic and electric coupling of electrons to nuclei, and also the °spin of nuclei. Such coupling constants are important for the °hyperfine effect in °electron spin resonance and the °spin-spin coupling in °nuclear magnetic resonance.

8. *X-ray spectra.* Spectra in the short-wavelength °X-ray region were the basis for Moseley's determination of the atomic numbers of the elements.

Further information. See *MQM* Chapter 8 for a description of the interactions that lead to the structure of atomic spectra and a more detailed description of their form. Introductory books on atomic spectra include those by Whiffen (1972), Barrow (1962), Herzberg (1944), Woodgate (1970), and White (1934). A book with many examples and with comprehensive coverage at a slightly more advanced level is that by Kuhn (1962). More detailed analysis will be found in Shore and Menzel (1968), Candler (1964), who gives much experimental data, Condon and Shortley (1963), Judd (1963, 1967), and Wigner (1959). The books by Condon and Shortley and Wigner are classics: the former was written before many of the impressive angular-momentum techniques were developed but has been a dominating influence on the development of the subject, and the latter is a classic and original exposition of atomic structure and spectra in terms of symmetry and °group theory. Both books may be regarded as ancestors of Griffith (1964), who, after his description of free atom spectra, develops the theory of the spectra of atoms in complexes: see °crystal-field theory. Data from atomic spectroscopy will be found in Moore (1949 et seq.), who lists energy levels. Applications to photochemistry are described by Wayne (1970) and Calvert and Pitts (1966).

atomic units. The appearance of many equations in quantum mechanics may be considerably simplified if mass is expressed as a multiple of the electron mass m_e (so that the mass of the electron is taken to be unity); charge as a multiple of the proton's charge e; length as a multiple of the °Bohr radius a_0; and energy in multiples of twice the ionization potential of the ground state °hydrogen atom. (Twice the ionization potential, 27·21 eV, or $e^2/4\pi\epsilon_0 a_0$, is generally employed, although some people use the energy itself; that is, 13·65 eV.) A consequence of this choice of units is that $\hbar = 1$. The units may be augmented by the choice $c = 1$ for the speed of light (and so all velocities are expressed as a fraction of the speed of light in a vacuum). The units so chosen eliminate many of the constants in the °Schrödinger equation, and the numbers that emerge for various properties can be translated

BOX 1: Atomic units (a.u.)

	quantity	value	
1 a.u. of	mass	m_e	$9{\cdot}109 \times 10^{-31}$ kg
	length	a_0	$5{\cdot}292 \times 10^{-11}$ m
	charge	e	$1{\cdot}602 \times 10^{-19}$ C
	energy	$e^2/4\pi\epsilon_0 a_0$	27·2 eV; 2625 kJ mol^{-1}
	velocity	c	$2{\cdot}998 \times 10^8$ m s^{-1}

Consequently $\hbar = 1$; $\mu_B = \frac{1}{2}$; $R_H = \frac{1}{2}$.

into conventional units by re-introducing the units of mass, length, charge, and energy; see Box 1.

aufbau principle. The *aufbau* or building-up principle is the statement about how electrons should be fed into the orbitals of an atom or molecule in order to construct the species. The principle states that an electron enters the lowest available orbital consistent with the requirements of the °Pauli exclusion principle. This implies that the first electron enters the lowest orbital, the second joins the first (but with opposite °spin); the third electron enters the next higher orbital, then the fourth pairs with it and so on. See Fig. A7. When a set of °degenerate orbitals is to be filled (for example, when the p-shell of an atom is being populated) the first electrons enter different members of the set with parallel spin, in accord with the °Hund rule, and only when each degenerate orbital contains one electron do the remainder enter with paired spins. The list of the orbitals populated by the application of the *aufbau* process constitutes the °configuration of the atom.

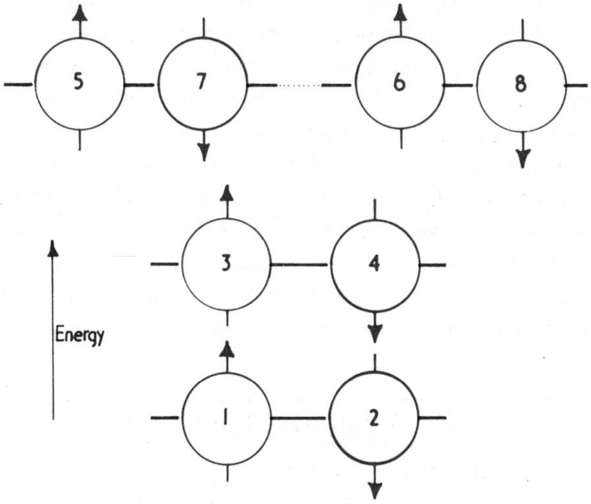

FIG. A7. The order of filling energy levels according to the *aufbau* principle.

Questions. What is the *aufbau* principle? In what way does it depend on the Pauli principle? How would the principle differ if the particles being filled into the orbitals were °bosons? What is the role of Hund's rule? Discuss the structure of the atoms He, Li, Be, B, C, and N in the light of the *aufbau* principle, and also the structure of the molecules H_2, N_2, O_2, F_2, and NO (get help from °molecular orbitals). Discuss what might happen when two energy levels lie close together, but are not degenerate: under what circumstances might each be half-filled before the lower is filled?

Further information. See *MQM* Chapter 8, Chapter 3 of Herzberg (1944), and Murrell, Kettle, and Tedder (1965). The *aufbau* principle is the basis of the periodic table; therefore see how it is applied in Puddephatt's *The periodic table of the elements* (OCS 3) and in Chapter 2 of Phillips and Williams (1965). For the application of the principle to molecular systems see *MQM* Chapter 9, Coulson's *The shape and structure of molecules* (OCS 9), and Coulson (1961). The *aufbau* principle is important in transition-metal chemistry because in complexes the metal ion has a number of close-lying energy levels, and the situation in the last question is common: see °crystal-field theory and °ligand-field theory.

Auger effect. Other names for this effect are *auto-ionization* and *pre-ionization.* The Auger effect is a *radiationless transition* (a transition between states that involves no emission or absorption of radiation) from an excited state into a dissociative state. Consider an atomic energy level scheme of the type shown in Fig. A8: in this atom one series of levels terminates (at an *ionization limit*) at a lower energy than the other. Suppose we monitor the absorption spectrum of the atom, and we concentrate on the series on the left (L). The spectrum observed consists of a series of sharp lines at increasing frequencies, but when the frequency corresponds to an energy above the ionization limit of the other series (R), for example when we observe the transition to the line A, a marked change appears in the spectrum. The most noticable difference is in the sharpness of the lines, for A,B . . . are blurred. They may also be slightly shifted. What is happening is that some °perturbation in the atom (for example, the spin-orbit coupling) is mixing the states of series L with those of series R, and therefore the states of L take a little of the character of R. But above the ionization limit of R this implies that the states of L have a tendency to ionize, the tendency

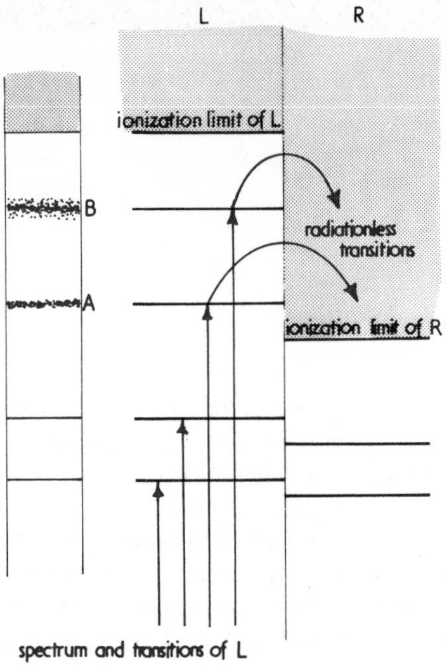

FIG. A8. The Auger effect: the broadening of the spectrum (on the left) occurs where the atom makes radiationless transitions from states on the left to the unbound states on the right.

increasing as the contamination increases. Since the lifetime of the levels A, B, . . . is diminished by this mixing, the width of the levels is increased (°uncertainty principle). The mixing of states R into states L may be expressed as a probability that an atom in a state of L makes an actual transition into a state of R, and the Auger effect is simply this type of radiationless transition into a dissociative state. The name *pre-ionization* reflects the fact that ionization occurs in series L before, on energetic grounds, it is expected, and the name *auto-ionization* reflects the 'self-induced' nature of the process in the sense that the perturbations within the molecule induce the ionization by flipping the bound state into the ionizing state.

The Auger effect was originally detected in °X-ray spectroscopy, where the bombardment of a solid with fast electrons excites a K-shell electron (let us say), and an X-ray is emitted when an L-shell electron falls into the vacant hole. A competing process is introduced by the Auger effect, because the excitation of the K-electron may induce auto-ionization, and another electron is boiled off the atom or out of the solid. The ionization process competes with the formation of X-rays and diminishes their intensities. The effect is not wholly bad for, if the energy of the Auger electron is measured, information may be obtained about the energy levels of electrons in solids. This is the basis of *Auger spectroscopy.*

For the sake of completeness, Auger is pronounced oʒe.

Questions. What is the Auger effect? How may it be detected in atomic spectra? Why do spectral lines become broadened by virtue of the Auger effect? What perturbations may cause auto-ionization? Describe the appearance of the spectrum showing pre-ionization. What is the role of the Auger effect in X-ray spectra? What effect does it have on the lines? Suppose we were looking at an atomic emission spectrum, what would be the influence of the Auger effect? In what sense may °predissociation of molecules be considered to be an Auger effect? What other processes can you think of that, however loosely, may be considered to be the manifestation of an Auger effect?

Further information. An account of the Auger effect in atomic spectra will be found in §4.2 of Herzberg (1944) and §4.5 and §5.3 of Kuhn (1962). The role it plays in the formation and appearance of X-ray spectra is described by Burhop (1952) and has been reviewed by Burhop and Asaad (1972). For a discussion of Auger spectroscopy, see Siegbahn (1973) and further references under °ionization potential. See also °predissociation.

B

band theory of metals. The theoretical description of the structure and properties of metals is based on the view that in gross terms they are composed of an array of positive ions held together and surrounded by a sea of electrons. The properties of this sea of electrons determine the typical characteristics of metals: their electrical conductivity, thermal conductivity, reflectivity, malleability, and ductility. The energy levels available to the electrons are of paramount importance, and

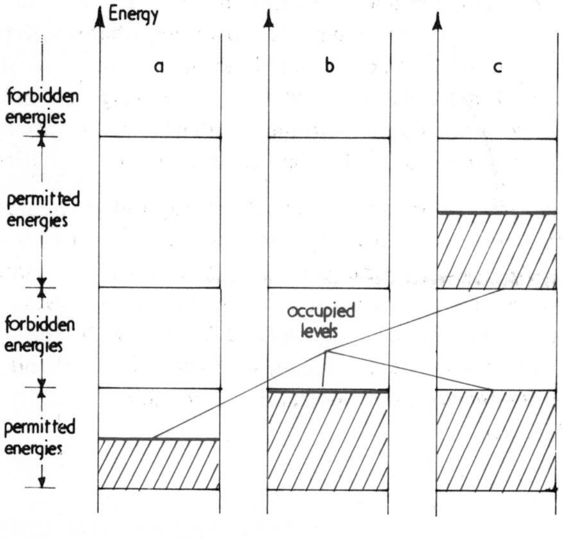

FIG. B1. The extent of occupation of bands separated by gaps determines whether a material is a conductor or an insulator. Occupied levels are coloured.

analysis of the problem shows that the available energies fall into *bands*, and that between these bands lie regions of energy which no electron can possess. If a band is less than full (Figs. B1a and c), the electrons in it can be induced to move under the influence of a small disturbance: hence the high conductivity of metals. If the bands are full, electrons can be induced to move only if they can be supplied with enough energy to excite them through the forbidden band gap into an empty upper band: this is an energetically unfavourable situation, and so such materials are electrical *insulators* (Fig. B1b).

The formation of energy bands in metals may be described in a number of ways: we shall discuss two. The first starts from the view that a metal may be envisaged as a massive molecule, a molecule of almost infinite extent. The molecule is composed of atoms in a regular lattice, and on these atoms there are °atomic orbitals which overlap with their neighbours' atomic orbitals. This situation of overlapping orbitals is encountered on a much smaller scale in conventional molecules, for it is the basis of the °molecular-orbital description of molecular structure. Let us pretend that only a single s-orbital is available on each atom, and for simplicity we consider a linear crystal (a single line of N atoms).

Concentrate first on two of the atoms in the chain: their orbitals °overlap and form a bonding and an antibonding pair of molecular orbitals with an energy separation determined largely by the amount of overlap (Fig. B2). Now bring up a third atom to a lattice distance and let it overlap with its immediate neighbour (and for simplicity, and as a good approximation, neglect its small overlap with its next-nearest

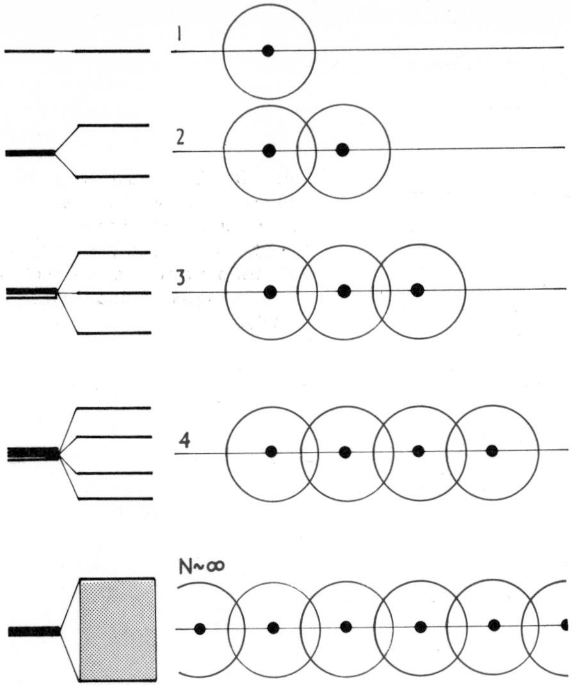

FIG. B2. As 2, 3, 4, . . . N atoms are added in a line the energy levels begin to fill a band; when N is very large the energy levels within the band virtually form a continuum.

neighbour). This adjusts the molecular orbitals and their energies so that three orbitals are obtained in the place of the former two; one is bonding, one is nonbonding, and the third is antibonding. This is illustrated in Fig. B2. The process of sliding an atom along the line up to a lattice point (rather like using an abacus) may be continued, and Figs. B2 and B3 show that the effect is gradually to fill in the energies until when N is very large the N energy levels form a virtually continuous band of energies of width Δ_s. Since the band has been formed from s-orbitals it is called the *s-band.*

If each atom contributes one electron (the atoms might be sodium atoms in a line), then since each energy level constituting the band may accommodate two electrons (°Pauli principle), in the metal half the band will be full of electrons, and the upper half will be empty, as in Fig. B1a. (This is just the application of the °*aufbau* process to a collection of energy levels.) The presence of the half-filled band means that the line of atoms behaves as a metal. If instead each atom were to contribute two electrons, the band would be filled, as in Fig. B1b, and an applied electric field would be unable to shift the electrons: the line of atoms is then an insulator. Why motion cannot occur in this case will be described below in more detail.

It is improper to restrict the formation of a band to the overlapping of s-orbitals. If the metal atoms have p-orbitals in their valence (outermost) shell these too should be allowed to overlap. Because of °shielding and penetration effect, p-orbitals lie higher in energy than s-orbitals, and so their overlap gives rise to a band (the *p-band*) above the s-band, and separated from it by a gap, the magnitude of which depends on the strength of bonding between the atoms and the s-p separation of the isolated atoms (Fig. B4). Here we see the reason for the appearance of the bands of energies, and the regions of forbidden energies.

The approach to the band structure just described is sometimes referred to as the *tight-binding approximation* (TBA) because it takes the view that electrons tend to stick to nuclei, and therefore are quite well described by atomic orbitals characteristic of the atoms. An alternative approach starts from the view that a good first approximation is to suppose that the electrons have no electrostatic interactions and are completely free to swim about in the bulk of the metal, and that the presence of a periodic lattice may be imposed as an improvement in a second step: this is the *nearly-free electron approximation* (NFE).

How does this alternative approach lead to band formation? Let us once again consider the one-dimensional metal, but begin by ignoring the presence of positive ions. The situation is now that of a collection of °particles in a box, or, since the line is of almost infinite length, the same as the free-electron system. The energies available to free electrons take a continuous range of values and depend on the momentum $\pm k\hbar$ according to k^2 (Fig. B5a). Pouring electrons into this continuum of energy levels fills them up to some energy E_F, the *Fermi energy,* and leaves vacant all the energy levels above. The filled levels constitute the *Fermi sea*, whose surface, the *Fermi surface,* is at E_F. On this model everything would be a

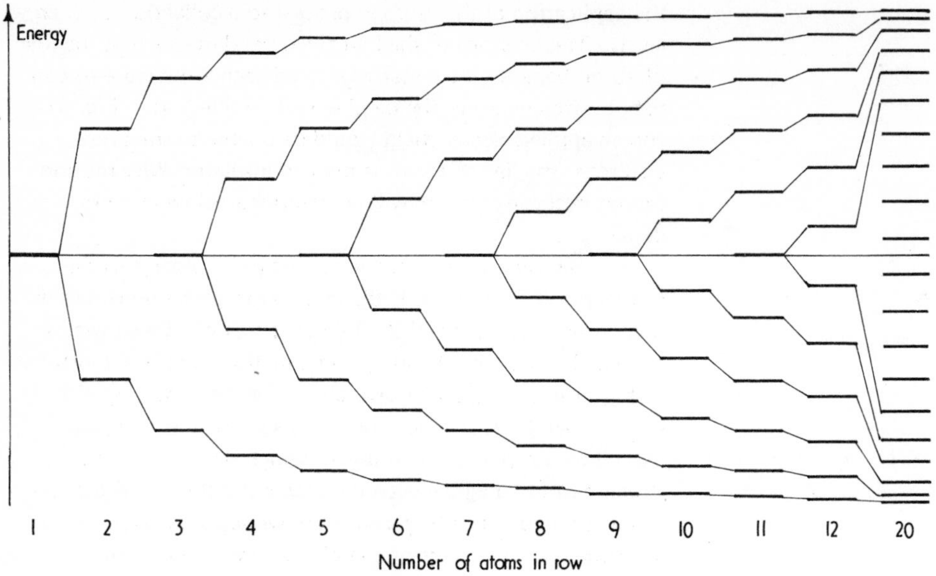

FIG. B3. The actual energy levels for a chain of N atoms, each interacting only with its nearest neighbour. Note that by $N = 20$ the band is getting dense, and that its width does not expand indefinitely.

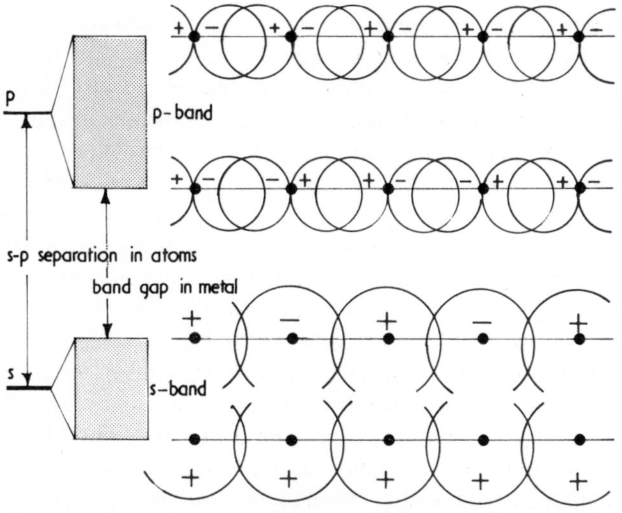

FIG. B4. Band-gap formation, s- and p-bands, and the orbital overlaps corresponding to the extreme energies of each band.

metal, for the 'band' has no upper limit, and so can never be filled. This emphasizes the central role that the periodic lattice plays in determining whether or not a material is a metal.

In order to see how the lattice imposes a band structure we remind ourselves that the states of the free electron are waves of definite length (wavelength $= 2\pi/k$), and the true system may be regarded in terms of these waves propagating through the periodic lattice. At wavelengths long compared with the lattice spacing a the waves slide through, but when the wavelength is comparable to a the lattice diffracts the waves. When the wavelength is equal to twice the lattice spacing a pattern of standing waves is set up because a wave that begins moving to the right is reflected by the lattice and moves to the left, where it is reflected to the right, and so on. These standing waves, with wavelengths in the vicinity of $2a$, have a stationary distribution in space, and we may envisage two types of arrangement. In one arrangement the standing wave has its amplitude maxima at the positions of the lattice points (positive ions), and in the other the maxima are between the lattice points. Whereas in the free-electron model these stand-

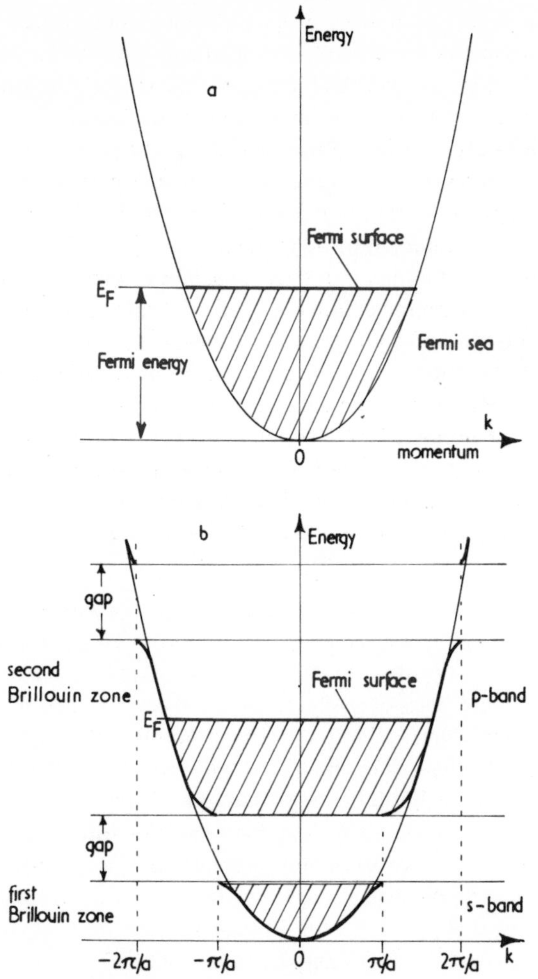

FIG. B5. (a) The free-electron energy levels and (b) the band structure imposed by the periodic lattice. Both contain a number of electrons that makes them metals.

ing waves had the same energy, the presence of the periodic lattice implies that they have different potential energies, and so we discover that at $k = \pm\pi/a$ there is an energy gap (see Fig. B6). Another gap is found at $k = \pm 2\pi/a$, and so on; therefore, we see that the periodic lattice splits the free-electron continuum of energy levels into a series of bands separated by gaps (Fig. B5). Into these bands, the *Brillouin zones,* may be inserted the electrons of the metal, and metallic properties are predicted only if there remain incompletely filled bands.

The relation of the NFE bands to the tight-binding bands may be discovered by comparing the form of the orbitals at the edge of the s- and p-bands with the waves at the edges of the first and second Brillouin zones. The immediate observation, from Fig. B6, is that the nodal structure is the same; only the details of the electron distributions differ, especially in the regions close to the nuclei.

Well below the Brillouin zone boundary (that is, for energy levels for which $|k| \ll \pi/a$ in the first zone) the states of the electron may be regarded as running waves (as opposed to the standing waves forced on us at the zone edge). In one dimension the waves run with momentum $+k\hbar$ to the right and $-k\hbar$ to the left; since they have energy proportional to k^2 these two running waves are °degenerate (have the same energy).

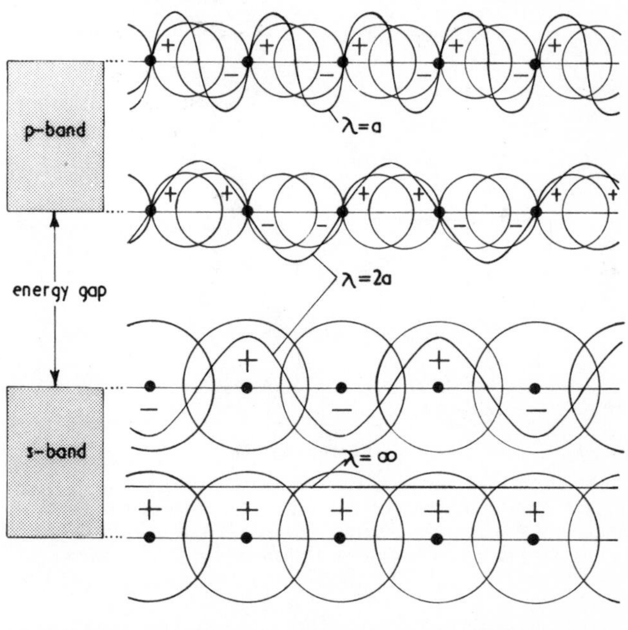

FIG. B6. Energy-gap formation due to a periodic lattice and its relation to the orbital (TBA) approach (in colour). Note that the uppermost level of the lower band and the lowermost of the upper have the same wavelength but one has nodes at the nuclei, the other between them. The lattice spacing is *a*.

Therefore, in a metal there are equal numbers of electrons running to the left and to the right, and in the absence of external stimuli no current flows. When an electric potential difference is applied, the energy of the electrons running to the right may differ from those running to the left (Fig. B7) and so the electrons redistribute themselves in order to attain the lowest energy: this means that more occupy states corresponding to the flow of electrons to the right, because a lower energy is attained thereby, and the equilibrium situation shows a steady flow of current. If however the band is full the electrons cannot reorganize themselves to give a net direction to travel (consider Fig. B7 with a full band), and so no current flows. Such a material is an insulator. A really enormous field might so affect the energies that an empty zone is brought down to the filled one: in this case of *dielectric breakdown* a current may flow, but often at a cost of disrupting the material.

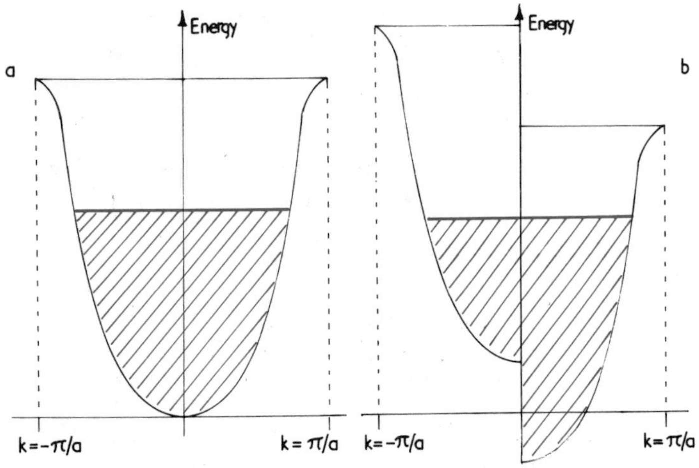

FIG. B7. When a suitable potential difference is applied to a material with an unfilled band the lowest energy distribution of electrons has more moving to the right (positive **k**) than to the left (negative **k**).

The band theory of metals is able to account for the *thermal properties* of metals. For example, the high *thermal conductivity* may be traced to the way in which an electron carries heat rapidly through the lattice. Applying heat to one end of a metal rod induces lattice vibrations: these lattice vibrations excite an electron with an energy close to the Fermi surface into an unfilled state just above the sea, and so it may skim through the lattice with its high energy. Sooner or later it will plunge back into the Fermi sea, and in the process will impart its excess energy to the lattice, but this part of the lattice might be some way from the heated end of the rod. Thus heat is conducted through the rod.

Pioneers of the theory of *heat capacities* of metals were worried by the presence of a great sea of electrons, all of which ought to be able to contribute to the heat capacity of a block of metal. Band theory dispelled this worry by drawing attention to the fact that when a metal is excited thermally an energy of the order of kT is supplied, and only those electrons within an energy kT of the Fermi surface can be excited into an empty level by such a stimulus. Consequently only a very small number of electrons are able to contribute to the heat capacity of a metal.

Questions. 1. A metal may be pictured as an array of positive ions embedded in a sea of electrons: how is this picture able to account for the malleability and ductility of metals? What other characteristics of metals must any theory of their structure explain? What is the role of energy bands in determining electrical and thermal conductivity? Why are clean, smooth metal surfaces highly reflecting? Describe the tight-binding approximation, and explain why bands may be formed. What is the difference between s- and p-bands? Consider a one-dimensional metal lattice, and let there be s- and p-orbitals in the valence shell. Describe the number of electrons that would give rise to metallic or insulating properties to the system (consider only p-orbitals along the line). What determines the width of the bands? Guess whether an s- or a p-band is the wider. Discuss the thermal conductivity of the lattice you have just considered. What is the nearly-free electron approximation? Why does the presence of a periodic lattice introduce discontinuities into the energy versus k dependence? Discuss how these bands are related to the tight-binding bands. What is a Brillouin zone? Discuss the conditions for a material to be a metal on the NFE theory. What is meant by the terms 'Fermi energy', 'Fermi surface', and 'Fermi sea'? What explanation of the heat capacity of metals is provided by the band theory?

Suppose that an empty band is within an energy kT of the upper edge of a completely filled band: discuss the dependence of the electrical properties on the temperature of this *semiconductor.*

2. Treat the one-dimensional chain of N atoms as a °Hückel problem and show that as atoms are added to the chain the levels gradually form a continuous band, but of finite width. Proceed by setting up a °secular determinant based on a resonance integral β between neighbours, and 0 between non-neighbours. Let there be N atoms in the chain. Show that the roots of the equation lie at $2\beta\cos[n\pi/(n+1)]$, $n = 1, 2, \ldots N$, and plot the energy levels for $N = 1, 2, 3, \ldots 12, \infty$.

Further information. A simple account of the structure of metals and insulators and the way the theory may be used to account for a wide range of properties is given in Chapters 6 and 7 of Solymar and Walsh (1970) and in Jennings and Morris, *Atoms in contact* (OPS 4). Then see Altmann (1970) for a more quantitative account, but still at a moderately elementary level, and Quinn (1973), who gives an account of the TBA and NFE approximations and their more sophisticated developments. See also Kittel (1971), Ziman (1972), and Dekker (1960). Semiconductors are simply described in Solymar and Walsh (1970). Amorphous materials are of immense technological importance, and a summary of this difficult field has been given by Mott and Davis (1971).

benzene. Benzene is the archetype of the °*aromatic* molecules in which the ring of carbon atoms is unusually stable when compared with other unsaturated systems. The °resonance theory of chemical structure is the °valence-bond (VB) attempt to explain this stability, and the delocalization picture is the °molecular-orbital (MO) attempt.

The classical picture of the structure of benzene is that of a hexagon of alternating single and double bonds. The energy of this *Kekulé structure* may be calculated by taking into account all the electrostatic interactions of the electrons and nuclei. But the interelectronic repulsions have the further effect of pushing the π-electrons into the vacancies between the double bonds; that is, there is a tendency for the molecule to turn itself into the other Kekulé structure (Fig. B8). If the transformation is not allowed the molecule has an energy E; if

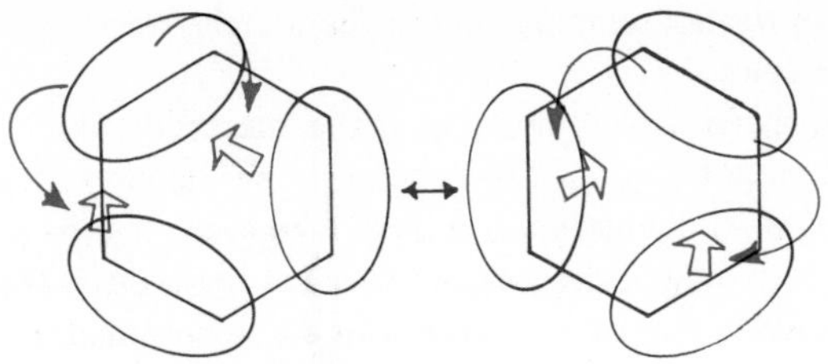

FIG. B8. Some of the electrostatic repulsions are relaxed by permitting resonance between two Kekulé forms.

the transformation is allowed the energy falls below E because the structure is more relaxed. The °resonance picture of the stabilization may therefore be interpreted in terms of the lowering of energy brought about by permitting the molecule to 'resonate' between the two Kekulé structures. This picture of two resonating Kekulé structures loses its edge when it is realized that these two structures contribute only about 80 per cent of the true total structure (which is a °superposition of resonating structures), the remaining 20 per cent being due largely to Dewar structures (Fig. B9). The 'resonance' picture gets rather muddy at these depths, although it

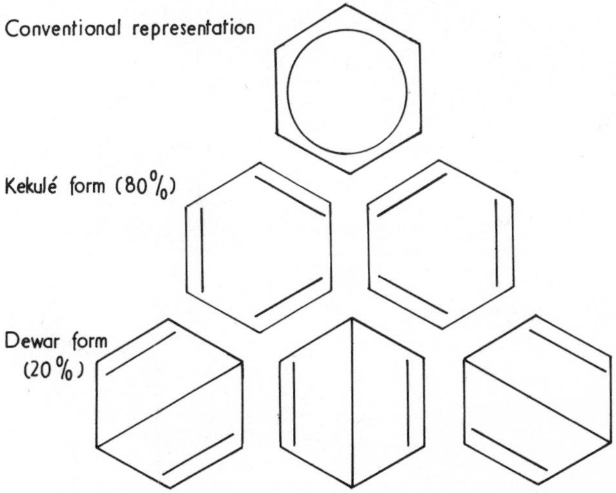

FIG. B9. Five resonating forms contributing to the VB structure of benzene. The true structure, designated by its conventional representation, is a superposition principally of these fundamental structures.

is valid when treated properly, and further details are given under °resonance.

The °molecular-orbital theory gives the impression of providing a more transparent description of the stability of the ring, based on the fact that benzene is an even °alternant molecule which may be described in terms of the orbitals and energies shown in Fig. B10. Six electrons are to be added to the delocalized π-system, and, as the first three orbitals are bonding, all the added electrons contribute to the stability of the molecule.

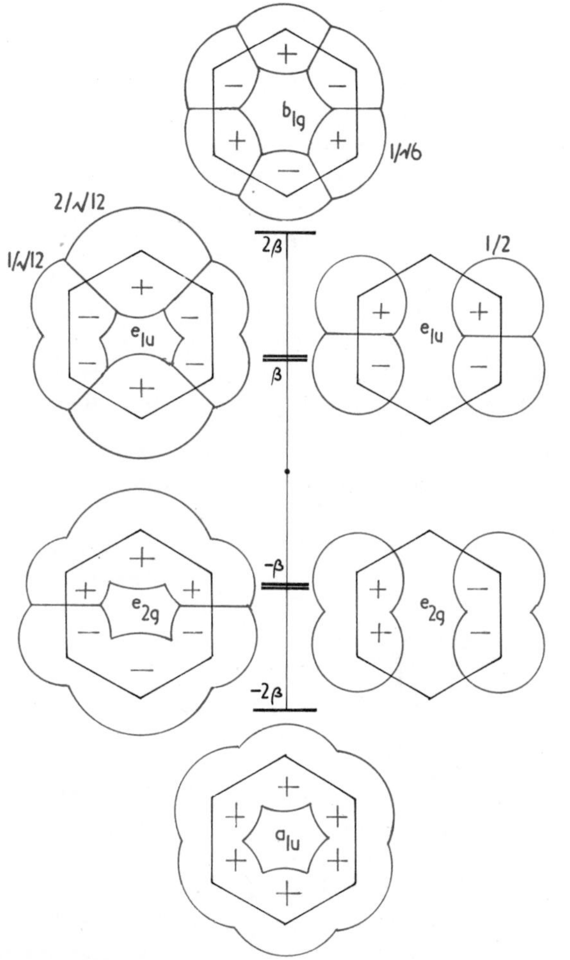

FIG. B10. Hückel energy levels and orbitals for benzene. The numbers are the coefficients of $2p_z$ for each atom; the sign of the coefficient is marked on the orbital. Obtain unmarked coefficients by symmetry.

The σ-electrons have an important role to play in both the VB and the MO descriptions because six carbon atoms sp^2-°hybridized (with lobes at 120°) form a six-membered ring (with angle 120°) without strain. Each of the six carbon atoms has its full share of its valence electrons, and so not only is there no energy arising from an imbalance of charge, but there are also no centres of charge excess or deficiency to provide a reactive site (see °alternant hydrocarbon). The hexagonal ring of carbon atoms is a very well poised system.

Questions. 1. Why does the °resonance of two Kekulé structures lend stability to the benzene ring? What structures must be taken into account in the full valence-bond treatment, and what proportion do they constitute of the total structure? Should ionic structures be included too? Draw some. What features of the hexagonal structure of benzene make the molecule stable in molecular-orbital terms? What features of this explanation are equally applicable to a valence-bond description?
2. Find combinations of the three occupied benzene molecular orbitals that may be interpreted as the three localized bonds of a Kekulé structure. (See °localized orbitals.) How may the other structure be obtained from the molecular orbitals? How may the Dewar structures be obtained?
3. Use the symmetry of the molecule to find the molecular orbitals in the Hückel scheme, and find their energies. Find the °resonance energy of the molecule. The experimental value is 150 kJ mol^{-1} (how would you determine this experimentally?).

Further information. See *MQM* Chapter 9 for the simple molecular-orbital description of benzene. A simple account of the structure of benzene is given by Coulson in his *The shape and structure of molecules* (OCS 9) and in Chapter 9 of Coulson (1961). For the valence-bond description see also Pauling (1960). For more mathematical details of the calculations see McGlynn, Vanquickenborne, Kinoshita, and Carroll (1972), Salem (1966), and Pilar (1968). For a recent review of the spectroscopy of benzene see Murrell (1971) and Hall and Amos (1969). Other entries of interest are °resonance,

°aromaticity, °Hückel method, and °alternant. Some physical properties of benzene are collected in Table 1.

birefringence: a synopsis. Birefringence denotes the presence of different °refractive indexes for the two polarization components of a beam of light. Birefringence may be a natural property of isolated molecules, or of a particular crystal form, or it may be induced electrically, magnetically, or mechanically. An important example of natural birefringence is *optical activity* in which the plane of polarization of light is rotated as it passes through the medium. This is an example of *circular birefringence,* because the effect depends on the different rates of passage of the left and right circularly polarized components (remember that the velocity of light in a medium is c/n). The *Faraday effect* is the induction of circular birefringence in a naturally inactive sample by the imposition of a longitudinal magnetic field. The rotation induced is proportional to the field strength, and the constant of proportionality is the *Verdet constant*; all molecules give a Faraday rotation. A magnetic field applied transversely induces a *linear birefringence* in which one plane-polarized component travels faster than the other: this induces an ellipticity into the beam, and is referred to as the *Cotton-Mouton effect.* The same phenomenon induced by a transverse electric field is called the *Kerr effect.* Because the °refractive index and the absorption coefficient are related (by the *Kramers-Krönig dispersion relations)*, and when one depends on the polarization so does the other, both the Kerr and the Cotton-Mouton effects may be observed by monitoring the different absorption coefficients for the polarization components. Birefringence may be induced by fluid flow if the molecules are sufficiently anisotropic: the alignment of long thin molecules introduces an anisotropy into the optical properties of the medium and the refractive indexes depend on the orientation of the polarization of the beam: this is *streaming birefringence.*

Further information. See *MQM* Chapter 11 for a discussion of the quantum-mechanical basis of natural optical activity. A further simple discussion has been given by Kauzmann (1957), and a thorough review, which also deals with induced birefringence, is in the book by Caldwell and Eyring (1971). See Fredericq and Houssier (1973) for a simple account of electric dichroism and electric birefringence, especially their applications. Other reviews containing interesting material are those of Moscowitz (1962), Tinoco (1962), Mason (1963), and Urry (1968). For a further discussion of the Faraday and Cotton-Mouton effects, see Buckingham and Stephens (1966). For the application of induced birefringence in liquid crystals to display devices, see the article by Elliott (1973). For the optical properties of solids, see the standard work on optics by Born and Wolf (1970), Landau and Lifshitz (1958a), and Wooster (1973). The dispersion (the frequency dependence) of optical activities is a basic research tool for the study of the stereochemistry of molecules: for an introduction to *optical rotatory dispersion* (ORD), see Crabbé (1965).

black-body radiation. A black body is one that absorbs all the radiation incident upon it. A practical example is a container completely sealed except for a tiny pinhole: this hole behaves as a black body because all light incident on it from outside passes through and, once in, cannot escape through the vanishingly small hole. Inside it experiences an indefinitely large number of reflections before it is absorbed, and these reflections have the result that the radiation comes into thermal equilibrium with the walls. Within the cavity we can imagine the electromagnetic field as having a distribution of frequencies characteristic of the temperature of the walls. The presence of the hole enables a small proportion of this equilibrium radiation to seep out and be detected, and the distribution of wavelengths in the black-body radiation is the same as the distribution within the equilibrium enclosure because the pinhole is a negligible perturbation. Black-body radiation is the radiation in equilibrium with matter at a particular temperature.

The general features of the distribution of frequencies are familiar from everyday experience: at low temperatures the hole does indeed look black, but a sensitive detector would show that a small amount of long wavelength radiation is present. At higher temperatures the amount of energy emitted is much greater, and its principal component lies in the infrared. At still higher temperatures the pinhole glows dull red, then white, and afterwards blue, and the total amount of energy radiated increases dramatically. As the temperature is raised further the peak of radiation passes through the ultraviolet, although the temperatures at which this occurs are too great to be conveniently accessible. Therefore we have made two observations: that the energy present in equilibrium increases dramatically as the temperature is raised, and that the wavelength of the light shifts towards the blue and beyond. The former observation is summarized by *Stefan's Law,* that the total energy emitted at a temperature T is equal to σT^4; the constant σ is Stefan's constant and has the value $5{\cdot}67 \times 10^{-8}$ W m^{-2} K^{-4}. The second

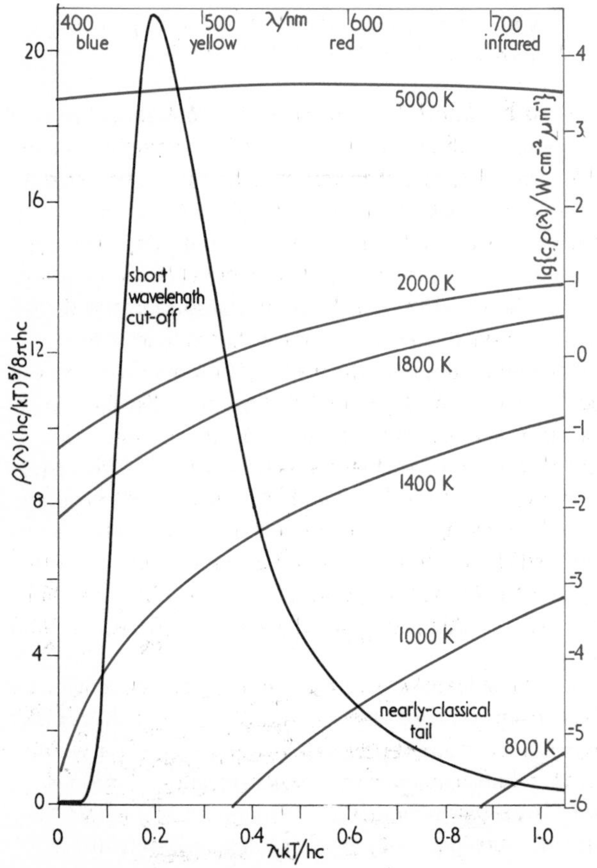

FIG. B11. Radiation density from a hot black body at different frequencies and temperatures.

observation is summarized by *Wien's displacement law,* that the wavelength of maximum intensity is inversely proportional to the temperature: $\lambda_{max} T = 2{\cdot}9$ mm K.

The notoriety of black-body radiation lies in its defeat of classical mechanics, and in its role in the inception of quantum theory. The *Rayleigh-Jeans law* was the result of applying the ideas of classical mechanics: Rayleigh, with Jeans's help, counted the number of oscillators of a particular wavelength that could be found in a cavity, and then applied °equipartition to associate an energy of kT with each mode of oscillation; the energy density at the wavelength λ was predicted to obey the rule $8\pi kT/\lambda^4$ (Fig. B11). This conforms with none of the observations mentioned above: it predicts an enormous energy density at short wavelengths (called, by Ehrenfest, the *ultraviolet catastrophe*) and an infinite energy in any enclosure (the integral of the energy over all wavelengths diverges). There is no maximum in the distribution, except the absurd one at zero wavelength. According to classical mechanics, even a glow-worm would devastate the surrounding countryside with its radiation.

Planck's quantum hypothesis was a device that saved the situation even though in the process it abolished classical mechanics. From thermodynamic arguments Planck was forced to the conclusion that he needed a single distribution law that yielded the Rayleigh-Jeans formula at low frequencies, and the Wien displacement law at high frequencies; therefore he found a formula which when approximated at low and high frequencies gave the two laws (see Box 2). On reflecting on the significance of his formula he was forced to the conclusion that it represented a situation in which a radiation mode of a specified frequency could not possess an arbitrarily small energy: a mode could be excited only in discrete amounts of energy, or *quanta*. Whereas the classical law said that if there is a mode of frequency ν in the container, then with it should be associated its due portion of energy according to equipartion, namely kT, the quantum law says that, if we have that mode, it shall be excited only if it is supplied with at least its due amount of energy, namely $h\nu$. The constant h is now referred to as *Planck's constant* ($6{\cdot}6256 \times 10^{-34}$ J s). This means that the very high frequency modes are not excited at normal temperatures because the thermal energy present in the walls of the container is insufficient to

BOX 2: Planck distribution law for black-body radiation

Energy density (energy per unit volume) in the range $d\lambda$ at the wavelength λ:

$$dU(\lambda) = \rho(\lambda)d\lambda$$

$$\rho(\lambda) = \left(\frac{8\pi hc}{\lambda^5}\right)\left\{\frac{\exp(-hc/\lambda kT)}{1-\exp(-hc/\lambda kT)}\right\}.$$

Energy density in the range $d\nu$ at the frequency ν:

$$dU(\nu) = \rho(\nu)d\nu$$

$$\rho(\nu) = \left(\frac{8\pi h\nu^3}{c^3}\right)\left\{\frac{\exp(-h\nu/kT)}{1-\exp(-h\nu/kT)}\right\}.$$

Rayleigh-Jeans law (long-wavelength, low-frequency limits of above):

$$\rho(\lambda) \sim 8\pi kT/\lambda^4 \qquad \lambda \gg hc/kT$$

$$\rho(\nu) \sim 8\pi\nu^2 kT/c^3 \qquad \nu \ll kT/h.$$

Stefan's law (total energy density $\propto T^4$):

$$U = \int_0^\infty d\lambda\rho(\lambda) = \int_0^\infty d\nu\rho(\nu) = (\sigma/c)T^4$$

$$\sigma = 5{\cdot}6697 \times 10^{-8}\ \mathrm{W\ m^{-2}\ K^{-4}}.$$

Wien's displacement law ($\lambda_{max}T$ = constant):

$$\lambda_{max}T = hc/5k = b$$

$$b = 2{\cdot}8978 \times 10^{-3}\ \mathrm{m\ K}.$$

supply them with adequate energy (see °quantum). This damping effect on the high-frequency oscillators quenches the rise of the Rayleigh-Jeans distribution at high frequencies (short wavelengths), and so it eliminates the ultraviolet catastrophe. Furthermore, it introduces a maximum into the energy distribution versus wavelength curve, and this is in accord with the Wien law at high frequencies (and the Wien constant for the maximum is found to be equal to $hc/5k$). Because of the elimination of the high-frequency excitations the total energy emitted at a temperature T is finite, and the Stefan-law dependence on T^4 is reproduced. Thus we are forced to accept the propriety of Planck's quantum hypothesis; and, since the interaction of matter and radiation is such a fundamental process, it should be no surprise that the ramifications of the hypothesis affected the whole of our appreciation of the nature of the world.

Questions. 1. What is a black body, and how may it be realized experimentally? Why is the radiation emitted through a pinhole in an otherwise closed cavity of fundamental importance? What are the changes in the frequency distribution of light emitted by a black body as its temperature is raised? State Stefan's law and Wien's law. What is the basis of the classical calculation of black-body radiation, and why is its form unacceptable? What was Planck's contribution, and what is the effect of quantization on the high-frequency oscillators? Discuss the differences between the excitation of a classical and a quantum °harmonic oscillator. Calculate the high-frequency form of the Planck distribution law (Box 2) and the short-wavelength form. From the latter show that the distribution passes through a maximum inversely proportional to T, and deduce an expression for the Wien constant, evaluating it numerically. Calculate the energy density radiated by a black body at wavelengths of 1 cm, 55 nm, and 200 nm when it is heated to 300 K, 1000 K, and 10^5 K. Suppose that the filament of an incandescent lamp is a black-body radiator (the approximation is not absurd) and calculate the temperature to which it must be raised to emit light predominantly in the visible region of the spectrum.

2. This question concerns the determination of the distribution function, and falls into two parts: the first (which we shall do) inserts the quantum hypothesis into the Boltzmann distribution to get the mean energy of a mode, and the second (which we shall not do) counts the number of modes of a particular frequency. If the energy of an oscillator is confined to the values $nh\nu$, then the probability that the oscillator has an energy $nh\nu$ is, according to Boltzmann, $\exp(-nh\nu/kT)/Z$, where Z is the partition function, or $\sum_{n=0}^{\infty}\exp(-nh\nu/kT)$. The mean energy is the sum of $[(nh\nu)\exp(-nh\nu/kT)/Z]$ over all the values of n (n = 0, 1, 2, . . .). First evaluate Z by realizing that it can be written as the sum over x^n, with x suitably chosen, and so it is a geometric progression; and then evaluate the sum over the numerator by realizing that it can be related to dZ/dT. Hence find the mean energy of a mode of wavelength $\lambda = c/\nu$. The number of modes of radiation in the range $d\lambda$ at the wavelength λ is $8\pi d\lambda/\lambda^4$; hence find the Planck distribution law. The answer is quoted in Box 2.

Further information. See *MQM* Chapter 1 for a derivation of the Planck distribution and the number of modes in a container. For the latter also see p. 41 of Heitler (1954), §2.1 of Power (1964), §1.4 of Bohm (1951), and p. 144 of Lin (1967). Black-body radiation is discussed in an historical perspective by Jammer (1966), and a recent review is that of Lin (1967). See also Ingram's *Radiation and quantum physics* (OPS 2) and §9.13 of Reif (1965) for a useful discussion. Numerical values of the Planck distribution over a wide range of temperatures and wavelengths, together with integrated intensities, will be found in the *American Institute of Physics handbook*, Gray (1972), p. 6.198 and in Abramowitz and Stegun (1965).

Bohr atom. Before the discovery of quantum mechanics, Bohr applied the principle of quantization to the problem of the structure of the °hydrogen atom. He asserted that:

(1) an electron remained in a *stationary state* until it made a transition;

(2) a transition from a stationary state of energy E_i to another of energy E_f was accompanied by the emission or absorption of radiation with a frequency ν determined by the condition $h\nu = E_f - E_i$ (this assertion is the *Bohr frequency condition*);

(3) the permitted stationary states were to be found by balancing the nuclear electrostatic attractive force against the centrifugal effect of the angular momentum of the electron in its orbit.

The quantum condition was imposed at the last stage, for Bohr asserted that

(4) the only angular momenta permitted were those whose magnitude was an integral multiple of $\hbar$.

The calculation of the energy levels done on the basis of these postulates led to an expression of the form $E = -R/n^2$, where R is the °Rydberg constant and n is the *principal °quantum number* ($n = 1, 2, \ldots$). This expression is in virtually exact agreement with experiment, and was cause for jubilation.

Refinement of this promising model proceeded in three steps. The first took into account the fact that the orbital motion occurred about the centre of mass of the system rather than about the nucleus itself: this merely involved replacing the mass of the electron in the Bohr formula by the *reduced mass* $\mu = m_e m_p/(m_e + m_p)$. The second step was taken by Sommerfeld: in the *Bohr-Sommerfeld atom* the orbits are allowed to be elliptical, and the degree of ellipticity is determined by a further quantum number k, the *azimuthal quantum number*: but the energy of the orbits was found to be independent of their eccentricity. The third improvement was also made by Sommerfeld: he incorporated relativity into the model, and found that its effect was to cause a mismatch of the ends of the elliptical orbits, so that the electron described an open orbit around the nucleus—a continuously evolving orbit that resembled a rosette. The inclusion of relativity caused the energies to depend weakly on k, and quite remarkable agreement with experiment was obtained (the numbers obtained are the same as those obtained in the °Dirac theory of the hydrogen atom).

Although the numbers are almost exact, the model of the hydrogen atom from which they are obtained is fundamentally wrong, and we are forced to the view that the agreement with experiment is an astonishing coincidence: this coincidence probably stems from the very peculiar properties of the Coulomb potential, properties that remain even in modern quantum-mechanical theories of the atom. The fallacy in the model was indicated by the later developments of quantum theory, for there it is discovered that the concept of trajectory is alien to phenomena on an atomic scale (see °uncertainty principle). Therefore it is wholly false to attempt to discuss the dynamics of a system in terms of the trajectories of its components: the Bohr orbits and the Bohr-Sommerfeld orbits are macroscopic concepts that have no meaning on the scale of the hydrogen atom. Furthermore, it is quite clear that the Bohr model is incomplete in the sense that in its postulates it virtually asserts the structure of the hydrogen atom and no justification is given for the stationarity of states and the quantization of angular momentum; these are provided much later by the theoretical structure of quantum mechanics. Nevertheless, Bohr's achievement was considerable, for it applied to a problem in mechanics a theory that had been constructed on the basis of the behaviour of radiation, and was therefore one of the first germs of the view that optical and mechanical phenomena were essentially identical.

Questions. 1. State the postulates of the Bohr theory of the hydrogen atom. Which of them conflicted with the requirements of classical mechanics? What is the form of the expression for the energy that is obtained on this model? Deduce an expression for the frequency of the transitions of the hydrogen atom: do these conform with the known °hydrogen atom spectrum? How was the original model refined? What is the significance of the quantum number k? The elliptical orbitals with $k = 0$ (which are straight lines swinging through the nucleus) were rejected as implausible: can you see the connexion of these rejected orbitals with the s-orbitals of the modern theory of the atom? The lower energy state of the Bohr theory requires the presence of an angular momentum to repel the electron from the nucleus: does the quantum-mechanical theory lead to the same conclusion? Why is the Bohr theory untenable? Discuss the role of the uncertainty principle in the Bohr theory. Why was the theory so important?
2. Deduce the energy of the hydrogen-atom stationary states on the basis of the Bohr theory. Set up an expression for the potential energy of the electron, and then relate the centrifugal force to the angular momentum. Balance the two, and then replace the angular momentum by $n\hbar$. Compare your result to the accepted expression for the °Rydberg constant.

Further information. See §1.2 of Herzberg (1944) and Chapter 2 of Pauling and Wilson (1935) for information about calculations on the hydrogen atom. For a view of the hydrogen atom in an historical perspective, see Jammer (1966).

bond. The nature of the chemical bond—the reason why atoms stick together and form molecules of a definite shape and energy—is one of the central topics and successes of the application of quantum theory to chemistry. Elementary chemistry distinguishes three kinds of bond between atoms: the *ionic* (where electrons are transferred between atoms and the bond is the electrostatic interaction between ions), the *covalent* (where electrons are donated by both partners, and shared more or less equally), and the *dative* (where one partner donates *both* electrons, which then are shared). Modern quantum chemistry shows how these three types may be considered to be special cases of a general form of bond. Elementary chemistry also ascribes the tendency to bond to the tendency of atoms to 'complete their octet' or to achieve an 'inert gas configuration'. Modern quantum chemistry interprets these rules of thumb in terms of the quantum-mechanical properties of electrons and nuclei.

Atoms group together and form molecules if by so doing the system attains a lower, more favourable energy; therefore we must seek the reason why energy is reduced when a molecule is formed. Generally the different stereochemical configurations of atoms differ considerably in energy from each other, and so the shape of the molecule is normally well defined, and corresponds to the stereochemistry that enables the system to attain its lowest energy. Conversely, a molecule falls apart into its components, or groups of components, if enough energy is injected into the structure (by a collision with another molecule or wall, or by the absorption of light), so that its total energy exceeds that of its separated components. Energy determines everything: to understand the shape and stability of a molecule we must study its energy. Why energy is important is of course a much deeper problem.

In order to assess the contributions that lead to a lowering of energy we should remember that the energy consists of two parts, kinetic energy and potential energy. A careful analysis of the contributions these make is very difficult, and quite often people ignore the contribution of kinetic energy by presuming that it can look after itself, or that the dominant contribution to binding energy is the lowering of the potential energy that occurs when electrons and nuclei are brought close together. Ignoring the kinetic energy is a dangerous game, and makes the description of chemical bonding look simpler than it really is. Nevertheless, we shall play the game because the situation has been fully analysed in only one place, to which we return later.

Given a kit consisting of two protons and one electron, where should the electron be put in an attempt to form a stable molecule (of H_2^+)? The conventional argument is that simple electrostatics suggests that the electron should be placed in the internuclear region; then the internuclear Coulombic repulsion will be overcome by the attraction between the electron and each nucleus, and the H_2^+ species will achieve stability on this account. Naturally the electron does not congregate solely on the midpoint itself, and the structure should be envisaged as a distribution of charge around the two nuclei, with a significant accumulation in the internuclear region. The addition of a second electron, to form H_2, will lead to a stronger bond if it too enters the same region of space, so that the nuclei can now stick to a double helping of opposite charge.

On the basis of the preceding analysis the structure of the hydrogen molecule may be envisaged as two nuclei surrounded by a charge cloud of two electrons, with an accumulation of charge density in the internuclear region, the bonding region. The characteristic bond length of H_2 is the point at which an equilibrium is reached between the repulsive interaction of the nuclei, which increases as the bond shortens, and the attractive interaction with the internuclear electrons; at very short bond lengths the electrons cannot accumulate in the bonding region and so the repulsion dominates. If a third electron is added to an H_2 molecule it attempts to cluster close to the nuclei, but cannot penetrate the bonding region because of the presence of the original pair of electrons (it is excluded by the °Pauli principle). It therefore congregates as a fuzzy accumulation outside the internuclear region. The force this electron exerts on the nuclei is disruptive, and so its presence tends to lengthen and weaken the bond. A fourth electron succeeds in breaking the bond.

On this description of the *covalent bond*, where the bonding electrons are provided equally by the two atoms, it is clear that two electrons give the strongest bond. Forming strong bonds is energetically favourable, and therefore atoms tend to form as many as they can without drawing on the inner, tightly bound electrons. This situation is what should be held in mind when one makes the remark that 'atoms share electrons in order to complete their octets'. Notice also that the two electrons have to occupy the same region of space to be effective in bonding, and in order to do so their spins must be opposed: this is a consequence of the °Pauli exclusion principle. This feature underlies the importance of the electron °pair in chemical bonding. Electrons do not seek to pair for some transcendental reason, nor because they lose repulsive energy by pairing—in fact it requires energy to push two electrons into the same orbital: they pair in order to attain a distribution that leads to the lowest energy for the system, and at the bottom of a stack of distributions often lies a molecule. This description of the role of an electron pair is seen very clearly in both the °molecular-orbital and °valence-bond theories of molecular structure.

In a *heteronuclear bond* (a bond between two different atoms) the situation is analogous, but is modified by the possibility that the energy will decrease if the bonding pair of electrons accumulates closer to one atom than the other: they congregate more in the vicinity of the more °electronegative atom. This situation may be envisaged in terms of prising off one of the valence electrons of the less electronegative atom (the atom with the smaller °ionization potential) and shifting it towards the atom with the larger °electron affinity. This process leads to a *polar bond,* and in one language (the valence-bond) it would be possible to say that the pure covalent bond is contaminated by ionic components. (Alternatively we might say that the molecular °wavefunction is a °superposition of covalent and ionic wavefunctions.) Atoms with the greatest electronegativity tend to be those that differ from a closed-shell configuration by only one or two electrons; and so once again we can understand that the tendency to form an octet is a manifestation of a search for the lowest energy distribution of the electrons.

When the electronegativities of the two atoms of a heteronuclear bond are very different, such as when an atom of low ionization potential (left-hand side of the periodic table) is next to an atom with a high electron affinity (right-hand side of the table) the stability gained by transferring a whole electron from one atom to the other may be very large, and the juxtaposition of the two atoms leads to the flow of an electron from one to the other, so that side by side there is a positive ion and a negative ion: these stay stuck together simply by a Coulombic interaction between the charges. This extreme case of a polar bond is the *ionic bond.* It is important to note that all ionization potentials are greater than all °electron affinities (for atoms), and therefore the Coulombic attraction between the ions provides the energy for the formation of ionic bonds.

Apart from the polarity of bonds the most significant difference between an ionic and a covalent bond is the directional properties of the latter in contrast to the lack of directional properties of the former. This arises because the Coulombic interaction between two charges is isotropic (the same in all directions), so the structures that can be formed, which are often extensive aggregates, are governed largely by the steric problem of packing together ions of various sizes: the ionic bond gives rise to rigid and extensive crystal lattices with characteristic packing patterns. In the pure covalent bond the interaction is by no means isotropic because its strength depends on the ability of an atom to provide electrons in the region between itself and its bonding neighbour. For a diatomic molecule there is no problem in principle, but as soon as three atoms are considered one encounters the reason why covalently bound structures have a geometry determined by the electronic structure of the bonding atoms rather than the geometrical problem of packing them together. Taking oxygen as an example we can understand that the molecule HO can be formed by the hydrogen and oxygen atoms each donating an electron to form a polar bond, and then a second hydrogen atom froms a second bond to yield HOH; the lowest energy configuration of this molecule occurs when the second bond is at 104·5° to the first because the oxygen atom can form the strongest bonds at that angle (see °hybridization). At this point the oxygen octet is complete, and the addition of another hydrogen atom leads to an unstable H_3O molecule (that is H_3O possesses more energy than separate $H_2O + H$). All that water can do is form a *dative bond*, where it supplies both electrons, and this it does to form H_3O^+ (in which the oxygen °lone-pair electrons donate towards a bare proton) or *aquo*-complexes with ions. The water molecule is therefore a well-defined, discrete entity. The *valence* of an atom, the number of bonds that it may form, is moderately well defined for most covalent compounds, and the stereochemistry is determined by the ability of the atom to provide electrons to attain this valence. This is very clearly brought out in the °molecular-orbital theory of molecular structure and the theory of °hybridization.

All the preceding discussion is based on the conventional view in the fourth paragraph; that, it seems reasonably certain, is a sweet seduction. There are few cases where the molecular structure has been studied in sufficient detail to enable the true source of bonding to be analysed critically, but with H_2^+ it has been possible to draw disconcerting conclusions. These conclusions run counter to most of the simple accounts of the chemical bond and, as far as I know, counter to anything to be found in textbooks. In H_2^+ the source of bonding appears to be a subtle interplay between the kinetic and potential energies of the electrons. As H^+ and H are brought together the accurate wavefunction shows that electrons are indeed shifted into the internuclear region, but that this leads to an *increase* in their potential energy, in contrast to the supposition that their potential energy would decrease if they could be shared by both nuclei. On reflection, of course, we should realize that an increase is more plausible than a decrease, because the lowest potential energy arises when the electrons are as close as they can get to one or other of the nuclei.

Where then does the bonding energy come from? First, we should note that the situation is slightly relaxed by virtue of the greater domain of freedom open to the electron when two protons are present, and consequently its kinetic energy due to its motion parallel to the bond falls; but only at first, for more complication is to come. A larger decrease in energy (increase in bonding energy) comes from a contraction which occurs in the atomic orbitals on each nucleus: this contraction enables the electron to approach the nuclei more closely, and so its potential energy falls: this contribution is very large and is the dominant change in the potential energy. On contraction there is a price to pay, because as the electron is confined to a smaller domain its °kinetic energy rises, and this almost cancels the decrease in potential energy; but not quite, and the earlier decrease in kinetic energy along the axis helps to counterbalance the change. Finally, the form of the wavefunction shows that there is also a shift of electron density from regions outside the nuclei into the bonding region as the atomic orbitals are polarized; this reduces the potential energy and increases slightly the kinetic energy. The net effect is a large decrease in the potential energy, which is dominated by the orbital contraction, and a large increase in the kinetic energy, also dominated by the orbital contraction, which does not quite succeed in winning. The overall effect is that H_2^+ has a lower energy than $H^+ + H$, and so is a stable species.

We stress that this complicated story has been elucidated on the basis of a careful study of the H_2^+ wavefunction, and might need to be modified for more complex species. But it is an excellent example of the power of myth in chemistry, and shows the importance of detailed and accurate calculations in discovering the true nature of the chemical bond.

Questions. What determines whether atoms will stick together and form a molecule? What thermodynamic quantity is the measure of the strength of a chemical bond? What happens when a large amount of energy is transferred to a molecule? How may the energy be transferred? What feature of the distribution of the electron in the hydrogen molecule accounts for its stability on a simple model? What contribution to the total energy does this description ignore? Why is the hydrogen molecule more stable than the hydrogen molecule-ion H_2^+, but H_2^- less stable than both? Can this argument be extended to the explanation of why two helium atoms do not form a stable molecule? Indeed, does it apply to the stability of bonds between all closed-shell species, for example the rare gases? What change in the distribution of the electrons occurs when a homonuclear bond is replaced by a heteronuclear bond? Is there an additional contribution to the binding energy? What determines the extent of polarization of the electrons in the bond? When does an almost pure ionic bond occur? What is the source of the stability of an ionic crystal: why does not a crystal of common salt blow apart into a gas of sodium and chlorine atoms? Why does the crystal have a definite structure? Why does covalency lead to discrete molecules, and ionic bonding to extended arrays of atoms? What determines the shape of ionic and covalent species? What determines the valency of atoms in covalent and ionic compounds? What other type of bonding leads to an extended array of atoms with a structure determined largely by packing considerations? Discuss the likely true cause of bonding in H_2^+.

Further information. See *MQM* Chapter 10 for a résumé of bonding theory and more details of its quantum theory. For a simple account of the structure of molecules see Coulson's *The shape and structure of molecules* (OCS 9) and Coulson (1961). See also Murrell, Kettle, and Tedder (1965), and for an original classic, well worth reading for the way it teaches one to think about the application of quantum theory to real chemical problems, see Pauling (1960). A close analysis of the nature of the reduction of energy when a bond is formed has been given by Ruedenberg (1962), and this is extended with a careful discussion of the structure of H_2^+ by Feinberg, Ruedenberg, and Mehler (1970). See in particular the analysis on p. 54 of this reference. For more information about the way that the concepts mentioned here are developed in quantum mechanics, and therefore made amenable to quantitative calculation, see the entries on °molecular-orbital theory, °valence-bond theory, °antibonding, °electronegativity, °hybridization. One type of bonding ignored in the discussion was that responsible for the structure of metals: see °band theory of metals for a short account.

bond order. The bond order is a measure of the single-, double-, or triple-bond character of a bond. In °valence-bond theory it is determined by calculating the proportion of single, double, and triple bonds in the contributing structures. In molecular-orbital theory, which now provides the more common definition, it is defined in a slightly more subtle manner. The basis of the definition (which is enough for a qualitative understanding) relies on the cancellation of the effects of occupied bonding and °antibonding orbitals. Thus in H_2, where one σ-bond is fully occupied, the σ-bond order is unity; in He_2, where the σ-bond and its antibonding counterpart are both fully occupied, the bond order is zero. In ethene a σ-bond and a π-bond are fully occupied, and so the overall bond order is 2 (a 'double bond'), and in oxygen one π-bond is cancelled by a π-antibond (see °molecular-orbital theory for details) and the rump, one σ- and one π-bond, gives an order 2. This idea may now be made more sophisticated in order to accommodate fractional bond orders.

In the °LCAO description of molecular orbitals a bond is formed when two atomic orbitals on neighbouring atoms overlap and interfere constructively. If the coefficient of the orbital on atom A is c_A and on atom B is c_B, then the contribution to the bonding will be proportional to the product c_Ac_B. The order of the bond between A and B is then defined as the sum of c_Ac_B over all the occupied orbitals. When c_A and c_B are simultaneously large for a particular orbital a large contribution to the total order results (but it cannot exceed unity); when c_A and c_B have opposite signs, corresponding to an °antibonding character between A and B, the product is negative—it subtracts from the overall result and so reduces the bond order. As an example, each C—C bond in °benzene has a contribution of $\frac{2}{3}$ from the π-orbitals, and 1 from the σ-orbitals, and so each bond is of order $1\frac{2}{3}$. The C—C bond in ethane is of order 1, in ethene 2, and in ethyne 3, in accord with a normal chemical appreciation of the order of the bonds.

One principal application of the quantitative definition of bond order is to the estimation of bond lengths, especially of C—C bonds. An empirical relation has been found between the length R and order b_{CC} of C—C bonds, and the length satisfies the rough rule $R_{CC} = 1{\cdot}665 - 0{\cdot}1398\,(1 + b_{CC})$, with R_{CC} in ångströms (see Table 2). The correlation should take into account the different hybridizations of the atoms involved in the bond; the effect of so doing is that for a given bond order the bond length decreases by 0·04 Å on going from sp^3 to sp^2 hybrids, and then by a further 0·04 Å on going to sp-hybrids. A further application of bond order is to the definition of °free valence.

Questions. What is the valence-bond definition of bond order? Calculate the bond order in °benzene on this basis, first on the assumption that only Kekulé structures contribute, and then on the assumption that 20 per cent of the total structure is Dewar-like. What is the molecular-orbital definition of bond order? What contribution does an antibonding orbital make? What is the bond order in H_2 and He_2? What is the bond order in H_2^+? On the basis of the molecular-orbital coefficients given in Fig. B10 on p. 20 calculate the bond order for benzene, benzene$^-$, and benzene$^+$. Estimate the bond length of naphthalene in which the π-bond orders are as follows: 0·725 (for 1-2), 0·603 (for 2-3), 0·554 (for 1-9), and 0·518 (for 9-10).

Further information. See Coulson's *The shape and structure of molecules* (OCS 9) and Coulson (1961). A helpful and lengthy discussion is provided in §6.7 of Streitweiser (1961). See also Coulson (1959) in the Kekulé symposium and Pilar (1968).

Born-Oppenheimer approximation. The Born-Oppenheimer approximation assumes that the electronic distribution in a molecule can be evaluated in a static nuclear framework. The assumption is based on the great differences of mass of the electrons and the nuclei: it is assumed that if the nuclei move the electrons can adjust their distribution instantaneously to take into account the new potential, and that the nuclei are insensitive to the rapid fluctuations of the electrons in their orbitals.

The practical effect of the approximation is that it is possible to simplify both the discussion and the calculation of molecular electronic structures. Instead of having to treat all the particles in the molecule on an equal footing, it is possible, according to the approximation, to set the nuclei into a frozen conformation, and then to calculate the electronic energy and distribution corresponding to it. The nuclei can then be moved to a new conformation, and the electronic calculation repeated. In this way it is possible in principle to calculate the energy for all possible arrangements of the nuclei, and then to find the one corresponding to the lowest energy—the stable conformation of the molecule.

The Born-Oppenheimer approximation makes the *molecular potential-energy curve* a meaningful quantity: as the nuclear conformation is changed the molecular energy also changes, and the dependence of the energy on the conformation is the molecular potential-energy curve. For a diatomic molecule the curve is a plot of energy against bond length, and for a polyatomic molecule the curve is a complicated potential-energy surface. Such a curve corresponds to a potential energy because if the molecule is released from a non-equilibrium conformation it will spring back into equilibrium (or at least vibrate around the equilibrium point), and so the rise of energy with changing conformation corresponds to the acquisition by the molecule of a potential energy. It should be clear that this description relies upon the validity of the Born-Oppenheimer approximation, for only then are we able to talk about the molecular energy as a function of the parameter determining the conformation of the molecule (bond length for a diatomic). If the Born-Oppenheimer approximation were to fail (if we were dealing with light or rapidly moving nuclei) the notion of a potential-energy surface would fail, and so too would the idea of bond length and bond angle. In practice, the approximation fails slightly, and small spectroscopic consequences are observed.

Questions. State the Born-Oppenheimer approximation. Upon what is it based? When might the approximation fail? What simplification does it introduce? Discuss the concept of a molecular potential-energy curve for a molecule. Calculate the relative velocities of an electron and a proton each with a kinetic energy of 100 kJ mol^{-1}.

Further information. See *MQM* Chapter 9 for a brief discussion; for an account of the approximation with some mathematics see p. 252 of Slater (1963). For spectral consequences of the failure of the approximation see King (1964). The original paper is Born and Oppenheimer (1927).

boson. A boson is a particle possessing an intrinsic °spin °angular momentum characterized by an *integral* spin quantum number, including zero. Examples include the deuteron ^2H ($I = 1$), the ^4He nucleus, or α-particle, the ^4He atom ($I = 0$), and the °photon ($I = 1$). Bosons are not restricted by the °Pauli *exclusion* principle (in contrast to °fermions), and any number may occupy a single quantum state. They do obey the °Pauli principle itself, which demands that a °wavefunction be symmetrical under the interchange of any pair of identical bosons. Because many bosons may occupy a single state, at low temperatures peculiar properties arise; these include superfluidity and superconductivity (where pairs of electrons, fermions, behave like bosons). The operation of °lasers depends on the °photon being a boson, for an intense monochromatic beam of light consists of a large number of photons in the same state.

Further information. See °spin and the °Pauli principle for a further discussion. The table of nuclear properties on p. 277 reveals at a glance which nuclei are bosons and which fermions. The way bosons occupy states is taken into account by the Bose-Einstein statistics which are discussed in Gasser and Richards' *Entropy and energy levels* (OCS 19), and in Chapter 6 of Davidson (1962), §9.6 of Reif (1965), and Chapter 22 of Hill (1960). For a discussion of the fundamental role of the distinction between fermions and bosons see the article by Peierls in Salem and Wigner (1972) and also see Pauli (1940). For accounts of superfluidity see Chapter 15 of Rice (1967), and for superconductivity see Chapter 11 of Kittel (1971) and Rose-Innes and Rhoderick (1969). The question of whether the fermion ^3He can show superfluid characteristics (if two stick together) is discussed by Osheroff, Gully, Richardson, and Lee (1972). Peierls (loc. cit.) also discusses the evidence for all particles being either bosons or fermions.

bracket notation; bra and ket. The bracket notation, which by virtue of the division $\langle bra|c|ket\rangle$ gives its name to the entities known as *bras* and *kets*, was introduced by Dirac. The state of a system whose wavefunction is $\psi_n(r)$ is represented by the ket $|n\rangle$, and the conjugate $\psi_n^*(r)$ by the bra $\langle n|$. The integral $\int d\tau\psi_m^*(r)\psi_n(r)$ is implied by the symbol $\langle m|n\rangle$, and the integral $\int d\tau\psi_m^*(r)\hat{\Omega}\psi_n(r)$ by the bracket $\langle m|\hat{\Omega}|n\rangle$, $\hat{\Omega}$ being some °operator. This elegant notation shows very clearly the connexion of wave mechanics with °matrix mechanics, and enables the whole of quantum theory to be put on deep structural foundations, for the kets may be interpreted as vectors in a special kind of space (Hilbert space).

Further information. See *MQM* Chapter 4 for the use of the notation. An account has been given in §6 of the book by Dirac (1958) and discussed further by Jauch in Chapter 9 of Salem and Wigner (1972). The subject is a component of the structure known as *transformation theory* or *representation theory*: see Chapter 4 of Davydov (1965), Roman (1965), von Neumann (1955), Katz (1965), Kaempffer (1965), and Jauch (1968).

branch. The °rotational transitions that occur when a molecule makes a °vibrational transition give rise to a structure in the spectrum which can be grouped into *branches*: when the rotational state of the molecule changes from J to $J-1$ the lines constitute the *P-branch;* when J is unchanged the lines constitute the *Q-branch*; and when J changes from J to $J+1$ the lines constitute the *R-branch*. In °Raman spectra the vibrational transitions may be accompanied by changes of ± 2 in the rotational quantum number: the resulting lines form the *O-branch* and the *S-branch* (for $J \longrightarrow J-2$ and $J \longrightarrow J+2$ respectively). The Q-branch of vibration-rotation spectra is absent when the molecule lacks a component of angular momentum about its symmetry axis: thus almost all diatomic molecules show no Q-branch (the exceptions are those with a component of orbital electronic angular momentum about the internuclear axis, such as NO). The appearance

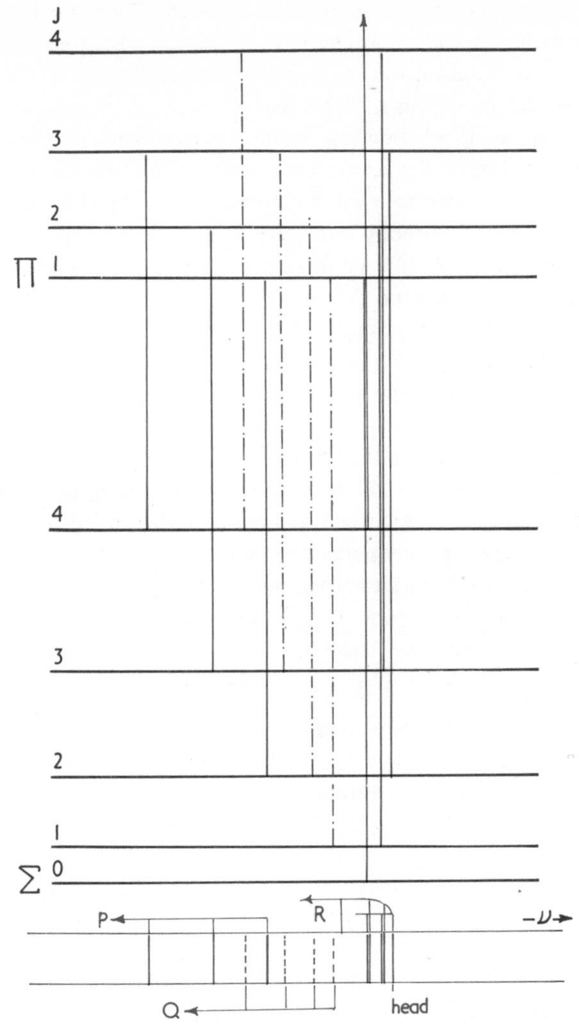

FIG. B12. Formation of P-, Q-, R-, branches; note the head on the R-branch which arises when the rotational constant in the upper level is smaller than in the lower.

and source of the P-, Q-, and R-branches are illustrated in Fig. B12, and the energies of the transitions are given in Box 3.

When the upper and lower vibrational states have different moments of inertia (which is especially likely when the upper vibrational state belongs to an electronically excited molecule), the spacing of the branch lines changes with the value of J. In a diatomic molecule it is common for the moment of inertia of the upper state to exceed that of the lower, and in this case the lines of the R-branch converge as J increases, and may even pass through a *head* at high frequency. The reason for this behaviour can be traced to the $(B' - B'')J^2$ term in Box 3, which outweighs $(3B' - B'')J$ at high J. An R-branch showing this behaviour is said to *degrade to the red.* When the moment of inertia is smaller in the upper state the P-branch shows the head and *degrades to the violet.*

The method of *combination differences* is used to extract the °rotational constants of the upper and lower states. Choosing the appropriate pairs of lines in the R- and P-branches (see Box 3) and plotting their energy differences against J'' gives B' or B'' from the slope of the line.

Questions. What is meant by a branch in a vibrational spectrum? What is the classification of the branches? To what rotational transitions do they correspond? When does a molecule show a Q-branch? Why should the Q-branch consist of a

BOX 3: Branches

Notation: J' rotational quantum number of upper states
J'' rotational quantum number of lower states
B' rotational constant of upper state
B'' rotational constant of lower state
$h\nu$ energy of vibrational transition.

R-branch (high energy; $\Delta J = +1; J' = J'' + 1$)

$$\Delta E = h\nu + 2B' + (3B' - B'')J'' + (B' - B'')J''^2 = h\nu + R(J'')$$

Q-branch ($\Delta J = 0; J' = J''$)

$$\Delta E = h\nu + (B' - B'')J' + (B' - B'')J'^2 = h\nu + Q(J')$$

P-branch (low energy; $\Delta J = -1; J' = J'' - 1$)

$$\Delta E = h\nu - (B' + B'')J'' + (B' - B'')J''^2 = h\nu + P(J'')$$

If $B' < B''$ the R-branch may form a head; if $B' > B''$ the P-branch may form the head.

Combination differences

$$R(J'') - P(J'') = 4B'(J'' + \tfrac{1}{2})$$

$$R(J'' - 1) - P(J'' + 1) = 4B''(J'' + \tfrac{1}{2}).$$

set of very closely spaced lines? On the basis that the energy levels of a rotating diatomic molecule are given by the expression $E(\nu, J) = (\nu + \frac{1}{2})\hbar\omega + B_\nu J(J+1)$, comment on why the rotational constant B should be labelled with the vibrational quantum number ν, and deduce expressions for the energy of the transitions of the P-, Q-, and R-branches of a rotating molecule. What spectral information can be obtained by a study of the branch structure? Now suppose that B depends on the electronic state of the molecule. Deduce the expressions given in Box 3 for a transition involving electronic, vibrational, and rotational excitation, and find the value of J for which a head may be formed (assume first $I' > I''$ and then $I' < I''$, I being the moment of inertia).

Further information. See *MQM* Chapter 10 for a discussion of rotational structure. For an account of the rotation-vibration spectra of molecules, examples of branch structure, and an account of the information that they can provide, see Chapter 4 of Wheatley (1968), Barrow (1962), Whiffen (1972), King (1964), and Herzberg (1950).

Brillouin's theorem. Singly excited states of closed-shell molecules do not mix directly with the ground state. (Like most statements, this can be made to sound more complicated; for those who enjoy such sounds we may state the theorem as follows: if a °matrix element of the electron-electron Coulomb interaction is calculated between a closed-shell °configuration of a molecule and a configuration differing by the excitation of a single electron, then that matrix element is zero.)

The delight of this theorem will be found in the simplification of °configuration interaction improvements to °self-consistent field calculations, because it implies that the singly excited configurations cannot contaminate closed-shell ground states by mixing directly into them. But do not interpret that as meaning that there is no mixing at all with singly excited configurations, because these may still mix by an indirect process involving interaction with an intermediate state. In some cases, indeed, it is found that the indirect route is so effective that the singly excited configurations are very important.

It should be appreciated that the existence of Brillouin's theorem implies the stability of the ground state as calculated by self-consistent methods: if it were false then the ground state could be strongly perturbed by close-lying singly excited configurations; but as it is true, direct mixing occurs with only relatively distant multiply excited levels, and only indirectly with the singly excited levels.

Further information. See §6·3 of Richards and Horsley (1970) for a simple introduction and proof of the theorem, and Slater (1963) p. 141 and Appendix 4 for a slightly longer discussion and proof. See Brillouin (1933).

C

character. In chemical applications of °group theory a °symmetry operation is generally represented by a °matrix. The *character* $\chi(R)$ of the operation R is the sum of the diagonal elements (trace or spur) of the matrix. (All these names are interrelated: *Spur* is the German for spoor, hence trace and character.) Those who know the basic features of group theory may wish to be reminded of the following facts:

(1) symmetry operations in the same class possess the same character in an irreducible representation of the group;

(2) the characters of different irreducible representations of a group are orthogonal (Note 2 in Box 4);

(3) the character of an operation is invariant under a similarity transformation;

(4) the character of a reducible representation of a group is equal to the sum of the characters of the irreducible representations into which it is decomposable (Note 3 in Box 4);

(5) the characters may be combined into the form of a projection operator which when applied to an arbitrary function projects out a component that is a basis for an irreducible representation of the group (Note 4 in Box 4);

(6) the character of the identity operation in a particular irreducible representation is equal to the dimension of that representation; the dimension of the representation is equal to the degeneracy of the basis of the representation.

These properties are summarized in mathematical terms in Box 4; further information is given in Further information, and a few useful character tables are listed in Table 3 on p. 266–267.

Further information. A sketch of the content of °group theory will be found under that heading; details of its content, method, and application will be found in *MQM* Chapter 6, and examples of the way it is applied to problems of molecular structure and properties in Chapters 9, 10, and 11. A list of character tables for all the common point groups, and some of the uncommon ones, with some simple notes on how to apply them, has been prepared by Atkins, Child, and Phillips (1970). For a thorough analysis see Cotton (1963), Bishop (1973), Tinkham (1964), and Bradley and Cracknell (1972), especially for solids. Books introducing the idea of group theory are listed under that heading.

BOX 4: Character

1. *Definition* $\chi^{(i)}(R) \equiv \mathrm{tr}\, \mathrm{D}^{(i)}(R) \equiv \sum_{\mu} D^{(i)}_{\mu\mu}(R)$

   $\chi^{(i)}(R)$ is the character of the operation R in the representation $\Gamma^{(i)}$, in which the operation R is represented by the matrix $\mathrm{D}^{(i)}(R)$.

2. *Orthogonality* $\sum_{R} \chi^{(i)}(R)^{*}\chi^{(j)}(R) = h\delta_{ij}$

   h is the order (the number of elements) of the group.

3. *Decomposition* of representation Γ

$$\Gamma = \sum_{i} a_i \Gamma^{(i)}, \quad a_i = (1/h)\sum_{R}\chi^{(i)}(R)^{*}\chi(R).$$

4. *Projection operator* for basis $f^{(i)}$ of $\Gamma^{(i)}$ from a general function f

$$p^{(i)}f = f^{(i)} \quad p^{(i)} = (\ell_i/h)\sum_{R}\chi^{(i)}(R)^{*}R$$

   ℓ_i is the dimension of $\Gamma^{(i)}$.

5. *Selection rules.* The integral $\int d\tau f^{(i)*}\Omega^{(j)}f^{(k)}$ disappears unless $\Gamma^{(i)}$ occurs in the decomposition of $\Gamma^{(j)} \times \Gamma^{(k)}$.

charge density. There are two sorts of charge density: one is the density of charge at a particular point in an atom or molecule, and the other is the charge that may be associated with a particular atom in a molecule. The former may be determined if the °wavefunction is known, for the probability of finding an electron in a small volume element $d\tau$ surrounding the point **r** is simply $|\psi(\mathbf{r})|^2 d\tau$. Since an electron carries the charge $-e$ it follows that the amount of charge in this region is $-e|\psi(\mathbf{r})|^2 d\tau$. The charge density (charge per unit volume) at the point **r** is therefore $-e|\psi(\mathbf{r})|^2$. This charge density may be used for a variety of purposes, for example in the evaluation of the °Coulomb integral or in the calculation of X-ray scattering properties of atoms.

The other definition lays a much coarser grid on the molecule: it does not seek to know all the intimate details of the distribution of the electron at each point of space. The charge density in a molecule generally means the amount of charge (or the density of electrons less the number of nuclear charges) on each atom in the molecule. Thus in a homonuclear diatomic there is zero charge density on each atom because the electrons are equally divided between the atoms, and the nuclear charge exactly cancels the electronic charge. In a polar molecule electrons may accumulate closer to the more °electronegative atom; then the charge density is not uniform.

Charge density is often calculated from a wavefunction that has been written as a °linear combination of atomic orbitals. If the amplitude of an orbital in a filled molecular orbital is c_A, so that the proportion of that atomic orbital in the molecular orbital is $|c_A|^2$, then that orbital contributes $-e|c_A|^2$ to the charge density on atom A if it is occupied by a single electron. The total charge density on atom A is calculated by summing all such terms for the occupied orbitals on the atom. The charge density may be used to calculate the °dipole moment of the molecule, and in discussions of its reactivity.

The analysis of the distribution of an electron in terms of its population of atomic orbitals is known as *population analysis.*

Questions. What are the two definitions of charge density? What is meant by population analysis? How may the charge density at an atom be calculated if the molecular structure is known? The wavefunction for the 1s-orbital of atomic °hydrogen is $\psi_{1s}(r) = (1/\pi a_0^3)^{1/2}\exp(-r/a_0)$: what is the charge density at a point r? What is the total charge density of the atom? The wavefunction for the hydrogen molecule ion is $(1/\sqrt{2})[\psi_{1s}(r_{a1}) + \psi_{1s}(r_{b1})]$, where r_{a1} is the distance of electron 1 from nucleus a and r_{b1} its distance from nucleus b (note that the molecular orbital is not accurately °normalized: does it matter?): what is the charge density on each atom? What is the charge density on each atom in the °benzene molecule?

Further information. See °alternant hydrocarbon for a further point concerning the Coulson-Rushbrooke theorem and charge density; see also °dipole moment for the way the concept is applied. °Bond order is a related concept of population analysis. A discussion of charge density will be found in Coulson (1961); Pilar (1968), McGlynn, Vanquickenborne, Kinoshita, and Carroll (1972). Tables of molecular-orbital parameters have been prepared by Coulson and Streitweiser (1965). See also Streitweiser (1961), Salem (1966), Pople and Beveridge (1970), and Murrell and Harget (1972).

closure approximation. The expressions that appear when in order to calculate a molecular property one indulges in second-order °perturbation theory normally contain sums over all the excited states of the system, and to incorporate them properly it is necessary to know the energy of every excited state and the wavefunction for each. Normally this is an impossible task because neither the excited-state energies nor the wavefunctions are known at all accurately. When an exact answer is not required, for example, when an order of magnitude of a physical quantity is sufficient or when it is desired to see in a general way how the property depends on various aspects of the molecule, it is possible to make the *closure approximation.* This consists of pretending that all the excited states that mix into the ground state have the same energy. The propriety of this we shall ignore for the moment; but its advantage is that expressions of the form $\sum_n M_{0n}N_{n0}/(E_n - E_0)$, which reference to Box 16 on p. 172 shows to be central to perturbation theory, are replaced by $(1/\Delta)\sum_n M_{0n}N_{n0}$ where Δ is the mean excitation energy. This expression may be developed further by recognizing that it has the form of a °matrix product (but see Questions); and so the second-order perturbation expression reduces to $(MN)_{00}/\Delta$. In order to evaluate this one needs to calculate only the ground-state °expectation value of the product MN, and no knowledge at all of the nature or the energies of the excited states is required. The step from the sum over $M_{0n}N_{n0}$ to $(MN)_{00}$ is the 'closure' that gives the approximation its name.

But what price have we paid? The error in the method is the absurdity that all the excited states have the same energy. When they all lie close together (as in some sense is true in the °hydrogen atom, see Fig. G3 on p. 86) the approximation is not ludicrous. In other cases the method can be justified weakly by saying that the value of Δ is to be chosen as a parameter which relates the true sum to the quantity we can evaluate $(MN)_{00}$; the parameter is then varied in a plausible way to simulate the effect of modifications to the molecular structure.

Questions. What is the source of the difficulty of using perturbation theory to calculate molecular properties, and how does the closure approximation circumvent it? When is the closure approximation plausible? The sum over the excited states in the perturbation expression is not really a true matrix sum because, according to Box 16 on p. 172, the ground state has to be omitted; show that the closure approximation really leads to an expression with $(MN)_{00} - M_{00}N_{00}$ in the numerator, and so only the ground-state properties are required even with this correction. When M and N are identical interpret the numerator in terms of fluctuations in the property M (interpret the numerator as a mean-square property). Discuss the closure approximation in terms of its application to the calculation of electric °polarizabilites, where more information will be found. Show, in particular, that the polarizability of a molecule should increase with its size.

Further information. See *MQM* Chapter 10 for a discussion and Chapter 11 for applications of the closure approximation to the calculation and discussion of the electric and magnetic properties of molecules. Further applications are outlined by Davies (1967), who underlines, on his p. 47, the remark made by McLachlan (1960) about possible limitations on the applicability of the closure approximation.

chemical shift. In a °nuclear magnetic resonance (n.m.r.) experiment an external magnetic field is adjusted until the energy required to invert a nucleus (to realign its magnetic moment) is equal to the energy of the °photons in the electromagnetic field bathing the sample: most efficient exchange of energy occurs when the nuclear energy levels are in °resonance with the radiation field. The nuclear magnetic energy depends on the *local* magnetic field rather than the applied field, and these may differ because the applied field is able to induce extra local fields in the vicinity of the nuclei. For a given applied field nuclei in different chemical environments experience different but characteristic local fields; therefore they come into resonance with the radiation at different values of the applied field. Different groups of nuclei therefore give rise to absorption lines at different magnetic fields, and since the n.m.r. spectrum is a plot of the absorption against applied field, different molecules, and even different groups on

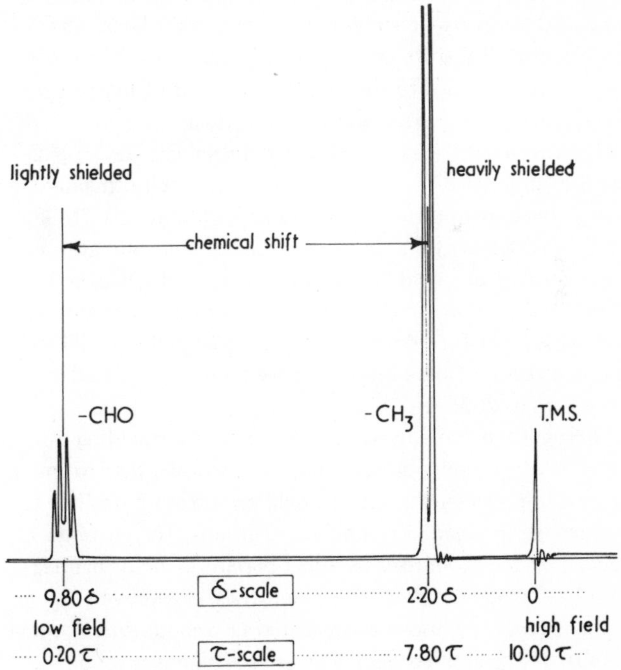

FIG. C1. The 60 MHz n.m.r. spectrum of acetaldehyde with TMS added as reference. The δ- and the τ-scales for the chemical shift of CHO and CH_3 are idicated. Note the fine structure.

the same molecule, give rise to absorptions in different regions of the spectrum (Fig. C1). The separation of the absorption lines is the *chemical shift.*

We deal first with the scales on which chemical shifts are measured. The separation of the resonances is measured in hertz (Hz, cycles per second), but, because the local field depends upon the strength of the applied field, to quote a separation is insufficient. Therefore the separation is divided by the mean frequency, or, what is effectively the same, the frequency of the stimulating field ν_0. If one proton resonates at a frequency ν_i and another at ν_j, the value of $\delta_{ij} = (\nu_i - \nu_j)/\nu_0$ is quoted as the chemical shift on the *δ-scale*. Since the separation is generally no larger than about 1 kHz, and the spectrometer operating frequency is of the order of 100 MHz, the chemical-shift scale extends up to about 10^{-5}. It is convenient therefore to express chemical shifts as parts per million (p.p.m.), and so a value of 1 p.p.m. implies that two lines are separated by 100 Hz in a spectrometer operating at 100 MHz, and by 60 Hz in a spectrometer operating at 60 MHz. The absolute chemical shift, the shift of the resonance of a proton in a molecule relative to the bare proton, is of little practical interest, and a scale often adopted sets the protons in tetramethyl silane (Me_4Si, TMS) at the origin of the chemical-shift scale ($\delta = 0$, by definition); heavily shielded protons have small δ values and resonate close to the TMS line; lightly shielded protons have large δ values and resonate well to low-field of the TMS line. Another scale is the *τ-scale*, in which TMS is set at $\tau = 10$; it follows that the scales are related by $\tau = 10 - \delta$. When the τ value is large the nuclei are heavily screened. Some representative τ values are listed in Table 4 on p. 268.

What are the contributions to the chemical shielding of a proton? All the contributions may be ascribed either to the currents induced by the applied field on the atom itself or to the currents induced in neighbouring groups. The currents induced on the atom may be either paramagnetic or diamagnetic (see °magnetic properties), and these respectively augment (*deshield*, move to smaller τ) or oppose (*shield*, move to larger τ) the applied field. The general explanation of °magnetic properties shows that the paramagnetic current is small when the excited states of an atom are high in energy, and this is the case in the hydrogen atom. For other atoms in molecules there are several states that lie quite close to the ground state, and in them the paramagnetic effects can dominate the diamagnetic. Diamagnetic currents are independent of the availability of excited states and so always contribute to the shielding (but might not dominate it).

When the currents are induced in a neighbouring group the proton experiences an additional field which may be ascribed to the induced magnetic dipole moment on the neighbour. Thus if the susceptibility of the neighbouring group is χ_m in the direction of the applied field, the latter induces a magnetic moment $\chi_m B$ which is a source of field at the neighbouring proton. Such a dipolar field has a $(1-3\cos^2\theta)/R^3$ dependence (see Fig. C2), and so the orientation of the proton and the induced moment are of crucial importance in determining whether the interaction is shielding or deshielding; the sign of the shift also depends on the sign of the susceptibility. Furthermore, for a tumbling molecule the local-field correction disappears unless the magnetic susceptibility of the neighbouring group is anisotropic, and so the shift is proportional to this anisotropy. Two famous cases are illustrated

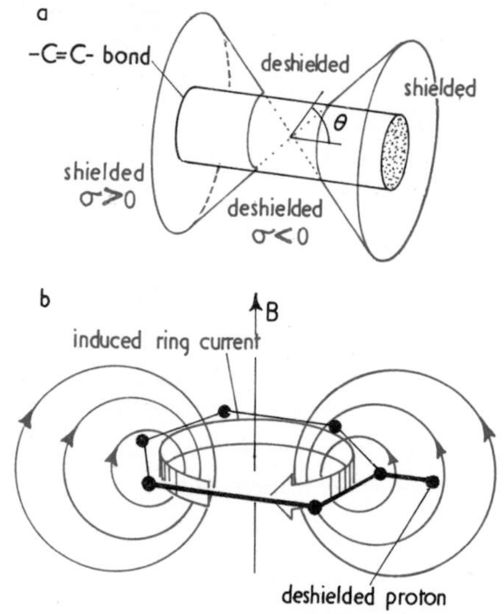

FIG. C2. (a) Shows the regions of positive and negative chemical shift in the neighbourhood of a double bond. If $\chi_{\parallel}$ and $\chi_{\perp}$ are the magnetic susceptibilities parallel and perpendicular to the bond the shielding constant varies as $\sigma \simeq (\chi_{\parallel} - \chi_{\perp})(1-3\cos^2\theta)/3R^3$. (b) Shows the ring current contribution to the chemical shift of ring protons in benzene.

in Fig. C2: the position of the resonance in the protons near a C=C double bond is determined largely by the magnetic moment induced in the π-electrons of the bond. The effect of the field this moment generates is to shield or deshield protons in the vicinity, depending on whether they lie respectively inside or outside a double cone of half-angle $54^\circ\ 44'$ (at which angle $1-3\cos^2\theta = 0$). The other example is benzene, where the proton shift to low field arises largely from the ability of the applied field to generate a *ring current* when it is perpendicular to the plane of the molecule.

The calculation of the chemical shift normally concentrates on the calculation of the ***shielding constant***. This relates the local field to the applied field B through $B(\text{local}) = (1-\sigma)B$. When σ is negative the local field exceeds the applied field (deshielding), and the nucleus resonates at low field; when σ is positive the local field is less than the applied, the nucleus is shielded, and the resonance occurs to high field. Just a little care is needed to relate a positive or negative shielding constant to a diamagnetic or paramagnetic current because the neighbouring-group effect depends, as we have seen, on the orientation of the molecule, and, depending on the orientation, either sign of the shielding constant can arise from either sign of the current.

Questions. 1. What is the meaning of the term 'chemical shift'? Is it dependent on the magnitude of the applied field? Is the separation of the lines due to protons in different chemical environments likely to be smaller or greater in a large applied field than in a small field? What happens to the separation when the field is changed from 14 kG to 50 kG? Is there any advantage in doing n.m.r. spectroscopy at high magnetic fields? What is the significance of the statements 'the protons resonate at $\delta_{TMS} = 2$' and 'the protons resonate at 2τ'? What is the significance of a high τ value? Put the following proton resonances in order of increasing field: C_6H_6, CH_3I, CH_3OH, C_6H_{12} (see Table 4). What is the source of the differences between the local field and the applied field? Under what circumstances is there a deshielding effect at the proton? What is the role of the neighbouring group of a proton? Why is it possible to get both positive and negative chemical shifts from both paramagnetic and diamagnetic currents in the neighbouring group? The magnetic susceptibility of the benzene ring in a direction perpendicular to the plane is $-9{\cdot}5 \times 10^{-5}$ and parallel to the ring it is $-3{\cdot}5 \times 10^{-5}$; calculate the chemical shift at the benzene protons using the formula in the caption of Fig. C2; calculate the shift of a proton at a point 3 Å above the centre of the ring. What is the shielding constant in each case?
2. Derive an expression for the chemical shift of the protons in benzene that takes into account the anisotropy of the magnetic susceptibility of the ring and the free rotation of the molecule, and show that the effect of the ring current would vanish if the anisotropy were zero. Assume that the field induces a magnetic dipole moment at the centre of the ring.

Further information. See *MQM* Chapter 11 for a detailed account of some of the steps that are needed to calculate the chemical shift of molecules in terms of the fields and currents induced by applied fields. For an account of the role of the chemical shift in n.m.r. see McLauchlan's *Magnetic resonance* (OCS 1). Further details will be found in Lynden-Bell and Harris (1969), Carrington and McLachlan (1967), Pople, Schneider, and Bernstein (1959), Memory (1968), Emsley, Feeney, and Sutcliffe (1965), and Abragam (1961). All these books deal with the calculation and interpretation of n.m.r. spectra in terms of the chemical shift; see also Further information in °nuclear magnetic resonance. The calculation required in Question 2 is done on p. 59 of Carrington and McLachlan (1967). The nature of the ring current is discussed by these authors and by Davies (1967).

colour. A material is coloured if it is able to absorb a band of wavelengths from incident white light or if it is able to scatter light of one frequency more effectively than another. If we discount the blue of the sky the more common mechanism is the former. Visible light spans the region from 700 nm (red) through yellow (at about 580 nm), green (530 nm), blue (470 nm) to violet (420 nm). The energies of the photons vary from 1·7 eV to 3·0 eV over this range (see Table 5), and therefore for a system to absorb in the visible it must possess excited states within this distance from the ground state. When red is absorbed (by virtue of the presence of low-lying excited states) the object appears blue; when blue or violet is absorbed it appears red. Low-lying energy levels are not particularly common among living systems, and so the predominant colours of naturally occuring substances tend to be towards the red end of the spectrum. This is part of the reason for the relative scarcity of purple cows, or bright blue dogs, plants, etc. Furthermore, if living systems had low-lying excited states they would be uncomfortably liable to photolysis. Chlorophyll, however, is specially constructed to cope with this situation, and so green is ubiquitous. The most intense colours are due to °electric dipole transitions. A *chromophore* is a group whose presence endows colour on a molecule. An important organic chromophore is the C=C double bond, in which the relevant transition is of an electron from the π-bond to the °antibonding π^*-orbital (a $\pi^*\leftarrow\pi$, 'pi-to-pi-star', transition). The carbonyl group (C=O) is also important: the relevant transition is from a nonbonding °lone pair on the oxygen to the π^*-orbital (an 'n-to-pi-star', $\pi^*\leftarrow$n, transition). This transition is electric-dipole forbidden (see °selection rules and °oscillator strength), and so is generally weaker than the $\pi^*\leftarrow\pi$ transition.

Transition-metal complexes are often coloured: this is a consequence of the presence of the d-electrons and their small energy splittings arising from the °crystal field of the surrounding ligands.The intensity of the colour is low because d-d transitions are forbidden by the °selection rules in operation, and the intensity is due to a °vibronic transition. More intense colours in the same systems (such as the characteristic intense purple of permanganate, or manganate (VII) ion, MnO_4^-) are often due to *charge-transfer transitions,* in which electrons migrate from the metal ion to the ligand or vice versa. Such transitions possess a large °transition dipole moment.

Insulators are often colourless and, when crystalline, transparent: think of diamond. This is because the electrons are tightly bound to the atoms and are available neither for conduction nor for light absorption (the conduction °band of diamond can be attained only by supplying 5·3 eV of energy). As the binding gets less tight, or as the conduction band approaches the filled band, colour begins to appear: the band gap in CdS_2 is 2·42 eV, and hence it is a yellow-orange solid (absorbing in the blue); silicon, with a band gap of only 1·14 eV, absorbs all frequencies and has a metallic lustre.

Metals are characterized by a shining surface when freshly cut, and this hardly seems compatible with the remark that they absorb all the incident light. The answer lies in the fact that they also radiate all the incident light. This can be envisaged in terms of the high mobility of the electrons in a metal—an oscillating light wave approaches the surface, its electric field drives the surface electrons back and forth, and the incident light is quenched. But the oscillating surface electrons themselves give rise to a radiated light field, and so almost all the light is reflected. In the case of some metals (copper and gold are familiar examples) there are true absorption bands in the visible region, and both these metals extract some blue light (and get hotter in the process).

Two examples of colouring arising through scattering may be mentioned briefly. The sky is blue because blue light is scattered more strongly than red; therefore more of the sun's blue radiation is scattered down to us than is its red (except in the late evening, when the sun appears ruddy because someone further west is getting its blue light for his daytime sky). The reason why clouds appear white even though their presence is also seen by a scattering of incident light is to be found in the size of the scattering particles (see Further information). The other example is the classical colouring of glass by the precipitation of colloidal gold: these minute particles scatter away the blue component of transmitted light, and to the glass there is imparted a rich ruby hue.

Further information. See Murrell (1971) for an account of the electronic spectra of organic molecules and Chapter 17 of Kittel (1971) for a good survey of the optical properties of insulators. A most pleasing account of the physical basis of colour has been given in a simple article by Weisskopf (1968). The photochemical aspects of the absorption of light are described by Wayne (1970) and Calvert and Pitts (1966), on which is based Table 5. The chemical aspects of light are also described by Bowen (1946). The intensity of the absorption of light depends, for °electric dipole transitions, on the °oscillator strength, and experimentally it is expressed in terms of the °extinction coefficient: see *MQM* Appendix 10.2 and Wayne (1970). Concepts, methods, and data concerning colour are described in Wyszecki and Stiles (1967).

commutator. A commutator of two °operators $\hat{A}$ and $\hat{B}$ is the difference $\hat{A}\hat{B}-\hat{B}\hat{A}$; it is normally denoted $[\hat{A},\hat{B}]$. ($\hat{A}\hat{B}$ means that operation $\hat{B}$ is performed first, and is followed by operation $\hat{A}$; $\hat{B}\hat{A}$ implies that $\hat{A}$ precedes $\hat{B}$.) Two operators are said to *commute* if their commutator is zero. The non-vanishing of a commutator of two operators indicates that the final result of performing two operations depends on the order in which the operations are done: operation $\hat{A}$ followed by operation $\hat{B}$ and $\hat{B}$ followed by $\hat{A}$ lead to different results. For example, multiplication of a function $f(x)$ by x followed by differentiation is different from differentiation followed by multiplication: $(d/dx)xf(x) \neq x(d/dx)f(x)$. The commutator of (d/dx) and x, $[d/dx, x]$, is 1 because from the rule for the differentiation of a product $(d/dx)xf(x)$ is equal to $f(x) + x(d/dx)f(x)$.

The importance of the commutator in quantum mechanics lies in the theory's dependence on °operators: the manipulations of quantum mechanics must take the possible lack of commutation into account; indeed, the very fact that commutators do not disappear is the feature responsible for the differences between quantum and classical mechanics (see °matrix mechanics). The °uncertainty principle applies to observables whose operators do not commute.

The commutator of quantum theory is related to the Poisson bracket of classical mechanics, and the recognition of this connexion is reputed to have been the cause of one of the most jubilant moments of Dirac's life.

The technical importance of the commutator lies in the fact that the °eigenfunctions of one operator are also eigenfunctions of any other operator with which it commutes.

Questions. What is a commutator? Calculate the commutator of (d/dx) and x, of d/dx and d/dy, of d^2/dx^2 and x^3, and of $x(d/dy) - y(d/dx)$ and $z(d/dx) - x(d/dz)$. Demonstrate the validity of the following relations:

$$[A,B] = -[B,A]$$

$$[A+B,C] = [A,C] + [B,C]$$

$$[A,[B,C]] + [B,[C,A]] + [C,[A,B]] = 0 \quad \textit{(Jacobi identity).}$$

Prove that a necessary and sufficient condition for two operators to have simultaneous eigenfunctions (that is, for the eigenfunctions of one operator to be eigenfunctions of the other) is that they commute.

Further information. See *MQM* Chapter 4 for a discussion and proof of some of the consequences of the lack of commutation of operators. The final Question is answered there (p. 108). See the standard texts on quantum theory for a further account; for example, Davydov (1965), Landau and Lifshitz (1958a), Messiah (1961), Schiff (1968), and Dirac (1958). For deeper accounts see Jauch (1968) and Salem and Wigner (1972). The consequences of noncommutation for *exponential operators* of the form $\exp\Omega$ are developed by Wilcox (1967).

complementarity. The wave and corpuscular properties of 'particles' are complementary in the sense that an experiment designed to determine the value of a wave-like property automatically eliminates the precision with which a corpuscular-like property may simultaneously be determined: see °uncertainty principle. *Complementarity* is the mutual exclusiveness of these two types of property: it is impossible to demonstrate simultaneously the wave and corpuscular attributes of a particle.

Further information. See °duality, °uncertainty principle, and °wave packet for a more detailed discussion. See p. 158 of Bohm (1951), Kramers (1964), and Jammer (1966).

Compton effect. Light scattered from electrons shows an increase in wavelength which is independent of its initial wavelength but characteristic of the angle through which it is deflected.

On the basis of classical theory it is surprising that only one value of the wavelength shift is observed for a particular angle of deflection, and the result strongly suggests that a collisional process is involved. If it is assumed that a °photon of energy $h\nu$ and momentum h/λ is in collision with a stationary electron, and that both energy and momentum are conserved in the collision of the two particles, then it is a simple matter to deduce the expression $\delta\lambda = (h/m_e c)(1-\cos\theta)$. $\delta\lambda$ is the wavelength shift (always an increase), and θ is the deflection of the light. This expression is indeed independent of the initial wavelength, and gives a unique value of $\delta\lambda$ for a given θ. The agreement shows the essential validity of the collisional model, and so it is excellent evidence for the quantization of light into °photons, and for their behaviour as particles.

The quantity $h/m_e c$ is the *Compton wavelength* λ_c and its numerical value is 0·024 Å, or 2·4 pm (to be precise: $2{\cdot}426\,309\,6 \times 10^{-12}$ m). Therefore even in the backward scattering direction ($\theta = 180^\circ$) the wavelength shift is only 4·8 pm, and this smallness indicates why it is necessary to use X-rays or γ-rays, for only then is the shift a significant proportion of the wavelength: the effect is independent of the wavelength, but it is easier to detect.

Questions. 1. What are the characteristics of Compton scattering? What features are inconsistent with a classical view of the process as an interaction of a charged particle with an electromagnetic wave? Why is the effect unimportant at large wavelengths? Calculate the Compton wavelength of a proton. 2. Deduce the Compton formula. Take an initial photon wavelength λ and a final wavelength $\lambda + \delta\lambda$; let the electron be at rest initially and after the collision have a kinetic energy $\frac{1}{2}mv^2$ and momentum mv (do everything non-relativistically). Write the expression for the conservation of energy during the collision (it is an *elastic* process), and then do the same for the linear momentum on the basis that the light is deflected through θ. Expand the quantities to first order in $\delta\lambda$ and eliminate v to get the final expression.

Further information. See §2.8 of Bohm (1951) for a discussion of the differences between the classical and quantum situations and Chapter 4 of Jammer (1966) for an historical perspective. The original work is described by Compton (1923). More complicated treatments of the Compton effect are to be found in §22 of Heitler (1954), Chapter 11 of Jauch and Rohrlich (1955), and Schweber (1961). Note that the non-relativistic limit of Compton scattering is normally called *Thomson scattering*, and the *Klein-Nishina formula* was the result of the first calculation of the cross-section for relativistic photon-electron scattering. These matters are discussed in the cited references.

configuration. The electronic configuration of an atom or molecule is the description of the way the electrons are distributed among the available orbitals. Thus the configurations of the first row atoms are H 1s; He $1s^2$; Li $1s^22s$; Be $1s^22s^2$; B $1s^22s^22p$, and so on up to Ne $1s^22s^22p^6$. Sometimes the inner complete shells are abbreviated to K,L,M, etc.. Thus the ground configuration of sodium could be written either as $1s^22s^22p^63s$ or as [KL] 3s. In a similar fashion the configurations of molecules may be written in terms of the occupied orbitals. Thus we have H_2 $1s\sigma_g^2$; O_2 $1s\sigma_g^2\,1s\sigma_u^{*2}\,2s\sigma_g^2\,2s\sigma_u^{*2}\,2p\sigma_g^2\,2p\pi_u^4\,2p\pi_g^{*2}$, and the latter is often abbreviated by the weak but wise to ... $\sigma_g^2\pi_u^4\pi_g^2$. If the electronic configuration is known (for example, by applying the °*aufbau* principle) the spectroscopic °terms may be deduced and spectra predicted.

Questions. What is a 'configuration' of an atom? What may be deduced if the configuration is known? Write down the configurations of the atoms He, B, C, O, F, Al, Si, Cl, Cu, Fe, U, and Cf in an economic fashion. Do the same for the molecules H_2, HD, N_2, F_2, Ne_2, FeO, and °benzene.

Further information. The standard collection of atomic energy levels, which perforce contains lists of configurations, is that of Moore (1949 et seq.). Standard works on atomic structure are those of Herzberg (1944) and Condon and Shortley (1963). Candler (1964) is helpful. See also *MQM* Chapter 8, the synopsis of °atomic spectra, and the °*aufbau* principle.

configuration interaction. A °configuration tells us how electrons are distributed among the available °atomic or °molecular orbitals, and the simplest description of the structure of an atom or molecule consists of a statement of its configuration. Thus molecular hydrogen could be described as having the structure $1s\sigma^2$. The energy of the molecule corresponding to this configuration could then be quoted as the 'molecular energy'. Such a description might not be particularly good, for a true description of the molecule ought to allow for the contamination of the configuration by some others: we know that a molecular wavefunction is inaccurate for a variety of reasons, and so it is certain that the single-configuration description of its structure will be inaccurate in some fashion. For example, the single-configuration description of the molecule of hydrogen is deficient in as much as it permits both electrons to be localized on the same nucleus to too great an extent.

The situation can be improved by modifying the wavefunction by permitting *configuration interaction* (CI): we permit the wavefunction of the molecule to be described by a mixture (a °superposition) of wavefunctions corresponding to different configurations. Admixture of some excited state configurations distorts the ground-state function, and if the mixture lowers the energy of the ground state then the °variation principle states that we have an improved description of the molecule. In the case of H_2 it turns out that a major improvement in the energy, and therefore the wavefunction, can be brought about by mixing in some of the configuration $1s\sigma^{*2}$: when the effect of this admixture is analysed (see Questions) it emerges that the effect of allowing configuration interaction is to reduce the contribution of situations in which both the electrons are at the same nucleus. Those who like the language of electron correlation theory will realise that CI has achieved a certain amount of *charge correlation*: simple molecular-orbital theory underestimates electron correlations, and the admission of CI goes some way to repair the defect.

What configurations can be mixed into the ground state? The first requirement is that they have the same symmetry: for example, H_2 is improved by the admixture of $^1\Sigma$ rather than $^3\Sigma$ or $^1\Pi$. The second requirement stems from °Brillouin's theorem, and is that singly excited states do not interact directly with the ground state if proper °self-consistent field configurations are being considered.

The effect of CI may extend beyond improvement to the molecular energy, because the fact that excited-state configurations are mixed into the ground state means that the ground state of the molecule possesses some of the characteristics of these excited states. Such contamination may influence the predictions of the °Hund rules, for instance.

The simplest way of doing a CI calculation in practice is to calculate the orbitals and their energies, and then feed in electrons to form various configurations. The ground state corresponds to the configuration with the lowest energy. Then the actual wavefunction of the molecule is expressed as a °linear combination of these configurations (using the symmetry criteria to decide which configurations one should bother about), and then the variation principle is used to determine the best mixture. A better, but much more complicated, procedure is the *multiconfigurational calculation* in which the best structure for each configuration is calculated separately (rather than by applying the °*aufbau* principle to a single set of levels), and then the variation principle is applied to these optimized components.

Questions. 1. Why is a single-configuration description of a molecular state possibly a poor description of its actual structure? In what respect is a single-configuration description of the hydrogen molecule a poor object in simple molecular-orbital theory? What is configuration interaction, and why does it overcome some of the defects of the single-configuration method? What effect does it have on the interpretation of the wavefunction of the ground state of H_2? What other influences on molecular properties may CI have? Suggest the influence of CI on the stability, dipole moment, magnetic susceptibility, and polarizability of molecules. Will spectral selection rules be modified by CI? What are the criteria for selecting the configurations able to interact with the ground state?
2. The energy of a configuration A lies at ΔE above the ground state configuration of energy E_g. Suppose that there is an interaction between the configurations (that is, there is a matrix element V between the configurations). Use the variation principle to show that the revised ground-state energy with CI is given by the smaller root of a quadratic equation (obtained from the °secular equations). Make a rough estimate for ΔE in H_2 and use a value of $V = 1$ eV to compute the modifications to the curves on CI. Is it reasonable to use the same value of V at all internuclear distances? What is the source of the interaction responsible for the magnitude of V?
3. Extend the results of Question 2 to compute the wavefunctions of the two states. Show that the configuration σ^2, with σ proportional to $1s_a + 1s_b$, is modified by the admixture of the configuration σ^{*2}, with σ^* proportional to $1s_a - 1s_b$, in a way that can be interpreted as an improvement of the distribution of the electrons. Discuss the role of CI on the products of dissociation of the H_2 molecule.

Further information. See *MQM* for a short discussion of molecular hydrogen in terms of CI, and see also Coulson (1961). A simple pragmatic approach to the subject will be found in Richards and Horsley (1970), and a lengthier, but helpful, account is given by McGlynn, Vanquickenborne, Kinoshita, and Carroll (1972); both work through some examples.

conserved property. A conserved quantity or property is one whose value does not change with time. A familiar example is the total energy of a system (first law of thermodynamics); another is the angular momentum of an electron in an atom, or the component of angular momentum about the internuclear axis in a diatomic molecule. An example of an unconserved quantity is the angular momentum about an axis perpendicular to the internuclear axis in a diatomic molecule: this can be envisaged as the electron beginning its journey about the perpendicular axis, but colliding with a nucleus before it has completed its rotation. This collision changes the value of the angular momentum about the perpendicular axis, and so it is not a conserved quantity. A conserved quantity is also called a *constant of the motion.*

The definition of a conserved property can be made quantitative by defining it as an observable whose corresponding °operator °commutes with the °hamiltonian of the system. For example, the linear momentum of a system is conserved if the linear momentum operator commutes with the hamiltonian for the system. In the Questions you are asked to show that the commutator of the linear momentum and the hamiltonian is proportional to the gradient of the potential energy of the system. From classical mechanics we know that the gradient of the potential is a force, and so we arrive at the pleasing conclusion that the linear momentum is a conserved quantity only in the absence of a force. Alternatively, we may conclude that in the presence of a force the linear momentum is not conserved, or that the linear momentum changes. This is essentially the content of Newton's second law of motion.

Questions. What is meant by the term 'conserved property'? Give some examples other than those mentioned in the text. Consider the °expectation value of the °operator corresponding to some observable Ω. By invoking the time-dependent form of the °Schrödinger equation, show that the rate of change of the expectation value, $(\mathrm{d}/\mathrm{d}t)\,\langle\hat{\Omega}\rangle$, is equal to $(\mathrm{i}/\hbar)\,\langle[H,\hat{\Omega}]\rangle$. This shows that if the commutator of H and $\hat{\Omega}$ disappears, then the expectation value of $\hat{\Omega}$ remains constant in time. Now let Ω be the linear momentum in the x-direction and let H be the operator composed of the °kinetic energy plus some potential energy $V(x)$. Deduce an expression for the rate of change of the expectation value of the linear momentum in terms of the expectation value of a force. Recognize and, if your spirit is of that kind, be thrilled by the fact that you have deduced Newton's second law of motion. Reflect on it by considering the fact that, in the light of this result, Newton's law may be regarded as an equation for average values, and so realize that classical mechanics is a treatment of averages and so ignores the finer details of motion. What are the conditions that must be satisfied in order that energy, angular momentum, and linear momentum be conserved in mechanical systems?

Further information. See *MQM* Chapters 4 and 6 for a short discussion of conservation laws. More detailed information will be found in Chapter 5 of Roman (1965), and Feynman, Leighton, and Sands (1963). On p. 195 *MQM* discusses the fact that the conservation of energy, momentum, and angular momentum are features of the symmetry of space.

correlation energy. If it is well done, a °self-consistent field calculation of an atomic or molecular structure in the Hartree-Fock scheme generally gives a good answer; but even if the calculation is done exactly within the scheme the calculated energy differs from the true energy. A part of the discrepancy lies in the neglect of relativistic effects, which might be very large for inner-shell electrons possessing a high kinetic energy; but even when this is allowed for there remains a discrepancy. The magnitude of this residual difference is the *correlation energy*, and its presence reflects the approximations inherent to the Hartree-Fock scheme. A basic approximation of the Hartree-Fock scheme is the neglect of the *local* distortion of the distribution of electrons, and the averaging of its effect over the whole orbital: instead of an electron's orbital being distorted in the vicinity of another electron, the whole orbital is modified in an averaged way (Fig. C3). Therefore the scheme neglects local electron-electron effects—it neglects electron correlations.

The effect of the neglect of correlations is to cause the calculated molecular potential-energy curve (see °Born-Oppenheimer approximation) to lie above the true curve. Nevertheless, the true shape is approximately reproduced, except that it is too narrow in the region around the minimum (the equilibrium bond length). The minimum of the Hartree-Fock curve occurs at about the same position of the true curve. Thus the equilibrium geometries are quite well predicted

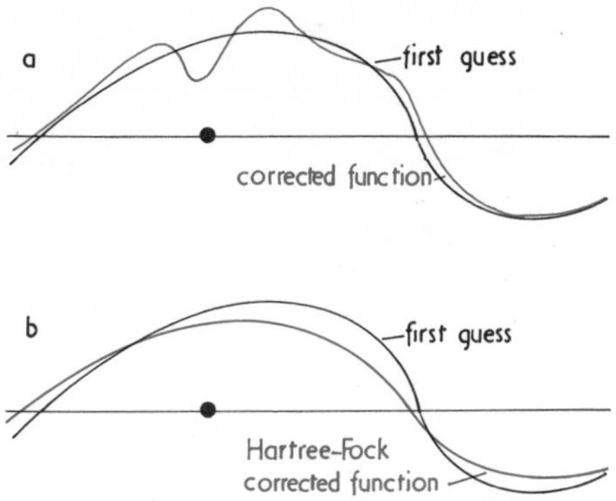

FIG. C3. (a) The actual distortion and (b) the Hartree-Fock pretence.

if correlation effects are neglected, but the °force-constants, and hence the molecular vibration frequencies, are exaggerated.

Questions. Even the best Hartree-Fock calculation does not give the exact electronic energy of an atom or molecule: what are the reasons? What is the correlation energy, and why is it so called? How must the Hartree-Fock scheme be improved in order to regain more accurate results? If a molecular potential-energy curve is calculated on the basis of the Hartree-Fock scheme, in what way should it be expected that the equilibrium bond lengths and vibration frequencies will differ from their actual values? Would you expect the neglect of correlation effects to be more or less important as the bond between two atoms lengthens? What features would you think of incorporating into a wavefunction of the helium atom in order to reflect the tendency of the electrons to remain apart?

Further information. A simple account of the methods that are employed to deal with the calculation of atomic and molecular structures, and the role of correlation effects, is contained in Richards and Horsley (1970) and in McGlynn, Vanquickenborne, Kinoshita, and Carroll (1972). For some of the ways the problem has been tackled, see Pauncz (1969), Berry (1966), Sinanoğlu (1961), Clementi (1965), and Sinanoğlu and Brueckner (1970).

correspondence principle. At large °quantum numbers the mean motion of a system becomes identical with its motion calculated on the basis of classical mechanics.

The principle implies that the rules of quantum mechanics contain the structure of classical mechanics when the fine details of the situation are ignored. An example of its application is provided by the construction of a °wave packet to represent the motion of a free particle when the energy or momentum is only coarsely specified: the packet moves along the same trajectory that the same mass point would have in classical mechanics. But as the energy becomes more precisely specified, so that fewer quantum states contribute to its representation, the distribution becomes less classical and more quantal. Another example is provided by the Planck distribution of energy in a °black-body radiator: as Planck's constant dwindles to zero (in a hypothetical classical world) the energy distribution becomes that of a classical system and agrees with the Rayleigh-Jeans distribution law. Likewise, the momentum of a °photon (a light quantum) is transmitted to the object that absorbs or reflects it; and when a sufficiently large number of photons is involved this impulse is interpreted as the steady radiation pressure of classical electromagnetic theory.

The correspondence principle was of profound importance in the early days of quantum theory for it acted as a guide through the exciting gloom of those days: any calculation based on quantum theory had to correspond to a classical result in all details when sufficiently large quantum numbers were involved and quantum fluctuations ignored. As an example of this kind of development we may consider the radiation emitted by an harmonically oscillating electron: the existence of an array of equally-spaced quantized energy levels in a °harmonic oscillator suggests that a very wide range of frequencies could be emitted because of the indefinitely large number of different energy separations that may be obtained. Nevertheless, a classical oscillator, to which the quantum harmonic oscillator must correspond, emits only a single frequency, that of its natural classical motion. In order to reproduce this result it is necessary to impose restrictions at the quantum level on the transitions that can occur; thus the correspondence principle leads to the °selection rule that an oscillator may make a transition only to a neighbouring level.

Such rules emerge naturally from the later quantum mechanics, but even there the correspondence limit is often a very good check on the validity of a calculation. Finally it should be noted that purely quantum phenomena disappear in the correpondence limit; in particular, all effects due to °spin are eliminated.

Further information. Various classical limits of quantum situations are discussed in *MQM* Chapter 3. For an historical perspective and an account of the way the principle was used to disentangle the old and discover the new quantum theory see Jammer (1966). Applications of the principle are described in Kemble (1958) and Kramers (1964).

Coriolis interaction. The Coriolis interaction is the interaction between the rotation and vibration of a molecule. Think first of a diatomic molecule rotating about an axis perpendicular to its internuclear axis. If we regard it as a classical problem we may imagine the bond lengthening and shortening as it vibrates, and this vibration changes the moment of inertia of the molecule. °Angular momentum is conserved for the molecule, and so for the same angular momentum, but smaller moment of inertia I, in order to preserve the product $I\omega$ it is necessary for the angular velocity ω to increase. Conversely, as the bond lengthens and the moment of inertia increases, the angular velocity must fall in order to conserve the angular momentum. Therefore the rotation accelerates and decelerates as the bond vibrates. (This is the same mechanism whereby managing directors on rotating chairs, and ice skaters, speed or slow their rotational motion.) This picture shows that there is an interdependence between the rotation and the vibration of a molecule, and it may appear in modifications of the spectral lines.

An important application of the Coriolis interaction is encountered in the case of a vibrating, rotating, linear, triatomic molecule. There are four °normal modes of vibration of this molecule; one is a symmetric stretch in which both A—B bonds vibrate in phase, another (named ν_2) is the asymmetric stretch in which as one A—B bond shortens the other lengthens, and the other two are the bending motions which may occur in two perpendicular planes (see °normal modes for pictures). Consider the effect of the ν_2 vibration

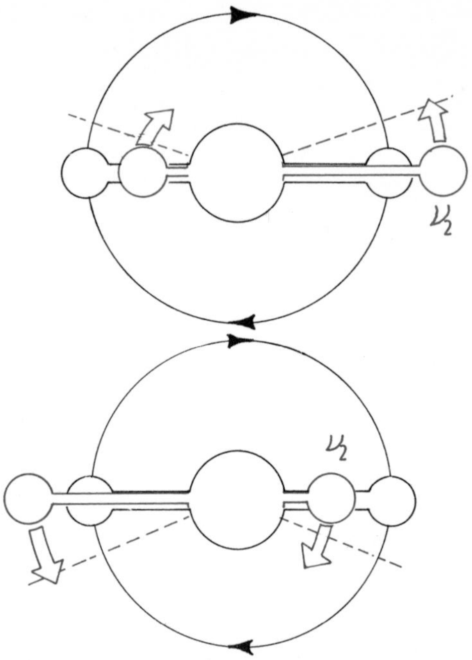

FIG. C4. The asymmetric stretch (labelled ν_2) and the molecular rotation interact and induce a bending vibration in the plane of rotation.

interacting with the rotation by the Coriolis mechanism (Fig. C4). As one A—B bond shrinks there is a tendency for that half of the molecule to speed up; therefore that bond tends to bend forward relative to the rest of the molecule. Meanwhile the other bond is getting longer, and the Coriolis interaction requires that half of the molecule to decelerate; therefore it tends to lag behind in the rotation of the molecule. The net effect is that the molecule tends to bend in the plane of the rotation. But having got this far the stretching motion is at the end of its swing, and it begins to swing back: the long bond shortens and the short lengthens. The Coriolis interaction comes into operation and the faster rotating bond becomes the laggard and vice versa. This induces the molecule to bend the other way. The net effect of the continuing process is that the bending vibration is stimulated by the combined antisymmetric stretch and the rotation of the molecule. This means that the two vibrations are not independent and that the effect of the Coriolis interaction has been to mix different vibrations together. This appears in the spectrum as ℓ-type °doubling.

Questions. What is the Coriolis interaction? Why is it able to cause an interaction between the vibrational and rotational motion of a molecule? Discuss the changes brought about by the change in the moment of inertia of a molecule by virtue of the latter's vibration on the angular speed, frequency, momentum, and rotational energy of the molecule. Discuss the effect of the Coriolis interaction on the vibrations of a linear triatomic molecule. What is it unable to mix? What is the consequence of the mixing on the spectrum? Apply the same reasoning to a planar triangular molecule of the form AB_3. Which vibrations of this molecule is the rotation able to mix? Consider the effect of rotations about the axis perpendicular to the plane, and about an axis in the plane of the molecule. What other manifestations of the Coriolis force can be observed in macroscopic phenomena?

Further information. See *MQM* Chapter 10. The classical basis of the Coriolis interaction, which is concerned with the way mechanical systems behave in rotating axis systems (*rotating frames*) will be found in §4.9 of Goldstein (1950). Applications to spectroscopy will be found in King (1964), Herzberg (1945, 1966), Sugden and Kenney (1965), Wilson, Decius, and Cross (1955), and Townes and Schawlow (1955). A helpful theoretical discussion is to be found in Allen and Cross (1963).

Coulomb integral. The Coulomb integral is the contribution of the classical electrostatic interaction between charge distributions to the total energy of an atom or molecule; although there are some frills which must be added to this basic description.

In atoms the frills are fewer and we deal with them first. Consider an electron distributed in an °atomic orbital ψ_a: knowing the mathematical form of the orbitals we are able to say that in the small volume element $d\tau_1$ surrounding the point $\mathbf{r}_1$ the probability of finding the electron is $|\psi_a(\mathbf{r}_1)|^2 d\tau_1$; therefore the charge in that region is $dq_1 = -e|\psi_a(\mathbf{r}_1)|^2 d\tau_1$. Another electron present in the atom may occupy the orbital ψ_b; by the same argument the charge in some little volume element $d\tau_2$ surrounding the point $\mathbf{r}_2$ is $dq_2 = -e|\psi_b(\mathbf{r}_2)|^2 d\tau_2$. If the charges dq_1 and dq_2 are separated by a distance r_{12} the potential energy of their interaction comes from the expression for the Coulomb potential, namely $dq_1 dq_2/4\pi\epsilon_0 r_{12}$. It follows that the two charges at $\mathbf{r}_1$ and $\mathbf{r}_2$ will give a contribution of this form to the total energy of the atom. The total contribution to the energy can be obtained by summing over all the volume elements $d\tau_1$ and $d\tau_2$, or, since these are infinitesimal volume elements, by integrating over them. The procedure leads to the *Coulomb integral J* as illustrated in Fig. C5a. As the charges are the same, J is positive, and so leads to an increase in the energy of the atom. This means, of course, that the Coulomb interaction is repulsive. The frills to tack on to this description are concerned with the intrinsic tendency of electrons to correlate their motion: the correction to the Coulomb energy arising from this effect is termed the °exchange energy.

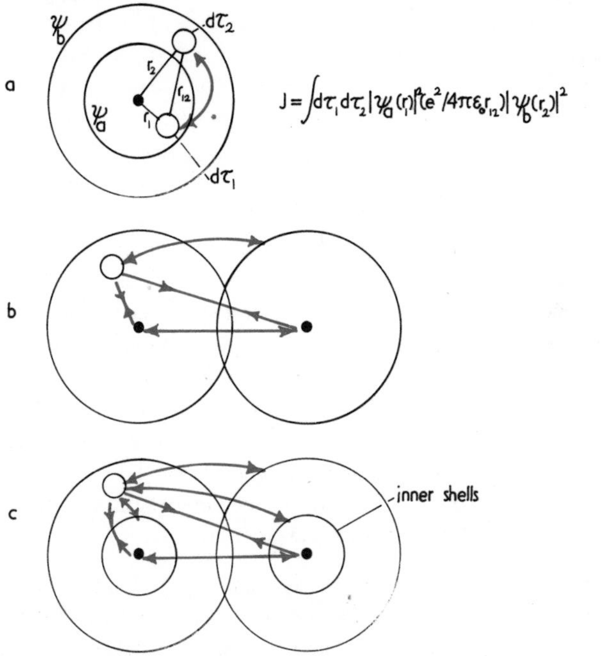

FIG. C5. The contributions to the Coulomb integral (a) in an atom, (b) in the VB theory of a diatomic molecule, and (c) in MO theory of the same. Arrows like →← represent attractive interaction, and ←→ repulsive.

In molecules the situation is complicated by the variety of interactions possible when several nuclei are present. It is further complicated by the existence of two different descriptions of the chemical bond: the °molecular-orbital and the °valence-bond theories. Nevertheless, in each one the term 'Coulomb integral' signifies the type of energy that arises by virtue of the classical electrostatic interaction between charges.

In the *valence-bond method* the Coulomb integral is composed of three parts: the electrostatic repulsion between the two nuclei in the bond, the repulsion between the charge distributions on the two nuclei, and the attraction between the charge distribution on one nucleus and the opposite charge of the other nucleus (see Fig. C5b). This integral is also called J, but we note that it may be negative if the last of the three contributions exceeds the others. It too must be corrected to allow for electron exchange: details are given under °valence-bond.

In the *molecular-orbital method* the Coulomb integral, which especially in the °Hückel method is often denoted α, generally consists of four parts. The first is the energy of the electron as if it were in an orbital of the isolated atom (this therefore contains the attraction of the electron to its own nucleus, its repulsion from the other electrons on the atoms, and its kinetic energy); the second is the nucleus-nucleus repulsion in the bond; the third is the electrostatic attraction between the charge distribution and the neighbouring nucleus; and the fourth is the repulsion of the electrons on the two nuclei. These interactions are illustrated in Fig. C5c and discussed further in the entry on °molecular-orbital theory. It too must be corrected for °exchange interactions.

The feature common to all these Coulomb integrals is the way they select, from all the interactions within the molecule, the ones that would be selected on a simple classical electrostatic picture of the interactions; they ignore the way that the °spin of the electrons correlates their motion.

Questions. What is meant by the expression 'Coulomb integral'? How does the Coulomb integral appear in the theory of atoms: present a simple argument on the basis of the expected electrostatic interactions, and demonstrate how the expression emerges from the proper °hamiltonian for the energy of a many-electron atom. Express the energy of the helium atom in terms of the Coulomb integral J. Can J (for atoms) ever be negative? What additional complications are there in molecules? What are the components of the electrostatic energy in the valence-bond description of a chemical bond between two atoms? What are the corresponding contributions in the molecular-orbital description of the same bond? What features are common to both? What features are unique to each? May the molecular Coulomb integrals be negative? What would that signify? What additional contributions to the Coulomb integral might be expected when a molecule containing more than two nuclei is being considered? What is the maximum number of different atomic orbitals that need be considered inside a Coulomb integral?

Further information. See *MQM* Chapters 8 and 9 for the role of the Coulomb integral in atomic- and molecular-structure calculations. See also Coulson (1961). A helpful account of the calculation of Coulomb integrals will be found in McGlynn, Vanquickenborne, Kinoshita, and Carroll (1972). Applications to the determination of molecular structure will be found there and also in Richards and Horsley (1970). See the entries on °exchange energy, °spin correlation, °self-consistent fields, and the °molecular-orbital and °valence-bond theories.

crystal-field theory. The five d-orbitals of a free transition-metal ion are °degenerate (have the same energy), but when the ion is complexed the ligands remove the spherical symmetry of the atom and replace it by a field of lower

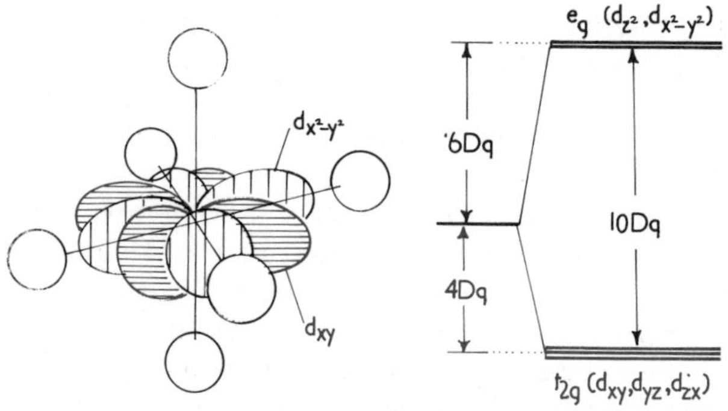

FIG. C6. The effect of an octahedral crystal field on the energy of an electron in the d-orbitals of the central atom.

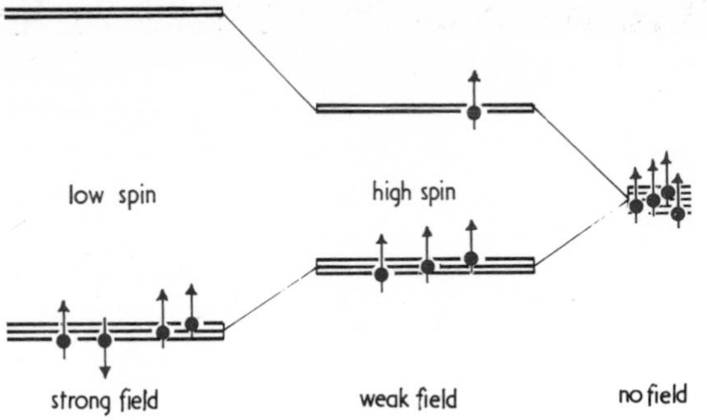

FIG. C7. The competition between spin-pairing and $10Dq$ leading to low-spin or high-spin complexes.

symmetry. The immediate environment of the ion may be octahedral, tetrahedral, and so on. The ligands may be regarded as a source of electrical potential, the *crystal field*, and the d-orbital energies adjust accordingly. In an octahedral complex the d_{z^2} and $d_{x^2-y^2}$ orbitals point directly towards the ligands (Fig. C6), whereas the other three d-orbitals point in mutally equivalent directions between them. It follows that the former pair possess one energy and the latter trio a different energy, and so the degeneracy of the orbitals has been removed. The energy separation is conventionally called $10Dq$.

Electrons may be fed into the array of atomic orbitals so formed, and the structure, spectra, stability, and magnetic properties of the complex discussed on the basis of the °*aufbau* process. The competition that governs the configuration of an ion in a complex is between the tendency of the electrons to enter the lowest-energy orbitals, which more than three can do only if their spins pair, and the tendency for electrons to enter a set of orbitals with parallel spins (°Hund rules). Which tendency wins is governed largely by the separation of the two sets of orbitals, and therefore by the strength of the crystal field. A *high-spin complex* results when the tendency not to pair wins, and a *low-spin complex* results when the electrons achieve lowest energy by pairing and entering the low-lying orbitals (Fig. C7).

The crystal-field theory is an approximation because it supposes that the energy of ligand-metal bonding is due solely to electrostatic effects, and ignores both the covalent nature of the bonding and the role that π-bonding might be expected to play: these deficiencies are repaired in the broader °ligand-field theory. Nevertheless, the crystal-field theory is successful in so far as it expresses the importance of the symmetry of the complex in determining the electric, magnetic, and chemical properties, and provides a simple rule for predictions of these properties.

Further information. See *MQM* Chapter 9 for a more detailed account. An introduction to the idea of the crystal field is provided by Earnshaw and Harrington in *The chemistry of the transition elements* (OCS 13). A pleasing introduction to crystal-field theory is provided by Orgel (1960), developed by Ballhausen (1962), and consummated by Griffith (1964). See °ligand field for further directions.

D

de Broglie relation. According to the de Broglie relation a particle travelling with a linear momentum p has associated with it a wavelength $\lambda = h/p$. As the particle's momentum increases the associated wavelength decreases. The relation can be understood in terms of the interpretation of the °wavefunction of the particle, and the connexion between the function's curvature and the particle's °kinetic energy. As the kinetic energy of the particle increases, the curvature of its wavefunction increases; but increasing curvature implies that the wave swings from positive to negative amplitude more often in a given length: its wavelength decreases. But the kinetic energy is proportional to the square of the momentum, and so the inverse relation between momentum and wavelength emerges.

A more direct demonstration of the quantum-mechanical basis of the de Broglie relation is to observe that the wavefunction for a particle with °momentum $p = k\hbar$ is $\exp(ikx)$. If this is written as $\cos(2\pi px/h)+i\sin(2\pi px/h)$ it can be seen immediately that the function corresponds to a superposition of real waves each with wavelength h/p.

Questions. What is the de Broglie relation? How can it be justified quantum mechanically? Why does the wavelength of a particle decrease as its momentum increases? How could the existence of the de Broglie wave be demonstrated experimentally? Calculate the de Broglie wavelength for the following particles: an electron accelerated from rest by a potential of 10 V, 1 kV, 100 kV; a proton travelling at 1 km s^{-1}, 1000 km s^{-1}; a mass of 1 g travelling at 100 km h^{-1}; a car of mass 1500 kg travelling at 50 km h^{-1}. Which of these species would be expected to show pronounced quantum-mechanical behaviour?

Further information. See Feynman, Leighton, and Sands (1963) and Chapter 3 of Bohm (1951). For an account of the de Broglie relation by two students of de Broglie, and an account of the way that some people are attempting to interpret it, see Andrade e Silva and Lochak (1969). A pleasing account of de Broglie's contribution to quantum theory is given in §5.3 of Jammer (1966).

degeneracy. When two or more different °wavefunctions of a system correspond to the same energy they are said to be degenerate. Thus the three np-orbitals of any free atom constitute a triply degenerate set of functions, and the π-orbitals of diatomic molecules are doubly degenerate. When only one wavefunction corresponds to a particular energy the state is said to be non-degenerate ('singly degenerate' is sometimes used in this case, but this seems to be an illicit extension). 'Razing the degeneracy' of a state means removing the degeneracy (for example, by applying an electric field to an atom).

The degeneracy of a system is related intimately to its symmetry, and whenever a wavefunction can be changed into another by a °symmetry operation the functions are degenerate. Thus rotating a free atom through 90° about z is a symmetry operation, and as it rotates an np_x-orbital into an np_y-orbital these are degenerate. In a similar fashion np_z may be generated by rotation about another axis, and so it too is degenerate with np_x (and np_y). A 3p-orbital cannot be generated by rotating a 2p-orbital, and so, according to the symmetry definition, they are not degenerate in atoms—and this accords with common sense.

When two functions correspond to the same energy by a numerical coincidence and not by virtue of the existence of a symmetry operation they are said to be *accidentally degenerate.* As an example, it is possible that the $2s\sigma^*$ and the $2p\pi$ orbitals of some diatomic molecule have the same energy to a few significant figures; they are then accidentally degenerate. A widely quoted example of accidental degeneracy is that of the °hydrogen atom, in which all the orbitals of a given principal quantum number (that is, the *n*s, *n*p, *n*d, . . . orbitals) have the same energy; but this is a fallacious example because it is possible to find a cunningly hidden symmetry operation by which it is possible to rotate an *n*s-orbital into an *n*p-orbital, etc., and so the degeneracies are true rather than accidental. The same 'hidden symmetries' can account for the apparently accidental degeneracies of a °particle in a box whose sides are in rational proportion (see Question 2), and all *exact* 'accidental' degeneracies can be explained in terms of a deeper scrutiny of the symmetry of the system.

Questions. 1. When does a degenerate state occur? How is degeneracy related to the symmetry of a system? What is accidental degeneracy? How many-fold degenerate are the ground states of the sodium atom and the boron atom (neglect spin-orbit coupling)? What is the degeneracy of the °hydrogen atom when the electron occupies a state with principal quantum number 1, 2, *n*? What is the degeneracy of the spin state of an electron in zero magnetic field, and what is its degeneracy when the field is applied? What can be said about the degeneracy of an electron in the d-shell of a transition-metal ion when an octahedral ligand field is present? Discuss the last problem by symmetry arguments.
2. Take the energy levels for a °particle in a two-dimensional rectangular well (Box 15 on p. 166) and consider the case where the sides are equal. Show that the lowest energy state is non-degenerate, and that the next-highest state is doubly degenerate. Show that the two wavefunctions for the first excited state can be interrelated by a rotation of the square through a right-angle. Can any of the states be triply degenerate? Can any state of a cubic box be triply degenerate? Now let the well have sides *a* and *ca*, where *c* is a rational number: find some degenerate states. Are these truly degenerate or accidentally degenerate? Is there a hidden symmetry? What happens when *c* is irrational?

Further information. The best way of discussing degenerate situations is in terms of °group theory: see *MQM* Chapter 5, Cotton (1963), Bishop (1973), and McIntosh (1971). For a discussion of the hydrogen atom degeneracy see *MQM* Chapter 3, Englefield (1972), McIntosh (1971), and Bander and Itzykson (1966). The razing of degeneracy is the basis of the crystal-field description of transition-metal ions; therefore read Earnshaw and Harrington's *The chemistry of the transition elements* (OCS 13), Orgel (1960), Ballhausen (1962), and Griffith (1964). Accidental degeneracy is discussed in detail by McIntosh (1958, 1971).

density matrix. In elementary applications of quantum mechanics calculations are based on the °wavefunction ψ; but whenever an actual observable is calculated one encounters formulae which involve the wavefunction as its square $\psi_n^*\psi_n$ or in a bilinear combination of the form $\psi_m^*\psi_n$; see, for example, °expectation value or °transition probability. Why not set up a formulation of quantum mechanics that deals with the bilinear combinations $\psi_m^*\psi_n$ directly rather than introducing them only when an observable is being calculated? Furthermore, the absolute phase of the wavefunction is immaterial, for if both ψ_m and ψ_n are multiplied by the arbitrary phase factor $\exp i\phi$ the product $\psi_m^*\psi_n$ remains unchanged, and so all observables are independent of the absolute phase; it appears that in dealing with the wavefunction one is carrying around a piece of useless information. The final preliminary point to make is that the state of a system is only very rarely pure: normally an actual system has to be treated as a statistically large collection of sub-systems, and the result of an experiment is determined by some average (actually one of the *ensemble averages* of statistical mechanics) of the products $\psi_m^*\psi_n$; this statistical average we denote $\overline{\psi_m^*\psi_n}$, and interpret the averaged product as the *n*, *m* element of a matrix, the *density matrix* ρ. The °matrix of elements ρ_{mn}, which are by definition $\overline{\psi_n^*\psi_m}$, should contain all the information about the system: it carries all the pertinent information of the wavefunction, and all the information about the role of the statistical averaging. It is not difficult to find an equation of motion of the density matrix (corresponding to the °Schrödinger equation for the wavefunction), but it is often quite difficult to solve. Nevertheless, powerful methods exist for dealing with the density matrix, and it is a common way of performing calculations dealing with the time-evolution of complex systems.

Further information. For a gentle introduction, see Chapter 5.4 of Slichter (1963). Then see Chapter 4 of Ziman (1969), Chapter 1.8 of Roman (1965), and Fano (1957). For applications to molecular and atomic structure, see McWeeny and Sutcliffe (1969).

dipole moment. A positive $(+q)$ and a negative $(-q)$ charge separated by a distance R constitutes an electric dipole moment $\mu = qR$. On a molecular scale a separation of the order of 1 Å (0·1 nm) is a typical magnitude, and the charge of the electron a typical charge ($4{\cdot}80 \times 10^{-10}$ e.s.u., $1{\cdot}60 \times 10^{-19}$C); therefore molecular dipole moments should be expected to have a magnitude of approximately 10^{-18} e.s.u. cm ($3{\cdot}3 \times 10^{-30}$ C m). Dipoles do indeed have this size in many systems, and so the unit *debye* (1D = 10^{-18} e.s.u. cm, $3{\cdot}3 \times 10^{-30}$ C m) is frequently used when magnitudes are quoted. Some typical molecular dipole moments are listed in Table 6. A dipole moment is a directed quantity because at one end is a positive charge and at the other a negative; in order to denote the direction of the dipole in a molecule the convention is employed of representing it by an arrow with the head at the negative end: $+\!\longrightarrow\!-$. Expressions for the energy of a dipole when it is in an electric field, and related information, are recorded in Box 5.

The vectorial nature of electric dipole moments is taken into account when the overall moment of a substituted molecule is considered: with each group can be associated a directed dipole moment of a magnitude which to a good approximation is reasonably independent of the nature of the rest of the molecule. The resultant of the vectorial addition of the dipole moments for all such groups in the molecule yields the overall dipole moment. In this way it is easy to appreciate that the dipole moments of chlorobenzene and the *o*-, *m*-, and *p*-dichlorobenzenes are 1.70 D, 2.25 D, 1.48 D, and zero respectively (Fig. D1).

The computation of electric dipole moments is a surprisingly complicated business, and its success depends critically on the accuracy of the molecular wavefunctions. The difficulty can be appreciated by considering the simplest possible approach to their calculation. In this the electron charge density on each atom in the molecule, plus the positive nuclear charge of the atom, may be represented as a point charge at each nucleus. It is then simply a matter of computing the

BOX 5: Dipole-moment formulae

Energy of a dipole μ in an electric field **E**

$$\mathcal{E} = -\boldsymbol{\mu}.\mathbf{E} = -\mu E\cos\theta.$$

Electric field at a point **R** due to dipole at origin

$$\mathbf{E} = \left(\frac{1}{4\pi\epsilon_0}\right)\frac{1}{R^3}\,[\boldsymbol{\mu} - 3\hat{\mathbf{R}}(\hat{\mathbf{R}}.\boldsymbol{\mu})]$$

$\hat{\mathbf{R}}$ is a unit vector along **R**: $\hat{\mathbf{R}} = \mathbf{R}/R$.

Energy of interaction of two dipoles (general case)

$$\mathcal{E} = -\left(\frac{1}{4\pi\epsilon_0}\right)\frac{1}{R^3}\,[\boldsymbol{\mu}_1.\boldsymbol{\mu}_2 - 3\boldsymbol{\mu}_1.\hat{\mathbf{R}}\hat{\mathbf{R}}.\boldsymbol{\mu}_2]$$

R is the vector from μ_1 to μ_2.

Energy of interaction of two parallel dipoles

$$\mathcal{E} = -\left(\frac{1}{4\pi\epsilon_0}\right)\frac{1}{R^3}\,\mu_1\mu_2(1 - 3\cos^2\theta)$$

R makes an angle θ with μ_1 (and μ_2).

Mean dipole moment of freely rotating polar molecule in a field **E** (Langevin function)

$$\langle\mu\rangle = \mu\mathcal{L}(\mu E/kT)$$

$$\mathcal{L}(x) = \coth x - \frac{1}{x}, \text{ the Langevin function}$$

$$\langle\mu\rangle \sim \mu^2(E/3kT) \quad kT \gg \mu E.$$

Molar orientation polarization (Langevin-Debye equation)

$$P_M = \left(\frac{\epsilon - 1}{\epsilon + 2}\right)\frac{M}{\rho}E = \frac{4\pi L}{3}(\alpha + \mu^2/3kT)E,$$

ρ is the density, α the polarizability, ϵ the relative permittivity, M is the molecular weight.

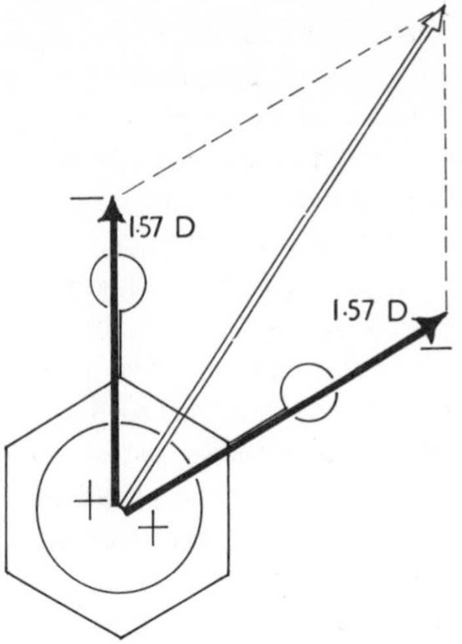

FIG. D1. Vectorial addition of dipole moments illustrated for 1, 2-dichlorobenzene. The experimental moment is 2·25 D.

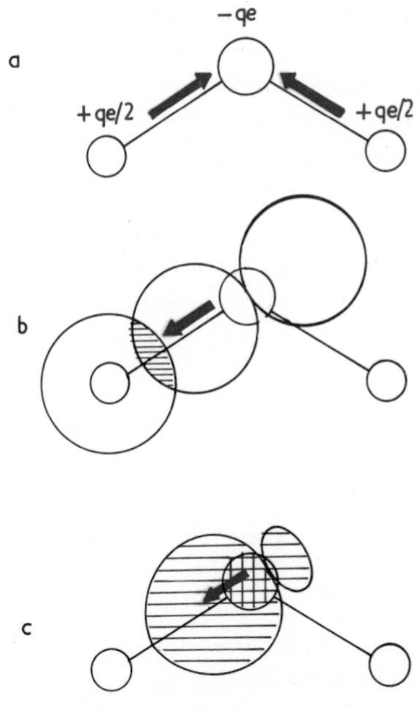

FIG. D2. Contributions to the dipole moment of H_2O: (a) point charge, (b) asymmetry dipole, (c) atomic (hybridization) dipole.

dipole moment of an array of point charges, distributed according to the molecular geometry. This *point charge* model (Fig. D2a) gives bad results because it is a poor approximation to assume that all the electronic charge is located at an array of points. One factor omitted is the *asymmetry dipole*. This arises from the charge distortion due to the °overlap of orbitals of unequal size. Consider the case when an occupied orbital is formed from the overlap of a large p-orbital on one atom and a small s-orbital on another. The region of maximum overlap lies closer to the small atom, and so instead of it being reasonable to regard the charge as residing on one atomic nucleus or the other, there is a considerable accumulation of charge in the overlap region close to the smaller atom (Fig. D2b): the asymmetry dipole moment is the contribution to the overall moment of this extra charge distribution. It is by no means negligible, for it may amount to about 1 D. Another major contribution is the *atomic dipole*, which is also called the *hybridization dipole* and which arises, as the latter name suggests, when an electron occupies a °hybridized atomic orbital. When this is so the centroid of electronic charge on an atom no longer necessarily coincides with the centre of nuclear charge (Fig. D2c). This separation of charge centroids is especially important when the hybridized orbital is a °lone pair, and the atomic asymmetry it is responsible for is reflected in a contribution to the total dipole moment of the order of 1 D. The contributions to the total moment of the water molecule are illustrated in Fig. D2.

Methods of measuring molecular dipole moments include the °Stark effect in molecular spectroscopy and the measurement of the dielectric constant (electric relative permittivity) of solutions (see °polarizability).

Questions. 1. What does a non-vanishing dipole moment represent in a molecule? Why is the debye a convenient unit to use? Why does a molecule with a centre of symmetry possess no dipole moment? From Table 6 estimate the dipole moments for *o*-, *m*-, and *p*-dibromobenzene. What are the deficiencies of the point-charge model? What is the asymmetry dipole? What is its direction? What is the atomic dipole?
2. The energy of a dipole in an electric field E is determined by $-\mu\cdot\mathbf{E}$. Calculate the energy (in J and in J mol^{-1}) required to reverse the orientation of a dipole of magnitude

1 D($3{\cdot}3 \times 10^{-30}$ C m) in a field of 100 V m^{-1}. Which orientation has the lowest energy? Consider a dipole moment on a freely rotating molecule; set up the Boltzmann distribution for the orientation of the molecule in an electric field, and show that the mean dipole moment does not vanish. (In fact, show that the mean dipole moment is given by the Langevin function (Box 5).) Show that at low applied fields (how low?) the mean dipole moment is inversely proportional to kT. Calculate the degree of ordering, and the energy of the optimum configuration, when a polar molecule is in the vicinity of an ion. Choose several separations for the species, which may be taken to be water and the sodium ion.

Further information. See Coulson (1961), and Chapter 10 of McGlynn, Vanquickenborne, Kinoshita, and Carroll (1972) for a thorough discussion and examples of calculations, and also §8.10. See also Streitweiser (1961) for accounts of the computation of dipole moments for organic molecules. Tables of moments, their determination and use are given by Smyth (1955), Smith (1955), Sutton (1955), McClellan (1963), and Minkin, Osipov, and Zhdanov (1970). See §15.18 of Moore (1972), and Gasser and Richards' *Entropy and energy levels* (OCS 19) for a simple deduction of the Langevin expression. Wheatley (1968) gives a simple introduction to the determination and application of dipole moments. The energy of interaction between two dipoles, the mean *orientation polarization* (the dipole moment of a collection of freely rotating molecules in the presence of an electric field, as determined by the Langevin function), and related information are given in Box 5. See °polarizability for related concepts.

Dirac equation. The Dirac equation describes the behaviour of an electron in a way that combines the requirements of quantum mechanics with the requirements of relativity. The trouble with the Schrödinger equation is that it is unsymmetrical in space and time (it contains first derivatives with respect to time and second derivatives with respect to space). One way out would be to find an equation which had second-order time derivatives; but the unfortunate quality of the solutions of such an equation (which was proposed by Schrödinger and named after Klein and Gordon) is that the total probability of the particle being anywhere in the universe is predicted to be a function of time; and so the equation allows the number of particles in the universe to vary. At the time this seemed unacceptable, and Dirac repaired it by keeping the equation first-order in time, and, like Procrustes, forcing the space derivatives to be first derivatives too. He could not do this arbitrarily, and the conditions he was forced to impose led him to conclude that he had to deal with wave-functions with four components. Two components corresponded to an embarrassing negative energy, but, instead of forgetting the whole thing, Dirac had sufficient confidence to propose that all the negative energy states were filled up throughout the universe and that we experience only the extra particles added to the overlying positive energy solutions. How satisfying it was then when it was shown experimentally to be possible to excite the particles out of their negative energy states, leaving a hole. Such a hole will have a positive charge and positive mass, and is referred to as the *positron* (e^+). It was then shown by Dirac that the two positive-energy solutions had the same energy, but that when a magnetic field was applied this degeneracy was removed, one level rose and the other dropped. This can be interpreted in terms of the electron having a magnetic moment that can take two orientations; in other words it is a particle with °spin $\frac{1}{2}$. The magnitude of the splitting was characteristic of a charged spin-$\frac{1}{2}$ particle, but with a moment twice as large as would be anticipated on the basis of a classical model of a spinning charge. Thus the anomalous °g-value of the electron emerges as a natural consequence of the Dirac equation.

Further information. Dirac (1958), of course. A simple account of the construction of the Dirac equation is given by Moss (1973) and by Bjorken and Drell (1964); see also Landau and Lifshitz (1958a), Schiff (1968), Messiah (1961), and Schweber (1961) for accounts of increasing sophistication. See the Dirac *Festschrift*, edited by Salem and Wigner (1972), for recent developments.

dispersion forces. The induced-dipole—induced-dipole contribution to the van der Waals °intermolecular force is the *London dispersion force.* It is a kind of self-generating bootstrap force, and arises by virtue of the correlation of fluctuations in the electron-density distribution of neighbouring molecules. The fluctuation in the electron density on molecule A causes it to possess instantaneously a dipole moment (if it is a polar molecule the fluctuation makes an extra ephemeral contribution to the permanent dipole). This instantaneous dipole polarizes the electrons on a neighbouring molecule; the accumulation of electrons on molecule A drives the electrons from the neighbouring region of B and so induces there, as in Fig. D3, a region of positive charge. Likewise, the region of relative positive charge on A matches the region of negative charge it induces in B. Such a correlation of charge distributions lowers the energy and corresponds to a binding force. Note that it is essential that there be a correlation between the charge fluctuations, for otherwise the effect would disappear.

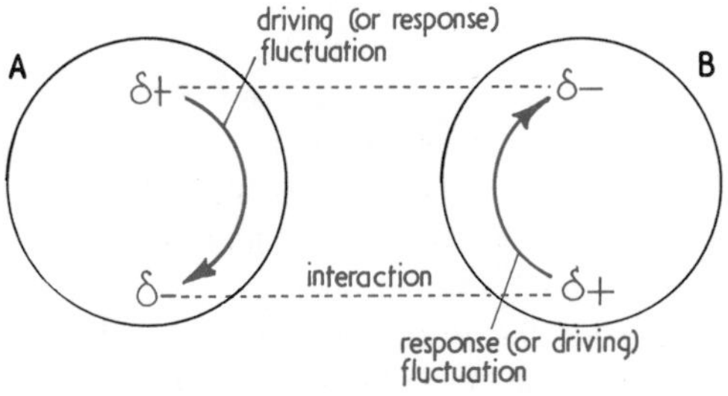

FIG. D3. The induced-dipole—induced-dipole (dispersion) interaction.

The dispersion energy has a characteristic R^{-6} dependence (which is reflected in the Lennard-Jones 6-, 12- °intermolecular potential) whose source is easy to detect in the model: the field arising from the initial dipole on A has an R^{-3} dependence (see Box 6), and the return interaction, where the dipole on B interacts with the dipole already on A, contributes another R^{-3}. The interaction energy also depends upon the °polarizability of the molecules, for it is a measure both of the ease with which an electric field may distort the molecule and of the extent of its charge fluctuations. The energy of interaction of two spherical molecules separated by a distance R and with polarizabilities α_A and α_B and ionization potentials I_A and I_B is given by the *London dispersion formula,* quoted in Box 6. Its magnitude is of the order of a few kJ mol^{-1}. The °ionization potential enters the formula because the extent of fluctuation depends on the ease with which a molecule can be excited.

BOX 6: Dispersion energy between spherical molecules

Energy of interaction of a and b separated by R:

$$\mathcal{E}(R) = -\left(\frac{1}{24\pi^2\epsilon_0^2}\right)\left(\frac{1}{R^6}\right)\sum_{m,n}\Delta_{mn}^{-1} \times [\mathbf{d}(a)_{0m}.\mathbf{d}(a)_{m0}][\mathbf{d}(b)_{0n}.\mathbf{d}(b)_{n0}],$$

where $\Delta_{mn} = (E_m - E_0)_a + (E_n - E_0)_b$ the excitation energies of a and b,

$\mathbf{d}_{0m}(a) = \int d\tau\,\psi_0^*(a)\mathbf{d}\psi_m(a)$, the transition dipole of a,

$\mathbf{d}_{0n}(b) = \int d\tau\,\psi_0^*(b)\mathbf{d}\psi_n(b)$, the transition dipole of b.

London formula

$$\mathcal{E}(R) \sim -\left(\frac{3}{32\pi^2\epsilon_0^2}\right)\left(\frac{\alpha(a)\alpha(b)}{R^6}\right)\left(\frac{I(a)I(b)}{I(a)+I(b)}\right),$$

where α is the polarizability of the atom and I is its °ionization potential.

If α is in cubic ångströms, R in ångströms, and I in electronvolts.

$$\mathcal{E}(R) \sim -\left(\frac{3}{32\pi^2}\right)\left(\frac{\alpha(a)\alpha(b)}{R^6}\right)\left(\frac{I(a)I(b)}{I(a)+I(b)}\right)\ \text{eV}$$

$3/32\pi^2 \sim 0{\cdot}0095$.

Retardation. When $R\Delta/\hbar c \gg 1$

$$\mathcal{E}(R) \sim -\left(\frac{23\hbar c}{64\pi^3\epsilon_0^2}\right)\left(\frac{\alpha(a)\alpha(b)}{R^7}\right).$$

At great distances the dispersion formula fails on account of the time it takes the information that a fluctuation has occurred to travel between the atoms: this is the *retardation effect.* When R is large ($R \gg hc/\Delta$, Δ a typical molecular excitation energy) the R^{-6} dependence is replaced by R^{-7}, and the interaction falls off more rapidly that the London formula predicts.

Questions. What are the dispersion forces, and how do they arise? What is the dependence on the separation of the molecules? Why does the interaction energy depend on the polarizability of the molecules? On what other properties does it depend? What does the distance-dependence become at large distances, and what is the change due to? Why are hydrocarbons volatile? Why does I_2 dissolve readily in liquid ammonia? Why is it difficult to liquefy helium?

Further information. See *MQM* Chapter 11 for the deduction of the quantum-mechanical expression for the dispersion interactions, and of the London formula. See also Kauzmann (1957), Chapter 18 of Eyring, Walter, and Kimball (1944), Chu (1967), § III of the book of Hirschfelder, Curtiss, and Bird (1954). A brief survey has been given by Longuet-Higgins (1965); see also Rowlinson (1969) and Curtiss (1967). The subject of °intermolecular forces is reviewed under that heading, and more references will be found there.

doubling. In a spectrum 'doubling' refers to a situation in which the °degeneracy of a level is removed by some hitherto neglected interaction; each two-fold degenerate level is split into two distinct nondegenerate levels—hence 'doubling'. The doubling shows up in the spectrum either as an actual doubling of the number of lines, when other states can make transitions

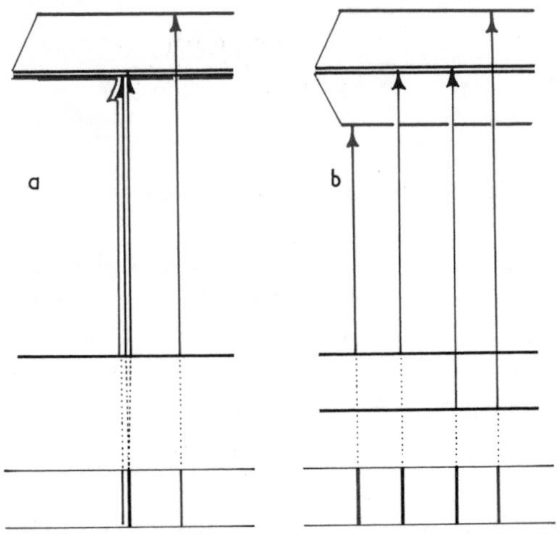

FIG. D4. Different types of doubling in a spectrum: (a) the originally degenerate level combines with one level; (b) the originally degenerate level combines with two different levels. Unperturbed levels are in black, perturbed levels are in colour.

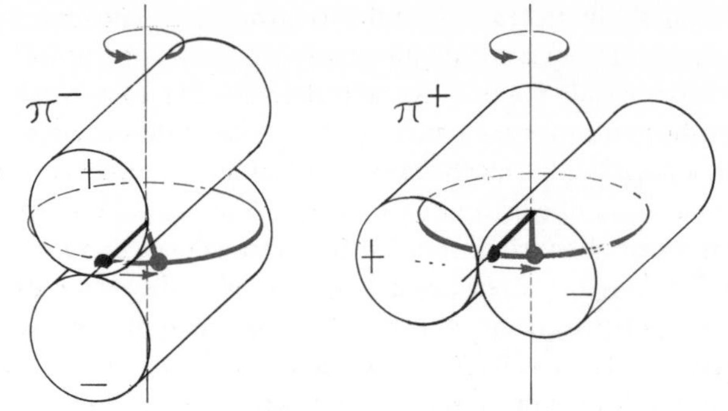

FIG. D5. Λ-doubling: the mechanism in a diatomic molecule.

to the now separated levels (Fig. D4a), or there occurs a situation in which some states combine with (which means make transitions to) only one of the components of the doublet, and others combine with the other component (Fig. D4b).

An example of doubling in atomic spectroscopy is the °fine structure in the spectra of the alkali metals. Take sodium as an example, and consider an excited configuration in which the valence electron occupies a 3p-orbital, then drops down into the 3s-orbital, and in the process emits the characteristic yellow sodium light (589 nm). Close inspection of the spectrum shows that the yellow light is slightly impure, for it consists of two components, one at 588.99 nm and the other at 589.59 nm; this splitting can be ascribed to a doubling of the excited-state levels. More details will be found under °fine structure; but, briefly, the excited state is ^2P, this has two °levels $^2P_{1/2}$ and $^2P_{3/2}$, which are degenerate in the absence of spin-orbit coupling but differ in energy when the coupling is taken into account. Transitions from these two levels to the ground state $^2S_{1/2}$ yield the two spectral lines separated by $17{\cdot}2\ cm^{-1}$.

An example of doubling in molecular spectroscopy is *Λ-doubling* (lambda doubling) in which the rotation of a linear molecule removes the degeneracy of the two components of a Π °term (or, less importantly, of a Δ or a Φ term). It is possible to identify the interaction responsible by considering a diatomic molecule in which a single valence electron occupies a π-orbital. In Fig. D5 we illustrate the situation in which the electron occupies either the orbital π^+ or the orbital π^-, where the superscript is based on the behaviour of the sign of the orbitals when they are reflected in the plane of molecular rotation. If the electrons were able to follow the rotation of the nuclei exactly, with no lag or slip, the two π-orbitals would have precisely the same energy; this is well-known to be the case when a static molecule is considered, as in the usual discussion of bonding theory. But the electrons do not follow the motion of the nuclei exactly (see °electron slip and the °Born-Oppenheimer approximation), and there is a tendency for the electrons to lag behind the nuclei. In the case of π^- the lag has virtually no effect, for to the lowest approximation the nuclei slide a little forward in the orbital's nodal plane and so remain surrounded by roughly the same electron density as in the static case. But the nuclei slide from the vertical nodal plane of π^+ into a region of non-zero electron density, and so it is entirely plausible that the energy of π^+ is modified by the rotation. It follows that the two orbitals move apart in energy and that the energy separation, or doubling, depends on the rate of rotation.

The effect of Λ-doubling on a spectrum may be seen by considering the °rotational structure of an °electronic transition in which a diatomic molecule changes from a Σ state to a Π state. (For the technical, we are considering the transition ${}^1\Pi \leftarrow {}^1\Sigma^+$.) The Λ-doubling of the upper state is illustrated in Fig. D6: the separation of the components of the state increases with °rotational quantum number J according to the rule $qJ(J+1)$, where q is a constant. Transitions of the P- and R- °branches of the spectrum are allowed to take place from the rotational states of the lower electronic state to only one of the components (the one labelled +) of the upper electronic state, but the Q-branch transitions may take place only to the other component. From an analysis of the shift of the Q-branch from the centre of the P- and R-branches it is possible to extract the value of the parameter q (see Questions) and to relate this value to the separation of electronic states in the molecule.

Two other examples of doubling are important. The first is *ℓ-type doubling*, in which the degeneracy of a bending vibrational level of a linear triatomic molecule is removed by the effects of molecular rotation (see °Coriolis interaction). The second is °*inversion doubling*, where the ability of a molecule to invert from one conformation to another doubles its vibrational spectrum. *Ω-doubling* (omega doubling) is the analogue of Λ-doubling when °Hund's case (c) is the appropriate coupling scheme.

Questions. 1. What is the meaning of the term 'doubling'? How does its presence show in the spectrum of an atom or

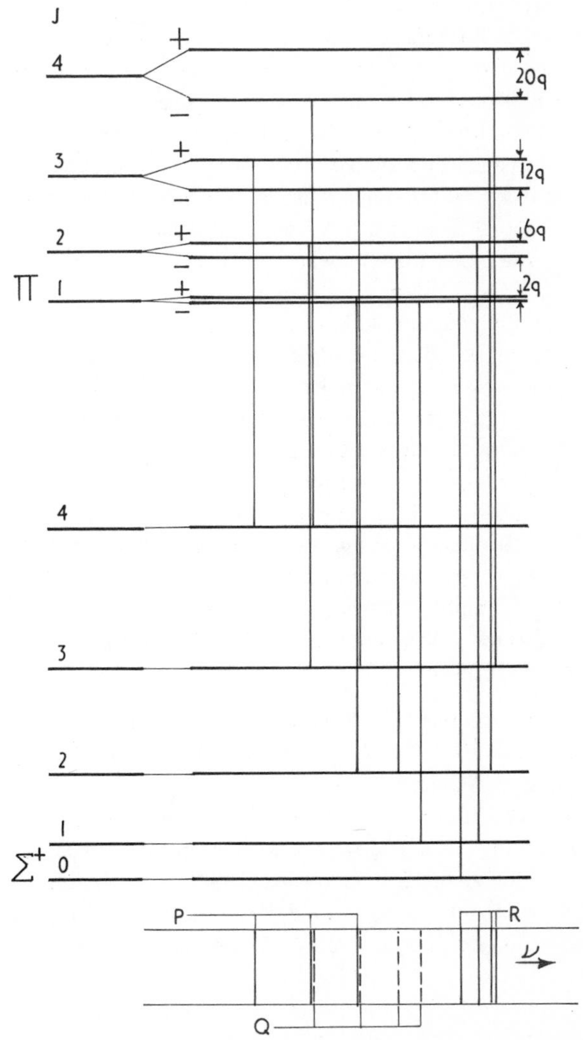

FIG. D6. Λ-doubling: selection rules and spectra. A large Λ-doubling of the upper state has been selected. Compare Fig. B12, which is based on the same parameters.

molecule? Discuss the doubling that arises in the spectra of the alkali metals: what is the interaction responsible for the doubling; how does the doubling change as the atom is changed from Na to Cs; are the °selection rules satisfactory for the explanation? If the two lines are at 588.99 nm and 589.59 nm, what is their separation in cm^{-1}? Deduce a value of the spin-orbit coupling parameter of Na from these data. What is the origin of Λ-doubling? Why should the doubling increase with rotational quantum number? By inspection of Fig. D5 deduce that the orbital mixed into the π^*-orbital by the effect of rotation is a σ-orbital. Is the orbital mixed in a bonding or an antibonding orbital? What mixing is expected in the case of an °antibonding π-orbital? (It should be stressed that the actual calculation of Λ-doubling effects should be done on the basis of overall states rather than one-electron orbitals.)
2. The Λ-doubling interaction varies as $qJ(J+1)$; show that in the spectrum of a diatomic molecule the R- and P-branches correspond to a diatomic molecule with a modified rotation constant $B+b$, where B is the true rotational constant, and the Q-branch corresponds to a molecule with a different rotational constant $B+b'$. Find expressions for b and b' in terms of q and show how the displacement of the branches may be used for the determination of the true B. Construct the first few lines of the rotational structure of the electronic transition in which a ${}^1\Sigma^+$ molecule changes to ${}^1\Pi$; in the lower state take $B = 6{\cdot}020\ cm^{-1}$, in the upper $B = 6{\cdot}000\ cm^{-1}$, and in the upper $q = 0{\cdot}008\ cm^{-1}$.

Further information. See *MQM* Chapter 10 for a more detailed discussion, Whiffen (1972), and Barrow (1962). A detailed discussion of Λ-doubling with worked examples is given in Herzberg (1950): see especially pp. 252–5; the basic theory is laid down on p. 226. Sugden and Kenney (1965) discuss ℓ-type doubling in § 3.1c, and King (1964) gives a helpful discussion of Λ-doubling in § 6.7, ℓ-type doubling in § 9.15, and inversion doubling in § 9.17. The detailed algebra of Λ-type doubling is described by Kovacs (1969). See also Townes and Schawlow (1955).

duality. Classical physics dealt with waves and with particles, and it was quite clear which was which. Quantum mechanics introduced the view that matter and radiation have a dual character and that either aspect of behaviour may be exhibited by the same entity. Thus what for historical reasons had been classified as particles showed behaviour that hitherto had been characteristic of waves: it was discovered, by Davisson and Germer, that crystal lattices could diffract beams of electrons, and Thomson showed that the same effect could be brought about by passing the beam through a thin gold foil. Conversely, it was discovered that what had been classified for historical reasons as waves showed behaviour that hitherto had been characteristic of particles: both the °Compton effect and the °photoelectric effect require the energy or momentum of the radiation to move around in localized bundles. The conclusion to which one is forced is that 'waves' and 'particles' have been so classified because at the level of the experiments done until the beginning of the present century one type of behaviour dominated and the other was concealed. Looking more closely at each type of entity reveals the duality of their character, and so the nature of matter and radiation is neither just one nor the other, but a composition of the two. Which aspect dominates depends on the experiment; no experiment can exhibit both aspects of the duality simultaneously (principle of °complementarity).

Further information. See Jammer (1966) for the way that the idea of duality emerged as a fundamental property of matter, and Bohm (1951) for an illuminating discussion. The quantum-mechanical basis of duality may be investigated by dealing with °wave packets and studying the role of the °uncertainty principle in limiting our view of Nature. We have mentioned the duality of matter and radiation; further aspects will be found under °excitons, °phonons, °photons, and °polarons.

E

eigenfunctions, etc. When some mathematical operation (such as multiplication, division, or differentiation) is done on a function the result is generally some different function. Thus differentiation of the function x^2 yields the different function $2x$. But some combinations of operations and functions are such that when the operation is done the same function is regenerated, but perhaps multiplied by a number. Thus differentiation of the function exp $2x$ gives 2exp $2x$, which is the same function multiplied by the number 2. When this occurs the function is referred to an an *eigenfunction* of the operator (in this case the differential operator d/dx), and the numerical factor (2 in the example) is called the *eigenvalue* of the operator. *Eigen* is the German word meaning 'own' or 'particular'.

The importance of these names in quantum mechanics can be recognized by noting that the Schrödinger equation may be written as $H\psi = E\psi$, where H is a differential operator (the °hamiltonian) and ψ is the °wavefunction. This has the form of an *eigenvalue equation,* with the energy E playing the part of the eigenvalue and the wavefunction as the eigenfunction. The wavefunction represents a state of the system, and so ψ is often termed the *eigenstate*, or, because it also shares some properties with vectors, the *eigenvector.* The result of an experiment done on a system in a given eigenstate is the eigenvalue of the °operator corresponding to the observation.

Questions. 1. Define the terms eigenfunction, eigenvalue, eigenstate, eigenvector, and eigenvalue equation. Why are these terms important in quantum mechanics? If you knew the state of a system, and knew the mathematical form of the operation corresponding to the observable you wanted to determine, how could you predict the result of an experiment?
2. Which of the following functions are eigenfunctions of the operation d/dx: ax, ax^2, exp ax, exp ax^2, ln ax, sin ax? Which are eigenfunctions of d^2/dx^2? The operator corresponding to the component of angular momentum about the z-axis is $(\hbar/i)(\partial/\partial\phi)$: if you knew that the state of the system is described by the function $f(r, \theta)\exp im\phi$, what experimental result could you predict? What if the state were $f(r, \theta)\cos m\phi$? Here is a tricky but important question: what is the eigenfunction of the operation 'multiplication by x'?

Further information. See *MQM* Chapter 4 for a discussion of operators and eigenvalues. For a deep view of eigenstates and an explanation of why they are called eigenvectors see Dirac (1958), von Neumann (1955), and Jauch (1968). See Davydov (1965) for a helpful summary and examples, including (on p. 28) the answer to the final question.

Einstein A and B coefficients. The rate of an absorptive transition between two states is proportional to the density of radiation present at the frequency of the transition, and the coefficient of proportionality is the *Einstein coefficient of stimulated absorption B.* The rate of emission depends on two factors. One contribution is proportional to the energy density at the transition frequency, and the coefficient of proportionality is termed *Einstein's coefficient of stimulated emission.* Since it is equal to B it is also denoted B. Another component of the transition rate is independent of the amount of radiation already present and is termed *Einstein's coefficient of spontaneous emission* and denoted A.

The necessity for this extra coefficient A stems from the equality of the rates of upward and downward stimulated transitions: if these stimulated processes were the only ones to occur the distribution of populations between the upper and lower states would be equal at equilibrium, whereas the Boltzmann distribution requires the upper population to be less than the lower. The spontaneous emission process comes to the rescue because it provides a way of permitting the upper states to leak into the lower at a rate independent of the radiation already present. Thus if the equilibrium population of the upper state is n_+, and of the lower is n_-, then the rate of upward, absorptive, transitions is $n_- B\rho(\nu)$, where $\rho(\nu)$ is the radiation density at the frequency of the transition of energy $h\nu$, and the rate of the downward transitions is $n_+ B\rho(\nu) + n_+ A$. Equating the two rates at equilibrium, and insisting with Boltzmann that $n_+/n_- = \exp(-h\nu/kT)$, enables us to deduce that the equilibrium radiation density must be of the form $\rho(\nu) = (A/B)\,[\exp(h\nu/kT) - 1]^{-1}$. Simply looking at this expression shows that A cannot be zero if the equilibrium radiation density is to be non-zero, and so the spontaneous process is essential. But one can go even further, and find an expression for A in terms of B by recognizing that at equilibrium the radiation density will be that of a °black-body radiator, and therefore that ρ should be given by the Planck distribution. By comparing the expression above with that in Box 2 on p. 23 it is easy to deduce that $A = 8\pi h(\nu/c)^3 B$.

An expression for B may be obtained from °time-dependent perturbation theory, and for °electric dipole transitions one finds that $B = d^2/6\epsilon_0\hbar^2$, where d is the magnitude of the °electric transition dipole between the two states of interest.

An important conclusion emerges from the expression for the ratio A/B, for we see that it increases as the cube of the frequency of the transition; therefore the spontaneous processes become very important at high frequencies, but can be ignored at low frequencies. A consequence of this is the inherent difficulty of constructing high-frequency °lasers, for these rely on the co-operative effect of stimulated transitions; if the spontaneous processes are too important the excited states decay too quickly and do not contribute to the co-operative laser process.

Questions. 1. What is the significance of the Einstein B coefficient? What is the rate of transition from a ground state occupied by N atoms? What is the rate of transition from an upper state occupied by N' atoms? If A were absent, show that the equilibrium populations of the upper and lower levels are equal and in conflict with the Boltzmann requirement. Deduce an expression for the Einstein A coefficient on the basis of a Boltzmann distribution of populations, equal rates of transition at equilibrium, and the Planck distribution of radiation at equilibrium (p. 23). At what frequencies are the spontaneous emission processes important? Confirm that the dimensions of B are those of (volume $\times$ frequency) per (energy $\times$ time), and that since the dimensions of ρ are energy per (frequency range $\times$ volume) the transition rate comes out with the correct dimensions. The dimensions of A should be those of time^{-1}: check that this is so.
2. From the Planck distribution (Box 2, p. 23) estimate the radiation density of light of wavelength 1 cm (microwave radiation) and 500 nm (visible light) emitted by a black body at 1000 K; deduce a value of B that corresponds to unit °oscillator strength and compute the relative importance of the emissive and absorptive processes at equilibrium.

Further information. See *MQM* Chapter 7. A discussion of the A and B coefficients is given in § 12.8 of Davidson (1962), in § 8d of Eyring, Walter and Kimball (1944), in § 7.2 of Hameka (1965), in Chapter 5 of Heitler (1954), and, implicitly, by Dirac (1958). Their importance in the discussion of laser radiation processes is reflected in books on laser technology; therefore see °laser and references therein.

electric dipole transition. The most intense transitions of atoms and molecules are those caused by the interaction of the electric component of an electromagnetic field with the electric dipole moment of the system. A simple example is the interaction of a permanent dipole moment of some molecule with the light beam; when this happens the rotational motion of the molecule is accelerated and it makes a transition between two °rotational energy levels. Conversely, a rotating electric dipole moment behaves like an oscillating electric charge, and an electromagnetic wave is generated and transmitted by the rotating system. The wave carries away energy, and so the molecule drops down the ladder of rotational energy states. The same kind of electric dipole transitions occur in vibrating systems if accompanying the vibration there is a net motion of charge. Thus electric dipole transitions can be induced in the °vibrational energy levels of the polar HCl molecule because an observer on the side of the molecule will see a changing charge distribution as it vibrates. The same observer viewing the chlorine molecule (Cl_2) will detect no such change, and so that mode of the molecule cannot interact with the electromagnetic field by an electric dipole mechanism; it can neither accept energy by absorption nor generate energy in the field and emit.

Electric dipole transitions may also occur between the electronic states of atoms, and once again it is necessary to assess whether the transition involves a motion of charge which can be interpreted as an oscillation of a dipole. It should be clear that a transition from a spherically symmetrical 1s-orbital to a spherically symmetrical 2s-orbital involves a symmetrical redistribition of charge, and so no net dipole moment can be associated with the transition. Therefore this transition cannot occur via an electric dipole-moment mechanism. If however we envisage an s-to-p transition, then a dipole can be identified. If the transition is from s to p_z the oscillating dipole lies along the z-axis, and so the emitted radiation is transmitted plane-polarized with its electric vector in the z-direction (the intensity would appear greatest to a viewer stationed in the xy-plane). If the transition is from s to p_x (or p_y) the polarization lies in the direction of x (or y), and the radiation emerges in a belt largely in the yz (or zx)-plane.

When transitions are made between orbitals with definite values of the °quantum number m_ℓ the radiation is circularly polarized; when m_ℓ decreases by unity the emitted radiation is left circularly polarized, and when it increases by unity the radiation is right circularly polarized; when m_ℓ is unchanged the light is plane polarized. (We use the convention that the electric vector of left circularly polarized light rotates anticlockwise to the observer towards whom the light is travelling.) This behaviour can be understood by considering the transitions s–p; p_x and p_y may be expressed as superpositions of states of different m_ℓ, and so the radiation emitted is the appropriate superposition of the plane polarized radiation already described.

The °selection rules for electric dipole radiation may be understood in terms of the above discussion and also by virtue of the °photon's possession of an intrinsic °spin angular momentum. The first view leads to the *Laporte selection rule* which states that the *parity* of an orbital (see °*gerade* and *ungerade*) must change in an electric dipole transition. Thus in an s–p transition an even orbital (even with respect to inversion through the atomic nucleus) changes to an orbital odd under inversion. The same is true of d–p transitions. The rule forbids s–s, p–p, and d–d transitions, for with these there is associated no transition dipole moment. The existence of a photon angular momentum coupled with the principle of conservation of angular momentum provides an alternative view of the situation, because the labels s, p, and d imply that electrons in the orbitals possess different °angular momenta, and when a photon is emitted or absorbed the angular momentum of the atom must change in order to conserve the total momentum. A photon impinging on an s-orbital must turn it into a p-orbital, and is unable to turn it into a d-orbital because it brings insufficient angular momentum. When an incident photon interacts with a p-orbital the final state can be either a d-orbital or an s-orbital, depending on the relative orientation of the angular momenta in the collision.

The connexion between the change in the value of m_ℓ and the polarization of the light can also be understood on the basis of the photon spin, because left circularly polarized light corresponds to one orientation of the photon spin with respect to its propagation direction and right circularly polarized light corresponds to the opposite projection. Therefore in order to conserve the total amount of angular momentum of the total system about a particular direction, m_ℓ must change appropriately if a photon is absorbed or emitted. If the light approaches the atom along the negative z-axis (from $z = -\infty$) and is left circularly polarized (spin projection +1 on the propagation direction, moving like a *right*-handed screw) when it is absorbed the atom must change from a state m_ℓ to $m_\ell+1$ if the angular momentum about the z-axis is to be conserved. The same argument applies to emission.

If an optical transition is observed when the preceeding rules forbid it, the reason may be that the atom lacks a centre of symmetry by virtue of its environment, or there may be a coupling between the electronic and vibrational modes: see °vibronic transitions. Or it may be that a °magnetic dipole or electric quadrupole transition is responsible for the intensity. To a very good approximation the electric field of the light cannot interact directly with the spin of an electron, because that is an internal mode of motion, and so spin is conserved in electric dipole transitions; when that rule fails it is by virtue of the spin-orbit coupling interaction.

Questions. 1. What are the most common and intense optical transitions due to? Why is an electromagnetic field able to accelerate a rotating molecule? To do so what must the molecule possess? Can an electric dipole transition increase the amount of angular momentum about the figure axis (the symmetry axis) of a symmetric top molecule (a cylindrical or disc-like molecule)? Is the light polarized in rotational electric dipole transitions? Under what circumstances can a vibrational mode emit or absorb light by electric dipole transitions? Which modes of vibration of carbon dioxide are able to interact with an electromagnetic field, and which are not? (It might be helpful to revise °normal modes and °vibrational spectra.) Why is it possible to regard the transitions between states of atoms as involving an electric dipole moment? What is the name given to the moment involved? How is the polarization of the light involved in a transition related to the orientation of the electric dipole? Discuss the polarization of the transitions $s-p_z$, $s-p_x$, $s-(p_x+ip_y)$, where by (p_x+ip_y) is meant the p-orbital with $m_\ell=+1$. Consider the effect of a magnetic field on an atom, as in the °Zeeman effect: discuss the polarization of the light that you would see as your detector, sensitive to the three transitions $s-p_z$, $s-p_{+1}$, $s-p_{-1}$, was moved over the whole sphere of possible orientations. State the Laporte selection rule: how can it be justified and under what circumstances will it fail? What role does the spin of a photon play in determining which electric dipole transitions are allowed? How may such a description be brought into line with the Laporte selection rule? Discuss the polarization of the transitions in the preceeding questions in terms of the angular momentum of the photon and the conservation of total angular momenta. Why may the angular momentum of an atom either increase or decrease when a photon is absorbed or emitted? If electric dipole transitions forbid a transition, what might account for its intensity?
2. Discuss the sense in which an electric transition dipole moment may be said to oscillate at the frequency of the radiation it transmits (the °correspondence principle requires some such sense to exist). Consider the time-dependence of the transition dipole moment by expressing the matrix element $\int d\tau \Psi_e^* \mathbf{d} \Psi_g$, where Ψ_e is the excited state, Ψ_g is the ground state of the system, and **d** is the electric dipole moment operator, in terms of the explicit time-dependence of the states; that is, write $\Psi_g = \psi_g \exp(-iE_g t/\hbar)$. Apply group theory (see °character) to the matrix element to deduce the Laporte selection rule.

Further information. See *MQM* Chapter 8 for a discussion of electric dipole transitions. For applications in organic chemistry see Murrell (1971) and Sandorfy (1964), and for applications in inorganic chemistry, especially in the electronic spectra of transition-metal compounds see Orgel (1960), Ballhausen (1962), and Griffith (1964). The basis of the selection rules is the calculation of transition probabilities by time-dependent perturbation theory: therefore see *MQM* Chapter 7, Herzberg (1940), and Eyring, Walter, and Kimball (1940).

electron affinity. The electron affinity of an isolated atom is the energy evolved when an electron is brought up from infinity and the anion formed. Therefore the electron affinity is the difference in energy of the neutral atom and its negative ion: $E_a(X) = E(X) - E(X^-)$. A *positive* electron affinity implies that the anion is *more* stable than the neutral atom. Since an amount of work $E_a(X)$ must be done on the ion X^- in order to regain the neutral atom and the infinitely separated electron it should be clear that $E_a(X)$ is the same as the °ionization potential $I(X^-)$ of the anion: $E_a(X) = I(X^-)$.

The determination of electron affinities is often somewhat devious. A direct method is to measure the ionization potential of the anion. The other methods are:

(1) electron impact, in which one tries to identify the appearance potential of the negative ion in the reaction $XY + e \rightarrow X^- + Y$;

(2) electron attachment measurements (so-called electron affinity spectroscopy);

(3) polarography;

(4) application of the Born-Haber cycle for the lattice energy of an ionic crystal.

One application of electron-affinity values is to the construction of the Mulliken °electronegativity scale, and it is of use wherever the stability of an anionic species is required.

Further information. A review of methods for determining electron affinities has been written by McDowell (1969). Further information and tables of affinities will be found in Prichard (1953), Vedeneyev, Gurvich, Kondrat'yev, Medaredev, and Frankevich (1966), and Briegleb (1964). For applications in chemistry, see Puddephatt's *The periodic table of the elements* (OCS 3) and Phillips and Williams (1965).

electron slip. Electrons slip not because they are slippery but because in a rotating molecule they may be unable to follow the rapid motion of the nuclei: electron slip is a manifestation of the breakdown of the °Born-Oppenheimer approximation. Think of a rotating hydrogen molecule: the electrons may lag behind the motion of the nuclei as the nuclear framework rotates. That is, the electrons and the nuclear framework have slightly different angular momenta.

There are two important consequences of electron slip. The first is that the distinction between σ and π orbitals (and between Σ and Π states) becomes blurred: this is manifest in the electronic spectra of linear molecules as *Λ-type °doubling.* The other consequence is that all molecules possess a magnetic moment by virtue of their rotation: this is the *molecular magnetic moment.* This moment can be traced to the different rates of rotation of the positively-charged nuclear framework and the negatively-charged electron cloud of the molecule. There is a net current, and therefore a net magnetic moment. All molecules possess such a moment when they rotate, and the magnitude of the moment increases with the °rotational quantum number J.

Further information. See *MQM* Chapter 10 for a more detailed account of the way that electron slip mixes Σ and Π states, and °doubling for a picture; for a quantitative treatment see King (1962), Herzberg (1950), and Kovačs (1969). For molecular magnetic moments see °g-value, §11.6 of Townes and Schawlow (1955) and p. 299 of Herzberg (1950).

electron spin resonance: a synopsis. The electron spin resonance (e.s.r.) experiment is the observation of the energy required to reverse the direction of an electron °spin in the presence of a magnetic field. The electron possesses a °magnetic moment by virtue of its spin, and in the presence of an applied field the two permitted orientations (α and β) have different energies (in a field of 3 kG the α-state lies 0·3 cm^{-1} above the β-state). An electron can be induced to reverse its orientation (make a transition from β to α) if electromagnetic radiation of the appropriate frequency is applied, and in a 3 kG magnetic field the 0·3 cm^{-1} radiation (wavelength 3 cm, frequency 9 GHz) lies in the microwave region of the spectrum. The apparatus therefore consists of a magnet capable of providing a homogeneous field in the vicinity of 3 kG, a source of 3 cm microwaves (a *klystron*), and a device for detecting whether the incident radiation is absorbed. The e.s.r. experiment is performed by maintaining a constant microwave frequency and sweeping the applied field until the incident radiation is absorbed (Fig. E1): at this field the separation between the α and β orientations exactly matches (is in °resonance with) the radiation frequency. The

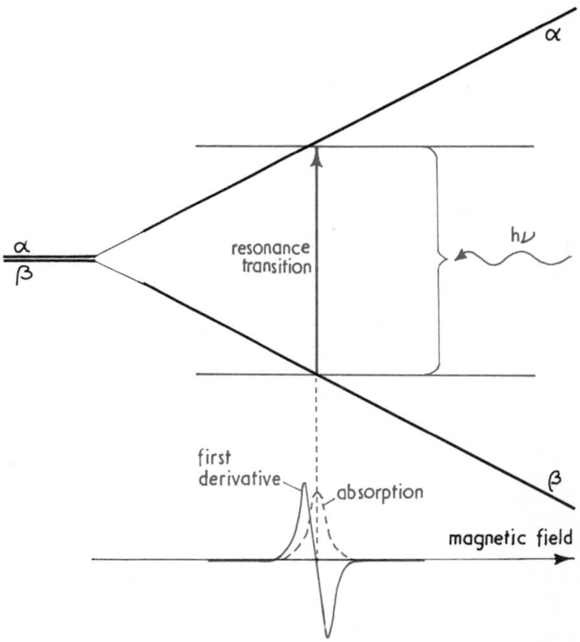

FIG. E1. The electron spin resonance transition, and the resulting spectrum.

sample, which must be paramagnetic, may be a solid, a liquid, or (more rarely) a gas.

Three principal pieces of information emerge from the experiment:

1. *The position of the spectrum*. The magnetic field experienced by the electron might differ from the applied field because the latter is able to induce local fields. For a given microwave frequency the resonance condition will be attained at the same *local* field, and therefore at slightly different applied fields in different species. If the microwave frequency is ν, so that each photon carries the energy $h\nu$, and the applied field is B, the resonance condition is $g\mu_B B = h\nu$, where g is a factor (which, by lack of inspiration, is called the °*g*-factor) which takes into account the possibility that the local field is not exactly equal to B. Measuring the position of the spectrum

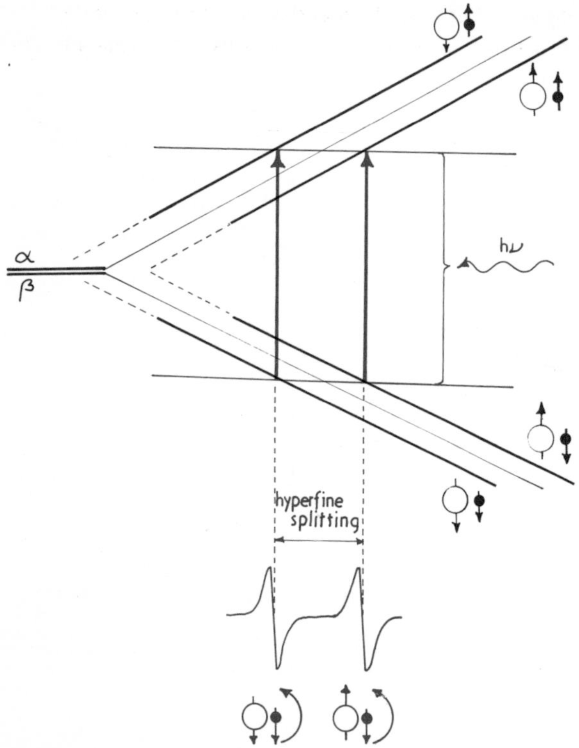

FIG. E2. The source of hyperfine splitting in a radical containing one spin-½ nucleus (denoted by the larger circle).

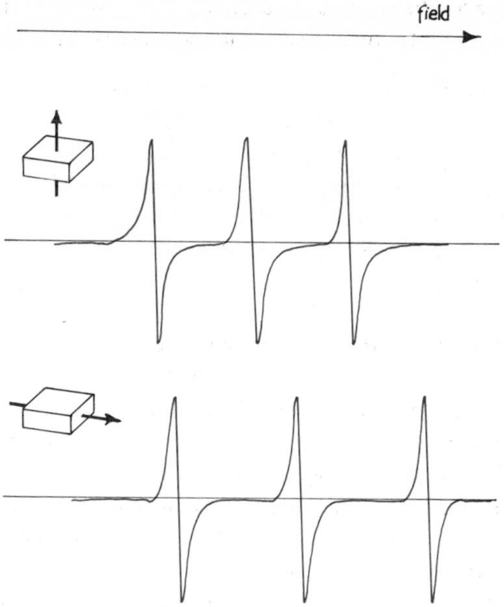

FIG. E3. A typical electron spin resonance spectrum of a radical (with one spin-1 nucleus) trapped in a crystal. Two orientations of the crystal are shown: note that the centre of the spectrum shifts (g anisotropic) and the splittings change (anisotropic hyperfine interactions).

enables g to be determined, and as g depends on the electronic structure of the paramagnetic species some deductions may be made about it. In organic and inorganic radicals g is most useful for the identification of the species; wider variations in its value are found in transition-metal ions, and there it can give useful structural information, particularly about the separation of energy levels and the spread of electrons on to ligands. g may be anisotropic, in which case the position of the spectrum depends on the orientation of the paramagnetic species (when it is trapped in a crystal, and the crystal rotated, the resonance position changes).

2. *The hyperfine structure of the spectrum.* Generally the spectrum does not consist of a single line: the structure observed is due to the °hyperfine interaction of the electron and any magnetic nuclei present. A magnetic nucleus (such as a proton) gives rise to a local magnetic field, which, depending on the relative orientation of the nuclear spin and the applied field, can increase or decrease the local field experienced by

the electron spin. This implies that radicals with different nuclear spin orientations resonate at different applied magnetic fields, and the spectrum from a large collection of radicals consists of lines at all these applied fields (Fig. E2). For example, N radicals each containing one proton will constitute a sample consisting of $\frac{1}{2}N$ radicals with proton spins aligned along the magnetic field and $\frac{1}{2}N$ proton spins aligned against it. The electrons in the first set of radicals experience one local field and resonate at the appropriate applied frequency, and the electrons in the other set resonate at another applied field. The spectrum therefore consists of two lines separated by several gauss: this °*hyperfine splitting* (h.f.s.) may be interpreted in terms of the probability that the unpaired electron will be found in the vicinity of the magnetic nucleus in question, and so a study of the h.f.s. enables the electron distribution to be mapped over the molecule. The h.f.s. has both isotropic and anisotropic components (see Fig. E3): the former is due to the °Fermi contact interaction and is characteristic of s-orbital character of the electron, the latter is due to the dipole-dipole interaction and is characteristic of p-orbital character. Therefore

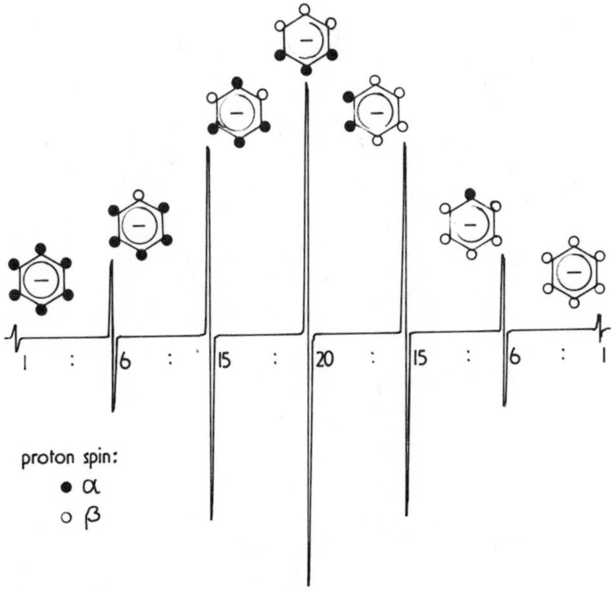

FIG. E4. A typical solution electron spin resonance spectrum (of benzene^{-}), and its interpretation.

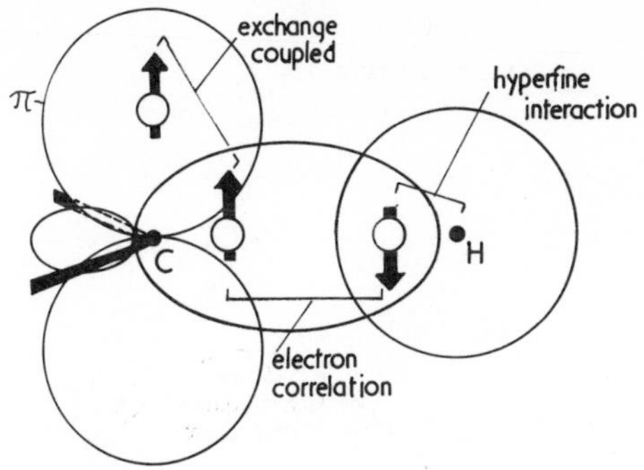

FIG. E5. The spin-polarization mechanism in CH.

a study of the angular dependence of the h.f.s. yields information on the °hybridization of the unpaired electron's orbital, and this can be used to discuss the shape of the radical (the methyl radical, for instance, is shown to be planar). In fluid solution only the isotropic h.f.s. is observed (see, for example, Fig. E4), and a principal application is its use to map spin density in organic radicals. In aromatic radicals the h.f.s. is due to a spin-polarization mechanism along a C—H bond, as illustrated in Fig. E5. The π-electron (with, we choose, α-spin) causes the α-spin in the C—H σ-bond to be predominantly in its vicinity (electrons prefer to be parallel in atoms: see the °Hund rules) so that the β-spin predominates in the vicinity of the proton. Therefore, although in the bond the spins are paired, the proton sees predominantly one spin, and there is a net interaction.

3. *The shape of the spectral lines.* The shape of the lines depends on the type of motion that the radicals undergo, for it is determined by *relaxation processes*. Two types of relaxation process may be distinguished: the *spin-lattice* and the *spin-spin*. The former arises by virtue of the motion of the radical giving rise to fluctuating magnetic fields at the unpaired electron; if these fluctuations happen to have a component that oscillates at the transition frequency, then a transition can be induced. The lifetime of the upper state is shortened, and, by what passes for the °uncertainty principle, the energy of the state is blurred. This spin-lattice relaxation process is feeble when the motion of the jitterbugging molecule is slow (because there are no oscillations in the fluctuating field with

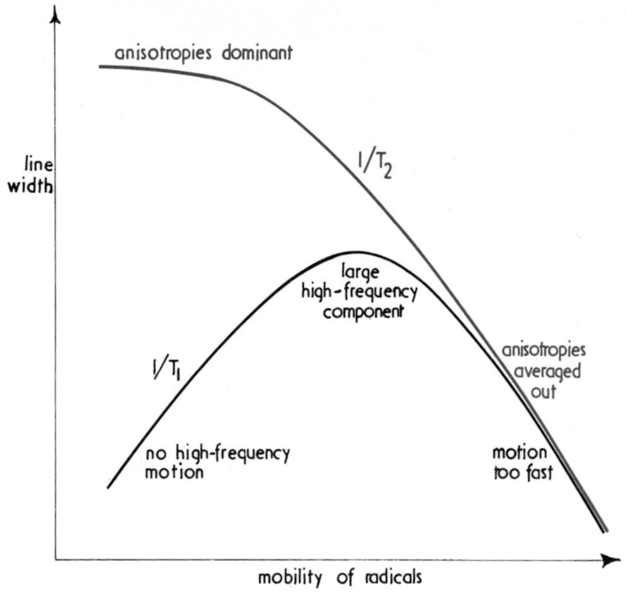

FIG. E6. The dependence of the relaxation time on the rapidity of molecular motion.

the correct frequency 10^{10} s^{-1}), passes through a maximum when a typical time scale for molecular motion is 10^{-10}s, and then declines in extremely mobile liquids when many of the fluctuations occur at very high frequencies (Fig. E6). The lifetime of the spin state is called T_1, the *spin-lattice relaxation time,* or the *longitudinal relaxation time.* The longer T_1 the narrower the line.

The other relaxation process is the spin-spin process: in a fluid but viscous solution each radical is in a particular magnetic environment or at a particular orientation, and so the local fields are all slightly different; consequently the radicals resonate at slightly different applied fields, and the spectrum is a collection of broadened lines. As the motion of the molecules increases the differences in the magnetic environments, or the anisotropic interactions, are averaged out, and the lines narrow. The effect of this broadening process is characterized by the *spin-spin relaxation time,* or the *transverse relaxation time*, T_2; the longer T_2, the narrower the line. The broadening effect disappears as the radical mobility increases (by raising the temperature or reducing the viscosity).

Note that only T_1 reduces the number of radicals in the upper spin state, and so only it is a true energy relaxation mechanism (the direction of energy flow, which is out of the spin system and into the lattice, or environment, is determined by the thermodynamics of the system: the entropy increases for heat flow out of the small spin system into the virtually infinite lattice). The T_2 process is a different kind of relaxation process: it relaxes the relative phase of the precessing electron spins (Fig. E7).

A study of the line widths and *saturation behaviour* (the reduction of intensity at high microwave powers as a result of the equalization of the α and β populations) of the spectrum gives information about the motion of molecules in liquids, because details of the rapidity of the motion can be inferred from the shape of the lines. Information can also be obtained about the rate of chemical processes, for example tautomerism, because these also modulate the environment of the electron spins.

Further information. See *Magnetic resonance* by McLauchlan (OCS 1) for a simple account of the principles and applications.

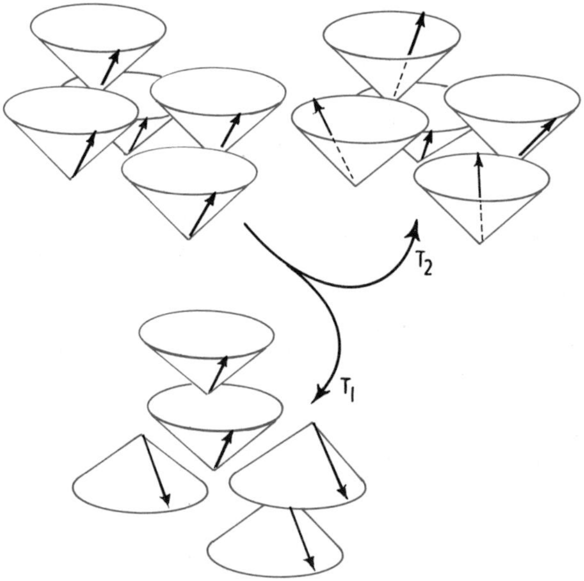

FIG. E7. The relaxation processes characterized by T_1 and T_2.

See also Lynden-Bell and Harris (1969), Carrington and McLauchlan (1967), Wertz and Bolton (1972), Slichter (1963), Abragam and Bleaney (1970) for general accounts. Instrumentation is described by Poole (1967). The application of e.s.r. to organic systems is described in some of these and in Ayscough (1967); the application to inorganic, non-transition-metal systems is described in Atkins and Symons (1967); the application to transition-metal ions is described by Carrington and McLachlan (1967), Wertz and Bolton (1972), Slichter (1963), calculation of the *g*-factor for simple systems is outlined in *MQM* Chapter 11, so too is the source of the hyperfine structure. See also Memory (1968). Relaxation processes are described by Carrington and McLachlan (1967), Poole and Farach (1971), and Standley and Vaughan (1968); and a collection of important papers has been published by Manenkov and Orbach (1966). Detailed theoretical exposition will be found in Muus and Atkins (1972).

electronegativity. The electronegativity of an element in a molecule is the measure of its power to attract electrons; the greater its electronegativity the greater its drawing power. Two definitions of electronegativity are in general use and are due to the efforts and insight of Pauling and Mulliken.

The Pauling electronegativity scale is based on the lowering of the calculated energy of a diatomic molecule when ionic structures are admitted into its description. Suppose the energy of the molecule AB is truly $E(\text{AB})$ but that a calculation based only on purely covalent structures yielded $E_{\text{cov}}(\text{AB})$, the *ionic* °*resonance energy* would be $E_{\text{ion}}(\text{AB}) = E(\text{AB}) - E_{\text{cov}}(\text{AB})$. Pauling found that the square root of $E_{\text{ion}}(\text{AB})$ could be set proportional to the difference of two numbers, one characteristic of the element A and the other of B, and that the expression $[E_{\text{ion}}(\text{AB})]^{½} = |\chi_A^P - \chi_B^P|$ was valid for a wide range of combinations. In order to set up the scale it is necessary to estimate $E_{\text{cov}}(\text{AB})$: Pauling proposed that a reasonable approximation would be the mean of the energies of the molecules A_2 and B_2. This was justified by the view that they are manifestly nonpolar and that the energies of A_2, AB, and B_2 should form a simple sequence if polar structures in AB are omitted. Pauling used both an arithmetic mean and a geometric mean to set up his table (see Table 7).

Having set up the electronegativity scale it is possible to deduce a number of molecular properties. First, one can use it to estimate bond energies if the A_2 and B_2 bond energies are known: this is just a reversal of its definition, but energies may be predicted of molecules other than those used to construct the scale. Next one may use it to predict the *ionicity* of a bond (the percentage ionic character), and for a scale expressed in electronvolts the ionicity is given by the expression $16|\chi_A^P - \chi_B^P| + 3{\cdot}5|\chi_A^P - \chi_B^P|^2$. From the percentage ionic character it is possible to give a rough estimate of the °dipole moment if the bond length is known.

The other scale, that due to Mulliken, is rather more fundamental, for instead of defining it in terms of unmeasurable but estimable quantities he defines it as the mean of the °ionization potential and the °electron affinity of the atom, and both these quantities are measurable. Thus the Mulliken scale is based on $\chi_A^M = \frac{1}{2}[I(\text{A}) + E_a(\text{A})]$. A further advantage of this scheme is that it is possible to take into account the differences in electronegativities of different orbitals on the same atom or the dependence of the electronegativity on its state of °hybridization.

It is not surprising that the two scales are related: at a numerical level it is possible to equate $\chi_A^M - \chi_B^M$ with $2{\cdot}78\,(\chi_A^P - \chi_B^P)$; at a deeper level it is possible to show that to a good approximation the value of $E_{\text{ion}}(\text{AB})$ is determined by the energy required to move an electron from A to B, which is $E_a(\text{B}) - I(\text{A})$, and the energy to move it from B to A, which is $E_a(\text{A}) - I(\text{B})$, and that as in a nonpolar molecule these are equal (because neither tendency wins) on rearranging the equality in this case of vanishing electronegativity difference we find that $E_a(\text{A}) + I(\text{A})$ is equal to $E_a(\text{B}) + I(\text{B})$. Consequently the difference between these quantities should be proportional to the difference of the electronegativities of the two atoms.

Questions. What does the electronegativity of an element measure? Why is it a plausible approximation that $E_{\text{cov}}(\text{AB})$ is the mean of $E(A_2)$ and $E(B_2)$? Given that the bond energies of the halogens X_2 are 2·17 eV for F_2, 2·475 eV for Cl_2, and 1·971 eV for Br_2, that the energy of H_2 is 4·476 eV, and that of O_2 is 5·080 eV, estimate the bond energies of the various heteronuclear diatomic molecules that may be formed.

Estimate the ionic character of each molecule. Deduce an expression for the dipole moment of a diatomic combination in terms of the electronegativities of its components. Why should you expect poor agreement with experimental values (even if you derive a decent expression)? What is the Mulliken definition of electronegativity? In what sense is it superior to the Pauling scale? On what grounds would you expect the Pauling and the Mulliken scales to be related? What molecular energy terms are ignored in this argument?

Further information. See §5.8 of Coulson (1961) and §2.11 of Pauling (1960) for a detailed discussion of the role and deduction of electronegativities. For Mulliken's analysis see Mulliken (1934) and Moffitt (1949b).

electronic spectra of molecules: a synopsis. A natural progression into complexity is from the electronic spectra of diatomic molecules into polyatomic molecules, then to the consideration of chromophores in complex molecules, and then to the spectra of molecules in solids.

The electronic spectrum of a diatomic molecule contains a number of *bands*, each resulting from a transition from the ground electronic state (X) into an excited electronic state (A, B, . . .), and the structure of the bands is due to the simultaneous excitation of vibration; the intensity of these °progressions is determined by the °Franck-Condon principle and the other °selection rules. On the vibrational structure there is a further structure due to the excitation of rotation, and P- and R- °branches are generally visible, and Q-branches in some cases. Since the moment of inertia is different in the two electronic states the branches tend to a head (see Fig. B12 on p. 31): when the moment of inertia is larger in the upper state than in the lower the R-branch, the branch to high frequency, has the head. The vibrational lines get closer to high energy because the vibrational levels converge towards the dissociation limit: the dissociation energy may be determined by observing the dissociation limit or by a careful extrapolation from lower frequencies (a *Birge-Sponer extrapolation* is often used). In some cases the rotational and vibrational structure disappears and then reappears before the dissociation limit is reached: this is a manifestation of °predissociation. From the spectrum may be determined the °force-constants, dissociation energy, and °anharmonicity of the electronic states of the molecule, and the parameters in the molecular potential-energy curves.

The electronic spectrum of a polyatomic molecule is more complicated, but the same principles apply and analogous information obtained. The return to the ground state is an additional subject of interest in polyatomics, especially when the molecule loses its energy by °fluorescence or °phosphorescence. In a condensed phase the rotational structure of the spectrum is lost, and the vibrational spectrum becomes so diffuse that the absorption spectrum is often just a series of broad bands. The electronic spectra of transition-metal complexes is of particular importance, and the transitions may often be associated with the °crystal-field splitting of the d-electrons: see °crystal-field theory and °ligand-field theory. In other cases the transition is a charge transfer transition from the metal ions to the ligands: see °colour. In organic molecules the absorption can often be associated with the presence of a *chromophore* such as the carbonyl group ($\pi^* \leftarrow n$ electric dipole transition) or a double bond ($\pi^* \leftarrow \pi$ transition): see °colour.

When a molecule is a part of a crystal lattice other effects may be observed; one especially important phenomenon is the formation of an °exciton, in which the excitation hops through the lattice.

Further information. See *MQM* Chapter 10 for a discussion of molecular electronic spectra. Books that summarize the applications of electronic spectra to the study of a molecular structure include Barrow (1962), Whiffen (1972), Dixon (1965), King (2964), Jaffé and Orchin (1962), Rao (1967), Stern and Timmons (1970), Herzberg (1950, 1966), Murrell (1971), and Gaydon (1968). Further information about the detailed topics will be found in the appropriate sections. Gaydon (1968) is a very good source of information about how to interpret electronic spectra of small molecules and how to extract potential-energy curves and dissociation energies. Murrell (1971) is concerned with larger, organic molecules, and discusses individual chromophores and their interaction in solids. Herzberg (1950, 1966) is a mine of detailed information, and is a brilliant example of the application of theoretical concepts to the detailed examination of molecular properties.

electronvolt. The electronvolt (eV) is the energy acquired by an electron when it is accelerated by a potential difference of 1 V. Since the charge on the electron is $-1{\cdot}602 \times 10^{-19}$ C the energy is equivalent to $1{\cdot}602 \times 10^{-19}$ J or 96·49 kJ mol^{-1}. Another useful conversion is 1 eV $\approx$ 8023 cm^{-1}.

equipartition theorem. The mean energy of each mode of motion of a classical system in thermal equilibrium is $\frac{1}{2}nkT$, where n is the number of quadratic terms (of displacement or momentum) needed to specify its energy. As an example, the energy of an atom in free space arises from its kinetic energy which can be expressed as the sum of the three quadratic terms $p_x^2/2m$, $p_y^2/2m$, and $p_z^2/2m$; and so the mean energy of an atom in equilibrium at a temperature T is $\frac{3}{2}kT$, and 1 mol of monatomic gas will have an internal energy $\frac{3}{2}RT$. A molecule that can °rotate around three axes will have a mean energy of $\frac{1}{2}kT$ associated with each mode, and so a mean rotational energy of $\frac{3}{2}kT$. A °harmonic oscillator has an energy $(p^2/2m) + \frac{1}{2}kx^2$, where x is the displacement from equilibrium, and so with each oscillatory mode of a body there will be associated a mean energy kT because two quadratic terms appear in the expression for its vibrational energy.

The theorem is a deduction from the Boltzmann distribution for the population of energy levels at thermal equilibrium, and the assumption that the modes concerned are classical. When the modes of motion are quantized the theorem fails, and so it is not applicable to the vibration of molecules nor to small rotating molecules at low temperatures.

Questions. 1. State the equipartition theorem. Calculate the total mean energy of a diatomic molecule, a linear triatomic molecule, a bent triatomic molecule, and methane, on the basis that the translational and rotational motion are classical and the vibrational motion quantized and not excited. Derive an expression for the molar °heat capacity of these species. In terms of the equipartition theorem discuss the contribution to the total energy and the heat capacity of a methyl group in a molecule which at high temperatures is able to rotate freely about one axis, and at lower temperatures can execute only classical torsional motions about the axis.
2. From the Boltzmann distribution at a temperature T show that components in the total energy of the form x^2 and p_x^2 both contribute an amount $\frac{1}{2}kT$ to the mean total energy. What would happen to the equipartition theorem in the event of quartic terms (x^4 and p_x^4) being involved in the energy? What effect has °anharmonicity of the form x and x^3?

Further information. This subject is really within the realm of statistical mechanics; therefore see Gasser and Richards' *Entropy and energy levels* (OCS 19) for some of its elementary applications. See also §7.5 of Reif (1965) for a helpful discussion with applications and §10.3 of Davidson (1962) for a deduction and discussion. §332 of Fowler and Guggenheim (1965) and §44 of Landau and Lifshitz (1958*b*) are worth looking at. See Fowler (1936) and Tolman (1938) for erudite discussion.

equivalent orbital. A molecular orbital is one of a set of equivalent orbitals if a °symmetry operation applied to the molecule transforms the orbital into another member of the set. As an example consider one of the C—H bonds in methane, CH_4: this is formed from the overlap of an sp^3-hybrid orbital on the central carbon and a 1s-orbital of the hydrogen. If the tetrahedral molecule is rotated into another equivalent position another of the sp^3—1s bonds is rotated into the original position. The four σ-bonds constitute a set of equivalent orbitals. The concept of equivalent orbitals is closely related to °hybridization and °localized orbitals.

Further information. See Appendix 9.2 of *MQM* and Chapter 8 of Coulson (1961). Further information can be traced through °localized orbitals.

exchange energy. The Coulombic interaction between two electron distributions is repulsive, and its magnitude may be calculated by dividing both regions into minute charged volumes, calculating the Coulomb energy of interaction between each of the charged volume elements, and then summing over all the elements to obtain the result which we shall write J (see °Coulomb integral). Unfortunately this gives the wrong answer because we have omitted the effect of °spin correlation, which can cause electrons of the same spin orientation to stick together and those of opposite spin to stay apart. Thus if the two electrons have the same spin the true average repulsion energy will be less than J, because of the intrinsic tendency of such electrons to avoid each other. The correction we should make changes the average repulsion energy to $J-K$, the correction term K being the *exchange energy.* The name reflects the source of the correction which lies in the °Pauli principle and the behaviour of wavefunctions when electrons are exchanged.

Further information. See Chapters 8 and 9 of *MQM* for a more detailed account and examples of the application of the concept in atoms and molecules. Good discussions will be found in §19.16–19 of Bohm (1951) and §10.89 of Davydov (1965). For applications to molecules see Coulson (1961), Richards and Horsley (1970), and McGlynn, Vanquickenborne, Kinoshita, and Carroll (1970), who give, in Appendix E, a guide to the computation of the exchange integrals.

exciton. Imagine an array of identical molecules in a crystal, and let one be excited. This excitation hops from molecule to molecule, and slides throughout the crystal until it decays. The excitation moves like a particle, and this notion is conveyed by the word *exciton*, which is the name given to this migrating excitation. If we think of the excitation as being caused by the removal of an electron from one orbital of a molecule (or atom or ion) and its elevation to a higher orbital, then the excited state of the molecule can be envisaged as the coexistence of an electron and a hole. The hopping of this *electron-hole pair* from molecule to molecule is the migration of the exciton. When the electron and the hole jump together from molecule to molecule as they migrate we have the *tight-binding case*, and the migrating excitation is a *Frenkel exciton.* It is also possible for the electron and hole to be on different molecules, but in each others vicinity; this is the *weak-binding case* and the migrating excitation, now spread over several molecules (more usually ions), is a *Wannier exciton.* In molecular solids the Frenkel exciton is more common, and that will be our interest.

The formation of an exciton affects the spectrum of a species in a solid. This should not be surprising, for the migration of an exciton implies that there is an interaction between the species composing the crystal (for otherwise the excitation on one unit could not move to another), and this interaction should affect their energy levels. The strength of the interaction governs the rate at which an exciton moves through the crystal: strong interaction implies fast migration; vanishing interaction implies that the exciton is localized on its original molecule, in which case it is an ordinary excitation of an 'isolated' molecule. Exciton formation causes lines to shift, split, and change in intensity. The reasons for this we shall understand when the mode of interaction between the molecules has been explained.

An electronic transition in a molecule involves a shift of charge (see °transition probability and °electric dipole transition). A shifting charge on one molecule exerts a force on a neighbour, which can respond with a shift of its charge. This process of transition dipole interaction can continue, and the excitation can rattle through the crystal (Fig. E8).

The process can be looked at in a slightly different way by considering all possible relative orientations of the transition dipole moments of the molecules of the crystal, and then seeing what combination a light wave can excite. Let us consider a linear array of molecules with transition moments perpendicular to the line (the arrows indicate the effective direction of motion of the charge when a molecule is excited). On the basis of simple electrostatics the energy of the array with all transition dipoles parallel is higher than any other phasing (Fig. E9), and so a transition to this arrangement of dipoles throughout the crystal appears at an energy higher than the transition to any other arrangement, and indeed higher than the transition in the separated molecules. But it is only this arrangement that the incident light is able to excite. This is because the wavelength of light is so long in comparison with the molecular spacing that its electric field has the same phase over a large number of molecules; therefore it stimulates a whole domain of transition dipoles to move in phase. This means that the presence of the exciton coupling appears in the spectrum as a shift of the absorption band to high energy. If

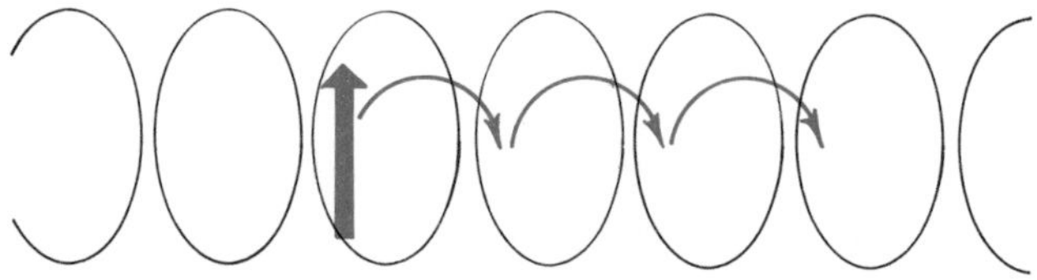

FIG. E8. An excitation migrating through a crystal as an exciton.

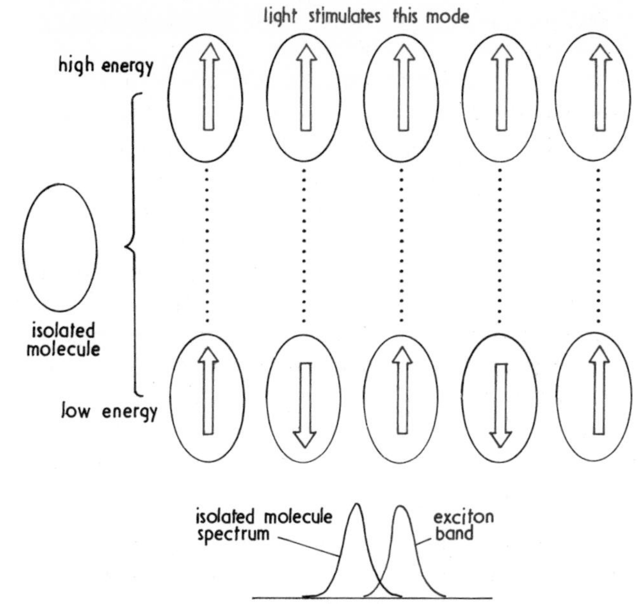

FIG. E9. Transition dipoles with various phasings. The alternating alignment lies lowest, the parallel (the one excited by incident light) lies highest.

the transition dipole moments were along the line of the molecules we should get the opposite shift; this follows from the fact that the in-phase excitation of the transition dipoles gives a head-to-tail array, which has a low energy.

If there is more than one molecule per unit cell it is possible to obtain several lines: N molecules per unit cell give N absorption lines, or *exciton bands.* The splitting between the bands is the *Davydov splitting.* To see how it arises consider the case when $N = 2$ and the molecules are arranged as shown in Fig. E10. Let the transition dipoles be along the length of the molecules. The light field stimulates the in-phase excitation of the transition dipoles, but they need be in-phase only in so far as neighbouring unit cells are concerned. Within each unit cell the transition dipoles may be arrayed as in Fig. E10 a or b, and these have different interaction energies. This will appear in the spectrum as two bands split by the energy of interaction between the transition dipoles within the unit cell.

Questions. 1. What is implied by the term 'exciton'? What is the difference between a Frenkel and a Wannier exciton? Would you expect excitons to contribute to the conduction of electricity in the medium? How may excitons be recognized spectroscopically? Why is it reasonable to consider only the in-phase excitation of transition dipoles? What will happen to the spectrum as this approximation fails? Assess the wavelength at which it might be expected to be seriously in error for the 380 nm band of anthracene.
2. Estimate the interaction energy between two transition dipole moments separated by 0.3 nm and each of magnitude 1 D ($3{\cdot}3 \times 10^{-30}$ C m). Suppose the °oscillator strength of the transition in the free molecule is $f = 0{\cdot}2$; estimate the exciton shift. What is the source of the Davydov splitting? What is the polarization of the split bands?

Further information. A simple account of the formation of molecular excitons will be found in Murrell (1971), who also discusses *hypochromism* (the reduction in intensity of absorption) and *hyperchromism* (the increase in intensity). (Further

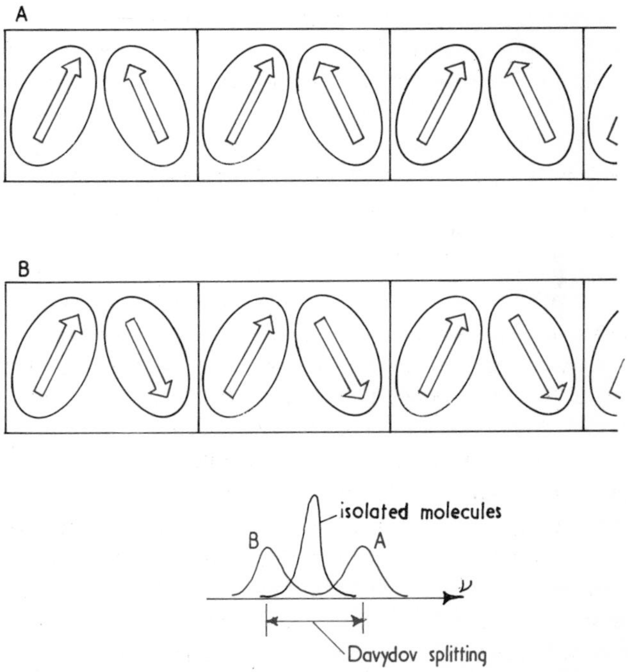

FIG. E10. Davydov splitting for exciton bands for two molecules per unit cell.

confusion may be encountered with the names *hypsochromism*, which implies the lightening of a colour, as in dyeing, and its opposite, *bathochromism*, the deepening of a colour.) An introduction to the mathematical theory of excitons will be found in Craig and Walmsley (1968) and Kittel (1971), and further development is given by Davydov (1962, 1965).

expectation value. The expectation value of an observable is its mean value for the state of the system, and is the mean result of a set of experiments designed to determine the value of the observable for that state. Thus the expectation value of the energy is the mean energy that would be measured in a set of suitable experiments on a collection of identical systems; the expectation value of the position is the mean position that would be measured, and the expectation value of momentum or angular momentum is that mean value.

If the system is in a *pure state* with respect to one of the observables (in other words the state is an °eigenstate of the °operator corresponding to that observable) all identical experiments give identical results, and the expectation value is the result that would be measured in all the experiments; such results are *dispersion free.* An example would be the determination of the energy of an atom or a molecule when it is in a definite energy state; it is then in an eigenstate of the energy operator for the system, and the expectation value of this operator is the energy that would be measured in all experiments.

Quite often the system is not in a pure state but is better described by a °superposition of pure states; performing one experiment to measure a property of such a system gives a result which can be identified as *one* of the eigenvalues of the operator corresponding to the property, and the *mean* result of a set of identical results performed on a set of identical systems will be the expectation value for the system in that state. An example could be the determination of the linear momentum of a system which is described by a °superposition of states of different momentum (for example, if the particle is described by a °wave packet): if the state with momentum $k\hbar$ occurs in the superposition with weight $|c_k|^2$ then the experiment will yield the answer $k\hbar$ with a probability $|c_k|^2$, and will yield other values with a corresponding probability. The average of all such measurements is the expectation value of the linear momentum, written $\langle p\rangle$.

If the state of a system is ψ_n the expectation value $\langle\Omega\rangle$ of an observable Ω is equal to the integral $\int d\tau\psi_n^*\hat{\Omega}\psi_n$, where $\hat{\Omega}$ is the appropriate °operator for the observable, and it is supposed that the state ψ_n is °normalized. Therefore we may predict the result of a set of experiments by calculating the expectation value by evaluating the integral. But in one experiment we can expect to observe the value of the integral only if the state ψ_n is an eigenstate of the operator corresponding to the experiment we are attempting to perform. If it is not an eigenstate, the value of the integral tells us only the mean value of a large number of experiments; this is the only information we are able to calculate, and we are unable to predict, except as a probability, precisely what result we shall get from a single experiment.

Questions. What is meant by the expression 'expectation value of an observable'? In which sense does it determine the result of an experiment? What interpretation should be put on the expectation value when the state of interest is a mixture (a superposition)? What is meant by a pure state? A beam of light is constituted from two plane-polarized orthogonal components and the resulting beam can be described as the superposition $c_X\psi_X + c_Y\psi_Y$, where X and Y refer to the two polarization directions. Discuss the result of an experiment designed to measure the polarization of the beam. Using the expressions in Box 15 on p. 166 calculate the expectation value of the kinetic energy and the linear momentum for a °particle in a one-dimensional square well, and discuss the results of an experiment to confirm the result.

Further information. See *MQM* Chapter 4 for a discussion of operators, observations, and expectation values. See also Feynman, Leighton, and Sands (1963), Kauzmann (1951), Pauling and Wilson (1935), and Bohm (1951). For deeper discussions of the measurement process see Dirac (1958), von Neumann (1955), and Jauch (1968).

extinction coefficient. The intensity of a beam of light is diminished as it passes through an absorbing medium, and since the amount each molecule absorbs is proportional to the intensity of the light present, the intensity falls exponentially. The rate of decay of the intensity is determined by the extinction coefficient. The actual intensity follows the *Beer-Lambert law* $I = I_0 \exp(-c\epsilon\ell)$, where I_0 is the initial intensity, c is the molar concentration of the absorbing species, ℓ the path length (which by convention is normally expressed in centimetres), and ϵ is the *extinction coefficient.* The extinction coefficient depends on the frequency of the incident light, and is often written $\epsilon(\tilde{\nu})$, where $\tilde{\nu}$ is the corresponding wave number in cm^{-1}.

The extinction coefficient is a measure of the °transition probability at the appropriate frequency, and is therefore a measure of the strength of the °transition dipole and the °oscillator strength of a transition, and in turn is related to the °Einstein coefficient of stimulated absorption. Molar extinction coefficients for a few representative materials are recorded in Table 8. The product $c\epsilon(\tilde{\nu})\ell$ is called the *optical density* of the material at that frequency.

Further information. See *MQM* Chapter 10, Appendix 10.2 for the relation of extinction coefficient and oscillator strength; for this relation see °oscillator strength. A discussion of the Beer-Lambert law and its applications and limitations will be found in Wayne (1970). A compilation of extinction-coefficient data and a discussion of its analytical applications are given by Mellon (1950).

F

Fermi contact interaction. A magnetic nucleus and an electron may have a magnetic interaction by virtue of their contact: this magnetic interaction is the Fermi contact interaction, and it is a special case of a °hyperfine interaction. But what is the nature of the interaction on 'contact'? It is possible to give a variety of explanations, of varying sophistication, of the actual mode of interaction; the most pictorial is as follows. Consider the magnetic moment of the nucleus as arising from the circulation of a current: we replace the magnetic moment by an equivalent current loop. At distances far from the nucleus the field due to this loop is indistinguishable from the field from a point magnetic dipole; but close to the nucleus, or loop, the point-source nature of the field is invalid and the magnetic field is characteristic of a circular loop of non-vanishing diameter (Fig. F1). Now bring in the electron with its spin °magnetic moment. Far from the nucleus it experiences a pure dipolar magnetic field, but if it can penetrate the nucleus it enters a quite different region, where the field flows in only one direction. The magnetic interaction between this non-dipolar field and the electron's magnetic moment is the contact interaction.

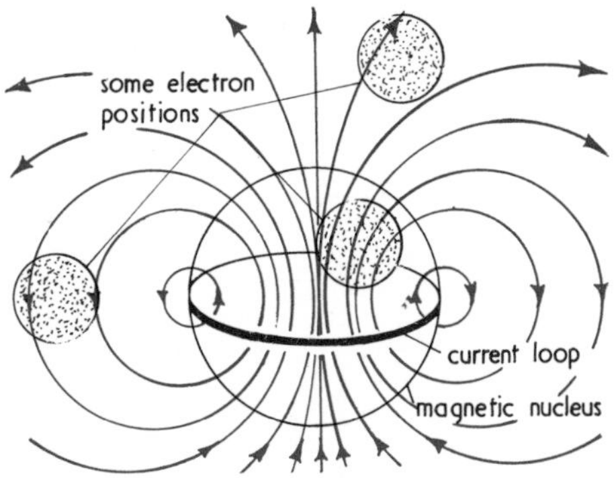

FIG. F1. An interpretation of the Fermi contact interaction: only an electron in an s-orbital can penetrate the nucleus.

The electron must come into contact with the nucleus if the interaction is to operate. Can an electron come into contact with the nucleus? If it is a p-electron, or a d-electon, etc. it cannot, because all such orbitals have a °node at the nucleus. An s-orbital has no node at the nucleus, and an electron occupying one has a non-vanishing probability of being at the nucleus. It follows that only s-electrons can show a Fermi contact interaction. Since s-orbitals are spherically symmetrical it also follows that the interaction should show no directional characteristics, and indeed it is found to be isotropic.

How strong is the interaction? A measure of its strength is the extra magnetic field that an s-electron experiences by virtue of its interaction with the nucleus. For the 1s-orbital in the hydrogen atom the contact interaction (of energy 1420 MHz) is equivalent to a magnetic field of 508 G acting on the electron; for an electron in a 2s-orbital of fluorine the field is as strong as 17 kG. The inner electrons of heavier elements can possess tremendously large interactions, amounting to megagauss. Some representative values are listed in Table 9.

The Fermi contact interaction plays an important role in °electron spin resonance spectra, because the extra local field appears in the spectrum as °hyperfine structure. The contact interaction, being isotropic, does not vanish in fluid media. It also plays an important role in °nuclear magnetic resonance because it is a contribution to one of the mechanisms of °spin-spin coupling.

Questions. 1. What is the Fermi contact interaction? In what sense does it depend on the non-vanishing size of the nucleus? Why is the contact interaction characteristic of an s-electron? Why is the interaction isotropic? Where does the interaction play an important role?
2. The energy of the Fermi contact interaction is given by the expression $-(2\mu_0/3)[\gamma_N\gamma_e|\psi(0)|^2]\,\mathbf{I}.\mathbf{s}$, where γ_N and γ_e are the magnetogyric ratios of the nucleus and electron respectively (see °magnetic moment), $\mathbf{I}$ and $\mathbf{s}$ their spins, μ_0 the vacuum permeability, and $|\psi(0)|^2$ the probability that the electron is at the nucleus. Show that this interaction has the form suggestive of a magnetic field $(\mu_0/3)\gamma_N|\psi(0)|^2\,\mathbf{I}$ arising from the nucleus and affecting the electron magnetic moment, and from the expression for the hydrogen atomic orbitals given in Table 15 on p. 275 compute the magnetic field (actually the magnetic induction) experienced by an electron in a 1s- and 2s-orbital of hydrogen. Repeat the calculation for a selection of °Slater-type atomic orbitals for the first-row elements. In each case replace $\mathbf{I}$ by its maximum projection $m_I\hbar$.
3. An electron in an orbital centred on a neighbouring nucleus may have a Fermi contact interaction whatever the nature of the orbital, provided the orbital has a non-vanishing amplitude at the nucleus of interest (thus a 2p-orbital on B may have a non-zero amplitude at the nucleus of its neighbour A). The strength of the interaction is determined by the expression in Question 2 but with $|\psi(0)|^2$ replaced by $|\psi(\mathbf{R})|^2$, where $\mathbf{R}$ is the position of the nucleus relative to the nucleus on which the orbital is centred. Calculate the strength of the interaction for a proton as it is brought towards the position of another proton surrounded by a 1s-electron. Ignore the distortion that the second proton induces.

Further information. See *MQM* Chapter 11 for a further discussion of the interaction. An account of the role the interaction plays will be found in McLauchlan's *Magnetic resonance* (OCS 1) and in Atkins and Symons (1967), Carrington and McLachlan (1967), Slichter (1963), and Abragam and Bleaney (1970). Magnitudes of the interaction for a variety of nuclei are given on p. 21 in Atkins and Symons (1967). Calculations involving the contact interaction are described by Memory (1968) and Freeman and Frankel (1967). The derivation of the contact interaction is described in a simple manner in *MQM* Chapter 11, and performed in §4.5 of Slichter (1963); a derivation from the Dirac equation is given in Griffith (1964) and Bethe and Salpetre (1957).

fermion. A fermion is a particle possessing an intrinsic °spin angular momentum characterized by a half-integral spin quantum number (s or I). Examples include the electron ($s=\frac{1}{2}$), the proton ($I=\frac{1}{2}$), the neutron ($I=\frac{1}{2}$), the neutrino ($s=\frac{1}{2}$), ^{35}Cl nucleus ($I=\frac{3}{2}$), ^{13}C ($I=\frac{1}{2}$), and ^{17}O ($I=\frac{5}{2}$). Fermions obey the °Pauli exclusion principle, and so no more than one can occupy any single quantum state. This has a profound influence on their behaviour, and distinguishes them sharply from °bosons, any number of which may enter a given state. The °Pauli principle requires a wavefunction to be °antisymmetrical under the interchange of any pair of identical fermions.

Further information. See °spin and the °Pauli principle for further discussion. The occupation restriction of fermions is taken into account by *Fermi-Dirac statistics* when large collections are under consideration: these are described by Gasser and Richards in *Entropy and energy levels* (OCS 19), in Chapter 6 of Davidson (1962), and in §9.7 of Reif (1965).

fine structure. The fine structure in an atomic spectrum is the splitting between different levels (different values of J of a particular °term). In atomic sodium the energy of $^2P_{1/2}$ differs from the energy of $^2P_{3/2}$, and so the emissions $^2P_{1/2}\rightarrow{}^2S_{1/2}$ and $^2P_{3/2}\rightarrow{}^2S_{1/2}$ occur at slightly different frequencies (and give rise to the two closely-spaced yellow D-lines of the sodium spectrum); this is an appearance of fine structure.

Fine structure is a manifestation of spin-orbit coupling and is best introduced by considering a one-electron atom. Suppose that the electron in the atom has an orbital angular momentum $\mathbf{l}$: by virtue of its charge it also has a °magnetic moment, which by Ampère's law may be considered to be a dipole at the centre of the orbit. This magnetic moment gives rise to a magnetic field which interacts with the spin magnetic moment of the electron, and the interaction energy depends on the relative orientation of the electron's spin and orbital magnetic moments. This implies that the energy also depends on the relative orientations of the angular momenta **l** and **s** (see Fig. F2). The low-energy orientation corresponds to the opposition of μ_L and μ_S, and therefore it also corresponds to the opposition of **l** and **s**; consequently the lower value of the total angular momentum **j** ($\mathbf{j} = \mathbf{l} + \mathbf{s}$) corresponds to the lower energy.

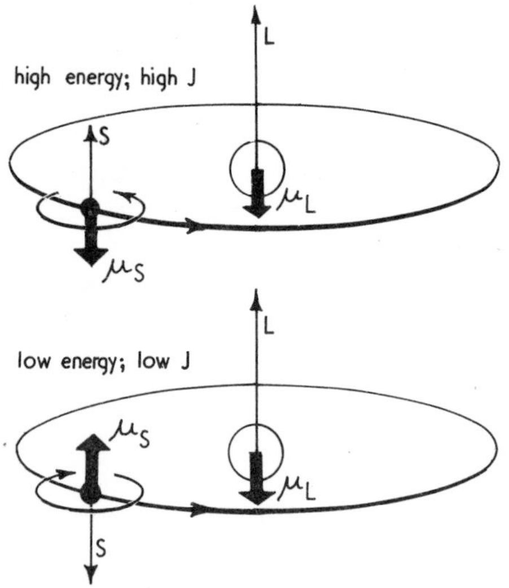

FIG. F2. The magnetic interaction resulting in fine structure. A high total angular momentum corresponds to a parallel alignment of moments, and therefore to a high energy.

We see that different values of j (and of J in many-electron atoms) correspond to different energies by virtue of the magnetic spin-orbit interaction. This is the basis of the third °Hund rule: when an electron shell is less than half full, low values of J have lower energy than high values of J (the opposite is true when the shell is more than half full). °Terms in which high-j levels have higher energies than low-j levels are called *regular*; when low-j levels lie highest the term is *inverted.* Since a term with several j values (for example, a ^2P term which has the two levels $^2P_{1/2}$ and $^2P_{3/2}$) is called a °multiplet term, we arrive at the names *regular multiplet* and *inverted multiplet*.

Within a given multiplet the spacing of the levels obeys the *Landé interval rule* which states that the energy interval between pairs of adjacent levels is in the ratio of the j-values of the upper level of each pair. Thus the ratio of the $^3P_2$—$^3P_1$ interval to the $^3P_1$—$^3P_0$ interval is 2:1.

As the spin-orbit coupling increases with atomic number we both expect and observe the fine structure to be very important in heavy atoms.

Further information. The fine structure is discussed in more detail in *MQM* Chapter 8. See especially §III A.5 of Kuhn (1962), where the mathematics is developed in a simple way; atoms more complex than hydrogen conform to the same principles, and are discussed by the same author in §III D.3 and Chapter V. See especially Chapter 2 of Herzberg (1940). Discussions of the multiplet structure and fine structure of atoms is also described in detail by Woodgate (1970), Condon and Shortley (1963), Griffith (1964), and Shore and Menzel (1968).

fine-structure constant. The fine-structure constant is a measure of the strength of interaction between a charged particle and the electromagnetic field: it is given by the expression $\alpha = e^2/4\pi\epsilon_0\hbar c$; it is dimensionless and has the numerical value 1/137·03602, or approximately 1/137. The smallness of this number is of great importance, for it determines the size of atoms and the stability of matter. If α were much larger the distinction between matter and radiation would be much less clear; if it were much smaller, matter would have virtually no electromagnetic interactions.

These considerations can be elucidated by considering how the fine-structure constant (that is, the strength of the coupling between charged matter and the electromagnetic field) determines the size of atoms and the magnitude of some of their properties. Consider an atom of radius r in which the potential energy of the electron is of the order of $Ze^2/4\pi\epsilon_0 r$: it is tempting to express this in terms of α, and falling into temptation we obtain $Z\alpha\hbar c/r$. The kinetic energy of the atom is of the order of $p^2/2m_e$; if we use the °uncertainty principle to assess the order of magnitude of this term on the basis of an electron being confined to a region of radius r we may use $p \sim \hbar/r$. This enables the total energy to be expressed in terms of the parameter r, roughly the size of the atom, and to seek r by minimizing the total energy (finding the value of r for which $dE/dr = 0$). The answer we get is $r \sim \lambda_C/Z\alpha$, where λ_C is the °Compton wavelength of the electron ($\lambda_C = h/cm_e \sim 2{\cdot}4 \times 10^{-12}$ m). This shows that the size of an atom is roughly this characteristic 'size' of an electron times 137. It is interesting to note that the °Bohr radius can be expressed as $\lambda_C/4\pi\alpha$, or as r_e/α^2, where r_e is the classical radius of the electron. If the interaction strength were much less the atom would be much larger, and if α were much larger, and comparable to the analogous coupling constant for the nucleon interaction (the 'strong interaction' as opposed to the electromagnetic interaction), then atoms would be of roughly the same size as their nuclei. The minimum energy can be found by substituting the size of the atom back into the energy expression, and rather pleasingly we find $-\frac{1}{2}Z^2\alpha^2(m_ec^2)$: this is pleasing because m_ec^2 is the relativistic expression for the rest energy of a particle of mass m_e, and so the energy of an atom is of the order of $Z^2/137^2$ of this value. This is a small proportion when Z is small, but it may approach unity as Z gets large (in heavy atoms). This implies that ordinary non-relativistic quantum mechanics is good for light atoms, but fails progressively through the periodic table. Another amusing deduction is the order of magnitude of the velocity of an electron in an atom or molecule: simple consideration of the energy expression (see Questions) gives the answer $v \sim Z\alpha c$: since α is so small, electrons move at non-relativistic velocities except in the case of heavy atoms. Another place where the fine-structure constant enters is in the magnitude of the °spin-orbit coupling which determines the °fine structure of spectra: in hydrogen-like atoms the strength of this interaction is proportional to α^2R, where R is the Rydberg constant, and it is from this relation that α gets its name.

The stability of atoms is determined at several levels by the small size of α. One important role played is the way that the °transition probability for °electric dipole radiation (essentially a mechanism whereby an atom emits or absorbs a photon) depends on α: an analysis of the situation shows that an electron has to oscillate about $1/\alpha(\alpha Z)^2$ times before it is virtually certain to emit a photon: this accounts for the moderate stability of the excited states of atoms and molecules. The probability that two photons are thrown off by an excited atom is of the order of the square of the probability that one will be emitted, and so this process is of very low probability and is indeed only rarely observed. But matter can also decay into radiation: matter can be annihilated and appear as electromagnetic energy. The probability of an electron disappearing in this fashion is proportional to its strength of coupling to the electromagnetic fields, and varies as α. Put another way, an electron spends α of its time as electromagnetic radiation. Fortunately α is small; if it were closer to unity, matter and radiation would be indistinguishable.

Questions. 1. Of what is the fine-structure constant a measure? What would be the consequences of it being zero? Evaluate its magnitude from the values of the fundamental constants, and confirm that it is dimensionless. What features of atomic and molecular structure does it determine? Express the spin-orbit coupling parameter, the °Bohr radius, the °Rydberg constant, and the °Einstein coefficients in terms of α, and attempt to interpret the form of the expressions. Carry through the calculation of the hydrogen-atom energy as described in the text: find the lowest energy as a function of atomic size r, the size of the atom in this case, and the velocity of the electron (from the kinetic energy).

Further information. A very good and quite simple account of the way that the fine-structure constant determines the magnitude of atomic properties is given in Chapter 1 of Thirring (1958).

fluorescence. Light when absorbed by a molecule may be degraded into thermal motion or it may be re-irradiated. Light emitted from an excited molecule is *fluorescence* or *phosphorescence.* The two types of radiation may be distinguished by the mechanism that generates them and, more ambiguously, by the general observation that fluorescence ceases as soon as the exciting source is removed, whereas phosphorescence may persist. See °phosphorescence for an account of its mechanism.

The mechanism of fluorescence is illustrated in Fig. F3. The incident light excites a ground-state molecule into a state which we shall label S_1; assuming the ground state is a °singlet state (all electrons are normally paired in molecules) and we are interested in a strong initial absorption, the upper state is also a singlet. The molecule is also excited vibrationally during the

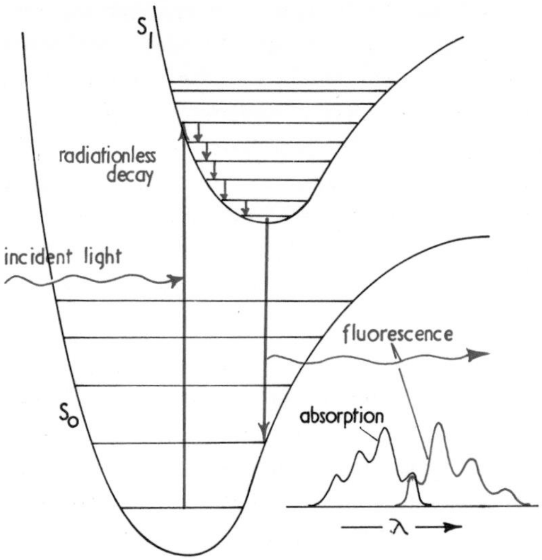

FIG. F3. The processes leading to fluorescence, and the 'mirror-image' relation of the absorption and fluorescence spectra. Note the shift of the latter to longer wavelengths.

transition (see °Franck-Condon principle). Collisions with the surrounding medium, which may be a gas, a solvent, or a solid lattice, induce vibrational transitions because the surrounding molecules may be able to carry away the moderately small amounts of vibrational energy of the molecule, and so to lower it down the ladder of vibrational states in the upper electronic state. When the molecule has reached its lowest vibrational state two things may occur. One is that the solvent may be able to carry away the electronic energy and so deactivate the molecule: this the solvent may do if it has an energy level that matches the energy of the excited molecule, for there may then be a °resonant transfer of radiation to the solvent, which then fritters away its excitation into thermal motion. An alternative mode of decay, and the one that concerns us at present, is the fluorescent decay of the excited electronic state: the molecule deactivates by emitting a photon and falling back into the lower electronic state. This emitted light is the fluorescence.

Whether or not fluorescence appears depends on competition between the radiationless deactivation, involving energy transfer to the surrounding medium, and the radiative emission. In a gas a molecule receives about 10^{10} collisions per second, and in a liquid the continuous jostling by the solvent amounts to about $10^{12}-10^{13}$ collisions per second. Observed lifetimes of fluorescent radiation are of the order of 10^{-8}s, and so in a gas we have to consider the effectiveness of about 100 collisions, and in a solvent 10^4-10^5 collisions. If the collisions are strong in the sense that they are effective in absorbing energy then the molecule will be deactivated by the radiationless processes, especially when the molecules are in a liquid. If the collisions are unable to extract much energy, then even in a solvent they may be able to lower the electronically excited molecule down only the vibrational ladder, and they will be unable to extract an electronic excitation energy. In this case the radiation decay dominates and the molecule fluoresces.

Two characteristics of the fluorescence should be noted. The first is that the fluorescence should appear at lower frequency than the incident light. This may be seen immediately from Fig. F3, which shows that the energy of the emitted photon differs from that absorbed by the amount of vibrational energy lost to the surrounding medium. Therefore we might expect objects irradiated with blue or ultraviolet light to fluoresce more in the red. Bright-red fluorescent clothing is a part of the modern scene, and a manifestation of this effect. The second point is that there may be vibrational structure in the spectrum of the fluorescent light: this vibrational structure is a °progression formed by the decay of the ground vibrational state of the upper electronic level into different vibrational levels of the lower electronic level. Its study can provide information about the °force-constant of the molecule in its ground state, and this is in contrast to normal electronic spectra which provide information about the stiffness of the bonds in the upper electronic level. It follows that the absorption spectrum and the *fluorescence spectrum* of a molecule should resemble each other: this is normally expressed by saying that one is the 'mirror image' of the other (see Fig. F3); but that description should not be taken literally, because the vibrational splittings and intensities are not quite the same.

A number of details may be added to this basic description. The first is that the initial absorption might not take place to the lowest excited singlet state of the molecule. In this case an *internal conversion* occurs in which the higher singlets S_2, S_3, etc. are induced, by a collision, to make a radiationless transition into the lowest excited singlet S_1, which then fluoresces (see °Auger effect). A famous rule due to Kasha reflects this effect: the fluorescent level is the lowest level of that multiplicity (for example, the lowest excited singlet level). The intensity of fluorescence depends strongly on the physical state of the sample because of the deactivating collisions in competition with the fluorescence; pure, undiluted liquids generally have a very low fluorescent efficiency because the excitation may hop from one molecule to an identical neighbour by a resonant process (see °exciton for the analogous effect in solids). Conversely, it is possible to enhance fluorescence by having present a molecule that can absorb the incident light and then transfer it (by a matching of energy levels, and a collision) into a molecule that may then fluoresce: this is *sensitized fluorescence* and is made use of in some kinds of °laser. Another term often encountered is *resonance fluorescence*: this signifies that the fluorescent radiation has the same frequency as the incident light; when this is so the fluorescence may be brighter because the transition is stimulated. Light of exactly the same frequency is rare in fluorescing molecules because the presence of the solvent slightly shifts energies, and so the (0—0) vibrational upwards transition (that is the transition from the lowest vibrational level of one state to the lowest of the other) might differ in energy from the (0—0) downwards transition because the solvent may solvate the upper state differently before the fluorescence occurs. Fluorescence is generally extinguished as soon as the incident illumination ceases: this is because all the transitions of interest are allowed, and therefore occur very quickly. Nevertheless, there is the phenomenon of *delayed fluorescence* (not to be confused with phosphorescence) which may persist for several milliseconds. The mechanism for this depends upon the excitation of a molecule from the ground state S_0 into the singlet S_1, and then this molecule migrating to another molecule to which it sticks by sharing its excitation. Thus we have the reaction $S_0 + S_1^* \rightarrow (S_0S_1)^*$. This *excimer* (if the two molecules are the same) or *exciplex* (if they are different) then falls apart, after a short life, with the emission of fluorescent radiation.

Questions. What are the characteristics of fluorescent radiation? How may it be distinguished from phosphorescent radiation? What electronic processes are responsible for fluorescence? What other alternative paths of energy degradation are open to atoms and molecules in gases and solutions? What properties of the solvent determine the rate of non-radiative decay? What differences would you expect in the fluorescent behaviour of a molecule dissolved first in a strongly interacting solvent with high-frequency bending and stretching vibrations, such as water, and then in a weakly interacting solvent with flabby bonds, for example selenium oxychloride? What is a fluorescent spectrum of a molecule? How does this information complement the absorption spectrum? In what sense is the fluorescent spectrum a mirror-image of the absorption spectrum? What is the role of the °Franck-Condon principle in determining the structure of the fluorescence spectrum? What is meant by the term 'internal conversion', and what is its significance in the study of fluorescence? In what sense is fluorescence an °Auger process? Why is fluorescence largely quenched in the pure liquid? How may fluorescence be enhanced? What is resonance fluorescence? In what sense does the operation of some types of °laser depend on the mechanisms described here? Why does the fluorescence spectrum show a *shift* from the position of the absorption spectrum, even allowing for the mirror-image symmetry? To answer this, consider a molecule surrounded by a polar solvent; and then excited by a transition that changes the molecule's polarity (for example, a $\pi^* \leftarrow n$ °electric dipole transition). Let the polar solvent *relax* about the excited state, and consider the energy of the emissive transition. What is meant by the terms excimer and exciplex, and what is a consequence of their formation? How may delayed fluorescence be distinguished from °phosphorescence?

Further information. See *MQM* Chapter 10 for more discussion. A simple account of some of the relaxation processes described has been given by Heller (1967) in connexion with liquid lasers. See also Haught (1968). A good account of fluorescence and related processes has been given by Bowen (1946), Wayne (1970), and Calvert and Pitts (1966). The generation of light in chemical reactions (*chemiluminescence*) is a phenomenon related to fluorescence, the difference being that the excited state of the emitting molecule is formed as the product of a chemical reaction. This subject is described by Wayne (1970). Energy-transfer processes are at the root of the fluorescence efficiency; therefore see Levine and Bernstein (1974).

force-constant. The force-constant k is the constant of proportionality between the restoring force and the displacement x of a simple harmonic oscillator: force $= -kx$. Large force-constants imply stiff systems (strong restoring forces even for small deviations from equilibrium). The frequency of a classical simple harmonic oscillator is related to k by the expression $\omega_0 = (k/m)^{1/2}$, where m is the mass of the oscillating system (with k expressed in newtons per metre and mass in kilograms, the frequency will be in radians per second; to get hertz divide by 2π). The lesson taught by this expression is that the frequency of oscillation is determined by the mass as well as the force-constant, for the heavier the mass the less effective will be the restoring force. In the quantum-mechanical treatment of the °harmonic oscillator the energies are given in terms of the fundamental frequency ω_0 calculated in the same way as the classical case: the energy of the nth quantum level is $(n+\frac{1}{2})\hbar\omega_0$.

The importance of the force-constant in quantum theory is that it is a measure of the stiffness of bonds between atoms, and therefore governs (together with the atomic masses) the °vibrational frequencies of molecules.

Table 10 lists typical values of force-constants for some molecules and the corresponding frequencies and quantum energy-level separations.

Questions. 1. What is the force-constant? What is the physical significance of a large force-constant? Would you expect the force-constant for the C—C bond in diamond to be less than that for the Pb—Pb bond in metallic lead? A mass of I kg hangs from a spring with force-constant 1 N m^{-1}: what is its natural frequency in radians per second and in hertz? To what should the mass be changed in order to oscillate at IHz? What force-constant would be needed if the mass were that of a proton and the frequency that typical of a molecular bond ($\sim 10^{14}$ Hz)? What wave number (cm^{-1}) does this correspond to in the infrared absorption spectrum? Where is the absorption shifted to on deuteration?

2. By a Taylor expansion of the bond energy about its equilibrium value, show that the force-constant is proportional to the curvature of the molecular potential-energy curve at the equilibrium separation.

Further information. See *MQM* Chapter 10 for more information about molecular vibrations. A good, simple, but detailed account is given by Woodward (1972), who reveals how to determine k from vibrational data, and a standard work is that of Wilson, Decius, and Cross (1955). See also Whiffen (1972), King (1964), and Gans (1971). A complication of molecular vibrational data has been made by Adams (1967, 1971).

Franck-Condon principle. The Franck-Condon principle governs the intensity of spectral transitions between the vibrational levels of different electronic states of molecules. By recognizing the great difference in mass between the nuclear framework and the electron being excited, it states that the electronic transition occurs so rapidly that during it the nuclei are static. A *vertical transition* occurs, which begins with the nuclei in some arrangement in the lower electronic state and ends with them in the same arrangement in the upper electronic state. But as the molecular energy curves might be displaced (see Fig. F4) this nuclear arrangement might correspond to a highly compressed or stretched state of the excited molecule, and so the molecule immediately starts to vibrate. It follows that a vibrational excitation of the molecule generally accompanies an electronic transition.

Which of the vibrational levels is most populated by the transition is governed by the relative positions of the upper and lower energy curves: if the curves were of the same shape and one lay directly over the other (Fig. F4a), the transition would be from the ground vibrational level of one to the ground vibrational level of the other, and so the electronic transition would occur without vibrational excitation. In general, we may envisage the transition as occuring from the most probable conformation of the ground state—which is the static, equilibrium arrangement of the nuclei. The electronic transition occurs, and during it the nuclei do not change their arrangement. At the completion of the electronic transition the nuclei are static, but in a new force-field because of the

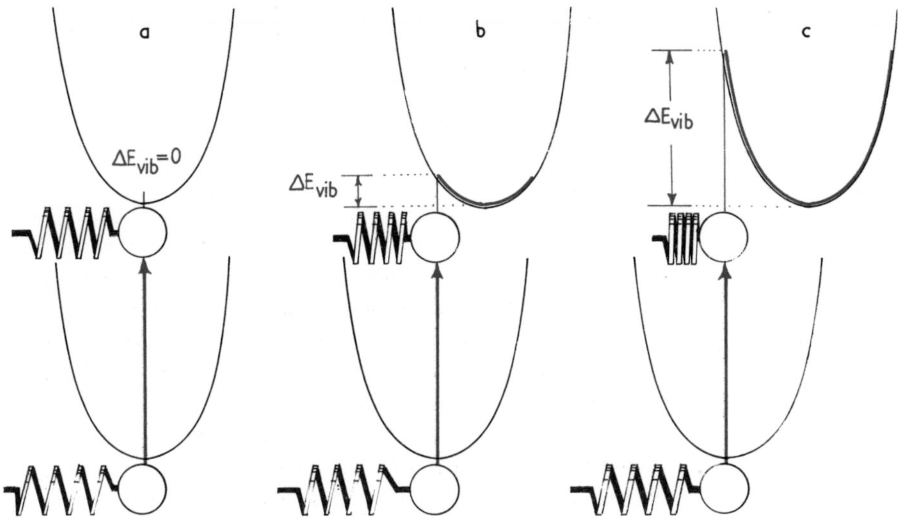

FIG. F4. The classical basis of the Franck-Condon principle. The bob remains static during the excitation, and the amount of vibrational energy simultaneously excited depends on the relative disposition of the potential-energy curves.

new electronic distribution. They therefore begin to move, and swing harmonically away from and back to their initial arrangement (Fig. F4b and c). It follows that the original arrangement is a turning point of the new motion, and that vibrational energy is stored by the molecule. A line drawn vertically from the initial ground state intersects the upper potential-energy curve at the point which will be the turning point in the excited state, and which shows how much energy is absorbed in the transition. (Remember that the energy of a °harmonic oscillation is constant: what potential energy it loses as the spring decompresses is turned into kinetic energy which is used to recompress the spring. Therefore the potential energy at the turning point, E_{vib} in Fig. F4, determines the energy at all displacements for that mode of oscillation.)

The quantum-mechanical basis of the principle is the °overlap between the °vibrational wavefunctions of the two electronic states: transitions occur most strongly between vibrational states that overlap most, because two states that overlap strongly have similar characteristics. The ground vibrational wavefunction is a bell-shaped curve with its maximum at the equilibrium nuclear conformation (Fig. F5). Many of the vibrational wavefunctions of the excited electronic states overlap this function, but the greatest overlap occurs with functions that peak in the same region of space. If the energy curves are displaced, the peaks of importance are those that occur at the edge of the potential well (see Fig. F5), and so the vibration excited will be that predicted by the simple device of drawing a vertical transition from the equilibrum separation in the ground state (the most probable conformation, and where the vibrational wavefunction peaks strongly) to the point where it intersects the edge of the upper potential curve. In the vicinity of this intersection the vibrational wavefunctions have moderately strong amplitudes, and so overlap most strongly with the ground vibrational state. The observed distribution of vibrational intensities then reflects the different overlaps between the ground and excited vibrational state wavefunctions.

Questions. 1. State the Franck-Condon principle. On what does its validity depend? What is the 'classical' explanation of the principle? What is the quantum-mechanical explanation, and how is the classical explanation related to it? What is a vertical transition? Construct a diagram similar to that in Fig. F5 in which the Franck-Condon principle is applied to determine the intensity distribution of °fluorescent transitions (from the ground vibrational level of the upper electronic state to various levels of the lower electronic state).
2. Demonstrate the quantum-mechanical basis of the principle by considering the °transition dipole moment between the

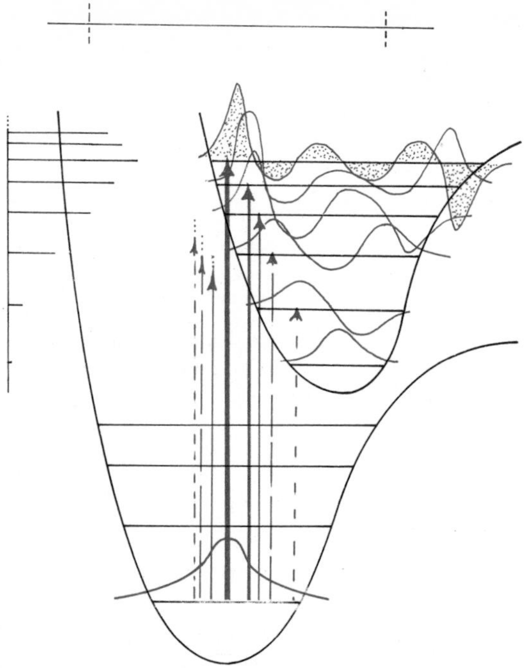

FIG. F5. The quantum basis of the Franck-Condon principle. The strongest transition occurs to the state with which the lowest vibrational level of the lower state has the greatest overlap; this is shown shaded. The resulting spectrum is shown on the left.

two states. Proceed by supposing that the state of the molecule can be written as the product of the vibrational state and the electronic state, and then think about the transition moment $\langle e^*, \nu^* | \mathbf{d} | e, \nu\rangle$. Show that this may be approximated by an expression of the form $\langle e^* | \mathbf{d} | e\rangle \langle \nu^* | \nu\rangle$, and recognize the presence of the overlap integral between the vibrational levels of the electronic states. Calculate the °overlap integral between the ground states of two °harmonic oscillators whose equilibrium conformations are displaced by a distance R, and plot the (0–0) transition intensity (the transition $\nu = 0$ to $\nu = 0$) as a function of R.

Further information. See *MQM* Chapter 10 for a further account, and a deduction of the principle. See also §6.16 of King (1964), Whiffen (1972), and Barrow (1962). A thorough discussion of the basis of the principle is given in §IV.4 of Herzberg (1950) and developed in even more detail in Herzberg (1966). The original formulation of the principle was by Franck (1925), and this was turned into mathematics by Condon (1928). A useful summary of modern work involving the principle has been given in Nicholls (1969).

Franck-Hertz experiment. In the Franck-Hertz experiment a beam of electrons was passed through a gas at low pressure and the current arriving was monitored; in later experiments the energy of the electron arriving was also monitored. As the energy of the incident electrons was increased it was found that the current arriving at a collector dipped sharply when the incident energy was equal to some excitation energy of the atom or molecule. It was observed that the sample simultaneously emitted light of a frequency corresponding to the energy of the incident beam. This can be rationalized in terms of the quantization of energy, for the electrons are able to donate their kinetic energy to an atom only if the atom can be excited by that amount; therefore the current will dip each time the energy can be imparted to the quantized system. This is confirmed by the observation of the emitted radiation at the corresponding frequency ($h\nu = \Delta E$).

One of the important features of the experiment is that it is an illustration that energy is quantized even when it is imparted from mechanical motion, as opposed to electromagnetic radiation.

Further information. See Chapter VI of White (1935) for a useful introduction. More discursive accounts are given in §2.15 of Bohm (1951) and p. 85 of Jammer (1966). The original papers are those of Franck and Hertz (1914, 1916, 1919).

free valence. An atom may be linked to its neighbours by bonds of various order (°bond order); the free valence of the atom is the difference between its maximum possible total bond order and the actual total bond order, and it therefore reflects the lack of saturation of the valence requirements of that atom. If triple bonds are discounted, for carbon the maximum total bond order is 4·73 (or $3 + \sqrt{3}$). As an example, in the °benzene molecule each carbon atom has a bond of order 1 to its hydrogen atom, two σ-bonds to the neighbouring carbons, and two π-bonds of order $\frac{2}{3}$; therefore the total bond order of each carbon is 4·33 and the free valence is 0·40. In butadiene the C—C bond orders are 1·89, 1·45, and 1·89 along the chain, and so the free valences are 0·84 for the two outermost atoms and 0·39 for each of the inner pair.

The magnitude of the free valence is a quantitative measure of Thiele's early theory of *partial valence*, which allows some predictions to be made about the relative reactivity of atoms in conjugated chains. Thiele supposed that because only one bond was sufficient to hold two carbon atoms together each carbon atom in the chain had a partial valence which could be used for reacting: the remaining part of the double bond was superfluous. Nevertheless he took the view that the two central partial valences got tangled up, leaving only the outer atoms with available valencies. Now, however, we can interpret the reactivity in terms of the different free valencies on the atoms. Free valencies also occur at the surfaces of metals, and the chemical consequences of this include the immensely important role of catalysts.

Further information. See §9.11 of Coulson (1961), and §2.9 and several other sections in Streitweiser (1961). See also Daudel, Lefebvre, and Moser (1959), and Pullman and Pullman (1958). For lists of bond orders see Coulson and Streitweiser (1965). For a discussion of the reactivity of molecules in terms of the concepts of free valence, and other quantities, see Chapter 11 of Streitweiser (1961). For a discussion of catalytic activity see Bond's *Heterogeneous catalysis: principles and applications* (OCS 18). Why 4·73? See Moffitt (1949a).

G

g-value. The °magnetic moment of an electron that arises from its °orbital angular momentum is $\gamma_e \mathbf{l}$, where γ_e is the magnetogyric ratio; but the magnetic moment of an electron due to its spin angular momentum is $g\gamma_e \mathbf{s}$, where g is an additional 'anomalous' factor to which experiment ascribes the value 2·0023 (often approximated to 2). Like most 'anomalous' quantities an explanation can be found in a deeper theory, and indeed it should not be surprising to find an extra factor of 2 appearing in connexion with spin (which, after all, has no classical analogue, and involves *half*-integral quantum numbers). The deeper theory required is that of °Dirac: his relativistic quantum mechanics leads naturally to the deduction that $g = 2$; but the theory is too strict, for it requires g to be equal to the *integer* 2. This shows the Dirac theory to be incomplete: the extra 0·0023 required for the observed value can be found from the even deeper theory of °quantum electrodynamics. In this theory the electron is continuously buffetted by stray electromagnetic fields which are always present, even in an ideal vacuum: these fields affect the spin of the electron in such a way that the magnetic moment is increased from its Dirac value. The calculation of the g-value of the free electron is one of the triumphs of quantum electrodynamics.

The *Landé g-factor* is closely related to the g-value we have just described; indeed, they are identical in the limit of vanishing orbital angular momentum. The Landé g-factor determines the effective magnetic moment of an electron or atom possessing both spin and orbital angular momenta, which are combined together to give a total angular momentum J. For an atom described by the quantum numbers S, L, and J the Landé g-factor is $g_J = 1 + \frac{1}{2}([J(J+1) + S(S+1) - L(L+1)]/J(J+1))$. When $L = 0$ we obtain $g_J = 2$ because J can then equal only S; and when $S = 0$ we obtain $g_J = 1$, which is the normal value for a spinless system. In terms of the Landé factor the magnetic moment of a system with angular momentum $\mathbf{J}$ may be written $g_J\gamma_e\mathbf{J}$.

The peculiar form of g_J arises from the anomalous g-value as follows. The vector-coupling picture of a system with spin momentum $\mathbf{S}$ and orbital momentum $\mathbf{L}$ coupled to give a resultant $\mathbf{J}$ is shown in Fig. G1. $\mathbf{L}$ and $\mathbf{S}$ both °precess around $\mathbf{J}$, and $\mathbf{J}$ precesses around some other axis z. Antiparallel to both $\mathbf{L}$ and $\mathbf{S}$ we may draw vectors representing the corresponding magnetic moments, but the spin magnetic moment must be drawn twice as long in proportion to the orbital moment because of the factor $g = 2$. The resultant of μ_L and μ_S, denoted μ'_J, does not lie along the direction of $\mathbf{J}$ (it would if $g = 1$, as shown in Fig. G1b), but will precess about it because of the precession of $\mathbf{L}$ and $\mathbf{S}$ about $\mathbf{J}$. Only the component along $\mathbf{J}$ does not average to zero during this precession, and so the effective magnetic moment of $\mathbf{J}$, which we write μ_J, depends on this component, and therefore on the value of L and S. When $L \gg S$ or $S \gg L$, μ'_J lies almost completely along $\mathbf{J}$ and g_J is approximately 1 or 2 respectively, because either the orbital or the spin moment is dominant; but when L and S are similar, the effective part of μ'_J may be much smaller than its true magnitude. Because $\mathbf{J}$ precesses around the z-direction so too does μ_J; therefore if the projection of $\mathbf{J}$ on z is J_z, the projection of μ_J on z is $g_J\gamma_e J_z$, where g_J is some

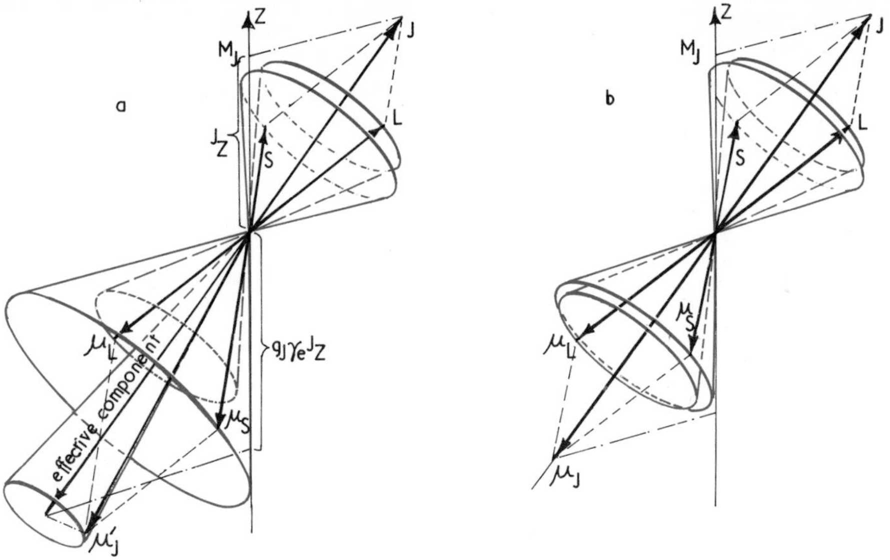

FIG. G1. In (a) is illustrated the source of the Landé g-factor; (b) is a hypothetical situation in which $g_e = 1$.

factor to be determined from the geometry of the situation depicted in Fig. G1a. It turns out that this factor is the Landé factor already quoted.

The *g-value in °electron spin resonance* is related to both these g-values. In this technique, which is described in more detail in the appropriate section, an oscillating field of frequency ν is brought into °resonance with a spin system held in a magnetic field B. The energy of the oscillating field is $h\nu$, and the energy separation of the electron spin levels (that is, the energy separation between $m_s = +\frac{1}{2}$ and $m_s = -\frac{1}{2}$) is equal to $g\mu_B B$: the resonance condition is therefore $h\nu = g\mu_B B$. The g-factor in this expression would be the free-electron value g_e if the electrons under consideration were free, or the Landé g_J-value if they were bound to an atom. In fact the electron investigated is normally part of a molecular system, and so neither situation holds. To a very good approximation (except in some transition-metal ions) an electron in a molecule possesses no orbital angular momentum; therefore we can expect the g-value of a radical to be very close to 2·0023. Nevertheless, the orbital angular momentum is not completely °quenched because of the presence of the spin-orbit coupling interactions. Normally there is sufficient spin-orbit coupling to leak some of the spin angular momentum into orbital angular momentum, and so we should expect the g-value to fall slightly below 2·0023 towards the value it would have if the momentum were all orbital and not spin (that is, towards 1). This is widely observed, and g-values of the order 2·0000 and thereabouts occur frequently. Furthermore, the deviation from the free-spin value increases with the magnitude of the spin-orbit coupling constant for the radical, and this accords with our interpretation. For a rough order-of-magnitude estimate one may write the deviation from 2·0023 as ζ/Δ, where ζ is the spin-orbit coupling constant and Δ a typical excitation energy of the radical (see °perturbation theory and °fine structure; some ζ-values are listed in Table 9). This mechanism can also account for the observations of g-values exceeding the free-spin value, which is the case when the electron is a member of a shell more than half full, but the argument is slightly more involved. Basically it is connected with the reversal of the order of levels when a shell is changed from being less than half full to more than half full. We know that according to the °Hund rules the levels become inverted (low-j levels lie above high-j) because the sign of the spin-orbit coupling changes. This can be interpreted in terms of changing from a system in which electrons are orbiting to one in which holes in an otherwise completed shell are circulating. A hole carries, in effect, a charge opposite to an electron's, and the inversion of the j-levels, and the deviation of g to values above the free-spin value can be traced to this.

A final kind of g-value is the *molecular g-value*, which relates the rotational °angular momentum of an entire molecule to the magnetic moment that arises from its motion. Even a closed-shell molecule, such as H_2 or methane, possesses a magnetic moment by virtue of its rotational motion; it arises because of °electron slip and the consequent imbalance of the rotating negative and positive charges leading to a net circulating current, and thence to a magnetic moment. The imbalance increases as the rotational motion quickens, and so the magnetic moment is proportional to **J**, the rotational angular momentum. It is normally written $\boldsymbol{\mu} = g\gamma_N \mathbf{J}$, and g, which depends on the details of the molecular electronic structure, is the molecular g-value. Note that it is common to use the nuclear magneton ($\mu_N = e\hbar/2m_p$) to define the molecular g-value: molecular magnetic moments are so small that this is more appropriate than using the Bohr magneton (using μ_N makes g of the order of unity). For ammonia $g \sim 0{\cdot}53$, and so the magnitude of μ when the molecule is in a state with $J = 10$ is approximately $5{\cdot}3\mu_N$.

Questions. 1. What electronic property does the g-factor determine? In an atom it is appropriate to label g with the value of J: why does the atomic magnetic moment depend on J, L, and S? Evaluate the Landé g-factor for atoms with $S = 0$, $L = 1$; $S = \frac{1}{2}$, $L = 1$; $S = 1$, $L = 1$; $S = 0$, $L = 2$: evaluate it for all possible values of J in each case. The energy for a magnetic moment with z-component μ_z in a magnetic field B in the z-direction is $-\mu_z B$: evaluate the energies of the states of the atoms for which you have just calculated the Landé g-factors. Now repeat the calculation with the false assumption that the g-factor for the free electron is 1 and not 2. Draw your results on a ladder energy-level diagram in order to see how the coupling of L and S modifies the magnetic properties of a system. Turn to °Zeeman effect for further development of this point. What does the g-factor measure in electron spin resonance? Why can g differ from 2 when the electron is a part of a radical? What information about the electronic structure of a radical can g reveal? Calculate the magnetic field for resonant absorption of 9 GHz radiation of (a) a free electron, (b) a radical with $g = 2{\cdot}0057$, and (c) a radical with $g = 1{\cdot}9980$. Quote results in gauss (G). What is the role of spin-orbit coupling in determing the g-value of a molecule? Why can some g-values be more than the free-spin value? What is the molecular g-value, and how does it arise?

2. This question invites you to deduce the form of the Landé g-factor. We consider the geometry set out in Fig. G1a with a magnetic field along z. We seek to express the energy of the system as $-g_J\gamma_e\mathbf{J.B}$, whereas in fact we know that the magnetic energy is really $-\gamma_e\mathbf{L.B} - 2\gamma_e\mathbf{S.B}$ (that is, the sum of the orbital and spin interactions with the field). We also know that $\mathbf{J} = \mathbf{L} + \mathbf{S}$. Consider **L**. This vector precesses about **J**, and the only time-independent, and therefore non-vanishing, component is the one parallel to **J**; this has the value $\mathbf{L.J}/|\mathbf{J}|$. This component now behaves like the vector $[(\mathbf{L.J})/|\mathbf{J}|](\mathbf{J}/|\mathbf{J}|)$, swinging round the z-axis as **J** itself precesses ($\mathbf{J}/|\mathbf{J}|$ is a unit vector along **J**). This vector has a projection along the magnetic-field direction which we may write $[(\mathbf{L.J})/|\mathbf{J}|]\ [\mathbf{J.B}/|\mathbf{J}|]$, and so the only time-independent component of $-\gamma_e\mathbf{L.B}$ is $-\gamma_e[\mathbf{L.J}/|\mathbf{J}|^2]\ \mathbf{J.B}$. This has the form $-g'_J\gamma_e\ \mathbf{J.B}$, which is what we require. A similar expression for $-2\gamma_e\mathbf{S.B}$ can be written as $-g''_J\gamma_e\mathbf{J.B}$ (find it), and so now we must show that $g'_J + g''_J = g_J$, the Landé factor. Do this by noting that $-2\mathbf{L.J} = (\mathbf{J}-\mathbf{L})^2 - \mathbf{J}^2 - \mathbf{L}^2 = \mathbf{S}^2 - \mathbf{J}^2 - \mathbf{L}^2$, and similarly for **S.J**, and then finally replace operators of the form $\mathbf{J}^2$ by their quantum-mechanical values $J(J+1)\hbar^2$. Find a more exact form of the Landé factor using $g_e = 2{\cdot}0023$ instead of $g_e \sim 2$.

Further information. An account of the deduction of the Landé g-factor will be found in Chapter 8 of *MQM*, and a further discussion is given in §11.3 of Herzberg (1940), and §IIIF and §VA3 of Kuhn (1969). The factor plays an important role in the °Zeeman effect and in determining the magnetic properties of transition-metal ions. For references to the latter see °crystal-field theory, and °ligand-field theory. A detailed account will be found in §5.6 of Griffith (1964) and §11.3 and subsequent chapters of Abragam and Bleaney (1970). For the g-value of electron spin resonance see *MQM* Chapter 11 for a detailed discussion, including something more about g exceeding 2·0023, and an account of the calculation of g-values for molecules. This topic is also taken up in Chapter 2 of Atkins and Symons (1967), in Chapter 9 of Carrington and McLachlan (1967), in Chapter 7 of Slichter (1963), and in

Chapter 12 of Griffith (1964). McLauchlan describes the dependence of the appearance of an electron spin resonance spectrum on the g-value in *Magnetic resonance* (OCS 1). Molecular magnetic moments are discussed in Chapter 11, especially §11.6, of Townes and Schawlow (1955).

gaussian atomic orbitals. The bore about molecular-structure calculations is the complexity of many of the electron-electron interaction-energy integrals which must be calculated. In a °self-consistent field calculation many of the integrals involve atomic orbitals based on more than one centre, and may involve orbitals on as many as four centres. These multi-centre integrals are complicated to evaluate and consume a great deal of time on an electronic computer. One simplification is to express the atomic orbital in terms of gaussian functions, which are basically of the form $\exp(-ar^2)$, instead of as the °Slater type of atomic orbital, which are basically exponential functions of the form $\exp(-a'r)$. The advantage of this procedure arises from the fact that the product of two gaussians based on different centres is itself a gaussian based on a point lying between the centres. Therefore a complicated 3- or 4-centre integral can be expressed as a relatively simple 2-centred integral, and this can be evaluated speedily. The disadvantage of the method lies in the fact that an atomic orbital is not well represented by a simple gaussian function, and so each atomic orbital has to be expressed as a sum of several gaussians. Therefore, although each integral is simpler, very many more of them need to be evaluated.

Questions. What advantages stem from employing gaussian atomic orbitals, and what are the disadvantages? Show that the product of two gaussian functions $\exp(-a_1r_1^2)$ and $\exp(-a_2r_2^2)$ may be expressed as a gaussian function centred on a point between the two centres, and find the appropriate position in terms of a_1 and a_2. Confirm that the procedure cannot be applied in the case of two exponential functions. By the °variation principle determine the best gaussian atomic orbital for a hydrogen atom; repeat the calculation using a trial function composed of the sum of two gaussians. In each case compare the true 1s-orbital with the best gaussian orbital by comparing the energies, and by plotting the radial dependence of the functions.

Further information. See §9.2(i) of Richards and Horsley (1970), and §1.6F of McGlynn, Vanquickenborne, Kinoshita, and Carroll (1972). The method was originated by Boys (1950). For calculations based on the method see the bibliography prepared by Richards, Hinkley, and Walker (1971).

gerade and ungerade (g and u). The German words *gerade* (even) and *ungerade* (odd) are added as labels to states and °wavefunctions to denote their behaviour under inversion (their *parity*). A simple example is the classification of the orbitals of the hydrogen molecule: there is a point of inversion symmetry of the molecule at the middle of the bond. Consider the amplitude of the 1sσ-bonding orbital at an arbitrary point of the molecule and project a straight line from this point through the inversion centre, and travel an equal distance to the other side (Fig. G2). The sign and magnitude of the amplitude of the σ-bond at the new point is unchanged, and so the orbital is even (g) under this symmetry operation, and is

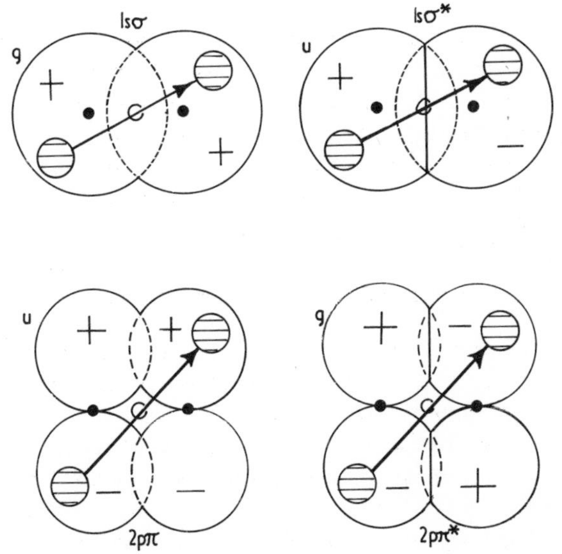

FIG. G2. *Gerade* and *ungerade* symmetry.

written σ_g. On the other hand, the same journey in the °antibonding orbital ($1s\sigma^*$) begins at a point of positive amplitude, passes through a °node, and ends at a point of negative amplitude. This orbital is odd (u) and is labelled σ_u^*. The $2p\sigma$-orbitals behave similarly, but the π-orbitals behave differently (see Fig. G2): the bonding π-orbital is u and the antibonding orbital is g.

The g, u classification also applies to states: the appropriate label is obtained by determining whether the state is even or odd overall by considering the product of the inversion behaviour of its components. Thus H_2 is g because (even) × (even) is even; the excited °configuration $\sigma_g\sigma_u^*$ is u because g × u = u.

When there is no centre of inversion symmetry the classification is inapplicable: g and u labels may be added to the states and orbitals of homonuclear diatomics and to centrosymmetric octahedral complexes, but not to heteronuclear diatomics or to tetrahedral complexes.

The classification is useful in a discussion of °selection rules because the only °electric dipole transitions allowed are those involving a change of parity; thus g ⟶ u and u ⟶ g transitions are allowed, but g ⟶ g and u ⟶ u are forbidden.

Questions. What is the significance of the labels g and u? Why are they not applicable to heteronuclear diatomics? Which of the following molecules could have orbitals and states distinguished by g and u: O_2, NO, NO_2, CO_2, CH_4, He, NH_3? Classify the following orbitals into g or u type symmetry: s-, p-, d-, f-orbitals on free atoms; $1s\sigma$, $2p\pi^*$, $3d\sigma$, $3d\pi$, $3d\pi^*$, $3d\delta$ in homonuclear diatomics. Apply g and u labels to the ground states of He, H_2, and O_2. Which electric dipole transitions are allowed under the g, u classification?

Further information. The g, u labelling is a group-theoretical classification of the parity of a state; therefore see *MQM* Chapter 5, Cotton (1963), Bishop (1973), and Tinkham (1964). Also see books on molecular structure, such as Coulson's *The shape and structure of molecules* (OCS 9), Coulson (1961), and Murrell, Kettle, and Tedder (1965). King (1964) and Herzberg (1950) both discuss the role of g, u classification in the electronic spectra of molecules.

Grotrian diagram. In a Grotrian diagram the energy levels of an atom are displayed as a ladder of lines classified into convenient groups. Spectral transitions are represented by lines connecting the °terms between which they take place, and the frequency (or wave number) of the transition can be added if desired. Sometimes the relative intensities of the transitions are indicated by the thickness of the connecting lines. An example of a very simple Grotrian diagram is shown in Fig. G3: this is for the °hydrogen atom. The levels are classified according to the principal °quantum number, and the classes correspond to different values of the °orbital angular momentum quantum number ℓ. The different transitions giving rise to various °series of lines are indicated.

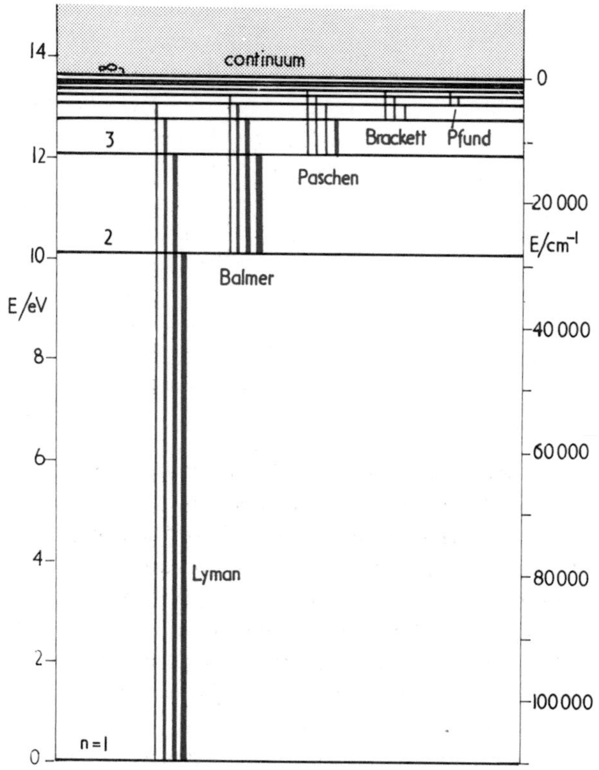

FIG. G3. Grotrian diagram for atomic hydrogen.

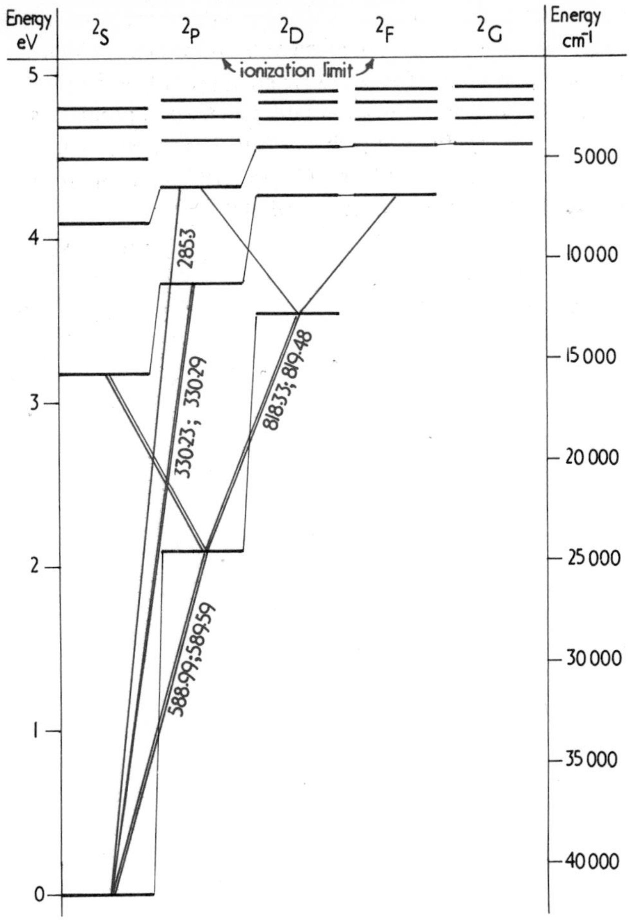

FIG. G4. Grotrian diagram for atomic sodium.

The Grotrian diagram for sodium is shown in Fig. G4. When there is more than one electron confusion sometimes arises in the labelling of the energy levels because in some cases the orbital occupied by the excited electron is used as the label, and in others the °term symbol, the label of the state of the atom. Thus in some cases the lowest state of the sodium atom is labelled 3s, in others it is labelled 3s ^{2}S, in others 3^2S, and in others, reasonably but dangerously, 1^2S, denoting that the ground state is the first of the doublet states. It is the penultimate of these labels that we shall employ.

The energy is generally referred to the ground state as zero. Fragments of the diagrams may be magnified if it is desired to display the °fine structure.

Further information. See *MQM* Chapter 8 for further examples and further discussion. Grotrian diagrams are discussed in King (1964), Candler (1964), who gives many examples, Kuhn (1962), and Condon and Shortley (1963). A collection of them is given in the *American Institute of Physics handbook*, p. 7–12, Gray (1972). The standard collection of energy-level data for atoms is that of Moore (1949 et seq.). Other aspects of the use of the diagrams is described under °fine structure, °series, and the °hydrogen atom.

group theory. In quantum theory, group theory is the mathematical theory of symmetry. It puts on a formal mathematical basis our intuitive notions about the symmetry of objects, and so enables unambiguous deductions to be drawn about the consequences of their symmetry. Taking full advantage of the symmetry of a system reduces the amount of labour involved in calculations, and it often enables conclusions to be drawn without the need for elaborate manipulations.

Group theory is used to find the appropriate °linear combination of atomic orbitals for the °molecular orbitals of a molecule, to classify atomic and molecular states, to determine the °selection rules that govern the transitions between these states, and to find the °normal modes of °vibration of molecules. °Angular-momentum theory can be regarded as a branch of group theory. The language of group theory is concerned with °symmetry transformations of molecules and solids: with their °matrix representations, with their °character and their class, and with the manipulation of the irreducible representations.

A brief summary of the properties of °characters, which are the most useful aspects in most chemical applications of group theory, is given in Box 4 on p 33 for those who already know some theory.

Further information. See *MQM* Chapter 5 for a discussion of basic group theory, and the remainder of the book for extensive applications. Its connexion with angular-momentum theory is discussed at the end of Chapter 6 in *MQM*. Helpful elementary introductions to group theory are the books by Jaffé and Orchin (1965) and Cotton (1963), and an introductory book with many of the details filled in is Bishop (1973). Other helpful introductions include those by Tinkham (1964), Schonland (1965), McWeeny (1963), and, for solids, Wooster (1973). For advanced treatments see Wigner (1959), Hamermesh (1962), Weyl (1930), and Judd (1963). An exhaustive treatment of the symmetry properties of solids has been prepared by Bradley and Cracknell (1972), and a small handbook containing character tables and group properties to act as a notebook for group theory calculations has been prepared by Atkins, Child, and Phillips (1970). An entertainment has been written by Weyl (1952).

H

hamiltonian. The name of Sir William Rowan Hamilton (1805–65), who was Astronomer Royal of Ireland as an undergraduate, was a devotee of pork chops, but not the husband of her who entertained Horatio Lord Nelson, is commemorated in quantum mechanics because he set up a system of classical mechanics ideally suited to the structure of quantum mechanics, and because he almost discovered quantum mechanics itself, and quite possibly would have done if during his life experiment had required it. For the systems that concern us the *hamiltonian* is the sum of the kinetic T and potential V energies (but like most things, it can be defined more generally, more subtly, and more powerfully). We give it the symbol H (some prefer $\mathcal{H}$) and so write $H = T + V$. In quantum mechanics it is necessary to interpret observables as °operators, and interpreting the observables T and V as operators we see that the hamiltonian is the operator for the total energy of the system. The total hamiltonian for a system consists of a sum of terms corresponding to different contributions to the total energy. A selection of such terms is listed in Box 7 (overleaf).

The °Schrödinger equation is often written in the form $H\psi = E\psi$, and so it can be interpreted as an °eigenvalue equation, the energy E of the system being the eigenvalue of the hamiltonian operator, and the °wavefunctions the corresponding eigenstates.

Questions. What is a hamiltonian? What is a hamiltonian operator? How may the Schrödinger equation be expressed in terms of the hamiltonian, and how may it be interpreted? Write the hamiltonian, and analyse the significance of each term, for the following species: a free electron; a hydrogen atom; a hydrogen molecule-ion; a hydrogen molecule; a helium atom; a carbon atom; an harmonic oscillator; an harmonically oscillating charge in an electric field; a mass on the end of a spring; and the hydrogen atom in a magnetic field.

Further information. See *MQM* Chapters 3 and 4 for an introduction to simple ideas about hamiltonians, and Pauling and Wilson (1935) for another discussion. All books on quantum theory discuss hamiltonians, and for the classical background see Goldstein (1950). For further information, see °operators. Most hamiltonians are very complicated, and their eigenvalues cannot be found exactly: the three major approximation techniques are °perturbation theory, °variation theory, and °self-consistent field techniques. A bibliographical note about Hamilton, and his behaviour at breakfast, will be found in *Scientific American*—Whittaker (1954).

harmonic oscillator. Harmonic oscillations occur in classical mechanics when the restoring force on a body is proportional to its displacement from equilibrium. A force $-kx$, where k is the °force-constant, implies the existence of a potential $\frac{1}{2}kx^2$ (because $F = -\partial V/\partial x$). An harmonic oscillator in quantum mechanics is a system with such a parabolic potential, and its properties can be determined by solving the °Schrödinger equation with a potential $\frac{1}{2}kx^2$. The conclusions this leads to are as follows.

1. The energy is quantized and limited to the values $(v + \frac{1}{2})\hbar\omega_0$, where $\omega_0 = (k/m)^{1/2}$ and v is confined to the

BOX 7: Hamiltonians

In general

$$H = T + V.$$

Free particle

$$H = -(\hbar^2/2m)\nabla^2$$

°Particle in a box (one-dimensional square well)

$$H = -(\hbar^2/2m)\left(\frac{d^2}{dx^2}\right) \quad 0 \leqslant x \leqslant L.$$

°Hydrogen atom

$$H = -(\hbar^2/2m)\nabla^2 - e^2/4\pi\epsilon_0 r.$$

Helium atom

$$H = -(\hbar^2/2m)\nabla_1^2 - (\hbar^2/2m)\nabla_2^2 - 2e^2/4\pi\epsilon_0 r_1 - - 2e^2/4\pi\epsilon_0 r_2 + e^2/4\pi\epsilon_0 r_{12}.$$

Hydrogen molecule-ion (H_2^+); fixed nuclei

$$H = -(\hbar^2/2m)\nabla_1^2 - e^2/4\pi\epsilon_0 r_{1A} - e^2/4\pi\epsilon_0 r_{1B} + + e^2/4\pi\epsilon_0 r_{AB}.$$

°Harmonic oscillator

$$H = -(\hbar^2/2m)\left(\frac{d^2}{dx^2}\right) + \tfrac{1}{2}kx^2.$$

Rigid °rotor

$$H = -(\hbar^2/2I_{xx})J_x^2 - (\hbar^2/2I_{yy})J_y^2 - (\hbar^2/2I_{zz})J_z^2.$$

°Magnetic dipole moment μ in field **B**

$$H = -\boldsymbol{\mu}.\mathbf{B};\ \text{for example, } \boldsymbol{\mu} = g\gamma_e \mathbf{s} \text{ or } \gamma_e \mathbf{l}.$$

Electric dipole moment μ in field **E**

$$H = -\boldsymbol{\mu}.\mathbf{E}.$$

values 0, 1, 2, ... This implies the existence of a *zero-point energy* of $\frac{1}{2}\hbar\omega_0$ when the oscillator is in its lowest energy state with $v = 0$: all the energy cannot be removed from an oscillator. The zero-point energy may be viewed in the light of the °uncertainty principle: eliminating all energy, and therefore momentum, would imply an infinite uncertainty in position; but the particle is confined by the potential. The other implication is that the spacing between energy levels is $\hbar\omega_0$, and the energy of oscillation can be increased only by absorbing integral multiples of the vibrational °quantum $\hbar\omega_0$. The consequences of this are discussed further in °heat capacity and °quantum.

2. The wavefunctions are simple polynomials in the displacement (the *Hermite polynomials*) multiplied by a gaussian function. The explicit form of some of the functions is given in Table 11 together with some of their more important technical properties. The shapes of a few of them are drawn in Fig. H1. In the lowest state the polynomial is simply the trivial factor 1, and so the wavefunction is the bell-shaped gaussian curve which has its maximum at the equilibrium position. As the °wavefunction gives the distribution of the particle it follows that, in the ground state, the particle clusters close to its equilibrium position but possesses both °kinetic and potential energy by virtue of the wavefunction's

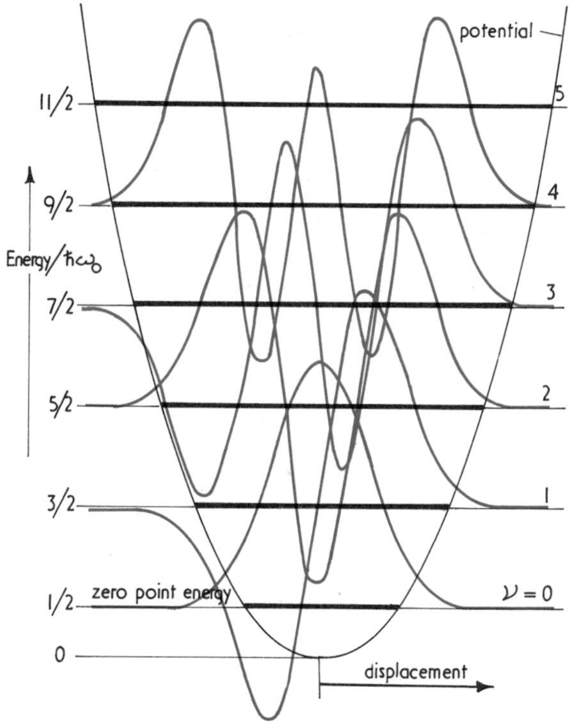

FIG. H1. The wavefunctions and energy levels of a harmonic oscillator. The classically accessible domains are shown by the strong lines confined by the potential. View this in relation to the upper half of Fig. F4.

shape and the presence of the potential. The next polynomial is essentially the factor x, and so the product of this and the gaussian is a wave with a °node in the centre (at $x = 0$). This corresponds to a higher energy because the wave is more sharply curved (higher °kinetic energy) and penetrates more deeply into the potential (in classical terms it swings both faster and further). The next function again peaks in the middle, but has significant accumulations of probability in the regions of higher potential. As the excitation increases the principal peaks of the probability distribution appear more dominantly at the limits of the distribution, at what in the classical treatment are the turning points of the oscillation. This is in accord with the classical distribution, for at the turning points the kinetic energy, and therefore the velocity, is least, and the probability of finding the particle there the greatest.

3. A °wave packet may be formed when the energy state of the oscillator is imprecise. A wave packet with a gaussian shape moves from one side of the well to the other with a frequency ω_0 in a manner that resembles the classical motion (Fig. H2);

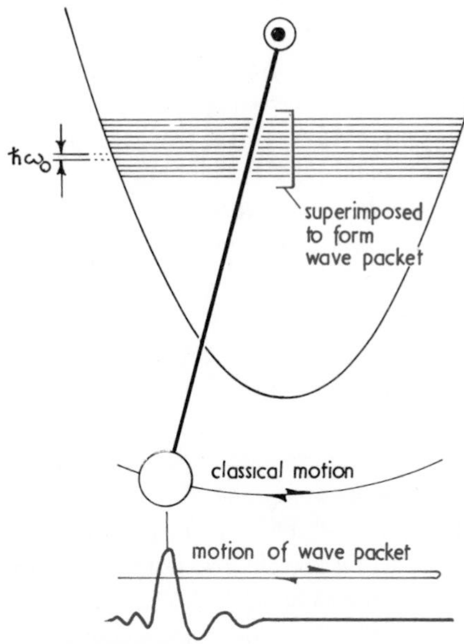

FIG. H2. Classical limit of the harmonic oscillator.

therefore we see that the quantum spacing ω_0 becomes the frequency of the classical oscillator. This is a very good example of the way that quantum-mechanical principles underlie classical mechanics (see °correspondence principle). An oscillator behaves more closely in accord with classical mechanics as a °superposition of states becomes more justifiable: this increases as the quantum separation decreases. Therefore it can be appreciated that oscillators with frequencies of the order of 1 Hz (or 2π rad s^{-1}), such as a classical clock, behave essentially classically, whereas periodic processes in atoms and molecules, with frequencies in the range 10^{12} - 10^{15} Hz, behave quantum-mechanically.

The importance of the harmonic oscillator is based on a number of features. First, oscillations in Nature are often harmonic to a very good approximation, and therefore the theory of the harmonic oscillator can be used in the description of the vibration of molecules and of atoms in solids. This leads on to its application in the theory of °heat capacities and to many other properties of solids. Next, just as in classical mechanics, the algebra of harmonic oscillations is closely related to the algebra of °rotational motion, and therefore it is not surprising to see harmonic-oscillator algebra appearing in some discussions of °angular momentum. Finally, the harmonic oscillator is a remarkably simple creature to deal with because the expression for its energy is symmetrical in the space and momentum coordinates (both are quadratic functions). This feature makes it very simple to handle and is responsible, for example, for the equal spacing of the energy levels of the oscillator. The harmonic-oscillator algebra is the basis of the technique of °second quantization.

Questions. 1. Under what circumstances are oscillations harmonic? What potential does this imply? What values of the energy are permitted to the quantized oscillator? What is its minimum permitted value? Why is it plausible that a zero-point energy exists for an harmonic oscillator? What is the separation between any pair of adjacent levels? What is the mathematical form of the wavefunctions? Discuss the form of the distribution of displacements when the oscillator is in its ground state, and compare it with the ground state of a classical oscillator and with the state of a classical oscillator containing the same amount of energy. How does the dis-

tribution of displacements change as the oscillator is excited? What is the motion of a suitably-formed wave packet? Under what circumstances may such a packet be formed, and how does it relate to the motion of a classical oscillator with the same force-constant and mass? Calculate the energy separation for an oscillator of frequency 1 Hz, 10^{14} Hz (remember to convert these frequencies to rad s^{-1} by multiplying by 2π). Calculate the energy difference between 1 mol of each kind of oscillator in its ground and excited states, and express the result in J mol^{-1} and in cm^{-1}.
2. Use the properties of the Hermite polynomials in Table 11 to deduce the selection rules for °electric dipole transitions in an harmonic oscillator. See °anharmonicity for a further development of this question. Show that the harmonic-oscillator Schrödinger equation can be written in the form $a^{+}a\psi_{\lambda} = -(\lambda - 1)\psi_{\lambda}$, where a is the differential operator $(d/dy) + y$, a^{+} is $(d/dy) - y$, $y = (m\omega_0/\hbar)^{1/2}x$, x the displacement from equilibrium, and λ is related to the energy by $E = \lambda(\hbar\,\omega_0/2)$. The lowest energy corresponds to $\lambda = 1$, and so $a^{+}a\psi_1 = 0$; therefore a solution is $a\psi_1 = 0$. Solve this first-order differential equation, and show that it is indeed the gaussian function in Table 11.

Further information. See *MQM* Chapter 3 for a discussion of the properties of the harmonic oscillator and the solution of the harmonic-oscillator Schrödinger equation by the method of factorization (in terms of *annihilation* and *creation operators*), and see §III.11A of Pauling and Wilson (1935) for the solution by the polynomial-expansion method. The oscillator solution is also described in Landau and Lifshitz (1958a), Schiff (1968), and Messiah (1961). The properties of the Hermite polynomials are listed in §22 of Abramowitz and Stegun (1965), where numerical values will also be found; the manipulation of the polynomials is described in §3.10 of Margenau and Murphy (1956). The relation of harmonic-oscillator algebra to angular momenta is described in Lipkin (1965), Mattis (1965), Englefield (1972), and by Schwinger (1965).

heat capacity. The theory of heat capacities of crystalline solids began with Dulong and Petit's 'law' that all metals had a heat capacity of 6 cal deg^{-1} mol^{-1} (25 J K^{-1} mol^{-1}). Unfortunately most metals do not have this heat capacity, and none do at low temperatures. Nevertheless it is helpful to understand the reasoning that 'justifies' Dulong and Petit assertion, because the quantum theory is then more easily understood. A block of metal contains N atoms, and each can vibrate against its neighbours in three perpendicular directions; therefore the block behaves like a collection of $3N$ oscillators. The °equipartition theorem states that with each oscillation at thermal equilibrium can be associated an amount of energy kT; therefore the total energy of the block at the temperature T is $3NkT$, or $3RT$ if the block is 1 mol of metal. Thermodynamics tells us that the heat capacity at constant volume is $(\partial U/\partial T)_V$, where U is the internal energy of the sample. In our case $U = 3RT$ and so the heat capacity is $C_V = 3R$, the numerical value of which accords with Dulong and Petit's rule.

Quantum theory warns us that the equipartion rule applies to a classical system and may fail for systems that, like the vibrations of atoms in crystals, ought to be treated by quantum mechanics. The root of the discrepancy lies in the inability of an oscillator to accept less than its full °quantum of energy: this has the effect of quenching the effectiveness of the oscillators that constitute the sample, and therefore of lowering its heat capacity.

The *Einstein model* pretends that every oscillator in the block has the same fundamental frequency ν_E, and we shall begin with this simplified version of the true situation. Imagine a source of heat of temperature T in contact with a collection of oscillators all having the same frequency. If the oscillators behaved classically each one would be activated when the sample was in thermal equilibrium with the source. Each would swing with its natural frequency, but with an amplitude such that its mean energy was kT. But as the oscillator is governed by quantum mechanics, if heat is transferred to the metal at a low temperature it can be used to activate only a very small number of oscillators, for no oscillator can possess an energy less than $h\nu_E$ if it is to be excited at all. A little energy must reside in a few oscillators, and the remainder must be quiescent. Therefore there is an effective reduction in the number of oscillators in the sample, and a consequent reduction of its heat capacity. At higher temperatures the energy may be distributed over many more oscillators and so more

BOX 8: Heat capacities of solids

Dulong and Petit

$$C_v = 3Lk = 3R\,.$$

Einstein

$$C_v = 3R\left(\frac{\theta_E}{T}\right)^2\left\{\frac{\exp(\theta_E/T)}{[1-\exp(\theta_E/T)]^2}\right\}$$

$$\theta_E = h\nu_E/k\,.$$

Debye

$$C_v = 9R\left(\frac{T}{\theta_D}\right)^3\int_0^{\theta_D/T} dx\left\{\frac{x^4\exp x}{(1-\exp x)^2}\right\}$$

$$\sim (12\pi^4R/5\theta_D^3)T^3 \qquad T \ll \theta_D$$

$$\theta_D = h\nu_D/k.$$

ν_D and θ_D may be related to the speed of sound v:

$$\nu_D^3 = 3Nv^3/4\pi V,$$

where N/V is the number density of atoms in the sample.

are able to accept energy: therefore the heat capacity is greater than at lower temperatures. At very high temperatures, when the energy of the block greatly exceeds the excitation energy of the oscillators, all oscillators are effective, and may be stimulated to high quantum levels, and the sample attains its classical heat capacity of $3R$. Box 8 gives the Einstein expression for the heat capacity, and Fig. H3 shows the predicted temperature-dependence.

The *Debye model* is a modification of the Einstein model and takes into account the fact that the oscillators have a range of fundamental frequencies from zero up to a limit ν_D. One may understand this situation in two different ways. The first way is to regard the solid as a continuum (as a jelly). The jelly can vibrate at all frequencies from zero up to a very high value and the number of modes of oscillation that have a given frequency can be calculated quite simply. But the total number of oscillatory modes cannot exceed the total number of vibrational modes of the atoms that constitute the jelly. This number is $3N$; therefore there must be an upper limit to the frequency of vibration of the jelly such that the total number of oscillators is equal to $3N$. (If the jelly were a true con-

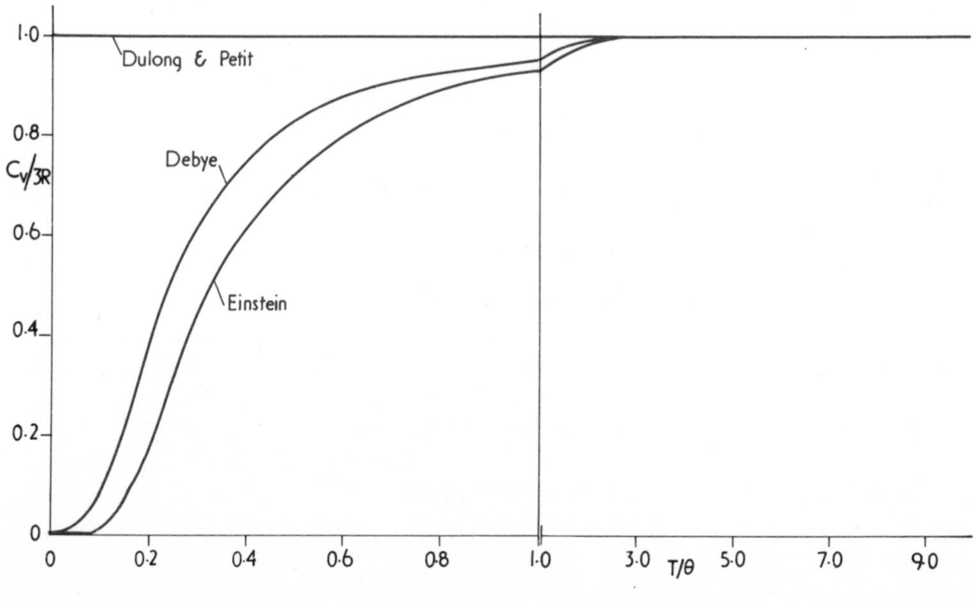

FIG. H3. Calculated heat-capacity curves.

tinuum, like the vacuum, there would be no upper limit to the frequencies because a continuum corresponds to a system with an infinite number of oscillating components: for this reason the vacuum can support all frequencies of light.)

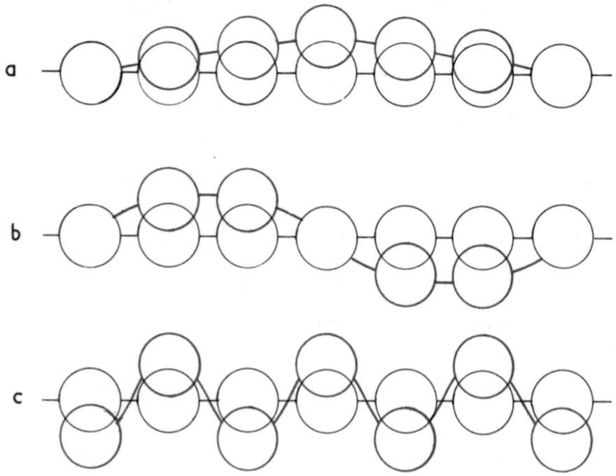

FIG. H4. Oscillations in a chain of atoms. (a) the lowest frequency, (b) an intermediate frequency, and (c) the highest frequency.

The other method of seeing that an upper frequency limit must exist is to consider Fig. H4, which shows the chain of atoms in a crystal vibrating relative to each other. If we consider only transverse vibrations (those perpendicular to the line of atoms) it should be clear that the vibration with the highest restoring force is the one in which neighbouring atoms are displaced in opposite directions, and the vibration with least restoring force is the one where all the atoms are displaced in the same direction (but by different amounts; if they were all displaced by the same amount we should obtain a translation of the block). There will also be intermediate modes of displacement, and therefore we can expect a range of restoring forces, and so a range of fundamental frequencies; but there will be a maximum frequency because it is impossible to obtain a higher restoring force than that in the situation where the direction of displacement changes between neighbours. This situation is illustrated in Fig. H5.

The Debye model takes the distribution of oscillations into account by assessing the number of fundamental oscillations of each frequency ν between 0 and ν_D and calculating the

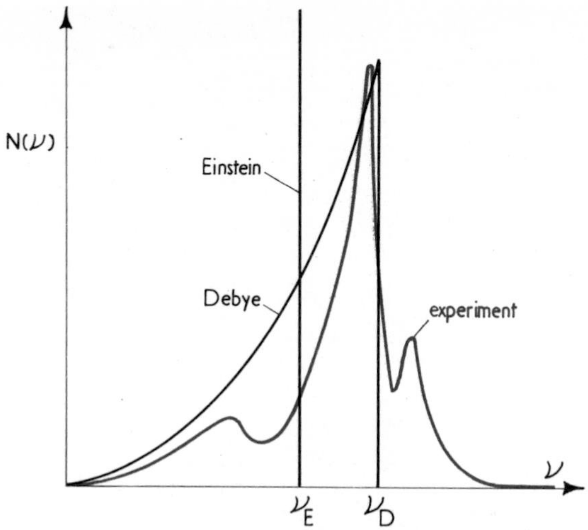

FIG. H5. The Einstein, Debye, and experimental distribution (for Cu) of the number of oscillators of a frequency ν.

total contribution to the heat capacity (see Box 8 and Fig. H3). Since there are oscillators at lower frequency than in the single-frequency Einstein model the heat capacity of the Debye model exceeds that of the latter, but the difference disappears at high temperatures when the behaviour is virtually classical. The heat capacity depends on the temperature and a characteristic constant known as the *Debye temperature* $\theta_D = h\nu_D/k$; since the cut-off frequency is higher in rigid materials so too is the Debye temperature. Some representative values of θ_D are listed in Table 12. A high Debye temperature tends to lower the heat capacity at a given temperature. At low temperatures the Debye model predicts that the heat capacity should be proportional to $(T/\theta_D)^3$, and this is often employed in entropy calculations.

Further information. Chapter 1 of *MQM* gives details of the calculation of the Einstein heat-capacity formula, and some information about the Debye calculation. For an account of the Einstein calculation, and a discussion of Debye's, see Gasser and Richards' *Entropy and energy levels* (OCS 19). A very good discussion of heat capacities, with full details of calculations, will be found in Chapter 6 of Kittel (1971) and Chapter 2 of Dekker (1960). For further information consult Chapter 16 of Davidson (1962). A compilation of numerical data, including the numerical values of the Einstein and Debye functions and the Debye temperatures of many materials, will be found in §4 of Gray (1972). For the Debye function also see §27 of Abramowitz and Stegun (1965). Some Debye temperatures are given in the other books mentioned.

Hellmann-Feynman theorem. The theorem states that the gradient of the energy with respect to some parameter $\mathrm{d}E/\mathrm{d}P$ is equal to the °expectation value of the gradient of the °hamiltonian with respect to that parameter, $\partial H/\partial P$. In order to calculate $\mathrm{d}E/\mathrm{d}P$, where P is the parameter (which might be a molecular bond length or angle, a nuclear charge, or the strength of some applied field), it is sufficient first to calculate $\partial H/\partial P$, which might turn out to be a very simple operator, and then to calculate its expectation value. The simplicity of this statement conceals a severe limitation (there has to be some catch): in this case it is the not unreasonable requirement that the wavefunctions used to calculate the expectation value must be exact. All the work lies in their evaluation, and faint hearts often apply the Hellmann-Feynman theorem even when only scruffily inaccurate functions are available. This misuse can introduce significant errors when the wavefunctions are only slightly bad; so beware.

When is the theorem used? One application is to the calculation of the response of molecules to electric and magnetic fields: see °polarizability. Another very interesting application is to the study of the geometry and °force-constants of molecules. This application stems from the remarkable consequence of the theorem that the force on a nucleus in a molecule may be calculated as a simple problem in classical electrostatics if the exact (quantum-mechanical) charge distribution is known. This deduction from the theorem is often called the *electrostatic Hellmann-Feynman theorem*. If we know the electron density everywhere, and that is known if the °wavefunction is known, then the force on a nucleus can be calculated by considering the Coulombic force that the same classical charge distribution exerts on a point nucleus. The °force-constant for any distortion of the molecule can then be calculated by working out the restoring force on a nucleus when the geometry is distorted. Note that this derivation treats the equilibrium geometry as a problem for classical electrostatics; but do not be misled into thinking that all the nonsense about °exchange energy, and so on, is an unnecessary nonsense after all. The complication of exchange interactions is hidden, of course, in the difficult task of determining the correct electron density for a given nuclear configuration. Nevertheless, the theorem does enable one to remove some of the mystery about the shape of molecules, for in some sense the geometry can be understood in terms of a balance of electrostatic forces, even though the distribution responsible for the balance is governed by quantum mechanics.

Questions. 1. State the Hellmann-Feynman theorem. Under what conditions is it untrue? Propose several possibilities for the parameter P in the calculation of various molecular properties. What use may be made of the theorem in the discussion of molecular structure? Why do problems of exchange energy remain even though the molecular shape may be understood in terms of the forces exerted on the nuclei? Given that the theorem enables the forces exerted on nuclei to be calculated, what conditions on the forces lead to the determination of the equilibrium geometry of the molecule? What might the parameter P represent in a diatomic molecule? What is the influence of the °exchange energy on the determination of molecular shape according to the theorem?
2. Prove the Hellmann-Feynman theorem by considering the expression $E(P) = \langle\psi(P)|H(P)|\psi(P)\rangle$, where the energy depends on the parameter P and so do both the hamiltonian and the exact normalized wavefunctions (so that $\langle\psi(P)|\psi(P)\rangle = 1$). Differentiate both sides with respect to P and use the fact that $\psi(P)$ is the eigenfunction of $H(P)$ with eigenvalue $E(P)$.

Further information. A simple account of the theorem in its application to electric and magnetic problems is given in *MQM* Chapter 11. For molecular applications see a thorough review of the subject by Deb (1973), where many more references will be found. More information is given in §2.6 of Slater (1963). For the original exposition of the theorem see Hellmann (1937) and Feynman (1939).

hermitian operators. An °operator $\hat{\Omega}$ is hermitian if the integral $\int\mathrm{d}\tau f^*\hat{\Omega}g$ is equal to the integral $\int\mathrm{d}\tau(\hat{\Omega}f)^*g$. In the

Dirac °bracket notation the requirement would be for $\langle f|\hat{\Omega}|g\rangle$ to equal $\langle g|\hat{\Omega}|f\rangle^*$. Hermitian operators are important in quantum theory because their °eigenvalues are real; therefore operators corresponding to physical observables must be hermitian. Another consequence of hermiticity is the °orthogonality of °eigenfunctions corresponding to different °eigenvalues of hermitian operators.

Questions. 1. What is the meaning of 'hermiticity'? What properties stem from the hermitian nature of an operator, and why are hermitian operators important in quantum mechanics? Is the operator 'multiply by x' hermitian? Is the operator d/dx hermitian? Is the operator $(\hbar/i)(d/dx)$ hermitian? (In investigating the hermiticity of d/dx use integration by parts and the property that the functions f and g disappear at sufficiently distant boundaries.) Which of these operators might correspond to what physical observables?
2. Prove that the eigenvalues of an hermitian operator are real, and that eigenfunctions corresponding to different eigenvalues are °orthogonal. Demonstrate these results specifically in the case of the operator $\hat{\ell}_z = (\hbar/i)(\partial/\partial\phi)$ which occurs in the theory of °angular momentum.

Further information. See *MQM* Chapter 4 for a further discussion of hermiticity, its consequencies, and the proof of the properties mentioned. See also Dirac (1958), von Neumann (1955), Jordan (1969), and Jauch (1968) for detailed accounts of the quantum-mechanical aspects of hermiticity.

Hückel method. By taking into account the symmetry of a molecule in a wise way, and by making foul assumptions that no referee would pass nor examiner condone, Hückel developed a simple scheme for calculating the energy of the π-electrons in conjugated systems. The approximations, which we label 1–6, are extreme, for they neglect every complicated aspect of the exact problem.

1. The σ-electrons are ignored; they are present implicitly because they are largely responsible for determining the shape of the molecule, but their interaction with the π-electrons is neglected.

2. All overlap is neglected. Since the overlap integral between neighbouring carbon π-orbitals is about 0·25 the propriety of this approximation can be appreciated. (In the event it turns out that overlap can be included quite simply, and it does not affect the answers savagely.)

What about all the complicated integrals that occur in the exact problem? They are classified as too difficult; but to eliminate all integrals would eliminate the problem. Therefore:

3. All the integrals involving only one atom (roughly corresponding to the energy of an electron occupying a carbon 2p-orbital) are set equal to α: this is called the °*Coulomb integral.*

4. All the integrals involving atoms separated by more than one bond are ignored as far too difficult.

5. All the integrals involving neighbouring atoms are set equal to the same value β: this is called the *resonance integral.*

6. After all these approximations it does not seem worth °antisymmetrizing the wavefunction; so it isn't. (But it should be realized that in a rather ill-defined sense the effect of antisymmetrization—the role of °exchange energy—has been taken into account by the parameters α and β.)

With these approximations in hand the °variation method is applied to determine the best °linear combination of atomic π-orbitals to describe the structure of the molecule; this leads to a °secular determinant whose roots give the energy of the orbitals. (Each diagonal element of the determinant is $\alpha - E$ and every off-diagonal element is zero except those corresponding to neighbouring atoms, which are set equal to β.) When the secular determinant is solved and the molecular-orbital energies are known the coefficients for the atomic orbitals may be discovered. This is essentially the complete solution to the problem in the Hückel approximation, and it is possible to deduce a number of molecular properties. These include the delocalization or °resonance energy, the energy of electronic transitions within the π-system, the °charge density on the carbon atoms, and the π-electron contribution to the °dipole moment, the °bond order, and the °free valence. In calculations of delocalization energy a reasonable value of β is $-0{\cdot}69$ eV (-67 kJ mol^{-1}), but for spectral transitions a better value is $-2{\cdot}71$ eV ($-21\,900$ cm^{-1}). A sample calculation is illustrated in Box 9.

BOX 9: Hückel calculation; an example

In general:

1. Write MO as $\psi = \sum_i c_i \phi_i$.
2. Set up °secular determinant $|H_{ij} - ES_{ij}|$ as follows:

$$S_{ij} = \begin{cases} 1 & \text{if } i=j \\ 0 & \text{if } i \neq j \end{cases}$$

$$H_{ij} = \begin{cases} \alpha & \text{if } i=j \\ \beta & \text{if } i \neq j \text{, but } i,j \text{ are neighbours} \\ 0 & \text{otherwise.} \end{cases}$$

3. Solve $|H_{ij} - ES_{ij}| = 0$ for energies E.

For butadiene $\psi = c_1\phi_1 + c_2\phi_2 + c_3\phi_3 + c_4\phi_4$, where $\phi_1, \ldots \phi_4$ are the 2pπ-orbitals on the carbon atoms in CH_2:CH·CH:CH_2. The secular determinant is

$$\begin{vmatrix} \alpha-E & \beta & 0 & 0 \\ \beta & \alpha-E & \beta & 0 \\ 0 & \beta & \alpha-E & \beta \\ 0 & 0 & \beta & \alpha-E \end{vmatrix} = 0$$

If $x\beta = \alpha - E$ this reduces to $x^4 - 3x^2 + 1 = 0$. Therefore the roots are

$$E = \alpha \pm 1{\cdot}6\beta \quad \text{and} \quad E = \alpha \pm 0{\cdot}6\beta$$

and these are the energies of the four molecular orbitals of butadiene. The secular determinant can usually be simplified (factorized) by using symmetry arguments. See Further information.

The Hückel method is moderately satisfactory because of its reliance on the symmetry of the molecule: the orbitals are essentially classified according to their symmetry, and then the number of bonding and anti-bonding juxtapositions of overlapping π-orbitals is counted by the coefficient of β; in this way one obtains a rough guide to the ordering of the energies.

There is obviously enormous room for improvement in the method, and an enormous amount of work has been done with that in mind. A simple improvement is the inclusion of overlap between neighbours: this squashes the lower, bonding orbitals together and separates the upper, °antibonding levels without significantly affecting their order. The next improvement often employed in simple calculations is to realize that the energy of an electron on a carbon atom, measured by the magnitude of α, depends on the charge density on that atom. The Hückel method ignores this dependence and gives the same value of α to all the atoms irrespective of the local accumulation of electron density. (See °alternant hydrocarbon in this connexion.) The *ω-technique* seeks to repair this deficiency by making α depend, through a constant of proportionality ω, on the charge density. This is a simple example of a °self-consistent calculation: a Hückel calculation is first done to find the charge density, then each α is modified appropriately, and the calculation repeated with the new set of αs: the scheme is repeated until the charge density remains constant through a cycle of the calculation.

Beyond these trivial modifications of the original theory one encounters the *semi-empirical* methods which are at the centre of much of present-day research. These attempt to relax the bold assumptions of the Hückel method and to approach the accuracy of an exact calculation. They proceed by neglecting electron-repulsion integrals in a more-or-less rational fashion, and expressing the magnitude of the remaining molecular integrals in terms of some empirical quantity, or in terms of quantities calculated for atoms, or leaving them as adjustable parameters. Virtually all of them deal with the valence electrons only, and acknowledge the existence of the core electrons only in terms of the final choice of the parameters. Most do not make the Hückel distinction between the σ- and π-electrons except in so far as their symmetry is concerned; therefore the methods can be applied to molecules lacking planes of symmetry. Popular methods at one time included the Pariser-Parr-Pople (or PPP) method, which is only a slight improvement on the Hückel method and ignores virtually all the electron repulsion integrals between atoms. The CNDO (complete neglect of differential overlap) method neglects fewer integrals and is the basis of many modern calculations. Other initials, such as INDO (intermediate neglect of differential overlap) and MINDO (modified INDO), represent schemes of neglecting different integrals and choosing the value of those remaining. Details of the actual choices and approximations in these schemes will be found under Further information.

Questions. 1. List the approximations that constitute the Hückel scheme for calculating π-electron energies. What is the significance of the parameters α and β? Why should α be expected to depend on the charge of the atom? What molecular properties may be calculated in the Hückel scheme? What improvements may be made quite simply? What improvement is it much more difficult to introduce? What is the major limitation on the accuracy of the semi-empirical methods? Why are they inferior to the best Hartree-Fock °self-consistent field calculations?
2. Using the calculational scheme set out in Box 9, set up and solve the Hückel equations for the molecules $CH_2{=}CH{-}CH{=}CH_2$, $CH_2{=}C{=}CH_2$, cyclopropene, and benzene, and calculate the delocalization energy and charge distribution in each. In the case of cyclobutadiene investigate the effect of including overlap between nearest neighbours: let the overlap integral be S in each case (set $S = 0{\cdot}25$ at the end of the calculation).
3. The ω-technique supposes that the Coulomb integral on atom r is related to the charge density q_r on r by the formula $\alpha_r = \alpha + (1 - q_r)\,\omega\beta$, with the coefficient ω being about 1·4. Apply the technique to the allyl cation starting with the Hückel approximation and proceeding through three cycles of the ω-method. What is the role of the ω-technique in the case of °alternant hydrocarbons?

Further information. See *MQM* Chapter 9. Many books deal with the Hückel method in detail, and work through many examples. See Coulson's *The shape and structure of molecules* (OCS 9) and §9.6 of Coulson (1961). See also Murrell, Kettle, and Tedder (1965), Streitweiser (1961), Pilar (1968), Salem (1966), McGlynn, Vanquickenborne, Kinoshita, and Carroll (1972), and Dewar (1969). Accounts of the developments of the theory will be found in these books and also in Pople and Beveridge (1970), Doggett (1972), and Murrell and Harget (1972). A compilation of the results of such calculations has been prepared by Coulson and Streitweiser (1965). Streitweiser (1961) works through many calculations on organic molecules, and shows how the results may be applied to the prediction of chemical properties. Roberts (1961*b*) works through the bare bones of the method. Parr (1963) has reviewed the modern theories of molecular structure, and his book contains a collection of some of the important original papers.

Hund coupling cases. In a diatomic molecule there are several sources of angular momentum, notably the °spin of the electrons, their °orbital motion about the axis, and the °rotation of the nuclear framework. The total angular momentum is the vector sum of all these momenta, but there is a variety of ways of coupling them together. The Hund cases are a sensible selection of a few of the possible ways of performing the coupling; we shall deal with the four simplest and most common schemes.

(a) In *Hund's case (a)* the strong electrostatic effect of the nuclei is respected: the axial field allows only circulation about the axis to survive and be a source of °orbital angular momentum. Through the °spin-orbit coupling any resultant spin of the electrons is also coupled to the surviving component of the orbital momentum; that is, the spins are coupled to the axis by a two-step process. All the electronic angular momentum is along the axis: the orbital component is $\Lambda\hbar$ and the spin component $\Sigma\hbar$ giving a total momentum along the axis of $\Omega\hbar$ with $\Omega = \Lambda + \Sigma$. But the nuclear framework is also rotating with a momentum which can be represented by a vector **O** perpendicular to the axis (Fig. H6 a). It follows that the total angular momentum of the molecule is represented by the resultant vector **J**.

(b) *Hund's case (b)* deals with the situation in which the coupling of the spin momentum to the axis disappears. This may occur in the case where there is no electronic orbital angular momentum (so there is no guidance via the spin-orbit interaction for the alignment of the spin) or when the spin-orbit coupling is so weak that the orbital angular momentum does not succeed in fastening it to the axis. This situation may arise in the diatomic molecules formed from the first-row atoms, especially in their hydrides. The orbital momentum is still coupled electrostatically to the axis, but the spin swims loosely around. Therefore the electronic orbital momentum

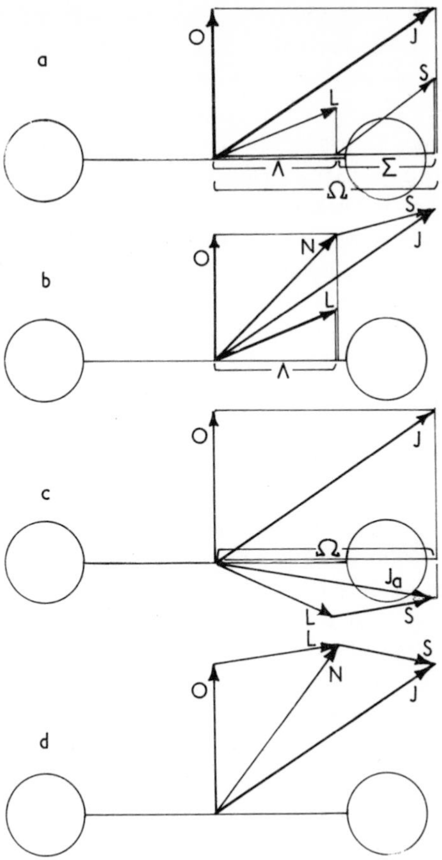

FIG. H6. The Hund coupling cases (a)–(d).

and the nuclear framework momentum couple into a resultant **N**, and only then, in order to get the total momentum of the system, is the spin coupled in to give a resultant **J** (see Fig. H6 b).

(c) In *Hund's case (c)* we go to the other extreme and encounter a situation in which the spin-orbit coupling is so strong that the spin and orbital momenta couple strongly at every opportunity. This passion couples them into a resultant total electronic angular momentum $\mathbf{J}_a$. This $\mathbf{J}_a$ °precesses around the internuclear axis, on which it has a component $\Omega\hbar$. To this resultant couples the rigid rotation of the nuclear framework, and the whole system yields a total momentum **J** (Fig. H6 c). The spin-orbit interaction is strong in heavy atoms, and it is for these that case (c) is important.

(d) In *Hund's case (d)* we encounter a peculiar situation in which the electrons are virtually independent of the orientation of the nuclear framework. The pair of nuclei churn around inside the molecule but the outermost electrons do not respond. Such a situation arises when the electron has been excited to an orbital outside the valence shell (into a °Rydberg state), for it is then so far away that the pair of nuclei resemble a single point nucleus. In this case the electronic orbital angular momentum vector combines with the nuclear-framework vector to yield a resultant **N**; with this combines the spin (there is very little spin-orbit coupling in such diffuse states) to give the total resultant **J** (see Fig. H6 d).

It should be clear that these four cases are only a few of the many possible; and even more are possible if the nuclei themselves possess °spin. Furthermore, the cases are extreme, ideal, or pure cases; in any real molecule there are various competitions between different angular momenta, and for none can there be complete victory. The contamination of one of the pure Hund's cases by another is referred to as a *decoupling.*

Questions. What different sources of angular momentum exist in a diatomic molecule? Under what circumstances does Hund's case (a) dominate? What happens when there is a vanishing orbital angular momentum in the molecule? What is an appropriate coupling scheme when the spin-orbit coupling is small? What is appropriate when it is large? What scheme is appropriate when an electron occupies a very diffuse orbital? What is actually meant by the term 'coupling'? (Consider what a particular coupling scheme represents in terms of energy; review °precession.) The quantum numbers Λ and Σ represent well-defined situations in case (a) (they are *good quantum numbers*); is that also true in case (c)? What of the quantum number Ω? What do these quantum numbers represent?

Further information. See *MQM* Chapter 10 for another look at the coupling schemes. See Barrow (1962), King (1964), and Herzberg (1950) for an account of the way the coupling cases are employed. There are a few more cases of interest: find them all splendidly discussed in Chapter 5 of Herzberg

(1950). One important application is in the discussion of the °selection rules that govern electronic transitions in diatomic molecules.

Hund rules. The Hund rules provide a simple guide to the ordering of the energies of atomic states. They state the following:

(1) for a given °configuration the °term with the highest °multiplicity lies lowest in energy;

(2) for a given configuration and multiplicity the term with the highest °orbital angular momentum lies lowest in energy;

(3) for a given configuration, multiplicity, and orbital angular momentum the °level with the lowest value of the total angular momentum J lies lowest in energy if the configuration represents a shell less than half-filled; and the state with the largest value of J lies lowest if the shell is more than half full.

As an example consider the configuration $1s^2\,2s^2\,2p^2$ and the terms ^3D, ^1P, and ^1S to which it gives rise. What is the order of energies? Application of the first rule yields the order $^3D < (^1P, {}^1S)$. Application of the second yields $^1P < {}^1S$, and so we can conclude that the terms should lie in the order $^3D < {}^1P < {}^1S$. The third rule enables us to order the three levels of the triplet term (^3D). Since $L = 2$ in ^3D, and $S = 1$, the levels correspond to $J = 3, 2, 1$. Since the p-shell is less than half full (it can hold six electrons) the appropriate order is $^3D_1 < {}^3D_2 < {}^3D_3$, and so we have a complete ordering.

The basis of the rules lies in electrostatic interactions for the first two, and magnetic interactions for the third.

1. The first rule has an explanation that is rather more subtle than is found in most books. First, we can say that if their spins are parallel, the electrons must be in different orbitals (°Pauli principle), and therefore must be further apart than if they were crammed into the same orbital; their repulsion will be diminished on this account. But if we have a configuration $p_x p_y$, where the electrons are in different orbitals, it is possible for them to have either parallel or antiparallel spins: which lies lower, and why? The conventional, mythical explanation of why the triplet (parallel) configuration lies lower is that, because electrons with parallel spins tend to keep apart (see °spin correlation), their repulsion is less than in a singlet (paired) configuration. This is not so. Detailed calculation on some cases has shown that the repulsion between the electrons is *greater* in triplet states than in singlets, and that the lowering of the energy is due to the modification of the electron-nucleus interaction. Thus, in a triplet atom the electron distribution contracts, and is stabilized by the improved nuclear attraction: the electron repulsion rises because the electrons are closer together, but this increase does not defeat the improvement in the nuclear attraction. Presumably the °spin correlation helps to stop the electron-electron repulsion rising faster than the nuclear attraction.

2. The second rule reflects the tendency for electrons to stay apart if their orbital angular momentum carries them in the same direction. Electrons circulating in the same direction, and therefore leading to a large total orbital angular momentum, can stay apart; but electrons orbiting in opposition will meet frequently, and so have a large Coulombic repulsive interaction.

3. The third rule is of magnetic origin because the order of levels is determined by the °spin-orbit coupling interaction. When the spin °magnetic moment is opposed to the orbital moment the magnetic energy is least; but such an arrangement of moments implies that the two momenta are also in opposition, which corresponds to a low total angular momentum (see °fine structure, and especially Fig. F2 on p. 74). The *inversion* of the levels when the shell is more than half full reflects the change in the sign of the spin-orbit coupling constant.

Questions. State the three Hund rules. Which depend on electrostatic interactions and which on magnetic? In which does the spin-orbit interaction play an important role? What is the reasoning that explains the first rule? And the second? And the third? Why does an inversion of the levels occur when the shell is more than half full? Put the following terms in order of increasing energy: ^2S, ^2P, ^4S, ^4D. Order their levels appropriately on the assumption that they arise from a more than half-filled shell.

Further information. See *MQM* Chapter 8 for a discussion. The Hund rules are discussed by Kauzmann (1957), King (1964), and Herzberg (1944). Tables of term and level energies have been prepared by Moore (1949 et seq.). The rules, of course, sometimes fail: this may be due to °configuration interaction, where the presence of another configuration depresses a term below the position where the rules predict it should lie. The view that conventional explanations of the first rule are all wrong (including that in *MQM*) is based on work of Lemberger and Pauncz (1970), Katriel (1972), and Colpa and Islip (1973). See Walker and Waber (1973) for a modification to the rules in the case of *jj*-coupling.

hybridization. If an electron occupies an °orbital that has mixed s-, p-, d-, . . . character on an atom, it is said to occupy a *hybrid orbital*, and the process of forming that orbital is known as *hybridization.* An sp-hybrid orbital, for example, is one composed of equal proportions of s- and p-character, and the electron that occupies it may be considered to have 50 per cent s-character and 50 per cent p-character.

What does a hybrid orbital look like? We know that an s-orbital may be regarded as a spherically symmetrical standing wave, and that a p-orbital is a wave with two regions, one with a positive amplitude and one with a negative amplitude. The hybrid orbital is a °superposition of these two standing waves, and where their amplitudes are both positive there is constructive interference, and where one is positive and the other negative there is more or less complete destructive interference. The superposition is lop-sided, and as shown in Fig. H7 a. An sp^2-hybridized orbital contains 33 per cent s-character, and an sp^3-orbital 25 per cent. These orbitals are also illustrated in the figure, and it should be clear that the amount of lop-sidedness increases through the series. Note how the node shifts as the hybridization changes (it passes through the nucleus in the case of an unhybridized p-orbital, but not for the hybrids because of their s-component).

What is the point of hybridization? It will occur in molecules if there results a reduction in the energy of the molecule. Is the energy of a molecule reduced when its atoms hybridize? On first glance it might be thought unlikely. Consider, for example, the carbon atom. In its ground state its °configuration is s^2p^2 (we ignore the deep 1s-electrons), and the 2s-electrons lie some way in energy below the 2p. It is natural to think that carbon will form bonds with its 2p-orbitals and be divalent. If,

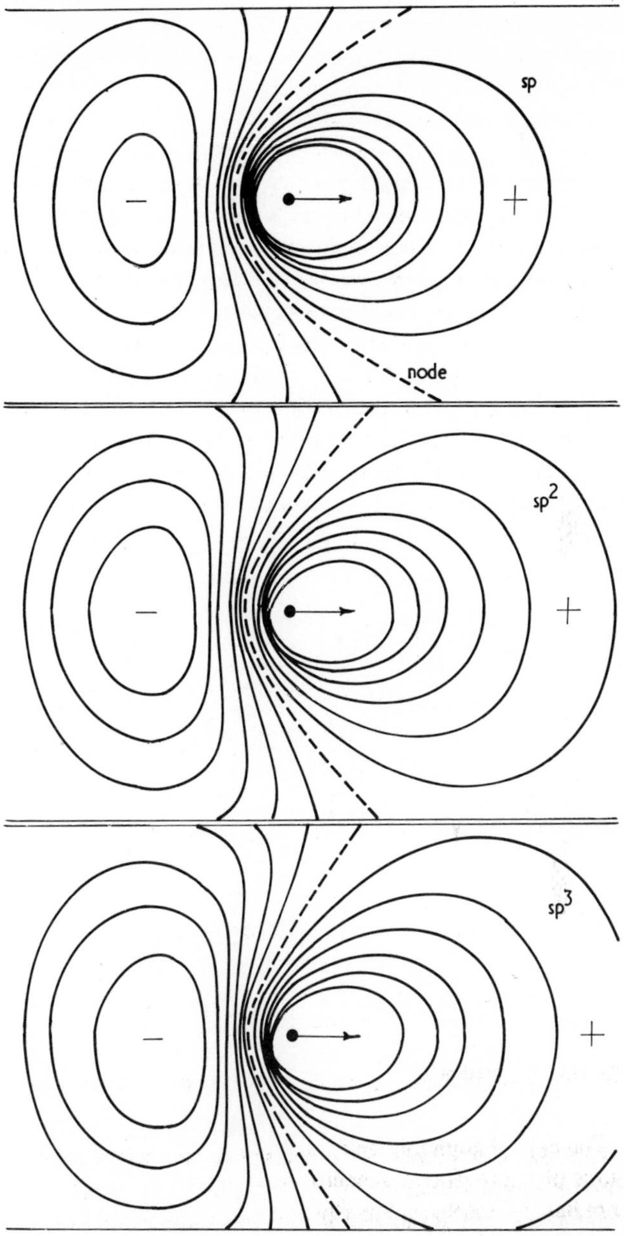

FIG. H7. sp^n-hybrid orbitals. Computed contours for hydrogenic 2s-, 2p-orbitals. Note that the nodal surface is shifted from the nucleus.

however, we can find enough energy to promote one of the s-electrons into the p-shell the atom attains the configuration sp^3: if each of the four s- and p-orbitals hybridize to form four sp^3-hybrids we can envisage a situation in which each electron occupies one of the hybrids. The form of these is clear from Fig. H7: they are strongly directional, and a little calculation shows that they are directed towards the four apices of a tetrahedron (Fig. H8) (see °equivalent orbitals). Nevertheless we still have not recovered our initial energy investment which was used to promote one of the s-electrons. At this point we can appreciate that where we shall recover the energy is in the *four* bonds that we are able to form. Because of the strong directional properties of the hybrids they will have a very efficient overlap with the four neighbouring atoms, and we can expect four *strong* bonds. This is where we draw our reward: more than the initial promotional energy is regained by the formation of four strong (and °equivalent) bonds.

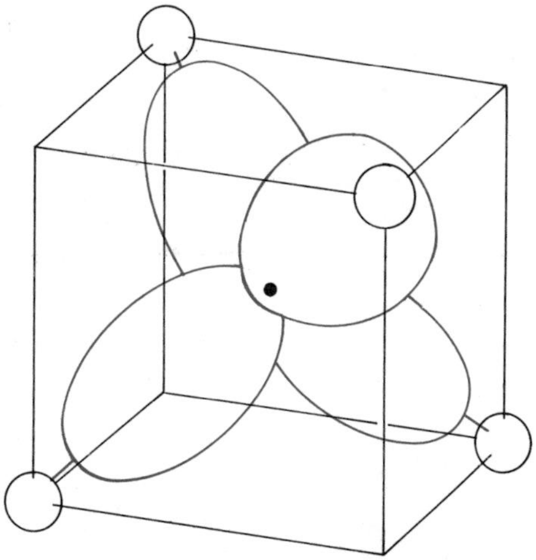

FIG. H8. Tetrahedral sp^3-hybridization (for example, in CH_4).

The case of ammonia (NH_3) helps us to appreciate another source of improvement in energy (Fig. H9). The nitrogen atom has the configuration s^2p^3, and so we can expect to form a pyramidal ammonia molecule by attaching one hydrogen atom to each half-filled nitrogen 2p-orbital. Suppose an s-electron were promoted into the p-shell; would the energy of the molecule be lowered? First we invest promotion energy by agreeing to treat all the s- and p-orbitals on the same footing. We form sp^3-hybrid orbitals with a tetrahedral disposition and strong directional properties. Then we feed in five electrons and add on three hydrogen atoms. The resulting structure consists of three σ-bonds, each formed from a strongly overlapping sp^3-hybrid and a hydrogen 1s-orbital (and each containing two electrons), and a further two electrons to form a °lone pair. With three of the bonds we get a return on the

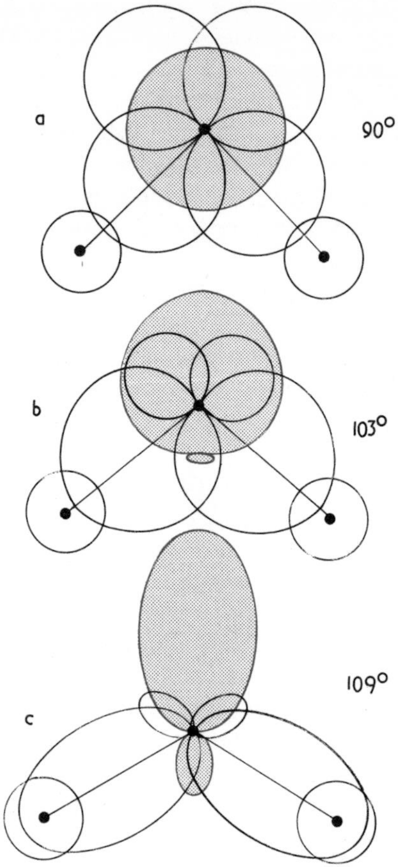

FIG. H9. Ammonia and hybridization; the lone pair is drawn in colour. In (a) there is no promotional energy, but high repulsive interactions and moderate overlap; in (c) low repulsive interactions, strong overlap, but high promotional energy; in (b) is illustrated the compromise. Only two bonds are illustrated.

energy invested because of the excellent overlap; but we also recover some energy from the lone pair, because it is concentrated in a region where its electrostatic repulsive interaction with the three σ-bonds is minimal; furthermore, the larger bond angles yield a reduced H-H repulsion. The actual structure of ammonia is a compromise between the amount of energy required to promote an s-electron into a p-orbital, and the energy that can be obtained by improving overlap and diminishing nonbonding interactions. In the event it turns out that the molecule is some way between the two extreme structures. (This can be determined by measuring the bond angles: in the pure p-orbital case the H—N—H angle is 90°, and in the pure sp^3-orbital case it is 109° 28′; the experimental value is 103°.)

Carbon is well suited for hybridization because its promotional energy is quite small (the promoted s-electron can enter an empty p-orbital); therefore it shows a range of hybrids, depending on the demands made under the reaction conditions. In CH_4 and its homologues the hybridization is almost pure sp^3; in alkenes and in aromatic molecules there is a planar, triangular array of sp^2-hybrids and the remaining 2p-orbital of this promoted state forms the π-bond. In acetylenic compounds (alkynes) the σ-bond is sp-hybridized, the remaining two 2p-orbitals forming the π-bonds.

A list of the symmetries of hybrid orbitals is given in Table 13. A discussion of the formation of hybrid orbitals will be found under °valence state.

Questions. 1. What is meant by the term 'hybridization'? Sketch some hybrid orbitals (especially sp, sp^2, sp^3, sd, sd^2). Why can hybridization lower the energy of a molecule? Describe the formation of CH_4, NH_3, and H_2O, and explore the contributions to the energy which are modified by hybridization of the central atom. Why is hybridization of special importance in carbon?
2. The four sp^3-hybrid orbitals may be expressed as $s + p_x + p_y + p_z$; $s + p_x - p_y - p_z$; $s - p_x - p_y + p_z$; $s - p_x + p_y - p_z$. Show that these are directed towards the apices of a regular tetrahedron, and that they are mutually °orthogonal. Express a hybrid orbital in the form $\alpha s + \beta(\ell p_x + m p_y + n p_z)$, where ℓ, m, n are the direction cosines of the bond that we hope to form, and $\alpha^2 + \beta^2 = 1$. Take another equivalent orbital pointing along the direction ℓ', m', n' and otherwise of the same composition. From the condition that the functions are °orthogonal and °normalized deduce that α and β are related to the angle θ between the bonds by $\alpha^2/\beta^2 = -\cos\theta$, and $1/\beta^2 = 2\sin^2\frac{1}{2}\theta$. Discuss the form of the hybrids when θ is 180°, 90°, and the angle of a tetrahedron. Plot s-character as a function of θ. Show that the effect of hybridization is important only when the orbitals involved are of approximately the same size. Proceed by writing α and β in the preceeding expression as $\sin\xi$ and $\cos\xi$ respectively (so that $\alpha^2 + \beta^2 = 1$ is satisfied automatically), and write $\ell p_x + m p_y + n p_z$ as the orbital p. Find an expression for the overlap with a neighbouring orbital φ in terms of the overlap integrals $S_s = \langle s|\varphi\rangle$ and $S_p = \langle p|\varphi\rangle$, and find the expression for the maximum value of S as a function of ξ. The answer is $S_{max} = (S_s^2 + S_p^2)^{1/2}$. This shows that S differs appreciably from S_s or S_p only if $S_s \sim S_p$; in the event of these overlaps being equal $S_{max} = 2^{1/2}S_s$.

Further information. See *MQM* Chapter 9, and especially Appendix 9.2 where a fuller discussion of hybridization, equivalent orbitals, and localized orbitals is given, together with the solution to Question 2. The importance of hybridization in molecular structure is described by Coulson in *The shape and structure of molecules* (OCS 9) and in Chapter 8 of Coulson (1961). See also Murrell, Kettle, and Tedder (1965), Pilar (1968), Kauzmann (1957), and McGlynn, Vanquickenborne, Kinoshita, and Carroll (1972). The last book describes the formation of hybrids in some detail and evaluates a number of useful overlap integrals. The group-theoretical formation of hybrid orbitals is described in *MQM* Chapter 9.

hydrogen atom. The hydrogen atom, consisting of an electron surrounding a proton, was one of the fences that classical mechanics failed to take, and one of the remarkable successes of quantum mechanics and its later developments.

The spectral observations on the hydrogen atom showed that it emitted and absorbed light at a series of well-defined frequencies (Fig. H10). In 1885 Balmer spotted a relation satisfied by the frequencies that lie in the visible region of the spectrum. This *Balmer series* (Fig. H10) fitted the formula

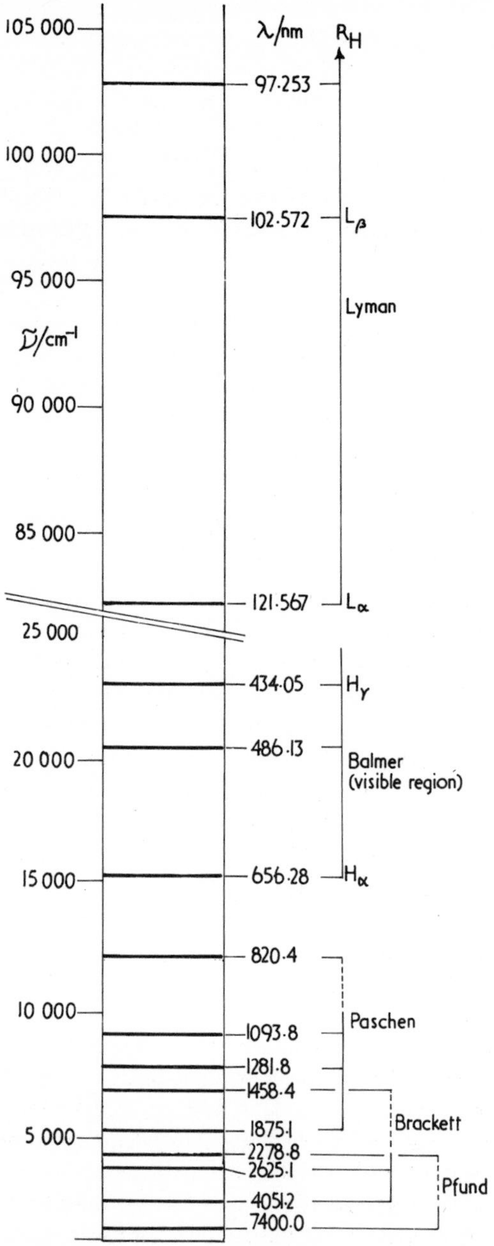

FIG. H10. The spectrum of atomic hydrogen.

$\tilde{\nu} = R(1/2^2 - 1/n_1^2)$, with n_1 an integer greater than 2. It is tempting to speculate on the existence of other series of lines in which 2^2 is replaced by n_2^2, n_2 another integer, and in due course *Lyman* discovered his series (in 1914 and the ultraviolet) corresponding to $n_2 = 1$, *Paschen* his ($n_2 = 3$; in 1908 and the infrared), *Brackett* his ($n_2 = 4$, in 1922 and the infrared), and *Pfund* his ($n_2 = 5$, in 1924 and the far infrared). Those, for the moment, are the facts.

∘Bohr constructed a theory of the hydrogen-atom structure which drew on Rutherford's nuclear model and the quantum hypothesis; but the model had defects, and it was replaced by a deduction of the structure from the ∘Schrödinger equation by Schrödinger himself in 1926. A principal feature of this theory is that the energy of the atom is ∘quantized and limited to values given by $-R_H/n^2$, where n is an integer greater than zero (the principal ∘quantum number) and R_H the ∘Rydberg constant, which is a collection of fundamental constants having the value 109 677 cm^{-1}. A transition from the level n_1 to the level n_2 involves an energy change in splendid accord with observation (see the ∘Grotrian diagram, Fig. G3 on p. 86).

The features of the structure are as follows:

1. The electron is distributed around the nucleus in ∘orbitals. Each atomic orbital can be distinguished by a set of three ∘quantum numbers. These are the *principal quantum number n*, the ∘*angular-momentum quantum number* (occasionally called the *azimuthal quantum number*) ℓ, and the *magnetic quantum number* m_ℓ. The principal quantum number may take any integral value greater than zero, the azimuthal quantum number may take any integral value from zero to $n - 1$, and the magnetic quantum number can take any integral value between ℓ and $-\ell$. The *energy* of the state is determined solely by the value of the principal quantum number and is given by $-R_H/n^2$. (More concerning the ∘Rydberg constant will be found under that heading.) The angular-momentum quantum number determines the magnitude of the ∘orbital angular momentum of the electron about the nucleus through the formula $[\ell(\ell + 1)]^{1/2}\hbar$. The magnetic quantum number determines the orientation of this angular momentum in space, and, in accord with the general properties of ∘angular momentum, the component of angular momentum of the electron about an arbitrarily selected axis is equal to $m_\ell\hbar$.

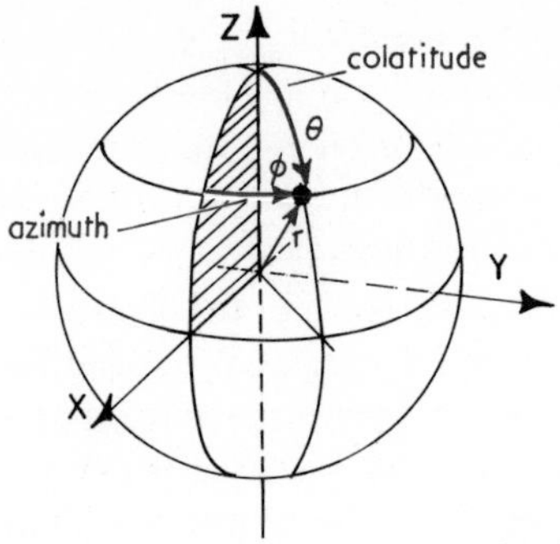

FIG. H11. The spherical coordinates used to discuss the position of the electron in hydrogen.

2. The *orbital* corresponding to the state with quantum numbers n, ℓ, and m_ℓ is in general a function that depends on the distance r of the electron from the nucleus, the colatitude (the angle away from the atom's north pole), and the azimuth (the electron's longitude) (Fig. H11), and may therefore be written $\psi_{n\ell m_\ell}(r, \theta, \phi)$. This orbital function may be expressed as a product of a function dependent solely on the radius and of one dependent solely on the angles: $\psi(r, \theta, \phi) = R_{n\ell}(r)Y_{\ell m_\ell}(\theta, \phi)$. The angular functions $Y_{\ell m_\ell}(\theta,\phi)$ are the °spherical harmonics.

2(a) When $\ell = 0$ the orbital is isotropic because $Y_{00}(\theta, \phi)$ is a constant $(1/2\pi^{1/2})$ and independent of the angles. The orbital in this case is known as an *s-orbital*, and an electron that occupies it is distributed symmetrically around the nucleus (Fig. H12). Since $\ell = 0$ the angular momentum of an electron in this orbital is zero; and in this connexion it is also important to note that there no angular °nodes in the orbital (the number of such nodes determines the °angular momentum).

2(b) When $\ell = 1$ the orbital is a *p-orbital*, and its angular dependence is given by the function $Y_{1m_\ell}(\theta, \phi)$. This is not a constant, but has its maximum amplitude along particular axes in space. When $m_\ell = 0$ the function is $Y_{10}(\theta, \phi)$, which might look fearsome, but in fact is simply the function $\cos\theta$; this has its extrema along the z-axis, where $\theta = 0$ or $180°$, and so an electron that occupies this orbital is most likely to be found in regions concentrated along the z-axis (Fig. H 12):

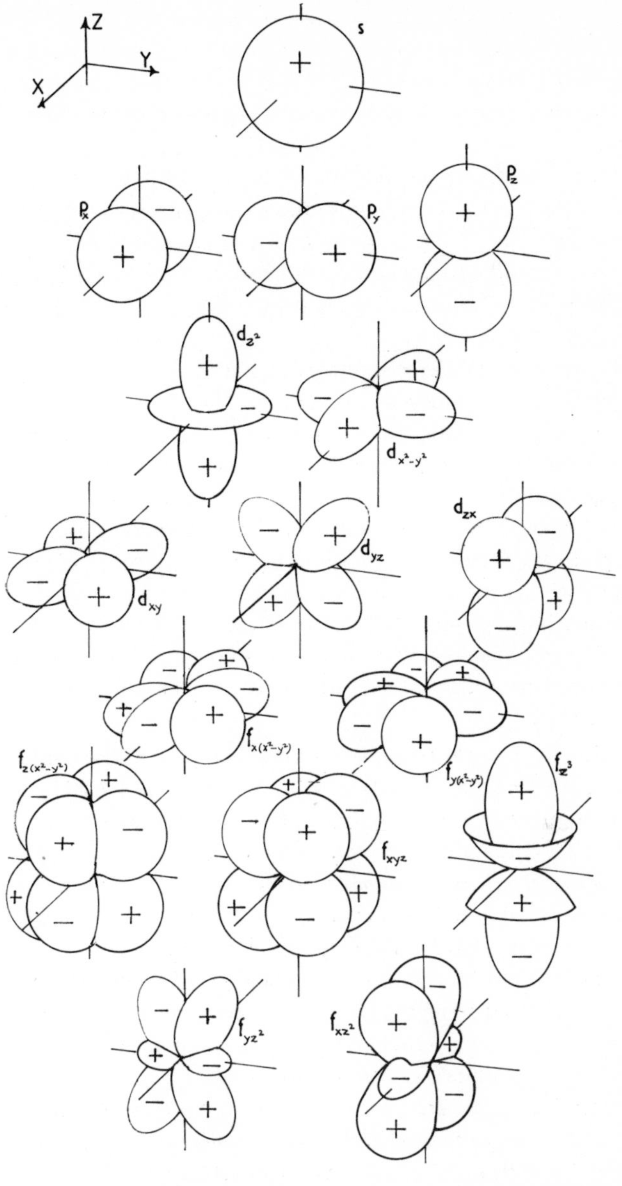

FIG. H12. Representation (by approximate boundary surfaces) of s-, p-, d-, and f-orbitals.

for this reason it is referred to as a p_z-*orbital*. The other possible values that m_ℓ may have (when $\ell = 1$) are ± 1, and in both these the dependence on θ is as $\sin\theta$: this implies that both are concentrated predominantly in the xy-plane and have zero amplitude anywhere on the z-axis. Both $Y_{1,1}$ and $Y_{1,-1}$ are complex functions, (see Table 23 on p. 282), but the sums and differences are real, and so these combinations are easier to depict. $Y_{1,1} + Y_{1,-1}$ is the simple function $\sin\theta\cos\phi$, and so it is a standing wave concentrated along the x-axis, because there both $\sin\theta$ and $\cos\phi$ are maximal: this is a p_x-*orbital*. The other combination $Y_{1,1} - Y_{1,-1}$ is the function $\sin\theta\sin\phi$, which is a standing wave concentrated along the y-axis, and therefore is referred to as a p_y-*orbital*. These have the same shape as p_z, but differ in orientation (Fig. H12). With each p-orbital there is associated an angular momentum of magnitude $[1(1+1)]^{1/2}\hbar$, or $(\sqrt{2})\hbar$, and it should be clear how the different values of the quantum number m_ℓ distinguish the different orientations of the distributions of the electron, and therefore the different orientations of the °orbital angular momentum of the electron occupying that orbital (for example, when $m_\ell = \pm 1$ the electron is largely in the xy-plane and so most of its angular momentum is about the z-axis).

2(c) Next up the scale of ℓ values lie the *d-orbitals* with $\ell = 2$. Of these there are five ($m_\ell = 2, 1, 0, -1, -2$), and although the five functions $Y_{2m_\ell}(\theta, \phi)$ are complex it is possible to select five real combinations (although it is not possible to choose five similar shapes). The d_{z^2}-orbital is concentrated in the z-direction, and the notation z^2 may be construed as implying a stronger concentration along z than that of the p-orbital denoted p_z. The d_{xz}-orbital has its major concentrations along the bisectors of the x- and z-axes, hence the notation, and so there are four lobes (Fig. H12). The d_{yz}- and the d_{xy}-orbitals are similar in form to d_{xz} but, as the notation suggests, are concentrated along the bisectors of the y- and z-axes and the x- and y-axes, respectively. The fifth d-orbital is $d_{x^2-y^2}$, and this peculiar notation implies that the lobes resemble the lobes of the preceding three orbitals but are directed along the x- and y-axes.

2(d) The seven *f-orbitals*, corresponding to $\ell = 3$, and therefore to a high angular momentum of magnitude $(\sqrt{12})\hbar$, are the spherical harmonics $Y_{3m_\ell}(\theta, \phi)$, and seven possible real combinations are illustrated in Fig. H12. It is very uncommon to encounter orbitals of higher momentum, but their form may be deduced quite simply because the angular dependence of all the °spherical harmonics is known.

3. The *radial dependence* of the orbitals is contained in the function $R_{n\ell}(r)$, and it reveals how closely the electron clusters around the nucleus. It is of major, but not of sole, importance in determining the potential energy of the electron and therefore the energy of the atom. The mathematical form of the functions had been encountered long before the Schrödinger equation was solved, for they are essentially the *associated Laguerre functions*. Do not be put off by the complexity of the name: they are simple polynomials in r (Table 14).

All the radial functions tend rapidly towards zero as the radius becomes large, and this reflects the improbability of discovering the electron at great distances from the nucleus. All except the functions $R_{n,0}(r)$ vanish at the nucleus, and so if the electron occupies an orbital with $\ell \neq 0$ there is zero probability of discovering the electron actually at the nucleus. The $R_{n,0}(r)$ functions are peculiar because all are non-zero at the nucleus, and so all predict a non-vanishing probability of finding the electron there. Since $\ell = 0$ for these functions we conclude that only for s-orbitals is there a non-zero probability of discovering the electron at the nucleus. The physical basis of this difference can be understood by recalling that an electron in an s-orbital has zero orbital angular momentum, and so drifts in toward the nucleus, whereas for all other orbitals ($\ell > 0$) the angular momentum provides a source of centrifugal force that flings the electron away from the nucleus so strongly at short distances that the attractive Coulombic potential is overcome. Between the nucleus and infinity the radial wavefunction oscillates a varying number of times: the number of °nodes in the function $R_{n\ell}$ is $n - \ell - 1$. The radial behaviour of the functions is depicted in Fig. H13, and it is helpful to remember that the 1s-orbital ($n = 1, \ell = 0$), which is the lowest-energy orbital, is simply a decaying exponential function which falls towards zero from a finite and non-zero value at the nucleus.

4. *The complete orbitals* are depicted in a few cases in Fig. H14 and listed in Table 15. The shapes of the orbitals

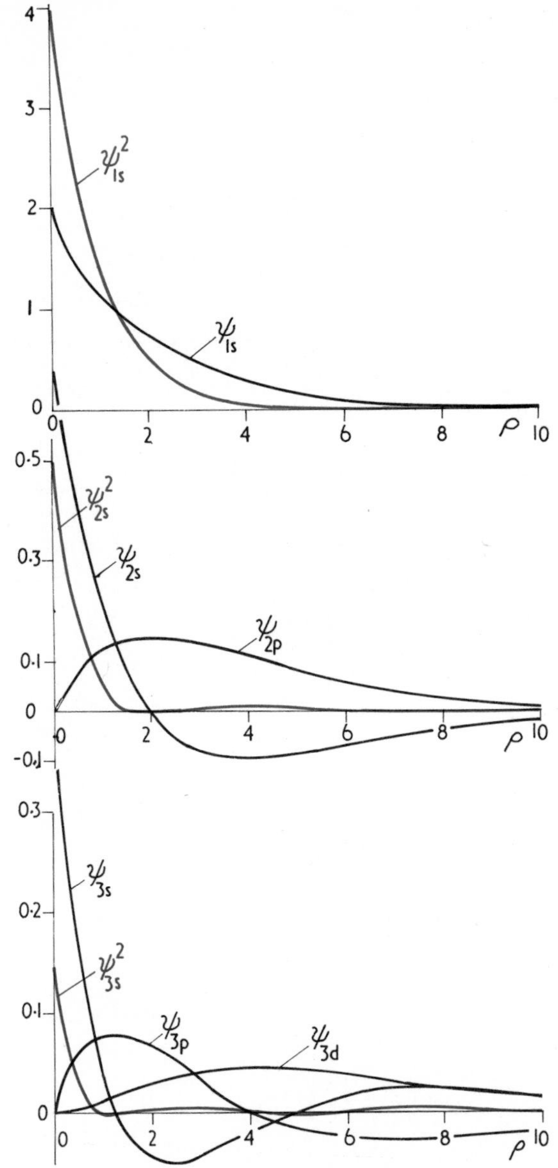

FIG. H13. Radial wavefunctions for some states of hydrogen. Probabilities (not radial-distribution functions) are shown in colour.

themselves and the probability distributions (which, according to the Born interpretation, are the squares of the orbital functions) have more-or-less the same shape, but the directional dependence is more pronounced. It is inconvenient to draw such complicated diagrams to illustrate aspects of atomic and molecular structure and, in accord with the discussion of °orbitals, it is common to draw a boundary surface within which there is a high probability of finding the electron; this was done to obtain Fig. H12. Note that the shape of the surface depends on whether one is attempting to catch a particular proportion of the amplitude or of the probability. Beware. The connexion of the boundary surfaces drawn here should be compared with the depiction of the spherical harmonics by a similar device on p. 221. The details of the shape of the orbitals are generally of small importance, and so boundary surfaces, which are normally drawn with scant regard for precision, like those in Fig. H12, should be interpreted as rough boundaries for regions of concentrated amplitude.

5. The most remarkable feature about the structure of the hydrogen atom is the dependence of the *energy* on only the principal quantum number and its independence of the orbital angular momentum quantum number ℓ. This means that every state of the atom with principal quantum number n has the same energy irrespective of the values of ℓ and m_ℓ. Since for a given n the value of ℓ may range from 0 to $n-1$, and for each ℓ the value of m_ℓ may range from $-\ell$ to ℓ, it follows that a state with quantum number n is n^2-fold °degenerate. This peculiar degeneracy, called by the shallow accidental, is a consequence of the very high symmetry of the central Coulomb potential, and is lost when the purity of the potential is destroyed by the presence of the other electrons in a many-electron atom (see °penetration and shielding).

6. The *energy of the ground state* is worth discussing in greater detail. On classical grounds one expects the electron to spend as much time as possible in the vicinity of the nucleus, because by so doing its potential energy is minimized. The ideal position of the electron is that of contact with the nucleus. But the ground state of the hydrogen atom, an electron in a 1s-orbital, has an electron distributed in regions close to the nucleus, but certainly not wholly confined to it.

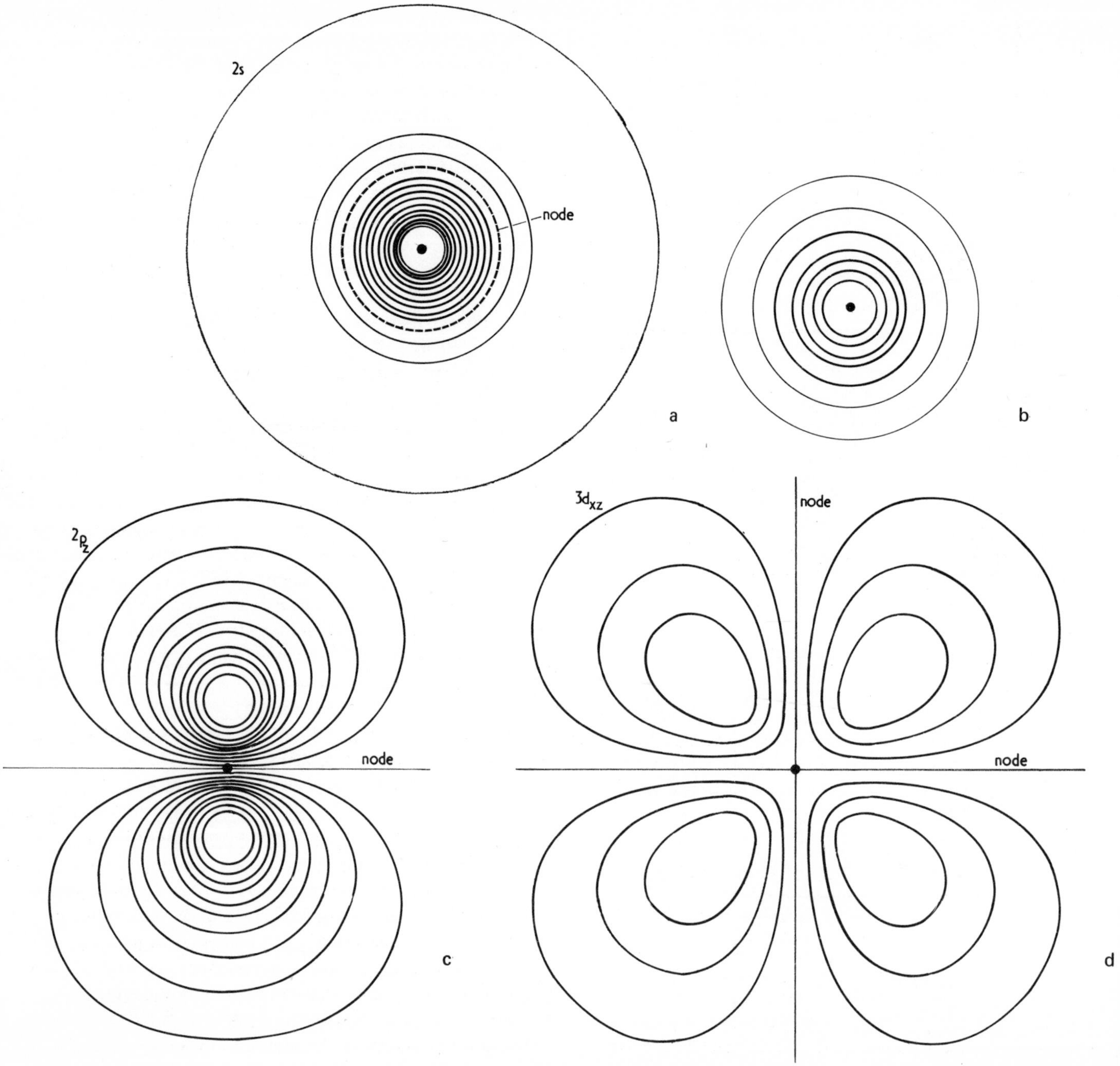
2s
node
a
b
$2p_z$
node
c
$3d_{xz}$
node
node
d

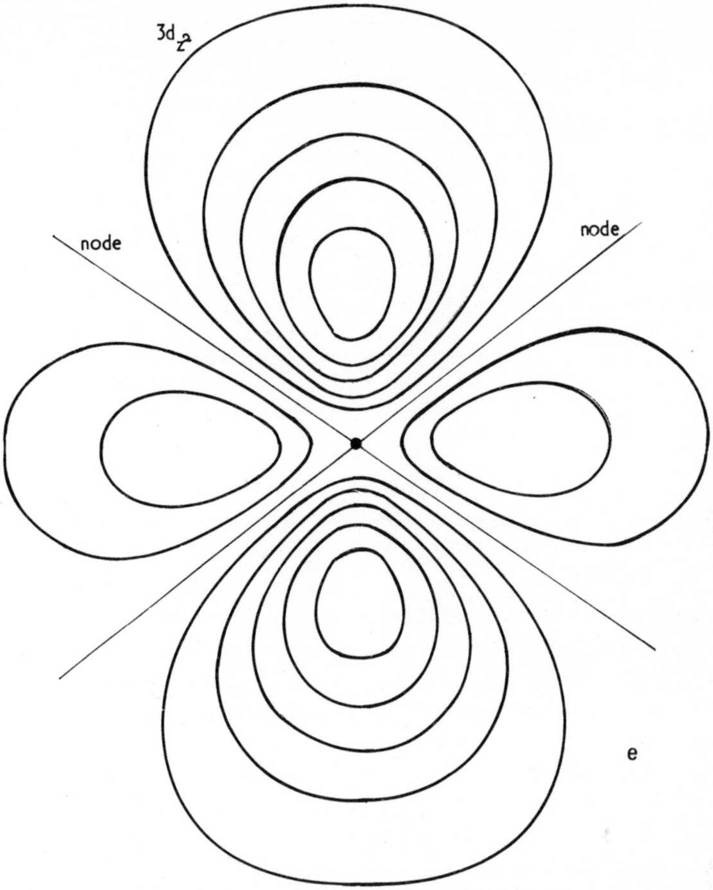

FIG. H14. Amplitude contours of some hydrogen atomic orbitals.

What repels the electron? The classical answer is its angular momentum and the concomitant centrifugal force, and this was the basis of °Bohr's model. But with the s-orbital there is associated no angular momentum, and so this cannot be the explanation. The answer is found in the implication of the shape of the radial wavefunction and the connexion between its curvature and the °kinetic energy.

In Fig. H15 are shown three possible distributions of the electron in a 1s-orbital. In Fig. H15c the electron is strongly confined to the vicinity of the nucleus, but the expense of doing so is discovered in the sharpness of the curvature of the wavefunction: this corresponds to a very high component of kinetic energy associated with the radial direction. Fig. H15a shows a situation in which the kinetic energy has been lowered by permitting the electron a more diffuse domain; but here the expense arises in the high potential energy of a situation in which it is allowed to be at a considerable distance from the nucleus. It is clear that there exists a compromise distribution, as shown in Fig. H15b, in which the electron achieves a balance between a moderate kinetic energy and a moderate potential energy: this is the ground state of the hydrogen atom. This situation may also be interpreted in terms of the °uncertainty principle (see Questions).

The major features of the structure and spectrum of the hydrogen atom are well explained by quantum mechanics; but complications are normally discovered when stones are over-

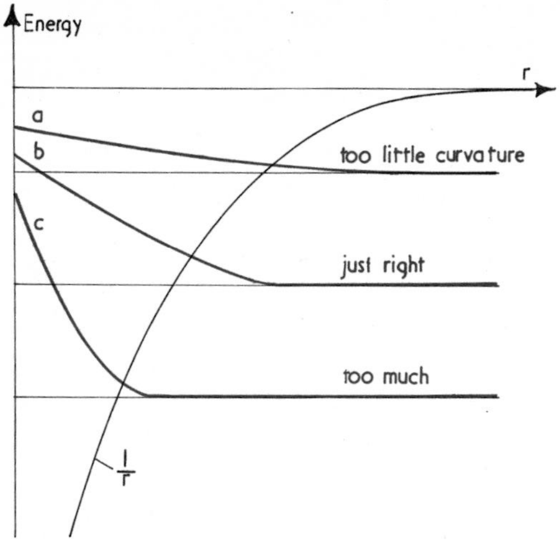

FIG. H15. Curvature, potential energy, and compromise determining the ground state of atomic hydrogen.

turned and the ground inspected in more detail. A closer scrutiny of the spectrum reveals that the lines depicted in Fig. H10 do in fact have a very fine structure, appropriately known as °fine structure. This can be explained, as described in that section, in terms of the coupling of the spin and orbital momenta, and the energy of the interaction, and the splitting, emerged naturally as a consequence of the °Dirac equation. Nevertheless, a slight discrepancy remained even after the application of that beautiful theory, and the *Lamb shift*, a splitting between the levels $^2S_{1/2}$ and $^2P_{1/2}$ (which on the Dirac theory are strictly degenerate), was accounted for only when the hydrogen atom was treated in terms of °quantum electrodynamics. Nevertheless, the closeness of the predictions of quantum theory and the experimental results was a triumph of the theory, and in its turn the explanation of the minute Lamb shift (a discrepancy of only 0·033 cm^{-1}) is a triumph of the more recent modifications of quantum theory.

Questions. 1. What is the evidence concerning the structure of the hydrogen atom? Estimate the highest frequency transition in each of the five spectral series. Street lamps containing sodium often glow red before they turn yellow on account of the hydrogen they contain: what transition is responsible? Calculate the °ionization potential of the hydrogen atom from the frequency of the lines in the Lyman series (Fig. H10). What is the significance of the quantum numbers n, ℓ, and m_ℓ used to denote an orbital in the hydrogen atom? What is the general form of the orbitals? What are the features of the s-orbitals? What distinguishes them from all the other orbitals? How many p-, d-, f-, and g-orbitals are there in the case of $n = 1, 2, 3, 4$? How many nodes does each orbital have? How many radial nodes, angular nodes, and total nodes does an orbital n, ℓ, m_ℓ possess? What is the connexion between the number of nodes and the orbital angular momentum? What is the significance of the number of radial nodes? What is represented by the curves that are often drawn to denote atomic orbitals? How many different orbitals correspond to the energy $-R_H/n^2$? Does the value of m_ℓ affect the energy? What is the physical interpretation of the structure of the hydrogen atom in its ground state? How would the argument be modified to account for the structure of the similar species He^+? Discuss the ground state in terms of the °uncertainty principle: consider the effect on the °momentum, and therefore on the °kinetic energy, as the electron is confined more severely to the vicinity of the nucleus. Discuss the effect on the atomic orbitals of modifying the nuclear charge: what happens to the orbitals as the atomic number of the nucleus increases from 1 to 4? What deficiencies are there in the quantum-mechanical description of the hydrogen atom?
2. From the Tables (p. 275) plot the radial wavefunction for the 1s-, 2s-, 2p-, and 3d-orbitals of the atom. Demonstrate explicitly that these functions are °normalized. Plot the probability distribution as a function of r and note that the most probable position for finding the electron in an s-orbital is at the nucleus. Plot the °radial distribution function for the 1s- and 2s- orbitals. Calculate the most probable radius for finding the electron in the 1s-, 2s-, and 2p-orbitals. Interpret the different values physically. Calculate the most probable radius of the atom as a function of Z. At what radius does the 1s-electron lie, most probably, in the atoms He, C, F, and U?

Further information. See *MQM* Chapter 3. For the explicit solution of the hydrogen atom see Pauling and Wilson (1935) for the series solution, and Kauzmann (1957), Davydov (1965), Messiah (1961), and Schiff (1968). For an account by the much more elegant method of factorization of the Schrödinger equation, see Infeld and Hull (1951), Green (1965), and Englefield (1972). For a discussion of why the degeneracies are not accidental, see *MQM* Chapter 3, Englefield (1972), Bander and Itzykson (1966), McIntosh (1959, 1971), and Fock (1935). For further depictions of the orbitals, and their relation to the classical orbits, see White (1935). See also Herzberg (1944). For a discussion of the spectrum of atomic hydrogen, see *MQM* Chapter 3, King (1964), Kuhn (1962), Herzberg (1944), and Series (1957). Through its bibliography the article by McIntosh (1971) will set you on a path through abundant fascination: through accidental °degeneracy, projections of hydrogen atoms on to hyperspheres and hyperhyperbolas, and the four- and two-dimensional atom. Theoretical and experimental data for the hydrogen atom are collected in Table 16.

hyperconjugation. The °overlap of σ-orbitals and π-orbitals such as the overlap of the methyl C—H σ-bonds with the aromatic π-orbitals in toluene, is called hyperconjugation, or the *Baker-Nathan effect*. It constitutes a mechanism whereby the methyl group can behave as an electron donor, and its consequences include increased electron density at *ortho* and *para* sites, and concomitant effects on aromatic reactivity.

The quantum-mechanical description considers the three σ-bonds of the methyl group, or, what is equivalent for the present purpose, the three hydrogen 1s-orbitals, as a unit from which three *group orbitals* may be constructed (Fig. H16). If the in-phase combination of the three orbitals is taken, an orbital embracing all three may be formed; this orbital has cylindrical symmetry about the C—C bond direction, and so has no net °overlap with the π-system. Two other combinations of the three atomic orbitals may be made, and both have a single °node. One has its node perpendicular to the ring, but the other's lies in the plane of the ring, and therefore has the same symmetry with respect to the C—C bond as the π-orbital on the ring carbon atom. It can therefore overlap it, form a very weak bond, and provide a means of mixing the C—H bond electrons with the π-electrons.

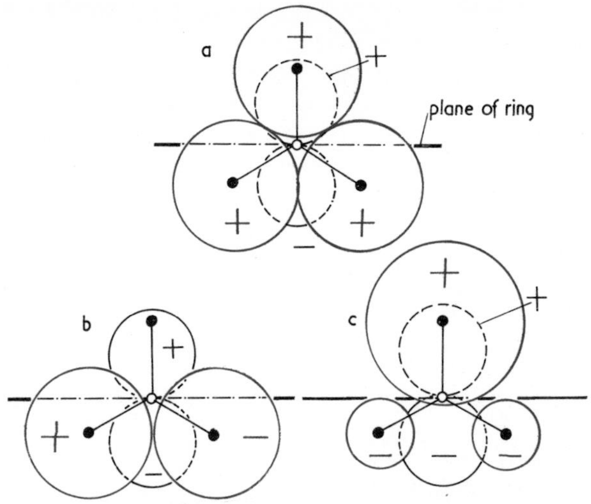

FIG. H16. Group orbitals on CH_3. Only (c) has non-zero net overlap with the π-orbital on the neighbouring aromatic ring.

Further information. See §2.3 of Coulson (1961) and §5.7 of Streitweiser (1961) for many references. See also Murrell, Kettle, and Tedder (1965) and Salem (1966). A discussion of the evidence and consequences for hyperconjugation are described by Baker (1952) and in a conference proceedings on the subject, Baker (1958). Group orbitals are discussed by McGlynn, Vanquickenborne, Kinoshita, and Carroll (1972), especially §2.8. Good evidence for hyperconjugation comes from °electron spin resonance: see Symons (1963), Ayscough (1967), and Bolton, Carrington, and McLachlan (1962).

hyperfine interactions. A hyperfine interaction is an interaction between an electron and a nucleus other than their point-charge Coulombic interaction. One may distinguish between electric and magnetic hyperfine interactions: the former arises because the nucleus may have an electric °quadrupole moment, and the latter because it may have a °magnetic dipole moment. We consider them separately.

Magnetic hyperfine interactions. A nucleus with non-zero °spin possesses a magnetic dipole moment; this dipole gives rise to a magnetic field in its vicinity, and with this field the magnetic moments of the electrons of the molecule may interact. Consider the important case where the molecule contains a single unpaired electron. This electron possesses a °magnetic moment by virtue of its spin, and this moment interacts with the dipolar field of the nucleus by a conventional *dipole-dipole* interaction. The interaction energy depends on the relative orientations of the spin magnetic moments (just as in the case of two small bar magnets) and also on the relative disposition of the two spins.

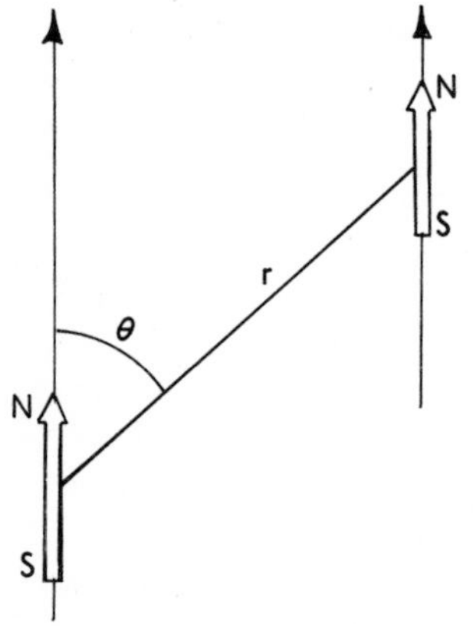

FIG. H17. Dipole-dipole interaction of parallel moments.

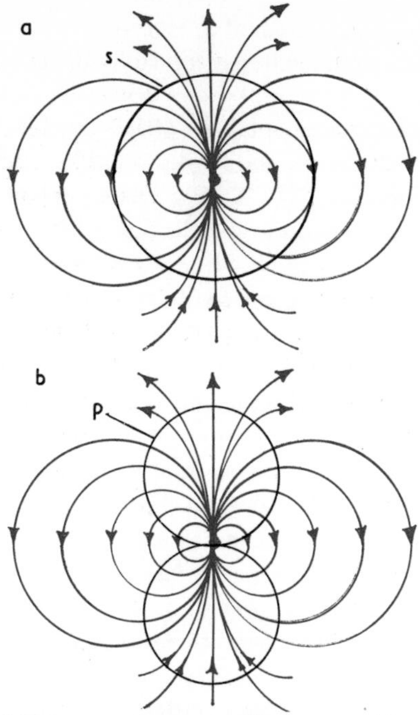

FIG. H18. Field from a nuclear magnetic moment: (a) an s-electron samples positively and negatively directed field equally; (b) a p-electron samples the positive field more than the negative (in this orientation).

Suppose that there is present an externally applied magnetic field (as in the °electron spin resonance experiment) which is strong enough to hold parallel the two magnetic moments of interest. The magnetic interaction energy now has the classical form for the interaction of two parallel dipoles, and this depends on r as r^{-3} and on the angle θ as $1-3\cos^2\theta$ (Fig. H17 and Box 5 on p. 50). If the unpaired electron occupies an s-orbital on the magnetic nucleus it is spread isotropically about it (Fig. H18 a): the net field it experiences is zero, and so there is no dipole-dipole interaction in this case. If the electron occupies a p-orbital on the magnetic nucleus its distribution would not be isotropic, and in fact it would sample some regions of the nuclear dipole field more strongly than others (Fig. H18 b). In such a case the energy of interaction does not vanish.

For a given electron spin orientation (expressed by the value of the °quantum number m_s) the energy of interaction depends on the nuclear spin orientation m_I. Since a nucleus of spin I may have $2I+1$ orientations the electron may experience one of $2I+1$ different values of the local magnetic field. In an °electron spin resonance experiment this leads to a splitting of the spectrum into $2I+1$ lines with a separation determined by the strength of interaction between the two magnetic dipoles. If the molecule (radical) is rotated relative to the applied magnetic field, and the moments retain their original projections m_s and m_I, the electron samples different regions of the nuclear hyperfine field because the p-orbital distribution is carried around by the rotating nuclear framework. It follows that the dipole-dipole hyperfine interaction is anisotropic (depends on orientation of the molecule). If the rotation is very fast, as it is for a molecule in a liquid, the rotation causes the electron spin to sample all the different nuclear hyperfine fields: this spherical average is zero and so the hyperfine structure disappears from the spectrum.

Hyperfine fields at the position of an electron may amount to tens of gauss. Typical values are given in Table 9. These values are for a p-electron confined completely to the atom containing the magnetic nucleus; therefore if a smaller value is measured in an experiment the ratio gives the contribution of that orbital to a molecular orbital extending over the molecule.

Although the above analysis predicts that the magnetic hyperfine structure of electron spin resonance spectra should disappear in fluid solution, experimental observation shows that this is far from the truth, for there usually remains a splitting of lines which is in many cases considerably larger than the anisotropic hyperfine structure just described (see, for instance, Fig. E4 on p. 63). The interaction responsible for this is the °*Fermi contact interaction.* It was an approximation in the preceeding discussion that the nucleus gave a truly dipolar field. That would be sufficiently accurate if the nucleus were vanishingly small or if an electron could never approach it sufficiently closely to realize that it was not an infinitesimal point. The nucleus does have an extension (its diameter is of the order of 10^{-14}m) and if the electron is in an s-orbital it may approach the nucleus very closely. When it gets there it discovers that the field is not a pure dipolar field (see Fig. F1 on p. 72). Let us take the view that the electron actually penetrates the nucleus, and let us replace the nuclear magnetic moment by an equivalent current loop with the same radius as the nucleus. Outside the loop the field does average to zero when the electron spin samples it spherically; but inside the field is all in the same direction, no cancellation occurs, and the spin magnetic moment interacts with the non-vanishing average of the field. This interaction is isotropic because it is independent of the orientation of the remainder of the nuclear framework. It is unique to s-electrons because all others have a °node running through the nucleus and so cannot penetrate it.

The Fermi contact interaction may be very large: some typical magnetic fields experienced by the electron by this mechanism are also listed in Table 9. Since it is characteristic of s-orbital character the magnitude of the observed isotropic splitting may be used to determine the amount of s-electron character in a molecular orbital.

Now let us turn off the external magnetic field, and let all the competition for magnetic coupling be between interactions within the molecule. The nuclear magnetic moment may couple to the magnetic fields from various sources within the molecule, and the energy of this interaction will appear in the spectrum (particularly the rotational spectrum) as a splitting of lines; molecules with different nuclear spin states will give rise to slightly shifted spectra, and therefore the observed spectrum will be the collection of lines from all the different molecules in the sample. The other sources of magnetic moment in the molecule include the electron spin (which now couples differently because there is no applied field holding it parallel to some laboratory axis), the electron orbital magnetic moment, and the °molecular magnetic moment.

Electric hyperfine interactions. It is not possible for a nucleus to have an electric dipole moment (on grounds of symmetry), but it may have an electric °quadrupole moment if its spin quantum number I is 1 or larger. The presence of an electric quadrupole moment implies an asymmetry in the distribution of charge in the molecule, and there are two possibilities. These are illustrated in Fig. H19. In one, the *prolate* case, there is an excess of positive charge in the polar regions of the nucleus (with respect to the axis of spin), and a compensating slight relatively negative band in the equatorial zone. In the *oblate* case the distributions are reversed. An electric °quadrupole moment interacts not with an electric field itself but with the field gradient. If, therefore, there is an electric field gradient at the quadrupolar nucleus, the energy of the molecule will depend on the orientation of the nucleus in the molecular framework, and so we arrive at another hyperfine interaction.

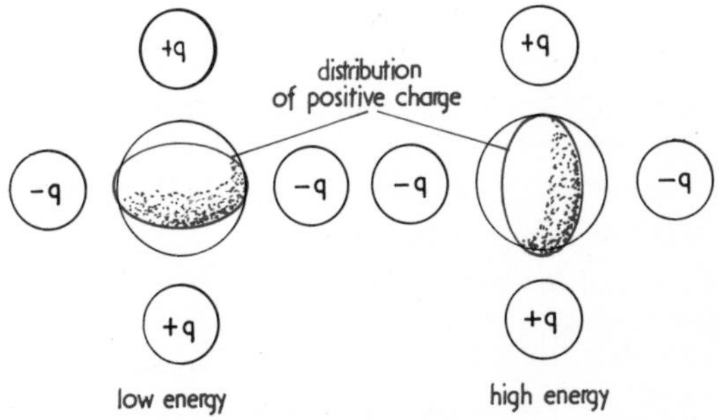

FIG. H19. A nuclear electric quadrupole in a field gradient.

Is there a field gradient at a nucleus in a molecule? If the surrounding electrons are in an s-orbital, or constitute a closed shell, there is no field gradient. If however the electrons do not form a closed shell and are not s-electrons there may be a very strong field gradient (see Fig. H19 and Fig. Q2 on p. 187). Therefore the magnitude of the electric quadrupole interaction in a spectrum gives information about the state of °hybridization of the orbitals occupied by the electrons surrounding it (that is, the amount of p-orbital character in the surrounding electrons). There are, of course, complications. One especially important nuisance is that the valence electrons may distort the underlying closed shells. This distortion gives rise to a field gradient at the nucleus and therefore increases or decreases the strength of the quadrupole coupling: these are the *Sternheimer anti-shielding* and *shielding effects.* The distribution of charges in the vicinity of the nucleus may also be estimated by pretending that the molecule consists of an array of point charges (see °dipole moment): ionicity has been estimated in this fashion.

Questions. What is meant by the term 'hyperfine interaction'? What two classes of interaction are there? What is the nature of the magnetic coupling between an electron spin and a nuclear spin? Why does this interaction disappear (when there is an external field present) when the electron is distributed in an s-orbital, or when it is in a p-orbital but the molecule is rotating rapidly in a liquid? What information can be obtained from the magnitude of the anisotropic hyperfine interaction? Why does there remain an interaction in fluid solution? Of what is the Fermi contact interaction diagnostic? In the radical NO_2 the hyperfine interaction to the nitrogen nucleus is 55 G for the isotropic component and 13 G for the maximum of the anisotropic component: what is the s- and p-character of the nitrogen orbital contributing to the molecular orbital occupied by the unpaired electron? (Use Table 9.) What is the source of the electric hyperfine interaction? What nuclei may possess a quadrupole moment, and what does such possession signify? With what electronic property does the quadrupole interact? What information may be obtained from a study of the interaction? What is the complicating feature?

Further information. See *MQM* Chapter 11 for a more detailed account of the magnetic hyperfine interactions. The way that they are employed in °electron spin resonance and °nuclear magnetic resonance (especially for °spin-spin coupling constants) is described by McLauchlan in *Magnetic resonance* (OCS 1). See also Lynden-Bell and Harris (1969), Carrington and McLachlan (1967), Atkins and Symons (1967), Ayscough (1967), Bolton and Wertz (1972), Slichter (1963), and Abragam and Bleaney (1970). The role of hyperfine interactions in spectra, and the structural information they may be used to obtain, are described in Sugden and Kenney (1965), Herzberg (1950), and Townes and Schawlow (1955). See Freeman and Frankel (1967) for a basic discussion. Magnetic and electric properties of nuclei are listed in Table 17.

I

ionization potential. The ionization potential (IP) is the energy required to remove to infinity an electron from the orbital it occupies in an atom or molecule. The more tightly bound the electron the greater its ionization potential. The energy is normally expressed in electronvolts (1 eV is equivalent to 96·49 kJ mol^{-1}), and its value depends on the orbital involved and the state of ionization of the atom. The *first IP* is the energy required to remove the least tightly bound electron from the neutral atom, the *second IP* is the energy required to remove the least tightly bound electron from the singly charged ion, and so on. IPs are a good guide to the chemical properties of elements, and the periodic table can be discussed in their light. A useful exercise of this nature is the discussion of the IP of the atoms from He to Ne along the first row of the periodic table (see Table 18). These can be rationalized in terms of °penetration and shielding effects.

Questions. What is an ionization potential? The ionization potential of atomic sodium is 5·14 eV; how much heat is evolved when 1 mol of sodium atoms is formed from a gas of Na^+ ions and electrons? Could an atom have a negative ionization potential? Account for the IPs of the elements of the first row in terms of penetration and shielding effects.

Further information. Lists of ionization potentials will be found in Kaye and Laby (1956) and §7b of Gray (1972). In Puddephatt's *The periodic table of the elements* (OCS 3) will be found a discussion of their dependence on penetration and shielding effects, and the role they play in determining chemical properties. This aspect is developed in detail by Phillips and Williams (1965). The ionization potential is used to calculate °electronegativities, and is a basis of the experimental technique of *photoelectron spectroscopy* (see °photoelectric effect).

intermolecular forces: a synopsis. The principal classification of the forces between molecules is according to their range. The *short-range forces* are repulsive, and reflect the increase in energy that occurs when two electron clouds are forced into contact and penetration. As two closed-shell species approach each other some of the electrons may be able to adjust their distribution so that they occupy energetically favourable regions, but the °Pauli principle does not permit all the electrons to settle into these regions, and the remainder are forced to occupy regions that tend to raise the energy of the approaching pair (they enter the °antibonding orbitals in the °molecular-orbital theory). This disruptive effect overcomes the attractive effect of the more favourably sited electrons, and so the energy of the pair of species rises sharply as the distance diminishes: this may be interpreted as a force that drives the molecules apart, and so we see the repulsive force to be rooted in the operation of the Pauli principle.

Long-range attractive forces between molecules must exist, for otherwise no condensed phases would exist. The simplest attractive interactions are between charged species (ion-ion interactions, the ionic °bond), where the Coulomb force draws the components together until repulsive forces supervene. Most molecules are uncharged, but attractive forces still operate. In polar molecules these can be identified with the attractive interaction between the permanent electric moments of the molecules (the °*dipole-dipole interaction,* or the *dipole—*

BOX 10: Intermolecular potentials

Rigid spheres:

$$V(R) = \begin{cases} \infty & R < \sigma \\ 0 & R > \sigma. \end{cases}$$

Point centres:

$$V(R) = DR^{-\delta}$$

$9 < \delta < 15$ usually. *Maxwellian* molecules have $\delta = 4$.

Square well:

$$V(R) = \begin{cases} \infty & R < \sigma \\ -\epsilon & \sigma < R < r\sigma \\ 0 & R > r\sigma. \end{cases}$$

Sutherland:

$$V(R) = \begin{cases} \infty & R < \sigma \\ -CR^{-\gamma} & R > \sigma. \end{cases}$$

Lennard-Jones:

$$V(R) = DR^{-\delta} - CR^{-\gamma}$$

special case: (6, 12)-potential

$$V(R) = 4\epsilon \left\{ \left(\frac{\sigma}{R}\right)^{12} - \left(\frac{\sigma}{R}\right)^{6} \right\}.$$

Buckingham:

$$V(R) = Be^{-bR} - CR^{-6} - C'R^{-8}.$$

Modified Buckingham (6-exp):

$$V(R) = \begin{cases} [\epsilon/(1-6/\alpha)]\,[(6/\alpha)\exp(\alpha - \alpha R/R_m) - R_m^6/R^6] \\ \infty & R < R_m \end{cases}$$

R_m is the value of R for which the upper expression for $V(R)$ attains a maximum.

Stockmayer:

$$V(\mathbf{R}) = V_{LJ}(R) + \mathscr{E}(\mathbf{R}, \mu_1, \mu_2),$$

where $V_{LJ}(R)$ is the Lennard-Jones potential, and $\mathscr{E}(\mathbf{R}, \mu_1, \mu_2)$ is the dipole-dipole interaction energy given in Box 5.

point-charge interaction if one is charged, or the *dipole–induced-dipole interaction* if one is polar and the other not: in the last case the strength of interaction depends on the °polarizability of the nonpolar molecule). Then there are the forces between nonpolar molecules: the most important of these is the *London* °*dispersion force* which is also termed an *induced-dipole–induced-dipole interaction* because it depends on the fluctuation of the electron density of one molecule leading to an instantaneous dipole moment which may in turn induce an instantaneous dipole moment in the other, these two dipoles then sticking together. This interaction depends on the polarizability of both molecules and its energy depends on their separation as R^{-6}.

The name *van der Waals forces* is a general term applied to these intermolecular interactions. The term *Keesom force* is reserved for the interaction between polar molecules, and *London force* refers specifically to the dispersion force.

The *distance-dependence* of the forces and the angular dependence of those between non-spherical species are normally expressed in terms of an empirical formula which has more-or-less the correct qualitative form and contains only a few adjustable parameters. Some of the more common intermolecular potentials are illustrated in Fig. 11 and Box 10. All make a crude approximation to the repulsive interaction which, in reality, because it depends on details of molecular °wavefunctions and °overlap, has a complicated behaviour. The most cavalier approximation is to replace the repulsive part by an impenetrable hard sphere. The *Lennard-Jones potential* assumes that the potential rises sharply at small separations according to R^{-n}; when, for mathematical convenience, n is chosen to be 12, we have the (6, 12)-Lennard-Jones potential (the R^{-6}-dependence [see Box 10] reflects the presence of the dispersion forces). The *Buckingham exp-6 potential* retains the R^{-6} component but pretends that the repulsive forces vary exponentially. The *Keesom potential* is an expression for the interaction of non-spherical molecules which treats them as cylinders capped by hemispheres. The *Stockmayer potential* adds to the Lennard-Jones potential a term representing the interaction of two dipoles placed at the centres of the molecules.

Intermolecular forces must be taken into account if the properties of real gases and liquids are to be understood, and if

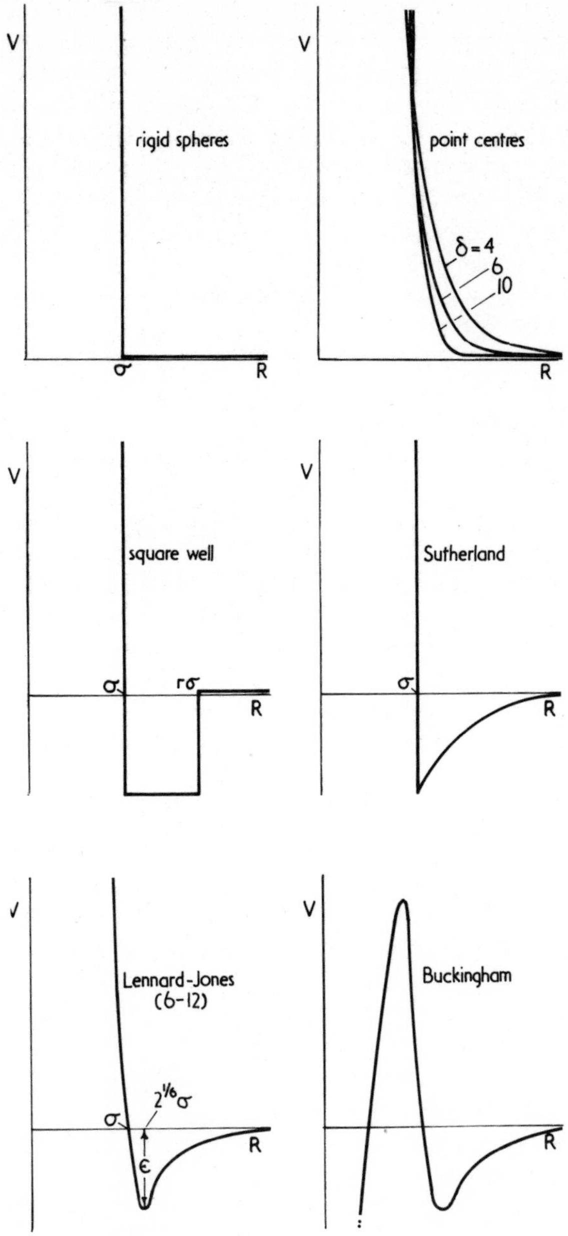

FIG. 11. The shape of some empirical intermolecular potentials.

quantitative calculations are to be made. One important route to thermodynamic quantities is through the virial equation of state, where PV is expressed as an expansion in $1/V$; the coefficents in this expansion, the *virial expansion,* are the *virial coefficients.* Expressions for these may be obtained from the intermolecular potentials and the coefficients used to calculate the properties of the gas. The structure of liquids depends on the form of the intermolecular forces. The forces (and the parameters in the empirical expressions) may be determined by fitting calculated virial coefficients to experimentally determined values, from transport properties, and, best of all, from scattering experiments in *molecular beams,* where individual molecules are used both as targets and projectiles and their deflexion is determined by their interaction.

Further information. An excellent book on the subject, which has a synoptic review in an early chapter and detailed accounts in later chapters, is that by Hirschfelder, Curtiss, and Bird (1954). A helpful account of Debye's contribution has been given by Chu (1967), and details of the quantum-mechanical equations involved, and their derivation, will be found in *MQM* Chapter 11, Kauzmann (1957), and Margenau and Kestner (1969). The determination of intermolecular potentials is described by Hirschfelder, Curtiss, and Bird (1954), Curtiss (1967), and Dymond and Smith (1969). Molecular beams and their application to the determination of intermolecular potentials are described by Levine and Bernstein (1974) and Ramsey (1956), and reviewed in a collection of articles edited by Ross (1966). Experimental and theoretical aspects of intermolecular forces have also been reviewed by Hirschfelder (1967).

inversion doubling. Inversion doubling can be discussed in terms of the specific and important example of the ammonia molecule. This pyramidal molecule can vibrate in a symmetrical bending mode, rather like an umbrella being shaken dry. And, like an umbrella, there is some probability that it can be inverted into another configuration where it continues to vibrate. The original and inverted configurations are physically indistinguishable, and vibrate with the same frequency; this situation can be pictured as in Fig. 12, where the molecule vibrates in one of the two potential wells. But

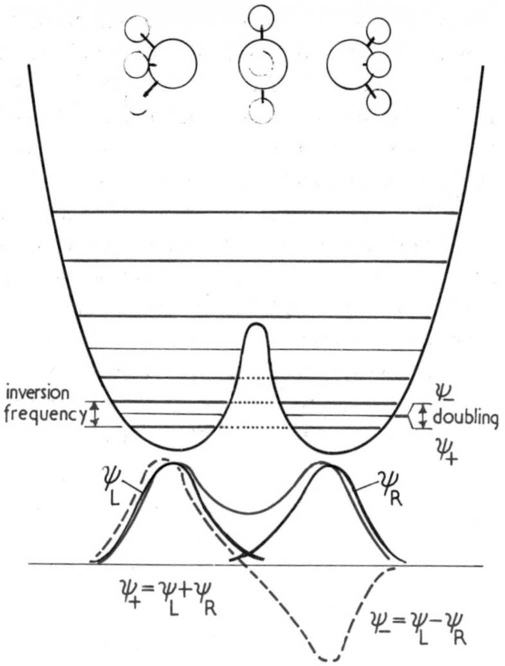

FIG. 12. Inversion doubling in ammonia: black lines are the 'confined' states of the two wells; coloured lines are the true, interacting states.

the fact that the molecule has some chance of inverting, or of °tunnelling from one well into the other, implies that the °vibrational wavefunctions of one well (which represent the displacement of the nuclei) seep through into the other. If the vibrational wavefunctions were wholly confined to one well the molecule would not be able to invert. Since the wavefunctions seep through the potential barrier their amplitudes overlap, and, just as in the case of the formation of a °molecular orbital, the correct description of the vibrational state of the molecule is in terms of a °superposition of the functions. Thus we take either their sum or their difference. The two new functions so formed correspond to different energies, because one is concentrated more within the barrier than the other. It is important not to conclude that the lower state is the one with the node within the barrier, even though this has the lower potential energy. We must also, as always, take into account the °kinetic energy, and discuss the total energy. When a °node is introduced into a function it becomes more curved, and its kinetic energy rises. This is the case for the tunnelling states of ammonia, and an analysis shows that the kinetic energy dominates and that the unbuckled, nodeless, symmetrical function corresponds to the lower total energy. In this connexion see °torsional barrier. It follows that, instead of having pairs of °degenerate vibrational states in the ammonia molecule, the inversion causes the degeneracy to be removed and each pair splits into two: each level is °*doubled.*

The energy separation depends on the difference in amplitude (and therefore probability) that the nuclei will be found within the potential barrier: this depends on the strength of the overlap between the vibrational wavefunctions in the two wells, and this in turn depends both on the height of the potential barrier above the interacting levels (the higher it is the smaller the penetration) and on the mass of the °tunnelling species (the greater the mass the less the tunnelling). In NH_3, the splitting, which is known as the *inversion frequency,* is 23 786 MHz (0·793 cm^{-1}) for the lowest level. On a classical picture of the process this frequency would be identified with the frequency with which the inversion actually occurred. In quantum mechanics that concept is untenable in detail, but a °wave packet localized in one well (and representing one configuration of the molecule) would wriggle through the barrier and emerge on the other side, with more or less the observed 'inversion frequency'.

Questions. 1. Why is inversion doubling so called? What is its source? Why do the positive and negative combinations of the vibrational levels correspond to different energies? Which has the lower energy? What determines the separation? Discuss the dependence of the separation as the barrier height is reduced from infinity to zero. How does inversion doubling affect the spectrum of ammonia? What changes would you expect to observe on deuteration of ammonia? Discuss inversion doubling in the other Group V hydrides.
2. Consider a double square-well potential with a rectangular potential barrier; take the potential V to be infinite for $x < 0$ and $x > L$, to have the value B between $x = \frac{1}{2}L - b$ and $\frac{1}{2}L + b$, and to be zero elsewhere. Set up and discuss the solutions of the °Schrödinger equation for a particle of mass m in this system, and discuss the doubling of the energy levels that is

brought about by lowering the height of the barrier from infinity. Discuss the effect of changing the mass of the particle.

Further information. See *MQM* Chapter 10. For the spectroscopic consequences of inversion doubling see §9.19 of King (1964), §8.2 of Sugden and Kenney (1965), various parts of Herzberg (1966), and Chapter 12 of Townes and Schawlow (1955). The inversion process is the basis of maser action (a microwave °laser process) and so has been studied in considerable detail: for applications of this nature see the references under °laser, Vuylsteke (1960), and Troup (1963).

J

J. The letter *J* is worked hard in quantum theory, but the context normally eliminates confusion. *J* and *j* are °quantum numbers used to denote the *total* °*angular momentum* of a system: the former is used in a many-electron system, or for the overall °rotation of molecules, and the latter is used when only a single particle is involved. As a consequence of this use both *J* and *j* are used to distinguish the °*levels* of °terms. *J* is also used to denote the °*spin-spin coupling constant* in °n.m.r. and the °*Coulomb integral* for the electrostatic interaction of electrons. **J** or **j** is used for the *current*, be it the current of electrons induced by applied fields in metals, atoms, and molecules, or the flow of matter, heat, and entropy.

Jahn-Teller effect. To those for whom the natural tendency of Nature is to states of highest symmetry, the Jahn-Teller theorem is a bitter pill, for its contention is that in a variety of situations a molecule of high symmetry is intrinsically unstable and will attain a lower energy by distorting into a lower symmetry configuration. To be more precise, the theorem states that no non-linear molecule can be stable in a °degenerate electronic state. Therefore, if the molecule is found, by calculation, to be degenerate, that form of the molecule will not be the stable form in Nature, and a less symmetrical and non-degenerate form will be its natural state. The theorem does not apply to linear molecules, and so these may exist in an undistorted degenerate state; but there is an analogous higher-order effect, the °Renner-Teller effect, which takes care of that loophole.

As an example of the Jahn-Teller effect we shall consider the case of a Cu^{2+} ion in an octahedral environment. We proceed to deduce its electronic structure on the basis of °crystal-field theory (which is good enough for our present purpose), and discover that its configuration is t^6e^3. This is a degenerate configuration because the two configurations $d^2_{z^2}d_{x^2-y^2}$ and $d^2_{x^2-y^2}d_{z^2}$ have the same energy. The molecule is non-linear, and so the Jahn-Teller theorem predicts that the molecule must distort and eliminate its degeneracy.

The physical reason for this may be understood by considering the forces operating on the ligands: in the first configuration there is more electron density along the *z*-axis than in the equatorial plane, whereas the opposite is true in the second configuration. In the first case there is a tendency for the ligands along the *z*-axis to move away from the central ion, and for the equatorial ligands to move in; in the second configuration the opposite shifts are to be expected. If the molecule does distort by stretching along the *z*-axis, the electronic configuration $d^2_{z^2}d_{x^2-y^2}$ will have a lower energy than the other electronic configuration *in the same environment* (Fig. J1 a). If the complex flattens along the *z*-axis, for that conformation the second configuration will have the lower energy (Fig. J1 b). Therefore we see that there does indeed exist a distortion of the molecule that removes the degeneracy of the electronic states, and we should expect the molecule to be found in either the elongated or the compressed form. (Which form it attains is very difficult to predict.)

Several electronic configurations are predicted to produce Jahn-Teller distortions in octahedral complexes: we simply have to seek cases in which degenerate configurations can arise.

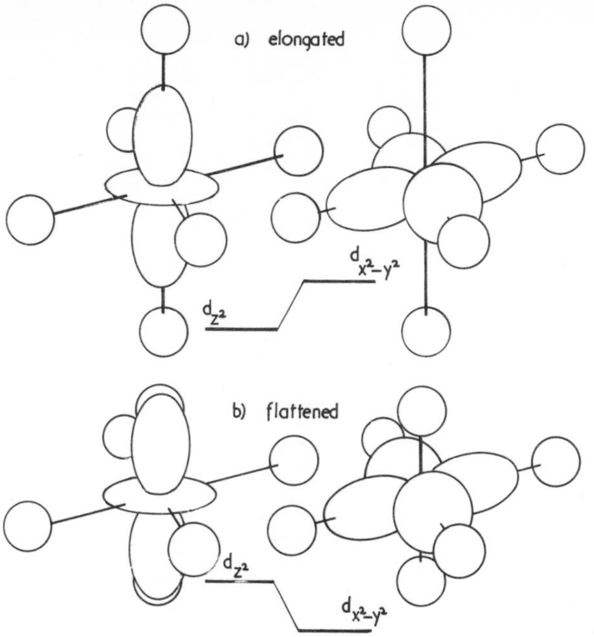

FIG. J1. The effect of (a) elongation and (b) flattening an octahedron on the energy of electrons in d_{z^2} and $d_{x^2-y^2}$.

The high-spin d^4 configurations t^3e^1, the low-spin d^7 configurations t^6e^1, and the d^9 configurations t^6e^3 are all cases in which there is degeneracy because a single electron or a single hole has to occupy the two degenerate e-orbitals (d_{z^2} and $d_{x^2-y^2}$). Examples are Cu^{2+} (d^9) and Cr^{2+} (d^4), whose compounds often have closely related distorted structures, Mn^{3+} (d^4), and the rare low-spin Co^{2+} (d^7), low-spin Ni^{3+} (d^7), and Ag^{2+} (d^9). Jahn-Teller distortions are not expected for d^3, high-spin d^5, low-spin d^6, or d^8.

Jahn-Teller distortions might be predicted also for configurations that give rise to degeneracy in the t-orbitals, such as d^1, d^2, high-spin d^6, and high-spin d^7. In practice the t-orbitals are directed between (rather than along) the metal-ligand axes, and uneven electron occupation therefore fails to produce observable distortions.

The d^8 configuration is rather special in the sense that small distortions are not expected; if a distortion does occur it is large. Because the spins are parallel, one electron must occupy d_{z^2} and the other must occupy $d_{x^2-y^2}$; therefore in a small distortion the energy of one electron increases, the other falls, and so overall there is no change in the energy. If the distortion is great enough, however, the energy difference between the d_{z^2} and $d_{x^2-y^2}$ orbitals can exceed the energy required to cram both electrons into either d_{z^2} or $d_{x^2-y^2}$ (that is, to overcome the first °Hund rule). Strictly speaking, this is not a Jahn-Teller distortion because it does not lower the degeneracy of the system.

Two effects complicate the analysis of the effect. The first is the *dynamic Jahn-Teller effect*, in which the centre of attention is the motion of a molecule in which a degeneracy may arise at certain nuclear conformations. The second is the role of °spin-orbit coupling, which generally reduces the effect's magnitude. The experimental detection of a true Jahn-Teller distortion is very difficult as there are other reasons why a complex may be distorted. In particular it is difficult to distinguish it from a distortion due to the packing requirements on formation of a crystal.

Questions. What is the Jahn-Teller theorem? What molecules are excluded? When a molecule is predicted by calculation to have a degenerate electronic state, what are the consequences of the theorem? Account for the content of the theorem in terms of the crystal-field model of transition-metal complexes: why may a lower energy be attained when an octahedral complex is distorted? What numbers of electrons must such a complex possess in order for this description to apply? Why is the Jahn-Teller effect much less important in tetrahedral complexes? What situation arises when the configuration of the central ion is d^8? What are the methods for distinguishing the Jahn-Teller effect, and what are the complications? When is the dynamic Jahn-Teller effect important? What is the °ligand-field (MO) explanation of the Jahn-Teller effect?

Further information. See *MQM* Chapter 10. A simple account of the Jahn-Teller effect is given in §4.2 of Orgel (1960) and Coulson (1961). Some of the mathematics is put in a simple way in §8d of Ballhausen (1962), and a full and interesting discussion of the spectroscopic consequences is given in §1.2 of Herzberg (1966). A discussion of both the static and dynamic effects is given in a book devoted to the subject by Englman (1972), and a simple example is worked on p. 45 of Herzberg (1966) and on p. 194 of Ballhausen (1962).

K

kinetic energy. The kinetic energy of a particle is the energy it possesses by virtue of its motion. In quantum mechanics the kinetic energy is related to the curvature of the °wavefunction. As the wavefunction becomes more sharply curved, so the kinetic energy of the state it represents becomes greater. Conversely, a state represented by an almost flat function has virtually no kinetic energy.

In the case of a free particle the wavefunction is of infinite extent and has a wavelength that decreases as the kinetic energy increases. The reason for this can be grasped quite easily from the connexion between curvature and energy: as the curvature of the wavefunction increases it becomes more buckled, and swings more rapidly from positive amplitude to negative; but increasing the rapidity with which the function changes sign is simply another way of saying the wavelength shortens. This connexion of wavelength and kinetic energy, and thence momentum, of free particles is the explanation of the °de Broglie relation.

In cases where the particle is bound to a potential centre the wave may not be sufficiently extensive for a wavelength to be discernible or meaningful, but the relation between curvature and kinetic energy remains. An example of this situation is the °hydrogen atom: the ground state arises from the balance of the kinetic and potential energies; the 1s-orbital is a simple exponentially decaying function which never passes through zero, yet an electron in it possesses kinetic energy by virtue of the non-zero mean curvature of the exponential function.

Questions. 1. What properties of the wavefunction determine the kinetic energy of a system? What is the connexion between the wavelength of a free particle and its kinetic energy? How is the wavelength related to the momentum? Calculate the wavelength of an electron with an energy equivalent to 1 eV, 1 keV, 1 MeV (eV is °electronvolt). Discuss the role that the curvature of the wavefunction plays in determining the structure of the ground state of the °hydrogen atom; what would happen to the energy of the atom if the electron were pinched more closely towards the vicinity of the nucleus in order to lower its potential energy?
2. The kinetic energy of a one-dimensional system is calculated by evaluating the °expectation value of the °operator $-(\hbar^2/2m)(\mathrm{d}^2/\mathrm{d}x^2)$, and the corresponding operator for a three dimensional system is $-(\hbar^2/2m)(\partial^2/\partial x^2+\partial^2/\partial y^2+\partial^2/\partial z^2)$, or $-(\hbar^2/2m)\nabla^2$ in terms of the °laplacian. Evaluate the kinetic energy of a particle with the following wavefunctions: $\exp ikx$, $\sin kx$, $\sin nkx \sin mky$, $\exp(-kx^2)$, $\exp(-nr/a_0)$. Plot the kinetic energy of a particle with the last wavefunction as a function of n, and so see the connexion between the curvature of a hydrogen-like exponential function and the kinetic energy.

Further information. See *MQM* Chapters 3 and 4 for some more specific examples. All standard books on quantum theory bring out the connexion of the curvature and the kinetic energy: therefore see Chapter 5 of Davydov (1965), Landau and Lifshitz (1958*a*), and Messiah (1961). An interesting account that emphasizes the optical-mechanical analogy is given in Chapter 3 of Bohm (1951). Scattering phenomena are excellent examples of the wavelength's connexion with kinetic energy; therefore see books on scattering theory, such as Rodberg and Thaler (1967) and Goldberger and Watson (1964), as well as the appropriate sections in the other books referred to above. Levine (1969) applies scattering theory to the discussion of molecular reactions; and this is presented in a more pictorial form by Levine and Bernstein (1974).

Koopmans' theorem. 'Theorem' is a name too grand for this approximation; Koopmans' rule would be better, for it is transgressed frequently, and is never obeyed to the letter. The rule states that the °ionization potential of an electron is equal to the energy of the orbital from whence it came. This apparently trivial statement is based on the fact that the energy that has to be supplied in order to ionize an atom or molecule must be expended in overcoming the combined effect of nuclear attraction energy and the electron's repulsive interaction with the other electrons present, and these factors determine its energy in its orbital.

The rule is an approximation because it assumes that the remaining electrons will not reorganize themselves in order to take advantage of the absence of the electron which is being removed. Therefore, when one-electron energies are calculated in the Hartree-Fock °self-consistent field manner, the ionization potentials calculated by Koopmans' rule are often in error because it is assumed that the electrons in the ion occupy the same orbitals as they did in the atom. Furthermore, the Hartree-Fock scheme neglects electron °correlation effects, and is non-relativistic: the latter approximation can be seriously in error for electrons that are strongly bound and so subject to strong forces.

Questions. 1. State Koopmans' rule. What is its justification? Why is it only an approximation? Would you expect it to overestimate or underestimate ionization potentials? For which electrons should it be a better approximation? For what species is the rule exact?
2. The one-electron energies of the CO molecule are as follows: 4σ, 21·87 eV; 5σ, 15·09 eV; 1π, 17·40 eV. Estimate the ionization potential for the molecule when an electron is removed from these orbitals (experimental values are 19·72 eV, 14·01 eV, 16·91 eV). Discuss the structure of the molecule in the light of these values (which are taken from p. 36 of Richards and Horsley, loc. cit. infra).

Further information. Koopmans' rule is now of interest because of the development of photoelectron spectroscopy: for an account of this see Turner, Baker, Baker, and Brundle (1970). Molecular energies are listed in the bibliography compiled by Richards and Horsley (1970).

L

laplacian. Pierre Simon de Laplace (1749–1827) was a notable French mathematician, and to his work his formidable *Mécanique céleste* is a profound and worthy memorial. Among its many notable pages of mathematics is the Laplace equation, $(\partial^2 f/\partial x^2) + (\partial^2 f/\partial y^2) + (\partial^2 f/\partial z^2) = 0$, where f is some function. Although the equation was set up in order to account for the properties of gravitational fields it has turned out to be applicable to a wide variety of phenomena. That it governs properties like the flow of incompressible fluids, gravitational and electromagnetic fields, and heat flow is probably due to the fact that it is an equation that expresses the tendency of natural phenomena towards uniformity: to the elimination of curvature in the distributions. So important is it that the differential operator $(\partial^2/\partial x^2) + (\partial^2/\partial y^2) + (\partial^2/\partial z^2)$ is given a special symbol ∇^2 the *laplacian*, and read 'del-squared'. Laplace's equation then becomes simply $\nabla^2 f = 0$.

It is not always convenient, and often foolish, to work with the laplacian expressed in cartesian coordinates; for systems of a predominantly spherical nature the spherical polar form is more convenient, and both forms are collected in Box 11. The part of the laplacian involving the angular derivatives is referred to as the *legendrian* and written Λ^2.

BOX 11: The laplacian and the legendrian

Cartesian form (x, y, z as coordinates)

$$\text{laplacian: } \nabla^2 = \frac{\partial^2}{\partial x^2} + \frac{\partial^2}{\partial y^2} + \frac{\partial^2}{\partial z^2}.$$

Spherical polar form (r, θ, ϕ as coordinates)

$$\text{laplacian: } \nabla^2 = \frac{1}{r}\left(\frac{\partial^2}{\partial r^2}\right) r + \frac{1}{r^2}\Lambda^2$$

$$\text{or } \nabla^2 = \frac{\partial^2}{\partial r^2} + \frac{2}{r}\frac{\partial}{\partial r} + \frac{1}{r^2}\Lambda^2;$$

$$\text{legendrian: } \Lambda^2 = \left(\frac{1}{\sin\theta}\right)^2 \frac{\partial^2}{\partial \phi^2} + \frac{1}{\sin\theta}\frac{\partial}{\partial\theta}\sin\theta\frac{\partial}{\partial\theta}$$

$$\text{or } \Lambda^2 = \left(\frac{1}{\sin\theta}\right)^2 \frac{\partial^2}{\partial \phi^2} + \frac{\cos\theta}{\sin\theta}\frac{\partial}{\partial\theta} + \frac{\partial^2}{\partial\theta^2}.$$

Cylindrical polar form (r, θ, z as coordinates)

$$\text{laplacian: } \nabla^2 = \frac{1}{r}\frac{\partial}{\partial r} + \frac{\partial^2}{\partial r^2} + \frac{1}{r^2}\frac{\partial^2}{\partial\theta^2} + \frac{\partial^2}{\partial z^2}.$$

Further information. The laplacian occurs widely in quantum mechanics because it is the °operator for the °kinetic energy; it therefore appears as a component of the °hamiltonian and is the differential part of the °Schrödinger equation. For an account of its transformation from cartesian coordinates to spherical polars see §6.8 of Kyrala (1967) for swift methods and Appendix 5 of Moelwyn-Hughes (1961) for slow. A brief biography of Laplace has been written by Newman (1954).

laser. The word laser is an acronym formed from 'light amplification by stimulated emission of radiation' and is a development of the maser, where the m denotes microwave, according to some, or molecular according to others. A laser operates by absorbing energy and emitting it at a well-defined wavelength by a stimulated emission process (see °Einstein *A* and *B* coefficients). As a simple example, consider a sample of material in which most of the atoms are in an excited state, and let the sample be contained in a cavity with reflecting walls. One atom will emit a photon as it falls spontaneously into the ground state, and this photon will rattle around inside the cavity. Its presence stimulates another atom to emit, and so a second photon appears in the cavity and travels in phase with the first. The pair of photons stimulates another emission, and very rapidly a cascade of emission occurs and an intense light field grows inside the cavity. The process ceases when the population of the excited state has fallen to its equilibrium value. If one of the walls of the cavity is semi-transparent, light will leak through it and an intense, monochromatic burst of phase-coherent light will emerge.

How is the process realized in practice? The cavity is normally in the form of a long thin tube, if the sample is a gas, or a cylinder of material if it is a crystalline solid; this configuration implies that the emitted radiation will have a very small lateral divergence because only those photons ricocheting backwards and forwards along or very close to the axis contribute to the amplification cascade: the remainder pass through the side walls and drain away from the system before their intensity amplifies. Thus the geometry of the system leads to a beam with very little divergence.

The principal problem that remains is how the population-inversion necessary for stimulated emission, and therefore for laser action, is achieved. Two basic systems may be envisaged. In the first (Fig. L1 a) the laser action takes place between an excited state and the ground state: the difficulty of this primitive arrangement is that it is necessary to remove more than 50 per cent of the atoms from their ground state into the excited state. The second method obtains laser action between two excited levels: the population-inversion is much easier to attain, especially if the lower excited state can relax rapidly into the ground state. In such a three-level laser (see Fig. L1 b) intense radiation excites the absorbing atoms or ions into the uppermost level, and if this pumping step is sufficiently effective the population in that level (E_2) is significantly, and even enormously, greater than that in the lower excited level E_1. If the E_2 population does not leak away into the lower levels by non-radiative processes, laser action may take place between E_2 and E_1 because photons passing back and forth within a reflecting cavity stimulate the $E_2 \longrightarrow E_1$ emission; a leaky mirror at one end of the cavity permits a highly collimated (non-divergent), coherent (all waves in phase, because they are generated by stimulation), polarized (because of the polarization of the transition or because the cavity has polarizing windows), and monochromatic radiation of frequency $\nu = (E_2 - E_1)/h$ to emerge.

An example of the laser process is the helium-neon laser in which the active material is a mixture of the two gases in the ratio 1:5. A radio discharge, being no respecter of °selection rules, excites the helium atom, and although many of the excited states decay very rapidly, the first excited singlet state is relatively long-lived (because s-s transitions are forbidden), and atoms in this state swim around in the sample for some time because they cannot return to the ground state except by a forbidden transition. Whilst swimming an excited helium atom may collide with a neon atom in its ground state, and by a coincidence (a coincidence at the heart of this laser system) the energy that the helium atom possesses almost exactly matches the energy of an excited state of neon. There occurs °resonant transfer of energy, the helium is deactivated and the neon is in an excited state E_3 (Fig. L2). This state has two unpopulated energy states below it which do not resonate with excited helium. Therefore it is in a configuration typical of a three-level system; laser action occurs between E_3 and E_1, and red light is emitted at 632·82 nm.

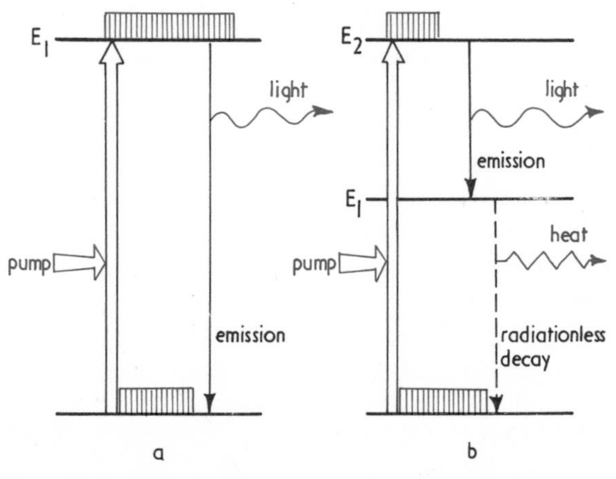

FIG. L1. (a) A two-level laser and (b) a three-level laser.

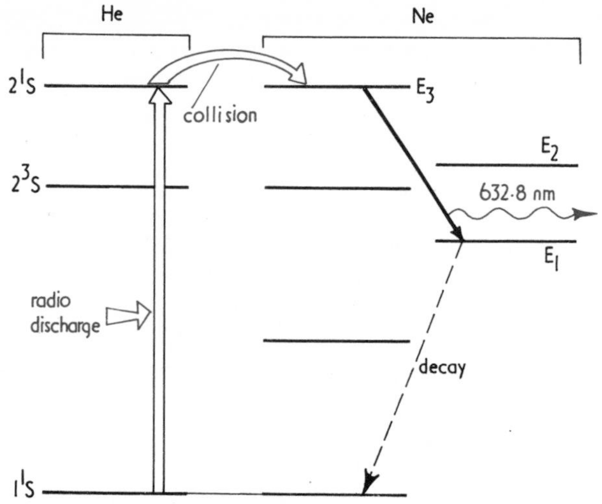

FIG. L2. The He–Ne laser (for the 632·8 nm mode).

Ruby is a famous laser, and is an example of a sort of three-level system involving four levels, but acting like a two-level system in so far as laser action involves a transition to the ground state. These somewhat perplexing remarks can be resolved by a glance at Fig. L3. Ruby, which the prosaic know to be Al_2O_3 with about 5 per cent of the Al^{3+} ions replaced by Cr^{3+}, gives delight to poets by virtue of its two intense transitions in the green (to E_2) and the violet (to E_3). Having pleased poets, ruby proceeds to please physicists as its chromium ions drop from E_3 and E_2 into E_1: this is a *radiationless decay* and relies on the transfer of the electronic excitation energy into the vibrations of the surrounding lattice (which gets hot). The initial absorption is so efficient that when intense illumination is used the population of E_1 may exceed that of the ground state, and laser action occurs with the emission of red light (694·3 nm).

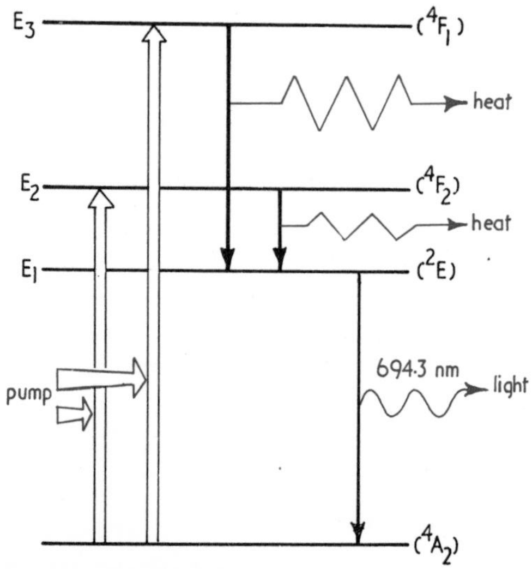

FIG. L3. The ruby laser transitions.

Lasers may be either continuous wave (CW), when the light emerges in a continuous flow so long as the pumping operation is in progress, or pulsed, as in the case of ruby, when the laser light emerges in a short burst as the stimulated emission occurs. The emergence of the light in short bursts means that very high powers may be obtained, albeit only for very short times. A typical procedure in a ruby laser is to employ a brilliant pumping flash emitting about 2·5 kJ of energy. Much of this is absorbed by the ruby rod, and although much of the absorbed energy appears as heat, about 25 J appears as laser radiation. But the pulse of light lasts for only about 5×10^{-4} s, and so the power that emerges is a splendid 50 kW, but of course this power is maintained for only 5×10^{-4} s. It is possible to increase the *power* output by shortening the length of the pulse in which the same amount of energy is delivered: the technique of effecting this is *Q-switching.* A crude way of describing this is to imagine a cavity with one of the mirrors removed; then pumping radiation is applied in a flash and the population of the upper level attains its maximum value and is not depleted by stimulated emission. Then the lost mirror is hurriedly slapped back into place while the population is still inverted, and it all drops out, by stimulation, and a giant pulse is obtained in about 10^{-8} s. The power of the laser, if the pulse carries 25 J, is a massive $2{\cdot}5 \times 10^9$ W, which is roughly the output of a massive power station (but power stations have the economical advantage of working for some years at that level, rather than for 10^{-8} s). The removal and replacing of the mirrors was done mechanically in early models but now the Kerr cell or Pockels cell is an electrical substitute.

Some of the common laser materials and their wavelengths are listed in Table 19.

Further information. See *MQM* Chapter 10 for a further discussion of the ruby system. A simple account of lasers is given by Schawlow (1969), Wayne (1970), and Lengyel (1971), and in review articles by Jones (1969) and Haught (1968). The last gives information about the expressions *mode-locking* (a manner of achieving short, picosecond flashes), *Q-switching,* various laser systems, and many pertinent references. A simple account of liquid lasers has also been given by Heller (1967). The stimulating source need not be radiation: chemical reactions that leave product molecules in excited states are also the basis of laser action—a chemical laser is a remarkable device that turns chemical energy directly into coherent light. For an account see Haught (1968) and Levine and Bernstein (1974). Chemical applications of lasers reviewed by Jones (1969) and Haught (1968). See Pressley (1971) for a compilation of data on lasers, and Levine and DeMaria (1966 et seq.) for recent advances.

level. In atomic structure and spectroscopy the name *level* denotes a particular value of the total °angular momentum J. For example, from the °configuration $1s^2 2s^2 2p$ arises a doublet P °term written ^2P. The two levels of this doublet correspond to $J=\frac{3}{2}$ and $J=\frac{1}{2}$, for only these angular momenta may be constructed from $L=1$ and $S=\frac{1}{2}$ (see °angular momentum). The two levels of the term therefore are written $^2P_{1/2}$ and $^2P_{3/2}$.

The number of levels of a particular term is its °*multiplicity*. Thus in ^2P there are two levels, and in ^3D there are three levels ($^3D_1$, $^3D_2$, and $^3D_3$). The levels differ in energy because of the °spin-orbit coupling, and their order can be predicted on the basis of the °Hund rules. The angular momentum J may have $2J+1$ different values of its component on some arbitrary axis; in common with the practice of angular momenta these are distinguished by the value of M_J. The *state* of a level of a term is denoted $^2P_{1/2}^{M_J}$, etc.

Questions. Define the use of the term 'level' in atomic spectroscopy. Write down the levels that may arise from the following terms: ^1P, ^3F, ^3S, ^4D, ^6D. Under what circumstances does the superscript not denote the mutiplicity? (See °term symbols.)

Further information. See Chapter 8 of *MQM* for more detail about atomic spectra. Levels, multiplicity, and fine structure are discussed by Kuhn (1969) and Herzberg (1940). Turn to °atomic spectra and °fine structure for further information.

ligand-field theory: a synopsis. The ligand-field theory of the structure of complexes of transition-metal ions is an

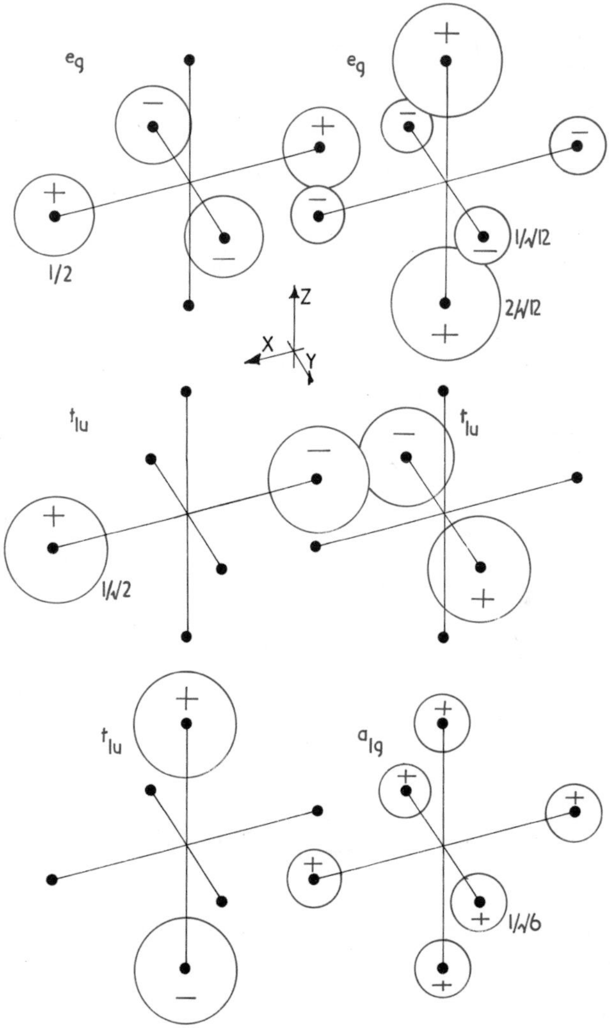

FIG. L4. The 6 ligand orbitals and the 6 symmetry-adapted combinations.

extension of the °crystal-field theory which takes into account the known delocalization of the electrons of the ion into the orbitals of the surrounding ligands; at the same time it makes use, like the crystal-field theory, of the very high degree of symmetry of the complexes normally encountered. The ligand-field theory is essentially a °molecular-orbital theory of complexes, and begins by concentrating its attention on the d-electrons of the central ion. We shall illustrate the method by considering an octahedral complex in which the central ion possesses *n* d-electrons.

Consider the ligands as bearers of σ-orbitals which approach the central ion with a °lone pair of electrons. We denote these by the spheres in Fig. L4. From these six orbitals six combinations may be formed: the six chosen have well-defined symmetry properties (For those who know °group theory, we select °linear combinations that span irreducible representations of the octahedral point group.) The six combinations are illustrated in the figure: they fall into three groups. Only one of the groups, that labelled e, has a net °overlap with the d-orbitals of the central ion, and so only this combination can form bonding and °antibonding molecular orbitals with the d-orbitals. It follows that a molecular-orbital diagram of the type shown in Fig. L5 may be anticipated. The energies of the ligand and ion orbitals are such that the lower-energy combination is largely ligand in nature, and the antibonding combination is nearly metal ion in character.

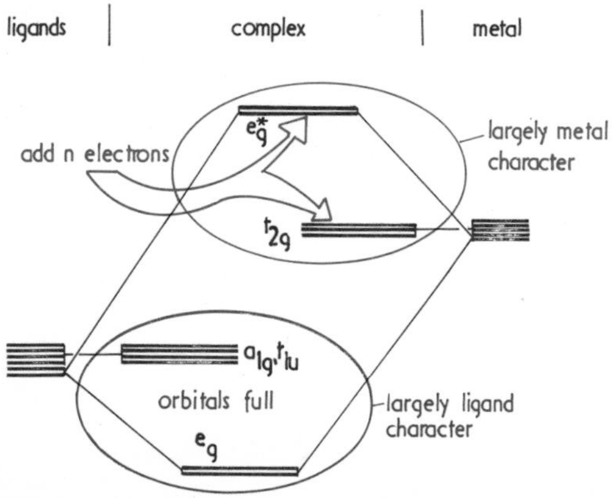

FIG. L5. The ligand-field splitting in an octahedral complex.

Into this set of eleven orbitals (a doubly °degenerate bonding-orbital labelled e_g, four degenerate nonbonding-orbitals confined entirely to the ligands and labelled t_{1u} and a_{1g}, three triply degenerate nonbonding-orbitals confined entirely to the metal ion and labelled t_{2g}, and an antibonding combination labelled e_g^*) we must insert $(12+n)$ electrons (2 from each ligand and *n* from the ion). Applying the °*aufbau* principle it should be clear that the first 12 electrons will occupy the orbitals e_g, t_{1u}, a_{1g}, and that these are of predominantly ligand character. The next *n* electrons have to compete for places in the orbitals t_{2g} and e_g^*: this is just the situation encountered in the °crystal-field theory and Figs. C6 and C7 should be consulted; there we see that if the energy gap between the orbitals is large (the ***strong-field case***) all the electrons attempt to enter the t_{2g} set, and enter the upper e_g set only if the °Pauli principle forbids them entry into the lower set. If the orbital separation (there called $10Dq$) were small (the ***weak-field case***) it might be energetically favourable for the electrons to enter the t_{2g} and the e_g^* orbitals, but to do so with their spins parallel (°Hund rules).

The distinction between the strong- and weak-field cases, and their generation of low- and high-spin complexes, is carried over from the crystal-field theory into the molecular-orbital theory: the difference lies in the source of the splitting. Another difference is the fact that the e_g^*-orbital is not wholly confined to the metal ion: since it is formed from the overlap of metal and ligand orbitals it contains some ligand character. This means that any electrons that occupy it may spread over on to the ligands. The evidence that this happens comes from spectroscopy, especially °electron spin resonance (where °hyperfine structure due to the ligands has been observed).

The other important improvement of ligand-field theory over crystal-field theory is the natural way that the former permits π-bonding between the metal and the ligands. This is especially important when the ligands are species such as CO or NO. In order to see the effect of permitting π-bonding consider the octahedral complex again, and this time, in addition to the σ-bonds, let each ligand possess two orbitals that are perpendicular to the metal-ligand bonds. From these 12 orbitals, which are illustrated in Fig. L6, 12 combinations may be constructed. Three of the combinations have the same symmetry as the d_{xy}-, d_{xz}-, d_{yz}-orbitals of the central ion

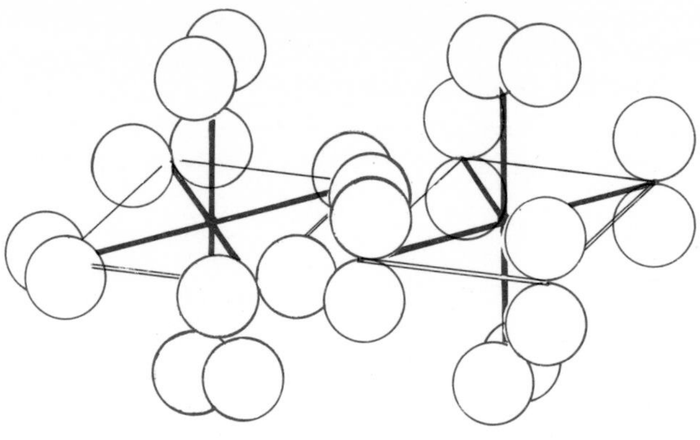

FIG. L6. The 12 π-orbitals of octahedrally disposed ligands.

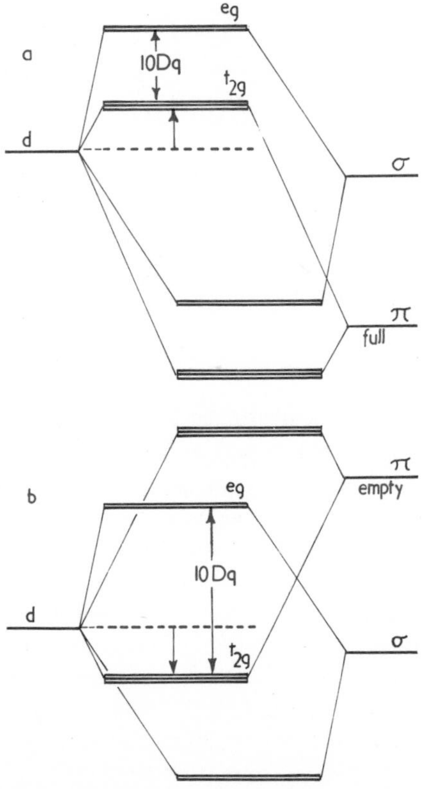

FIG. L7. π-bonding: the effect on energies. In (a) the ligand π-levels are initially full; in (b) they are empty.

(which so far have formed the nonbonding t_{2g} set of orbitals confined to the metal). When we permit this overlap to occur the molecular-orbital energy-level diagram is modified. Two situations need to be distinguished: in the first the π-orbitals of the ligands are full (and lie below the σ-orbitals); in the second they are empty (and lie above the σ-orbitals). The two cases are illustrated separately in Fig. L7. In the former case the ligands bring up their π-electrons and fill all the bonding combinations of π-orbitals. This leaves the n electrons from the metal to be distributed between the antibonding π combination (t_{2g}^*) and the untouched e_g^* combination. Since the previously nonbonding orbitals have become slightly antibonding, the gap (10Dq) has been reduced by the presence of the π-electrons. The opposite is the case when the π-orbitals of the ligands are empty, for now the n electrons compete for places between the bonding t_{2g} combination and the antibonding e_g^* combination. Thus the splitting has been increased by the presence of unfilled π-orbitals.

The size of the splitting 10Dq determines the spectroscopic, magnetic, and chemical properties of the complex in the same way as there are determined by the °crystal-field theory, but the distribution of the electrons on to the ligands gives them some of the latter's °spin-orbit coupling energy.

Further information. See *MQM* Chapter 9 for an account of ligand-field theory. A simple introduction to the ideas of ligand-field theory is provided by Earnshaw and Harrington in *The chemistry of the transition elements* (OCS 13); this is developed further in Coulson's *The shape and structure of molecules* (OCS 9). The effect of these ideas on the explanation of the magnetic properties of complexes is described by Earnshaw (1968). For spectral consequences see Jørgensen (1962, 1971). A simple and good introduction to ligand-field theory has been given by Orgel (1960), Coulson (1961), and Murrell, Kettle, and Tedder (1965), and developed more mathematically by Figgis (1966), Ballhausen (1962), and Griffith (1964). See also °crystal-field theory and the °Jahn-Teller effect.

linear combination of atomic orbitals (LCAO). An LCAO is a method of describing a molecular orbital covering several nuclei in terms of a sum of atomic orbitals centred on each nucleus. Thus the bonding orbital in the hydrogen molecule is really a complicated function spreading round both nuclei, but since it is expected to resemble the 1s-atomic orbitals on each nucleus the orbital is expressed as the LCAO formed by the °superposition of the two 1s-orbitals (Fig. L8).

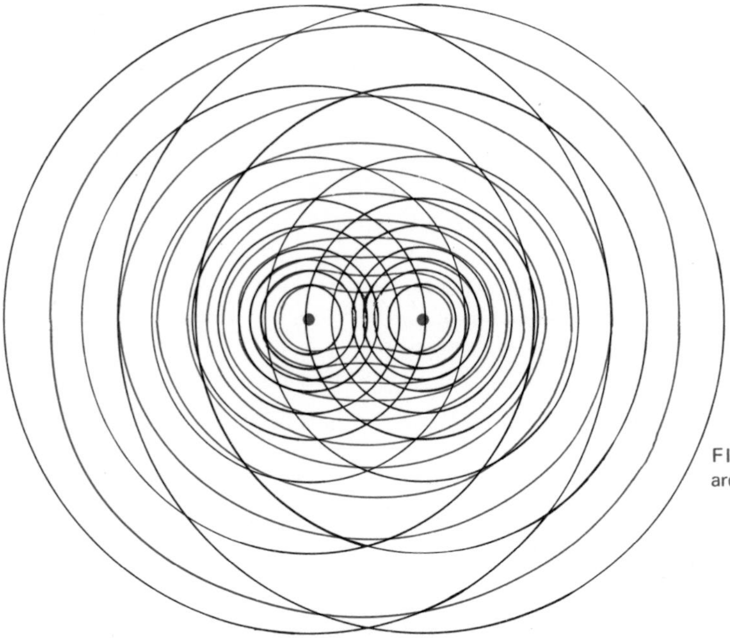

FIG. L8. In the LCAO method the wavefunctions of the atoms (black) are superposed to give a molecular orbital (colour).

If all the atomic orbitals were used in order to reconstruct the true molecular orbital the LCAO procedure would be exact, but this task is too heavy and normally a small number of atomic orbitals is selected as the *basis set*; used in this way the LCAO procedure is an approximation. In the elementary discussion of the °hydrogen molecule the basis set consists of the two 1s-atomic orbitals, and this gives a reasonably good description of the bond, but it can be improved considerably by expanding the basis to include the 2s- and 2p-orbitals, and others. The use of a small basis set in the LCAO description of molecular bonding is one of the gravest sources of error in the method, and the selection of too small a set can make a nonsense of an otherwise elaborate calculation.

The use of the LCAO method has a theoretical justification that lies deeper than the mathematical device of being able to expand any function in terms of a sufficiently complete set of simpler functions. This deeper justification is provided by the °superposition principle. When one has the possibility that a variety of processes can occur the superposition principle demands that one should consider the probability *amplitudes* for the individual processes rather than the probabilities themselves. The total, composite process is described by the total, composite amplitude, and all manipulations and thought must be applied to this object, and the probability for an individual process extracted only at the end of the calculation. In the case of a molecule we have an example of such a composite situation, for there is a probability that an electron is on one of a number of nuclei. Our problem is the distribution of this electron in the face of these various possibilities, and the superposition principle tells us that in order to find this distribution we should construct the overall amplitude (molecular-orbital wavefunction) by superimposing the amplitudes of the individual processes (the atomic-orbital wavefunctions). But this is precisely the line taken by the LCAO method in its attempt to construct the molecular orbital from the individual atomic orbitals.

Questions. What is the LCAO procedure? Is it accurate? What is the worst source of error in the method? Can the method be justified? What is the basis set in the simplest description of molecular oxygen (that is, we require the *minimal basis set*)? How can a simple description of molecular hydrogen be improved? What guidance can the physical nature of the problem provide in the problem of extending the minimal basis set? (Think about energy, size, and orientation of the orbitals, and how the polarization of an atom by neighbouring nuclei can be taken into account.)

Further information. The LCAO method is at the foundations of molecular-bonding theory, and more information will be found under appropriate entries. See in particular Coulson's *The shape and structure of molecules* (OCS 9) and *MQM* Chapter 9. See also Coulson (1961), Murrell, Kettle, and Tedder (1965), and McGlynn, Vanquickenborne, Kinoshita, and Carroll (1972). For a simple introduction to °self-consistent field calculations on molecules see Richards and Horsley (1970). The choice of orbitals to combine into a particular molecular orbital must conform to the symmetry of the molecule, and °group theory can be extremely useful for determining appropriate combinations. See *MQM* Chapters 5 and 9, Cotton (1963), Tinkham (1964), and Bishop (1973).

localized orbitals. The chemistry of many molecules suggests that to a significant extent electrons may be regarded as belonging to different parts of the molecule; °molecular-orbital theory gives the impression of predicting that all electrons are spread throughout each molecule, and therefore it seems to run counter to the chemical evidence. The deficiency is apparent rather than real. It is possible to manipulate the form of molecular orbitals (by taking various sums of them) and to generate localized orbitals, orbitals that are localized almost wholly in the vicinity of different groups of the molecule. This procedure is illustrated in Fig. L9 (which is based on the calculation in Question 2).

It is possible to take the appropriate linear combinations because the actual many-electron wavefunction of a molecule

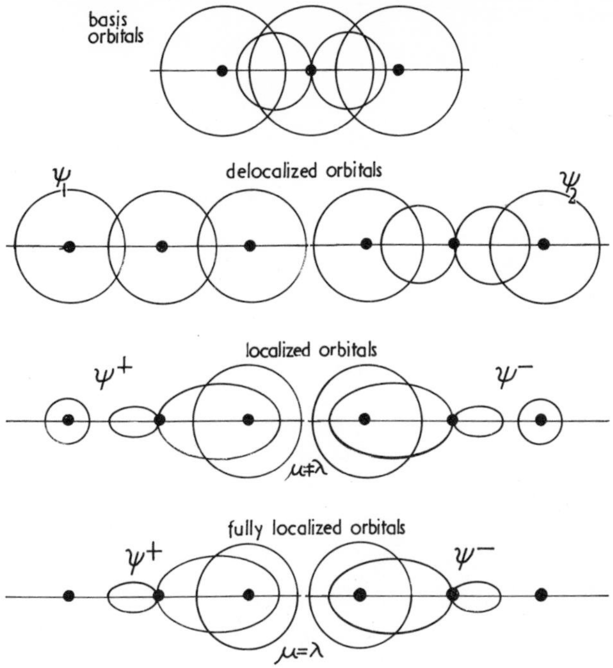

FIG. L9. The formation of localized orbitals. Only when $\mu = \lambda$ is full localization obtained.

must satisfy the °Pauli principle, and this is ensured if it is written as a °Slater determinant. It is an elementary feature of a determinant that rows or columns may be added to other rows or columns without changing its value. Therefore similar manipulations applied to the Slater determinant do not change the total wavefunction, and the localized description is mathematically equivalent to the original delocalized description. An example of the procedure is set as a Question.

Questions. 1. What is the aspect of the molecular-orbital theory that seems to conflict with chemical evidence? What evidence supports the view that electrons are indeed delocalized throughout the molecule? How are localized orbitals generated? What do they succeed in achieving? Why is it a permissible procedure? Why are delocalized and localized descriptions equivalent? Suppose we have an orbital which is a sum of an s-orbital on atom a, an s-orbital on atom b, and an s-orbital on atom c, and we call this ψ_1, then the orbital is $\psi_1 = c_a s_a + c_b s_b + c_c s_c$; and let there be a similar orbital in which the

central atom b contributes a p-orbital—then the bonding orbital is $\psi_2 = c'_a s_a + c'_b p_b + c'_c s_c$. Show that the combinations $\psi_1 + \psi_2$ and $\psi_1 - \psi_2$ are largely localized in the a–b and b–c regions respectively, and sketch the resulting localized orbitals. The reason why it is correct to take these combinations is treated in the next, harder Question.
2. Consider a linear triatomic AB_2 molecule (BAB), and let the occupied orbitals be of the form $\psi_1 = s + \mu(a + b)$ and $\psi_2 = p + \lambda(a - b)$ (for the notation see Fig. L9). These orbitals contain four electrons, and so the antisymmetrized wavefunction is the °Slater determinant $\psi = (1/4!)^{1/2} |\psi_{1\alpha}(1)\psi_{1\beta}(2)\psi_{2\alpha}(3)\psi_{2\beta}(4)|$, where α and β denote the spins. Show that this determinant may be manipulated, without change of value, into the determinant $\psi = (1/4!)^{1/2} |\psi^+_\alpha(1)\,\psi^+_\beta(2)\,\psi^-_\alpha(3)\,\psi^-_\beta(4)|$, where $\psi^\pm = (\frac{1}{2})^{1/2}(\psi_1 \pm \psi_2)$. Form these orbitals from the original pair and show that they are localized, but that the localization is complete only in the case where $\mu = \lambda$. The procedure is illustrated in Fig. L9. Discuss your result in terms of the °hybridization of the central atom.

Further information. See *MQM* Appendix 9.2 for an account of localization and a worked example. See also Coulson's *The shape and structure of molecules* (OCS 9) and Coulson (1961). See also Murrell, Kettle, and Tedder (1965), Streitweiser (1961), Salem (1966), and Pilar (1968). Good accounts in the literature on the formation of localized bonds are those of Lennard-Jones and Pople (1950), Boys (1960), and Edmiston and Ruedenberg (1963, 1965).

lone pair. A lone pair of electrons is a pair of electrons of the valence shell not engaged in bonding. As an example, consider the tetrahedral distribution of electrons around the oxygen atom in H_2O: two electrons stick one proton to the atom, two stick the other, and the remaining four form two lone pairs sticking out like rabbit's ears on either side of the molecular plane. We may consider the last four to be electrons in °localized, *nonbonding* orbitals.

Lone pairs are important both structurally and chemically. They influence the structure of a molecule by exerting large repulsive effects on the electrons in neighbouring bonds: for example, the pyramidal shape of ammonia may be traced partly to the effect of the single lone pair on nitrogen exerting a repulsive force on the six electrons in the three N—H bonds. This analysis of molecular structure in terms of the lone-pair interactions is the basis of the *Sidgwick-Powell rules* which state that lone pairs dominate the repulsive interactions in molecules. In chemistry the lone pair is a nucleophilic centre because it can so readily form a dative bond to an electropositive centre: lone pairs act as a base (in the Lewis sense).

Since lone pairs are not tied into place by a parasitic nucleus they also contribute strongly to spectra, and the $\pi^* \leftarrow n$ (read 'n to pi star') transition in carbonyl compounds is a major mode of excitation (see °colour). The n stands for a lone-pair (nonbonding) orbital, and the transition takes the electron from the oxygen lone pair and spreads it over the carbonyl group by depositing it in the °antibonding π-orbital. Note that this transition changes the charge distribution in the carbonyl group and so is strongly responsive to solvent effects.

Further information. See *MQM* Chapter 10. For a discussion of the Sidgwick-Powell rules and their modern development see Bader (1972). For references to the role of lone pairs in spectra see °colour.

M

magnetic dipole and electric quadrupole radiation. The most intense transitions in molecules are due to °electric dipole transitions, but when these cannot operate (when they are forbidden by °selection rules) other mechanisms may have sufficient strength to cause a transition, albeit at a much lower intensity. One such mechanism is the *magnetic dipole transition*, which relies for its operation on the magnetic component in the light field; the other mechanism, of similar strength, is the *electric °quadrupole transition*, which relies for its operation on the variation of the electric field of the light over the space occupied by the molecule (that is, there must be a field gradient on a molecular scale if the quadrupole transition is to operate).

The *magnetic dipole transition* generates the magnetic component of a light field just as an electric dipole transition generates an electric component (but, of course, in each case the other component is forced to accompany the generated component). There are two principal differences.

The first is the weakness of the interaction of the molecule and field via the magnetic dipole. Pictorially, this can be traced to the rotational nature of the magnetic dipole transition: if during a transition charge is displaced in a curved path it will possess a magnetic transition dipole (Fig. M1). But in a region as small as the extent of a molecule the curvature of the displacement will be only weakly apparent: if D is the diameter of the molecule and λ the wavelength of the emitted or absorbed light, it is plausible to suppose that the efficiency of the coupling is of the order of D/λ. Since the intensity of a transition is proportional to the square of its °transition dipole moment, this suggests that the intensity should be only about $(D/\lambda)^2$ of the intensity of an electric dipole transition, where curvature need not be detected. For typical molecules and wavelengths $(D/\lambda)^2 \sim 10^{-5}$, and this is the order of magnitude of the intensities observed in practice.

The other difference between electric and magnetic dipole transitions is in the selection rules: a magnetic dipole transition is akin to a rotational displacement of charge; a rotation is not reversed when it is inverted through a point (Fig. M1); therefore a magnetic dipole transition has even *parity* (see °*gerade* and *ungerade*). Unlike an electric dipole transition (which is a translation of charge, and which is therefore of odd parity,

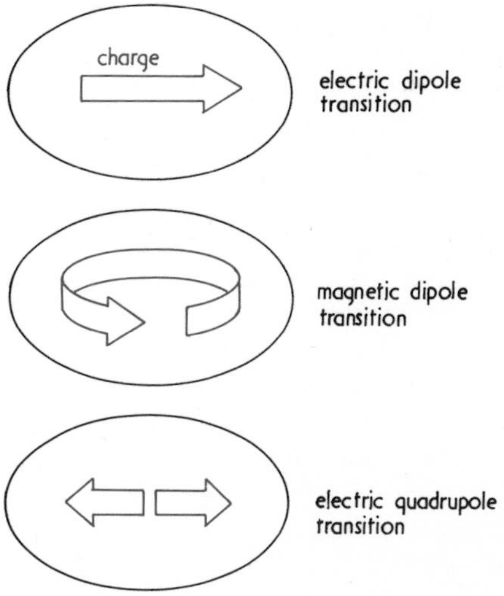

FIG. M1. The charge displacement in transitions of different type.

and where the selection rules $\Delta L = \pm 1$ and $g \rightarrow u$ emerge) in a magnetic dipole transition $\Delta L = 0$, $g \rightarrow g$, and $u \rightarrow u$. The over-all selection rule $\Delta J = \pm 1$ applies to both the electric and magnetic dipole transitions, because both are dipolar. (See °electric dipole transition, and the account of the role of photon angular momentum.)

The *electric quadrupole transition* arises from a displacement of charge that has a °quadrupolar nature. This somewhat subtle (but simple) type of charge displacement, which is illustrated in Fig. M1, can be detected with an efficiency of the order of D^2/λ^2 (in intensity), and so we expect magnetic dipole and electric quadrupole transitions to be of comparable intensity. But detailed analysis shows that the latter also depends on the square of the frequency, and for visible light the intensity is reduced by a further two orders of magnitude. Therefore, an electric quadrupole transition has an intensity of only 10^{-7} that of an electric dipole transition.

Since we are now dealing no longer with a dipole but with a quadrupole, the selection rules differ. A quadrupole can be envisaged as two dipoles in opposition: therefore we expect it to be of even parity. Consequently $g \rightarrow g$, $u \rightarrow u$ transitions are allowed. More detailed analysis shows that the angular momentum selection rules are $\Delta L = 0, \pm 1, \pm 2$ and $\Delta J = 0, \pm 1, \pm 2$. One might ask what has happened to our arguments concerning the unit spin of the °photon? The answer lies in the quadrupolar nature of the transition: as the photon is flung off the radiating molecule the spatial variation of the transition endows it with an orbital angular momentum. The total angular momentum of the photon may exceed unity, and so a selection rule of $\Delta J = \pm 2$ can still be understood in terms of the conservation of angular momentum.

Further information. Magnetic dipole transitions are nicely discussed in §IIID 2b of Kuhn (1962), in §3.2.2 of Griffith (1964), and in §7.6 of Hameka (1965). See also Heitler (1954) and Berestetskii, Lifshitz, and Pitaevskii (1971). The transitions that are responsible for °electron spin resonance and °nuclear magnetic resonance, where a magnetic moment couples with an oscillating electromagnetic field, are important examples of magnetic dipole transitions. If a molecule can be excited to the same state by an electric and a magnetic dipole transition it is optically active (see °birefringence).

magnetic moment. The magnetic moment of an electron due to its °orbital angular momentum (which may be pictured as arising from a circulating current) is $\mu_L = \gamma_e \mathbf{l}$, where $\mathbf{l}$ is the orbital angular momentum and γ_e a constant of proportionality known either as the *magnetogyric ratio* or as the *gyromagnetic ratio* (the former name is more helpful). Simple calculation shows γ_e to be equal to $-e/2m_e$; the negative sign of γ_e (which arises from the negative charge of the electron) shows that the direction of μ_L is opposite to the direction of $\mathbf{l}$, but they are collinear (see Fig. M2).

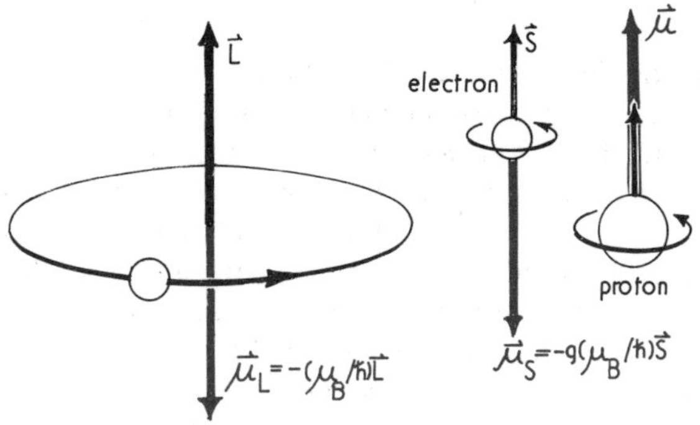

FIG. M2. Orbital and spin magnetic moments.

The °spin angular momentum also gives rise to a magnetic moment (as a simple picture of a rotating charge would suggest) but its magnitude is 'anomalous' (which means that people could not explain it when it was first encountered), and in order to express the moment in terms of the magnetogyric ratio γ_e an extra factor (the °*g* factor, is introduced: then $\mu_S = g\gamma_e \mathbf{s}$. Experiment, and later theory, showed that $g = 2{\cdot}0023$, and this is frequently approximated as $g = 2$. The spin magnetic moment and the spin momentum are collinear but antiparallel.

The magnetic moment is often expressed in terms of the *Bohr magneton* $\mu_B = e\hbar/2m_e$, which is a positive quantity and may be considered to be a basic unit of magnetic moment (its magnitude is $9{\cdot}273 \times 10^{-24}$ J T^{-1}, or $9{\cdot}273 \times 10^{-28}$ J G^{-1}). In terms of the magneton we have $\gamma_e = -\mu_B/\hbar$ and so $\mu_L = -(\mu_B/\hbar)\mathbf{l}$ and $\mu_S = -g(\mu_B/\hbar)\mathbf{s}$.

Just as the electron is the elementary negative charge and representative of the lighter fundamental particles (the *leptons*, but note that the class lepton contains neutrinos and muons) and μ_B is the elementary unit of magnetic moment, it is convenient to consider the proton as the elementary positive charge and representative of the heavier fundamental particles (the *baryons*; the proton and neutron, a subset of this class, are called *nucleons*). The corresponding elementary unit of magnetic moment is the *nuclear magneton*, $\mu_N = e\hbar/2m_p$, and it has the magnitude $5{\cdot}051 \times 10^{-27}$ J T^{-1} or $5{\cdot}051 \times 10^{-31}$ J G^{-1}. The enormous difference in magnitude between the Bohr and nuclear magnetons is due to the difference in mass of the electron and the proton (to achieve the same spin angular momentum as an electron, the heavier proton needs a much smaller angular velocity, and so the equivalent current loop carries much less current, and the magnetic moment is smaller). The nuclear magneton is of a size convenient for the expression of the magnetic moments of nuclei (and, incidentally, of the magnetic moments of rotating molecules: see °*g*-value). If a nucleus has a spin angular momentum **I** its magnetic moment is $g_n(\mu_N/\hbar)\mathbf{I}$, where the nuclear *g*-value, which depends on the nucleus, is defined by this relation and is determined by experiment (and in the future, one hopes, by calculation in terms of the nuclear structure). It is found that g_n may be positive or negative, depending on the element and the isotope, and it should be food for thought to be told that even the uncharged neutron has a magnetic moment. Typical values of the magnetic moments of some common nuclei are listed in Table 17. Note that $\gamma_n = g_n(\mu_N/\hbar)$.

Further information. See *MQM* Chapters 8, 9, and 10 for a discussion of magnetic moments. The classical electromagnetic theory concerning magnetic moments is well described in Corson and Lorrain (1970). The Maxwell equations are summarized in Table 20. The quantum-mechanical theory of magnetic moments is described further under °spin, °*g*-value, and °magnetic properties. See also °Dirac for his contribution. See °electron spin resonance and °nuclear magnetic resonance for one way of harnessing magnetic moments into useful employment.

magnetic properties. When a substance is immersed in a magnetic field it has an effect which may be visualized (Fig. M3) in terms of the distortion of the lines of force of the field. In a *diamagnetic* material the number of lines of force is reduced (or the magnetic *induction B* is less within the body than in free space), and in a *paramagnetic* material the number (and induction) is increased. An alternative way of expressing this behaviour is to regard a diamagnetic sample as magnetized in opposition to the direction of the applied field, and so to give rise to an opposing field which partially cancels the applied field; conversely, a paramagnetic sample is magnetized in the same direction as the applied field, and the field that this induced moment generates augments the applied field. A physical manifestation of paramagnetism and diamagnetism is that a paramagnetic sample tends to move into a magnetic field, and a diamagnetic sample tends to move out of it.

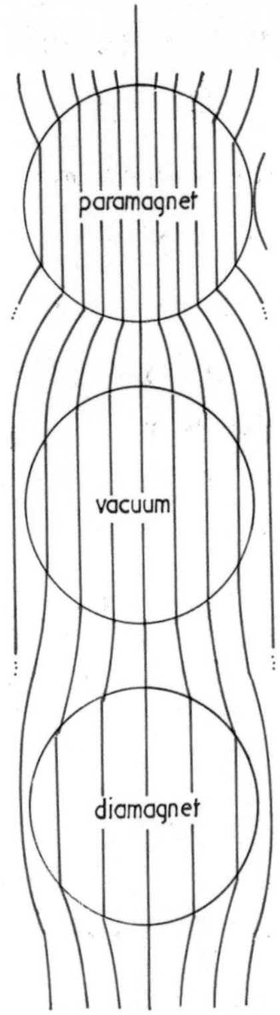

FIG. M3. A schematic indication of the magnetic induction (magnetic flux density) in magnetic materials of different kinds.

The ratio of the induced magnetic moment to the strength of the applied field is the *magnetic susceptibility* of the sample,

BOX 12: Magnetic properties

Magnetization $\mathbf{M} = \chi_m \mathbf{H}$

χ_m is the magnetic susceptibility and $\mathbf{H}$ the field strength.

$$\chi_m = \chi_m^p + \chi_m^d$$

paramagnetic susceptibility $\chi_m^p > 0$

diamagnetic susceptibility $\chi_m^d < 0$.

Magnetic induction (flux density)

$$\mathbf{B} = \mu_0 \mathbf{H} + \mu_0 \mathbf{M} = \mu_0 (1 + \chi_m)\mathbf{H}.$$

Curie law

$$\chi_m = C/T;\ C = \mu_0 L \mu^2/3k$$

(μ is the magnetic moment; for example, $\mu^2 \sim g^2 \mu_B^2 S(S+1)$ for spin-only paramagnetism).

Curie-Weiss law

$$\chi_m = C/(T - \theta).$$

Brillouin function

$$M = N\mu \mathcal{B}_J(\mu B/kT)$$

$$\mathcal{B}_J(x) = \left(\frac{2J+1}{2J}\right) \coth\left(\frac{2J+1}{2J}x\right) - \left(\frac{1}{2J}\right) \coth\left(\frac{x}{2J}\right).$$

Perturbation theory expression for the molar susceptibilities:

$$\text{TIP:}\ \chi_m^p = L\left(\frac{e^2\mu_0}{6m_e^2}\right) \sum_n{}' \left\{\frac{\langle 0|\mathbf{l}|n\rangle \cdot \langle n|\mathbf{l}|0\rangle}{(E_n - E_0)}\right\}$$

$$\chi_m^d = -L\left(\frac{e^2\mu_0}{6m_e}\right)\langle r^2\rangle$$ (Langevin-Pauli equation).

See Table 20 for the Maxwell equations.

and it is normally denoted χ_m (see Box 12 and Table 20). For a diamagnetic material the susceptibility is negative, and for a paramagnetic material it is positive (in accord with the different directions of the induced magnetization). The susceptibility of all materials can be written as the sum of a paramagnetic susceptibility χ_m^p and a diamagnetic susceptibility χ_m^d: $\chi_m = \chi_m^p + \chi_m^d$ (remember that $\chi_m^d < 0$ and that for most molecules the diamagnetic term dominates the paramagnetic). When the molecule possesses unpaired electrons the paramagnetic susceptibility dominates, and it is generally found that χ_m^p diminishes as the temperature is raised and that in the vicinity of room temperature it is proportional to $1/T$ (the *Curie law*). In a few cases the paramagnetic term dominates the diamagnetic even though all the electrons are paired; in such cases it is also found that this weak paramagnetism is independent of temperature; for this reason it is referred to as *temperature-independent paramagnetism* (*TIP*) (an alternative name is *high-frequency paramagnetism*).

1. *Diamagnetism*. All molecules have a diamagnetic component of their magnetic susceptibility which arises by the applied field exerting a torque on the electrons present. The torque tends to drive the electrons in circles within the molecular orbitals (Fig. M4 a), and the circulating current so produced

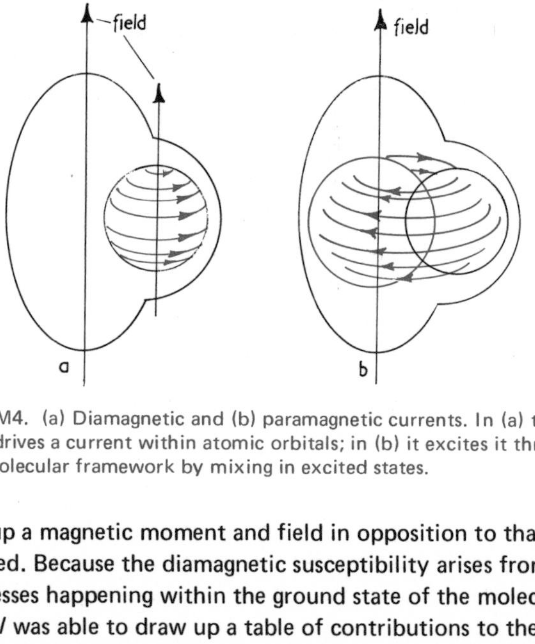

FIG. M4. (a) Diamagnetic and (b) paramagnetic currents. In (a) the field drives a current within atomic orbitals; in (b) it excites it through the molecular framework by mixing in excited states.

sets up a magnetic moment and field in opposition to that applied. Because the diamagnetic susceptibility arises from processes happening within the ground state of the molecule, *Pascal* was able to draw up a table of contributions to the total diamagnetic susceptibility of a molecule in terms of its structural features which could be transferred between molecules. Aromatic molecules, in which there is a cyclic path for the electrons of the π-system, show anomalously large susceptibilities, which are ascribed to *ring currents*. These ring currents are of particular importance in determining the form of °nuclear magnetic resonance spectra, but there has been some quarrel over their existence.

2. *Paramagnetism*. The spin paramagnetism is easily understood in terms of the °magnetic moment associated with the electron's °spin angular momentum. In a magnetic field the energy of a magnetic moment depends on its orientation; since an electron may have one of only two orientations with respect to a selected axis, the application of a magnetic field to a collection of molecules, each with a single unpaired spin, lowers the energy of those with β-spin ($m_s = -\frac{1}{2}$) and raises by an equal amount those with α-spin ($m_s = +\frac{1}{2}$). Very quickly the collection of molecules relaxes into thermal equilibrium, and the sample then contains more β-spins than α-spins, (Fig. M5) (the proportions are determined by the

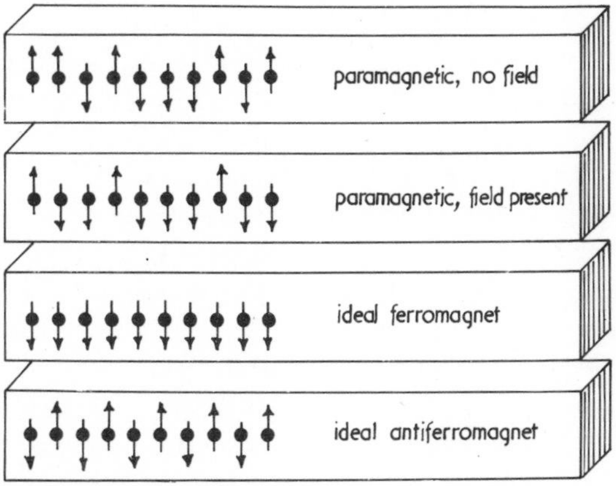

FIG. M5. Magnetic materials dependent on electron spin.

Boltzmann distribution). The spin magnetic moment lies in a direction opposite to the spin angular momentum (because the electron is negatively charged), and so at equilibrium there is a net moment parallel to the applied field. The field it generates augments the applied field and the sample is paramagnetic. As the temperature is raised the Boltzmann distribution becomes more even between the two spin orientations because the thermal motion jostles the spin alignment, and consequently the net induced moment falls; a simple calculation applicable to room temperatures (see Question 2) leads to the Curie law, and a simple extension that leads to an expression valid at all temperatures may also be deduced (so long as the material does not turn ferromagnetic, see below): this is the *Brillouin function*. Both these expressions may be calculated for molecules with arbitrary spin. (For instance, molecular oxygen is a paramagnetic species with $S = 1$, and so there are three orientations with different energies.)

An important point about the role of the magnetic effects of the orbital angular momentum should always be remembered: in many molecules this motion is °quenched and so makes no contribution to the magnetic susceptibility—the magnetic behaviour is then referred to as *spin-only paramagnetism*. When the orbital motion is not fully quenched the situation is more complicated; so too is it when the °spin-orbit coupling energy is large, and then the magnetic susceptibility cannot be calculated simply by counting spins and applying the Brillouin or the Curie formulas.

Temperature-independent paramagnetism is a property of the °orbital angular momentum of the electrons. If there are low-lying excited states the magnetic field can make use of them to induce a migration of electrons through the molecular framework, and the orbital angular momentum of this motion gives rise to an orbital magnetic moment. This orbital motion differs from the diamagnetic current in so far as it arises from a distortion of the electronic distribution by the field, whereas the diamagnetic current occurs within the undistorted molecular orbitals. This difference leads to a current which percolates through the molecule in the direction opposite to the diamagnetic drifts within the molecular orbitals (Fig. M4), and so it gives rise to a magnetic moment that enhances the applied field. The magnetic field determines the sense of circulation of the current, and therefore the direction of the magnetization. It follows that the latter is independent of the jostling motion that randomizes the spin magnetic moments, and so this paramagnetism is temperature-independent.

3. *Ferromagnetism and antiferromagnetism*. At sufficently low temperatures many paramagnetic materials undergo a transition to a state where all the spins align co-operatively and strongly enhance the magnetic properties of the material (Fig. M5). When the neighbouring spins align in the same direction throughout a reasonably extensive region (a *domain*)

of the sample, a strong magnetization is obtained and remains after the magnetizing field is removed. This is the *ferromagnetic* phase, and a common examples are those of iron with a transition temperature (known as the *Curie temperature*) of 1043 K, and of cobalt, with a Curie temperature of 1403 K (these high temperatures explain why 'permanent' magnets are made of these materials). Their magnetic susceptibility above the Curie temperature follows the *Curie-Weiss* law (Box 12), in which the $1/T$ of the Curie law is replaced by $1/(T_C+T)$, T_C being the Curie temperature (more accurately, $1/(\theta_C+T)$, where θ_C is the *paramagnetic intercept*, which is slightly larger than T_C: for Fe, $\theta_C = 1100$ K and for Co, $\theta_C = 1415$ K). Another group of materials, of which NiO is a famous but far from unique example, shows a transition to an *antiferromagnetic* phase, in which neighbouring spins are aligned in opposition (Fig. M5); therefore the spin paramagnetism is strongly quenched in this co-operative state. The transition temperature is known as the *Néel temperature*. The spin-spin interactions responsible for the alignment in both kinds of phase are electrostatic in origin and related to the °exchange energy; see Further information.

Questions. 1. How could you recognize diamagnetism and paramagnetisim in a material? How is the susceptibility related to the induced moment? What are the dimensions of χ_m? Consider the work necessary to insert a magnetic sample into a magnetic field: which is easier to insert, a paramagnetic or a diamagnetic sample? What is the source of paramagnetism? What is the difference in energy between 1 mol of electron spins in the β-orientation and 1 mol in the α-orientation when a field of 5 kG (0·5 T) is present? What is the population difference when the spins are in thermal equilibrium at 300 K? What is the magnetization of this sample, and what is its susceptibility? (Try to get your units right: magnetization has units of A m^{-1}, so does the field strength; magnetic induction, or flux density, has units of Wb m^{-2}, or kg s^{-2} A^{-1}, or T; see Table 20.) What is the difference between the currents giving rise to diamagnetism and those giving rise to TIP? How can you justify Pascal's rules? What is the difference between ferromagnetism and antiferromagnetism? What are the transition temperatures called in each case? What is the nature of the interaction between the spins that gives rise to the co-operative phenomena?

2. Deduce the Curie law as follows. The magnetization (magnetic moment) of a sample in a magnetic field B is equal to the magnetic moment of an α-spin multiplied by the number of α-spins, plus the moment of a β-spin multiplied by the number of β-spins. The numbers of α and β spins are determined by the Boltzmann distribution at a temperature T, the energy of the spin with magnetic moment m being $-m_zB$ as the field lies along z. When this energy is small the exponential in the Boltzmann distribution may be expanded. Your answer should be the Curie law exhibited in Box 12.

3. Repeat the calculation for a general spin S, and find the expression for the temperature dependence of the magnetization at all temperatures: this is the Brillouin function. The answer is shown in the Box. Plot this function's dependence on $g\mu_B B/kT$.

Further information. The standard work on magnetic susceptibilities is by van Vleck (1932), but as it was written so long ago it uses rather old-fashioned language. See *MQM* Chapter 11 for an account of the calculation of magnetic properties and their interpretation in terms of currents. Earnshaw's book (1968) gives a discussion of many of the points mentioned in the preceeding paragraphs, and other volumes of interest are those by Davies (1967) and Selwood (1956). A good introduction to co-operative phenomena is provided by Stanley (1971), and a tough but good introduction to co-operative magnetic phenomena is given by Mattis (1965). Much interest in magnetic properties arises from the application of °ligand-field theory to transition-metal ions; therefore you should look at Earnshaw and Harrington's *The chemistry of the transition elements* (OCS 13), Earnshaw (1968), Orgel (1960), and Griffith (1964). More information about magnetic properties will be found under °electron spin resonance, °nuclear magnetic resonance, and °chemical shifts. The controversy over the existence of ring currents may be traced by referring to Musher (1966). An excellent compilation of magnetic properties of a wide variety of materials is in §5 of Gray (1972). The Maxwell equations are summarized in Table 20.

matrix. A matrix is a rectangular array of numbers. It may be regarded as a generalization of the concept of 'number' in the sense that an ordinary number is a 1×1 matrix and is therefore a special case of the general $n \times m$ matrix of numbers. In an $n \times m$ matrix (which we denote **M**) the numbers that constitute it (the *matrix elements*) may be labelled according to the row and column they occupy. Thus each element may be denoted M_{rc}: the first subscript labels the row, the second the column. In a square $n \times n$ matrix the number of rows is equal to the number of columns, and there are n^2 elements. Square matrices are very important in quantum mechanics (although oblong matrices also occur), and our comments will be confined to them.

BOX 13: Matrices

A square matrix **M** is the array of n^2 elements M_{rc}; M_{rc} is the element in row r, column c:

$$\mathbf{M} \equiv \begin{bmatrix} M_{11} & M_{12} & M_{13} & \dots & M_{1n} \\ M_{21} & M_{22} & M_{23} & \dots & M_{2n} \\ \cdot & \cdot & \cdot & & \cdot \\ \cdot & \cdot & \cdot & & \cdot \\ \cdot & \cdot & \cdot & & \cdot \\ M_{n1} & M_{n2} & M_{n3} & \dots & M_{nn} \end{bmatrix}$$

Addition $\mathbf{M} + \mathbf{N} = \mathbf{P}$, where $P_{rc} = M_{rc} + N_{rc}$.

Multiplication $\mathbf{MN} = \mathbf{P}$, where $P_{rc} = \sum_q M_{rq} N_{qc}$.

Examples: if $\mathbf{M} = \begin{bmatrix} a & b \\ d & c \end{bmatrix}$ and $\mathbf{N} = \begin{bmatrix} e & f \\ h & g \end{bmatrix}$,

$$\mathbf{M} + \mathbf{N} = \begin{bmatrix} a+e & b+f \\ d+h & c+g \end{bmatrix} \quad \mathbf{MN} = \begin{pmatrix} ae+bh & af+bg \\ de+ch & df+cg \end{pmatrix};$$

n.b. $\mathbf{NM} = \begin{bmatrix} ae+df & be+cf \\ ah+dg & bh+cg \end{bmatrix} \neq \mathbf{MN}$ in general.

Special matrices (and illustrations using the example of **M** defined above)

Diagonal matrix

$A_{rc} = 0$ unless $r = c$, for example, $\mathbf{A} = \begin{bmatrix} a & 0 \\ 0 & c \end{bmatrix}$.

Unit matrix

$$\mathbf{1} \begin{cases} \text{all elements on diagonal} = 1 \\ \text{all elements off diagonal} = 0 \end{cases}$$

for example, $\mathbf{1} = \begin{bmatrix} 1 & 0 \\ 0 & 1 \end{bmatrix}$. 1_{rc} is often denoted δ_{rc} and then called the *Kronecker delta*.

Inverse matrix $\mathbf{M}^{-1}$: $\mathbf{MM}^{-1} = \mathbf{M}^{-1}\mathbf{M} = 1$ (see below)

Transposed matrix

$\tilde{\mathbf{M}}$: $\tilde{M}_{rc} = M_{cr}$, for example, $\tilde{\mathbf{M}} = \begin{bmatrix} a & d \\ b & c \end{bmatrix}$.

Complex conjugate

$\mathbf{M}^*$: $(M^*)_{rc} = (M_{rc})^*$, for example, $\mathbf{M}^* = \begin{bmatrix} a^* & b^* \\ d^* & c^* \end{bmatrix}$.

Adjoint matrix $\mathbf{M}^\dagger$: $\mathbf{M}^\dagger = \tilde{\mathbf{M}}^*$; that is $(M^\dagger)_{rc} = M^*_{cr}$,

for example, $\mathbf{M}^\dagger = \begin{bmatrix} a^* & d^* \\ b^* & c^* \end{bmatrix}$.

Unitary matrix $\mathbf{M}^\dagger = \mathbf{M}^{-1}$.

Hermitian or self-adjoint matrix $\mathbf{M}^\dagger = \mathbf{M}$.

Determinant of matrix: $|\mathbf{M}|$ or det **M**;

for example, $|\mathbf{M}| = ac - bd$;

n.b. if $\mathbf{P} = \mathbf{MN}$, $|\mathbf{P}| = |\mathbf{M}|\,|\mathbf{N}|$.

To find the inverse.

1. Find $|\mathbf{M}|$; if $|\mathbf{M}| \neq 0$ the inverse may be found; if $|\mathbf{M}| = 0$ the matrix is *singular* and has no inverse.
2. Form $\tilde{\mathbf{M}}$.
3. Form $\mathbf{M}'$, where the element M'_{rc} is the cofactor (the signed minor) of $(\tilde{M})_{rc}$.
4. Form the matrix $\mathbf{M}'/|\mathbf{M}|$; this is the inverse $\mathbf{M}^{-1}$.

For example, 1. $|\mathbf{M}| = ac - bd$.

2. $\tilde{\mathbf{M}} = \begin{bmatrix} a & d \\ b & c \end{bmatrix}$.

3. $\mathbf{M}' = \begin{bmatrix} c & -b \\ -d & a \end{bmatrix}$.

4. $\mathbf{M}^{-1} = \left[\dfrac{1}{ac - bd}\right] \begin{bmatrix} c & -b \\ -d & a \end{bmatrix}$. (contd.)

Check: $\mathbf{M}\mathbf{M}^{-1} = \left(\frac{1}{ac-bd}\right)\begin{bmatrix} a & b \\ d & c \end{bmatrix}\begin{bmatrix} c & -b \\ -d & a \end{bmatrix}$

$= \left(\frac{1}{ac-bd}\right)\begin{bmatrix} ac-bd & -ab+ab \\ cd-cd & -bd+ac \end{bmatrix}$

$= \mathbf{1} = \mathbf{M}^{-1}\mathbf{M}.$

To solve a set of linear simultaneous equations

If the equations for n unknowns are

$$\begin{aligned} M_{11}x_1 + M_{12}x_2 + \ldots M_{1n}x_n &= c_1 \\ M_{21}x_1 + M_{22}x_2 + \ldots M_{2n}x_n &= c_2 \\ \vdots \quad\quad \vdots \quad\quad\quad \vdots \quad &\quad \vdots \\ M_{n1}x_1 + M_{n2}x_2 + \ldots M_{nn}x_n &= c_n \end{aligned}$$

write them as $\mathbf{Mx} = \mathbf{c}$ where $\mathbf{x}$ and $\mathbf{c}$ are the $n \times 1$ matrices

$$\mathbf{x} = \begin{bmatrix} x_1 \\ x_2 \\ \vdots \\ x_n \end{bmatrix} \qquad \mathbf{c} = \begin{bmatrix} c_1 \\ c_2 \\ \vdots \\ c_n \end{bmatrix}$$

Then as $\mathbf{M}^{-1}\mathbf{M} = \mathbf{1}$ and $\mathbf{1x} = \mathbf{x}$

$$\mathbf{x} = \mathbf{M}^{-1}\mathbf{c}.$$

Therefore, find $\mathbf{M}^{-1}$ by the preceding rule, and form $\mathbf{M}^{-1}\mathbf{c}$ to find the n unknowns $x_1, \ldots x_n$.

Matrices may be combined together by following certain simple rules. If two matrices have the same dimension (number of rows or columns) they may be added and multiplied together: the rules for each type of combination are given in Box 13. Some matrices have special properties: these are also given in Box 13. Note especially that the rule of matrix multiplication differs from that for the multiplication of ordinary numbers (or *c-numbers* as they still are occasionally called): for matrices it is not generally true that the product **MN** is equal to the product **NM**: matrix multiplication is *non-commutative* in general. The difference **MN**–**NM** is known as the °commutator of **M** and **N**: the fact that the commutator does not necessarily disappear leads to the most significant differences between matrices and ordinary numbers, and, at a different level, is a manifestation of the differences between classical and quantum mechanics: see °matrix mechanics.

The language of matrices has spread into ordinary Schrödinger quantum mechanics, for there one encounters integrals over wavefunctions having the form $\int d\tau \psi_r^* \hat{\Omega} \psi_c$, where $\hat{\Omega}$ is some °operator. A convenient notation for this integral is Ω_{rc}, and all the objects that may be formed from the wavefunctions of the system, where the labels r and c run over all its states, may be arranged into the matrix Ω (see, for example, °perturbation theory).

Questions. Many of the techniques of matrix algebra may be illustrated with two-dimensional square matrices. The following simple problems are based on the three matrices

$$\mathbf{A} = \begin{bmatrix} 1 & 2 \\ 3 & 4 \end{bmatrix} \quad \mathbf{B} = \begin{bmatrix} 5 & 6 \\ 7 & 8 \end{bmatrix} \quad \mathbf{C} = \begin{bmatrix} 3 & 2+4i \\ 5 & 6 \end{bmatrix}.$$

1. Identify the elements $A_{11}, A_{12}, B_{21}, C_{11}, C_{12}$.
2. Form **A**+**B**, **A**–**B**, **A**+**B**+**C**, **AB**, **BA**, **A**(**BC**), (**AB**)**C**, **AB**–**BA**, **AC**–**CA**.
3. Form **A**, $\mathbf{A}^+$, $\mathbf{A}^*$, $\mathbf{A}^{-1}$, det **A**, $\mathbf{C}^*$, $\mathbf{C}^+$.
4. Form $\mathbf{B}^{-1}\mathbf{AB}$, $\mathbf{B}^{-1}\mathbf{B}$, $\mathbf{BB}^{-1}$.
5. Using the rule for matrix multiplication and identifying the 2×1 matrix $\mathbf{x}$ as $\begin{bmatrix} x \\ y \end{bmatrix}$, express the set of simultaneous linear equations $x + 2y = 2$ and $3x + 4y = 5$ as a matrix equation. This equation will be of the form $\mathbf{M}\,\mathbf{x} = \mathbf{N}$; show that x and y may be found if $\mathbf{M}^{-1}$ may be found. Find it and them.

Further information. See *MQM* Chapter 6 for a summary and simple matrix manipulations. See Chapter 10 of Margenau and Murphy (1956) for a moderately complete account. Ayres (1962) is a good source of accounts of application of matrices and the way that they can be used to solve a large number of mathematical and physical problems. Matrices are the basis of the formulation of quantum mechanics known as °matrix mechanics and are indispensable for any thorough discussion of °group theory.

matrix mechanics. The formalism of quantum mechanics due to Heisenberg is based on the observation that the position of a particle along a coordinate q and its linear momentum along that coordinate, p, must obey the rule $qp-pq = i\hbar$, where $\hbar$ is Planck's constant h divided by 2π. If one assumes that the observables of position and momentum obey this rule, then one obtains quantitative agreement with all experimental observations. Yet the rule is quite remarkable in content because it goes counter to all we have been brought up to believe in classical physics.

In classical physics we may assign a number to the position (for example, a distance of 4 m from some origin) and a number to the momentum (for example, 2.5 kg m s^{-1}). The product of the numbers for the values of these observables, 10 J s, is the same whether we calculate $p \times q$ or $q \times p$, and so the difference $qp-pq$ is zero. Heisenberg's contribution was to assert that the difference is not zero, but is equal to the imaginary and very small number $i\hbar$. It follows that q and p cannot be regarded as conventional numbers. Born pointed out to Heisenberg that the non-vanishing of the difference $qp-pq$ would hold if the observables q and p were regarded as °matrices, for in general the product of two matrices depends on their order. This is the basis of matrix mechanics: instead of treating observables as ordinary numbers (so-called *c-numbers*, the 'c' denoting something classical) they should be regarded as matrices (so-called *q-numbers,* 'q' denoting something quantal) which satisfy the rule of matrix multiplication such that $qp-pq = i\hbar$. When mechanical calculations are carried through on this basis one finds excellent agreement with experiment. Note that the error introduced by using the wrong rule $qp-pq = 0$, and therefore of treating q and p like ordinary numbers, is only of the order of $\hbar$; therefore classical calculations are good enough when inaccuracies of the order of Planck's constant can be tolerated.

Heisenberg's matrix mechanics preceeded °Schrödinger's wave mechanics by an insignificantly short time, and very quickly they were seen to be equivalent mathematical theories by Schrödinger himself. Today the languages of each formulation are used as convenient. The Heisenberg formulation, dealing as it does with the matrices, or what is equivalent, the °operators that represent physical observables, is often more convenient for formal manipulations, and the Schrödinger formalism (which is more easily visualizable in terms of its °wavefunction description of the state of a system) is often used for the actual calculation of the energy levels and states of complicated systems.

There is a well-defined meaning to the terms *Heisenberg picture* and *Schrödinger picture* (or *representations* as they are often too loosely called) of quantum mechanics. The difference between the pictures is in where the time-dependence of the description of a system is taken to lie. In the Heisenberg picture the time-dependence is borne by the operators (or matrices): the state remains constant but the operators that extract the physical information change with time. Therefore we observers are presented with a changing view of the system, and conclude that it is evolving. In the Schrödinger picture the operator for the desired information remains unchanging in time, but the wavefunction squirms around beneath it, and once again we are presented with a view of the system as it evolves in time. The difference between the pictures is simply one of mathematical formulation and is not of physical significance. There is an intermediate picture standing between the Heisenberg and Schrödinger viewpoints: this is the *interaction picture*, or *Dirac picture*. In this picture the motion is divided between the state function and the operator: the simple motion (often a harmonically varying motion) is carried by the operator, and the wavefunction carries the extra, complicated, but often slow, motion. This picture is very useful in the formulation of time-dependent °perturbation theory.

Further information. An account of quantum mechanics entirely in terms of matrix mechanics has been provided in a short book by Green (1965). The original papers are Heisenberg (1925), Born and Jordan (1925), and Born, Hensenberg, and Jordan (1926), and English translations have been published by van der Waerden (1967). Born's involvement is nicely illustrated in the collection of correspondence between him and Einstein (Born 1970). For more mathematics see Dirac (1958), Kemble (1958), Kramers (1964), and von Neumann (1955). A fourth picture, to complete those of Schrödinger, Heisenberg, and Dirac, has been described by Marcus (1970). The mathematics of the first three of these pictures are well and simply described in §3.2 of Ziman (1969), §5.4 of Slichter (1963), and Roman (1965).

molecular orbitals. The molecular orbital (MO) method gives a popular theoretical description of the chemical °bond, and is an extension of the idea of °atomic orbital to a collection of nuclei. An electron in a molecule may be found in the vicinity of all the nuclei, and therefore we can regard it as

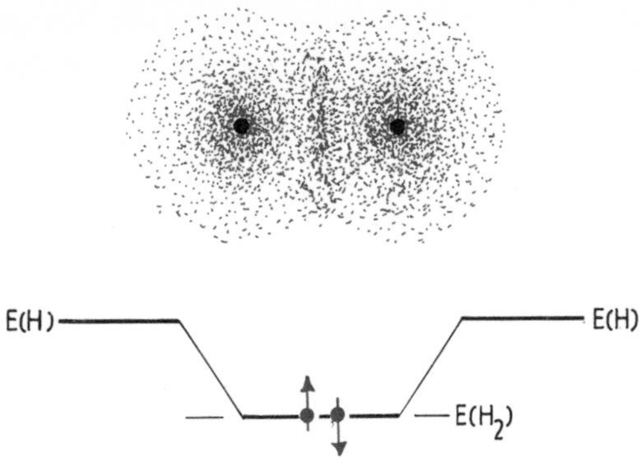

FIG. M6. The molecular orbital responsible for bonding in H_2.

being distributed with varying density over the nuclear framework. The °wavefunction of an electron in a molecule contains information about its distribution, for according to the Born interpretation the square of the wavefunction at any point is proportional to the probability of finding the electron there. Therefore the wavefunction for the electron in the molecule may be regarded as a function spreading throughout the nuclear framework, and its square at any point is proportional to the electron density. This wavefunction is the *molecular orbital*.

The distribution of the molecular orbital should account for the nature of the bond: we should expect a high amplitude of the orbital, and therefore a high density of the electron, to appear where our understanding of the chemical °bond shows such density to be desirable, namely between the nuclei the electron is attempting to stick together. Think about diatomic compounds. In a *homonuclear bond* (a covalent bond between two identical atoms) we should expect the orbital to spread equally over the two nuclei; and as the bond becomes increasingly polar (in a *heteronuclear bond* between different atoms) we should expect the molecular orbital to have increasingly greater amplitude on one of the nuclei. In the limit of a pure *ionic bond* the molecular orbital is wholly localized on one nucleus.

It is common practice to treat molecular orbitals in the same way as atomic orbitals are used to discuss the structure of atoms: the °*aufbau* process is applied to a set of molecular orbitals in order to build up the molecular electronic structure. As an initial example of this basic idea consider the hydrogen molecule. The molecular orbital responsible for the bonding is a symmetrical orbital extending over the two nuclei and having a considerable density in the region between the nuclei (Fig. M6). Into this orbital we insert one electron, and then follow it with a second; according to the °Pauli principle the latter must enter with its spin opposed to the first (Fig. M6), and no others can be accommodated. Therefore we see that in a very natural way the molecular-orbital theory accounts for the importance of spin °pairing in the formation of a chemical bond. This idea of the *aufbau* principle will be enlarged on when we have discussed the common approach to the formation and calculation of molecular orbitals.

In principle, it is possible to imagine an extension to the hydrogen molecule of the calculation of the solution of the °Schrödinger equation for the °hydrogen atom, and even the direct calculation of molecular orbitals for a polynuclear molecule. This is horribly difficult, and about the only place where it has been done is in the case of the hydrogen molecule-ion (H_2^+), but even in that apparently simple one-electron case the calculation is not at all easy. Since chemists tend to be interested in molecules more complicated than H_2^+ a scheme of approximation of the true molecular orbitals has been devised: this involves first the °Born-Oppenheimer approximation (of freezing the nuclei into chosen geometrical arrangements), and then the application of the method of °linear combination of atomic orbitals (LCAO). More details will be found under those entries; for the moment we shall simply discuss the application of the LCAO approach to the case of the hydrogen molecule and one or two other simple molecules.

In the LCAO approximation it is supposed that the true, complicated molecular orbital can be expressed as a sum of the atomic orbitals on the constituent atoms of the molecule. This provides a remarkably good approximation because it reproduces a number of the essential features of the exact solution. In the case of H_2 the atomic orbitals of principal importance are the 1s-orbitals on each nucleus. The molecular orbital is then expressed as the sum $\psi_{1s_a} + \psi_{1s_b}$. This obviously treats the nuclei equally, and so the electron is spread among them equally. It also reproduces the significant accumulation of charge in the internuclear region. This arises from the wave nature of the two atomic orbitals: one 1s-orbital

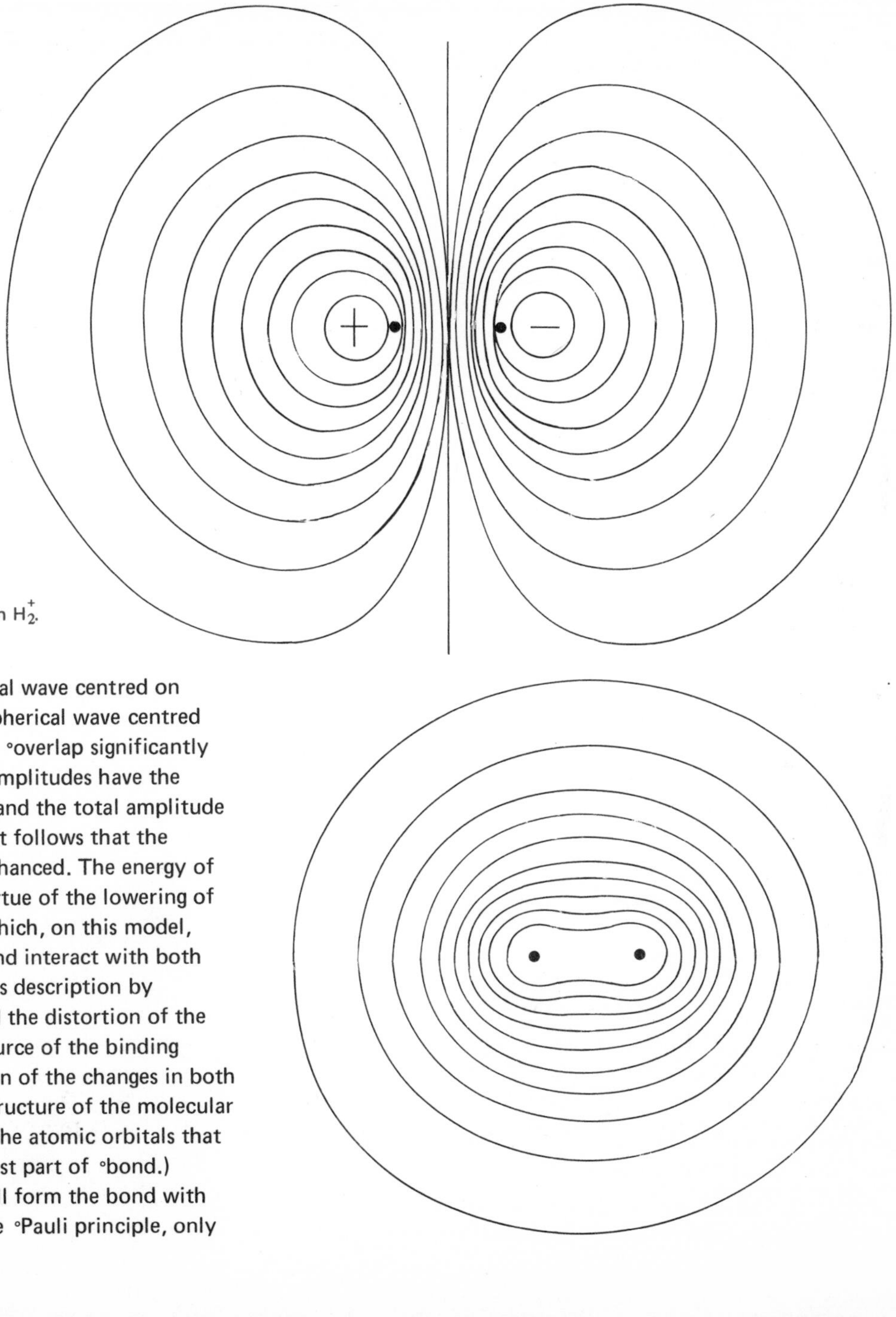

FIG. M7. Bonding and antibonding orbitals in H_2^+.

may be considered as a standing spherical wave centred on nucleus a, and the other as a standing spherical wave centred on nucleus b, (Fig. M7). The two waves °overlap significantly in the internuclear region, and if their amplitudes have the same sign they interfere constructively and the total amplitude in the internuclear region is enhanced. It follows that the electron density in this region is also enhanced. The energy of the molecule therefore is lowered by virtue of the lowering of the potential energy of the electrons, which, on this model, accumulate in the internuclear region and interact with both nuclei. (I do not want to complicate this description by invoking the role of °kinetic energy and the distortion of the atomic orbitals themselves. The true source of the binding energy must be sought in a consideration of the changes in both potential and kinetic energy, and the structure of the molecular orbitals must reflect the distortions of the atomic orbitals that occur when a bond is formed; see the last part of °bond.) Finally, it is clear that two electrons will form the bond with maximum stability for, according to the °Pauli principle, only two electrons may occupy the bonding orbital, and then they must have opposed spins.

The method of linear combinations for the construction of a molecular orbital leads both to bonding and to °antibonding orbitals: the latter are formed when the atomic orbitals overlap with opposite phase (sign of their amplitude), so that destructive interference occurs and electrons are eliminated from the bonding region between the nuclei (Fig. M7); electrons that occupy these orbitals tend to drive the bond asunder. A third electron added to H_2 would have to enter the antibonding orbital, and so the bond would be weakened.

These ideas can be extended very easily to more complex molecules, and a diatomic molecule of considerable interest and importance, and to which it is instructive to apply the method, is oxygen O_2. Our kit of parts consists of two nuclei, sixteen electrons, and, since this is a beginners' kit, one 1s-orbital, one 2s-orbital, and three 2p-orbitals on each nucleus. The structure may be deduced as follows:

1. The tightest-bound orbitals are the 1s-orbitals; if the two nuclei are pinned down at the known interatomic distance of O_2, these two orbitals overlap to a negligible extent; therefore the bonding orbital they give rise to is exceedingly weakly bonding, and the antibonding orbital is weakly antibonding. This situation is illustrated in Fig. M8.

2. The 2s-orbitals are the next tightest bound, but are much larger and overlap significantly. Like the orbitals in H_2 they form a bonding and an antibonding molecular orbital at roughly the energies marked in Fig. M8.

3. Next we encounter the 2p-orbitals, and here two quite distinct possibilities arise: the orbitals may overlap head on, or broadside on.

(a) In the former case the enhanced electron density is accumulated in the internuclear region, and we can expect a strong bond when the orbitals are in phase and a strong antibond when they are out of phase. We note that the electron distribution in such an orbital is cylindrically symmetrical about the internuclear axis (Fig. M8), and so it is termed a σ-orbital, or a σ-bond (this takes its name by analogy with the spherically symmetrical s-orbital of atoms).

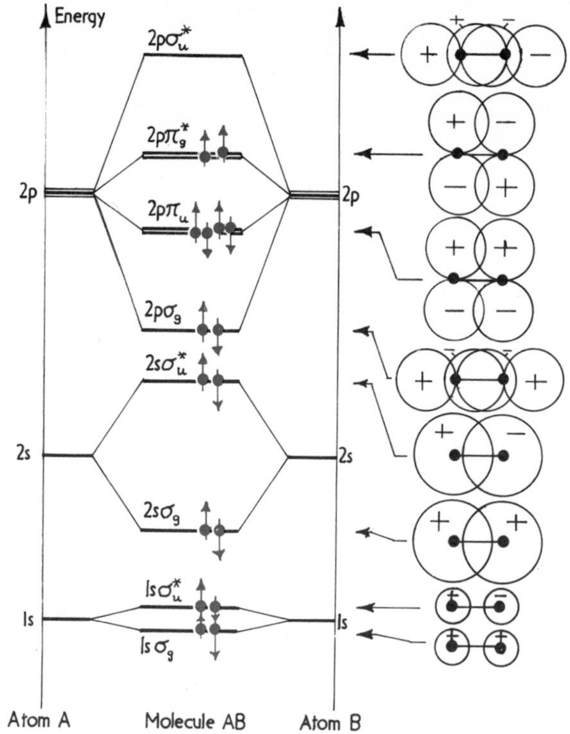

FIG. M8. Schematic energy levels and orbitals of homonuclear diatomic molecules of the first row elements; occupation as for O_2.

(b) The other possibility is for the broadside overlap of two p-orbitals. The overlap is not particularly extensive, and it is greatest in regions outside the internuclear axis; nevertheless, electrons accumulated in these regions can exert attractive forces on the nuclei and a moderately strong bond can result (and a moderately effective antibond if the overlap is destructive). This distribution is a π-orbital, or π-bond (by analogy with p-orbital in atoms).

The complete range of orbitals for molecular oxygen constructed in this way is shown in Fig. M8. Into these receptacles we now inject our 16 electrons, and play the game according to the rules of °*aufbau*. The first tumbles down and down in energy until it enters $1s\sigma$. The next joins it with opposed spin, the next enters $1s\sigma^*$, and so it goes on, and we encounter no ambiguity until we have inserted 14 electrons. (A slight hesitation might be noticed at the filling of $2p\pi$, which takes 4 electrons; but we should remember that $2p\pi$ is really two molecular orbitals, one formed from $2p_x$ overlap and the other from $2p_y$ overlap. Electron 15 we insert into the antibonding $2p\pi^*$-orbital. Electron 16 may enter the same orbital with opposed spin, or it may enter the other $2p\pi^*$-orbital of the pair with either the same or the opposite spin (Pauli allows either). What determines the outcome? The first °Hund rule informs us that in this situation the lower-energy arrangement is that with parallel spins in different orbitals; therefore we conclude that the °configuration of O_2 is $1s\sigma^2\ 1s\sigma^{*2}\ 2s\sigma^2\ 2s\sigma^{*2}\ 2p\sigma^2\ 2p\pi^4\ 2p_x\pi^*\ 2p_y\pi^*$. Is there a way of testing whether this configuration is plausible? A powerful way is by °electronic spectroscopy, but another more immediate way is to note that the presence of the two unpaired spins leads us to predict that O_2 is paramagnetic: see °magnetic properties. It was an early triumph for molecular-orbital theory that O_2 is in fact paramagnetic.

How does this structure fit in with a more elementary view that O_2 is a molecule with a *double bond*, O=O? Looking at Fig. M8 we can imagine that the bonding due to the 1s-electrons is cancelled by the antibonding nature of the electrons in $1s\sigma^*$; likewise the occupied $2s\sigma$ and $2s\sigma^*$ cancel in effect; $2p\sigma$ is occupied but $2p\sigma^*$ empty, and so we notch up 1 on our bonding tally; $2p_x\pi$ and $2p_y\pi$ are fully occupied, but $2p_x\pi^*$ and $2p_y\pi^*$ are both half-occupied, and so we can cut another notch. In total the net bonding can be ascribed to two net bonds, and this we can signify by O=O, as in elementary chemistry. It should stimulate profound respect for the early chemists each time their views on molecular structure—views formed more by introspection than by calculation—are confirmed by modern quantitative theory. Note too that we also see why a 'double bond' is less strong than two 'single bonds'. A single bond is generally a full σ-orbital plus a full π-orbital, and we have seen that a π-orbital does not have its extra accumulation in the prime bonding region. Earlier chemists ascribed this to 'strain': how right they were. A triple bond, which is also depicted in Fig. M9, is formed from one σ- and two π-orbitals. The stability of double bonds to twisting (torsion) can also be understood in MO terms: rotating a CH_2 group in ethene relative to the other reduces the overlap between the $2p\pi$-orbitals, the π-bond weakens, and the energy of the molecule rises (Fig. M10).

What orbitals contribute best to the formation of molecular orbitals? First, they must have the right symmetry: it is no good attempting to form a molecular orbital from the sideways overlap of an s-orbital and a p-orbital, for there is no net °overlap. (Head-on overlap of s and p can, of course, occur.) That criterion satisfied we then require the orbitals to have about the same energy (the *energy-matching criterion*) and to be roughly the same size (to have significant net overlap). These criteria are explored in the Questions. The extent of overlap can be increased by permitting °hybridization of the available atomic orbitals, and the study of hydridization and the formation of molecular orbitals is the basis of the

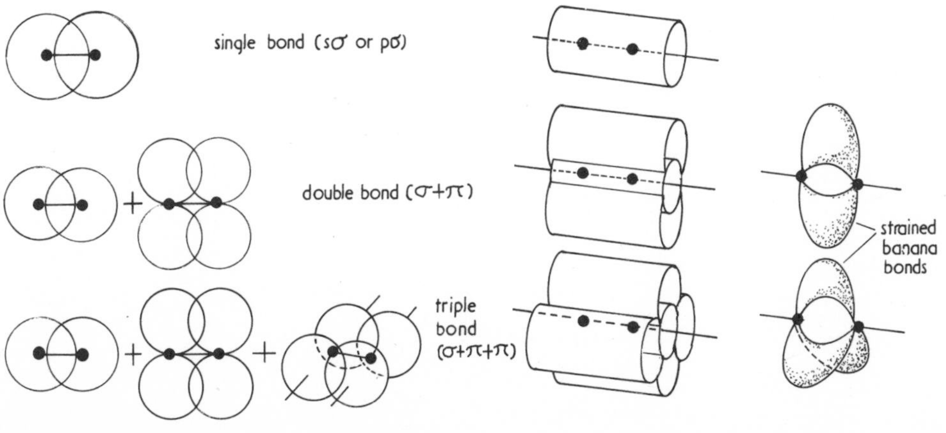

FIG. M9. The formation, and two representations of their appearance, of single, double, and triple bonds. The bananas (which resemble the classical picture of strained bonds) are formed by taking appropriate sums of the σ, π representations of the bonds.

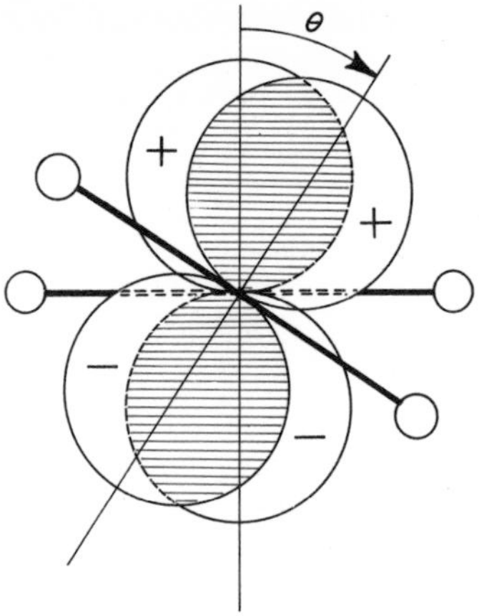

FIG. M10. Overlap and the torsional rigidity of a double bond.

molecular-orbital approach to the discussion of molecular shape.

All that has gone before suggests that molecular-orbital theory is a modern triumph. Is it? In a word, yes. One can level a number of criticisms at it, but at the expense of losing the conceptual simplicity of the theory these can all be overcome. At a basic level the molecular-orbital method underestimates the tendency of electrons to stay apart: the simple theory of H_2, for example, ascribes too much importance to structures like H^+H^-. This can be repaired by doing some °configuration interaction. The method is also poor at large distances: the separation of the hydrogen atoms in H_2 yields H^+ and H^- in the products instead of just 2H; but this too can be overcome by permitting configuration interaction. At a different level lies the criticism that the molecular-orbital method does not reflect the chemist's view that different regions of the molecule can be considered for many chemical purposes as separate, isolated entities. The proponent of molecular-orbital theory can retort quickly that it is possible to take the molecular-orbitals we have discussed, and which spread throughout the nuclear framework, and manipulate them into a set of °*localized orbitals* which can be ascribed to different regions of the molecule. Therefore the criticism can be circumvented by the application of a mathematical transformation.

The molecular-orbital theory can be adapted to quantitative calculation according to the method of °self-consistent fields; an enormous amount of effort has been put into the calculation of accurate molecular wavefunctions and energies by an extension of the methods used for atoms, and for more information see °Hückel method and semi-empirical methods. See also °*ab initio*.

Questions. 1. What is meant by the term 'molecular orbital', and what information does such an orbital contain? What features should we expect a molecular orbital to possess: where is its maximum amplitude expected, and what can we say about its symmetry? Describe the changes that occur in the distribution of a molecular orbital as the bond it describes changes from pure covalent to pure ionic. What is the bonding energy due to over this range? What commonly used approximation is resorted to in order to set up a molecular orbital? What are the deficiencies of this method? Discuss the formation of the hydrogen molecule in terms of molecular-orbital theory. Account for the instability of the molecule He_2 on this basis. Set up a molecular-orbital scheme like that for O_2 shown in Fig. M8 for all the diatomic molecules of the first row of the periodic table. Put the following molecules in order of increasing stability by referring to the diagrams you have just deduced: C_2^+, C_2, C_2^-; N_2^+, N_2, N_2^-; O_2^+, O_2, O_2^-; F_2^+, F_2, F_2^-; Ne_2^+, Ne_2, Ne_2^-. What is the major defect of a simple molecular-orbital treatment? How may it be overcome?
2. Take the molecular orbital $1s_a + 1s_b$ and show that when it is occupied by an electron the distribution can be interpreted in terms of a large proportion of H^+H^- in the wavefunction (think about the square of the function). Now consider two electrons in $1s_a + 1s_b$ and two in $1s_a - 1s_b$, as in the structure of He_2: what is the electron distribution in this molecule? Take the orbital $1s_a + 1s_b$ and insert one electron. Write the °hamiltonian for the molecule, and deduce an expression for the energy of the molecule in terms of integrals over the wavefunctions. Some of these integrals can be identified with the integrals that occur in the description of the hydrogen atom, therefore the energy of the molecule can be expressed as the energy of the atom plus a part that can be ascribed to the formation of the bond. Analyse the expression in that way. Now insert two electrons into the orbital and so consider H_2. Repeat the exercise, using the appropriate hamiltonian, and attempt to analyse your expression. What you have probably forgotten to do is to allow for the °antisymmetrization of the

electrons: you should write the wavefunction as a °Slater determinant, and you will discover an extra enjoyable contribution due to °exchange. Analyse this new result.
3. Consider an orbital ϕ_a on atom a and ϕ_b on atom b, with energies E_a and E_b respectively. Allow them to overlap and interact, and make the approximation that the extent of interaction is proportional to the amount they overlap. Show by solving the °secular determinant that, of the two linear combinations that may be formed, one moves down in energy, and the other moves up; that the energy change is greater when the energies E_a and E_b are similar and when the overlap is greatest; that the bonding orbital is more localized on the atom with lower-energy atomic orbitals. These calculations illustrate the criteria mentioned in the text, and also show how the polarity of a bond reflects the relative energies of the contributing orbitals.

Further information. See *MQM* Chapter 10 for a discussion of the molecular-orbital method. A simple account of molecular-orbital theory which fills in the details of the present discussion and gives many applications to chemically important molecules is given by Coulson in *The shape and structure of molecules* (OCS 9) and by Coulson (1961). See also Murrell, Kettle, and Tedder (1965), Streitweiser (1961), Salem (1966), Pilar (1968), Slater (1963), and Doggett (1972). Many drawings of molecular orbitals for numerous molecules will be found in Jorgensen and Salem (1973). Calculations of molecular orbitals will be found referred to in °self-consistent field, °*ab initio*, and °Hückel method. Accounts of °hybridization, °equivalent orbitals, °antibonding, and °bond extend this discussion. An alternative account of molecular structure is provided by the °valence-bond theory, which should be referred to, and the two methods are compared under °molecular-orbital and valence bond: a synopsis.

molecular-orbital and valence-bond: a synopsis. The details of these techniques are given under their separate headings. In this synopsis an attempt is made to emphasize their similarities and differences.

1. Both molecular-orbital (MO) and valence-bond (VB) theories seek to describe the structure of molecules, their shape and their energy, and the valence of the atoms that compose them.

2. Both theories, at least in their simplest interpretation, achieve their object by leading to an accumulation of electron density in regions where it is most effective in interacting with the nuclei. This region is in the vicinity of, or actually in, the internuclear region. This common interpretation neglects the contribution to the total energy of the °kinetic energy: in both the MO theory and the VB theory significant contributions to both the potential and the kinetic energies may be ascribed to the distortion of the orbitals of the atoms constituting the molecule. This additional, but important contribution is often neglected in an elementary analysis of the theories: we neglect it here, but refer to sources in Further information.

3. Both theories achieve the object of accumulating electron density in the internuclear region by recognizing that electrons cannot be localized on a single atom when that is part of a molecule. The MO theory says that if an electron can be on atom a with wavefunction $\psi_a(\mathbf{r}_1)$, which we abreviate to $a(1)$, and can also be on atom b with wavefunction $b(1)$, then, according to the °superposition principle, its actual distribution must be determined from the wavefunction $a(1) \pm b(1)$. The case of two electrons is obtained by dropping two electrons into this orbital to form $[a(1) \pm b(1)]\ [a(2) \pm b(2)]$. The VB theory approaches the problem in a different way, and says that if atoms a and b were well separated the state of the electrons (one on each atom) would be well described by the wavefunction $a(1)\,b(2)$, because that is the quantum-mechanical description of such a situation; it then pretends that the only difference in the function when the two atoms are at a bonding separation is that the electron originally on atom a may be on atom b, and vice versa. According to the °superposition principle this state of the two electrons is described by the function $a(1)\,b(2) \pm b(1)\,a(2)$. Analysis of the expression for the energy in both the MO and VB cases leads to the conclusion that the + sign in the composite functions gives the lower energy. The implication of this is that the electrons that form the bonds must enter these wavefunctions with paired spins (this is required by the °Pauli principle); therefore both the MO and VB theories account for the importance in chemical bonding of the electron pair.

4. Although both methods emphasize the role of the electron pair, in practice they do so in different ways. The MO theory starts by ignoring the way that the electrons enter the molecule and calculates the molecular orbitals that may be formed from the available atomic orbitals. At the end of that work it inserts the electrons in accord with the °*aufbau* principle and, perforce, the °Pauli principle. The VB method concentrates on electron pairs from the outset, and calculates the energy of various ('canonical') structures that have all the electrons in the molecule paired in all possible ways. Then having set up all these 'perfect pairing' structures it allows them to interact (that is, the true wavefunction is expressed as a °superposition of them), and then calculates the energy of the best combination. This process introduces the concept of °resonance.

5. Electrons are allowed to spread over the whole molecule automatically in the MO method, but these delocalized orbitals may be transformed into a collection of °localized orbitals. In VB theory attention is concentrated on individual bonds right from the beginning, and this feature is largely preserved in the final superimposed wavefunction. Complete delocalization, of the sort found in °benzene, has as its counterpart strong °resonance, as between equivalent Kekulé structures.

6. Although both methods give a similar distribution of electrons, there are notable differences. Expansion of the two-electron MO given in Note 2 leads to $a(1)\,a(2) + b(1)\,b(2) \pm a(1)\,b(2) \pm b(1)\,a(2)$. This differs from the VB function in the occurrence of the first two terms. These can be interpreted as the contribution to the total state of the situation in which both electrons are on the same atom, either on a or on b. As these extra terms appear with the same weight as the other terms, we conclude that the MO theory does not take into account the effect of *electron correlation*, the tendency of electrons to keep apart. There must be some probability of finding both electrons simultaneously on a or on b, and so we should expect the true function to be of the form $a(1)\,b(2) + b(1)\,a(2) + \lambda a(1)\,a(2) + \mu b(1)\,b(2)$ with $\lambda, \mu < 1$. This modification can be introduced by the method of °configuration interaction. The VB theory moves to the opposite extreme and forbids both electrons to be on a or b simultaneously; therefore it overestimates the role of electron correlation. It can be improved by adding ionic terms to the original covalent wavefunction (ionic-covalent °resonance).

7. The MO method is applied quantitatively by feeding the electrons into approximate wavefunctions, and then permitting the orbitals to distort in response to the electron-electron repulsions. This is taken care of by doing a °self-consistent field (SCF) calculation. The final answer is improved by permitting configuration interaction. MO theory has received far more attention than VB theory at this quantitative level because SCF methods are easily programmed for electronic computers; the difficulty of dealing with VB calculations has been the very large number of canonical and ionic structures that must be taken into account.

Further information. See MQM Chapter 9 for more details of the methods and their comparison. See especially Coulson's *The shape and structure of molecules* (OCS 9), which is mostly MO, Pauling (1960), which is mostly VB, and Coulson (1961) which compares them. A very careful scrutiny of the nature of the chemical bond has been given by Ruedenberg (1962) and Feinberg, Ruedenberg, and Mehler (1970). See Murrell, Kettle, and Tedder (1965) for another comparison of the methods. See the individual entries on °molecular orbitals and °valence bond for further information on each.

momentum. In classical mechanics the momentum plays a fundamental role, and the same is true in quantum mechanics. In accord with the rules of constructing quantum mechanics, the momentum, an observable, must be interpreted as an °operator. Once the form of this operator is known, other observables that depend on the momentum may also be expressed as operators, and so a complete scheme may be formed. The choice of the operator for linear momentum is of crucial importance in quantum theory, and one common and familiar choice for the component of linear momentum along the q-axis is the differential operator $(\hbar/i)\,(\partial/\partial q)$. It follows from this that the linear momentum of a system is related to the gradient of the °wavefunction that describes its state: steep gradients correspond to high momenta. This aspect of the wavefunction is compatible with the °de Broglie relation, which states that the wavelength of a wavefunction diminishes as the momentum of the particle increases ($p = h/\lambda$). When the system is described by a standing wave the average gradient is zero, and in such states it follows that the linear momentum is zero. For example, a °particle trapped in a one-dimensional square well is described by a standing wave, and its mean momentum is zero. (Classically that would be interpreted as multiple reflections from the walls of the container reversing the momentum so often that its mean vanished.)

If a particle's linear momentum along an axis is sharply defined, its position on the axis is indeterminate: this is an important consequence of the °uncertainty principle and is an aspect of the wave-particle °duality of matter. It can be understood by recognizing that a particle with definite momentum is described by a monochromatic wave of indefinite extent, and in such a wave, according to the Born interpretation (see °wavefunction), the position of the particle occurs with equal probability throughout space. Conversely, the formation of a °wave packet, which localizes the position of the particle, does so at the expense of superimposing so many waves of different wavelength that the momentum is broadly dispersed.

Questions. 1. What aspect of the wavefunction determines the momentum of a state? How may the de Broglie relation be justified in terms of this interpretation? Under what circumstances is the momentum of a particle zero? What is the momentum of a particle trapped in the ground state of a one-dimensional square well? Why may the °kinetic energy be non-zero even though the linear momentum is zero? In what sense are the linear momentum and the position of a particle °complementary?
2. By average value of the gradient is meant the °expectation value. Evaluate the expectation value of the linear momentum for particles described by running waves of the form exp ikx and exp($-ikx$). (Note that complex-conjugate wavefunctions correspond to opposite momenta.) Calculate the expectation value for the linear momentum of a particle in a one-dimensional square-well potential (see °particle in a square well for the wavefunction). Prove from the hermiticity of the linear momentum operator that the expectation value of the momentum for a state described by a real wavefunction is necessarily zero.

Further information. See MQM Chapters 3 and 4 for a detailed discussion of momentum in quantum mechanics. The fundamental role of linear momentum in quantum theory is described in Bohm (1951), Messiah (1961), Schiff (1968), Landau and Lifshitz (1958a), Dirac (1958), von Neumann (1955), and Jauch (1968).

multiplicity. The multiplicity of a °term is the number of °levels it possesses; that is, it is the number of different values of the °quantum number °J that may be ascribed to the term. When the values of the quantum numbers L and S of the term are such that $L \geqslant S$ the multiplicity is equal to $2S + 1$. This is because that number of values of the total angular momentum J may be formed by coupling the spin and orbital °angular momenta together (J may take the values $L+S, L+S-1, \ldots, |L-S|$). When $L < S$ the number of J values that may be formed is $2L + 1$, and so under these circumstances the multiplicity is equal to $2L + 1$.

The numerical value of $2S + 1$ is normally denoted by an upper left superscript on the term symbol, but it is important to note that this gives the true multiplicity of the level only when $L \geqslant S$. As an example a ^{2}D term ('doublet D') has two levels distinguished by $J = \frac{3}{2}$ and $J = \frac{5}{2}$ and written $^2D_{3/2}$ and $^2D_{5/2}$; likewise a ^{3}P term (a triplet P term) has a multiplicity of three, and its levels are distinguished as $^3P_2$, $^3P_1$, $^3P_0$. The ^{2}S term, with $L = 0$ and $S = \frac{1}{2}$ is referred to as a doublet term even though it has only one level ($J = \frac{1}{2}$). Beware of sloppy usage, and always think about the relative size of S and L.

Questions. What is meant by the multiplicity of a term? How can it be calculated from a knowledge of the values of L and S? What is the significance of the left superscript on a term symbol? Under what circumstances does the superscript indicate the multiplicity? How many levels do the following terms possess (that is, what is their multiplicity):

^2P, ^3P, ^4P, ^1S, ^5S, ^3D? In each case indicate the *J* labels of the levels.

Further information. The multiplicity of a term appears spectroscopically as the °fine structure. For the structural differences of singlet and triplet terms see the entry °singlet and triplet states. For general aspects see °angular momentum. For a further discussion see *MQM* Chapter 8 and books on atomic and molecular spectroscopy: Whiffen (1972), King (1964), Herzberg (1944), Kuhn (1962), White (1934), Candler (1964), and Condon and Shortley (1963). Stevenson (1965) gives a moderately simple and complete theoretical account of the multiplet structure of atoms and molecules. See Calvert and Pitts (1966) and Wayne (1970) for an account of the way that the multiplicity of a species determines its chemical behaviour.

N

node. A node is the place where a °wavefunction has zero amplitude (that is, no displacement). The node may be a point, a line, or a surface. For the °particle in a one-dimensional square well the wavefunction has a node at the walls and at a number of regularly spaced points within the box, and the higher the energy (or higher the harmonic of the fundamental wave) the more nodes are present. A 1s-orbital in °hydrogen has no nodes, apart from a rather special one at infinity (see °atomic orbital). A 2s-orbital has one node which should be visualized as a spherical surface surrounding the nucleus; as the position of this node depends only on the radius and is spherically symmetrical it is called a *radial node.* A 2p-orbital has no radial node (apart from the one at infinity), but it is divided into two lobes by an *angular node,* which is a plane running through the nucleus. A more complicated nodal structure occurs in the other °atomic orbitals, but an s-orbital always has no angular nodes, a p-orbital always has one, and a d-orbital always has two.

The significance of the nodal structure of a wavefunction stems from its connexion with the °momentum or the °kinetic energy of the system: the more nodes in a given region the greater the kinetic energy. The reason for this is as follows. A node occurs where a wavefunction changes sign, and the number of sign changes in a region increases as the wavelength shortens. Therefore as a shorter wavelength implies, through the °de Broglie relation, a greater momentum, it follows that the more nodes present the greater the momentum and the kinetic energy. The connexion is illustrated by the example already mentioned of a °particle in a square well.

In the case of angular nodes the relevant momentum is the °orbital angular momentum; so we can believe that as the number of angular nodes increases so too does the angular momentum. This is confirmed by calculation, for the number of angular nodes is equal to the numerical value of the °angular momentum quantum number ℓ, and the magnitude of the angular momentum is proportional to $\surd[\ell(\ell+1)]$. For this reason the angular momentum of a d-electron (2 angular nodes) exceeds that of a p-electron (1 angular node).

Questions. What is a node? What shape can it take? Can there be a nodal point (rather than a nodal line) for a particle in a two-dimensional well? How are the nodes in an atomic system classified? How many nodes are there in the wavefunction of atomic hydrogen corresponding to the principal quantum number n? Does the number of nodes depend on n and ℓ? Does the value of m_ℓ affect your conclusions? Why is there a connexion between the number of angular nodes and the orbital angular momentum of a state? Discuss the nodal structure and the physical significance of the nodal structure of the orbitals in diatomic molecules.

Further information. See *MQM* Chapter 3 for a variety of different systems showing nodes of various kinds. The nodes of functions, being places where the functions drop to zero, may be ascertained by locating the zeros of the function; the zeros of many mathematical functions are listed in Abramowitz and Stegun (1965). A general theorem on nodes states that the lowest energy level is nodeless: see §18 of Landau and Lifshitz (1958a). This theorem fails when many particles are present because Fermi holes occur in the wavefunction by virtue of °spin correlation.

non-crossing rule. Consider two states of an atom or molecule, and let their energy depend on some parameter P (for example, a bond length). As this parameter is varied the energies change, and it is conceivable that a variation of P takes the energy of the upper energy state below that of the lower; that is, the energy curves cross. The non-crossing rule asserts that this crossing cannot occur if the states have the same symmetry. It follows that a variation of P leads to the energy variation illustrated in Fig. N1.

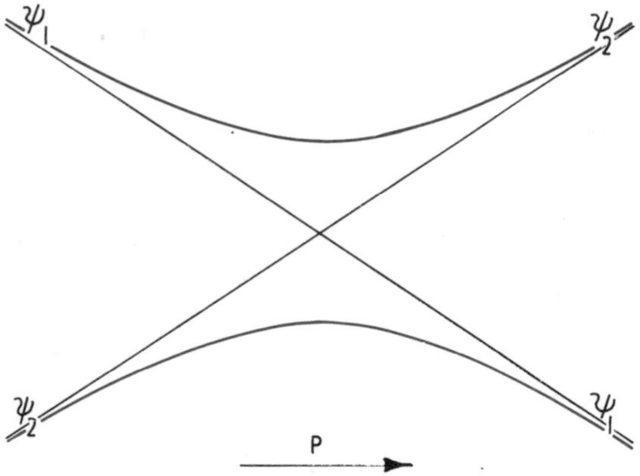

FIG. N1. The non-crossing rule. Black lines correspond to states of different symmetry (which may cross) and colour lines to states of the same symmetry (which may not).

The rule is of considerable importance in the construction of correlation diagrams (see °united atom), because its application enables the energy of states of molecules and atoms to be followed as bonds are formed.

Note that the non-crossing rule is an example of an °adiabatic process: if a system starts in ψ_2 (Fig. N1) and the parameter is varied slowly, it will be in state ψ_1 of the new system (corresponding to a different value of the parameter P on the right of the diagram). If the motion from left to right is done very rapidly, the system may be in ψ_2 at the final value of P: this corresponds to an excited state of the new system. Therefore we see that the non-crossing rule is applicable to time-dependent systems only if their motions are slow.

Further information. A diagram like Fig. N1 may be deduced from perturbation theory by solving the Schrödinger equation for a two-state system. This is done in Chapter 7 of *MQM*. Such an analysis formed the basis of Teller's deduction of the rule (Teller 1937). A more abstract and earlier deduction is that of von Neumann and Wigner (1929). Both approaches have been strongly criticized, and a more rigorous proof has been given by Naqvi and Byers Brown (1972), and extended to polyatomics by Naqvi (1972). For simpler and more conventional accounts, see Coulson (1961) and Herzberg (1950).

normal modes. The number of modes of vibration of a molecule containing N atoms is $3N-6$ in general, but $3N-5$ if the molecule is linear. The source of these numbers is the fact that to specify the position of an atom requires three coordinates, and so the specification of the position of all the N atoms in a molecule requires $3N$ coordinates. Changing any of the $3N$ coordinates corresponds to changing the molecule's shape (bending or stretching its bonds) or to moving or rotating it as a whole. Of the $3N$ coordinates, 3 may be chosen to be the position of the centre of mass of the molecule (that is, they specify the position of the molecule in the room), and so the remaining $3N-3$ must specify the position of the atoms with respect to the position of the centre of mass. Of these, three may be ascribed to the orientation of the molecule (if it is non-linear), and the remaining $3N-6$ must then specify the relative positions *within* the molecule of all the atoms, and changing them corresponds to a bending or stretching of the bonds, that is, to molecular vibrations. If the molecule is linear only two coordinates are required to specify its orientation, and so the number of internal coordinates is $3N-5$.

Consider now the case of carbon dioxide, a linear triatomic molecule having $9-5=4$ internal degrees of freedom (coordinates necessary to specify the configuration of the molecule other than its position or orientation in the world). Suppose we identify one of the degrees of freedom with the stretching of one of the C—O bonds, and investigate the vibration of that bond. When the vibration of the bond is excited the other equivalent C—O bond will very quickly pick up its energy, because of the motion of the shared carbon atom, and there will be a °resonant transfer of the vibration from one bond to the other. The process will continue, and the vibrational motion transfers back and forth between the bonds until some external process quenches the molecular vibration. Suppose now that instead of exciting just one of the bonds we were more canny and excited both equally, we should expect an equilibrium situation in which the vibration continued smoothly until it was quenched. Take, for example, the excitation of the *symmetrical stretching mode* O←—C—→O ⇌ O—→C←—O: the carbon atom is buffeted equally from both sides, and there is no way (unless °anharmonicities are present) for the alternative combination, the *antisymmetrical stretching mode* ←O–C→←O ⇌ O→←C–O→, to be excited. Nor can energy in these modes be transferred to the bending modes, because to do so a perpendicular force is needed (this can be provided by the °Coriolis interaction arising from molecular rotation). Thus we see that by a judicious choice of the modes of vibration of the molecule we may obtain a set of independent motions: these are the *normal modes.* The four internal (vibrational) modes of CO_2 may be chosen as four normal (independent) modes, and because only four internal modes exist, any vibration of the molecule, however complicated, may be expressed as a superposition of the normal modes.

The independence of the normal modes makes their quantum-mechanical discussion very simple, since each of them may be considered to be equivalent to a single °harmonic oscillator of a particular mass and °force-constant vibrating along some equivalent coordinate, the *normal coordinate.* All the properties of °harmonic oscillators apply in the normal way to each normal mode, and the °selection rule that governs a vibrational transition applies to the modes too. In particular, a mode is *active in the infrared* region of the spectrum (and so gives a line in the ordinary °vibrational spectrum) only if there is a change of °dipole moment along the normal coordinate; that is, if the dipole moment of the molecule changes when it is distorted in a particular normal mode. Some of the normal modes of carbon dioxide and water are illustrated in Fig. N2.

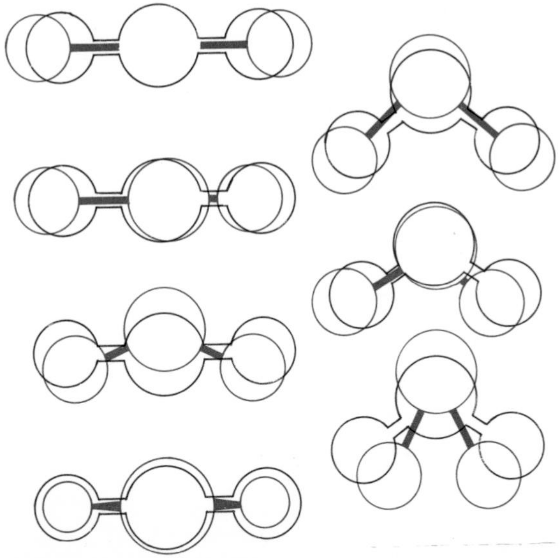

FIG. N2. Normal coordinates in CO_2 and H_2O (or other triatomic molecules).

Questions. Why does a non-linear molecule possess 3*N*–6 vibrational modes and a linear molecule 3*N*–5? What happens to the extra mode in the linear case when it is turned into a bent molecule? What happens when a single bond is stretched and then released in CO_2, H_2O, and CH_4? How is it possible to achieve a 'steady-state' vibration? Under what circumstances does the independence of the normal modes fail? What advantages stem from the use of normal modes? What is the basis of the quantum-mechanical calculation of the vibrational frequencies of the normal modes? What factors affect their frequency? If ^{12}C is replaced by ^{13}C in CO_2, would you expect all the normal-mode frequencies to change?

Further information. See Chapter 10 of *MQM* for a further discussion of the deduction and properties of normal modes and vibrations. See Chapter 6 of Brand and Speakman (1960) for a simple discussion of the classical and quantum mechanics of normal vibrations. A helpful introduction to normal-mode analysis is given by Woodward (1972), and more advanced sequels may be found in Wilson, Decius, and Cross (1955). See also Barrow (1962) and Ganz (1971). All these books describe the °group-theoretical analysis of normal modes of vibration.

normalized function. The Born interpretation of the °wavefunction views $\psi^*(\mathbf{r})\psi(\mathbf{r})d\tau$ as proportional to the probability of finding the particle in the volume element $d\tau$ surrounding the point $\mathbf{r}$; when the proportionality constant is unity the wavefunction is said to be *normalized* (or, more strictly, normalized to unity).

Suppose the wavefunction we are presented with is ψ; how do we proceed to normalize it? The basis of the method is the observation that, if the wavefunction is to be related to the probability distribution of the particle, then the probability of it being somewhere in the universe must be exactly unity. The probability of the particle being in the universe is the sum of the probabilities of it being in each of the volume elements $d\tau$ into which the universe may be shattered; this total probability is the integral $\int d\tau \psi^* \psi$, which must equal unity. Therefore if in fact we find it equal to N we may normalize the wavefunction by dividing it by the number $N^{\frac{1}{2}}$: the normalized function is $N^{-\frac{1}{2}} \psi$ and $N^{-\frac{1}{2}}$ is the *normalization constant.* When a function is both normal and °orthogonal it is *orthonormal.*

Questions. What is meant by the term 'normalized function'? Why is it convenient to deal with normalized functions in quantum mechanics? What is the procedure for normalizing an arbitrary function? Normalize to unity the following wavefunctions: the constant a in a universe stretching from $x = 0$ to $x = L$; the functions $\sin kx$ in the same short universe; the function $\exp im\phi$ in a universe stretching around a circle; the function $\exp(-r/a_0)$ in the whole of three-dimensional space.

Further information. Simple examples of normalizing wavefunctions are given in Chapter 3 of *MQM*. A particular problem arises with the normalization of functions that do not decay at large distances; for example, the function $\exp ikx$ oscillates for ever as $x \longrightarrow \infty$. Resort is then made to a special device (δ-function normalization): this is described in §5 of Davydov (1965), §4 of Mandl (1957), and §1.3 of Goldberger and Watson (1964).

nuclear magnetic resonance: a synopsis. The technique of nuclear magnetic resonance (n.m.r.) is the observation of the absorption of electromagnetic radiation by the magnetic nuclei of molecules, and in particular of protons, in the presence of an externally applied magnetic field.

In a magnetic field the two orientations of the °spin of a proton have different energy (α lies below β) and transitions between them (inversion of the orientation, or reversal of the direction of spin) can be induced by an electromagnetic field of the appropriate °resonance frequency. Typical spectrometers employ a 15 kG magnetic field, and the resulting energy separation corresponds to photons of frequency 60 MHz; recent developments have taken magnetic fields into the 50 kG region, where the radiation required is about 200 MHz. These figures imply that n.m.r. is a form of radiofrequency spectroscopy. The experiment is generally performed by applying a fixed radiofrequency field to the sample, and varying the applied magnetic field until the radiation is absorbed most strongly: this is the resonance condition. A typical spectrum is shown in Fig. N3.

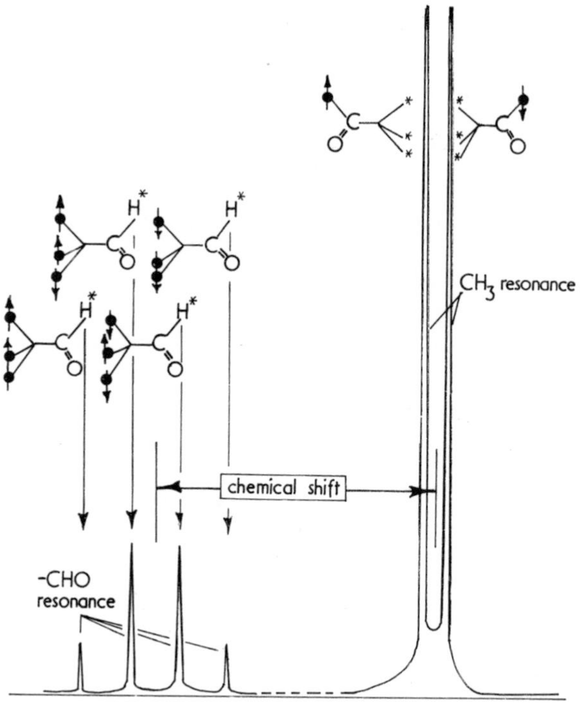

FIG. N3. The structure of an n.m.r. spectrum (of acetaldehyde). In each case the signal is due to resonance of the starred proton.

The information forthcoming from an n.m.r. spectrum is as follows:

1. *The position of the resonance.* Protons in different chemical environments resonate at different values of the applied magnetic field: this is the °chemical shift. It arises

because the applied field may induce local fields in the molecule, and the nuclei sense the total field. The applied field induces different fields in different types of chemical groups, and so different groups resonate with the fixed radiofrequency at different values of the applied field. More information will be found under °chemical shift. The simplest application of the chemical shift is to the recognition of different types of groups in an unknown molecule (see Fig. N3).

2. *The fine structure of the spectrum.* Under high resolution the lines of a spectrum are normally found to have a fine structure. This is due to *°spin-spin coupling*, in which the spins of the magnetic nuclei interact. As a first approximation the effect of the presence of the magnetic moments of the other nuclei is to modify the local magnetic field at the nucleus of interest, and the consequence of this is that it resonates at a value of the applied field which depends on the orientation of the neighbouring nuclear spins. The spin-spin coupling within a magnetically equivalent group of nuclei (a group with the same chemical shift) may be large, but it does not appear in the spectrum (this is a consequence of the selection rules that govern the spectrum). When the magnitudes of the spin-spin coupling and the chemical shift are comparable the spectrum may take on a very complicated appearance, but when they are markedly different the interpretation of the spectrum is simple (Fig. N3). The fine structure is an excellent fingerprint for the identification of an unknown molecule, or for the determination of structure.

3. *The width of the lines; the line shape.* The shape of the lines, and especially their width, is determined in solution by relaxation processes: these are described under the heading °electron spin resonance. The same effects operate in n.m.r., but as the nuclear magnetic moment is about 2000 times smaller than the electron spin magnetic moment its interaction with the environment is very much weaker and the relaxation times correspondingly longer (and line widths much less). Nevertheless, the determination of line widths and relaxation times is an important tool for the study of molecular motion in fluid solution. It is also important for the study of chemical motions; for example, tautomerism and proton exchange. The line shape is strongly affected by processes that occur on the n.m.r. time scale: if a motion modulates the chemical shift of a nucleus (for example, if a proton jumps between two inequivalent environments) then the line will be broadest when the frequency of the motion is of the order of the frequency difference between the two resonant positions.

Further information. See the entries on the °chemical shift and °spin-spin coupling for more information, and an idea of the magnitudes involved. The magnetic moments of nuclei are listed in Table 17. A description of n.m.r. will be found in McLauchlan's *Magnetic resonance* (OCS 1): this gives a description of the method and the way that it may be applied. For other simple accounts see Lynden-Bell and Harris (1969), Jackman (1959), Roberts (1959), Carrington and McLachlan (1967). More details will be found in Pople, Schneider, and Bernstein (1959), Emsley, Feeney, and Sutcliffe (1965), Slichter (1963), and Abragam (1961). Recent advances are described in *Advances in magnetic resonance, Progress in nuclear magnetic resonance spectroscopy, Annual review of n.m.r. spectroscopy,* and in the *Specialist periodical reports* of the Chemical Society. For a description of rate processes in terms of n.m.r. see the above books, especially Chapter 12 of Carrington and McLachlan (1967).

nuclear statistics. Nuclei, like electrons and other particles, must satisfy the requirements of the °Pauli principle: whenever any two equivalent nuclei are interchanged the overall wavefunction must change sign if they are °fermions, but not change sign if they are °bosons. This requirement has stringent consequences on the possible °rotational energy levels that a molecule may occupy, for the rotation of a molecule is a mode of motion that interchanges nuclei. Unfortunately, rotating a molecule also drags round the electrons, and so it is necessary to disentangle the exchange of the nuclei from the other effects that accompany rotation. We shall confine our attention to the hydrogen molecule, partly because it is pleasantly simple, and partly because it is important through the role that nuclear symmetry plays in the thermal properties of hydrogen gas.

Consider what happens when a molecule of hydrogen is rotated through 180°. The nuclei are interchanged, but so too is the orientation of the molecule as a whole, and the electrons. Inspection of Fig. N4 shows that it is a simple matter to return the electrons to their initial position in space by in-

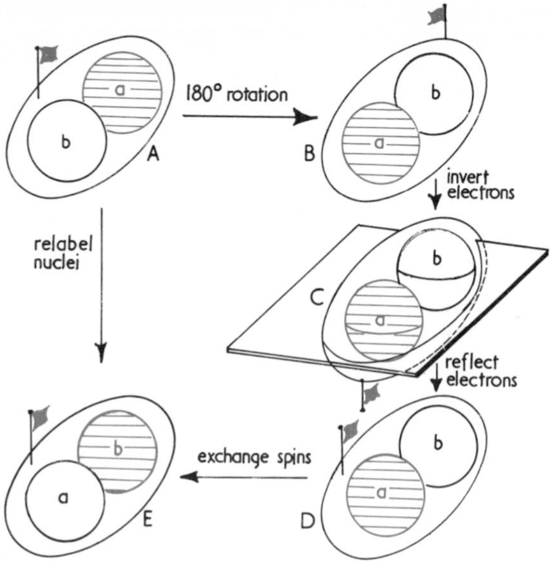

FIG. N4. Symmetry operations on nuclei and electrons in a homonuclear diatomic.

verting them through the centre of the molecule (no sign change on the electronic wavefunction for H_2 in its ground state), and then reflecting them back across the plane in which the molecule was rotated (also no sign change in the case of the ground state of H_2). A glance at the figure shows that the object of interchanging the nuclei without any net effect on the electrons has been achieved.

At this point we analyse the effect of each of the constituent operators on the wavefunction of the molecule.

The wavefunction is the product of the wavefunctions for the electronic state of the molecule ψ_{el}, the vibrational state ψ_{vib}, the rotational state ψ_{rot}, and the nuclear state ψ_{nuc} (of which more below). When the molecule is rotated through 180° the rotational wavefunction changes sign if the °rotational quantum number J is odd, but does not change sign if it is even (think of the similar behaviour of s-, p-, d-, f-, . . . orbitals). Therefore from the overall rotation of the molecule, the first step of the chain, we get a factor of $(-1)^J$. On the next two steps, the inversion and reflection of the electrons only, there is no change in the case of H_2 (although molecules in states other than Σ_g^+ may change sign), and so at stage D the wavefunction has changed sign by $(-1)^J$. Finally, the spin orientations of the nuclei are interchanged: this takes the molecule from D to E, and the last stage results in the same molecule that would have been obtained simply by relabelling the two nuclei.

When the two protons are relabelled the Pauli principle demands that the total wavefunction change sign; therefore going from A to E changes the sign of the function, and so the chain of operations A—B—C—D—E must also lead to a change of sign. So far a factor of $(-1)^J$ has been identified, but the step D to E may also lead to a sign change. This may be appreciated by considering the possible spin states of the two equivalent protons: the spins may be parallel or antiparallel, just as in the case of two electrons. The wavefunction for the spins in their antiparallel configuration is $\alpha_n(a)\beta_n(b) - \beta_n(a)\alpha_n(b)$ (see °singlet and triplet states), and if the projections α_n and β_n are interchanged this function changes sign. Conversely, the parallel spin arrangement (a nuclear triplet) is represented by the three states $\alpha_n(a)\alpha_n(b)$, $\alpha_n(a)\beta_n(b) + \beta_n(a)\alpha_n(b)$, $\beta_n(a)\beta_n(b)$, and none of these changes sign when the orientations are exchanged.

Suppose that the protons of H_2 are antiparallel, then the step from D to E introduces a factor of (-1) into the circuit, and so the overall phase in the trip from A to E is $(-1)^{J+1}$. But as the protons are fermions the wavefunction must change sign on going from A to E, and so we are forced to the conclusion that when the nuclear spins are antiparallel the molecule can occupy only the rotation states corresponding to even values of the quantum number J. Conversely, if the proton spins are parallel the step from D to E leaves the sign unchanged, and so overall a factor of $(-1)^J$ is obtained for the cycle from A to E; it follows that when the proton spins are parallel the molecule can occupy only the states with odd values of J.

The restrictions on the quantum numbers of the occupiable states have two principal effects. The first is the modification of the appearance of the spectrum of the molecule: in a thermal equilibrium mixture the odd-J states are occupied three times as heavily as the states with even J because three orientations of the nuclear spins are compatible with odd values of J, and only one orientation with even values. This intensity alternation is characteristic of the rotational structure of the spectra of molecules containing equivalent nuclei. Hydrogen molecules with paired nuclear spins (and therefore even J values) constitute *para-hydrogen*, and those with parallel spins (and therefore odd-J values) constitute *ortho-hydrogen*. At thermal equilibrium a sample of gas contains three times as much *ortho*-hydrogen as *para*-hydrogen, except at the lowest temperatures, where all the gas tends to occupy the lowest rotational level $J = 0$, in which case the thermal-equilibrium sample contains only *para*-hydrogen. *Ortho*- and *para*-hydrogen display different thermal properties at low temperature because of the differences in their available rotational energy levels.

The attainment of thermal equilibrium can be a very slow process because the relative orientation of the nuclear spins has to be changed. A pure *para*-hydrogen sample will change only slowly at room temperature to the thermal-equilibrium mixture, because many of the nuclear spins must be reorientated to make them parallel to their partners. This can be achieved more rapidly in the presence of a catalytic surface on which the molecules may dissociate and then recombine with random partners, or in the presence of a paramagnetic molecule (such as oxygen or a transition-metal ion) in which the magnetic field of the molecule can interact more strongly with one proton than the other and so drive them into new relative orientations (see Fig. S7 on p. 218).

The nuclear statistical effects are lost when the molecule is isotopically substituted, for then the nuclei are no longer equivalent. The molecule HD shows none of the properties of the kind just described. On going to D_2 a situation with equivalent nuclei is regained, but the deuterons are bosons and the intensity distribution is modified accordingly (see Questions). The effect of nuclear statistics on spectra and thermal properties may be discovered also in other molecules containing equivalent nuclei, such as O_2, HCCH, H_2O, CH_3CH_3, CH_4; the analysis gets quite complicated but depends on the same arguments.

Questions. 1. What is the basis of the effect of relative nuclear orientation on the rotational energy levels of molecules? Do the nuclei affect the energy levels or just their population? Why is it necessary to consider the peculiar complicated scheme depicted in Fig. N4? Why are even-J states associated with paired nuclear spins when the nuclei are fermions, and odd-J states associated with parallel nuclear spins? What effects does the demand of nuclear statistics have on the spectral and thermal properties of hydrogen? What is the significance of the classication of hydrogen into *ortho* and *para* states? What is the thermal-equilibrium concentration of the two species at elevated temperatures? Why is the interconversion a slow process, and what can be used to accelerate it?
2. Consider the molecule D_2, the spin of the deuteron being 1, and determine which nuclear states may be associated with even and odd J values. What is the lowest state of the molecule? Show that at elevated temperatures the even:odd J state ratio is 2:1.
3. Deduce that the ratio of even:odd nuclear spin states for a nucleus of spin I in a molecule containing two equivalent nuclei of spin I is $(I + 1):I$. Proceed by counting the number of odd and even combinations of the states $Im_a Im_b$ that may be formed.

Further information. See *MQM* Chapter 10 for a further discussion and a deduction of the general rule. A simple discussion will be found in §4.5 of Sugden and Kenney (1965), and §5.13 of King (1964), who also discuss the spectral consequences. The thermal consequences are described by Davidson (1962). See Townes and Schawlow (1955) for the extension of these arguments to more complex molecules.

O

operators. Classical mechanics deals with observables such as position and momentum as functions, sometimes of each other, or of time, and Newton's laws of motion enable these functions to be discovered. Quantum mechanics recognizes that all the information about the system is contained in its °wavefunction and that, in order to extract the information about the value of an observable, some mathematical operation must be done on the function. (This is analogous to the necessity of doing an act, an experiment, on the system in order to make a measurement of its state.) Quantum mechanics really boils down to making the correct selection of the operation appropriate to the observable.

In the simple quantum mechanics that concerns us it turns out that the right way to determine the momentum from a wavefunction is simply to differentiate it and then multiply the result by $\hbar/i$. Thus the gradient of the wavefunction at a particular point determines the °momentum. The operator that extracts the position turns out to be simply 'multiplication by x', but this, as you can imagine, is deceptively simple. Once we know what the operators are for the dynamical variables of position and momentum we can set up the operators for all observables, because these can be expressed as functions of the two basic variables. Thus the kinetic energy in classical mechanics is a function of the momentum, namely $p^2/2m$, with $p^2 = p_x^2 + p_y^2 + p_z^2$; therefore the corresponding operator can be obtained by replacing p_x^2 by $(\hbar/i)^2(\partial/\partial x)^2$, etc.; this shows that the curvature of the wavefunction determines the °kinetic energy.

How does one find the operators for p and x in the first place? The choice is severely limited by the requirement that the operators be such that the values of the observables they yield are real numbers (the result of an observation cannot be a complex number); this implies that the operators must have the mathematical property of hermiticity (they must be *hermitian operators*). Another requirement is that the operators must satisfy the rule that $(\hat{x}\hat{p}_x - \hat{p}_x\hat{x})\psi$ must be equal to $i\hbar\psi$. (We have denoted the operators corresponding to the observables x and p_x by $\hat{x}$ and $\hat{p}_x$.) Another way of putting this is that the °commutator of $\hat{x}$ and $\hat{p}_x$ must be $i\hbar$ (see °matrix mechanics). The latter is a very stringent requirement and has profound consequences; from it one may deduce the °uncertainty principle.

Having found the operator for the observable of interest, the value of the observable for the state of the system in question is an °eigenstate of the operator, if the state is not an eigenstate the result of the experiment is determined by the °expectation value of the operator.

Questions. 1. Why are operators important in quantum mechanics? What is the operator corresponding to linear momentum in the x-direction, and in the y-direction? What is the operator corresponding to the position along the z-coordinate? What is the operator corresponding to kinetic energy, and to the z-component of angular momentum? The state of a system is described by the function $\exp ikx$: what is the linear momentum of the state, and what is its kinetic energy? Another system is described by the function $\cos kx$: what is its linear momentum and kinetic energy?
2. What properties must operators possess if they are to be satisfactory in quantum mechanics? Confirm that the

°commutator of x and $(\hbar/i)(d/dx)$ is $i\hbar$. If we had chosen 'multiplication by p_x' to be the operator corresponding to the x-component of linear momentum, what would have been the necessary choice of operator for position? In the *momentum representation* of the operators just encountered, what would be the appropriate expression for the kinetic energy, and the Coulomb potential energy of two charges at a separation r?

Further information. Operators are at the very heart of quantum theory, and so books dealing with the fundamentals treat operators at length. For a simple account of the basic theory see *MQM* Chapter 4. The classical account of operators and observables is provided by Dirac (1958), and more mathematical accounts will be found in Mackey (1963), von Neumann (1955), Jordan (1969), and Jauch (1968). For a résumé, see Appendix 1 of Roman (1965). An introductory account of representation theory is given in Chapter 4 of Davydov (1965). The formulation of quantum mechanics as °matrix mechanics uses the properties of operators directly, and a succinct account is given by Green (1965).

orbital angular momentum. The orbital angular momentum is the contribution to the total angular momentum that in classical mechanics would be ascribed to the circular motion of a particle around a fixed centre. In quantum mechanics it is found that the orbital angular momentum is quantized, and its values are constrained in two ways.

1. The *magnitude* of the orbital angular momentum is confined to discrete values given by the expression $\hbar\sqrt{[\ell(\ell+1)]}$, where ℓ is the *orbital angular momentum quantum number*, or *azimuthal quantum number*, and is limited to positive integral values ($\ell = 0, 1, 2, \ldots$). Thus the angular momentum of any body is confined to the values $0, \hbar\sqrt{2}, \hbar\sqrt{6}, \ldots$. (Massive rotating bodies, such as a bicycle wheel, have angular momenta corresponding to $\ell \sim 10^{34}$.) In some situations (such as the °hydrogen atom) the maximum value of ℓ is limited by the value of other °quantum numbers.

2. The *orientation* of the direction of rotation is quantized (this is *space quantization*). The orientation of the plane of rotation is determined by the *magnetic quantum number* m_ℓ

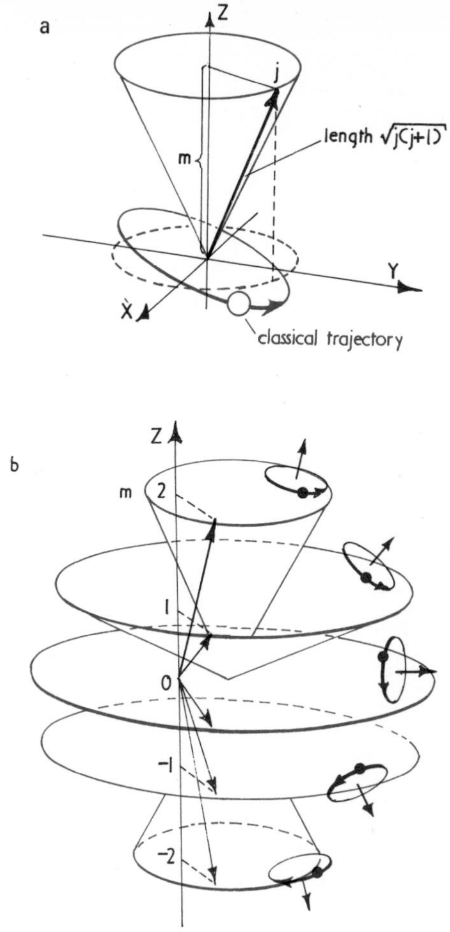

FIG. O1. (a) shows how a vector of length proportional to $[\ell(\ell+1)]^{1/2}\hbar$ is related to a classical trajectory; the component on the z-axis is $m\hbar$. In (b) is illustrated the discrete orientations (with respect to the z-axis) allowed by quantum theory to a particle with $\ell = 2$.

which can take all integral values between $+\ell$ and $-\ell$ (there are $[2\ell + 1]$ such values). The plane of rotation is determined in the sense that the component of the orbital angular momentum about a selected axis (conventionally the z-axis) is limited to the value $m_\ell\hbar$ (Fig. O1). Therefore if the magnitude of the angular momentum of a particular body is $\hbar\sqrt{6}$ (so that $\ell = 2$) the angular momentum about the z-axis may have one of the give values $-2\hbar, -1\hbar, 0, \hbar, 2\hbar$ (the different signs correspond to different (classical) senses of rotation) (Fig. O1b).

The component of momentum about either of the other axes (x or y) is indeterminate (according to the °uncertainty principle), and so if one denotes the angular momentum of a body by a vector $\mathbf{l}$ of length $\sqrt{[\ell(\ell+1)]}$ its projection on only one axis (the z-axis, by convention) may be determined at a particular instant: the simultaneous determination of either the x- or the y-component is excluded by the uncertainty principle. Therefore, if we still wish to represent angular momentum by a vector we have to draw it in a way that does not give the impression that we know more about its orientation than is permitted by the uncertainty principle. The best we can do is to draw a cone of all the possible (but indeterminate) positions of the vector (Fig. O1b), all of them of length proportional to $\hbar\sqrt{[\ell(\ell+1)]}$ and z-components proportional to $m_\ell\hbar$ (see °vector model). Sometimes the cone of possible positions is interpreted in terms of the °precession of the angular momentum; but see the appropriate entry before you believe in such a description.

The orbital angular momentum of a system is related to the number of °nodes in its wavefunction: the total number of angular nodes is equal to ℓ, and the number of angular nodes that one encounters on encircling the z-axis is equal to $|m_\ell|$. Thus a d-orbital has two angular nodes, and $\ell = 2$; the d_{xy}-orbital has both nodes in the xy-plane, and so one encounters both on a circuit about the z-axis, consequently $|m_\ell| = 2$.

This connexion between angular momentum and nodal structure is easy to understand if one recalls the °de Broglie relation or, what is equivalent, recalls that the °kinetic energy of a particle increases as the curvature of the wavefunction increases. Thus a shorter-wavelength wave (a more buckled function) has more nodes in a given length than one of longer wavelength. For angular momentum we are concerned with momentum on a circle or sphere; therefore a constant function (that is, a function independent of the angles θ and ϕ) has no nodes, is of infinite wavelength, has zero kinetic energy, and therefore zero (angular) momentum (or by the de Broglie relation has zero momentum). A function with one angular node (such a node lies on a diameter, and cuts a circle twice) corresponds to one wavelength wrapped round a circle, and one with two angular nodes (four nodal *points* on a circle) corresponds to two wavelengths confined to the same circumference, and so on. Therefore we see that the wavelength is shortened and the angular momentum is increased as we pack more nodes into the function. This picture of fitting waves on to a circle also makes clear the reason why angular momentum is quantized: only integral numbers of wavelengths can be fitted, for otherwise there would be destructive interference between waves on successive cycles of the ring (Fig. O2).

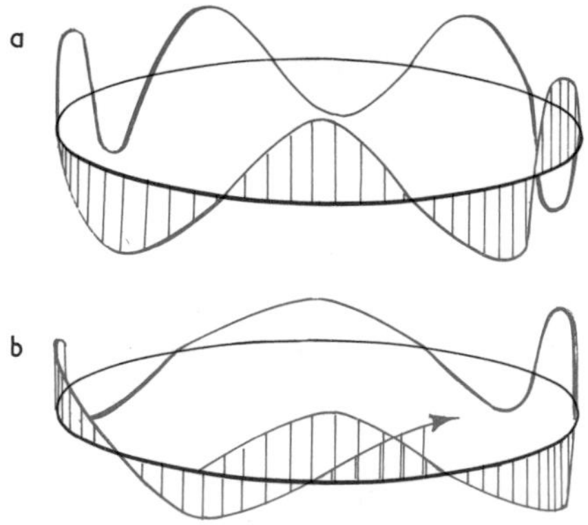

FIG. O2. (a) Acceptable and (b) unacceptable waves on a ring.

Questions. What is the classical definition of orbital angular momentum? How does quantization modify our view of the classical case? What values of the magnitude of the angular momentum of a rigid body are permissible? What orientations of a rotating body are permissible? Why is it not possible to represent an angular momentum by a vector in a fixed orientation? What is the connexion between the number of nodes in a wavefunction and its angular momentum (and which nodes do we count)? The number of nodes around the equator determines $|m_\ell|$: what is the significance of the difference between $+m_\ell$ and $-m_\ell$? How can the quantization of both the magnitude and orientation of orbital angular momentum be explained in terms of fitting a wave to a spherical surface? For more questions see °angular momentum Questions.

Further information. See Chapter 2 of *MQM* for a discussion of the quantum mechanics of a particle on a ring and on a sphere: this is an introduction to the quantum theory of

BOX 14: Orbital angular momentum

Classical definition $\mathbf{l} = \mathbf{r} \wedge \mathbf{p}$,

that is, $\ell_x = yp_z - zp_y$

$\ell_y = zp_x - xp_z$

$\ell_z = xp_y - yp_x$

with magnitude $\ell = (\ell_x^2 + \ell_y^2 + \ell_z^2)^{½}$.

Quantum definition

$$\hat{\ell} = \hat{\mathbf{r}} \wedge \hat{\mathbf{p}} = (\hbar/i)\mathbf{r} \wedge \nabla,$$

that is,

$$\hat{\ell}_x = (\hbar/i)\left(y\frac{\partial}{\partial z} - z\frac{\partial}{\partial y}\right)$$

$$\hat{\ell}_y = (\hbar/i)\left(z\frac{\partial}{\partial x} - x\frac{\partial}{\partial z}\right)$$

$$\hat{\ell}_z = (\hbar/i)\left(x\frac{\partial}{\partial y} - y\frac{\partial}{\partial x}\right).$$

In spherical polar coordinates these become

$$\hat{\ell}_x = -(\hbar/i)\left(\sin\phi\frac{\partial}{\partial\theta} + \cot\theta\cos\phi\frac{\partial}{\partial\phi}\right)$$

$$\hat{\ell}_y = (\hbar/i)\left(\cos\phi\frac{\partial}{\partial\theta} - \cot\theta\sin\phi\frac{\partial}{\partial\phi}\right)$$

$$\hat{\ell}_z = (\hbar/i)\frac{\partial}{\partial\phi}$$

$$\hat{\ell}^2 = -\hbar^2\Lambda^2$$

where Λ^2 is the legendrian (see Box 11).

Commutation relations

$$[\hat{\ell}_x, \hat{\ell}_y] = i\hbar\hat{\ell}_z \quad [\hat{\ell}_y, \hat{\ell}_z] = i\hbar\hat{\ell}_x \quad [\hat{\ell}_z, \hat{\ell}_x] = i\hbar\hat{\ell}_y$$

$$[\hat{\ell}^2, \hat{\ell}_q] = 0 \quad q = x, y, z.$$

Eigenvalues and eigenfunctions

$$\hat{\ell}^2\psi_{\ell m}(\theta,\phi) = \ell(\ell+1)\hbar^2\psi_{\ell m}(\theta,\phi) \qquad \ell = 0, 1, 2 \ldots$$

$$\hat{\ell}_z\psi_{\ell m}(\theta,\phi) = m\hbar\psi_{\ell m}(\theta,\phi) \qquad m = \ell, \ell-1, \ldots, -\ell.$$

$\psi_{\ell m}(\theta,\phi)$ are the °spherical harmonics: see Table 22.

Matrix elements. The only non-zero elements are:

$$\langle \ell, m|\hat{\ell}_z|\ell, m\rangle = m\hbar$$

$$\langle \ell, m \pm 1|\hat{\ell}_x|\ell, m\rangle = (\hbar/2)\surd[\ell(\ell+1) - m(m \pm 1)]$$

$$\langle \ell, m \pm 1|\hat{\ell}_y|\ell, m\rangle = \mp(i\hbar/2)\surd[\ell(\ell+1) - m(m \pm 1)].$$

Shift operators $\hat{\ell}_{\pm} = \hat{\ell}_x \pm i\hat{\ell}_y$

raising operator:

$$\hat{\ell}_+|\ell, m\rangle = \hbar\surd[\ell(\ell+1) - m(m+1)]\,|\ell, m+1\rangle$$

lowering operator:

$$\hat{\ell}_-|\ell, m\rangle = \hbar\surd[\ell(\ell+1) - m(m-1)]\,|\ell, m-1\rangle.$$

angular momentum. For a more general development, see Chapter 6. A summary of the properties of angular momentum is given in Box 14, and it should be observed that the wavefunctions for systems of given orbital angular momentum are the °spherical harmonics. In this connexion see Kauzmann (1957). For a detailed account of orbital angular momentum, see Brink and Satchler (1968), Rose (1957), and Edmonds (1957). Tinkham (1964) connects it with the rotational symmetry of systems. For the role of orbital angular momentum in chemical problems, explore °atomic orbitals, °hydrogen atom, and °atomic spectra and its ramifications.

orthogonal functions. Two functions ψ_1 and ψ_2 are orthogonal if the integral $\int d\tau\, \psi_1^* \psi_2$ vanishes; therefore they are orthogonal if their °overlap integral is zero. A trivial example would be the orthogonality of the 1s-orbital on two widely separated hydrogen atoms. Another example is the orthogonality of the 1s- and 2s- orbitals on the same atom, or the orthogonality of a 1s-orbital on one atom to a 2pπ-orbital on the neighbouring atom in a diatomic molecule.

A general result of °operator algebra is that eigenfunctions of an °hermitian operator are mutually orthogonal if they correspond to different °eigenvalues. When an eigenvalue has °degenerate eigenfunctions these need not be mutually orthogonal, but combinations that are orthogonal may be formed by the *Schmidt orthogonalization process.* In °group-theoretical terms, two functions are orthogonal if they belong to different irreducible representations of the point group of the system. Although orthogonality is a natural consequence of the type of operators one encounters in quantum mechanics, it is also a most desirable property because enormous numbers of potentially difficult integrals disappear automatically.

Questions. 1. What is meant by the term 'orthogonal function'? What are some examples of orthogonal functions? When can we be sure that a set of functions is mutually orthogonal? If they are not orthogonal, what process can be used to recover orthogonality? What group-theoretical property guarantees orthogonality?
2. Consider the functions exp $im\phi$ in the range $0 \leqslant \phi \leqslant 2\pi$: show that functions with different integral values of m are orthogonal. Show explicitly that the °hydrogen-atom 1s-orbital is orthogonal to the 2s- and 2p-orbitals. Show that the wavefunctions for a °particle in a one-dimension square well are mutually orthogonal. Consider the lowest-energy degenerate wavefunctions of a °particle in a two-dimensional square well and show that it is possible to find either orthogonal or non-orthogonal linear combinations of the two degenerate functions which continue to satisfy the Schrödinger equation with the same eigenvalue. Sketch the form of some of the combinations.
3. Orthogonalize the °Slater 2s-atomic orbital to the 1s-orbital by the Schmidt procedure. This involves forming the sum $\psi'_{2s} = \psi_{2s} + c\psi_{1s}$ and determining c so that the new 2s-orbital ψ'_{2s} is orthogonal to ψ_{1s}. How may the Slater 3s-orbital be made orthogonal to ψ_{1s} and ψ'_{2s}?

Further information. See *MQM* Chapter 4 for the proof that non-degenerate eigenfunctions of hermitian operators are orthogonal, and for other consequences of orthogonality. For the group-theoretical description of orthogonality see *MQM* Chapter 5, Tinkham (1964), Bishop (1973), and Wigner (1959). For the Schmidt orthogonalization process see McGlynn, Vanquickenborne, Kinoshita, and Carroll (1972).

oscillator strength. The oscillator strength f is a measure of the strength of a transition and is the ratio of the actual intensity to the intensity radiated by an electron oscillating harmonically in three dimensions. Thus for such an ideal electron the oscillator strength is unity, and for strongly allowed transitions it is found that f lies in the neighbourhood of unity. Oscillator strengths for several types of transition are recorded in Table 8.

The oscillator strength can be calculated from two directions, the theoretical and the experimental, and so its importance lies in the connexion it provides between theory and reality, as well as in its usefulness as a classification of the strength of transitions.

1. The *theoretical calculation* of °electric dipole oscillator strengths is based on the expression $f = 4\epsilon_0 mh\nu B/e^2$, where B is the °Einstein coefficient of stimulated absorption. For electric dipole transitions B is equal to $d^2/6\epsilon_0\hbar^2$, with d the transition dipole; this implies that $f = (2m_e/3e^2\hbar^2)h\nu d^2$. Therefore, if we can calculate the °transition dipole d for the pertinent transition we can find f.

2. The *experimental determination* of the oscillator strength is based on its relation to the °extinction coefficient $\epsilon(\tilde{\nu})$ at the wave number $\tilde{\nu}$, through the formula $f = 4{\cdot}33 \times 10^{-9} \int d\tilde{\nu}\epsilon(\tilde{\nu})$. Therefore, if the extinction coefficient is known over the range of wavenumbers the integral provides an experimental measure of f for the transition.

An important theoretical rule predicts that the sum of the oscillator strengths for all the electrons in an N-electron molecule is equal to N; this is the *Kuhn-Thomas sum rule.* Thus overall the hydrogen atom behaves like an ideal oscillator, because the sum of the oscillator strengths for all transitions away from the ground state is unity.

Questions. 1. What does an oscillator strength measure? What is the oscillator strength of a (three-dimensional) harmonic oscillator? What is the sum of oscillator strengths for all possible transitions from the ground state of the hydrogen atom? State the Kuhn-Thomas sum rule for an N-electron atom. How is the oscillator strength related to the extinction coefficient for a transition? How is the oscillator strength related to the transition dipole moment?
2. Calculate the oscillator strength for the transition from the nth to the $(n+1)$th level of an electron in a one-dimensional square well, and for a one-dimensional simple harmonic oscillator. Compute the integrated intensity of the absorption bands.

Further information. For the properties of the oscillator strength, its connexion with the extinction coefficient, and the derivation of the Kuhn-Thomas sum rule, see *MQM* Chapter 10. See also Kauzmann (1957) for a discussion and Eyring, Walter, and Kimball (1944). For applications in

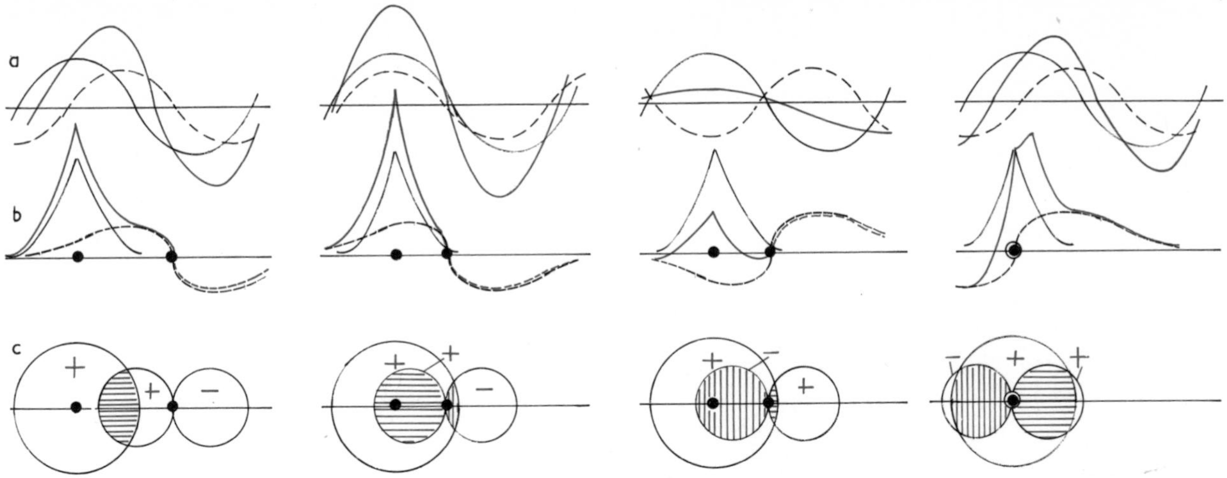

FIG. 03. (a) Interference of waves (in black) leads to the resultant drawn in colour (since the interfering waves have different wavelengths we have selected only a small domain). (b) Shows the analogous situation for overlapping s- and p-atomic orbitals and (c) denotes the regions of overlap pertinent to (b). Note that horizontal hatching implies constructive interference, and vertical hatching destructive.

photochemistry, see Wayne (1970) and Calvert and Pitts (1966).

overlap. When two waves lap into the same region of space they interfere and their superposition gives rise to a new wave with an increased amplitude in regions of constructive interference (where the two overlapping waves have amplitudes of the same sign) and diminished amplitude in regions of destructive interference (where the amplitudes have opposite signs and so tend to cancel) (see Fig. O3a). Since the electron distribution is determined by the square of the amplitude of the °wavefunction, the electron will be concentrated in regions of constructive interference and will be to some extent banished from the regions of destructive interference. Therefore the overlapping of two wavefunctions can strongly modify the distribution of the electron (or any other species).

When an s-orbital is brought up to a p-orbital along the latter's axis (Fig. O3b) the amount of interference increases as the separation decreases, and if they are brought up with the same sign of their amplitudes the constructive interference increases and the electron accumulates strongly in the region of overlap. As the orbitals move even closer together, the region of overlap increases further, but the net amount of overlap decreases because the s-orbital begins to overlap the region of negative amplitude of the p-orbital on the other side of the node. When the two nuclei are superimposed the s-orbital overlaps the positive and negative lobes of the p-orbital equally: on one side there is constructive interference and on the other there is an equal amount of destructive interference. As the s-orbital continues on its passage through the nucleus the overlap gradually becomes entirely destructive because the amplitudes tend to cancel, and over a fairly complicated surface do in fact cancel to give a node. As the s-orbital moves away the destructive interference disappears because where one orbital is large the other is small, and eventually goes to zero. Had the s-orbital been brought up along the line perpendicular to the axis of the p-orbital there would always have been an equal amount of destructive and constructive overlap at all distances.

A measure of the net amount of overlap is provided by the *overlap integral*, which is zero when there is no net overlap (either because there is no overlapping or because there is an equal amount of constructive and destructive interference in the regions of overlap) and is unity when there is perfect overlapping (when the overlap of an orbital with itself is considered). Orbitals with zero mutual-overlap integral are said to be °orthogonal. The overlap integral S is calculated by taking the two functions at some point $\mathbf{r}$, multiplying them together to give $\psi_a^*(\mathbf{r})\psi_b(\mathbf{r})$, and then integrating this product over all space: $S = \int d\tau \psi_a^*(\mathbf{r})\psi_b(\mathbf{r})$. It should be clear that this definition of the overlap integral conforms with the properties we have described.

Questions. 1. What happens when two orbitals overlap? Describe the change in the electron distribution that occurs when two 1s-orbitals approach each other, pass through each other, and then separate (let them approach with the same sign of their amplitudes). Sketch the approximate value of the overlap integral for this process as a function of separation. What is the behaviour of the overlap as a 1s-orbital is brought up to a $3d_{xz}$-orbital along (a) the y-axis and (b) the x-axis. Sketch the form of the °hybrid orbitals that arise in each case when the nuclei coincide.
2. The overlap of two hydrogen 1s-orbitals separated by a distance R is given by the expression

$$S(1s, 1s) = (1 + R/a_0 + R^2/3a_0^2)\exp(-R/a_0).$$

a_0 is the Bohr radius (53 pm, 0·53 Å). Plot this function as a function of R. At what separation is S a maximum? The overlap integral of a 1s-orbital and a 2s-orbital or a 2p-orbital approaching along the latter's axis is given by

$$S(1s, 2s) = (1/2\surd 3)(1 + R/a_0 + 4R^2/3a_0^2 + R^3/3a_0^3)\exp(-R/a_0)$$
$$S(1s, 2p\sigma) = (R/2a_0)(1 + R/a_0 + R^2/3a_0^2)\exp(-R/a_0).$$

Plot these functions, and find the position of maximum overlap in each case.
3. Suppose that on one of the nuclei we have a °hybrid orbital of the form $\psi_{2s}(\mathbf{r})\sin\xi + \psi_{2p}(\mathbf{r})\cos\xi$, where $\sin\xi$ and $\cos\xi$ are mixing coefficients, and we bring up a 1s-orbital along the axis of this hybrid. Discuss the form of the overlap integral; sketch its dependence on R for a mixture of 2s and 2p that gives the maximum overlap at all separations. Plot this optimum ξ as a function of R.

Further information. Overlap is of importance in all discussions of bonding; therefore see *MQM* Chapter 9, and especially Coulson's *The shape and structure of molecules* (OCS 9), Coulson (1961), and Murrell, Kettle, and Tedder (1965). The manner of calculating overlap integrals is described in Eyring, Walter, and Kimball (1944) and in more detail in McGlynn, Vanquickenborne, Kinoshita, and Carroll (1972). Extensive tables of overlap integrals have been published in a number of places: see the list of references on p. 421 of the book by McGlynn *et al* (1972). Overlap is considerably enhanced when the orbitals involved are °hybridized, and the strength of the bond so formed is increased. The occurrence of overlap, and the consequent interference effects, are aspects of the °superposition principle, which is one of the fundamental aspects of quantum mechanics.

P

pairing. Electrons pair when they enter an °orbital with opposed °spins. Electrons must pair if they are to enter the same orbital, for that is a requirement of the °Pauli principle.

Electron pairs are of prime importance in the theory of the chemical bond, and at an elementary level it is sometimes said that bond formation reflects the tendency of electrons to pair. That shorthand must be based on the deeper remark that electrons will sink to lower energy if they do pair, and the reason for this may be found by considering the formation of a °bond. The first electron of a bond enters the region of lowest potential energy (between the two nuclei), and the second can enter the same region only if it has opposed spin and pairs with the first; because of the Pauli principle a third electron cannot enter the same region, and so it will be much less effective in bonding. The basis of this description may be illustrated by °molecular-orbital theory, for in order to be most effective in bonding an electron must enter a bonding orbital (which is a distribution concentrated between the two bound nuclei); for two electrons to enter their spins must be opposed; three or more electrons cannot enter this best, bonding orbital and are forced to enter higher-energy orbitals, which may be °antibonding. Hence the great importance of electron pairs is merely a manifestation of the fact that only by pairing are two electrons able to enter the lowest-energy orbitals and be most effective in bonding, and more than two cannot get into the most favourable orbital; and the tendency of electrons to pair is a reflection of their tendency to seek lowest-energy situations.

A slightly different situation holds in atoms, for there the °Hund rules tell us that the outermost electrons tend not to pair: but here there is only one attractive centre, not two or more, and the important effect is the operation of °exchange and °spin correlation.

Further information. See °bond and °molecular orbital for a guide to the role of pairing, and the °Pauli principle for its basic source. The °valence-bond theory is an approach to chemical-bonding theory that recognizes the importance of pairing at the outset, and develops that point of view quantitatively; refer to its entry for details.

particle in a square well. A particle constrained to remain strictly within a particular region of space, with no seeping into or through the walls of the container, is a particle in a square well. It is so called because the confinement can be achieved by arranging a potential to be zero throughout the domain of freedom of the particle but to rise perpendicularly to infinity at the edges. The geometrical shape of the domain may take a variety of forms: a simple example is the one-dimensional square well, or box, where the particle can travel freely from 0 to L along the x-axis, but be nowhere else. The two-dimensional square well may take any shape in a plane, and the rectangle or the square are particular examples. The three-dimensional square wells include the cube and the sphere (which is sometimes called, without intention of paradox, a 'spherical square well').

In each case the energy of the particle arises entirely from its °kinetic energy, because it cannot penetrate the region where the potential energy differs from zero. Since the particle is confined its energy is °quantized, and the permitted

BOX 15: Particle in a square well

Linear (one-dimensional) box of length L:

$$E_n = n^2\left(\frac{h^2}{8mL^2}\right) \qquad \psi_n(x) = \left(\frac{2}{L}\right)^{1/2} \sin\left(\frac{n\pi x}{L}\right)$$

$n = 1, 2, \ldots$.

Rectangular, three-dimensional box of sides L_1, L_2, L_3:

$$E_{n_1n_2n_3} = \left\{\left(\frac{n_1}{L_1}\right)^2 + \left(\frac{n_2}{L_2}\right)^2 + \left(\frac{n_3}{L_3}\right)^2\right\}\left(\frac{h^2}{8m}\right)$$

$$\psi_{n_1n_2n_3} = \left(\frac{2^3}{L_1L_2L_3}\right)^{1/2} \sin\left(\frac{n_1\pi x}{L_1}\right) \sin\left(\frac{n_2\pi y}{L_2}\right) \sin\left(\frac{n_3\pi z}{L_3}\right)$$

$n_1 = 1, 2, \ldots$; $n_2 = 1, 2, \ldots$; $n_3 = 1, 2, \ldots$.

Spherical box of radius R

$$E_{n\ell} = f^2_{n\ell}\left(\frac{\hbar^2}{2mR^2}\right)$$

$f_{10} = 3{\cdot}142$, $f_{11} = 4{\cdot}493$, $f_{12} = 5{\cdot}763$, $f_{20} = 6{\cdot}283$, $f_{13} = 6{\cdot}988$, $f_{21} = 7{\cdot}725, \ldots$

$$\psi_{n\ell m} = N_{n\ell}\, j_\ell(kr)\, Y_{\ell m}(\theta, \phi)$$

$k = f/R$; j_ℓ is a spherical Bessel function. See §36 of Davydov (1965).

energies (which are set out in Box 15 for various box shapes) are obtained from the °Schrödinger equation for the problem and the boundary conditions characteristic of the well. From the requirements that the functions be continuous and the probability of finding the particle anywhere outside its domain of freedom be zero, one deduces that the wavefunction must always vanish at the walls. From this it follows that although the permitted functions are the same as free-particle functions within the box, their wavelength must satisfy $n\lambda/2 = L$, with n an integer greater than zero; otherwise their °nodes would not occur at both walls. Since the wavelength determines the momentum by the °de Broglie relation, and since the momentum determines the kinetic energy, it follows that the permitted energy levels are confined to the values given by n^2/L^2. This situation is a good example of the discussion of the quantum-theoretical significance of °kinetic energy and the curvature of the wavefunction for, as we attempt to cram more waves into a given length, the function has to be more buckled, and its curvature greater. The wavefunctions themselves are just ordinary sine waves of decreasing wavelength, and a few of them are illustrated in Fig. P1.

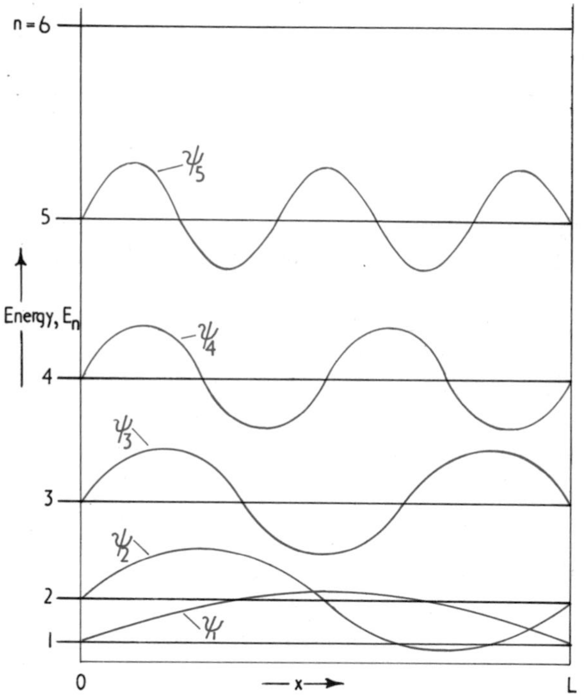

FIG. P1. Energy levels and wavefunctions for a particle in a one-dimensional square well.

We may summarize the properties of a particle in a square well in the following way.

1. In a *one-dimensional box* the energies are determined by a single quantum number n and are proportional to n^2/L^2 (see Box 15). n may take the values $n = 1, 2, 3, \ldots$, and since $n = 0$ is forbidden (the wavefunction with $n = 0$ would vanish everywhere) the lowest energy is greater than zero; therefore there is an irremovable *zero-point energy*. All the states are non-degenerate.

2. In a *three-dimensional box* the energies depend on three quantum numbers, and in a rectangular box of sides

L_1, L_2, L_3 are proportional to $(n_1^2/L_1^2) + (n_2^2/L_2^2) + (n_3^2/L_3^2)$, with n_1, n_2, n_3 allowed all integral values above zero. There is a zero-point energy corresponding to $n_1 = n_2 = n_3 = 1$.

3. The wavefunctions are simple sine functions of different wavelengths (and therefore of different °kinetic energies). The zero-point energy corresponds to a state in which the particle is most probably near the centre of the box, and furthest from the walls. At higher quantum numbers the probability density is spread more evenly throughout the region.

4. The energy levels move apart as the walls become more confining: an integral number of half wavelengths must be fitted into a decreasing length; therefore the wavelength must decrease, and so the kinetic energy increases. As the confining walls move apart the energy separation diminishes, and in the limit of infinite separation the levels form a continuum, and the system is unquantized.

5. Increasing mass has an effect similar to the effect of increasing the size of the domain: a particle of large mass behaves more classically than one of low mass for a box of given size.

6. A localized particle may be constructed by forming a suitable °superposition corresponding to a °wave packet at the point where the particle is located; the packet so formed moves in close accord with the predictions of classical mechanics for a particle confined to a region surrounded by infinitely rigid and perfectly reflecting walls.

Questions. 1. What is the meaning of the expression 'square well'? What is the effect of the presence of impermeable walls on the allowed energy levels of the system? Why is the energy proportional to n^2/L^2? From the classical expression for the kinetic energy in terms of the momentum, and the °de Broglie relation for the momentum in terms of the wavelength, deduce an expression for the energy of a particle in a one-dimensional square well, and compare your answer with Box 15. What is the lowest energy permitted to a particle in a box, and what is its dependence on the size of the box? What interpretation in terms of the °uncertainty principle may be put on this zero-point energy? What is the mean momentum in any single energy state of the box? In what limit does the particle behave in a classical manner? Calculate the lowest energy of an electron in a box of length 1 m, 1 nm, 0·1 nm, 10^{-15} m: what is the energy of transition to the first excited level in each case? Why is a fly in a room a classical particle, to all intents and purposes (if flies have intents or purposes)? An electron in a conjugated polyene may be considered to be a particle in a one-dimensional box: estimate the transition energy from the nth to the $(n + 1)$th level in a chain of N carbon atoms.
2. The °Schrödinger equation for a one-dimensional box is $-(\hbar^2/2m)(d^2/dx^2)\psi = E\psi$; solve this equation in terms of a function of the form $A\sin kx + B\cos kx$, and apply the boundary conditions that the function vanishes at $x = 0$ and $x = L$, the edges of the box. Show that A may be deduced from the fact that the functions should be °normalized, and show that states of different energy are °orthogonal. Show that a rectangular two-dimensional box may be solved in terms of 2 one-dimensional boxes by the method of separation of variables (see °Schrödinger equation).

Further information. See *MQM* Chapter 3 for detailed information about the solution of the Schrödinger equation for particles confined in boxes. The spherical square well is more difficult, but its solution is outlined in Kauzmann (1957), and, since it is a fair model of an electron in liquid ammonia (metal-ammonia solutions), see LePoutre and Sienko (1964) and Lagowski and Sienko (1970) for its applications and properties. When the barrier is not infinite the particle can seep into the walls, and if the potential falls outside to some finite value the particle might °tunnel through the barrier: situations of this kind are discussed and solved in §32 of Davydov (1965), Schiff (1968), Messiah (1961), and Landau and Lifshitz (1958 a). Gol'dman and Kryvchenkov (1961) work through a number of problems involving barriers. See also Chapter 11 of Bohm (1951) for a good discussion of square potentials.

Paschen-Back effect. The Paschen-Back effect is the decoupling of spin and orbital angular momenta by an applied magnetic field.

Consider an atom with both °spin and °orbital angular momenta, **s** and **l**; these are coupled together by the °spin-orbit coupling interaction and form a resultant angular momentum which is represented by the °vector **j**. Both **s**

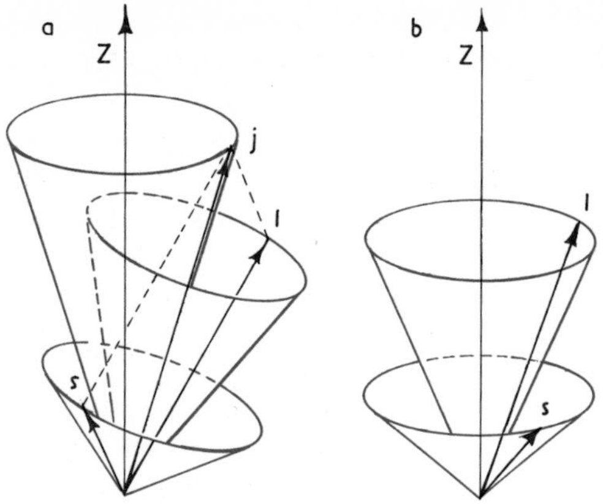

FIG. P2. Paschen-Back effect.

and l precess around their resultant, and in a magnetic field of moderate strength the resultant vector also precesses about the field direction (Fig. P2 a): the energy of this interaction gives rise to the °Zeeman effect. As the strength of the applied field is increased the strength of its interaction with the spin and orbital °magnetic moments becomes so great that it begins to overcome the spin-orbit coupling. At this point the spin and orbital moments begin individually to precess around the direction of the field, and the spin-orbit coupling is broken; the motion is complex because the spin-orbit coupling and the applied field are in competition for the two moments. If the field is made sufficiently strong (of the order of tens of kilogauss) the battle is resolved in its favour, and the state is one of almost *pure precession* of each type of momentum about the field's direction (Fig. P2 b). The Paschen-Back effect has succeeded in decoupling the momenta.

The spectral consequence of the effect is that the electronic transitions occur in a simple fashion: the optical field interacts with the orbital angular momentum and causes transitions which are independent of the spin direction. The anomalous °Zeeman effect, which depends on the interplay of spin and orbital moment effects, is replaced by the normal Zeeman effect, characteristic of systems without spin.

The term Paschen-Back effect is also used for other situations in which the spin and orbital momenta are decoupled by a field; one example is the effect of the axial nuclear Coulombic electrostatic potential on the momenta in a diatomic molecule; its effect is to modify the °Hund coupling case.

Questions. What is the Paschen-Back effect? Discuss the effect in terms of the °vector model of the atom. Why does the effect simplify the anomalous Zeeman effect and replace it by the normal effect? If the spin-orbit coupling energy in an atom is of the order of 100 cm^{-1} estimate the strength of the applied field required to decouple the angular momenta.

Further information. See the discussion of the °Zeeman effect and *MQM* Chapter 8. See also §II.3 of Herzberg (1944) and §III F3 of Kuhn (1962) for detailed accounts of its spectroscopic consequences.

Pauli principle. The *Pauli exclusion principle* states that no more than one electron may occupy a particular state: a consequence of this is the °*aufbau* principle which underlies the periodicity of the elements; for an atomic orbital labelled n, ℓ, m_ℓ, may be populated by no more than two electrons and these must differ in the quantum number m_s (and so must have opposite spin orientations).

The exclusion principle is a special case of the full *Pauli principle* which makes a general statement about all particles. The Pauli principle starts from the view that if two particles are indistinguishable, when they are interchanged the calculated properties of the system must remain unchanged. In particular, since the particle density is proportional to $|\psi|^2$ (see °wavefunction), when two indistinguishable particles are interchanged (the first put where the second was and vice versa) the particle density, and hence $|\psi|^2$, must not change. This implies that ψ itself can either change sign when the particles are interchanged, or not change sign; no more complicated change is permissible. The change of sign, or lack of it, must occur for all possible pairs of indistinguishable particles in the system when the two particles of each pair are interchanged. A fundamental distinction which determines whether or not the wavefunction changes sign is between °fermions (which are particles with half-integral spin, such as electrons, protons, neutrons, ^{13}C nuclei, and ^{3}He) and °bosons (which have integral spin, such as ^{2}H, ^{4}He, ^{12}C, and photons). The principle states that if a collection of identical particles 1, 2, . . . n is described by the wavefunction $\psi(\mathbf{r}_1, \mathbf{r}_2, \ldots \mathbf{r}_n)$ then the form of this function must satisfy a stringent requirement: *If the particles are fermions the function must change sign whenever the positions of any two particles are interchanged; whereas if the particles are bosons the function must not change sign.* Another way of saying this is that under particle interchange the total wavefunction for identical fermions must be °antisymmetric, and for identical bosons it must be symmetric.

The principle is adequately illustrated by considering a two-particle state $\psi(\mathbf{r}_1, \mathbf{r}_2)$, or $\psi(1, 2)$ for short: if the particles are fermions Nature demands that $\psi(2, 1) = -\psi(1, 2)$. The implication of this for electrons (fermions) is as follows. Suppose we have a state ψ_a which can be occupied by electron 1 and a state ψ_b which can be occupied by electron 2, then the total system is described by a function of the form $\psi_a(\mathbf{r}_1)\psi_b(\mathbf{r}_2)$, or $\psi_a(1)\psi_b(2)$ for brevity. But this function does not satisfy the Pauli principle because it is neither symmetric nor antisymmetric in the labels 1, 2 (it is unsymmetric). We can turn it into an acceptable function for electrons by replacing $\psi_a(1)\psi_b(2)$ by $\psi_a(1)\psi_b(2) - \psi_a(2)\psi_b(1)$, for when 1 and 2 are interchanged the sign of the function changes. This function demonstrates why only one electron can exist in a given state: if the states ψ_a and ψ_b were identical, so that both electron 1 and electron 2 were in the same state, the form of the function that satisfies the Pauli principle would be $\psi_a(1)\psi_a(2) - \psi_a(2)\psi_a(1)$, which vanishes: this shows that multiply-occupied states vanish and that the exclusion principle is a special case of the full principle. If instead of electrons we were dealing with bosons, the appropriate two particle state would be $\psi_a(1)\psi_b(2) + \psi_a(2)\psi_b(1)$, and this does not vanish if $\psi_a = \psi_b$; therefore bosons do not satisfy the exclusion principle because multiply-occupied states are permitted (a large number of photons may occupy the same state and give rise to an intense monochromatic light beam). Remember that the Pauli principle applies to the *total* state of the system, so that ψ_a and ψ_b represent space (orbital) and spin states.

The Pauli principle was introduced in order to account for the spectrum of helium, for an analysis of its spectrum showed that many expected °terms were absent, and their absence could be explained on the basis that two electrons on a given atom could not occupy the same state. The principle can be given a theoretical foundation, and Pauli, by considering the problem relativistically, and demanding that the energy of a system be positive, showed that all particles of half-integral spin must have antisymmetric wavefunctions and behave as we have described. Possible exceptions to the principle are quarks, which are peculiar particles used in one theory of elementary particles; but as they have not yet been observed experimentally they may be figments of the imagination, and particles, not figments, are required to satisfy the Pauli principle.

Without the Pauli principle matter would not be rigid; likewise, if electrons had no spin (and were bosons) matter would have less bulk, everything would be denser, nothing rigid, and everything very sticky.

Further information. The experimental basis of the Pauli principle is described in *MQM* Chapter 8. A product of functions may be made to accord with the principle by writing it as a °Slater determinant, and the discussion is taken further in that entry and in the one on °antisymmetric functions. Problems too will be found there and in Further information. Pauli deducing his principle may be observed in Pauli (1940); for quarks see °fermions.

penetration and shielding. Like Castor and Pollux, penetration and shielding seem inseparable twins: so they are in application but not in contemplation. Let us fix our ideas by considering the sodium ion Na^+, which consists of a strongly charged nucleus ($Z = 11$) surrounded by ten electrons filling the K and L shells (the °configuration is $1s^2 2s^2 2p^6$). Drop an electron into the 3s-°orbital and observe that, since the s-orbitals all have a non-vanishing probability of being at the nucleus, the electron penetrates the surrounding electrons to a small extent, and with a small but non-zero probability may be found in the vicinity of the nucleus. In that region it will have a low potential energy and be stabilized. If instead of dropping it into a 3s-orbital we contrive to deposit it in a 3p-orbital, the electron is unable to penetrate so closely to the nucleus (p-orbitals have °nodes at their nucleus), and so it does

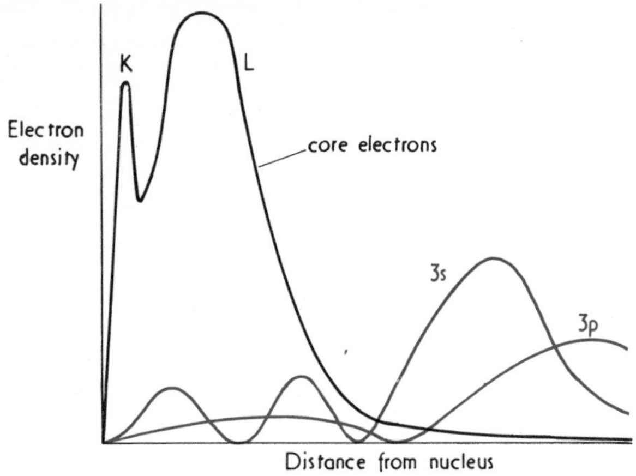

FIG. P3. The coloured lines show the 3s and 3p radial-distribution functions superimposed on K, L shell electron density.

not attain the region of lowest potential energy (Fig. P3). That, then, is *penetration*; we can believe that s-orbitals might lie lower in energy than p-, d-orbitals on account of their closer approach to the nucleus.

Close approach is not of itself sufficient to lower the energy, because in the °hydrogen atom all the orbitals with the same principal °quantum number carry the same energy, irrespective of whether they are s, p, or d. In order for penetration to have an effect it is necessary to eliminate the peculiar property of the pure Coulomb interaction which is responsible for the unique properties of the hydrogen atom. This is achieved by the *shielding* effect of the other electrons that are present in the case of many-electron atoms (see Fig. P3). In these the potential experienced by our extra electron is that of a nucleus of charge $Ze(Z = 11)$ at small radii, but at larger radii, when the test electron is outside the core, the potential is more characteristic of a nucleus of charge e, because the $(Z - 1)$ electrons have shielded all but one unit of positive charge. Therefore the potential of the shielded nucleus drops off far more rapidly than the Coulombic law would entail, and so the peculiar characteristics of the Coulombic potential are eliminated. Consequently the s-, p-, and d-electrons possess different energies.

It should be clear that the different orbitals have different energies on account of the shielding effects, and the order of their energies and their separation depends on the extent of their penetration of the core.

Questions. Which orbitals penetrate most closely to the nucleus? What is the essential role of shielding? What accounts for the fact that s-electrons generally lie lower in energy than p-electrons, and p-electrons lie lower than d-electrons? What is the order of °ionization potentials for s-, p-, and d-electrons?

Further information. See *MQM* Chapter 8 for a description of the extent and role of penetration and shielding. Simple diagrams are given there, and in White (1934) and Herzberg (1944), of the extent of penetration of various inner shells by various outer electrons. For a discussion of the screening constant see °Slater atomic orbitals. The effects of penetration and shielding are most important for the structure of the periodic table, for they influence the properties of the elements through the °*aufbau* principle and the °ionization potential. These matters are discussed by Puddephatt in *The periodic table of the elements* (OCS 3) and by Phillips and Williams (1965).

perturbation. Most systems of interest are described by °Schrödinger equations too difficult to solve exactly; but inspection of the problem often reveals that a simpler, solvable system closely resembles the true, intractable system. If the °wavefunctions and energies of this simpler system are known it is possible to adjust them so that they are distorted in the direction of the true wavefunctions and energies. If the true system resembles the simpler system very closely the amount of distortion required is very small, and is a mere *perturbation* of their form. The modification of the simple wavefunction can be achieved by mixing into it other wavefunctions of the simple system in the appropriate proportions, and *perturbation theory* provides the recipe for the mixture. At the same time, perturbation theory shows how to calculate the additional terms that must be added to the energy of the simple system to yield the energy of the true system.

First-order perturbation theory teaches that the wavefunction of the simple system ψ_0 should be modified to $\psi_0 + c_1\psi_1 + c_2\psi_2 + \ldots$, where the ψ_n are the various wavefunctions of the model system corresponding to the energies

E_n, and where the coefficients c_n are determined by the ratio of the strength of the perturbation (which is essentially the energy difference between the true and the simple systems, and is actually the °matrix element of the perturbation hamiltonian—the difference between the true °hamiltonian and the simple hamiltonian) to the energy separation E_0-E_n. The wavefunction obtained in this way is the *first-order wavefunction.*

An example to fix our ideas at this stage could be the distortion of the ground state of the hydrogen atom by an applied electric field (the °Stark effect): the simple system would be the hydrogen atom in the absence of applied fields (the wavefunctions and energies, of course, are known), and the distortion (°polarization) of the atom by the applied field could be taken into account by adding some $2p_z$-orbital into the ground state, and then some $3p_z$-orbital, and so on. The coefficient of each orbital is determined by the ratio of the perturbation energy (in this case the electrical interaction energy ezE, which comes from the expression $-\mathbf{d.E}$ for a dipole **d** in our electric field **E**) to the energy separation for each orbital ($E_{1s}-E_{2p}, E_{1s}-E_{3p}, \ldots$) . The *proportion* of the orbital in the mixture is determined by the square of the mixing coefficient (see °superposition principle), and so it is clear that only those orbitals lying fairly close in energy to the 1s-orbital will be mixed significantly. This is a general result of perturbation theory: *the greater the energy separation, the less the mixing.* It follows that if all the energy levels lie far above the ground state, the simple system cannot be distorted very much, and so it will resemble very closely the true system. Conversely, if the perturbation is too strong (the true and simple systems being very dissimilar) a large amount of mixing may occur and the first-order theory might be inappropriate: the solution is generally to choose a better model system.

It should be noticed that the form of the true wavefunctions emerges automatically from the perturbation-theory machinery, for the recipe generates the correct distortion. This is in contrast to the °variation approach to the approximation of wavefunctions, where the final form depends on the original guess of the form of a sufficiently flexible function.

The modification of the energy due to the perturbation may also be calculated, and although the *first-order energy* is sometimes sufficient, it is normally necessary to calculate the *second-order energy*. The former is calculated by taking the perturbation energy and calculating its average value over the *undistorted* wavefunctions of the simple system. The second-order energy correction takes into account the distortion of the simple wavefunctions by the perturbation: first the wavefunction is distorted by the application of the perturbation, and then the average value of the perturbation energy is calculated over this distorted wavefunction. The name 'second-order' indicates that the perturbation is involved twice.

A helpful analogy, which enables one to appreciate how perturbations operate, is the mutilation of a violin string by suspending from it a number of small weights. The weights hanging from the nodes affect neither its motion nor its energy, but those hanging from the antinodes (the points of maximum displacement) may have a profound effect on its vibrational energy and waveform. The first-order energy correction is found by averaging the effect of the weights (the perturbation) over the wavefunction (in this case the displacement) of the system. The weights also distort the waveform of the string: the nodes are slightly shifted and the pure sinusoidal shape lost. This distorted mode can be reproduced by taking a suitable superposition of the harmonics of the unladen string, and if the weights are not too big it should be clear that only a few of the harmonics need be incorporated to give a good representation of the distortion. The second-order energy correction to the vibrational energy of the string can be found by averaging the effect of the weights over the distorted waveform. This second-order correction should be added to the first-order correction, and their sum added to the original vibrational energy of the unladen string, in order to find a good approximation to the true energy of the modified string.

The order of magnitude of the correction to the energy brought about by a perturbation of energy P is $\sim P$ for the first-order correction, and $\sim P^2/\Delta$ for the second-order correction, Δ being a typical energy separation of the undistorted system. Often the first-order correction disappears identically (on grounds of symmetry). The first-order correction to the wavefunction yields coefficients of order P/Δ, and so the proportion of states admixed is of the order P^2/Δ^2. The application of perturbation theory is normally valid so long as P is much smaller than Δ: that is, so long as $|P/\Delta| \ll 1$. It is important to note that the second-order energy can be obtained from the first-order wavefunction (in general the nth-order energy can be obtained with knowledge of the $(n-2)$th-order function†); thus jubilation at obtaining a good energy should be tempered with the reflection that the wavefunction itself might still be very poor. Alternatively, the more sanguine will reflect with some satisfaction that such a good energy can be obtained from such a poor wavefunction. (For example, a wavefunction correct to within 10 per cent can give an energy correct to within 1 per cent.)

The algebraic recipes for perturbation theory are set out in Box 16.

Time-dependent perturbation theory allows the perturbation to vary with time and permits the calculation, as an important application, of the effect of the perturbation caused by a light wave. The distortions change with time and the admixture of the excited states of the system may be interpreted as transitions from the ground state to another state. See °transition probabilities.

Questions. 1. What is a 'perturbation'? What does it affect? How may the effect of the perturbation of the wavefunction be taken into account? What is the order of magnitude of the coefficients of the admixed functions, and in what proportion are they mixed? How is the first-order correction to the energy calculated? How is the second-order correction calculated? Why do they differ? What action should you take if you find that the wavefunction of the simple system has to be severely modified? What is the order of magnitude of the first- and second-order energy corrections and the first-order wavefunction distortion when a perturbation of energy equivalent to 10 J mol^{-1} is applied to a system in which the energy separations are of the order of 1 kJ mol^{-1}? A mass of 1 kg hangs from a spring of force-constant 1 N m^{-1}: how will its motion be modified by the addition of a 100 g mass ($g = 9{\cdot}8$ m s^{-2})? Now consider a similar quantum-mechanical problem: let a ^{210}Po atom be oscillating against an effective °force-constant of 40 N m^{-1}, and let it be in the vibrational

† Really, if the lower orders don't set us a good example, what on earth is the use of them? (Oscar Wilde, *The importance of being earnest,* Act 1.)

BOX 16: Perturbation theory

We suppose that we know the eigenvalues and eigenfunctions of the hamiltonian $H^{(0)}$:

$$H^{(0)}\psi_n^{(0)} = E_n^{(0)}\psi_n^{(0)},$$

and we require the energies and wavefunctions of a hamiltonian H:

$$H = H^{(0)} + H^{(1)} + H^{(2)},$$

where $H^{(1)}$ is a first-order correction (of order λ in some small parameter λ) and $H^{(2)}$ is a second-order correction (of order λ^2). The true energies and wavefunctions are written

$$E_m = E_m^{(0)} + E_m^{(1)} + E_m^{(2)} + \ldots$$

$$\psi_m = \psi_m^{(0)} + \psi_m^{(1)} + \psi_m^{(2)} + \ldots.$$

Zeroth-order energy and wavefunction

$$E_m^{(0)} = \langle\psi_m^{(0)}|H^{(0)}|\psi_m^{(0)}\rangle \quad \text{corresponding to } \psi_m^{(0)}.$$

First-order correction

$$E_m^{(1)} = \langle\psi_m^{(0)}|H^{(1)}|\psi_m^{(0)}\rangle$$

$$\psi_m^{(1)} = \sum_n{}' c_n\psi_n^{(0)}, \text{ where } c_n = \left\{\frac{\langle\psi_n^{(0)}|H^{(1)}|\psi_m^{(0)}\rangle}{(E_m^{(0)} - E_n^{(0)})}\right\}.$$

Second-order correction

$$E_m^{(2)} = \langle\psi_m^{(0)}|H^{(2)}|\psi_m^{(0)}\rangle + \sum_n{}'\left\{\frac{\langle\psi_m^{(0)}|H^{(1)}|\psi_n^{(0)}\rangle\langle\psi_n^{(0)}|H^{(1)}|\psi_m^{(0)}\rangle}{(E_m^{(0)} - E_n^{(0)})}\right\}.$$

Time-dependent perturbation theory

We suppose that $\quad H = H^{(0)} + H^{(1)}(t)$

and write

$$\Psi_m(t) = \sum_n c_n(t)\Psi_n^{(0)}(t),\ \Psi_n^{(0)}(t) = \psi_n^{(0)}\exp(-iE_n^{(0)}t/\hbar).$$

Then

$$c_n(t) = c_n(0) - (i/\hbar)\sum_k \int_0^t dt' c_k(t')H_{nk}^{(1)}(t')\exp i\omega_{nk}t',$$

where $H^{(1)}_{nk}(t') = \langle\psi^{(0)}_n|H^{(1)}(t')|\psi^{(0)}_k\rangle$

and $\hbar\omega_{nk} = E^{(0)}_n - E^{(0)}_k$.

For weak perturbations applied to a state in which initially $c_i(0) = 1$, $c_f(0) = 0$ (only state i occupied), then to first order:

$$c_i(t) = 1$$

$$c_f(t) = -(\mathrm{i}/\hbar)\int_0^t \mathrm{d}t' H^{(1)}_{fi}(t')\exp \mathrm{i}\omega_{fi}t'.$$

If $H^{(1)}(t) = 2V\cos\omega t$,

$$c_f(t) = V_{fi}\left[\frac{1-\exp[\mathrm{i}(\omega_{fi}+\omega)t]}{\hbar(\omega_{fi}+\omega)} + \frac{1-\exp[\mathrm{i}(\omega_{fi}-\omega)t]}{\hbar(\omega_{fi}-\omega)}\right]$$

and if $\omega_{fi} - \omega \ll \omega_{fi} + \omega$ the probability of being in state f is

$$P_f(t) = |c_f(t)|^2 \sim \left[\frac{4V_{if}V_{fi}}{\hbar^2(\omega_{fi}-\omega)^2}\right]\sin^2\tfrac{1}{2}(\omega_{fi}-\omega)t.$$

ground state. Let it emit an α-particle. What is the order of magnitude of the probability of finding the resulting ^{206}Pb atom oscillating in its ground state?

2. The quantum-mechanical expressions for the perturbation corrections to the energy and wavefunction are given in Box 16. Take a °particle in a one-dimensional square-well wavefunction and add to the system a perturbation of the form $-qx$, $0 \leqslant x \leqslant L$: find the first-order energies and wavefunctions. Using the same model, select a system that has a flat potential within the walls except for a small rectangular dip of depth D and width W. Set the centre of this dip at the centre of the well, and let $W \ll L$. Calculate the first-order energy correction to a particle in the ground state ($n = 1$), and then in the first excited state ($n = 2$). What do you notice about the extent of correction in each case? Is the difference also reflected in the correction to the wavefunction? Now slide the centre of the dip to $x = L/3$; what happens?

3. Estimate the extent of distortion and the correction to the energy that results when an electric field of 10^6 V m^{-1} is applied to a ground-state °hydrogen atom.

Further information. See *MQM* Chapter 7 for the details of perturbation theory. Perturbation theory is one of the most important methods for calculating atomic and molecular properties: therefore see *MQM* Chapter 11, Eyring, Walter, and Kimball (1944), Hameka (1965), Davies (1967), and Kauzmann (1957). The mathematics of perturbation theory and its recent developments are described by Hirschfelder, Byers-Brown, and Epstein (1964) and by Wilcox (1966). The last two references describe the differences between the *Rayleigh-Schrödinger* perturbation theory (which is the scheme set out in the Box), and the *Wigner-Brillouin* perturbation theory. The convergence of a perturbation expansion to the exact energy is a frisky problem, slightly tamed by the *Rellich-Kato theorem* described on p. 6 of Wilcox (1966). Time-dependent perturbation theory enables, among other things, the evolution of a wavefunction to be calculated as a function of time; see °transition probability, Chapter 7 of *MQM*, Davydov (1965), and Heitler (1954). An account of Heitler's theory has been given by Hameka (1965). A recent review of time-dependent perturbation theory is that of Langhoff, Epstein, and Karplus (1972).

phonons. Just as °photons are °quantized vibrations of the electromagnetic field so phonons are quantized vibrations of a crystalline lattice. Imagine first a linear chain of atoms which is vibrating in a low-frequency mode (Fig. P4): this vibration is quantized and may possess only discrete amounts of energy; if its frequency is ν its energy must be some integral multiple of $h\nu$. Instead of exciting a single vibrational mode through its successive evenly-spaced quantum levels it is possible to regard the rising energy of the system as resulting from the addition of hypothetical particles to that state; if n particles enter a state of characteristic frequency ν the energy of the system rises by $nh\nu$. This particle picture of excitation of vibrations is the basis of the concept of a phonon: a phonon is a quantum of excitation of a specified frequency, and may be envisaged as a particle of energy $h\nu$ added to the system.

In a complex solid, phonons of different frequency exist (just as in the electromagnetic field light of different frequencies exists). As in the case of light the phonons in a solid may be polarized, but as well as *transverse phonons*, in which the lattice atoms are displaced perpendicular to the propagation direction (Fig. P4 a), *longitudinal phonons*, in which the displacement is along the direction of propagation, as in a sound

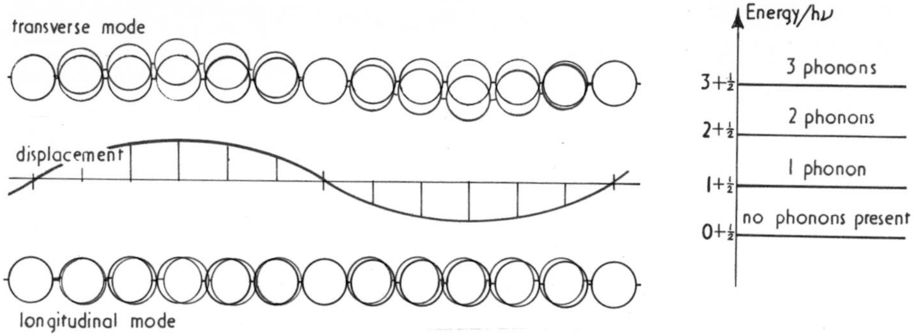

FIG. P4. Transverse and longitudinal modes of the same wavelength: the extent of excitation can be expressed as the number of phonons present.

wave in a fluid, may also exist (Fig. P4 b). A further complication may be illustrated by the case of an ionic lattice containing positive and negative ions. First imagine the vibrations of the two interpenetrating lattices as independent: now consider the combined system. Two situations may arise (see Fig. P5). In the first the lattice of positive ions moves in phase with the lattice of negative ions: this gives rise to the *acoustical branch* of the phonon spectrum. In the second the phase of the displacement of the two lattices is opposite: this gives rise to the *optical branch.* The latter name arises from the modulation of the lattice dipole moment during the out-of-phase movements of the two sublattices, and the fact that a light beam can interact with this oscillating dipole and so stimulate that particular branch of the lattice vibrations.

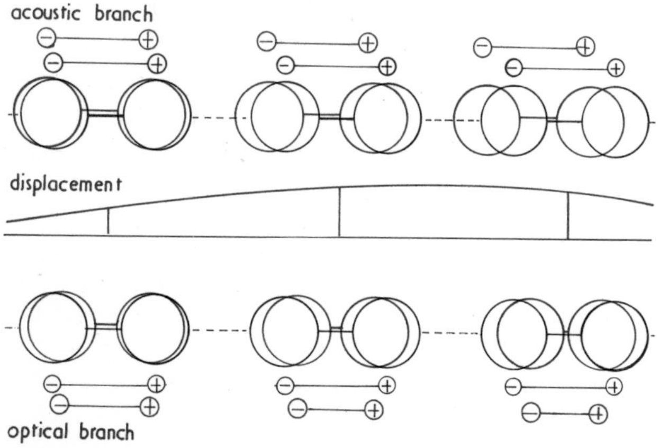

FIG. P5. Acoustic and optical branches of the same wavelength. Note that the dipole changes only in the latter.

Further information. A good introduction to lattice vibrations is given in Kittel (1971) and a more advanced one by Kittel (1963) and Ziman (1960, 1972). The role of phonons in determining the electrical, optical, and thermal properties of solids is discussed in these books. For a simple account of the matter see Jennings and Morris's *Atoms in contact* (OPS 5).

phosphorescence. When a phosphorescent material is illuminated it emits light, and the emission may persist for an appreciable time even after the stimulating illumination has been removed; in this sense phosphorescence differs from °fluorescence, for in the latter the emission ceases virtually instantaneously. There is also a mechanistic distinction between the two processes, and this is connected with the persistence of the emission.

Phosphorescence occurs by the following mechanism: the ground-state molecule, in which all the spins are paired (and which is therefore a °singlet state S_0), absorbs the incident light and makes a transition to an upper singlet level. The electronic excitation is accompanied by a vibrational excitation (see Fig. P6), and this vibrational energy is transferred to the surrounding molecules by the type of processes described in °fluorescence. Indeed, the molecule is well along the path that leads to fluorescence; but if the vibrational deactivation is not too fast another process may intervene. Let there be a triplet state of the excited molecule (in which two spins are unpaired): this is illustrated as the curve T_1 in the diagram. There is a non-vanishing probability that the molecule will switch from the singlet state to the triplet as

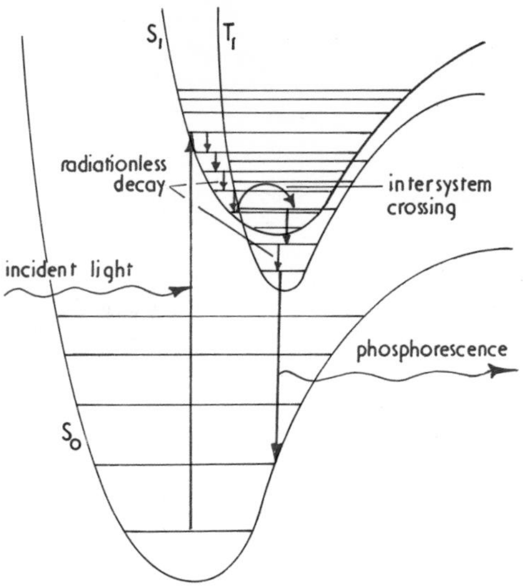

FIG. P6. The mechanism of phosphorescence.

it steps down the vibrational energy ladder (this is the *inter-system crossing*, ISC). At the foot of the ladder it finds itself trapped. It cannot radiate its electronic energy and drop to the ground state because that involves a singlet-triplet transition (which is forbidden by the °selection rules). It cannot clamber back to the crossing point and then step down the singlet ladder, because the collisions with the lattice cannot supply enough energy. It cannot give up its electronic energy to the surrounding molecules by a radiationless transition, because we have supposed that even the vibrational deactivation is weak, and that involved a smaller energy (which is easier to remove). If the foregoing description were true, the molecule would be stuck in the upper triplet. But the remarks are not strictly true, like most remarks, and the important fallacy is that the °singlet-triplet transition is forbidden. If it were strictly forbidden the molecule would have been unable to cross from the singlet state to the triplet. The fact that it did cross implies that there is enough °spin-orbit coupling present to break down the singlet-triplet selection rule, and so this becomes weakly allowed. But as it is only weakly allowed the transition $T_1 \longrightarrow S_0$ is slow, and may persist even after the illumination has ceased.

Phosphorescence involves a change of °multiplicity (an unpairing of spins) at an intermediate step, and this is its mechanistic difference from °fluorescence. From this point of view it follows that phosphorescence may occur if there is a suitable triplet state in the vicinity of the excited singlet states of the molecule and if there is a sufficiently strong spin-orbit coupling to induce ISC: a heavy atom enhances this crossing probability (the *heavy-atom effect*). Furthermore, there must be enough time for the molecule to cross from one curve to the other, and this means that the vibrational deactivation must not proceed so fast that the molecule is quenched and taken below the point where the curves intersect before the ISC interaction has time to operate. It is for this reason that many molecules which fluoresce in fluid solution are found to phosphoresce when they are trapped in a solid lattice, such as a gel or glass. We can also predict from Fig. P6 that the wavelength of the emitted light should be longer (further into the red) than fluorescent emission: the lowest vibrational level of the triplet lies below that of the lowest excited singlet. Finally, it is not impossible for some molecules to clamber back into the singlet S_1, and to fluoresce into the ground singlet: this is *slow fluorescence*, the triplet state acting merely as a reservoir.

What is the evidence that the triplet state is involved in phosphorescence? The first direct evidence came from the determination of the °magnetic susceptibility of a phosphorescent sample with and without illumination: it became paramagnetic when the light was on. The most sensitive procedure is to apply °electron spin resonance to the phosphorescent state: this shows unequivocally that a triplet state is involved.

Questions. How does phosphorescence differ observationally from fluorescence? Sketch the diagram corresponding to the formation of a fluorescent state and superimpose it on the diagram that leads to phosphorescence. What competitions determine which path is taken? How may phosphorescence be enhanced relative to the fluorescent and radiationless decay routes? What is meant by the term 'inter-system crossing', and how does it differ from 'internal conversion'? Why is phosphorescence a slow process? What perturbation is responsible for the ISC and the emission? How may this perturbation be enhanced? What is slow fluorescence, and how may it be distinguished from phosphorescence? How may it be distinguished theoretically and experimentally from delayed °fluorescence? What evidence is there that the triplet state is involved in phosphorescence? Discuss the reason why it is appropriate to think of the ISC as occuring at the intersection of the two potential curves.

Further information. See *MQM* Chapter 10, °fluorescence and °laser action. See also Bowen (1946), Wayne (1970), Calvert and Pitts (1966), and McGlynn, Azumi, and Kinoshita (1969). The electron spin resonance evidence for the role of the triplet state will be found in Hutchison and Mangum (1958) and Carrington and McLachlan (1967), and is reviewed in detail in McGlynn *et al*. (1969).

photoelectric effect. When short-wavelength light falls on a metal surface electrons are emitted. Three observations are very important:

(1) the emission occurs only if the wavelength of the incident light is smaller than a threshold value characteristic of the metal;

(2) emission occurs even at very low intensities so long as the threshold frequency is exceeded, and however dim the light there is no time-delay between its application and the appearance of photoelectrons;

(3) the kinetic energy of the emitted electrons depends linearly on the frequency of the light once the threshold is exceeded.

The first observation suggests that the energy that can be transferred to the metal surface in order to eject an electron is related to the frequency of the light, and that the metal surface cannot gradually accumulate energy until it has sufficient for the job. This behaviour is non-classical, because an incident wave would be expected to deposit its energy into the metal irrespective of its frequency.

The quantum theory and its concept of °photons can explain all the features of the effect in a simple and direct fashion. It recognizes that a light wave of frequency ν may be considered as composed of a collection of photons each bearing the energy $h\nu$. The explanation of the three observations is then as follows.

1. When a photon strikes the metal's surface it can eject an electron by imparting all its energy to it, but the ejection will be successful only if the energy transferred $h\nu$ is sufficient to overcome the energy that binds the electron to the metal (the °work function ϕ). If the frequency is less than the work function the electron will not be emitted, and the photon re-emerges from the surface as part of the reflected beam. Thus the threshold frequency of the photoelectric effect can be understood.

2. The intensity and time characteristics are explained on the same basis, because so long as the frequency exceeds threshold the photon is able to eject an electron; the effect depends on single photon-electron collision events rather than the accumulation of energy from a passing wavefront. At low intensities (few photons) only a few collisions occur, but each photon carries the same energy $h\nu$ as the photons in a heavily populated intense beam of the same frequency.

3. The third point can be explained on the grounds that a successful photon is annihilated in the collision that ejects the electron, and, by the conservation of energy, all its energy must appear in the electron; of this energy an amount corresponding to the work function is expended in prising the electron out of the metal and setting it in free space, and the remainder $h\nu - \phi$ must be ascribed to the kinetic energy of the electron $\frac{1}{2}m_e v^2$. It follows that the kinetic energy of the electron is proportional to the frequency of the incident light.

The importance of the photoelectric effect, other than its technological value for light-sensitive devices, lies in its historical value in the development of the idea that radiation is °quantized and in its application to the study of the °work function, for the latter can be determined from the threshold frequency. A modern development of this is *photoelectron spectroscopy* (PES), where electrons are ejected from molecules by a high-energy photon (from a short-wavelength source). The 'work function' in this case is the energy required to extract the electron from the °orbital it occupies in the molecule, and so the appearance of electrons with a variety of different kinetic energies under the influence of monochromatic radiation implies that they are being ejected from a corresponding range of orbitals of various binding energies (Fig. P7). Analysis of the kinetic-energy spectrum of the

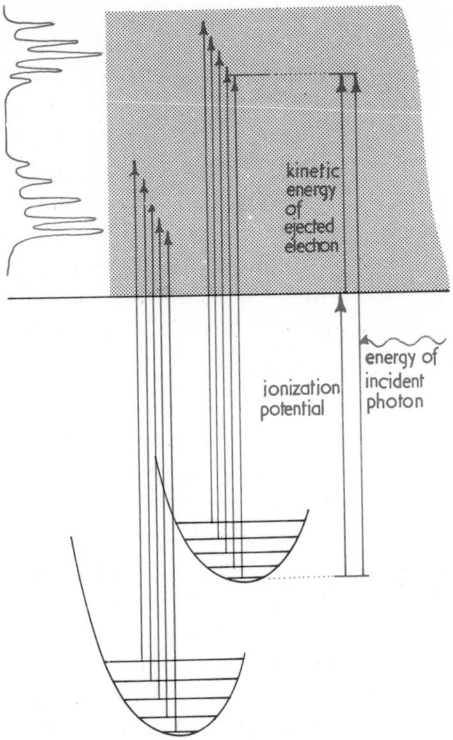

FIG. P7. Formation of a photoelectron spectrum.

ejected electrons provides detailed information about the energy levels of molecules. When the photon source is in the X-ray region each photon carries sufficient energy to eject electrons from the innermost shells of atoms, and so their energies can also be studied (Fig. P8). This X-ray technique is known by the inglorious name of *electron spectroscopy for chemical analysis* (ESCA). See also °Auger effect.

Questions. State the significant features of the photoelectric effect. Why cannot the classical wave theory of light account for these phenomena? What is the role of photons in the photoelectric effect, and how do they enable the features of the effect to be explained? What is the role of the work function? Light of wavelength 750 nm, 500 nm, 200 nm falls on a surface composed of one of the following metals: Na (2·3 eV), K (2·2 eV), Cs (2·1 eV), W (4·5 eV); the number in brackets is the work function for the metal. Predict the

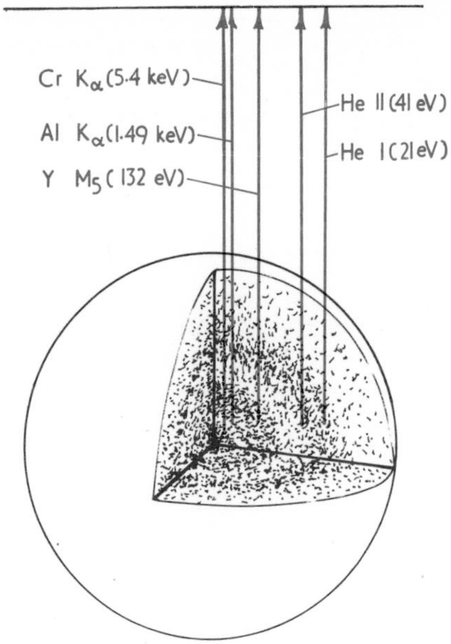

FIG. P8. Ejection of electrons from different regions of an atom.

kinetic energy of the ejected electron in each case where photoemission may occur. The kinetic energy of photoelectrons as a function of incident frequency was measured: at a wavelength of 625 nm the kinetic energy was 0·2 eV, at 416 nm it was 1·2 eV, and at 312 nm it was 2·2 eV. Calculate the work function for the metal. What is the relation of photoelectron spectroscopy to the photoelectric effect?

Further information. Analysis of the photoelectric effect will be found in Chapter 2 of Bohm (1951) and §1.3 of Jammer (1966). The implications of the phenomenon for the concept of photons is described by Born and Beim (1968). Photoelectron spectroscopy is described in Turner, Baker, and Brundle (1970), Baker and Betteridge (1972), and Siegbahn *et al.* (1969). Siegbahn (1973) has given a simple introduction to ESCA and Turner (1968) a simple introduction to PES.

photons. Light of frequency ν can impart energy only in discrete amounts (°quanta) of magnitude $h\nu$, where h is Planck's constant. A light beam of frequency ν therefore can possess an energy that is an integral multiple of $h\nu$, and so it is natural to imagine this successive excitation of a frequency mode as an addition of hypothetical particles to a state. Thus a beam of frequency ν and energy $nh\nu$ could be regarded as containing n light corpuscles. These quanta of excitation, or hypothetical corpuscles, are *photons.* Each photon of wavelength $\lambda = c/\nu$ carries an energy $h\nu$ and, according to the °de Broglie relation, a linear momentum $h\nu/c$. Low-frequency photons carry little energy and momentum; high-frequency photons carry much of both.

Does light exhibit any of the corpuscular features that this photon description suggests? Indeed it does, for the °photoelectric effect confirms that energy can be transferred only in discrete amounts (corresponding to the annihilation of a photon), and the °Compton effect shows that each photon carries a characteristic amount of momentum related to its frequency. Radiation pressure can be understood in terms of the pressure imparted to a surface by a steady stream of incident photons.

Photons may be polarized so that their electric component lies in a plane (plane-polarized light) or moves in a circle or ellipse; but in all cases the electric component must be perpendicular to the propagation direction. The photon possesses an intrinsic angular momentum (its °spin), and of this the existence of left and right circularly polarized light is a manifestation. The spin of a photon is unity: one projection (that corresponding to a *right*-hand screw along the direction of travel) corresponds to *left* circularly polarized light, one projection (the left-hand screw) to right circularly polarized light, and the third (remember that for °spin 1 there are three possible components on a selected axis) is forbidden to particles moving with the speed of light, which photons do.

The existence of the spin of a photon is the basis of the °selection rules for °electric dipole transitions. Since its spin is unity the photon is a °boson: this entails, through the °Pauli principle, that an indefinite number may occupy a single quantum state, and for this reason intense monochromatic beams may be prepared (see °laser).

Questions. What is meant by the term 'photon'? What is the energy of a photon in light of frequency ν, and what momentum does it carry? What is the energy of the photon of light corresponding to the microwave region of the spectrum (1 cm^{-1}) and infrared (500 cm^{-1}), the visible (~550 nm), the ultraviolet (300 nm), and γ-rays (10^{-11} m)? How many photons are emitted in a 1 mJ pulse from a 337 nm wavelength nitrogen-gas laser? How many photons are emitted from a tungsten 100 W lamp each second: assume all the radiation is at 450 nm? What frequency of light is the minimum that can be used to fracture a 100 kJ mol^{-1} bond in a molecule? What is the evidence for the corpuscular nature of light? Why is this view compatible with the existence of the typically wave phenomenon of diffraction?

Further information. The quantum mechanics of photons can be made very complicated; but it is very important now that lasers are ascendant. If you are really interested see Grandy (1970), Louisell (1973), Berestetskii, Lifshitz, and Pitaevskii (1971), Akhiezer and Berestetskii (1965), Levich, Mayamlin, and Vdovin (1973), Jauch and Rohrlich (1955), and Kaempffer (1965). The °uncertainty relation for the phase of photons and their number is discussed correctly by Carruthers and Nieto (1968), but rarely correctly elsewhere. The study of photons is helpful in the discussion of the interpretation of quantum mechanics: see Dirac (1958) and Feynman, Leighton, and Sands (1963). Quantum optics is the study of optics where the quantum, and therefore the photon, aspects are dominant. See Glauber (1969) for a review and Loudon (1974) and Louisell (1973) for a modern account. Are photons particles? See Born and Beim (1968) for a view. See p. 9 of Whittaker's *Stereochemistry and mechanism* (OCS 5) for a helpful picture of the decomposition of a plane wave into its circular components.

polarizability. When an electric field is applied to an individual atom or molecule the electron distribution and the molecular geometry are distorted; the polarizability is a measure of the ease with which this occurs. The *atomic polarizability* is the contribution to the overall polarizability due to the geometrical distortion. It is usually significantly smaller than the *electronic polarizability*, which is the contribution due to the displacement of the electrons. There is a third contribution to the polarizability of a bulk sample: this is the *orientation polarization.* It arises when the molecules have a

BOX 17: Polarizability

Energy of polarizable molecules in a field **E**

$$\mathcal{E}(E) = \mathcal{E}^{(0)} - \mu^{(0)}E - \frac{1}{2!}\alpha E^2 - \frac{1}{3!}\beta E^3 + \dots$$

Dipole moment in a field **E**

$$\mu = \mu^{(0)} + \alpha E + \frac{1}{2!}\beta E^2 + \dots$$

$\mu^{(0)}$ is the permanent dipole moment, α the polarizability, and β the first hyperpolarizability. (For magnetic properties, α is called the magnetizability, and written ξ.)

Quantum expressions

$$\mu^{(0)} = \langle\psi_0|\mathbf{d}|\psi_0\rangle$$

$$\alpha = -(\partial^2\mathcal{E}/\partial E^2)_{E=0} = \frac{2}{3}\sum_n{}' \Delta_n^{-1}\mathbf{d}_{0n}.\mathbf{d}_{n0}.$$

$\Delta_n = E_n^{(0)} - E_0^{(0)}$, the molecular excitation energy,

$\mathbf{d}_{0n} = \langle\psi_0|\mathbf{d}|\psi_n\rangle$, the °transition dipole moment.

Polarization of medium

Electric susceptibility (χ_e): $P = \epsilon_0\chi_e E$.

Relative permittivity (dielectric constant): $\epsilon_r = 1 + \chi_e$.

Refractive index: $n_r = \epsilon_r^{1/2}$.

Lorentz local field: $\mathbf{E}_{loc} \sim \mathbf{E} + \mathbf{P}/3\epsilon_0 = \frac{1}{3}(\epsilon_r + 2)\mathbf{E}$ (the factor 3 is approximate).

Lorentz-Lorenz or Clausius-Mossotti equation:

$$\left(\frac{\epsilon_r - 1}{\epsilon_r + 2}\right)\left(\frac{M}{\rho}\right) = \frac{L\alpha}{3\epsilon_0} = \alpha_M.$$

M is the molecular weight, ρ is the density, and L is Avogadro's number. $L\alpha/3\epsilon_0$ is referred to as the *molar polarizability* α_M.

Debye equation (for molar polarizability of polar dielectrics):

$$\alpha_M = \left(\frac{\epsilon_r - 1}{\epsilon_r + 2}\right)\left(\frac{M}{\rho}\right) = \frac{L}{3\epsilon_0}\left(\alpha_A + \alpha_E + \alpha_O\right)$$

α_A: atomic polarizability

α_E: electronic (molecular) polarizability

α_O: orientation polarizability, which is given by the *Langevin contribution* for a molecule with permanent dipole moment $\mu^{(0)}$, as

$$\alpha_O = \mu^{(0)2}/3kT.$$

See Table 20 for the Maxwell equations.

permanent dipole moment: the applied field orientates the molecules, and the entire sample acquires net polarization. The orientation effect is not complete because thermal motion disorganizes the sample: its magnitude may be calculated by applying the Boltzmann distribution to determine the mean dipole moment of the sample, and one deduces the *Langevin contribution* exhibited in Box 17. This mechanical contribution will not concern us further (although it is an important component of the total polarization); we shall concentrate on the source of the electronic contribution.

Highly polarizable molecules respond strongly to the application of the field; they become highly polarized, and the centroid of negative electronic charge is displaced. If the molecule is initially nonpolar the polarization leads to the formation of an electric °dipole moment; and if it is already polar it leads to an additional component of the dipole. The magnitude of the induced dipole is a good indication of the polarizability of the molecule, and the polarizability α may be defined as the constant of proportionality between the induced moment and the strength of the electric field: $\mu(\text{induced}) = \alpha E$. The dipole moment might depart from this linear relation if the applied field is very strong; in that case the dipole depends on E^2, and higher powers, and the coefficients of E^2, E^3, . . . are known as the first, second, . . . *hyperpolarizabilities.* We shall neglect these non-linear response terms and concentrate on the linear response, the polarizability α.

The quantum-mechanical calculation of the polarizability proceeds by calculating the energy of a polarizable molecule in an electric field, and relating this to a second-order °perturbation-theory calculation (see Box 17). It is found that the magnitude of polarizability can be interpreted in a variety of ways.

1. One interpretation shows that the polarizability increases with the size of the atom and with the number of electrons it contains; this can be understood in terms of it being easier for a field to distort the electronic distribution when the electrons are far from the nucleus, or well shielded from its charge.

2. Another interpretation, which is based on the view that the distortion of the molecule can be represented by an appropriate °superposition of wavefunctions, gives the expression for the polarizability as a sum of terms, each one of which represents an admixture of an excited state into the ground state. The amount of each state depends on its energy separation from the ground state and on the intensity of an optical, °electric dipole transition between it and the ground state: as the intensity of the transition increases the state may contribute more strongly, and as the energy increases it contributes less. A consequence is that it is reasonable to expect molecules that have intense transitions in the optical or lower-frequency region of the spectrum to be highly polarizable. On this basis it is understandable that the aliphatic hydrocarbons, which have weak optical transitions in the ultraviolet, are only weakly polarizable.

3. A third interpretation remarks that the polarizability formula can be understood in terms of the magnitude of the fluctuations in the instantaneous electric dipole moment of the species. It is possible to imagine local transient electronic movements in the molecule that give rise to a dipole moment which on the average is zero (for a nonpolar molecule); the greater these fluctuations the greater the polarizability. This interpretation is related to the first, because the fluctuations are greater in large, weakly-bound systems.

The polarizability of a sample is frequency-dependent. At low frequencies (below about 10^{12} Hz) the molecules, the atoms within the molecules, and the electrons of the molecules can follow the changing direction of the applied field. At higher frequencies (above 10^{12} Hz but below 10^{14} Hz) the molecules cannot reorientate themselves sufficiently quickly, and so the orientation polarizability ceases to contribute. At still higher frequencies the atomic nuclei are too sluggish to follow the oscillating field, and the atomic contribution is eliminated. This implies that at high frequencies (in the optical range) the only contribution to the polarizability is the electronic, but even this ceases at very high frequencies. The frequency-dependence (the *dispersion*) of the polarizability is a helpful property in distinguishing the contributions.

Polarizabilities of molecules are related to the relative permittivity (dielectric constant) of the medium they compose (see Box 17), and its °refractive index. Both properties enable the polarizability to be determined over a wide frequency range. (Since the refractive index is normally measured at optical frequencies it is related to the electronic polarizability.)

Questions. 1. What happens when a molecule is immersed in an electric field? How may the polarizability be defined? What is the dependence of the induced dipole moment on the applied field when the latter is very strong? Would you expect the polarizability of a molecule to depend on its orientation with respect to the field? Why should the polarizability increase as the species becomes larger and its electrons less strongly bound? Which is more polarizable, He or He^+? What is the role of the instantaneous fluctuations of the dipole moment of an atom in determining its polarizability? Can the polarizability be related to the strength and frequency of optical transitions? Why does the polarizability depend on the admixture of excited states? (Revise °perturbation theory and °virtual transitions.)
2. Apply the expression in Box 17 to calculate the polarizability of a charged simple °harmonic oscillator, an electron in a one-dimensional square well, and the °hydrogen atom. Where you feel it necessary apply the °closure approximation. Calculate the polarizability parallel and perpendicular to the axis of a $2p_z$-orbital in the carbon atom: use °Slater atomic orbitals and the closure approximation.

Further information. See *MQM* Chapter 11 for a derivation of the relations in the Box and for a further discussion. See also van Vleck (1932), Davies (1967), and Buckingham (1960). Polarizabilities are listed in Landolt-Börnstein. For further applications see °intermolecular forces and °dispersion forces. Hyperpolarizabilities and their measurement are discussed by Buckingham and Orr (1967). See also Kielich (1970).

polaron. A polaron is a defect in an ionic crystal that is formed when an excess of charge at a particular point polarizes the lattice in its vicinity. Thus if an electron is

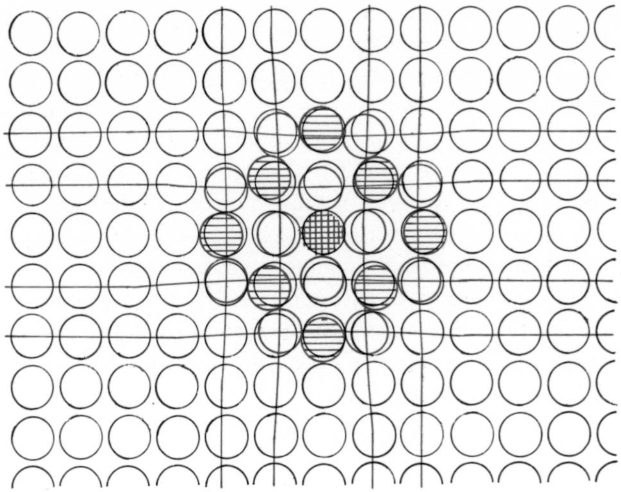

FIG. P9. A polaron in a simple lattice. The doubly hatched site is a doubly charged region; the singly hatched sites are singly charged with opposite sign.

captured by a halide ion in an alkali-halide crystal the metal ions move towards it and the other negative ions shrink away (Fig. P9). As the electron moves through the lattice it is accompanied by this distortion. Dragging this distortion around effectively makes the electron into a more massive particle, and this is intended to be implied by the name polaron: a lattice distortion moving through the lattice like a massive particle.

Further information. See Chapter 10 of Kittel (1971) and Kittel (1963). A good discussion is given in Chapter 4 of Mott and Davis (1971), and the subject is reviewed in Kuper and Whitfield (1963).

precession. In the °vector model of the atom and in the general theory of °angular momentum, an angular momentum of magnitude $[j(j+1)]^{1/2}\hbar$ and z-component $m\hbar$ is represented by a vector of length $[j(j+1)]^{1/2}$ making a projection m on to a z-axis. From the °uncertainty principle it is known that if the z-component of angular momentum is precisely specified then the x- and the y-components are completely uncertain. This situation may be represented in the vector diagram by indicating the range of possible orientations of the angular

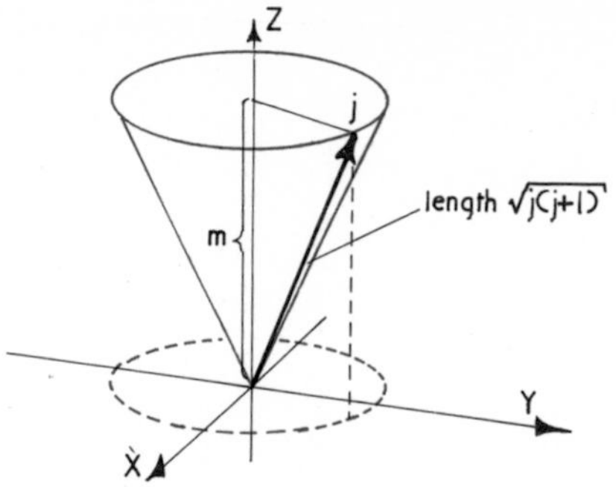

FIG. P10. Precession. The cone denotes the possible but indeterminate orientations of the vector.

momentum by a cone (Fig. P10, but see also Figs. A2 and A3): wherever the vector lies on this cone, it has the same z-component but its x- and y-components are completely undetermined. The cone is referred to as the *cone of precession.* Note that we avoided saying that the angular momentum actively precesses around z: the cone represents the possible array of orientations of the angular momentum, and at this stage we do not wish to imply that the tip of the vector moves round the mouth of the cone. In the absence of magnetic fields the vector is at rest at an indeterminate position on the conical surface.

When a magnetic field is applied along the z-axis the states with different projection m have different energies by virtue of the magnetic moment associated with the angular momentum: the energy of the state m is $m\mu_B B$ for orbital angular momentum (and $2m\mu_B B$ for °spin). This energy can be expressed as a frequency by dividing by $\hbar$: $\omega = m\mu_B B/\hbar$. The vector diagram is a symbolic code representing the quantum mechanics of the situation, and it can be augmented in a way that incorporates the energy of the state by adopting the convention that a state with energy $m\mu_B B$ is represented by a vector that revolves around the z-axis with a frequency ω (Fig. P11): this is *precession*, and the frequency is the *Larmor precession frequency.* As the field is made weaker the precession frequency slows, and in the limit of zero field the static, indeterminate distribition of vecots is regained. The state with the greatest value of $|m|$ precesses most rapidly, and

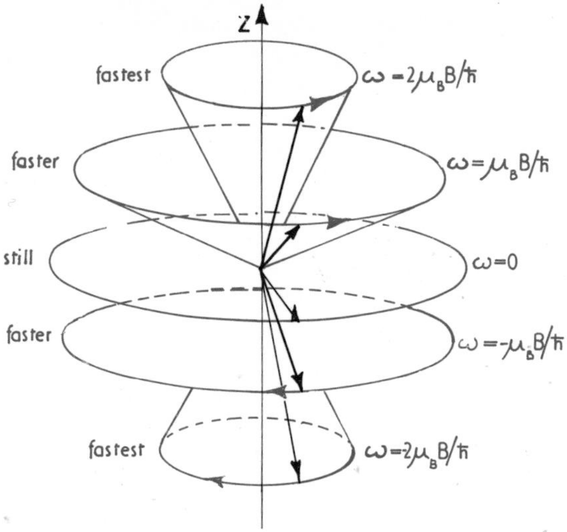

FIG. P11. Larmor precession in the presence of a magnetic field, and its connexion with the vector model.

that with zero m precesses not at all; opposite signs of m are interpreted as opposite senses of precession.

From this picture we see that the rate of precession about an axis represents the strength of coupling to that axis, and this view may be extended to situations where the energy arises from sources other than external magnetic fields. The

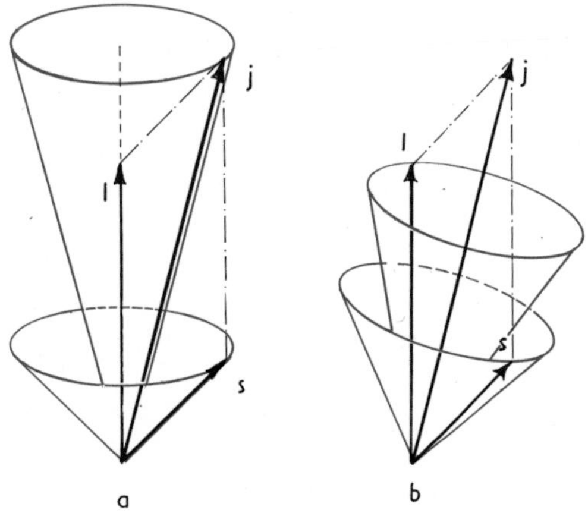

FIG. P12. Two points of view about the precession of coupled vectors. In (a) we sit on **l** and observe **s** and **j**; in (b) we sit on **j** and observe **s** and **l**.

case of °spin-orbit coupling is an example: **l** and **s** are coupled by the spin-orbit interaction, and form a vector **j**. If the spin-orbit coupling is strong the vector-coupling scheme involves a rapid precession of **s** about **l** (or, what is equivalent, a rapid precession of **l** and **s** about their resultant **j**): this is illustrated in Fig. P12. When the coupling is weak the precession is slow and the coupling can easily be broken by other influences.

The picture of precession is a superb example of the way that algebraic concepts of quantum mechanics can be represented by diagrams: each aspect of the 'picture' is a code for some aspect of the quantum-mechanical situation. But then, you might think, is the quantum-mechanical algebra not itself merely a code?

Questions. What does the cone of precession represent in the vector model of angular momentum when no field is present? Why is a cone forced on the model? What does it represent when a magnetic field is applied? Upon what does the precession frequency depend? Calculate the Larmor precession frequencies for a p-electron in a magnetic field of 1 G and 3 kG; what is the Larmor frequency for an electron °spin in a field of 3·4 kG and of a proton spin in a field of 15 kG? What in general does the rate of precession represent? Is it easy to decouple two momenta that are rapidly precessing about each other? The spin-orbit coupling energy of an electron in a first-row atom is about 50 cm^{-1}: compute the relative precession frequency for this situation, and estimate the external magnetic field that would be required to cause a significant decoupling of the momenta and a significant orientation of the individual momenta with the field. The conversion of a triplet state into a °singlet can be brought about by changing the relative phase of the two electron-spin orientations: thus if one spin precesses faster than the other its orientation is shifted by 180° with respect to the other, and a singlet is generated out of a triplet (see °singlets and triplets, especially Fig. S7). Suppose that the two electrons of a triplet molecule are in fields differing by 1G, either by virtue of inhomogeneities in the field or because they experience different internal fields. Calculate, by determining the different Larmor precession frequencies, the rate at which the singlet is formed. Can you see a connexion with the interconversion of *ortho*- and *para*-hydrogen (see °nuclear statistics)?

Further information. See *MQM* Chapters 6 and 8 for a discussion of the algebra beneath the picture, and the applications of the °vector model to atomic and molecular spectra. See also Candler (1964), Herzberg (1944), White (1934), and Kuhn (1962) for applications in atomic spectroscopy. The language of precession is used extensively in the discussion of magnetic-resonance experiments: therefore see McLauchlan's *Magnetic resonance* (OCS 1), Lynden-Bell and Harris (1969), Carrington and McLachlan (1967), and Slichter (1963). A good example of the decoupling of two precessing vectors is provided by the °Paschen-Back effect.

predissociation. Ordinary, well-behaved dissociation occurs when a molecule is excited to a state that possesses more energy than the separated fragments. A transition from curve X to curve A in Fig. P13 a provides such an example; the spectrum is blurred where the upper vibrational states are not °quantized (where they are really translational states). Predissociation is dissociation that occurs in a transition before the dissociation limit is attained, hence its name.

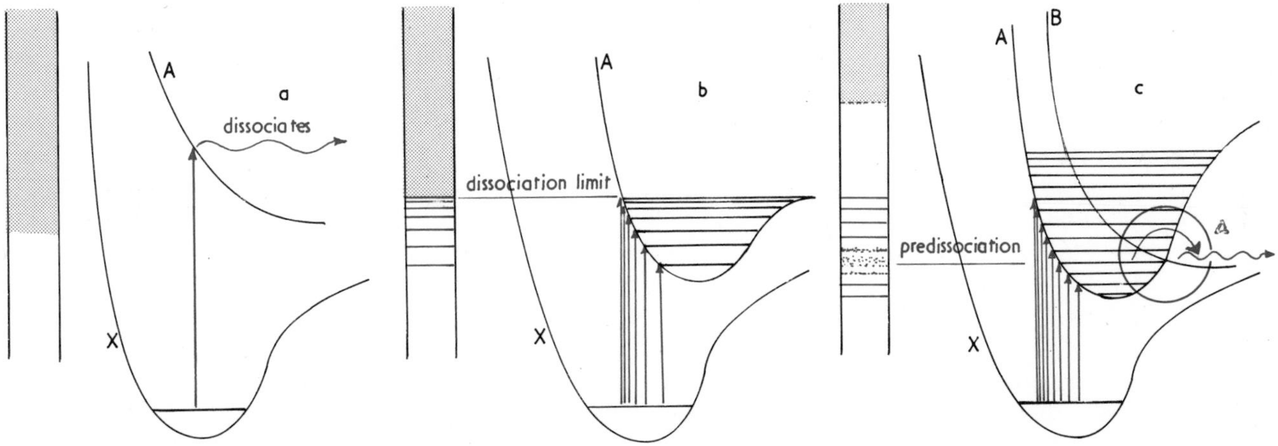

FIG. P13. (a) Dissociation by a transition to a dissociative state. (b) Dissociation when enough energy is added to disrupt the upper state. (c) Predissociation due to the presence of a dissociative state. The appearances of the spectra are indicated on the left.

Consider the transitions A ← X shown in Fig. P13 b. On the °electronic transition is superimposed a series of lines due to the transition to the vibrational states of A. At low frequencies (energies) the lines are sharp, and so we expect them to remain until enough energy is added to excite the molecule beyond the dissociation limit of the upper state. In Fig. P13 b we see that the vibrational structure disappears at this point. (Below this point it has the intensities characteristic of the °selection rules in operation and the °Franck-Condon principle.) In some cases it is observed that the vibrational structure of the spectrum disappears before the dissociation limit is attained. This may occur because another, dissociative state (B) crosses A, and because there exists an interaction (°perturbation) in the molecule that can flip the state of the excited molecule from A to B (Fig. P13 c). Put another way, this can be interpreted as the states in the vicinity of the region Δ in Fig. P13 c being a mixture: the vibrational states of A acquire some of the translational character of the states of B at that energy. Therefore a state within the region Δ has some propensity to dissociate even though its energy may be far below the dissociation energy for the state A. When the energy of the incident light is great enough to excite the vibrational state of A above the region Δ the lines are again observed to be sharp, for now the molecule is unable to switch into the state B. The presence of predissociation may be recognized therefore by a blurred region in the vibrational °progression of an electronic transition.

The mechanism of predissociation is closely related to the

°Auger effect, the principal difference being that the former dissociates a fragment of the molecule and the latter spits out an electron. In each there is a radiationless transition from a bound to an unbound state. Predissociation obeys certain °selection rules, and these will be found listed in that section.

Induced predissociation is predissociation that is induced by some external influence; in particular, collisions with a foreign gas ('collision-induced predissociation') or an applied field. The collisions are able to knock the excited molecule from A to B, and the applied field may relax some of the selection rules that govern the A ⇝ B transition (the wavy line denotes that the transition is radiationless).

Questions. 1. What is meant by the term 'predissociation'? How may it be recognized in a spectrum? Suppose the emission of light from a molecule were observed: what effect would predissociation have on the appearance of the emission spectrum? What causes the molecule to flip from one curve to another? How may the efficiency of this transition be enhanced? In what senses is predissociation a type of °Auger effect? What happens to the rotational structure of the electronic transition in the region close to the predissociation domain? Suppose that the state dissociates with first-order kinetics and lifetime τ, use the °uncertainty principle to find an expression in terms of τ which determines whether or not rotational structure will disappear from the spectrum, and then find an expression for the disappearance of vibrational structure. Choose typical values of the molecular properties you require, and assess the lifetimes of levels for which the rotational and vibrational structures disappear.
2. In the text it was remarked that outside the region Δ there was only insignificant mixing of the states A and B. On what grounds may that statement be justified? Provide a classical and a quantum-mechanical interpretation; for the latter consider the role of overlap in the same way as in the justification of the °Franck-Condon principle.

Further information. See *MQM* Chapter 10. See Herzberg (1950, 1966) for a thorough discussion of predissociation and many examples. See also Barrow (1962), Gaydon (1968), and King (1964). Induced predissociation is described by Wayne (1970).

progression. In the °electronic spectra of molecules the excitation of the electron is accompanied by excitation of the °vibrations, and so instead of a single line in the spectrum there may be a complicated band of transitions. A progression is a °series of lines that arise from transitions from the same vibrational level of one of the states (the ground electronic state if absorption is involved) to successive vibrational levels of the other state. Thus the $\nu'' = 0$ progression is the series of transitions starting in the $\nu'' = 0$ vibrational level of the ground electronic state of the molecule and terminating in the $\nu' = 0$, 1, 2, . . . vibrational levels of the upper electronic state (Fig. P14). The $\nu'' = 1$ progression is a similar series starting in the $\nu'' = 1$ vibrational level of the ground electronic state. The lines in a progression are labelled (ν', ν''); therefore the $\nu'' = 0$ progression consists of the transitions (0, 0), (1, 0), (2, 0), etc..

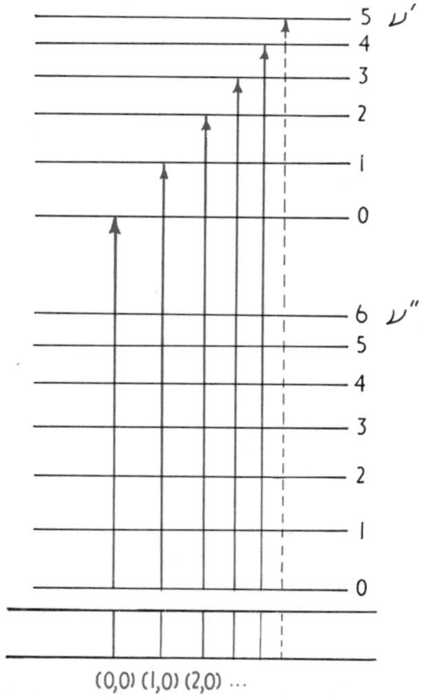

FIG. P14. A progression.

Questions. What is a progression? How does it differ from a °sequence? What information can you extract from the positions of the lines in a progression, and what information can you obtain by comparing the $v'' = 0$ and the $v'' = 1$ progressions? Would you expect the intensities of the progressions to be the same? Given that the energy of a vibrational level of the ground state depends on v'' through the expansion $\omega''(v'' + \frac{1}{2}) + x''\omega''(v'' + \frac{1}{2})^2$, with a similar expression for the upper state, calculate the frequencies of the $v'' = 0$ and the $v'' = 1$ progressions.

Further information. See *MQM* Chapter 10. Detailed information about the appearance, analysis, and formation of progressions will be found in Barrow (1962), Whiffen (1972), Gaydon (1968), King (1964), and Herzberg (1950).

Q

quadrupoles and other multipoles. The electric quadrupole moment is one of the series of *multipole moments* which are used to describe the way electric charge is distributed over a body. The first member of the series is the electric *monopole*, more commonly referred to as the point charge; then comes the electric °*dipole* moment, which may be regarded as the juxtaposition of two opposite charges, and so has no net charge (no monopole moment); then comes the electric *quadrupole* which may be regarded as being formed from four charges arranged in a way that leads neither to net charge (no monopole moment) nor net dipole moment. An arrangement that achieves this is shown in Fig. Q1. Higher multipoles may be constructed in an analogous way: for a *2^n-pole* ($n = 1$ is a dipole, $n = 2$ a quadrupole, $n = 3$ an octopole, $n = 4$ a hexadecapole) it is necessary to arrange 2^n electric charges in an array that possesses no lower multipole. Some of these are represented in Fig. Q1, but alternative arrangements may also be envisaged.

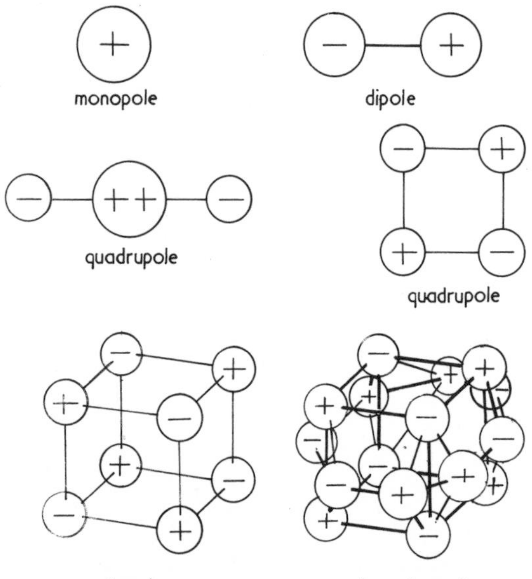

FIG. Q1. Various electric multipoles.

Often many multipoles vanish by virtue of the symmetry of the molecule. Consider, for example, the molecule CO_2 which has the linear structure O=C=O. As the molecule has no net charge, it has no electric monopole moment. It is symmetrical about the carbon atom, and so it has no electric dipole moment. The oxygen atoms are more °electronegative than the carbon, and so they bear a higher charge density than the central carbon; therefore the charge distribution has the form $(\delta -)-(\delta + \delta +)-(\delta -)$. This is of the form of a quadrupole, and so we can expect the quadrupole moment of CO_2 to be non-zero, as indeed is found.

The potential arising from a general charge distribution may be represented by a sum of potentials of the multipoles into which the distribution may be divided. The *electric potential due to a 2^n-pole* falls off with distance according to $1/r^{n+1}$; therefore the *electric field* due to a 2^n-pole falls off according to $1/r^{n+2}$ (the field is the negative gradient of the potential). It follows that the higher multipoles have a much shorter range than the lower: a monopole potential falls off according to the Coulomb law $1/r$, a quadrupole according to $1/r^3$. The more rapid decay of potential in the higher multipoles may be understood in terms of the way that a cluster of electric charges (as depicted in Fig. Q1), when viewed from great distance, is hardly distinguishable from having nothing at all: the cancellation at large distances occurs more effectively the higher the rank of the multipole.

BOX 18: Multipole fields

Field at r due to a point multipole at origin

$$E_n \propto 1/r^{n+2}.$$

Potential at r

$$\phi_n \propto 1/r^{n+1},$$

dipole: $\left(\frac{\mu}{4\pi\epsilon_0}\right)\left(\frac{1}{r^2}\right)\cos\theta$ $(q, -q$ separated by R, $\mu = qR)$,

linear quadrupole: $\frac{1}{2}\left(\frac{2qR^2}{4\pi\epsilon_0}\right)\left(\frac{1}{r^3}\right)(3\cos^2\theta - 1)$

(quadrupole formed with μ, μ head-to-head, $eQ = 2qR^2$).

Energy of multipole in a field E_z

(1) point charge (monopole) $\mathcal{E} = q\phi(r)$, where $E_z = -\mathrm{d}\phi/\mathrm{d}z$;

(2) dipole: $\mathcal{E} = -\mu.\mathbf{E}$
$= -\mu E_z \cos\theta = \mu(\partial\phi/\partial z)\cos\theta$;

(3) quadrupole: $\mathcal{E} = \frac{1}{8}eQ(\partial^2\phi/\partial z^2)(3\cos^2\theta - 1)$.

Different multipoles interact with different features of the electric field. An electric monopole interacts with the electric potential itself (see Box 18). An electric dipole interacts not with the potential but with its gradient; that is, the electric dipole interacts with the electric field. This can be understood in terms of the structure of the dipole as two juxtaposed point charges: at a general orientation of the dipole one charge interacts with the potential at its position and the other opposite charge interacts with the potential at its position. Only if the potential is different at the two points is there a net interaction; therefore there is an interaction only if the gradient of the potential does not vanish at the position of the dipole. Those to whom extension of analogies gives pleasure will be pleased to discover that the electric quadrupole moment interacts with the second derivative of the electric potential; or, what is the same thing, with the gradient of the electric field. This may be understood by considering the situations depicted in Fig. Q2. In the first, where the gradient of the potential (the field) is constant over the quadrupole, the energy of interaction is independent of orientation, and so there is no net interaction. In the second, where the potential has curvature (and where the field has a gradient), the energy depends on the orientation, and therefore we conclude that there is an interaction. The mathematical form of the interaction is given in Box 18.

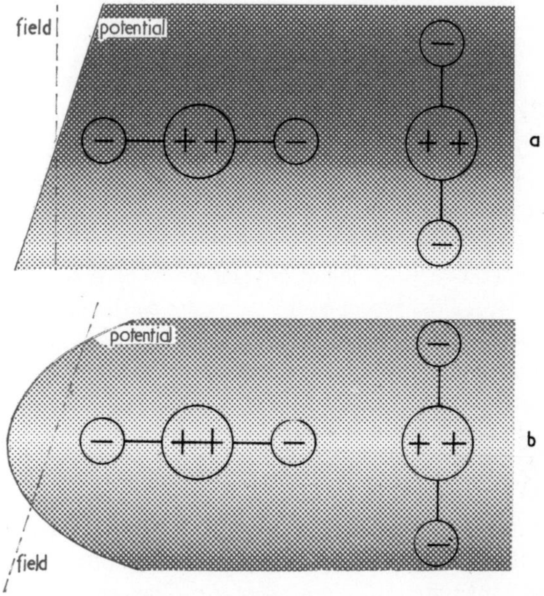

FIG. Q2. (a) A quadrupole in a constant field has an energy independent of orientation. (b) A quadrupole in a field gradient has an energy dependent on orientation. In each case the density of shading denotes the strength of the *potential*.

The typical magnitude of a molecular monopole is of the order of the magnitude of the electronic charge e (1.6×10^{-19} C). A single charged ion may be regarded, by the pedantic or the neat, as a monopole of this magnitude. The magnitude of a molecular dipole is of the order of eR, where R is a molecular diameter; for $R \sim 0.1$ nm (1 Å) the order of magnitude is 10^{-29}

C m (but see °dipole moment for debye). In the same way we may estimate the order of magnitude of the electric quadrupole moment of a molecule as eR^2, or roughly 10^{-39} C m^2. Part of the absurdity of the size of the unit is eliminated by defining the electric quadrupole moment as eQ, and calling Q the 'quadrupole moment'. It is normally expressed in square centimetres; therefore a molecular quadrupole moment might be expected to be of the order of 10^{-16} cm^2 (1 $Å^2$), and a nuclear quadrupole moment (see °hyperfine effects) of the order of 10^{-24} cm^2.

Questions. 1. Draw diagrams of charge distributions that represent an electric quadrupole, octopole, hexadecapole, 32-pole. Now draw alternative structures with similar multipoles. What is the dependence of distance of the potential due to a 2^n-pole? What is the dependence on distance of the field due to a 2^n-pole? Why is the electric quadrupole moment the most important multipole moment of CO_2? What is the first non-vanishing multipole moment of the helium atom? Of methane? Of water? Why does the potential of a quadrupole fall off more rapidly that that of a dipole? With what aspect of an electric field does a quadrupole interact? Why does a quadrupole not interact with a constant electric field? With what aspect of the field does an electric octopole interact? Draw a diagram to illustrate the physical basis of your answer. How may a molecular quadrupole be measured?
2. Take the quadrupole arrays of charges illustrated in Fig. Q1 and consider a point at a distance r from the centre of both arrays. Write an expression for the potential at that point due to the multipole (by regarding each point of the multipole as the source of a Coulomb field). Assume that r is much greater than the separation d of charges within the multipole, and expand the potential in powers of d/r; retain the leading term in the expansion. In this way find the electric potential due to a quadrupole. Then find the field at the point r. Compare your answer with the expression in Box 18.
3. Put a single electron at a distance r from the centre of a quadrupole of (a) molecular dimension and (b) nuclear dimension. Calculate the energy needed to rotate the quadrupole through 90°. What size quantum would be needed to invert a nucleus of this nature? To what frequency does that correspond? This calculation is the basis of the technique of *nuclear quadrupole resonance* (n.q.r.), where electric field gradients within molecules are determined by observing the energy required to rotate the orientations of nuclei with electric quadrupole moments.

Further information. Simple calculations on the electrostatics of multipole moments will be found in Corson and Lorrain (1970); tougher accounts are given by Jackson (1962) and Rose (1955, 1957). See Sugden and Kenney (1965) for a simple account with special attention paid to the way that quadrupole moments play a part in molecular spectroscopy. The calculation of molecular quadrupole moments is described by Davies (1967) and their measurement by Buckingham (1965), who also considers their role in intermolecular forces. The determination of nuclear quadrupole moments is described by Lucken (1969), who also gives a detailed account of nuclear quadrupole resonance spectroscopy; see also Das and Hahn (1958). A recent review of n.q.r. is that by Chihara and Nakamara (1972). See Carrington and McLachlan (1967) for a simple account of the effects of quadrupole moments in magnetic resonance, and Chapter 6 of Slichter (1963) for a more sophisticated, but well stated, account. Tables of nuclear quadrupole moments are given in §8 of Gray (1972), and a few will be found in Table 17.

quantum. A quantum of energy is the smallest amount of energy that may be transferred to or from a system. In classical physics there is no limitation to the smallness of permissible energy changes of a system, but quantum physics shows that only quantities of energy of a well-defined size can be transferred, the actual size depending on both the system and its state. A particularly simple example is provided by the °harmonic oscillator of natural period ν. In classical theory the oscillator may swing at its natural frequency with some energy, and its energy may be changed continuously. Quantum theory shows that the oscillator's energy can change only by some integral multiple of $h\nu$, where h is *Planck's constant*. Thus an attempt to change its energy by a fraction of $h\nu$ must fail.

The magnitude of quanta involved in the behaviour of macroscopic objects is so small that the changes in energy are virtually continuous, but at a microscopic level the quantization cannot be ignored. For example, the size of the quantum needed to transfer energy to and from the pendulum of a grandfather clock ($\nu \sim 0.5$ Hz) is only 3×10^{-34} J; but the oscillation of a bond in a molecule occurs at a frequency of the order of 10^{14} times larger at 6×10^{-20} J, or 36 kJ mol^{-1}.

When an atom falls from an excited state of energy E_e the change of energy $E_e - E_a$ is emitted as a quantum of light with a frequency ν given by the *Bohr frequency condition* $h\nu = E_e - E_g$. The size of the emitted quantum depends on the states involved in the transition: quantum changes of large energy appear as high-frequency radiation, and those of small energy as low-frequency radiation.

Planck's constant itself has the dimensions of *action* (J s) and so may be regarded as the fundamental *quantum of action.* The early approach to quantum theory proceeded by limiting the action of a system to multiples of h, and the *Bohr-Sommerfeld quantization condition*, which was the basis of the old quantum theory, was based on this quantization scheme. The dimensions of angular momentum are the same as those of action, and the natural quantum of angular momentum is also Planck's constant: the °angular momentum of a rotating body may be changed only in amounts of the order of h ($\hbar = h/2\pi$ is a better order of magnitude), and so a rotating wheel cannot be decelerated continuously and smoothly, but must deliver up its angular momentum (and its energy) in steps. Once again the angular-momentum quanta are so minute for macroscopic bodies that it can be varied virtually continuously, but on an atomic scale the effects of quantization are of profound importance.

Questions. What is a quantum of energy? Discuss the excitation of a simple pendulum in both classical and quantum terms. How is the energy of the quantum associated with the excitation of an oscillator of frequency ν? Calculate the size of the energy quantum for processes of natural frequencies 1 Hz, 10^{10} Hz, and 10^{15} Hz. Calculate the energy of a quantum of red, yellow, and blue light, of ultraviolet light, and of X-rays (get help from Table 5).

Further information. See *MQM* Chapter 1 for an historical account of the realization of the necessity of quantization, and Chapter 3 for some of its simpler manifestations. See Jammer (1966) for an historical perspective, and Hoffmann (1959), Heisenberg (1930), and Andrade e Silva and Lochak (1969) for gentle accounts. The experimental evidence is also reviewed in Moelwyn-Hughes (1961), Slater (1968), and Bohm (1951). See Feynman, Leighton, and Sands (1963) for a thorough and illuminating discussion of the whole subject. The *Josephson effect* provides an excellent method for measuring h: for a description of the effect, see Langenberg, Scalapino, and Taylor (1966), and for its application, see Taylor, Langenberg, and Parker (1970).

quantum defect. The spectrum of atomic °hydrogen (which is illustrated in Fig. H10 on p. 104) consists of several °series of lines which can be represented as the difference of two °terms, both of which have the form R/n^2, where R is the °Rydberg constant and n is an integer. The spectra of the alkali metals may also be grouped into series that can be expressed as the difference of two terms of the form R'/n^2; but on account of the repulsive effect of the core electrons the number n, the *effective quantum number*, is no longer an integer. It may be written as $n' - \delta$, where n' is an integer and δ is a correction called the *quantum defect*. This defect diminishes as the principal quantum number of the electron increases, for the electron is further away and the nucleus and its surrounding core electrons resemble quite accurately a single positive point charge, and the spectrum and the energies become more hydrogen-like. Since the quantum defect depends very strongly on the interaction of the valence electron and the core electrons it is not surprising that the greatest defects occur for s-orbitals, which °penetrate most closely to the nucleus. The quantum defect is a guide to the extent of penetration, but it has little other theoretical significance or importance.

Further information. The quantum defect occupied more of the older literature than it does of the modern. Mention of it will be found in §3.6 of King (1964), §I.5 of Herzberg (1944), and Chapter III of Kuhn (1962), who lists some values and discusses why they were of importance. In this connexion, see §8.5 of Hartree (1957) and §8 of Condon and Shortley (1963).

quantum electrodynamics. The apotheosis of present-day quantum mechanics seems to be quantum electrodynamics, although it is not entirely clear that the theory exists. What might exist is a unified view of particles and fields in which the electron is a manifestation of the electromagnetic field. Like Hamlet's ghost the electron momentarily slips back into the electromagnetic field, loses corporeality, and then regroups itself again as a recognizable particle. The electron spends 1/137 of its existence as radiation (which, incidentally, is about one-quarter of the proportion of the play Hamlet *père* spends as ghost), and the remainder as particle (see °fine structure constant). This intimate connexion between matter and radiation is emphasized by quantum electrodynamics, which treats the radiation field and the particle as the same object. One consequence of the electron being a manifestation of the electromagnetic field is that its motion cannot be smooth on a microscopic scale, but it should be envisaged as jitterbugging along: *Zitterbewegung* is the German with which the idea is elevated into respectability.

For the chemist there are two important manifestations of this jitterbugging. One is the *Lamb shift* and the other is the free-spin °*g*-value of the electron. According to the °Dirac theory of the °hydrogen atom the levels $^2S_{1/2}$ and $^2P_{1/2}$ should be exactly degenerate, but Lamb measured a very small splitting (of the order of 1057 MHz). Therefore the Dirac theory, good as it is, must be wrong.

In order to sketch the quantum-electrodynamic explanation of the Lamb shift we must first establish a crude picture of what is meant by the vacuum of the electromagnetic field. The picture of a light beam as a collection of °photons is based on the view that a mode of frequency ν of the electromagnetic field can be excited to an energy which is an integral multiple of $h\nu$. This is analogous to the way in which a harmonic oscillator can be excited, and it is tempting to extend the analogy, and to say that, when no excitation is present (no photons), the mode still possesses a zero-point energy. This zero-point energy may be traced to the unquenchable zero-point fluctuations of the electric and magnetic fields, just as in a harmonic oscillator the motion cannot be entirely eliminated. The field oscillations buffet the electron, and so it jitterbugs about an equilibrium position. This slight smearing of the position of the electron affects the energy of an electron in an s-orbital slightly more than one in a p-orbital because in an s-orbital an electron goes closer to the nucleus and the smearing effect is more important, and the consequence is that their energies diverge. This shift may be calculated by quantum electrodynamics, and almost exact agreement with experiment is obtained.

The °*g*-value of an electron measures its effective °magnetic moment arising from its spin. Once again we may envisage an electron as being buffeted by zero-point electromagnetic fields as it spins, and, instead of spinning smoothly, it rocks. If we imagine a vibration in the equatorial plane the magnetic moment may be calculated, and once again essentially exact agreement with experiment is obtained.

Further information. Books on quantum electrodynamics, disarmingly referred to as QED, are difficult to penetrate. See Grandy (1970), Power (1964), Feynman (1962*a*, 1962*b*), Roman (1969) (who gives a helpful guide to further reading), Bjorken and Drell (1965), Henley and Thirring (1962), Thirring (1958), and Schweber (1961). A collection of significant original papers has been prepared by Schwinger (1958). The existence of zero-point fluctuations in the vacuum is also related to the attractive force that two conducting sheets exert on each other at small separations: for details of this *Casimir-Polder interaction*, see p.142 of Grandy (1970) and §3.4 of Power (1964).

quantum numbers. Quantum numbers are labels that distinguish the state of a system and, in simple cases, enable the value of an observable to be calculated. Thus the state of a °particle in a box is labelled by the quantum number n, which may take all integral values greater than zero, and a particle in a state labelled n has an energy $n^2(h^2/8mL^2)$. The state of an electron in a °hydrogen atom is fully determined if we give the numerical values of the quantum numbers n, ℓ, m_ℓ, s, m_s: n is the *principal quantum number* and determines the energy through $E = -R_H/n^2$ (R_H being the °Rydberg constant); ℓ *the azimuthal quantum number,* or the *orbital angular momentum quantum number*, determines the magnitude of the orbital angular momentum through the expression $[\ell(\ell+1)]^{\frac{1}{2}}\hbar$ and the number of possible orientations of this momentum through $2\ell+1$; m_ℓ selects which of the orientations the orbital angular momentum does in fact have (and therefore which of the $2\ell + 1$ atomic orbitals of given n and ℓ the electron occupies) and is called the *magnetic quantum number* (because if a magnetic field is present the electron will have an energy $m_\ell \mu_B B$ on account of its orbital °magnetic moment); s is the °*spin quantum number* which determines the magnitude of the spin angular momentum through $[s(s+1)]^{1/2}\hbar$, and for an electron s is fixed at the value $s = \frac{1}{2}$; m_s, the *magnetic spin quantum number*, determines the orientation of the spin angular momentum relative to some axis, and if a magnetic field lies along this axis there will be an additional contribution to the energy of $m_s g \mu_B B$.

For atoms other than hydrogen the orbital energy also depends on the value of ℓ on account of the effect of °penetration and shielding, but it is no longer possible to give a simple analytical connexion between the values of the quantum numbers and the energy of the state (but see °quantum defect).

BOX 19: Quantum numbers

Capital letters are used for quantum numbers referring to many-particle systems.

F — *total angular momentum*, including the contribution of nuclear spin. Interpretation as for j.

I — *nuclear spin quantum number*, significance as for j. I may have integral or half-integral values, but one isotope of an element has a single, characteristic value of I. See Table 17.

j,J — *total angular momentum* (excluding nuclear spin), or designation of a *general angular momentum*. j,J is never negative, and may be integral or half-integral depending on the system.

magnitude of a.m.: $\hbar\sqrt{[j(j+1)]}$

number of projections on a specified axis: $2j+1$

magnitude of projection: see m.

If j is composed from j_1 and j_2, then permitted values are $j = j_1 + j_2, j_1 + j_2 - 1, \ldots |j_1 - j_2|$.

K — *component of a.m.* about symmetry axis of an axially symmetric molecule: $K\hbar$. K is restricted to the $2J+1$ values, $J, J-1, \ldots, -J$.

ℓ,L — *orbital a.m. quantum number* (also called the azimuthal quantum number). Interpretation as for j but ℓ,L can take only integral values.

m,M — *magnetic quantum number* (often appearing as m_ℓ, m_s, M_L, M_S, M_I, M_J, etc.)

component of a.m. on a particular axis (by convention the z-axis): $m\hbar$,

energy of a magnetic moment in a magnetic field B: $-m\hbar\gamma B$.

n — *principal quantum number*; the energy of an electron in the °hydrogen atom: $-R_H/n^2$ with $n = 1, 2, \ldots$. (Note that ℓ cannot exceed $n-1$.)

general quantum number in a variety of situations; for example, the °particle in a square well has $n = 1, 2, \ldots$ and energy $n^2(h^2/8mL^2)$.

N — *total angular momentum*, excluding electron and nuclear spin. Restriction and interpretation as for ℓ,L.

s,S — °*spin a.m. quantum number*. Significance and interpretation as for j,J, and s,S may have positive half-integral values. s is a single-valuded intrinsic property of a particle.

α,β — *spin projections* for a spin-$\frac{1}{2}$ object. α corresponds to $m_s = +\frac{1}{2}$ and β to $m_s = -\frac{1}{2}$.

λ,Λ — *component of orbital a.m.* about symmetry axis of a linear molecule: $\lambda\hbar$, $\Lambda\hbar$. λ,Λ are restricted to $\ell, \ell-1, \ldots, -\ell$ or $L, L-1, \ldots, -L$ respectively. $\lambda,-\lambda$ are degenerate to a first approximation.

v — *vibrational quantum number*. The energy of a °harmonic oscillator is $(v+\frac{1}{2})\hbar\omega_0$, where $v = 0, 1, 2, \ldots$.

σ,Σ — *component of spin a.m.* about symmetry axis of a linear molecule: $\sigma\hbar$, $\Sigma\hbar$. σ can lie at $s, s-1, \ldots, -s$, and Σ at $S, S-1, \ldots, -S$.

ω,Ω — *component of total electronic a.m.* about symmetry axis of a linear molecule: $\omega\hbar$, $\Omega\hbar$. Ω can take the $2J+1$ values $J, J-1, \ldots, -J$.

In Box 19 are listed some common quantum numbers and the properties they determine: for further information, consult the appropriate entry. The reader might care to reflect on why quantum numbers are always either integral or half-integral, and never fractions more vulgar nor numbers irrational.

quantum theory: a synopsis. The view that energy could be transferred between systems only in discrete amounts rather than continuously arose from observations on the interaction of matter and radiation and on the behaviour of solids at low temperatures. The evidence came from the study of °black-body radiation, the °photoelectric effect, the °Compton effect, °atomic spectra (especially the spectrum of atomic °hydrogen), and the °heat capacities of solids. The first quantum calculation was due to Planck, who deduced the distribution law for black-body radiation. The first quantum-mechanical calculation, where the quantum ideas were applied to a mechanical system, was °Bohr's calculation of the energy levels of atomic hydrogen. The early theory of quantum mechanics was displaced by a new quantum theory in 1926, when °Schrödinger proposed his equation, and Heisenberg his °matrix mechanics. These entailed a wholesale revision of classical physics, and gave a theoretical basis to the wave-particle °duality of matter. The incorporation of relativity into the theory was made by °Dirac, and relativistic quantum mechanics is now at the stage of °quantum electrodynamics and quantum field theory.

Further information. See *MQM* Chapter 1 for an outline of the observations that led to quantum theory. See also Heisenberg (1930) and Jammer (1966) for a historical perspective. An interesting introduction has been given by Andrade e Silva and Lochak (1969). A collection of the significant early papers (in translation) has been prepared by van der Waerden (1967).

quenching. The angular momentum of a system is quenched when it is eliminated by the presence of some electrostatic potential. In an atom, and for simplicity we fix our attention on a hydrogen atom, the energy of an electron is independent of the angular coordinates (its latitude and longitude), and so its angular motion can occur smoothly and without hindrance. In such a case the °orbital angular momentum remains constant, and is well defined. When the atom is surrounded by ligands the energy of the electron depends on its angular coordinates and it experiences a force that accelerates it in a complicated manner. In classical terms the acceleration continuously changes the direction of the electron's motion and the average angular momentum is zero.

One cannot use quite the same argument in quantum mechanics because the trajectory is an alien concept, but one can come to the same conclusion by considering the effect of the ligand potential on the wavefunction of the electron. The presence of the °ligand potential causes the electron to collect in pools of high probability, either close to the ligands if the potential is attractive or between them, if it is repulsive; but the formation of these pools implies that the original running wave has been turned into a standing wave (the stationary antinodes being the pools), and with standing waves there is associated no angular momentum. Therefore the momentum has been quenched by the anisotropic potential.

Questions. 1. What does 'quenching of angular momentum' mean? When does it occur? What causes it? What is its quantum-mechanical explanation? Can the same explanation account for the fact that in diatomic molecules only the angular momentum about the internuclear axis is well defined?
2. A wave running around the z-axis is described by the function $\exp im\phi$; the z-component of the angular momentum is found by calculating the °expectation value of the operator $(\hbar/i)\partial/\partial\phi$. Show that the z-component of the angular momentum for this state is $m\hbar$. Now quench the momentum by replacing the running wave, which has an even distribution of probability, by the standing wave $\cos m\phi$, which has accumulations of probability in the vicinity of $\phi = 0$ and π. What is the expectation value of the z-component of angular momentum for this wave?
3. Using the °hermiticity of the operator ℓ_z, prove that its °expectation value is necessarily zero for real states. This is a formal demonstration that angular momentum is quenched in states represented by real wavefunctions.

Further information. Angular-momentum quenching is described in more detail in *MQM* Chapter 6 and Question 3 is answered on p.417. Quenching profoundly affects the magnetic properties of materials, in particular those of transition-metal ions, for when the orbital motion is eliminated the paramagnetism can be ascribed solely to the spin magnetic moments. These aspects of quenching are also described in Earnshaw (1968), Ballhausen (1962), Figgis (1966), Jørgensen (1971), and Griffith (1964). See also Davies (1967), and van Vleck (1932).

R

radial distribution function. The radial distribution function (r.d.f.) determines the probability that a particle will be found somewhere within a spherical shell of thickness dr at the radius r. For a wavefunction depending on only the radius the radial distribution function $P(r)$ is $4\pi r^2\psi^*(r)\psi(r)$, and the probability of being in the shell of radius r and thickness dr is $P(r)$dr. The source of this function can be traced by recalling the interpretation of the °wavefunction and considering the response of a probe sensitive to the presence of the particle. The probability of finding a particle in the volume element dτ surrounding the point **r** is equal to $\psi^*(\mathbf{r})\psi(\mathbf{r})d\tau$, and a probe of volume dτ gives a response proportional to $\psi^*(\mathbf{r})\psi(\mathbf{r})$. Now let the sensitive part of the probe consist of a thin spherical shell of thickness dr and radius r. This probe is dipped into the atom so that the nucleus is at the origin of the shell, and the meter reading is indicative of the total probability of finding the particle anywhere on the shell. The volume of the shell is $4\pi r^2$dr, and so if the wavefunction is isotropic, the reading is proportional to $4\pi r^2\psi^*(r)\psi(r)$dr, or $P(r)$dr. This means that $P(r)$ tells us the probability of finding the particle anywhere on the shell of thickness dr at r.

The probe behaves in an odd manner, because its sensitive volume diminishes as it samples regions closer to the nucleus (the volume of the shell is proportional to r^2). The meter reading falls to zero at the nucleus, because there the shell becomes vanishingly small, and it also falls to zero at very great distances, because there the wavefunction vanishes. The decaying exponential wavefunction of the hydrogen atom therefore gives rise to a r.d.f. that rises from zero at the nucleus, passes through a maximum, and then falls to zero at infinity. This curve (see Fig. R1) shows the probability of finding the electron at a particular radius irrespective of the angular coordinates of the point: the square of the wavefunction itself gives the probability of finding the electron at a specified point, and the number of these points at a given radius increases as $4\pi r^2$.

Questions. What is the significance of the radial distribution function (r.d.f.)? What is the difference in interpretation of the r.d.f. and the square of the wavefunction? Discuss the form and significance of the r.d.f. for the electron in the 1s- and 2s-orbitals of the °hydrogen atom. Using the mathematical form of these two functions (Table 15) plot the

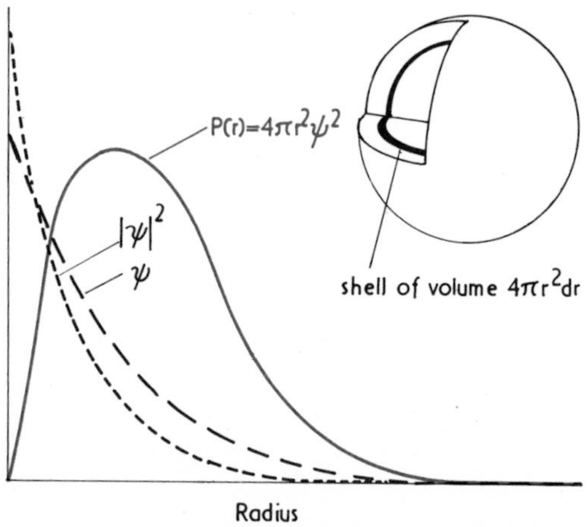

FIG. R1. The radial-distribution function for the ground state of hydrogen.

corresponding r.d.f.. Deduce an expression for the most probable radius of the charge distribution and discuss the nature of the r.d.f. for anisotropic orbitals (for example, the 2p-orbitals of hydrogen).

Further information. A discussion of the r.d.f. will be found in books that deal with atomic structure: see Chapter 2 of Coulson (1961), §I.4 of Herzberg (1944), §4.10 of White (1934), and §V.2 of Condon and Shortley (1963). Radial distribution functions enable one to think sensibly about a lot of inorganic chemistry, because they are the basis of °penetration and shielding and consequent discussions. For the trail through this matter see Puddephatt's *The periodic table of the elements* (OCS 3), pp. 34, 35 of Pass's *Ions in solution 3* (OCS 7), Earnshaw and Harrington's *The chemistry of the transition elements* (OCS 13), and Phillips and Williams (1965), particularly Chapters 1 and 2. Analytical expressions and references to the r.d.f. of numerous atoms will be found in McGlynn, Vanquickenborne, Kinoshita, and Carroll (1972), especially Appendix B. See also Herman and Skillman (1963) for numerical tables.

Raman spectra. The Raman process is the inelastic scattering of light by molecules. An inelastic process is one in which energy is transferred between the two colliding systems. In Raman scattering the light may deposit energy in the molecule by exciting one or more of its internal modes (of rotation or vibration), or it may collect energy from the molecules if a mode is already excited. Since the internal modes are °quantized the energy transfer is limited to well-defined amounts, and so the scattered light contains frequency components that are shifted from the incident frequency by discrete amounts. The detection and recording of the frequency composition of the scattered light constitutes the Raman spectrum of the species.

In practice a brilliant, monochromatic beam irradiates the sample and the light scattered in the perpendicular direction is analysed: the forward-scattered component would be obliterated by the intense incident beam (but see below). The spectrum consists of a strong component at the incident frequency, the *Rayleigh scattered* component, which represents the elastic collision of the light with the sample, and a series of lines to high and low frequency (Fig. R2). The low-frequency lines are the *Stokes lines*, and arise from inelastic collisions in which energy is transferred from the light to the molecule. The lines on the high-frequency side of the Rayleigh component are the *anti-Stokes lines*, and arise from inelastic collisions in which molecular excitation is transferred from the molecule to the light. The intensity of the Stokes lines is greater than the intensity of the anti-Stokes lines because the latter depend on the presence of molecules already in higher-energy states. It should be clear that the spacing of the Raman lines contains information about the vibrational or rotational levels of a molecule, but to determine the information we must first decide the significance of the transitions.

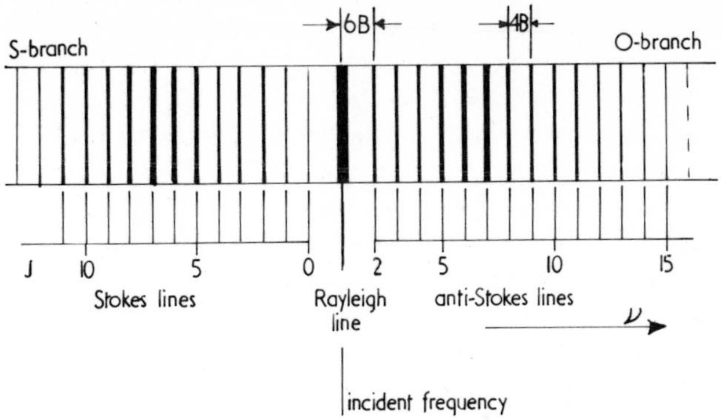

FIG. R2. Rotational Raman spectrum of a linear molecule.

The Raman effect depends on the properties of the °polarizability of the molecule. This can be understood when the scattering process is pictured in terms of the incident radiation inducing a °dipole moment in the molecule, and this dipole moment radiating electromagnetic radiation. The efficiency of the process depends on the ease with which the molecule can be distorted by the incident light, and hence it depends on its polarizability. It can be understood on this picture that the emitted light will not necessarily carry away from the molecule all the energy needed to excite it: discrete amounts of energy can stick to the structure. The molecule, then, must be polarizable; but that alone is insufficient.

If the molecule is to show a *rotational Raman spectrum* (where the inelasticity of the collision excites or deactivates rotational motion) its polarizability must depend on its orientation. A rotating hydrogen molecule is *Raman active* because it has different polarizabilities parallel and perpendicular to the bond. The methane molecule is rotationally *Raman inactive* because, being spherical, its polarizability is independent of its orientation and the field cannot couple to the nuclear framework. In the case of the elastic, Rayleigh scattering, the requirement is much less stringent: all a molecule need be is polarizable; therefore all molecules scatter elastically, but onl. molecules with anisotropic polarizabilities can exchange rotational energy with the light.

If the molecule is to show a *vibrational Raman spectrum* the polarizability must change as the molecule vibrates. A vibrating hydrogen molecule is Raman active because its polarizability depends on how greatly the bond is stretched; the antisymmetrical vibration of CO_2, which we can denote O→←C—→O ⇌ O←—C→←O, does not affect the polarizability of the molecule (it leaves it roughly the same size) and so this particular vibration is Raman inactive. As in the rotational case, we see that the change in the polarizability is the essential feature if energy is to be exchanged and the collision be inelastic.

An important rule, the *exclusion rule*, applies to the vibrational Raman spectrum of molecules having a centre of symmetry. If in such a molecule there is a mode of vibration active in the ordinary (infrared) vibrational spectrum, then that mode is inactive in the vibrational Raman spectrum; conversely, if the mode is infrared-inactive, it is Raman-active. It follows that the Raman effect is useful in the study of vibrations (and rotations) that are inaccessible to normal absorption spectroscopy.

The scattered radiation of the Raman effect is *polarized* even if the incident radiation is not. Fig. R3 illustrates the simpler case of *Rayleigh scattering*, which is the elastic scattering of light: the Raman scattering process is analogous, but slightly more involved. From Fig. R3 a it should be clear that if the molecule is isotropic and the incident light plane-polarized the scattered light is also plane-polarized. The scattered light is also plane-polarized if the incident light is unpolarized. If the molecule is anisotropic (Fig. R3 b), the scattered light has both polarization components, and so is not plane-polarized. A convenient measure of the degree of polarization is the *depolarization ratio* ρ, which is defined

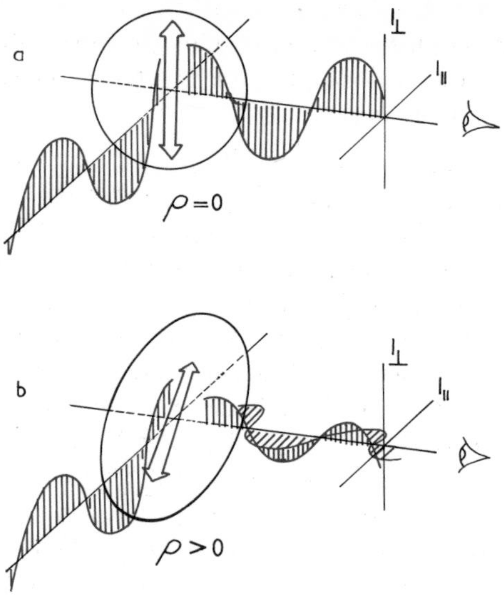

FIG. R3. Depolarization of Rayleigh lines and, by analogy, of Raman lines.

as the ratio of the intensities $I_\parallel$ and $I_\perp$ as defined in Fig. R3. In the isotropic molecule case there is zero intensity in the scattering plane, and so $\rho = 0$. In the anisotropic case there is intensity both in the plane and perpendicular to it, and the depolarization ratio is non-zero. For a freely rotating molecule the maximum value is $\rho = \frac{6}{7}$ for unpolarized incident light, and $\rho = \frac{3}{4}$ for plane-polarized incident light (for the polarization and geometry of Fig. R3). The polarization in *Raman scattering* is determined similarly, but it is necessary to consider the isotropy or anisotropy of the *changes* in the polarizability of the molecule. Thus a completely symmetrical vibration plays in the Raman case the role of the symmetric molecule in the Rayleigh case; therefore the Raman scattering from such a mode is fully polarized and $\rho = 0$. If a vibration is anisotropic the Raman scattered light is depolarized, and so $\rho > 0$. If the incident light is polarized ρ cannot exceed $\frac{3}{4}$, and if it is unpolarized ρ cannot exceed $\frac{6}{7}$. It follows that the determination of the polarization of the Raman scattered light is a valuable tool for determining the symmetry of the active molecular vibrations.

We still do not know what transitions the Raman lines represent apart from the qualitative remark that they represent modes involving a changing polarizability. The °*selection rules* for Raman-active transitions are that the °vibrational quantum number of a mode must change by ± 1; the °rotational quantum number must change by $\Delta J = \pm 2$. The two-quantum rotational-jump behaviour stems from the fact that the transitions depend on the polarizability rather than the °transition dipole moment (which determines the absorption spectrum). One approach to understanding the occurrence of 2 is to picture the scattering process as involving two dipole transitions, one for the photon coming in and one for the photon going out. A classical picture elucidates why the rotational quantum number changes by ± 2 but the vibrational quantum number changes by ± 1: in a rotation of a molecule the dipole moment is restored to an indistinguishable orientation after a complete rotation of the molecule, but the polarizability is restored to an indistinguishable orientation twice on a revolution. In a vibration the dipole moment and polarizability return at the same time and vibrational Raman and absorption spectra both have $\Delta v = \pm 1$.

The rotational Stokes and anti-Stokes lines are related to the °branches of a rotation-vibration spectrum; and analogously to the notation used there, they are referred to as the *O-branch* ($\Delta J = -2$; anti-Stokes) and the *S-branch* ($\Delta J = +2$; Stokes). Knowing what transitions the spectrum shows it is possible to relate the Raman lines to the energy levels of the molecule by the same analysis as in the corresponding absorption spectrum, and so to extract °force-constants, moments of inertia, and molecular geometry, and to identify unknown species.

An important experimental requirement in Raman spectroscopy is an intense monochromatic light beam; what is more natural than to apply °lasers, which have just this property? *Laser-Raman spectroscopy* is today a major branch of study; not only does it refine the conventional Raman technique by enabling frequencies very close to the exactly-defined incident frequency to be studied, but its unique properties give rise to a number of new effects. The properties put to work are the low divergence of the beam, which enables observations to be made close to the forward direction, and its exceedingly high intensity.

In the *stimulated Raman effect* an intense laser beam is focused on a sample, and the light scattered in the forward direction, or just off-axis, is observed. The light in the forward direction itself is the same as the incident frequency, but mixed with it is Stokes radiation of frequencies ν, $\nu - \nu_i$, $\nu - 2\nu_i$ etc., where ν_i is the frequency of an internal mode giving an intense Raman signal in a conventional experiment. Surrounding this narrow, forward-scattered beam are a series of concentric circles of light of increasing frequency; the first ring is of frequency $\nu + \nu_i$, the next ring has frequency $\nu + 2\nu_i$, the third $\nu + 3\nu_i$, and so on (Fig. R4 a). The effect arises from the fact that the initial Stokes scattered line is so intense that it can be scattered again, and an inelastic collision leads to a further Stokes line at $\nu - 2\nu_i$; and so the process continues as more quanta are chipped off the beam. Likewise the intensity of the anti-Stokes lines is due to successive scattering, and the initial high intensity of the anti-Stokes light at $\nu + \nu_i$ is due to the high intensity of the initial beam permitting the annihilation of two ν photons by one molecule, followed by the simultaneous generation of one of frequency $\nu + \nu_i$ and another of frequency $\nu - \nu_i$. Only for very high beam intensities is there a significant probability that two photons can simultaneously be in the region of the same molecule, which is necessary if the frequency-sharing is to occur. The angular

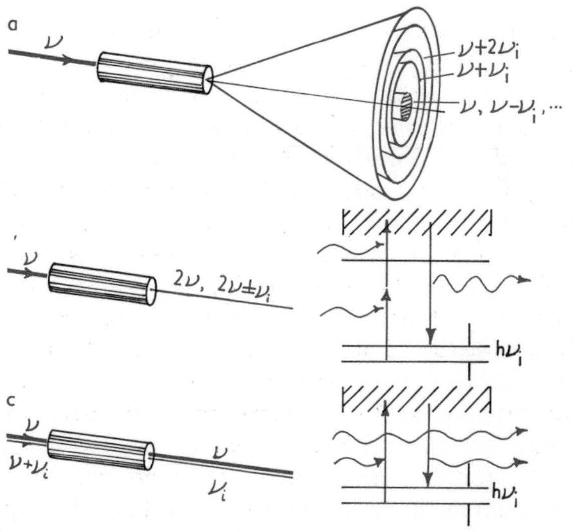

FIG. R4. (a) Stimulated Raman effect. (b) Hyper-Raman effect. (c) Inverse Raman effect.

dependence of the frequency of the scattered light is a consequence of the conservation of momentum in the collision.

In the *hyper-Raman effect* an intense beam of frequency ν is focused on a sample, and together with the normal Raman scattering there appear frequencies of 2ν and $2\nu \pm \nu_i$ (Fig. R4 b). Thus the hyper-Raman effect is the inelastic scattering structure on high-frequency photons generated by the annihilation of two low-frequency photons in a simultaneous event involving one molecule and two incident photons. As in the stimulated Raman effect, the efficiency of the hyper-Raman effect depends on the intensity of the light. One application is to the measurement of molecular hyperpolarizabilities (see °polarizability).

In the *inverse Raman effect* two beams of light are employed and focused on a sample. One has a continuous spectrum and the other is a highly intense monochromatic beam. It is found that transitions occur which appear as absorptions from the continuum at frequencies $\nu + \nu_i$. The process may be pictured as the arrival at the molecule of a photon of the continuum with a frequency $\nu + \nu_i$; simultaneously there arrives a laser photon of frequency ν which stimulates the excited molecule to shake off a photon of its own frequency, leaving behind an amount of energy corresponding to the frequency ν_i (Fig. R4 c).

Questions. 1. What is the difference between an elastic and an inelastic process? On which does the Raman effect rely? What experimental arrangement is employed in Raman spectroscopy? In what way can the use of a laser benefit the observations? What is meant by the Rayleigh component? Discuss the appearance of the Raman spectrum and indicate the significance of the Stokes and anti-Stokes lines. On what molecular property do the Raman and Rayleigh scattering rely? Why do they so depend? What is a necessary property of the molecule if it is to show a vibrational Raman spectrum, and a rotational Raman spectrum? State the exclusion rule. Which vibrations of carbon dioxide are Raman-active, and which are infrared-active? State the selection rules for vibrational and rotational Raman spectra: why does the latter rely on a double-quantum jump, but the former on a single jump? What information can be obtained from the splittings in the O- and S-branches of a rotational Raman spectrum?
2. Show that in a classical polarizable rotator the induced dipole moment will emit Stokes and anti-Stokes lines. In the calculation suppose that the polarizability of the molecule varies harmonically between $\alpha - \delta\alpha$ and $\alpha + \delta\alpha$ about a mean value α. Proceed by showing that the molecule possesses an induced dipole moment of the form $\alpha E + \delta\alpha E \cos\omega t$, where E is the imposed optical field; then take the time-dependence of E to be $\cos\omega_0 t$, and show by simple trigonometric manipulations that the overall induced dipole has components, oscillating at ω, $\omega \pm \omega_0$. This calculation leads to the prediction of equal intensities for the Stokes and anti-Stokes lines: why is that false?
3. °Group-theoretical arguments may be applied to the Raman problem in order to determine the vibrational selection rules. The transition operator is the polarizability tensor for the molecule: this transforms like xx, yy, and zz. Show, using Box 4 on p. 33, that in a centrosymmetric molecule the exclusion rule follows from the difference in symmetry of the polarizability and the dipole moment under inversion. From the characters in Table 3 confirm that the A_1, E, and T_2 vibrations are Raman active in a tetrahedral AB_4 molecule. What transitions are Raman active in water, carbon dioxide, and ammonia?

Further information. See *MQM* Chapter 10 for answers to Questions 2 and 3 and for further discussion. For applications see Woodward (1972), Wheatley (1968), Whiffen (1972), and Barrow (1962). Laser-Raman spectroscopy is described in Long (1971) and Gilson and Hendra (1970). See Herzberg (1945) for further details. Woodward's Chapter 19 is a good summary of depolarization processes.

Ramsauer effect. When a beam of electrons was passed through a sample of argon and the other noble gases, it was found that the scattering power of the sample decreased strongly at some energies of the electron beam (a *transmission resonance* is observed at about 0.7 eV). This effect may be understood in terms of the °wave nature of the electron, and its decreasing wavelength as its energy increases (°de Broglie relation). The system may be viewed as an electron wave incident on atoms, and these are regions of potential different from the surrounding vacuum. But in regions of different potential energy the wavelength of the electron is changed (see °kinetic energy). Just as in the case of an incident beam of light passing into a region where the refractive index changes, there are reflections from the front of the atom (where the potential changes abruptly), and reflections from the opposite inside surface where the potential drops back to the vacuum level. If the potential has a thickness equal to one quarter of the wavelength of the electrons the waves reflected backwards from the two surfaces interfere destructively, but the waves transmitted interfere constructively. It follows that the intensity of the electrons reflected by the atom is reduced and that the transmitted intensity is increased. (This of course is the role of a coating on a lens.)

Further information. A helpful discussion of transmission resonances is given in §11.8 of Bohm (1951) and applied to the Ramsauer effect in §11.9 and §21.54, where he explains that the effect is not quite the same as the square-well process we have described. See also §99 of Davydov (1965) and Mott and Massey (1965).

refractive index. The ratio of the speed of light *in vacuo* c to its speed in a medium v is the *refractive index* of the medium: $n = c/v$.

The size of the refractive index depends on the strength of the interaction between the light field and the medium, and as the electric field of the light has a stronger interaction than the magnetic field, we should expect the refractive index to depend on the electric °polarizability of the medium. The greater the polarizability, the stronger the interaction, and the greater the drag on the progress of the light. This guess is confirmed by calculation, for in a nonpolar medium the refractive index is related to the relative permittivity (dielectric constant) by $n^2 = \epsilon_r$, and the relative permittivity is related to the polarizability by $\epsilon_r = 1 + N\alpha(\omega)/\epsilon_0$, where N is the concentration of molecules and $\alpha(\omega)$ their polarizability. But we have to be just a little careful because the molecule on whose polarizability we might at one instant focus our attention is surrounded by other polarizable molecules. These other molecules respond to the electric field of the light and their polarization enhances the field experienced by the central molecule. Therefore we should apply a correction to take into account the presence of the surrounding molecules. This is the *Lorentz local-field correction*, and it involves increasing the strength of the field by a factor of $\frac{1}{3}(\epsilon_r + 2)$. ϵ_r is the relative permittivity, or n^2, and so the expression for the refractive index becomes rather more complicated. By an unlikely but helpful coincidence the indistinguishable Lorenz and Lorentz introduced this correction independently and simultaneously, and arrived at the *Lorenz-Lorentz formula* $(n^2 - 1)/(n^2 + 2)\rho = N\alpha(\omega)/3\rho\epsilon_0$, where ρ is the density. Since N is proportional to the density the right-hand side of the equation is independent of the density, and so too therefore is the term on the left, which is called the *refractivity* of the medium.

It should be noticed that the refractive index (and the refractivity) depends on the frequency of the light through the dependence of the polarizability on the frequency. This dependence is described in the section on °polarizability, but at optical frequencies is due to the high-energy photons being more able than low-energy photons to excite the molecules into their low-lying excited electronic states. Therefore, as the frequency gets greater (and approaches an absorption frequency of the molecule), the interaction gets stronger and the refractive index gets larger. For this reason the refractive index for blue light exceeds that for red light, and, as a consequence of this, a beam of white light is dispersed by a refracting medium. The name *dispersion,* which denotes the frequency-dependence of a property, is derived from this aspect of the refractive index.

Very close to absorption bands the refractive index varies strongly. If the behaviour of the refractive index throughout the frequency range is known it is possible to extract the absorption spectrum of the molecule and vice versa. The formula that enables this to be done is the *Kramers-Krönig dispersion relation*. A dispersion relation relates the overall frequency-dependence of a dispersion property (such as refractive index) to the absorption property and vice versa.

The refractive index for a composite molecule is the sum of the refractivities of its parts in so far as the polarizability of a molecule is itself an additive property.

Further information. See *MQM* Chapter 11 for an account in more detail of the derivation of the quantum-mechanical expression for the refractive index of the molecule. See

Corson and Lorrain (1970) for a derivation via the *Clausius-Mossotti equation* of the Lorentz local-field correction. See also van Vleck (1932) for a discussion. A simple introduction to the Kramers-Krönig dispersion relation will be found in Slichter (1963), and tougher accounts in Roman (1965, 1969). Pertinent information on refractive indices is contained in the polarizability Box (Box 17 on p. 179).

Renner effect. The Renner effect, or as it is sometimes more fairly called the *Renner-Teller effect*, is an interaction between the electronic and vibrational motions of a linear molecule (especially a triatomic linear molecule) which removes the degeneracy of the energy levels. Consider a Π-state of a linear triatomic; bending the molecule into a triangular conformation affects the two components of the electronic molecular orbital differently. For simplicity let the molecule have a single electron in a π-orbital; in the linear case the π_x -and π_y-orbitals are degenerate, but when the molecule is bent they diverge in energy: three possible types of behaviour are illustrated in Fig. R5. The Renner effect appears in the spectrum of the molecule because the bending vibrational levels are modified by their interaction with the electronic levels.

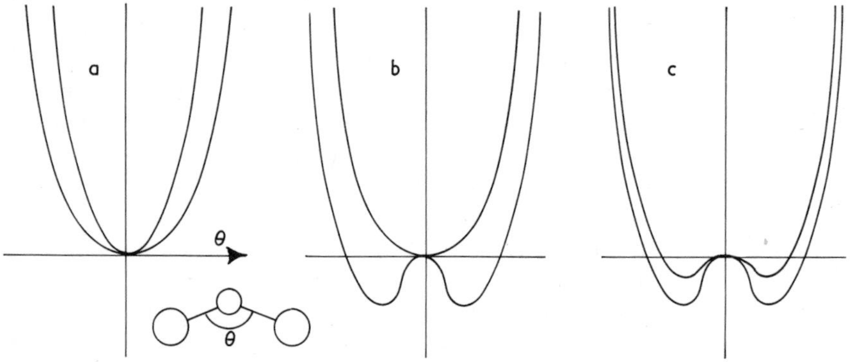

FIG. R5. Renner effect splitting of π-levels: three possible situations.

Further information. An account of the Renner effect in molecules is given in §1.2 of Herzberg (1966), who provides a number of examples, and gives expressions for the energies of the vibronic states of the molecules showing the effect. See also §10.13 of King (1964). A quantitative treatment has been given by Renner (1934), Pople and Longuet-Higgins (1958), and Longuet-Higgins (1961).

resonance. The concept of resonance has its roots in classical mechanics, and it is helpful to recall that application of the term. If two pendulums are weakly linked (for example, if they hang from the same slightly flexible axle, as in Fig. R6) the motion of one is experienced by the other. If one is initially still, and the other set in motion, the energy of the latter will be transferred to the first, which will begin to swing, and pass back to the second some of its acquired energy. This ebb and flow of energy continues indefinitely in the absence of damping forces. The exchange of energy is most effective when the pendulums have the same natural frequency, and this condition of equality is known as *resonance*; the energy, or amplitude, is then said to *resonate* between the two tuned systems.

It is possible to imagine a form of coupling where the energy of the system is lower if the pendulums swing in phase, and where the worst arrangement (in terms of energy) occurs when they swing in opposition. A flexible axle is an example: it might require less energy to twist the support in the same direction at each pivot than to twist it in opposition (Fig R6); if there is no coupling between the periodic systems their relative phase is immaterial.

With the preceding classical picture of resonance and coupled systems in mind we shall consider two examples of quantum-mechanical resonance. The first is the *interaction of*

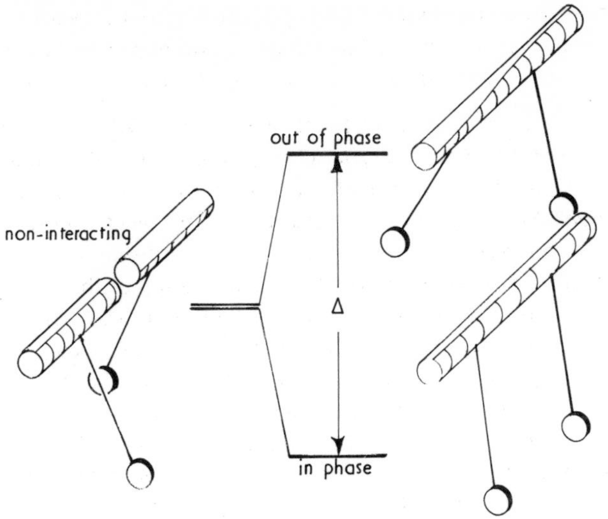

FIG. R6. Resonance of two coupled pendulums. The energy splitting Δ is greatest when the natural frequencies are identical.

light with atoms (or molecules). The atom and the electromagnetic field (light) play the roles of the two coupled periodic systems. The 'natural frequencies' of the atom are the transition frequencies, and we can imagine adjusting the 'natural frequency' of the electromagnetic field bathing the atom by changing the frequency of the incident light. There comes a point when the frequency of the light matches the frequency of a transition within the atom: the combined system behaves like the two coupled pendulums, and energy is transferred from the light field (resulting in absorption) or to the light field if the atom is already in an excited state (emission). These processes occur most effectively at resonance.

The other example of resonance is the type one encounters in theories of *molecular structure*, particularly in the °valence-bond theory, where one attempts to describe the true structure of a molecule by a superposition of simple, canonical structures. The best-known example is °benzene, where one attempts to describe the structure by the superposition of the two Kekulé structures. Let us suppose that there is a coupling between the Kekulé forms; then the superposition will have a lower energy than either form alone if the phase of coupling is correct (remember the second aspect of the classical idea of resonance). Thus each Kekulé structure behaves like a simple pendulum (by symmetry they correspond to the same frequency) and the presence of a coupling means that their energy is different in conjunction than separately. The nature of the coupling may be visualized as the tendency of the π-electrons in one C—C bond to push the neighbouring π-electrons into a neighbouring gap in the π-bonding structure: in this way one Kekulé structure is turned into the other (Fig. R7) (see °benzene and Fig. B8). Thus resonance stabilizes in the sense that the coupled system has a lower energy; the stabilization is greatest when the natural frequencies of the separate systems are the same (consequently the resonance stabilization of benzene is large). *Ionic-covalent resonance* also stabilizes, but as the contributing forms differ in energy the resonance is less exact and the effect less.

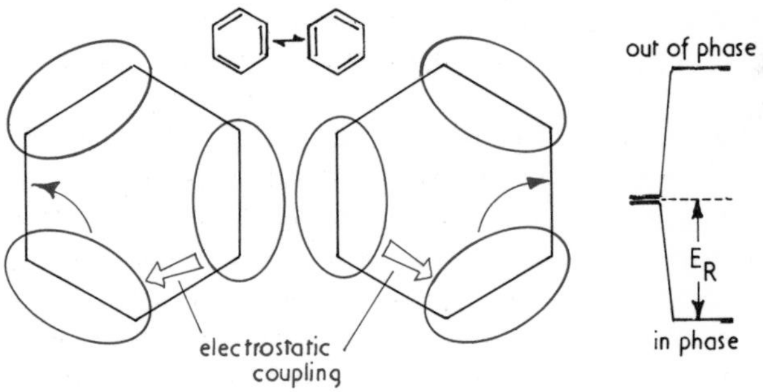

FIG. R7. Resonance in VB theory (of benzene). E_R denotes the resonance energy.

Further information. For discussions of the concept of resonance in molecular-structure studies, see §5.5 of Coulson (1961), §1.3 of Pauling (1960), and §13 of Eyring, Walter, and Kimball (1944). Resonance in light absorption is discussed in Chapter 7 of *MQM*, and very well illustrated by the phenomena of °electron spin resonance and °nuclear magnetic resonance. A *transmission resonance* is described under °Ramsauer effect. See also °benzene, °valence bond, and °resonance energy.

resonance energy. An °aromatic molecule is more stable than untutored speculation, confronted with a molecule bristling with double bonds, might predict. The difference between the true energy, which takes into account the stabilization of the molecule by °resonance among various structural possibilities, and some reference state of the molecule, is termed the *resonance energy* (see Fig. R7). (An alternative name, which reflects the analogous phenomenon in °molecular-orbital theory, is *delocalization energy*.)

The choice of reference is difficult and several suggestions have been made. The *Hückel definition* is the most elementary: it defines the resonance energy as the difference in energy between the true molecule and the hypothetical molecule in which there are localized ethene-type double bonds. Thus if the π-electron energy of °benzene is found to be $3\alpha + 4\beta$, and the energy of each of the three ethene bonds is $\alpha + \beta$, the resonance energy is β.

The difficulty with the Hückel definition is the arbitrariness of the comparison: would it not be better to attempt to find the energy of the unconjugated form of the molecule itself, and then use this as the reference? Why not take the hypothetical cyclohexatriene molecule, calculate its energy, and use it as the reference for benzene? This reference molecule has alternating short and long bonds, and it is argued that by its use the full effect of conjugation, delocalization, or resonance on both the π- and the σ-electrons is taken into account. This is the basis of the *Mulliken-Parr* definition of resonance energy.

A common method of measuring the resonance energy is to determine the heat of formation of the molecule (for example, by determining the heat of combustion of the molecule in a bomb calorimeter, and knowing the heats of formation of the combustion products, which are often carbon dioxide and water), and comparing this result with the value obtained on the basis of ascribing a bond energy to each bond in the structure (these bond energies may be found from tables): the difference of the two calculations is the resonance energy. For example, in benzene a Kekulé structure has six C—H bonds, three C—C bonds, and three C=C bonds; the energy of that structure is therefore $6E(\text{C—H}) + 3E(\text{C—C}) + 3E(\text{C=C})$. The difference of this value from the observed heat of formation is the resonance stabilization of the Kekulé structure (150 kJ mol^{-1}). Modern values are often obtained from the heat of hydrogenation, which is less in the presence of resonance stabilization (the more the molecule is stabilized the closer it lies to the fully hydrogenated energy). In this type of determination a molecule containing three (unconjugated) double bonds is expected to have a heat of hydrogenation three times that of cyclohexene; the observed heat of hydrogenation of benzene is less than that figure by 150 kJ mol^{-1}, and this difference is identified as the resonance stabilization of the Kekulé form.

Questions. What is meant by resonance energy? What are two possible definitions? Can you think of alternative definitions? How would you determine the resonance energy of a hydrocarbon? What changes in the value of the resonance energy might you expect on replacing the Hückel definition by the Mulliken-Parr definition? The heat of formation of the naphthalene molecule was measured and found to be 8623 kJ mol^{-1}. The following bond energies have been measured in other experiments: C—C, 333 kJ mol^{-1}; C=C, 593 kJ mol^{-1}; C—H, 418 kJ mol^{-1}. Calculate the resonance energy of naphthalene. On the basis of the Hückel molecular-orbital scheme, estimate the resonance energies of cyclobutadiene and butadiene (buta-1, 3-diene).

Further information. See Streitweiser (1961), Salem (1966), Dewar (1969), Murrell and Harget (1972), and McGlynn, Vanquickenborne, Kinoshita, and Carroll (1972) for further discussion. A short table of resonance energies will be found in Chapter 9 of Streitweiser (1961) and Chapter 4 of Murrell and Harget (1972). A book devoted to resonance in organic chemistry is that by Wheland (1955).

rotation of molecules. The rotational energy of a molecule arises from its °angular momentum, and because the latter is quantized, so too is the rotational energy. The energy separation of adjacent quantized levels is small, and transitions between them occur in the microwave region of the spectrum (10^8 - 10^{12} Hz, 10^2 - 10^{-2} cm). The separations are determined by the moments of inertia of the molecule, and so microwave spectroscopy gives information about molecular geometry. Rotational transitions are also observed in conjunction with the °vibrational, °electronic, and °Raman spectra of molecules, and these give the same kind of information. Molecules are normally classified into four groups in a discussion of their rotational energy levels: linear molecules, symmetric tops (molecules with an axis of symmetry), spherical tops (spherical, tetrahedral, and octahedral molecules), and asymmetric tops (anything else).

1. *Linear molecules*. A linear molecule has only two rotational degrees of freedom: these correspond to end-over-end rotation about two perpendicular axes. It is easy to see why the question of a third degree of rotational freedom does not arise: in a diatomic molecule the atoms have six degrees of freedom; three are ascribed to the overall translation of the molecule; one is ascribed to the vibration of the bond; and so only two remain for the rotations. A similar argument applies to any linear molecule. The classical kinetic energy of rotation of a body of moment of inertia I is $\frac{1}{2}I\omega^2$, and as the classical angular momentum is $I\omega$ this energy may be expressed as $(I\omega)^2/2I$. The transition to quantum mechanics is now trivial, for the quantum theory of °angular momentum tells us that the angular momentum of a body is limited to the values $[J(J+1)]^{1/2}\hbar$ with J confined to the integers 0, 1, 2, ... Therefore it is merely necessary to replace $I\omega$ by this expression to obtain the energy of the Jth quantized rotational level as $J(J+1)\hbar^2/2I$. The quantity $\hbar^2/2I$ is normally written B and called the *rotational constant* of the molecule. It is important to note that the separation of the rotational levels decreases as the moment of inertia of the molecule increases (for B then decreases) and that the level J lies at an energy $2BJ$ beneath its neighbour. Typical values of B are 60.809 cm^{-1} for H_2, 30.429 cm^{-1} for D_2, 10.5909 cm^{-1} for HCl, and 0.0374 cm^{-1} for I_2; more values are given in Table 10.

In accord with the theory of °angular momentum there are $2J+1$ possibilities for the orientation of the rotational angular momentum vector of the molecule, but in the absence of external fields the orientation of the molecule has no effect on its energy, and so $2J+1$ orientations all have the same energy (they are °degenerate).

Pure rotational transitions can be stimulated by an electromagnetic field of the appropriate frequency only if the molecule has a permanent dipole moment, for the dipole acts as a kind of lever for the interaction, and through it the field accelerates the molecule by exerting a torque. Molecules without dipole moments (including, for example, H_2 and CO_2) do not show a pure rotational spectrum. If a molecule has a permanent dipole the field can induce transitions only between neighbouring levels; that is, the °selection rule for rotational transitions is $\Delta J = +1$ (absorption) or $\Delta J = -1$ (emission). The rotational spectrum is therefore a set of lines spaced by $2B$,

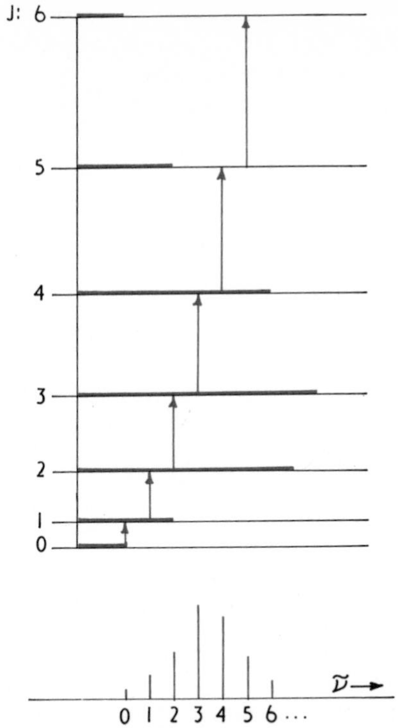

FIG. R8. Pure rotation spectrum of a linear molecule, showing population of levels and the intensity distribution (which is determined by the population and the size of transition dipole moments).

with an intensity distribution governed by their initial (thermal) population and, in a slightly complicated way, by selection rules which vary with J (Fig. R8).

2. *Symmetric tops*. Symmetric tops may be either *prolate* (cigar shaped) or *oblate* (disc shaped), and have three rotational degrees of freedom. As they have two distinct moments of inertia (one parallel to the figure axis $I_{\parallel}$, and two equivalent moments perpendicular to the axis $I_{\perp}$, the energy of rotation of the molecule depends on how the angular momentum is distributed about the three molecular axes. If the molecule rotates end-over-end the energy is determined by $I_{\perp}$ alone, but as the motion becomes more like the spinning of a top about its axis, so the energy becomes dependent more strongly on $I_{\parallel}$. The amount of rotation about the figure axis is determined by a quantum number K: $K\hbar$ is the component of the angular

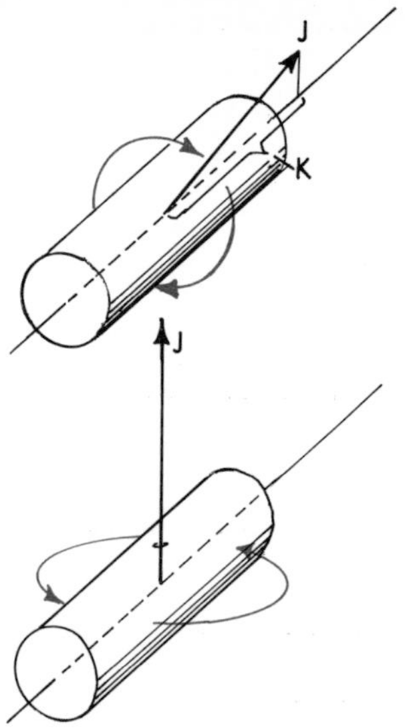

FIG. R9. Rotation of a (prolate) symmetric top. When K is large the motion is largely about the figure axis; when K is small it is largely about the perpendicular axis.

momentum on the axis, and can vary in integral steps from $+J$ to $-J$ (there are $2J+1$ such values) (see Fig. R9). When $K=0$ there is no rotation about the axis. It is quite easy to see how the quantum number K enters the problem: the classical energy of rotation depends on the angular momentum about each of the axes. If with the axis q there is associated a component of angular momentum $(I\omega)_q$ and a moment of inertia I_{qq} then the kinetic energy associated with this mode is $\frac{1}{2}(I\omega)_q^2/I_{qq}$. Therefore the total kinetic energy of our molecule is $\frac{1}{2}(I\omega)_x^2/I_\perp + \frac{1}{2}(I\omega)_y^2/I_\perp + \frac{1}{2}(I\omega)_z^2/I_\parallel$, where z is taken to be the figure axis. If we recognize that $(I\omega)_x^2 + (I\omega)_y^2 + (I\omega)_z^2$ is the square of the total angular momentum of the molecule, which can be identified with the quantum-mechanical value $J(J+1)\hbar^2$, it is possible to cast the energy expression into the form $J(J+1)B + \frac{1}{2}(1/I_\parallel - 1/I_\perp)(I\omega)_z^2$, where B is $\hbar^2/2I_\perp$.

Next we identify $(I\omega)_z$ as the component of the angular momentum on the figure axis, and from our knowledge of the quantum theory of °angular momentum recall that all components of angular momentum are quantized, and so set this component equal to some integral multiple of $\hbar$: thus we identify $(I\omega)_z$ with $K\hbar$.

The final form of the energy expression is given in Box 20. The form of the expression is as we anticipated, for when K is zero the energy is determined solely by $I_\perp$, and when $K=\pm J$ the energy is determined largely (but not solely) by $I_\parallel$. It is also satisfying to note that the energy depends on K^2 rather than K itself: this means, as common sense requires, that the direction of motion about the figure axis is immaterial. Remember that the molecule can still have $2J+1$ different orientations with respect to some space-fixed axis, but these are °degenerate in the absence of external fields.

The spectra of symmetric tops depend on the presence of a permanent dipole to act as a lever: by symmetry this dipole must lie along the axis and so a light wave is unable to exert a torque to accelerate the motion about the axis; consequently the °selection rules are $\Delta K = 0$ and $\Delta J = \pm 1$.

3. *Spherical tops*. The energy levels of spherical tops can be obtained very easily from the expression for the symmetric top because we may set $I_\perp = I_\parallel$. The resulting expression is given in Box 20. The energy is independent of K because all axes of the molecule are equivalent. Another way of saying this is that all the $2J+1$ states K for a given value of J are °degenerate. Therefore the rotational levels of the spherical top are $(2J+1)^2$-fold degenerate (because the $2J+1$ space orientations, labelled M, are also degenerate). A spherical top is invisible in microwave spectroscopy because it has no permanent dipole, and so cannot be accelerated by incident radiation. The rotational levels of this and the other types of molecule can, of course, be excited by collisions with other molecules, or the walls of a vessel, and so the large number of accessible rotational levels must be taken into account when the properties of the gas (such as its °heat capacity) are calculated.

4. *Asymmetric tops*. These are real horrors because the angular momentum cannot be distributed among the three axes in a tidy fashion. If we think of a prolate symmetric top with a bump added to one side we shall see the problem. If the top is spinning about its figure axis the effect of the bump will be to tip the molecule away from its original direction; that is, the bump induces the transfer of angular momentum from the figure axis to the other two axes. But the process continues,

BOX 20: Rotational energy levels

Diatomic (and linear) molecules

$$E(J) = BJ(J+1) \qquad B = \hbar^2/2I.$$

(B is in joules if I is in kg m^2; $B = \hbar/400\pi cI$ is the appropriate expression in cm^{-1}.)

Transition energy: $\Delta E(J) = E(J+1) - E(J) = 2B(J+1)$.

Symmetric tops

$$E(J, K) = BJ(J+1) + (A-B)K^2$$

$$B = \hbar^2/2I_{\perp} \quad A = \hbar^2/2I_{\parallel}.$$

Transition energy: $\Delta E(J) = E(J+1, K) - E(J, K)$

$$= 2B(J+1).$$

Spherical tops

$$E(J) = BJ(J+1) \quad B = \hbar^2/2I.$$

Moments of inertia:

diatomic molecule: (m_A, m_B separated by R)

$$I = \left(\frac{m_A m_B}{m_A + m_B}\right) R^2$$

linear triatomic molecule: (m_A, m_B, m_C separated by R_{AB} and R_{BC})

$$I = m_A R_{AB}^2 + m_C R_{BC}^2 - \frac{(m_A R_{AB} - m_C R_{BC})^2}{(m_A + m_B + m_C)}$$

pyramidal molecule: (AB_3, bond length R, BAB angle θ)

$$I_{\parallel} = 2m_B R^2 (1 - \cos\theta)$$

$$I_{\perp} = m_B R^2 (1 - \cos\theta) + \frac{m_A m_B R^2 (1 + 2\cos\theta)}{(3m_A + m_B)}.$$

and although the total angular momentum remains constant, the molecule rotates in a complicated, varying pattern. The energy levels can be obtained only by complicated techniques, and the rotational spectra are immensely complex. Nevertheless, information about molecular geometry can be extracted by a close analysis of the shapes of the spectral bands.

Questions. 1. What is the source of the rotational energy of a molecule? Why is it quantized? Is there a zero-point energy? In what region of the spectrum do rotational transitions occur? How do the transition energies depend on the size of the molecule? What information can be obtained from rotational spectra? What must a molecule possess if it is to absorb radiation by a rotational transition? What is a classification of molecular types? What is the significance of the quantum number K? When does the rotational energy of a molecule depend on the space projection M? How many-fold degenerate are the rotational states of linear molecules, and the various kinds of tops? Why does the energy of a symmetric top still depend weakly on $I_{\perp}$ when $K = \pm J$? Can the rotational energy of a symmetric top ever be ascribed solely to motion about its figure axis? What are the selection rules for rotational transitions? How do all the rotational modes come into thermal equilibrium even though some transitions are electric-dipole forbidden?

2. Calculate the energy-level separation (in cm^{-1}) for the rotational levels of H_2, HD, and D_2, taking the bond length to be 0·074 nm in each case. The pure rotational spectrum of HI consists of a series of equally spaced lines with a separation of 12.8 cm^{-1}; calculate the bond length of the molecule. Why are the lines equally spaced? (Draw an energy-level scheme and apply the appropriate °selection rules; or just think about $2BJ$ and ΔJ.)

3. Calculate the relative populations of the rotational levels of H_2, D_2, I_2 ($B = 0.0374$ cm^{-1}), CH_4 ($r_{CH} = 0.1094$ nm), and NH_3 ($I_{\parallel} = 4{\cdot}437 \times 10^{-47}$ kg m^2, $I_{\perp} = 2{\cdot}816 \times 10^{-47}$ kg m^2) at 300 K and at 1000 K. Use the Boltzmann distribution, include the degeneracy of the levels properly, and forget (if you already know) about °nuclear statistics.

Further information. A fuller discussion of molecular rotation and rotational spectra is given in *MQM* Chapter 10. See also Whiffen (1972), Barrow (1962), and King (1964). An introduction to microwave spectroscopy has been written by Sugden and Kenney (1965), and a standard work is that by Townes and Schawlow (1955); both books give a bibliography of molecules studied. Allen and Cross (1963) give a theoretical discussion. See Herzberg (1945, 1950, 1966) for further discussion and applications; in these volumes are useful collections of molecular data (such as bond lengths, °force-constants, and rotational constants). A useful collection of molecular structural data has been compiled by Sutton (1958). Rotational transitions can also be studied by observing the °vibrational and °electronic spectra of molecules, and by the use of °Raman spectra. The °heat capacity of molecules depends upon the accessibility of rotational states, and therefore on their energy. A complicating feature of rotational problems is that the occupation of rotational states is restricted by the °Pauli principle: for more information see °nuclear statistics.

Rydberg constant. The Rydberg constant relates the energy of an electron in a °hydrogen atom to its principal °quantum number n: $E = -R/n^2$. It is necessary to be just a little careful in recording values of R because it depends on the mass of the electron and the proton, and if some one-electron atom other than hydrogen itself is being considered it is necessary to correct it for the mass of the new nucleus. That having been said, we refer to the true *Rydberg constant* as the quantity R_∞ in Box 21. The Rydberg constant for the hydrogen atom, taking into account the finite mass of the proton, is $R_H = R_\infty/(1 + m_e/m_p)$; this is also recorded in the Box. The Rydberg constants for other nuclei can be obtained by replacing the mass of the proton in this expression by the mass of the nucleus of interest. These different expressions arise because the electron-proton system rotates around its centre of mass, which is slightly shifted away from the position of the nucleus by virtue of its finite mass and the electron's non-zero mass.

BOX 21: Rydberg constant

Rydberg constant

$R'_\infty = \mu_0^2 m_e e^4 c^3/8h^3$	$1{\cdot}097\,373 \times 10^7\ \mathrm{m}^{-1}$
	$1{\cdot}097\,373 \times 10^5\ \mathrm{cm}^{-1}$
$R'_\infty c$	$3{\cdot}289\,842 \times 10^{15}$ Hz
$R_\infty = R'_\infty hc = \frac{1}{2}m_e c^2\alpha^2$	$2{\cdot}179\,72 \times 10^{-18}$ J
	1313 kJ mol^{-1}
	13·60 eV.

Hydrogen-atom Rydberg constant

$R'_H = R'_\infty/(1 + m_e/m_p)$	$1{\cdot}096\,776 \times 10^7\ \mathrm{m}^{-1}$
	$1{\cdot}096\,776 \times 10^5\ \mathrm{cm}^{-1}$.

The value of R_∞ is referred to as a *rydberg* (1 Ry ~ 13·60 eV). Note that 1 Ry is half the °atomic unit of energy (the hartree E_a: $1E_a = 2$ Ry).

Further information. See °Bohr atom for the first calculation of the Rydberg constant in terms of fundamental constants, and °hydrogen atom for the basis of its quantum-mechanical deduction. Both entries give further information.

Rydberg level. An electronic transition in a molecule might lift the electron out of the valence-shell orbitals into an outer orbital: the state so formed is a *Rydberg state*, and the electron occupies a *Rydberg level.* An example of this would be the excitation of a 2p-electron of the fluorine atom in the fluorine molecule into a 3s-orbital, or something higher.

The Rydberg levels are of interest in so far as the important electron is in a very diffuse orbital; so diffuse, in fact, that in a diatomic molecule the two nuclei appear to the electron as a single nucleus. This implies that the Rydberg electron is only very weakly coupled to the nuclear framework, which is therefore able to rotate without dragging the electron round with it: see °Hund's coupling case (d). Rydberg electrons are characterized by small °quantum defects: since they are so diffuse they hardly interact with the inner electrons and their wavefunctions resemble those of the °hydrogen atom.

Further information. Rydberg levels and states are discussed in some detail in §10.3 of King (1964) and §VI.5 of Herzberg (1950). For a thorough discussion see Duncan (1971).

S

Schrödinger equation. The Schrödinger equation, which by one of those rare coincidences is named after him who did indeed discover it†, is a differential equation whose solution is the °wavefunction for the system under consideration. This implies that it is of central importance, for once we have the wavefunction all the properties of the system are, in principle, predictable, because the structure of quantum mechanics tells us how to elicit the information. The application of quantum mechanics to physical systems therefore boils down to solving the appropriate Schrödinger equation, and realizing that the mathematical function which is the solution is the wavefunction for the system.

Unfortunately the Schrödinger equation is not a simple algebraic equation (like $x^2 = 2$), but, as mentioned above, it is a *differential* equation. Except in a fairly small number of cases such equations are very difficult to solve. That, however, is not of much significance: what matters is that we believe we have the equation which, in principle, is the correct equation for the description of Nature. (Actually that is not really true, for the Schrödinger equation ignores relativity. Therefore it is only an approximation, bearing a similar relation to a correct description as Newtonian mechanics bears to Einsteinian. This is a difficulty which has been partly removed—see the °Dirac equation—but minor fundamental difficulties have in the past bred cataclysm.)

The Schrödinger equation is a second-order linear differential equation in space coordinates (it contains terms such as d^2/dx^2) and a first-order differential equation with respect to time. Various forms of it are illustrated in Box 22. Written in its full form it should be clear that it is not a *wave equation*, for such an equation has second-order derivatives with respect to time. It may be regarded instead as a type of *diffusion equation*; it is not unreasonable that the evolution of the 'wavefunction' in time should be akin to a diffusional process. This point is of considerable significance, for the diffusional form of the Schrödinger equation means that it is possible to to interpret the wavefunction in terms of a probability of discovering a particle in various regions of space (see Born interpretation in the section on °wavefunction). Had the equation been a true wave equation this interpretation would have been untenable. The time-dependence can often be shaved off by the method of *separation of variables* (see Question 2 and Box 22), and then we are left with the *time-independent Schrödinger equation* (see Box 22), which is of the same form as an equation for a standing wave. It is from this form of the equation that the name 'wave mechanics' derives.

The time-independent Schrödinger equation may be interpreted as an equation for the *curvature* of the wavefunction, and bearing this in mind enables one to anticipate some of the features of its solution. The second derivatives $\partial^2\psi/\partial x^2$, etc.

† 'While visiting Paris he (Victor Henri) received from Langevin a copy of "the very remarkable thesis of de Broglie"; back in Zürich and having not very well understood what it was all about, he gave it to Schrödinger, who after two weeks returned it to him with the words: "That's rubbish". When visiting Langevin again, Henri reported what Schrödinger had said. Whereupon Langevin replied: "I think Schrödinger is wrong; he must look at it again". Henri, having returned to Zürich, told Schrödinger: "You ought to read de Broglie's thesis again, Langevin thinks this is a very good work"; Schrödinger did so and "began his work".' Max Jammer (1966, p. 258).

BOX 22: The Schrödinger equation

Time-dependent form: $H\Psi = i\hbar(\partial\Psi/\partial t)$

H is the °hamiltonian.

Time-independent form: if H is independent of time, Ψ may be written

$$\Psi = \psi \exp(-iEt/\hbar),$$

where ψ is independent of t and satisfies

$$H\psi = E\psi.$$

Typical form of equation:

One-dimensional system; mass m in a potential $V(x)$:

$$-\left(\frac{\hbar^2}{2m}\right)\left(\frac{d^2\psi}{dx^2}\right) + V(x)\psi(x) = E\psi(x)$$

or

$$\frac{d^2\psi}{dx^2} + \left(\frac{2m}{\hbar^2}\right)[E - V(x)]\,\psi(x) = 0.$$

Three-dimensional system; mass m in a potential $V(\mathbf{r})$:

$$-\left(\frac{\hbar^2}{2m}\right)\nabla^2\psi(\mathbf{r}) + V(\mathbf{r})\psi(\mathbf{r}) = E\psi(\mathbf{r}),$$

where ∇^2 is the °laplacian.

Separation of variables. Write $\Psi = \psi\theta$, where ψ is a function of position and θ a function of time. Let H be independent of time. Then $H\Psi = i\hbar\dot{\Psi}$ becomes

$$\theta H\psi = i\hbar\psi\dot{\theta}, \text{ or } (1/\psi)H\psi = (i\hbar/\theta)\dot{\theta}.$$

The left-hand side is a function of position, not time, and if x is varied the right-hand side is invariant. Therefore l.h.s. = constant = r.h.s.

$$(1/\psi)H\psi = E = (i\hbar/\theta)\dot{\theta}.$$

Hence $\quad \theta = \exp(-iEt/\hbar)$ and $H\psi = E\psi$.

are what we normally interpret as the curvature of the function in elementary calculus, and we shall employ this interpretation here. Note that when ψ'' (as we shall denote the second derivative) is positive the curvature of ψ is like $\smile$, and when it is negative the curvature is like $\frown$. The essential feature to note is that the magnitude of the curvature (the sharpness with which the curve bends) increases as the total energy E exceeds the potential energy $V(x)$. This difference $E - V(x)$ is just the classical kinetic energy at the point x, and so we see that the °kinetic energy and the curvature are proportional. Note too that the sign of the curvature depends on the sign of the function ψ itself: if E is everywhere larger than V, the curvature has the sign of $-\psi$ at each point (Fig. S1). It is amusing to follow through the implication of this for a free particle where V is constant and $E > V$. Suppose we consider a point where $\psi > 0$, then the curvature is negative and so the function droops down towards zero like $\frown$ (Fig. S2). Sooner or later this droop causes it to fall through zero and become negative. The hitherto drooping function acquires a positive curvature (because still $E > V$ but $\psi < 0$) and so begins to curl up towards the value zero. This value it crosses and then again begins to droop back down. The dependence of the curvature on the function therefore forces the function to swing backwards and forwards across the axis, and so to describe a harmonic wave. It is also amusing to note that the rapidity with which it swings from positive to negative values increases as E exceeds V: therefore the wavelength of the motion decreases as the kinetic energy increases (see °kinetic energy and the °de Broglie relation). If the potential depends on position the wavelength is not a constant (and not really defined), but these arguments may be extended to account qualitatively for the form of wavefunctions for electrons in atoms and molecules.

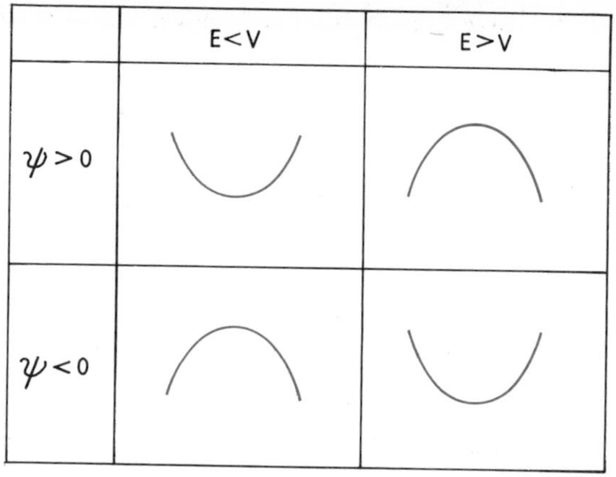

FIG. S1. Curvature of the wavefunction at a point for different signs of ψ and $E-V$ at that point.

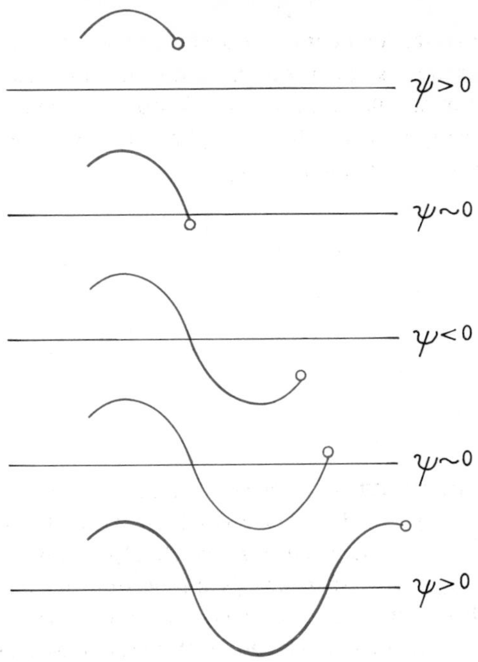

FIG. S2. Propagation of a wave when $E > V$.

The only adequate way of accounting for the quantitative form of the wavefunction in atoms and molecules is to solve the equation mathematically. The immediate problem that one encounters is that there exists an infinity of solutions for a second-order differential equation. The essential point at this stage is the recognition that only some of the solutions satisfy the stringent requirements of the Born interpretation: when *boundary conditions* are imposed (that is, when one states what conditions the function must satisfy at some point of space) only a few solutions are acceptable. The immediate consequence of this is that bounded systems are quantized.

Quite often it is impossible to find analytical solutions to the Schrödinger equation, or at least to find analytical solutions that are not too complex to use. Under these circumstances (which include the immensely important cases of the structure of atoms and molecules) it is necessary to resort to approximate methods: these include °perturbation theory, °variation theory, and the method of °self-consistent fields. Time-dependent perturbation theory is one way of dealing with the Schrödinger equation. Some of the standard solutions of the Schrödinger equation are discussed under the appropriate headings (see °particle in a square well, °harmonic oscillator, °angular momentum, and °hydrogen atom).

The fact that the Schrödinger equation is a *linear* differential equation implies the validity of the °superposition principle and all that flows from it.

Questions. 1. What is the importance of the Schrödinger equation? Why is the time-dependent form not a true wave equation, and how may it be manipulated into a form that looks like a wave equation? What basic local property of the wavefunction does the equation determine? Demonstrate qualitatively and then quantitatively that the wavefunction for a free particle is a wave of constant length. What is the connexion between the length of this wave and the linear °momentum and °kinetic energy of a particle described by such a wave? Sketch the form of the wavefunction for a particle of energy E in a potential field that decays linearly with distance. Can a particle be described by a wave in which at some point the energy E is less than the potential energy V at that point? Sketch the form of a wavefunction for a particle in which the potential rises linearly with distance (and crosses the point $V(x) = E$). Sketch a number of possible wavefunctions for a °particle in a square-well potential, and in a °harmonic potential (try to do this without looking at the answers, which will be found in the appropriate sections; if you cannot do it, attempt to interpret the answers there in terms of the discussion in this section).
2. Show, by the method of *separation of variables*, that the time-dependent equation can be separated into an equation for the time-dependence and an equation for the spatial dependence, and solve the former. Proceed by attempting to express the function $\Psi(x, t)$ as the product $\theta(t)\psi(x)$, and inserting this in the time-dependent equation. Divide through by $\theta\psi$, and realize that one block of terms depends only on x and the other depends only on t. Deduce that these two terms must each be equal to some constant, which write E (on the grounds that the constant has the dimensions of energy). Then solve the equation for the time, and compare your answer with that in Box 22.

Further information. See *MQM* Chapter 2 for a way of setting up the Schrödinger equation, and Chapter 3 for the method of obtaining some of its solutions in a number of important cases. A good account is also given in Pauling and Wilson (1935) and in Kauzmann (1957). All books dealing with quantum theory must, except for the most abstruse, mention the Schrödinger equation. For Schrödinger's original papers see Schrödinger (1926). See Chapter 5 of Jammer (1966) for a fascinating commentary, and in an English translation in Shearer and Deans (1928). The Schrödinger equation is only one of a number of possible equivalent formulations of quantum mechanics, and is not always the simplest to use, especially in formal manipulations. Therefore see also °matrix mechanics.

second quantization. Those who find quantization a sufficiently difficult topic will be distressed to encounter second quantization, and may have visions of a continuation yet more subtle than Chinese boxes. But second quantization is as far as things have gone, and is a device that enables one to conjure elegantly with problems involving many particles, including the problem of the electromagnetic field. It is a mathematical artifice; but is that not possibly true of all mathematical descriptions of Nature?

The mode of thought that leads to the introduction of the idea is as follows. *First quantization*, which in our naïvety we have referred to elsewhere simply as quantization, replaces observables by °operators, and the behaviour of a system, and the results of experiments, are calculated by allowing these operators to operate on the wavefunction obtained as a solution of the °Schrödinger equation for the system. Thus the dynamical functions have been replaced by operators operating on a function $\psi(x)$. But suppose by analogy with this development we interpret the function $\psi(x)$ as an *operator* on something; then we have gone beyond our formal procedure for quantization and are in the artificial realm of *second quantization.* In this realm it is discovered that the operator $\psi^*(x)$ operates (on something) to create a particle at x, and that the operator $\psi(x')$ operates to annihilate a particle at x'. It should be possible to appreciate that this power of summoning and dismissing particles provides a means of setting up equations that enable the quantum-mechanical properties of many-body problems to be calculated. Thus second quantization does not introduce a revolution into physics (as did first quantization), but it does introduce a new technique of calculation, and a new language—a language that includes words such as °photons, °phonons, °polarons, °excitons, magnons, and rotons.

Further information. An introduction to the ideas of second quantization will be found in a set of lecture notes by Atkins (1973), which are based on a book by Mattuck (1967). Other introductions of increasing sophistication will be found in Ziman (1969), Roman (1965), Davydov (1965), Bogoliubov and Shirkov (1959), and Schweber (1961). See also Kittel (1963).

secular determinant. In the construction of a °molecular orbital by the method of °linear combination of atomic orbitals one attempts to express the orbital as a sum $c_a\psi_a + c_b\psi_b + \ldots$, where the ψs are the atomic orbitals on atoms a, b, etc. and the *c*s are the coefficients to be modified until the best set of values is found: this is done by seeking the set that gives the lowest energy. Instead of idly toying with random different values of the *c*s until mental decay supervenes, it is desirable to have a short, sharp method for finding the best set, and this is the role played by the secular determinant.

In the Questions you are asked to show that the best combination of orbitals is given by one of the solutions of a set of simultaneous equations in which the coefficients c are the unknowns (see Box 23). These are the *secular equations.* In common with other sets of simultaneous equations they have a non-trivial solution when the determinant of the factors of the *c*s disappears (the trivial solution corresponds to all the *c*s themselves vanishing). This determinant is the *secular determinant.* See the Box. The secular determinant vanishes for N values of the energy of the system, if there are N atomic orbitals contributing, and the lowest *root* may be identified with the lowest energy of the system, that can be attained on this model. The values of the *c*s corresponding to this root may be found by the normal methods (brute force, or intelligence via the method of cofactors, see Box 23) and give the best wavefunction for the system. The other $(N-1)$ roots may be identified with higher-energy orbitals; for the

BOX 23: The secular determinant

Direct approach. Write the Schrödinger equation $H\psi = \mathcal{E}\psi$ in terms of the expansion

$$\psi = \sum_{j=1}^{N} c_j\psi_j \qquad (1)$$

and obtain

$$\sum_{j=1}^{N} c_j H\psi_j - \sum_{j=1}^{N} \mathcal{E}c_j\psi_j = 0.$$

Multiply from the left by ψ_i and integrate, to obtain

$$\sum_{j=1}^{N} c_j[H_{ij} - \mathcal{E}S_{ij}] = 0 \quad (i = 1, 2, \ldots N) \qquad (2)$$

with $H_{ij} = \int d\tau\psi_i H\psi_j$ and $S_{ij} = \int d\tau\psi_i\psi_j$. This is a set of N simultaneous equations for the coefficients c_j, and possesses non-trivial solutions when

$$\Delta \equiv \det |H_{ij} - \mathcal{E}S_{ij}| = 0. \qquad (3)$$

Expansion of this $N \times N$ determinant, and solution for $\mathcal{E}$ leads to the N eigenvalues of H. In general, if N is finite the eigenvalues are only approximate.
To each root $\mathcal{E}$ of (3) there corresponds a wavefunction ψ expressed as in (1). To find the coefficients c_j use *Cramer's rule*. (See Margenau and Murphy (1956, p. 313) or Irving and Mullineux (1959, p. 269).) Let $k_j = c_j/c_1$; then (2) becomes

$$\sum_{j=2}^{N} k_j[H_{ij} - \mathcal{E}S_{ij}] = (\mathcal{E}S_{i1} - H_{i1}) \quad (i = 2, 3, \ldots N).$$

Let D be the $(N-1) \times (N-1)$ determinant formed from this $H_{ij} - \mathcal{E}S_{ij}$, and $D^{(n)}(h)$ be the determinant formed by replacing the nth column in D by $(\mathcal{E}S_{21} - H_{21}, \mathcal{E}S_{31} - H_{31}, \ldots \mathcal{E}S_{N1} - H_{N1})$. Then according to Cramer's rule:

$$k_j = D^{(j)}(h)/D.$$

This gives the ratios $c_2/c_1, \ldots, c_N/c_1$. To complete the determination use

$$c_1^2 + c_2^2 + \ldots + c_N^2 = 1. \qquad (4)$$

This procedure gives the coefficients c_j corresponding to the root $\mathcal{E}$, and should be repeated for each root of (3).

Variational approach. Minimize $\mathcal{E}$ with respect to variations in the coefficients c_j:

$$\mathcal{E} = \int d\tau\psi H\psi / \int d\tau\psi\psi.$$

The condition $(\partial\mathcal{E}/\partial c_j) = 0$ is satisfied when

$$\sum_{j=1}^{N} c_j(H_{ij} - \mathcal{E}S_{ij}) = 0. \qquad (5)$$

(Confirm this by substituting (1), taking the derivative of $\mathcal{E}$, and using simple algebra.) This is identical to (2) and the procedure is as before. The lowest of the N roots of (2) is the minimum value of $\mathcal{E}$.

Example. Suppose $N = 2$, then the secular equations are

$$\left.\begin{aligned} c_1(H_{11} - \mathcal{E}S_{11}) + c_2(H_{12} - \mathcal{E}S_{12}) = 0 \\ c_1(H_{21} - \mathcal{E}S_{21}) + c_2(H_{22} - \mathcal{E}S_{22}) = 0 \end{aligned}\right\}$$

and the secular determinant is

$$\Delta = \begin{vmatrix} H_{11} - \mathcal{E}S_{11} & H_{12} - \mathcal{E}S_{12} \\ H_{21} - \mathcal{E}S_{21} & H_{22} - \mathcal{E}S_{22} \end{vmatrix}$$

The roots of Δ are the roots of

$$(S_{11}S_{22} - S_{12}S_{21})\mathcal{E}^2 + (H_{12}S_{21} + H_{21}S_{12} - H_{22}S_{11} - H_{11}S_{22})\mathcal{E} + $$
$$+ (H_{11}H_{22} - H_{12}H_{21}) = 0,$$

and the lower is the minimum of $\mathcal{E}$. The coefficients are determined from $D = H_{22} - \mathcal{E}S_{22}$ and eqn (4):

$$k_2(H_{22} - \mathcal{E}S_{22}) = -(H_{21} - \mathcal{E}S_{21})$$

and $$c_1^2 + c_2^2 = 1.$$

In the special case when $S_{11} = S_{22} = 1; S_{12} = S_{21} = 0$ the solution may be put into the form

$$\mathcal{E} = \begin{cases} H_{11} - H_{12}\cot\theta & \psi = \psi_1\sin\theta - \psi_2\cos\theta \\ H_{22} + H_{12}\cot\theta & \psi = \psi_1\cos\theta + \psi_2\sin\theta' \end{cases}$$

where $$\theta = \tfrac{1}{2}\arctan[2H_{12}/(H_{11} - H_{22})].$$

molecule, and the corresponding coefficients give the other $(N - 1)$ molecular orbitals.

The secular determinant crops up wherever one has several orbitals which one anticipates may interact. If there is a °perturbation that can mix one state with another the true ground state of the system is best found by a linear sum of the two unperturbed states. The energy of the new system is given by the lowest root of the secular determinant, and the set of coefficients corresponding to that root gives the best modification of the wavefunction. One example of this type of situation is provided by °configuration interaction, and another by the °Hückel method of conjugated molecules.

The name *secular* originates in the appearance of the same kind of determinant in classical mechanics, and especially in celestial mechanics. A secular variation in the motion of a body, and in particular the orbit of a planet, is one that gradually develops over a long period of time (*saeculum*: Latin for age or generation) as opposed to one that varies rapidly or periodically and is not cumulative. Why on earth, if you will forgive the allusion, does this have anything to do with molecular structure? The answer lies in the fact that variation theory may be related to perturbation theory, and that the perturbations of interest to variation theory are those that accumulate to give rise to a set of orbitals with well-defined and constant separation. This shows up especially clearly in degenerate-state perturbation theory, but that is a subject that deters unless it is called by some other name. One name that ought not to deter is °molecular-orbital theory, for when homonuclear systems are considered the molecular-orbital method is equivalent to degenerate-state perturbation theory. This can be appreciated by realizing that in the absence of interaction between the atoms all the atomic orbitals (of the same quantum numbers) which later are to be combined have the same energy (are °degenerate). The effect of the interatomic interaction is like a perturbation on the degenerate systems. If we imagine putting the atoms in a molecular conformation, forbidding interaction, and then gradually turning on the interaction, we can appreciate that the perturbation gradually accumulates and the different linear combinations of atomic orbitals diverge until they attain the separations characteristic of the molecule. Thus we are really considering a strong secular perturbation on the atomic orbitals, and the separation of the levels can be found by the application of the secular determinant.

The language of ordinary °perturbation theory also draws on the word secular. The expression for the energy to second order in some perturbation consists of a part involving only the original state of the system (see Box 16 on p. 172) and a part involving °virtual transitions to excited states. The former terms represent the effect of a secular term, or *secular perturbation*, whereas the latter represent the effect of the *non-secular* terms.

Questions. The °variation method considers a linear combination of orbitals of the form $\psi = c_a\psi_a + c_b\psi_b$ for a two-orbital system and then calculates the minimum value of $\mathcal{E} = \int d\tau\psi H\psi / \int d\tau\psi\psi$. Show that the extremal values of this expression correspond to the solutions of the two simultaneous equations $(H_{aa} - \mathcal{E}S_{aa})c_a + (H_{ab} - \mathcal{E}S_{ab})c_b = 0$ and $(H_{ba} - \mathcal{E}S_{ba})c_a + (H_{bb} - \mathcal{E}S_{bb})c_b = 0$, where H_{ab}, S_{ab}, etc. are various integrals. Set up and solve the secular determinant for this problem, and find expressions for the two sets of *c*s corresponding to the lower and higher energies. Apply this calculation to H_2 by identifying ψ_a and ψ_b with 1s-orbitals on nuclei a and b respectively, taking $S_{aa} = S_{bb} = 1$, $H_{aa} = H_{bb} = \alpha$, and $H_{ab} = H_{ba} = \beta$. Suppose that $S_{ab} = 0$. Now generalize the calculation to an orbital of the form $c_a\psi_a + c_b\psi_b + \ldots c_N\psi_N$ and show that the solution of the variational problem leads to an $N \times N$ determinant. Approximations are usually made as to the values of the integrals involved in these secular determinants: this is the realm of the °Hückel method and its analogues, and you will find more problems set there.

Further information. See *MQM* Chapters 7 and 10; the former deals with degenerate-state perturbation theory and the latter with the application of the secular determinant to various aspects of molecular structure. Further details will be found in §9.6 of Coulson (1961), §2.1 of Streitweiser (1961), §VI.24 of Pauling and Wilson (1935), §7b and §11b of Eyring, Walter, and Kimball (1944), Pilar (1968), and McGlynn, Vanquickenborne, Kinoshita, and Carroll (1972). See °Hückel method, °configuration interaction, and °perturbation theory.

selection rule. Spectral lines result when a system makes a transition from one state to another of different energy. All lines in a spectrum can be related to the difference between the energies of states of the system (each line can be expressed as a combination of °terms), but not all possible pairs of states give rise to spectral transitions: some transitions are *allowed* and some are *forbidden.* Selection rules tell us which are allowed and which are forbidden. They are generally quoted in terms of the changes that may occur in a °quantum number, but sometimes they are rules about the way that the symmetry of the state may change. Occasionally one encounters the term *gross selection rule*: this refers to a property that a molecule must possess in order for the remaining selection rules to come into operation. Selection rules for a variety of transitions are shown in Box 24.

There are various ways of understanding why the selection rules govern as they do. The gross selection rules refer to the fact that the molecule must have some way of interacting with the electromagnetic field: the presence of a permanent dipole, for instance, means that the electric field of a passing light beam may accelerate the molecule by exerting a torque and so induce a °rotational transition. The other selection rules can generally be understood in terms of the possession by the photon of a definite intrinsic angular momentum (a °photon has °spin). On absorption the photon is annihilated but angular momentum must be conserved, and this momentum appears in the electrons or in the nuclear framework. Rules

BOX 24: Selection rules

Atoms

Electric dipole transitions:

$\Delta J = 0, \pm 1$; but $J = 0 \not\leftrightarrow J = 0$

$g \rightarrow u$; $g \not\leftrightarrow g$, $u \not\leftrightarrow u$ (Laporte rule)

$\left.\begin{array}{l}\Delta S = 0 \\ \Delta L = 0, \pm 1;\ \text{but } L = 0 \not\leftrightarrow L = 0\end{array}\right\}$ in *LS*-coupling.

Magnetic dipole transitions:

$\Delta J = 0, \pm 1$; but $J = 0 \not\leftrightarrow J = 0$

$g \rightarrow g$, $u \rightarrow u$; $g \not\leftrightarrow u$

$\Delta L = 0, \pm 2$.

Electric quadrupole transitions:

$\Delta J = 0, \pm 1, \pm 2$; but $J = 0 \not\leftrightarrow J = 0$

$g \rightarrow g$, $u \rightarrow u$; $g \not\leftrightarrow u$

$\Delta L = 0, \pm 1; \pm 2$; but $L = 0 \not\leftrightarrow L = 0$.

Molecules

Electric dipole transitions:

electronic transitions:

$\Delta J = 0, \pm 1$; but $J = 0 \not\leftrightarrow J = 0$

$+ \rightarrow -$; $+ \not\leftrightarrow +$, $- \not\leftrightarrow -$

$g \rightarrow u$; $g \not\leftrightarrow g$, $u \not\leftrightarrow u$

$s \rightarrow s$, $a \rightarrow a$; $s \not\leftrightarrow a$

case (a): $\Delta\Lambda = 0, \pm 1$; but for $\Lambda = 0 \rightarrow \Lambda = 0$:

$$\Sigma^+ \rightarrow \Sigma^+,\ \Sigma^- \rightarrow \Sigma^-;\ \Sigma^+ \not\leftrightarrow \Sigma^-$$

$\Delta S = 0$

$\Delta\Sigma = 0$

cases (a) & (c): $\Delta\Omega = 0, \pm 1$; but $\Omega = 0 \not\leftrightarrow \Omega = 0$ if $\Delta J = 0$

cases (b) & (d): $\Delta N = 0, \pm 1$; but in (b) $\Lambda = 0 \not\leftrightarrow \Lambda = 0$ for $\Delta N = 0$.

vibrational transitions:

absorption (i.r.): dipole moment must change along °normal coordinate

$\Delta v = \pm 1$.

Raman: polarizability must change with vibration

$\Delta v = \pm 1$.

vibration-rotation transitions:

$$\Delta v = \pm 1;\quad \Delta J = \begin{cases} +2 & \text{S-branch (Raman, Stokes)} \\ +1 & \text{R-branch (i.r.)} \\ 0 & \text{Q-branch † (i.r.)} \\ -1 & \text{P-branch (i.r.)} \\ -2 & \text{O-branch (Raman, anti-Stokes).} \end{cases}$$

† Only if molecule has component of a.m. about axis.

rotational transitions:

absorption (microwave): molecule must possess permanent dipole moment

$\Delta J = \pm 1$, $\Delta K = 0$.

Raman: anisotropic polarizability of molecule

$\Delta J = \pm 2$ (Stokes: $+2$; anti-Stokes: -2).

such as $\Delta\ell = \pm1$ or $\Delta J = \pm1$ reflect this conservation of angular momentum, and are discussed further under °electric dipole transitions and in the sections on the different types of spectra (see also °magnetic dipole and electric quadrupole transition for a variant of this rule).

All the rules may be deduced from an examination of the form of the transition dipole moment (see °electric dipole transition). One very important way of examining this moment is by °group theory: those who know about group theory and irreducible representations should remember that the product of the irreducible representations of the initial state, the final state, and the transition moment operator must contain the totally symmetric irreducible representation for the transition not to be forbidden (Box 4 on p. 33). Those who do not know enough group theory to understand this important rule should learn some as soon as possible.

Further information. See *MQM* Chapter 5 for a discussion of the group-theoretical basis of selection rules, and Chapters 8 and 10 for their application to all the types of atomic and molecular transitions. Other group-theoretical discussions will be found in the references in the entry on group theory. The applications to spectra are also described under °electronic, °vibrational, °rotational, and °Raman spectra, and detailed accounts will be found in Barrow (1962), Whiffen (1972), King (1964), and Herzberg (1944, 1945, 1950, 1966).

self-consistent field. The self-consistent field (SCF) method of calculating atomic and molecular structures was originated by Hartree, improved by Fock, and used by almost everyone. The basis of the method is to guess the °wavefunctions for all the electrons in the system. Then one electron is selected and the potential in which it moves is calculated by freezing the distribution of all the other electrons and treating them as the source of the potential. The Schrödinger equation for the electron is solved for this potential, and so a new wavefunction for the electron is obtained. This procedure is repeated for all the other electrons in the system, using the electrons in the frozen °orbitals as the source of the potential. When the cycle is completed (Fig. S3) one possesses a set of orbitals for all the electrons of the system, and in general these will differ from the original, guessed set. Now the cycle is repeated, but improved wavefunctions generated by the first cycle are used as the initial guess: a complete cycle generates a new set of improved functions. This sequence is continued until passing a set of orbitals through the cycle leads to no change: the orbitals are then self-consistent.

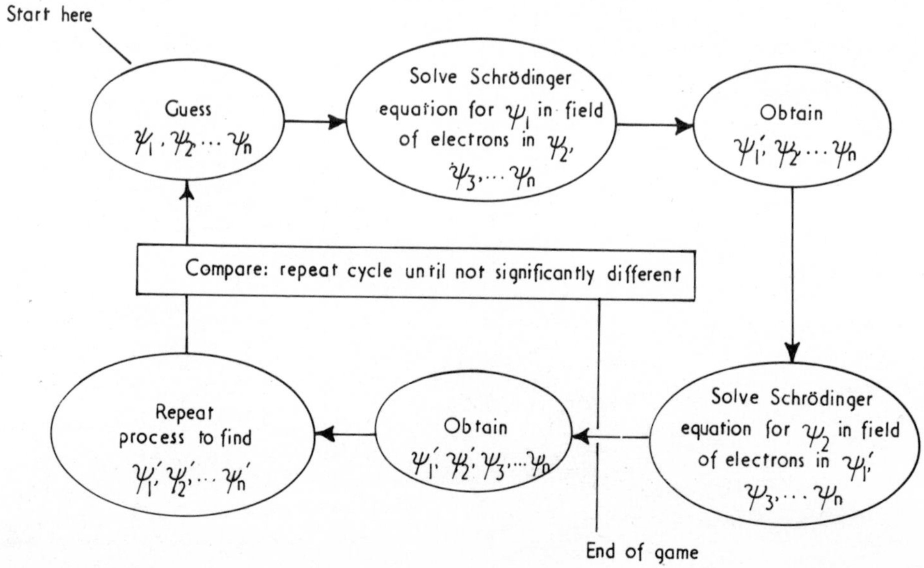

FIG. S3. The self-consistency cycle.

1. The *Hartree method* takes the view that the atom or molecule can be represented as a product of orbitals, one for each electron. Therefore it guesses a set of functions, and sets the self-consistent machinery in operation; after a number of cycles the solution has become stable, and so one has a function (still a simple product of one-electron orbitals) that describes the structure of the system, and a set of orbital energies from the solution of the Schrödinger equation. The calculation is actually done with the *Hartree equations* (see Box 25) in which the potential experienced by one electron is the sum of its interactions with all the other electrons. The presence of the electron is not allowed to distort the electron clouds locally: its effect is to distort the orbital as a whole. No possibility of the other electrons tending to keep away from the position of the electron of interest is admitted: *electron correlation* effects are ignored; see Fig. C3 on p. 43.

BOX 25: Self-consistent fields

Hartree equations

$$[H^{\text{core}}(1) + 2\sum_{j=1}^{n} J_j(1)]\,\psi_i(1) = \sum_{j=1}^{n} \epsilon_{ij}\psi_j(1),$$

where the Coulomb operator is

$$J_j(1) = \int d\tau_2\, \psi_j^*(2)\,\psi_j(2)\,(e^2/4\pi\epsilon_0 r_{12}).$$

Sum j runs over *occupied orbitals.*

Hartree-Fock equations (closed shell)

$$[H^{\text{core}}(1) + 2\sum_{j=1}^{n} J_j(1) - \sum_{j=1}^{n} K_j(1)]\,\psi_i(1) = \epsilon_i\psi_i(1),$$

where the exchange operator is defined through

$$K_j(1)\,\psi_i(1) = \int d\tau_2\, \psi_j^*(2)\,\psi_i(2)\,(e^2/4\pi\epsilon_0 r_{12})\,\psi_j(1)$$

$$E = \sum_{i,j}\,[2\epsilon_i - 2J_{ij} + K_{ij}]$$

with $J_{ij} = \int d\tau_1\, \psi_i^*(1)J_j(1)\psi_i(1)$

$K_{ij} = \int d\tau_2\, \psi_i^*(1)K_j(1)\psi_i(1)$

as the Coulomb and exchange integrals.

2. In the *Hartree-Fock method* the self-consistent field procedure takes into account the indistinguishability of the electrons as required by the °Pauli principle. That is, it allows for the possibility of °exchange. To do so it takes as the wavefunction a °Slater determinant, and then enters the self-consistency cycle of Fig. S3. The potential experienced by each electron is the Coulombic potential modified by the °exchange energy (which is the correction of the Coulombic repulsion energy required in order to take into account the tendency of electrons with like spins to avoid each other). The Schrödinger equation is cast into the form of the *Hartree-Fock equations* (Box 25), where the first part of the potential is the uncorrected Coulombic interaction of the electron with all the other electrons in their frozen orbitals, and the second part is the exchange-energy correction. The Hartree-Fock (HF) method also neglects the °correlation energy. The *unrestricted Hartree-Fock* (UHF) method allows more freedom to the form of the orbitals by permitting the spatial form of the orbital to depend on whether the electron has an α or a β °spin.

It is normal for the atomic and molecular orbitals used as a starting point in SCF calculations to be °linear combinations of atomic orbitals, and the accuracy of the calculation is severely curtailed if the functions chosen are too inflexible; this might occur if too few (too small a *basis set*) have been chosen. A convenient set of orbitals with which to commence a calculation are the °Slater atomic orbitals. The evaluation of molecular integrals is considerably simplified if °gaussian orbitals are used, but more of these must be used if the atomic wavefunctions are to be at all reasonably represented. When the labour of an SCF calculation appears to be too great, or is actually found to be too great, approximations are introduced in a more or less rational fashion: such methods constitute the semi-empirical SCF calculations (see °Hückel method) as opposed to the *a priori* or °*ab initio* SCF calculations which begin from scratch and proceed without approximation (apart from the approximations inherent to the HF scheme). In all cases the calculations can be improved by permitting °configuration interaction.

Questions. Outline the sequence of calculations involved in a self-consistent field calculation. When does the cycling procedure cease? What is the basis of the Hartree method? What does it neglect? What is the basis of the Hartree-Fock method, and why is it an improvement on the Hartree method? Why is the HF—SCF method unable to provide exact atomic wave functions and energies? What is the UHF—SCF method? What interpretation could be put on the letters HF—SCF—LCAO—MO, and what process of computation would you understand by it? What is the difference between an *ab initio* SCF calculation and a semi-empirical calculation? What errors are introduced by using too small a basis set, and what is meant by a 'basis set' in this context? Show that it is necessary to deal with electron repulsion and exchange integrals involving orbitals located on up to only four atomic centres. Why is it unnecessary to invent methods to deal with 5-centre integrals in HF calculations?

Further information. See *MQM* Chapter 8. A simple introduction to the methods of atomic and molecular energy calculations is given by Richards and Horsley (1970) and by McGlynn, Vanquickenborne, Kinoshita, and Carroll (1972). A classic account of atomic-structure calculations, which illustrates the headaches which Hartree must have suffered before electronic computers were available, is described in Hartree (1957). Both Richards and Horsley and McGlynn *et al.* work through sample calculations. The semi-empirical methods are described under °Hückel method.

sequence. First review and be quite clear about the meaning of a °progression in the °vibrational structure of the °electronic spectra of molecules. A *sequence* is a series of lines that have in common the same value for the difference of the vibrational quantum numbers for the upper and lower electronic states. If the upper vibrational quantum number is v' and the lower v'', then the lines that have $v' - v'' = 0$ form one sequence, those with $v' - v'' = -1$ form another, those with $v' - v'' = +1$ a third, and so on (see Fig. S4).

All the lines of one sequence would lie at the same frequency if the vibrational energy levels in both the electronic states were evenly spaced, but the °anharmonicity of the vibrations destroys the even separation of a truly °harmonic oscillator, and so the separation of the lines of a sequence yields information about the deviation of the molecular potential-energy curve from an ideal parabolic form.

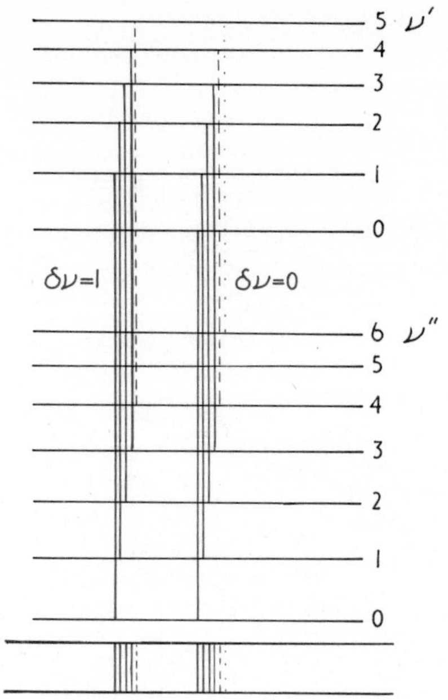

FIG. S4. Two sequences.

Questions. What is a sequence, and how does it differ from a progression? What information is it possible to extract from the positions of the lines in a sequence? When may all the lines of a given sequence be coincident? Would you expect the intensity of the lines in a sequence to be the same; if not, what is a major influence on the intensity? Given that the vibrational energy of the ground state depends on v'' through the expression $\omega''(v'' + \frac{1}{2}) + x_e''\omega''(v'' + \frac{1}{2})^2$, with a similar expression for the excited electronic state vibrational energies, calculate the frequencies of the 0, −1, and +1 sequences.

Further information. See *MQM* Chapter 10. Detailed information about the appearance, analysis, and formation of sequences will be found in Barrow (1962), Whiffen (1972), Gaydon (1968), and Herzberg (1950, 1966).

series. The frequency of any spectral transition may be expressed as the difference of two °terms, each term representing the energy of a state of the atom or molecule. Let us denote the terms T_n, where n is some index which is generally identified as a °quantum number or a collection of quantum numbers for the system. The frequency of each transition from a state n to a series of other states n' is simply $T_{n'} - T_{n'}$, and the series of lines in the spectrum for a fixed n and changing n' is called a *spectral series*.

Some of the most famous spectral series occur in the alkali metals and involve transitions of the single valence electron. The transitions in which an electron in a p-orbital drops down into the ground-state s-orbital (see Fig. S5) gives a series of lines known as the *principal series* (and hence the notation 'p' for the orbitals involved); the series formed by the light emitted as the electron falls from some upper s-orbital into the lowest p-orbital constitutes the *sharp series* (and hence 's'); the decay of electrons from the upper excited d-orbitals falling into the lowest p-orbital gives a *diffuse series* (thus it looks, and hence 'd'); and as electrons in f-orbitals drop to the lowest d-orbital so is generated the *fundamental series* (and hence 'f'). The transitions are illustrated in Fig. S5.

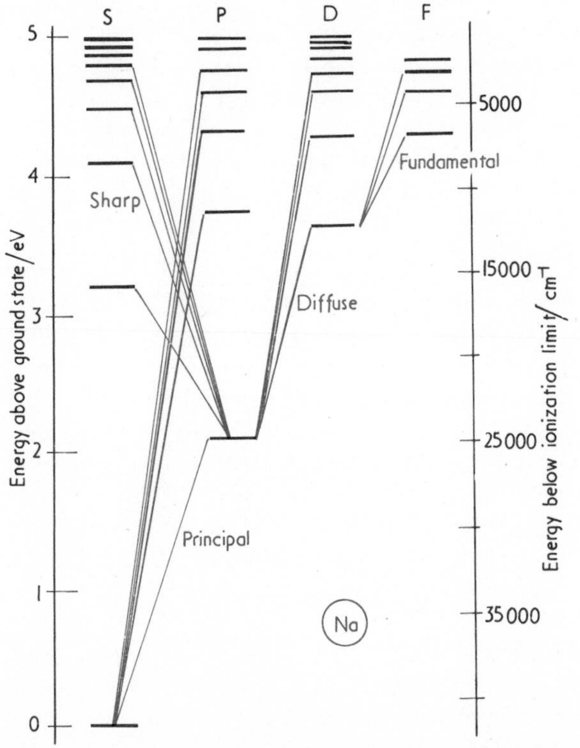

FIG. S5. S, P, D, F series in sodium.

Further information. See *MQM* Chapter 8 for more information about series. The structure of atomic spectral series is described by White (1934), King (1964), Herzberg (1944), Whiffen (1972), Kuhn (1964), and Condon and Shortley (1963). The °selection rules that led to the construction of Fig. S5 are described in that section. Molecular series are discussed in King (1964), Barrow (1962), Whiffen (1972), and Herzberg (1950, 1966).

singlet and triplet states. In a singlet state the net °spin of a many-electron system is zero ($S = 0$). In a triplet state the net spin is unity ($S = 1$). The spin °angular momentum °vector may have a series of projections on a selected axis. These projections are distinguished by the quantum number M_S which can range in unit steps from S down to $-S$. It follows that M_S may take on three values ($M_S = 1, 0, -1$) when $S = 1$, but only one value ($M_S = 0$) when $S = 0$: hence the names triplet and singlet.

The distinction is easiest to see in the case of a system composed of two electrons. As each electron can have a projection $m_s = +\frac{1}{2}$ or $-\frac{1}{2}$ (which we denote α or β) the combined system can be in any of the four states $\alpha(1)\alpha(2)$, $\alpha(1)\beta(2)$, $\beta(1)\alpha(2)$, and $\beta(1)\beta(2)$. The middle two choices do not correspond to a resultant spin vector of fixed length because the α and β vectors can make any azimuthal angle to each other. If we specify the azimuth of one with respect to the other we shall get a definite resultant: if $\alpha(1)$ and $\beta(2)$ are in phase they give a resultant corresponding to $S = 1$; if they are 180° out of phase their resultant is zero and corresponds to a state with $S = 0$ (see Fig. S6). It is worth emphasizing that when we say that spins are 'paired' in a singlet state we mean not only that one has α spin and the other β but also that they are relatively oriented so that they point in opposite directions. (In the $M_S = 0$ state of the triplet one electron has α spin and the other β but their resultant is not zero.) One can show from quantum mechanics that the appropriate form of the spin function for the triplet (in-phase) state with $M_S = 0$ is $\alpha(1)\beta(2) + \beta(1)\alpha(2)$, and for the singlet

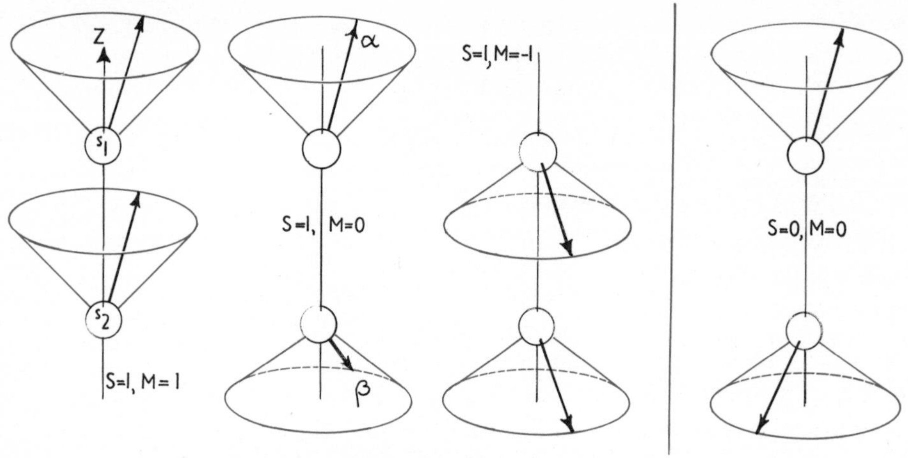

FIG. S6. Triplets and singlets: note the different phase of α and β in the $M_s = 0$ state of the singlet and the triplet.

(out-of-phase) state it is $\alpha(1)\beta(2) - \beta(1)\alpha(2)$. The other two states of the triplet ($M_S = \pm 1$) are $\alpha(1)\alpha(2)$ and $\beta(1)\beta(2)$.

It is possible to convert a singlet term into a triplet (and vice versa) by making one electron spin precess faster than the other. This may be brought about by applying different magnetic fields to the two spins so that their Larmor frequencies (see °precession) differ: an in-phase (triplet) orientation is thereby gradually turned into an out-of-phase orientation (Fig. S7). A field from a laboratory magnet cannot effect the interconversion (which is known as *intersystem crossing*, ISC) because it affects both spins equally (the magnet's field is homogeneous on a molecular scale). A magnetic field arising from within the molecule may be able to rephase the spins. For example, the °spin-orbit coupling to one electron might

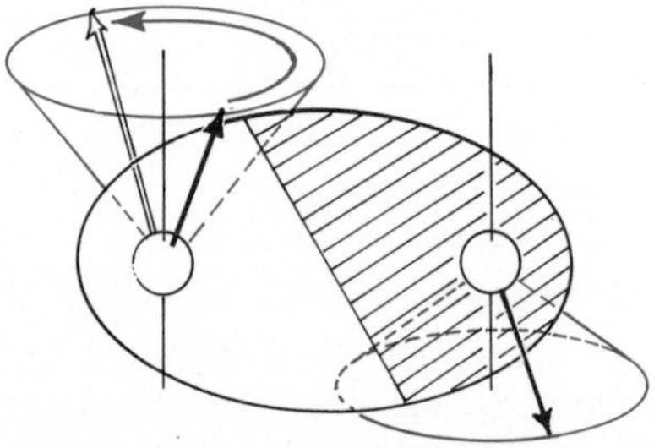

FIG. S7. Relative re-phasing of the spins lead to triplet-singlet interconversion. The hatching denotes a region of a different spin-orbit coupling.

differ from that to the other, and as this interaction is magnetic, we have a situation in which the Larmor frequencies differ. This is the reason why molecules containing heavy atoms (with large spin-orbit couplings) are efficient at intersystem crossing (see °phosphorescence).

The interconversion of *ortho*- and *para*-hydrogen (see °nuclear statistics) can be brought about by paramagnetic ions because the singlet and triplet phasing of the nuclear spins can be interconverted by the inhomogeneous field which such an ion may generate if it is closer to one nucleus than the other.

Further information. See Chapter 6 and Chaper 10 of *MQM* for a more detailed discussion of singlets and triplets, and their interconversion. The role of the triplet state in chemistry, and its detailed quantum mechanics, is discussed in McGlynn, Azumi, and Kinoshita (1969), who give many references. The photochemical consequences of the differences between singlet and triplet states are discussed by Wayne (1970) and Calvert and Pitts (1966). The difference is taken up in °Hund rules and °spin correlation, which you now should see. A manifestation of singlet-triplet ISC is °phosphorescence.

Slater atomic orbitals. Atomic orbitals in many-electron atoms have a complicated dependence on position which can be represented accurately only be listing their amplitude numerically. For many purposes it is desirable to have an analytical function rather than a table of numbers, and the

Slater atomic orbitals are analytical functions based on the numerical results, but designed to reproduce them with moderate accuracy. A set of simple rules has been devised which enable the Slater-type orbital (STO) to be written for any electron in any atom.

Each orbital has a radial dependence given by $Nr^{n^*-1}\exp(-\zeta r)$ and an angular dependence given by the °spherical harmonics corresponding to the appropriate values of the quantum numbers ℓ and m_ℓ (see Table 23). The rules for finding the effective principal quantum number n^* and ζ are as follows.

1. n^* is related to the actual principal number n by the correspondence $n \longrightarrow n^*$ using the rule $1 \longrightarrow 1$, $2 \longrightarrow 2$, $3 \longrightarrow 3$, $4 \longrightarrow 3{\cdot}7$, $5 \longrightarrow 4$, and $6 \longrightarrow 4{\cdot}2$.

2. ζ is related to the effective atomic number Z_{eff} by $\zeta = Z_{\text{eff}}/n^*$; Z_{eff} is related to the true atomic number by $Z_{\text{eff}} = Z - \sigma$; σ is the *screening constant.*

3. The screening constant is calculated by classifying atomic orbitals into the following groups: (1s); (2s, 2p); (3s, 3p); (3d); (4s, 4p); (4d); (4f); (5s, 5p); (5d); . . .. σ is the sum of a number of contributions arising from each group, and is calculated as follows. Let the atomic orbital of interest be in a group X and let it have a principal quantum number n. The contribution from the other electrons present is

(a) from electrons outside group X (that is, to the right of X in the list): 0;

(b) from electrons in group X; 0·30 if the electron is 1s but 0·35 from any other electron in X;

(c) if the electron of interest is ns or np
  (i) for each electron with principal quantum number number $n-1$: 0·85;
  (ii) for each electron with principal quantum number $n-2, n-3, \ldots$: 1·00;

(d) if the electron of interest is nd or nf, for each electron in a group preceding X in the list: 1·00.

Slater-type orbitals for the valence orbitals of the first-row atoms are given in Table 21.

Inspection of the form of the Slater orbitals reveals a serious defect: they possess no radial nodes. One consequence of this is that they are not °orthogonal. They may be made mutually orthogonal by the Schmidt orthogonalization procedure, and so this defect can be overcome (see °orthogonal functions for the procedure).

Questions. Deduce the form of the Slater-type atomic orbitals for the 1s-orbital in H, 2s in Li, 2s and 2p in C, N, O, and F, and the 3d in Fe^{2+} and Fe. Find the °normalization constant for the general STO. Find the mean radius of the electron distribution in each of the orbitals just set up. Show that it is possible to choose a sum of the 1s and 2s STOs that is orthogonal to the 1s-orbital: this is the Schmidt procedure for orthogonalizing 2s to 1s, and it may be extended to orthogonalize 3s to both 1s and 2s: do so (see °orthogonal functions). What effect does orthogonalization have (in this case) on the number of radial nodes, and for the C atom, the mean radius of the 2s-orbital?

Further information. See *MQM* Chapter 8 for a brief discussion. A useful discussion of Slater-type orbitals is given in §II.8 of Coulson (1961), Murrell, Kettle, and Tedder (1965), and McGlynn, Vanquickenborne, Kinoshita, and Carroll (1972). The last, in Appendix B, give many references to the expression of °self-consistent field orbitals in terms of sums of STO's and a table of orbitals. For the Schmidt orthogonalization see °orthogonal functions. °Overlap integrals involving Slater atomic orbitals are referred to under that heading.

Slater determinant. According to the °Pauli principle the wavefunction for a system of electrons must change sign whenever the coordinates of any two electrons are interchanged. It follows that a simple product of the form $\psi_a^\alpha(1)\psi_a^\beta(2)\psi_b^\alpha(3)\ldots\psi_z^\beta(N)$, where electron 1 occupies orbital ψ_a with spin α, and so on, is inadequate. It is possible to ensure that a product of this form does satisfy the Pauli principle by writing it as a determinant:

$$(1/N!)^{1/2}\begin{vmatrix} \psi_a^\alpha(1) & \psi_a^\alpha(2) & \psi_a^\alpha(3) & \ldots & \psi_a^\alpha(N) \\ \psi_a^\beta(1) & \psi_a^\beta(2) & \psi_a^\beta(3) & \ldots & \psi_a^\beta(N) \\ \psi_b^\alpha(1) & \psi_b^\alpha(2) & \psi_b^\alpha(3) & \ldots & \psi_b^\alpha(N) \\ \cdot & \cdot & \cdot & \ldots & \cdot \\ \cdot & \cdot & \cdot & \ldots & \cdot \\ \cdot & \cdot & \cdot & \ldots & \cdot \\ \psi_z^\beta(1) & \psi_z^\beta(2) & \psi_z^\beta(3) & \ldots & \psi_z^\beta(N) \end{vmatrix}$$

Expansion according to the rules of manipulating determinants leads to $N!$ terms, half occuring with a +ve sign and half with —ve. The factor $(1/N!)^{1/2}$ ensures that the determinantal wavefunction remains °normalized. That this Slater determinant satisfies the Pauli principle follows automatically from the property of determinants that interchange of any pair of rows or columns reverses its sign. Suppose that we interchange electrons 1 and 2, so that electron 1 is put into the orbital hitherto occupied by electron 2, and vice versa. The effect on the determinant is to interchange the first and second columns, and so the sign changes. The same happens when any pair of electrons are interchanged, and so the determinant is the appropriate combination of the one-electron orbitals.

It should be observed that the °Pauli exclusion principle follows from the disappearance of a determinant when any two rows or columns are identical. Suppose that electron 1 entered orbital ψ_a with spin α and that electron 2 joined it with the same spin. Then the first two rows of the determinant would be the same, and so it would vanish; therefore it is not possible to form a state in which more than one electron occupies the same orbital with the same spin.

A word on notation: the orbitals with their accompanying spin are known as *spin-orbitals.* A spin-orbital corresponding to spin α instead of being written ψ_a^{α} is sometimes written merely ψ_a with the α spin understood. In this notation the β spin-orbital is denoted $\overline{\psi}_a$. Much paper would be employed if a determinantal wavefunction were always written in full; therefore it is normally denoted by listing only the terms on the diagonal and ignoring (but remembering) the normalization constant. The determinant above becomes $|\psi_a\overline{\psi}_a\psi_b\ldots\overline{\psi}_z|$ in this notation.

It should be noted that only for closed-shell species can the wavefunction be represented by a single Slater determinant; when the shell is incomplete a linear combination of determinants must be used.

Questions. Why is a simple product of orbitals an inadequate representation of the state of a many-electron system? Why is a Slater determinant a suitable representation? Write the Slater determinant for the helium atom, expand it, and confirm by inspection that it satisfies the Pauli principle. Do the same for four electrons in the lowest-energy configuration of a one-dimensional square well. Confirm that the helium atom must have paired spins in its ground state, but that in an excited state they may be paired (a °singlet) or unpaired (a triplet). Repeat these considerations for the hydrogen molecule. Continuing with a two-electron system, write down the °hamiltonian and show that a simple (non-determinantal) product function leads to an expression for the energy in which the electronic interactions are represented solely by a °Coulombic repulsion term, but that when a Slater determinant is used an additional integral appears (the °exchange integral). What is the value of this exchange integral in the ground state of helium?

Further information. See *MQM* Chapter 8. See Richards and Horsley (1970) for a gentle introduction to the way of manipulating determinantal wavefunctions, and McGlynn, Vanquickenborne, Kinoshita, and Carroll (1972) for a more detailed version. The role of the Pauli principle in determining the energies of atoms and molecules is described under °Pauli principle, and aspects of the consequences are the °exchange energy, Fermi hole, and °spin correlation. The °localization of molecular orbitals into regions of a molecule can be demonstrated in terms of properties of a Slater determinant.

spectroscopic perturbations. The presence of a °perturbation generally muddles a system by shifting energy levels and causing states to take on to some extent the characteristics of other states. Spectra arise from transitions between energy levels, and therefore perturbations appear as shifts and changes in intensity of the spectral lines. For example, one might be following a series of spectral lines forming a regular array on a photographic plate, and then in the region of a particular frequency the lines lose their regularity and the spectrum seems distorted. This is a *spectroscopic perturbation* and has arisen because several states that can be mixed by a perturbation have come close together in energy.

Two classes of perturbation are often distinguished: a *homogeneous perturbation* is an interaction mixing vibrational and electronic levels, and in a linear molecule it mixes states with the same value of the °quantum number Λ. A *hetero-*

geneous perturbation is a rotational-electronic interaction (as in Λ- °doubling) and mixes states differing in Λ by ±1.

Further information. See §6.19 of King (1964) and §V.4 of Herzberg (1950). See also Herzberg (1966), Krönig (1930), and Kovács (1969). Revise °perturbation theory, °superposition principle, °resonance, and °predissociation.

spherical harmonics. The spherical harmonics are a set of functions of the angular coordinates θ and ϕ (as defined in Fig. S8), that satisfy the differential equation $\Lambda^2 Y_{\ell m}(\theta, \phi) = -\ell(\ell+1)Y_{\ell m}(\theta, \phi)$, where Λ^2 is the legendrian operator (see °laplacian). These may be expressed as simple polynomials of sin θ, cos θ, sin ϕ, and cos ϕ, or as polynomials in x, y, and z (Tables 22 and 23), and visualized as the vibrational modes of a spherical shell.

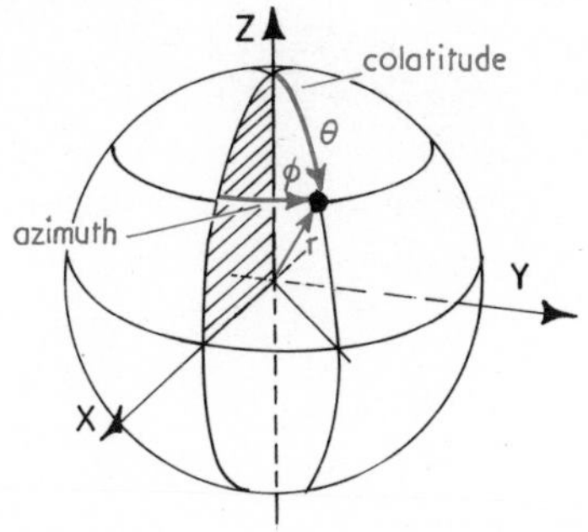

FIG. S8. Spherical polar coordinates.

Each function is distinguished by the labels ℓ and m: ℓ may take any positive integral value, including zero; and m, for a given value of ℓ, may vary in unit steps from $-\ell$ to ℓ. These properties of ℓ and m should be strongly reminiscent of the properties of °orbital angular momentum, and it is in fact the case that the spherical harmonics are the wavefunctions corresponding to states of angular momentum ℓ, m.

The function $Y_{0,0}(\theta,\phi)$ is a constant $(1/2\sqrt{\pi})$ and therefore has the same value at all points on the surface of the sphere: it can therefore be depicted by the function drawn in Fig. S9 a, where $Y_{0,0}$ is the surface at a constant height above the spherical surface. A convenient way of denoting this isotropy

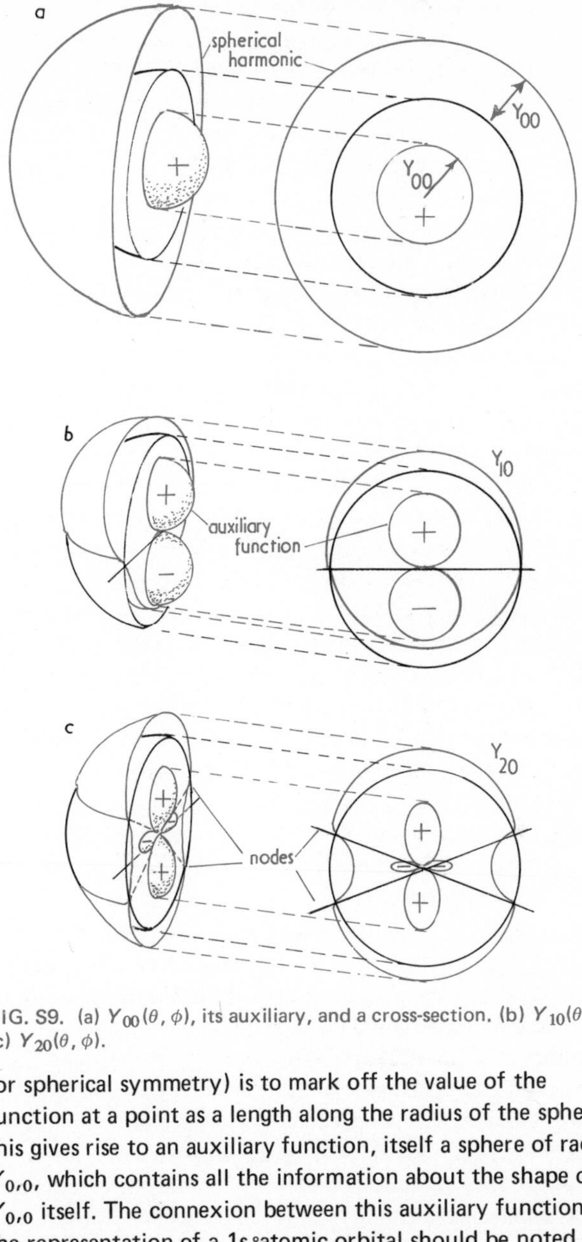

FIG. S9. (a) $Y_{00}(\theta, \phi)$, its auxiliary, and a cross-section. (b) $Y_{10}(\theta, \phi)$. (c) $Y_{20}(\theta, \phi)$.

(or spherical symmetry) is to mark off the value of the function at a point as a length along the radius of the sphere: this gives rise to an auxiliary function, itself a sphere of radius $Y_{0,0}$, which contains all the information about the shape of $Y_{0,0}$ itself. The connexion between this auxiliary function and the representation of a 1s °atomic orbital should be noted (see p. 108). There are no angular °nodes in $Y_{0,0}$, and so it corresponds to a wave with zero °orbital angular momentum.

The function $Y_{1,0}(\theta, \phi)$ is proportional to $\cos\theta$ and is independent of ϕ. It has extrema at the poles and is zero on the equator, and may be represented as in Fig. S9 b. The auxiliary function may be constructed in the same way as before, and it will be observed that in the northern hemisphere the wave has a positive amplitude, and that this is denoted by + in the auxiliary function; and that in the southern hemisphere the amplitude is negative. The resemblance of the auxiliary function to the boundary surface of a p_z-orbital should be noted. Since there is one angular node the wave represents a state of angular momentum with $\ell = 1$. An observer looking along the z-axis would not see the equatorial node, and so the component of momentum about the z-axis is zero (and that, it should be recalled, is the significance of the quantum number m being equal to zero).

The other spherical harmonics corresponding to $\ell = 1$ are those with $m = 1$ and -1: both these functions are complex (but not complicated) and correspond to waves running round the z-axis with their amplitudes predominantly in the equatorial zone. Combinations of the two functions may be constructed that are real, and correspond to standing waves: one combination is $Y_{1,1} + Y_{1,-1}$, which is proportional to $\cos\phi$ (inspect Table 23). This has the same shape as $Y_{1,0}$ but is orientated along the x-axis. The combination $Y_{1,1} - Y_{1,-1}$, which is proportional to $\sin\phi$, is also of that shape and is directed along the y-axis. The connexion of these combinations with the p_x- and the p_y-orbitals should be appreciated.

The procedure may be continued to include the five functions with $\ell = 2$, and the functions generated have a close resemblance to the d-orbitals of atomic theory (Fig. S9 c and Fig. H12 on p. 105). In each case the number of angular nodes is equal to ℓ (we count each plane surface as a node) and the connexion of the number of nodes and the angular momentum arises as a consequence of the °de Broglie relation and the connexion between the °kinetic energy of a state and its °wavefunction. The orbital shapes and the atomic-orbital boundary surfaces are not identical, because the latter are boundaries enclosing chosen amounts of amplitude or density and the dependence of these on the radius (as well as the angles) distorts the spherical harmonic shapes.

If it is desired to find the distribution of a particle sliding round the surface of a sphere with a particular angular momentum, then in accord with the Born interpretation (see °wavefunction) it may be calculated by taking the square of the appropriate function. Thus a particle with zero angular momentum ($\ell = 0$) is spread evenly over the surface; one with $\ell = 1$ is found either predominantly in the polar regions ($m = 0$) or in the equatorial ($m = \pm 1$); one with $\ell = 2$ is found strongly in the polar regions, but also with a significant density spread smoothly around the equator ($m = 0$), or in two bands concentrated at 45° N and 45° S ($m = \pm 1$), or in a band highly concentrated on the equator ($m = \pm 2$).

Questions. 1. What is the significance of the spherical harmonics in classical theory and in quantum theory? What values may the indices ℓ and m take, and how many values of m are permitted for a particular value of ℓ? What is the shape of $Y_{0,0}$, and why is it plausible that it corresponds to a state of zero orbital angular momentum? To what vibration of the surface of a sphere does it correspond? Construct the auxiliary function for a p_x-, a d_{z^2}-, and a d_{xy}-orbital. Draw the shape of the function that determines the probability distribution of the particle in each of these orbitals. To what vibrations of the sphere do these orbitals correspond? How could each vibration be stimulated? Repeat the exercise for an f-orbital ($\ell = 3$). Compare your answers with the representation of the °hydrogen atomic orbitals depicted in Fig. H12 on p. 105. Why should the contour diagrams there resemble (rather than be identical with) the auxiliary functions you have drawn? Suppose you took a spherical shell around the proton in the hydrogen atom and at each point plotted the value of the wavefunction in the various orbital states, might you expect the function so obtained to be identical to the functions you have been drawing in this section? Why is that? Calculate the latitude of the maximum concentrations of electron density in the orbitals d_{xy}, d_{xz}, f_{xyz}.
2. Confirm that the functions $Y_{0,0}$, $Y_{1,1}$, $Y_{4,3}$ do indeed satisfy the differential equation that defines the spherical harmonics. Use the legendrian operator in Box 11 on p. 124. Apply the operator ℓ_z (see Box 14 on p. 161) to the explicit expression for the general form of the spherical harmonics and confirm that $Y_{\ell m}$ is an eigenfunction of ℓ_z with eigenvalue $m\hbar$. Prove that the standing-wave solutions $Y_{\ell,m} \pm Y_{\ell,-m}$ are eigenvalues of the magnitude of the angular

momentum, but correspond to states with zero component of angular momentum about the z-axis (as should be expected for standing waves), and are not eigenfunctions of the operator ℓ_z (see °quenching).

Further information. See *MQM* Chapter 3 for a further discussion of the spherical harmonics, their connexion with angular momentum, and illustration of auxiliary functions. A pleasing account of the properties of the spherical harmonics and their relation to states of particular orbital angular momentum, to waves on a flooded planet, to tidal motion, and to the vibration of spheres is given by Kauzmann (1957). See Kauzmann (1957) also for the solution of the differential equation for the spherical harmonics, and Pauling and Wilson (1935). Alternative derivations are provided by *MQM* Chapter 6, Rose (1957), Brink and Satchler (1968), and Edmonds (1957). The mathematical properties of the spherical harmonics, and their components the associated Legendre functions, are given in detail by Abramowitz and Stegun (1965).

spin. The spin is the intrinsic, characteristic, and irremovable °angular momentum of a particle. A convenient fiction is to suppose that the spin is the angular momentum arising from the rotation of a body about its own axis: this model enables one to recall most of the properties of quantum-mechanical spin, and in particular to understand (albeit at only a shallow level) why charged particles with spin also possess an intrinsic magnetic moment. The quantum-mechanical description of the spin of a particle leads to the following conclusions.

1. *The magnitude of the spin angular momentum* of a particle is determined by the spin quantum number s which has a positive, unique, integral or half-integral value characteristic of the particle. If the value of s is known the magnitude of the spin can be calculated from the expression $[s(s+1)]^{1/2}\hbar$. As an example, the spin of an electron is $s=\frac{1}{2}$; this means that its spin angular momentum is $3^{1/2}\hbar/2$, or $0{\cdot}91 \times 10^{-34}$ J s, whatever its other state or condition (the spin is an ineluctable characteristic of the particle, like its charge). Each nucleus has a characteristic spin, and the letter I is used in place of s as the nuclear spin quantum number. See Table 17 for a list of the spins of some nuclei.

2. *The orientation of the spin angular momentum* is quantized (confined to particular angles) in the manner of all °angular momenta. The orientation is determined by the value of the magnetic quantum number m_s: $m_s\hbar$ is the value of the component of spin angular momentum on an arbitrary axis in space (conventionally the z-axis). As an example, two values of m_s are permitted for the electron ($s=\frac{1}{2}$), namely $m_s=+\frac{1}{2}$, corresponding to a component of magnitude $\frac{1}{2}\hbar$ on the z-axis, and $m_s=-\frac{1}{2}$, corresponding to a component $-\frac{1}{2}\hbar$ on the z-axis. The different signs are often referred to as denoting an 'up-spin' (or α-spin) or a 'down-spin' (or β-spin), and the good sense of this can be appreciated from a °vector model of the situation.

3. *Spin is a non-classical phenomenon* in the sense that if $\hbar$ were zero the spin angular momentum would vanish. Do not draw the conclusion that all angular momenta are non-classical in the same sense: an orbital angular momentum of magnitude $[\ell(\ell+1)]^{1/2}\hbar$ could survive the dwindling of $\hbar$ to zero in a classical world because ℓ can be increased without limit so that the product did not vanish; but the value of s is fixed.

4. *Spin is not a relativistic phenomenon* in the sense normally put on these words; thus although spin emerges naturally as a consequence of °Dirac's relativistic equation it is possible to arrive at its existence without referring to relativity.

5. *Spin is a fundamental classifier* and divides all matter into two camps with fundamentally different behaviour. Particles with half-integral spin are called °*fermions* and satisfy *Fermi-Dirac statistics*; particles with integral spin (including zero) are °*bosons* and satisfy *Bose-Einstein statistics.* The two classes satisfy different forms of the °Pauli principle, and because of this they show profoundly different behaviour. It is just possible that there exists a third camp containing the *parafermions* which are neither fermions nor bosons and might be needed to account for the properties of quarks, if these exist.

6. *The tendency of spins to °pair* is a term too often ill-used in fallacious accounts of chemical bonding, where it is quoted as the *reason* why bonds form. Energy considerations govern bonding, and if by pairing electrons are enabled to enter a low-lying orbital, and so reduce the energy of the molecular system below that of the separated atoms, then pairing will

occur. But rather than showing any transcendental mutual affection they are forced to pair (essentially by the °Pauli exclusion principle) in order to achieve this low-energy state.

Questions. What is spin? What do the quantum numbers s and m_s signify? What angle does the spin-momentum vector make to the z-axis in the α-spin state of an electron? What is the minimum angular momentum of a °photon? Why is spin non-classical? Which of the following species are fermions and which are bosons: e, p, n, ^{4}He, ^{3}He, ^{2}H$^+$, photon, H_2, and quark? Why do electrons seem to show a tendency to pair?

Further information. See *MQM* Chapter 6 for more information, especially information about coupling spins together. See Dirac (1958) for a horse's mouth account of spin, and Salem and Wigner (1972) for speculations on parafermions. For the angular momentum of spin see °angular momentum and references therein. For an account of the manifestations of spin see Wheatley (1970), and McWeeny (1970) for a more sophisticated version. For an account of other properties that behave like spin (for example, charge) see Lipkin (1965) and Lichtenberg (1970). Spin was introduced empirically by Uhlenbeck and Goudsmit (1925, 1926) in order to explain features of °atomic spectra, developed into a consistent theory by Pauli, and then shown to be a consequence of °Dirac's equation. The historical development of the idea is described in §3.4 of Jammer (1966), a book well worth turning to in order to see the emergence (and sometimes eclipse) of the unconventional. See also °Stern-Gerlach experiment for an earlier experiment proving the existence of spin, but not interpreted then as such. Why spin is not a necessarily relativistic phenomenon is described by Galindo and Sanchez del Rio (1961).

spin-correlation. Electrons with parallel °spins tend to stay apart, and those with opposite spins tend to bunch together. This remarkable phenomenon has nothing to do with the charge of the electron (although it affects the average Coulombic repulsion of two electrons and appears in the °exchange energy); nor is it, one presumes, supernatural. The tendency is an intrinsic property of electrons and is a consequence of the °Pauli principle. This may be seen by considering a wavefunction for two particles $\psi(\mathbf{r}_1, \mathbf{r}_2)$, and supposing that the particles have no interactions. Then the wavefunction can be written as the product $\psi_a(\mathbf{r}_1)\psi_b(\mathbf{r}_2)$, where particle 1 occupies orbital a and particle 2 occupies orbital b. If such a wavefunction is to accord with the Pauli principle it must be modified to $\psi_a(\mathbf{r}_1)\psi_b(\mathbf{r}_2) + \psi_a(\mathbf{r}_2)\psi_b(\mathbf{r}_1)$ if the spins are paired, and to $\psi_a(\mathbf{r}_1)\psi_b(\mathbf{r}_2) - \psi_a(\mathbf{r}_2)\psi_b(\mathbf{r}_1)$ if they are parallel. In the latter case we can investigate the probability of finding both electrons at the same point by

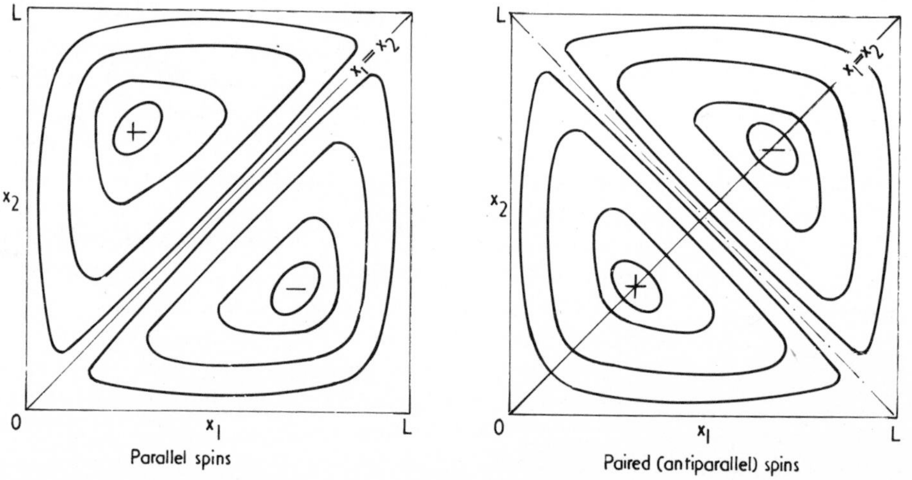

FIG. S10. Formation of a Fermi hole. Contours of total wavefunction for two non-interacting particles in a one-dimensional square well. Note that node at $x_1 = x_2$ when the spins are parallel.

letting $\mathbf{r}_1$ and $\mathbf{r}_2$ coincide: the wavefunction becomes $\psi_a(\mathbf{r}_1)\psi_b(\mathbf{r}_1) - \psi_a(\mathbf{r}_1)\psi_b(\mathbf{r}_1)$, and vanishes. Therefore we must conclude that there is a vanishing probability of finding both electrons at the same point if their spins are parallel.

In Fig. S10 is illustrated the situation for two particles (electrons, with their charge ignored) in a one-dimensional square well (a narrow wire). The contours depict the probabilities of finding the particles at points x_1 and x_2 in the wire when one particle occupies the ground state ($n = 1$, see °particle in a square well) and the other occupies the first excited level ($n = 2$). The mutual avoidance when the spins are parallel (Fig. S10 a) is manifest as the disappearing probability along the line $x_1 = x_2$. If one imagines an electron at some point, then one may imagine a small surrounding volume into which electrons with the same spin direction will tend not to penetrate: this region is referred to as a *Fermi hole.* An electron with a spin opposite to the first is described by the other wavefunction, and will have an enhanced probability of occurring within this small volume; although the resulting bunching of electrons is not, as far as I know, referred to as a *Fermi heap.* Thus we see that the relative positions of electrons tend to be correlated by virtue of their relative spins.

Further information. See *MQM* Chapter 8 for a further discussion and another picture. There is a brief account of the problem in §IV.6 of Linnett (1960), who gives pictures like Fig. S10 but for the helium atom: these are instructive. Linnett (1964) has emphasized spin-correlation effects in a theory of chemical bonding. Reviews of electron correlation in atoms and molecules include those by Pauncz (1969) and Hylleraas (1964). See °exchange energy and °self-consistent fields for more information.

spin-orbit coupling. An electron in an atom possesses a magnetic moment both by virtue of its °spin and its °orbital magnetic moments. Two magnetic moments in each other's vicinity interact, and the strength of the interaction depends on the magnitudes of the moments and their mutual orientation: this interaction energy appears in atomic spectra as °fine structure.

The source of the spin-orbit coupling energy can be visualized by taking up a position on an electron which is orbiting a nucleus of charge Ze. Such an observer will see a positive current encircling him, and a consequence of the current is a magnetic moment at his position. Thus we can conclude that the electron spin magnetic moment is bathed in a magnetic field arising from its own orbital motion. (There will also be magnetic fields arising at the electron by virtue of the orbital moments of the other electrons in the atom or molecule, but these *spin-other-orbit interactions* are generally less important.) It is in principle a simple matter to calculate the magnetic field $\mathbf{B}$ at the electron by virtue of its orbital motion, and therefore to deduce its magnetic energy from the expression $-g\gamma_e\,\mathbf{s}.\mathbf{B}$ (because the interaction energy is $-\mathbf{m}.\mathbf{B}$, and the spin °magnetic moment is $g\gamma_e\mathbf{s}$); then we could anticipate that $\mathbf{B}$ is proportional to $\mathbf{l}$, the orbital angular momentum, and so expect an energy of the form $(\zeta/\hbar^2)\mathbf{s}.\mathbf{l}$, where ζ is the *spin-orbit coupling constant.* Nevertheless, the calculation is not quite so straightforward, and the early, straightforward physicists, who first did it, were perplexed when they obtained disagreement with experiment.

The calculation proceeds by finding the magnetic field at a body moving in a electric field with a particular velocity. In this case the electric field is due to the nuclear Coulomb potential, and the velocity may be expressed in terms of the orbital angular momentum through $\mathbf{l} = \mathbf{r} \wedge m\mathbf{v}$. Then the resulting radius-dependent quantity is averaged over the radial part of the atomic orbital occupied by the electron, and the mean constant so obtained is identified with $\zeta/\hbar^2$. This approach gives an answer which is broadly correct (ζ is strongly dependent on Z, and varies as Z^4) but is wrong by a factor of 2. With °spin we know that factors of 2 are not unreasonable; but even so they must be justified. One justification for this extra factor may be found from the °Dirac equation; from this the correct expression emerges. Nevertheless, it is always pleasing to seek a more physical, visualizable explanation, and as usual one may be provided. When we step on to the orbiting electron in order to observe the current due to the central nucleus, we must do so with more circumspection than had Copernicus when he trod the opposite journey. In the atom the electron is moving so fast that it must be regarded relativistically, and watching an electron spin from the viewpoint of a nucleus is not the same as watching it spin from the viewpoint of an observer travelling with it. By a coincidence, or by design, the electron is moving in such a way that to an observer on the nucleus it appears to be spinning at only one-half its rate for a travelling observer. This modification of its motion, which is essentially *Thomas precession*, introduces an extra factor $\frac{1}{2}$ into the spin-orbit calculation, and so brings it into conformity with the °Dirac equation, and with experiment.

The strength of the spin-orbit coupling constant increases with the atomic number of the atom; the heavy atoms have large spin-orbit coupling constants (some are listed in Table 9 on p. 271). In one-electron atoms this dependence is Z^4 as mentioned above, and this reflects the dominant sampling by the electrons of regions close to the nucleus where the field is strong: as Z increases the orbital contracts and the electric increases, and both lead to a larger value of ζ. Outer electrons are further away, and in hydrogen-like atoms ζ falls as $1/n^3$: this also reflects the magnitude of the electric field sampled by the electron.

Further information. See *MQM* Chapter 8 for a detailed examination of the topics mentioned here, including the calculation of ζ for hydrogen-like atoms, and a further mention of Thomas precession. The latter is well-described in Moss (1973) and Hameka (1965). The role of shielding electrons is examined further in *MQM*. A thorough discussion of spin-orbit coupling effects, especially with respect to °singlet and triplet states and °phosphorescence, will be found in McGlynn, Azumi, and Kinoshita (1969): they explain how to do calculations involving spin-orbit coupling, and tabulate data. For applications in atomic spectroscopy, see °fine structure and its ramifications. See Table 9 for some spin-orbit coupling data.

spin-spin coupling. The interaction between nuclei that in °nuclear magnetic resonance (n.m.r.) gives rise to the splitting known as *fine structure* is called spin-spin coupling, and its magnitude is generally denoted J and quoted in hertz (Hz, cycles per second). The appearance of a spectrum showing fine structure is shown in Fig. N3 on p. 154. The coupling between most protons lies in the range -20 Hz to $+40$ Hz, although the commonly observed range is from 0 Hz up to 10 Hz. These energies are minute, and correspond to a magnetic field being induced at one nucleus by virtue of the presence and orientation of another.

One possible mechanism for the interaction is a direct °dipole-dipole interaction between the two nuclear °spin °magnetic moments; but the spherical average of such an interaction is zero, and so it cannot contribute to the fine structure in a molecule freely rotating in a fluid medium.

Another interaction involves the electrons in the bonds as intermediaries in transmitting the interaction between the nuclei. This mechanism may be illustrated by the example of the hydrogen molecule: the problem is to account for the fact that the energy of the molecule with the nuclear spins parallel is different from that of the molecule with the nuclear spins opposed. The key to the mechanism is the °hyperfine interaction between the nuclei and the electrons. Consider the case when an α electron is close to nucleus A; by virtue of the °Fermi contact interaction the electron and nuclear magnetic moments couple, and the lower-energy configuration is with antiparallel spins (parallel moments) (Fig. S11). But the °Pauli principle requires the other electron in the bond to be antiparallel to the first, and charge correlation suggests that the other electron, with β spin, will be predominantly in the vicinity of the other nucleus. With that nucleus the second electron has a hyperfine interaction by virtue of the Fermi contact term, and so the lowest-energy configuration for the other nucleus is with β spin. Therefore, overall we see that if one nucleus has a particular spin then the other attains the lowest energy if it has the opposite spin. It follows that the energy of the molecule with parallel nuclear spins lies very slightly above that with opposed spins; consequently it requires energy to turn the spins into a parallel alignment.

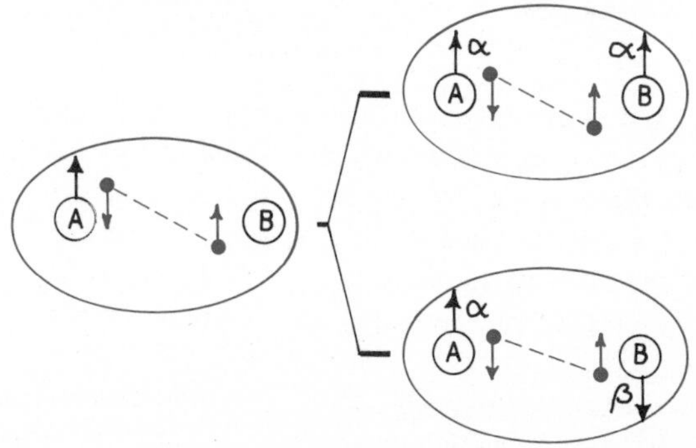

FIG. S11. Spin-spin coupling between protons.

The magnitude of the effect depends on the strength of the hyperfine interactions involved, and on the ease with which the electrons in the bond can be polarized to wash predominantly over the most favourable nuclei: the latter depends on the mean excitation energy of the bond, and since the tendency for the electron spins to be decoupled must be taken into account, it turns out that the mean energy required is the mean energy of excitation to *triplet* configurations of the bond (see °singlet and triplet states). The interaction does not average to zero as the molecule rotates because the contact interactions are isotropic and do not themselves average to zero.

No account of the external magnetic field was taken in the mechanism, and therefore it should be expected, and is indeed found, that the spin-spin coupling interaction is independent of the strength of the applied field.

We have shown that the interaction energy depends on the relative orientation of the two nuclear spins; therefore it is not unreasonable to expect an interaction proportional to the scalar product $\mathbf{I}_A \cdot \mathbf{I}_B$: this form of the interaction is found by detailed calculation, and the constant of proportionality is just the spin-spin coupling constant $J/\hbar$. (If J is positive, the antiparallel orientation of the spins is the more stable because $(J/\hbar)\mathbf{I}_A \cdot \mathbf{I}_B$ then gives a negative contribution to the total energy.)

The example we have provided is artificial in one sense: the spin-spin coupling can be detected in an n.m.r. spectrum only when the coupled nuclei are in different chemical environments (have different °chemical shifts). Thus although there is a coupling between the protons in H_2 (with a magnitude of 280 Hz), the n.m.r. spectrum consists of a single line because all the allowed transitions occur at the same energy (see °n.m.r.). It is more realistic to consider proton coupling in more complicated molecules, and the mechanism already described may be extended in a simple fashion by considering the chain of interactions through the bonds as well as the possibility of direct interaction by the overlap brought about by squashing two nonbonded atoms together.

In an obvious notation, using large and small arrows to denote electron and proton spins respectively, the interaction in H_2 can be represented by {↑ ↓ ↑ ↓} for the lower energy orientations, and {↑ ↓ ↑ ↑} for the upper energy. Analogously, in the CH_2 group the chain will be {↑ ↓ ↑ ⋮ ↑ ↓ ↑} where the parallel orientation of the middle electron pair is favoured by the °Hund rule of maximum multiplicity for atoms (which favours parallel arrangements of spins on atoms); the upper energy orientation for this group is {↑ ↓ ↑ ⋮ ↑ ↓ ↓}, and it is important to note that, because of the insertion of the atom in the chain of interactions, the parallel nuclear orientation lies below the antiparallel (corresponding to a negative J). This chain of interactions can be quite large: J can lie in the range $-21{\cdot}5\ \mathrm{Hz} < J < 42{\cdot}4\ \mathrm{Hz}$. An example is the coupling in HCHO (42·4 Hz). A coupling between two protons separated by three bonds proceeds through the chain {↑ ↓ ↑ ⋮ ↑↓ ⋮ ↓ ↑ ↓} and leads to an antiparallel arrangement as the low-energy state (J positive). Beyond three bonds the interaction is strongly attenuated—that is, much reduced—this is fortunate, for otherwise n.m.r. spectra would be impossibly complicated to disentangle.

The spin-spin coupling between protons separated by bonds depends on the conformation of the molecule. This is because the efficiency of alignment of the spins at the intervening atoms depends on the relative orientation of the bonds. Thus the predominance of {.... ↑ ⋮ ↑ ....} over {.... ↑ ⋮ ↓ ....} depends on factors like the °hybridization of the atoms. As an example, the *trans* coupling in ethene is 19·1 Hz whereas the *cis* coupling is 11·6 Hz.

Although we have dismissed the direct dipole-dipole interaction in fluids, the electron-nucleus dipolar °hyperfine interaction can contribute to spin-spin coupling. We have seen that the spin-transmission mechanism involves two hyperfine interactions, one at each end of the chain; the rotational average of the product of two dipolar interactions does not disappear, and so two electron-nuclear dipole interactions, one at each proton, can contribute. This type of interaction is important in atoms other than hydrogen where p-orbitals occur in the valence shell.

Questions. What is the significance of the term 'spin-spin coupling' in n.m.r.? Under what circumstances will a coupling not show in the spectrum even though it is non-zero? What is the range of proton coupling constants in n.m.r.? What dependence on the strength of the applied field do they show? Why is the direct dipole-dipole interaction between two spins unimportant in fluid media? Is it important in solids? What is a typical magnitude for the direct dipolar interaction between the two protons in the water molecule? Investigate how this interaction depends on the orientation of the molecule with respect to the applied field (assume that the proton moments align themselves with respect to this field and search Box 5, p. 50, for formulae). What structural information might you anticipate obtaining from a study of the direct interaction? What is the source of the spin-spin interaction between protons in liquids? Explain the sequence of interactions that transmits the orientation of the proton to its neighbour. What happens to the interaction when the protons are separated by 3, 4, and 5 bonds? What excited states should be mixed into the ground state in order to yield the spin polarization of the bond? Can a dipolar interaction give any contribution in fluids? What is the significance of a negative value of J?

Further information. See *MQM* Chapter 11 for a detailed discussion of the source of the spin-spin coupling. The role it plays in n.m.r. is described by McLauchlan in *Magnetic resonance* (OCS 1). Further details will be found in Lynden-Bell and Harris (1969), Carrington and McLachlan (1967), Slichter (1963), Memory (1968), and Abragam (1961). The analysis of n.m.r. spectra in order to extract coupling data, and its application, are described by these books and in Roberts (1961), Abraham (1971), Emsley, Feeney, and Sutcliffe (1965), Pople, Schneider, and Bernstein (1959), and Corio (1966). The reason why the spectrum exhibits coupling between non-equivalent nuclei can be seen by referring to the little piece of mathematics in §4.4 of Carrington and McLachlan (1967). Tables of J values will be found in Emsley, Feeney, and Sutcliffe (1965).

Stark effect. The modification of the energy levels, and therefore of the spectra, of atoms and molecules by the application of an electric field, is known as the Stark effect. It is possible to distinguish the first- and second-order effects (which are respectively linear and quadratic in the strength of the applied field) and the atomic and molecular effects.

The *first-order atomic Stark effect* is large but rare, for it depends on the presence of a °degeneracy which enables the atom to respond massively to the applied field. Such a situation occurs in atomic hydrogen: because the 2s- and 2p-orbitals are degenerate, when a field is applied the electron can easily reorganize itself by °hybridization. Thus the combination $\psi_{2s} + \psi_{2p_z}$ gives a distribution strongly biased towards the low-potential region, and the other possible combination $\psi_{2s} - \psi_{2p_z}$ is concentrated on the high-potential side of the nucleus (Fig. S12). Therefore the transitions involving the $n = 2$ shell of the atom are no longer degenerate and occur at different frequencies. The p_x- and p_y-orbitals are unaffected by the field.

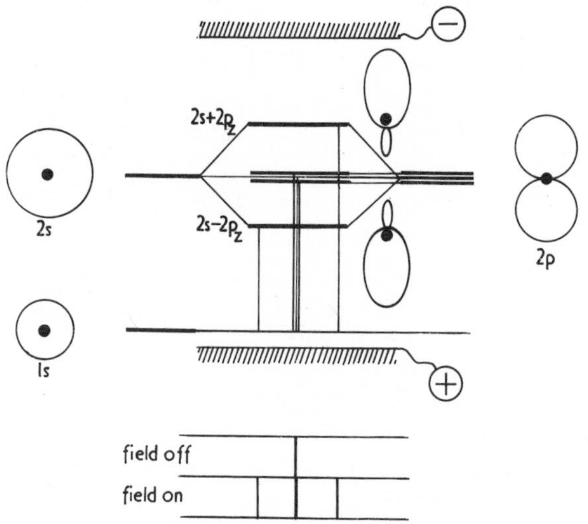

FIG. S12. Linear Stark effect in atomic hydrogen.

As in the °Zeeman effect the transitions are polarized. Two points follow from our discussion of °electric dipole transitions.

1. If m_ℓ does not change, the emitted light (forming the *π-lines*) is polarized parallel to the direction of the applied field (and so it would not be seen if viewed along the direction

of the field; it is radiated in a belt around the transverse direction).

2. If m_ℓ changes by ±1 the light (the *σ-lines*) is transversely polarized. When viewed perpendicular to the field the $\Delta m_\ell = +1$ component is right circularly polarized and the −1 component is left circularly polarized. When viewed along the field direction the light is unpolarized because the +1 and −1 transitions occur at the same frequency, and so the light emitted from different atoms gives an incoherent superposition of both circular polarization states.

Not only does the Stark effect cause a splitting of lines, it also causes them to broaden slightly, and shifts the series limits to lower frequency. Both effects are related to the presence of the low potential on one side of the atom, for it enables an electron to escape (Fig. S13). An electron in a state not far from the ionization limit may be able to °tunnel through the remaining potential-energy barrier and emerge into a region where the applied field can pluck it from the atom. This reduces its lifetime in the excited state, and so, by the °uncertainty principle, the energy of that state is made imprecise; this imprecision appears in the spectrum as a broadening of the appropriate lines. The electron need not be excited into so high an energy state for ionization to occur, and so the field also reduces the energy of the series limit (Fig. S13).

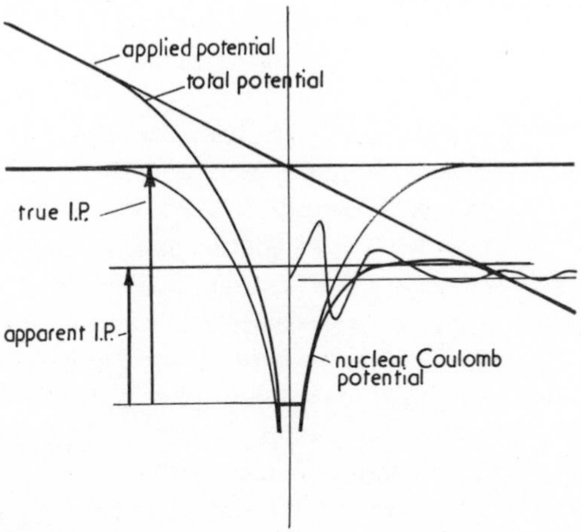

FIG. S13. Extra consequences of the Stark effect for hydrogen.

In atoms not having the degeneracies possessed by hydrogen, the first-order effect is absent and is replaced by the much weaker *second-order effect*. One power of the field is used in distorting the atom from spherical symmetry (°polarizing it), and the second power is used in the interaction with the dipole moment of the distorted atom, so causing the energy separation. Since normal fields can polarize atoms only slightly the induced dipole is small and its interaction with the field weak; therefore the second-order Stark energy shifts are small and huge fields ($\sim 10^5$ V cm^{-1}) must be used.

The *molecular Stark effect* may also be of first- or second-order. The first-order effect is shown by symmetric top molecules with permanent dipole moments: the applied field causes °rotational states of the same value of J but different values of M to have different energies (they are degenerate in the absence of the field), and the splitting is proportional to the permanent dipole moment of the molecule μ, as we explain below. Since fields of the order of 50 kV cm^{-1} give splittings of the order of 20 MHz, and this is easily and accurately detectable in a microwave spectrum, the method is a powerful way of determining dipole moments.

It is instructive and quite easy to understand why the energy of a state with quantum numbers J, K, and M is shifted by an amount $-\mu MKE/J(J+1)$ by a field E. From the theory of the °rotation of symmetric-top molecules we know that K is the projection of the °angular momentum **J** on the figure axis, and that **J** °precesses around this axis. An alternative view would be to consider the vector **J** as fixed and the axis as precessing around it. Since the dipole is directed along the axis the motion averages out its components except for one of magnitude $\mu\cos\theta$ along **J** (see Fig. S14). But **J** is also precessing about the field direction, and the component of dipole parallel to the field is $\mu\cos\theta\,\cos\theta'$; therefore the interaction energy is $-\mu E\cos\theta\,\cos\theta'$. From Fig. S14 we can use simple trigonometry to express $\cos\theta$ as $K/[J(J+1)]^{1/2}$ and $\cos\theta'$ as $M/[J(J+1)]^{1/2}$. Combining these results we obtain the energy as $-\mu MKE/J(J+1)$, as we anticipated. The application of the °selection rules $\Delta J = \pm1$, $\Delta K = 0$, and $\Delta M = 0$, ±1 enables the spectrum (and from the M changes, the polarization of the lines) to be predicted.

In the case of linear molecules, where the angular momentum is perpendicular to the dipole moment, and in

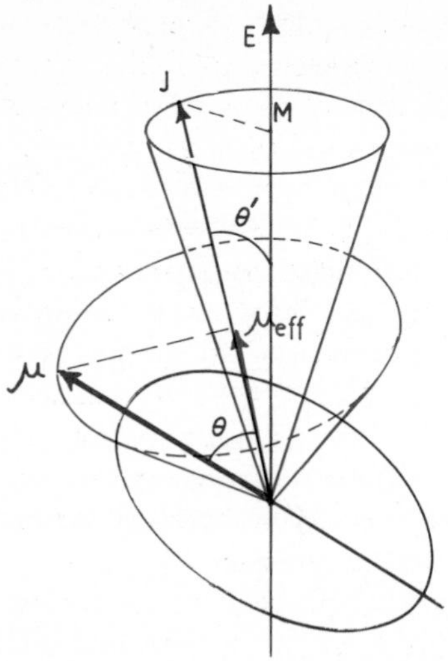

FIG. S14. Molecular Stark effect.

asymmetric tops, where the lack of symmetry causes the motion to be very complicated, there is no linear effect, but the orientating effect of the field (which, in classical terms, distorts the rotational path of the molecule) affects the energy of the states and induces energy shifts of the form $\mu^2E^2(A_1+A_2M^2)$.

The molecular Stark effect is of considerable importance in the study of permanent dipole moments of the molecules that can be examined by microwave spectroscopy, and it is also important in the technology of microwave spectrometers, for an oscillating electric field (usually of several 10 kV cm^{-1}) will modulate the position of spectral lines, and therefore the intensity of absorption or emission at a particular frequency. Detectors making use of this oscillation of the intensity are called *Stark-modulation spectrometers.*

Questions. 1. What is the Stark effect? What classifications of the effect are there? Why is the first-order atomic effect confined to hydrogen-like atoms? Would you expect it to be shown by helium in a highly excited state? What polarizations are observed for the permitted transitions in hydrogen? Take the hydrogen energy-level diagram (Fig. G3 on p. 86), modify it to show the effect of an electric field, and discuss the form of the spectrum. The shift of the energy of an electron in the $n=2$ shell results in a separation of the levels by an amount $6ea_0E$, where a_0 is the °Bohr radius. Compute the separation for an applied field of 20 kV cm^{-1} and 100 kV cm^{-1}. What separation would be expected for He^+ in the same state and in the same fields? What other effect does a strong field have? What effect has the field in the case of atoms that lack hydrogen-like degeneracy? Why is the second-order effect small? What effects occur in molecules? The permanent dipole moment of ammonia is 1·47 D; discuss the splitting of the $J=0, 1, 2$ states brought about by a field of 50 kV cm^{-1}; sketch the form of the spectrum and label the polarizations of the lines (ignore, if you are aware of them, the effects of °nuclear statistics).
2. Using the explicit orbitals given in Table 15 on p. 275 set up the 2 X 2 secular equation for the effect of an electric field along z on the energies of the 2s- and 2p-orbitals of hydrogen. Solve for the energies and states, and evaluate all integrals. The splitting of the 2s- and 2p-orbitals is, as stated in the preceeding question, $6ea_0E$, and this should be your answer.

Further information. See *MQM* Chapter 8. A nice, and occasionally anthropomorphic, discussion of the effect on atomic spectra is given in Chapter 17 of Condon and Shortley (1963); see also §III A4 of Kuhn (1962), Chapter 20 of White (1934), and §11.3 of Herzberg (1944). The molecular effect, together with accounts of how to determine dipole moments and build spectrometers using Stark modulation, is described in Chapter 7 of Sugden and Kenney (1965) and in Chapter 10 of Townes and Schawlow (1955).

Stern-Gerlach experiment. The Stern-Gerlach experiment consisted of the passage of a collimated beam of atoms (silver atoms boiled off hot metal through slits into a vacuum) through an inhomogeneous field, and the observation of the distribution of the atoms when the beam had been deposited on a glass plate. If the atoms possessed a magnetic moment the effect of the inhomogeneous field would be to drive in one direction those that had one orientation, and in the opposite direction those that had an opposite orientation, and, according to classical physics, to spread atoms with all intermediate orientations into the region in between. An inhomogeneous magnetic field is essential for this effect because a homogeneous field would not split the beam as it provides no directional information; an inhomogeneous field, one with a non-vanishing gradient, provides a sense of direction.

In their first experiment Stern and Gerlach observed that classically anticipated result. In their second, done with great care with a low pressure and a long exposure, they saw that the band of deposited atoms had two closely spaced components, separated by a clear region. This result is wholly at variance with classical physics but in full accord with quantum theory, for each silver atom possesses an unpaired electron with °spin, and therefore has a °magnetic moment. Quantum theory predicts that a spin-$\frac{1}{2}$ object can take only two orientations in a magnetic field, and so the Stern-Gerlach experiment confirms this in a striking fashion.

It is important to note that this was the first piece of evidence for the quantum theory that did not involve a thermal experiment or an experiment involving radiation: it provided a purely mechanical demonstration of quantization (*space quantization,* as the restricted number of orientations of an angular momentum is termed). The original explanation did not associate the magnetic moment with the intrinsic °spin of the electron; that came later (1925) when Uhlenbeck and Goudsmit introduced the concept from their study of atomic spectra. The experiment was also one of the first applications of molecular beams, a subject now in a dynamic phase.

Questions. Sketch the Stern-Gerlach experimental arrangement. Why is it necessary to use a very low pressure in the apparatus? Why is it necessary to use an inhomogeneous field? What is the result predicted by classical physics for the experiment? What is the result obtained? Why is the result consistent with quantum theory? Suppose the upper beam were passed through another inhomogeneous field with (a) the field in the same direction as the first, and (b) the field rotated about the direction of the beam by 90°: what would be the result of the experiment?

Further information. The Stern-Gerlach experiment is put into its historical context in §3.4 of Jammer (1966). For the details, see §134 of Richtmeyr, Kennard, and Lauristen (1955) and §VI.2 of Ramsey (1956). The original papers are by Stern (1921) and Stern and Gerlach (1922). An analysis will be found in §14.16 of Bohm (1951). For the philosophical discussion to which the result gave rise, see Einstein and Ehrenfest (1922) and Jammer (1966). The modern state of molecular beams is described in Ross (1966) and Ramsey (1956); see also Levine and Bernstein (1974).

superposition principle. The superposition principle states that when a situation is a composition of a number of elementary situations, its amplitude is the superposition of the amplitudes for the components. The significance of this principle, which is one of the fundamental principles of quantum mechanics and implies the notable features of the differences between classical mechanics and quantum mechanics, can be introduced by considering the classical situation.

Suppose that an event can be divided into a number of composite events; for example, the event might be the journey from a point p_1 to another p_2, and the elementary events might be the journeys by alternative paths through the points p_a or p_b. Classical theory ascribes a probability $P(a)$ to the path through p_a and a probability $P(b)$ to the path through p_b, and goes on to say that the total probability of making the journey from p_1 to p_2 is the sum of the probabilities of making the individual journeys: $P = P(a) + P(b)$ (Fig. S15).

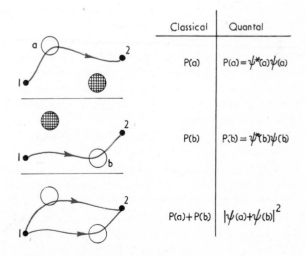

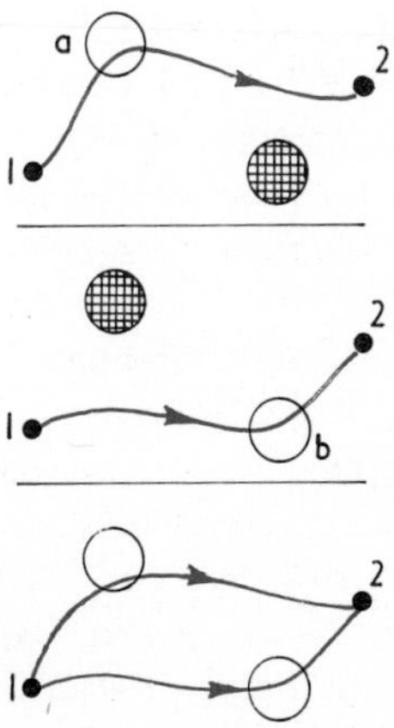

Classical	Quantal
P(a)	$P(a) = \psi^*(a)\psi(a)$
P(b)	$P(b) = \psi^*(b)\psi(b)$
P(a)+P(b)	$\lvert\psi(a)+\psi(b)\rvert^2$

FIG. S15. The superposition principle.

This discussion might seem trivial; but quantum theory shows that it is wrong. The superposition principle agrees that there is a probability of effecting the journey through p_a with a probability $P(a)$, and an analogous probability for the path through p_b, but it disputes the assertion that the joint probability is the sum of the probabilities. It implies that in order to compute the joint probability it is first necessary to find the *probability amplitude* (the °wavefunction) for the individual paths, then to find the probability amplitude for the composite situation, and from that to find the probability itself (Fig. S15). Let the probability amplitude for the journey through p_a be $\psi(a)$: by this we mean that the probability itself is $\psi^*(a)\psi(a)$. The corresponding probability amplitude for the journey through p_b is $\psi(b)$. The superposition principle tells us that the amplitude ψ for the composite process is the sum $\psi(a) + \psi(b)$. It follows that the probability for the joint process is $\psi^*\psi$, which may be expanded into $P(a) + P(b) + \psi^*(a)\psi(b) + \psi(a)\psi^*(b)$. This total probability differs from the sum of the individual probabilities by the interference term $\psi^*(a)\psi(b) + \psi(a)\psi^*(b)$.

First we should note that if one of the paths were forbidden its amplitude would be zero and the probability for the overall journey would reduce to $P = P(a)$ (for p_b closed). Next we should note that the interference term does not occur in the classical case, is characteristic of quantum processes, and arises from the insistence of the superposition principle that all basic manipulations are done on the amplitudes.

If the superposition principle is a true description of Nature we should be able to detect some direct physical consequences: one that might immediately spring to mind is the possibility of observing interference effects for particles that are able to travel from a gun at p_1 to a target at p_2 through a screen perforated with two holes: such interference effects of particles, which correspond to the analogous interference of light under similar circumstances, have been observed.

The superposition principle applies to all the processes of quantum mechanics. Wherever a compound situation is under consideration the calculations must be performed on the wavefunction (the state amplitude): that is why the °Schrödinger equation is a central formula of quantum theory—it enables the amplitude of a state to be calculated, and shows how to determine its time evolution.

The °LCAO method is an example of the working of the superposition principle. To see this, we can take the view that the probability of finding an electron at a particular point of the molecule depends on its probability of being in some of the atomic orbitals of the constituent atoms. Therefore to work out the probability of being at the point **r** we must know the probability amplitude for the electron to be there if it occupied each of the atoms separately. These probability amplitudes are just the atomic-orbital wavefunctions themselves, each evaluated at the point **r**. Therefore the total probability amplitude of the electron being at **r** is a sum of the atomic orbitals (at that point), and the probability is the square of this amplitude. This is precisely the interpretation of °molecular orbitals in terms of the LCAO approximation.

Questions. State the superposition principle. Discuss the process of travelling from Aix to Ghent through two gated roads, and take into account both classically and quantum mechanically the chance that the gates might be closed. Discuss the analogy between the propagation of particles and of light in terms of the superposition principle. Discuss the diffraction of particles in terms of the superposition principle. Why is the LCAO account of molecular structure plausible in terms of the superposition principle? Discuss, in its terms, the concept of °hybridization.

Further information. See Feynman, Leighton, and Sands (1963), §9.2 of Bohm (1951), and Chapter 1 of Dirac (1958). For a simple account of optical analogies see *MQM* Chapter 2. See Jammer (1966) for historical attitudes. See Feynman and Hibbs (1965) for a construction of quantum mechanics in terms of the superposition principle.

symmetry operation. A symmetry operation or symmetry *transformation* is a transformation of the coordinates of the system (*passive convention*) or transformation of the object itself (*active convention*) that, after its application, leaves the system in a configuration indistinguishable from its original.

The active convention is the more direct, and we illustrate it first. Consider an undecorated square object lying on a plane on which is drawn a coordinate system; close your eyes, rotate the object through 90° in the plane, and look at it again. It is impossible to tell that it has been rotated, and so this operation

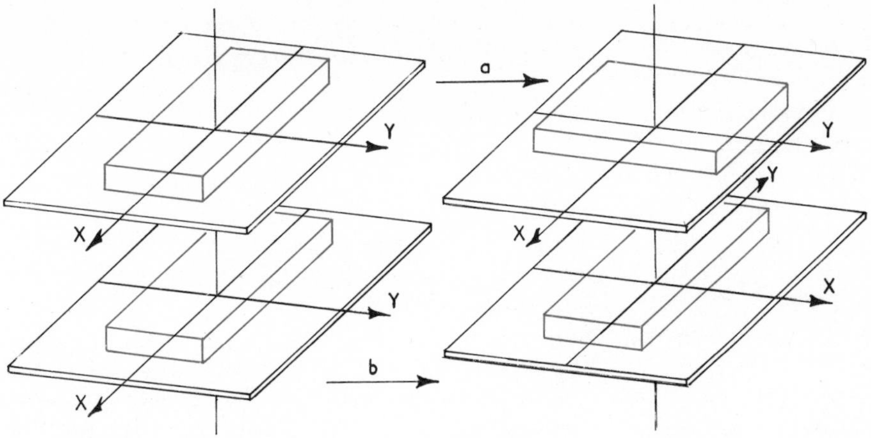

FIG. S16. (a) Active and (b) passive conventions for transformations.

is a symmetry operation. Had the rotation been through an angle less than 90° we would have noticed a new orientation. Similarly a rectangular (oblong) object can be rotated through 180° into an indistinguishable position, which rotation is therefore a symmetry operation; but rotation through 90° is not a symmetry operation (Fig. S16).

In the passive convention a coordinate system is drawn on the plane on which the square object is lying; if we move a units along x we arrive at the edge of the square (of side $2a$), and if we step a units along y we also come to an edge. Now rotate the coordinates (that is, the underlying plane rather than the object) until the x-axis lies along the direction

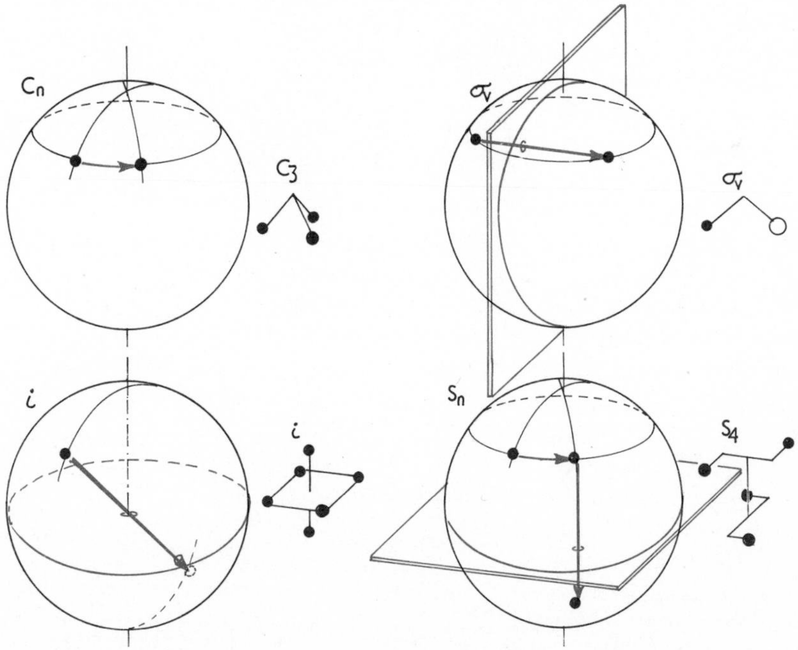

FIG. S17. The symmetry operations C_n, σ_v, i, and S_n and an example of a molecule possessing each.

originally occupied by the y-axis. Stepping along the new x-axis a units, we again encounter an edge; likewise for the new y-axis. This system is indistinguishable from the first, and so the 90° rotation is a symmetry operation. In the case of a rectangle of sides $2a$ and $2b$ stepping along the original x-axis a units will bring us to an edge, but if we step a units along the rotated x-axis we shall not be at an edge unless $a = b$ (Fig. S16). This is therefore not a symmetric situation, and so a 90° rotation of a rectangle is not a symmetry operation.

It is a matter of taste which convention one employs, although there are aesthetic advantages (at least to my muse) in the passive convention on the grounds that it is always possible to manipulate coordinates (they being a convenient mathematical fiction, and at our disposal), whereas it may not be possible to do the active act. This is especially true in the case of symmetry operations other than rotations: inversion through a point is difficult to effect actively (although it may, of course, be imagined), and so too is reflection.

The basic symmetry operations are those of translation (especially in periodic systems such as crystals or in free space), rotation through $2\pi/n$ rad (denoted C_n), reflection in a plane (σ)— a subscript v implying a vertical plane and an h implying a horizontal plane—inversion through a point (i), and rotary-reflection (S_n), which is a composite motion effected by rotating by $2\pi/n$ rad and then reflecting in the plane to which the rotation axis is perpendicular (see Fig. S17).

The study of the effect of symmetry operations is the basis of °group theory.

Questions. 1. What is a symmetry operation? What two conventions are employed? Discuss in the active and the passive conventions the operations denoted C_2, C_3, σ, i, S_4. Enumerate the symmetry operations of the following objects: a left hand, a right hand, a man, a chair, a cube, a triangle, a tetrahedron, a square pyramid, the molecules H_2O, CO_2, CH_4, SF_6, benzene.
2. Demonstrate that an alternative and consistent definition of a symmetry operation is that it is an °operation that °commutes with the system's °hamiltonian.

Further information. See *MQM* Chapter 5 for a further discussion of symmetry operations and the development of the structure of °group theory. See Atkins, Child, and Phillips (1970) for a simple enumeration of symmetry elements and some examples. Refer to the section on °group theory for further references, and see Weyl's book (1952) for an entertaining pictorial account of the appearance of symmetry in Nature.

T

tensor. To a mathematician a tensor is an object that transforms in a particular way when the coordinates he is using to describe a problem are transformed. A *scalar* quantity, which may be regarded as a zeroth-rank tensor, does not change when the coordinates are transformed. A *vector* does change when the coordinates change (at least, the 'object' remains the same, but its description in terms of the new axes is different from its description in terms of the original axes): it is a first-rank tensor. More complex objects may be given as examples of higher-rank tensors; for example, the object **rr**, where **r** is a vector, is a second-rank tensor. The mathematician distinguishes between *contravariant* and *covariant* tensors: for example, the set of coordinates $[x, y, z]$ of a vector transforms as a contravariant tensor of rank one, and the set of objects $[\partial f/\partial x, \partial f/\partial y, \partial f/\partial z]$, where f is a scalar function, transforms as a covariant tensor of rank one. Tensor calculus in its most powerful form is concerned with general transformations of coordinates, and is a powerful tool when non-euclidean geometry has to be studied: for instance, in general relativity. When the transformations are limited to *orthogonal transformations*, those preserving angles in the transformation (like a simple rotation of axes), the properties that an object must possess to be a tensor are less stringent, and the objects that comply are termed *cartesian tensors*. When the objects transform in a special way under rotations we encounter the *irreducible spherical tensors*; these are of considerable importance in the discussion of molecular and atomic properties.

To a chemist a tensor is a quantity that expresses the directional dependence of the properties of molecules and solids; he is normally on safe ground because usually, but not always, the properties that interest him transform in the same way as tensors, and so are tensors. As an example consider the effect of an electric field on a molecule. Let the field be along some axis Z, then the field °polarizes the molecule and induces a dipole moment. Usually the major component of this induced dipole lies in the same direction as the field, but in general the field and the induced dipole are not exactly collinear, and there are also X- and Y-components (Fig. T1). The magnitudes of the components are proportional to the strength of the applied electric field E_z, and so the dipole has components $\alpha_{xz}E_z$, $\alpha_{yz}E_z$, and $\alpha_{zz}E_z$, where the $\alpha_{QQ'}$ are the coefficients of proportionality, the °polarizability. If the field is applied

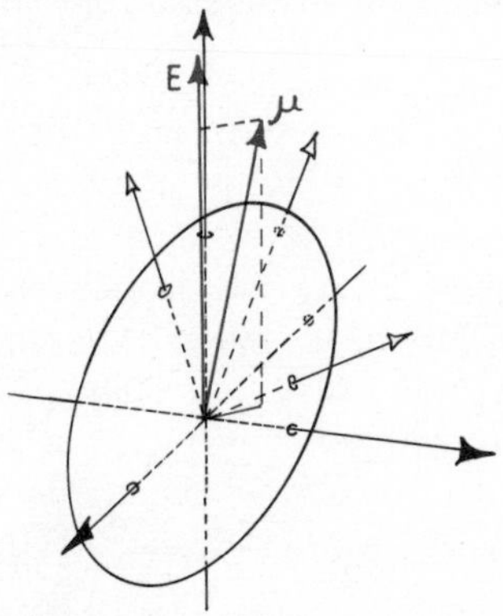

FIG. T1. The effect of off-diagonal elements of the polarizability tensor. When E is along an arbitrary direction it may induce a dipole which need not be parallel to E. The dipole is parallel if E lies along a *principal axis* (one of the axes marked on the molecule).

along the X- or Y-axes similar expressions could be set up to describe the induced dipole (which may have different components if the molecule is anisotropic). In all we get nine quantities of the form $\alpha_{QQ'}$. Recall that the quantity **rr**, with the nine components $XX, XY, XZ, \ldots ZZ$ is a second-rank tensor; then we see that by analogy we may call the nine quantities $\alpha_{QQ'}$ the components of a second-rank tensor α, the *polarizability tensor*. Knowing α we may predict the polarization in any direction when a field is applied in any direction.

Other physical quantities that behave like tensors include those representing a strain $\propto$ stress type of relation, and it is from this that the name tensor arose. In the example just described the stress is supplied by the applied field, and the strain is the resulting polarization. The °magnetic susceptibility is of the same type, and may be expressed as a second-rank tensor. The elasticity of a body is of this form, and it too may be expressed tensorially. For rather special reasons the g-tensor of °electron spin resonance is not a true tensor, and therefore we have called it the °g-value; this is a slight pedantry because most people do call it a tensor, which in many cases it very nearly is.

A *spinor* is a quantity that resembles a tensor, but has the peculiar property that when it is rotated through 360° it changes sign; therefore a rotation of 4π must be made to bring it back to its initial form. Objects such as this are involved in the mathematical description of spin; hence the name.

Further information. An excellent and moderately simple introduction to the general mathematical theory of tensors will be found in Synge and Schild (1949); see also Kyrala (1967) and Jeffreys (1931). The role that tensors play in the discussion of the physical properties of matter is described by Brink and Satchler (1968), Rose (1957), and Edmonds (1957). See Fano and Racah (1959) for a consolidated account. Why g is not a tensor is described in §15.6 of Abragam and Bleaney (1970).

terms. The word 'term' first entered spectroscopy with its colloquial meaning, and therefore without much fundamental significance. In the early days of atomic spectroscopy it was found that a considerable simplification of the description of the spectrum of an element could be obtained by expressing the frequency of every line as the difference of two terms: since one term contributed to a number of spectral lines it was necessary to list far fewer term energies than transition energies. The rule that the spectrum could be so expressed is known as the *Ritz combination principle* (terms are *combined*, by subtraction, to give the frequency or energy of a transition). Thus initially the 'terms' of a spectrum were just a collection of numbers which could be used to predict spectra; but, rather oddly, it was found that not all combinations $(T_1 - T_2)$ corresponded to an observable transition.

The quantum theory provided a natural interpretation of terms: it revealed that a term was an energy state of the atom, and the combination principle was elucidated partly by °Bohr's postulate and later by proper quantum-mechanical calculation which showed that a spectral line represented the transition of the atom from one stationary energy state to another, and that the frequency was determined by $h\nu = T_1 - T_2$. Quantum mechanics also permitted the calculation of °selection rules, which tell whether a given combination of terms is observable.

A term is now interpreted as an energy state of an atom, and a *term symbol*, which labels the energy state, may be constructed from the quantum numbers that define the energy state. A typical term symbol looks like ^{2}S or ^{3}P (but other indices are often attached for a finer description of the state, as we shall describe). The symbol, illustrated in its full glory in Box 26, is constructed as follows.

BOX 26: Term symbol

multiplicity $\longrightarrow (2S+1)$ $M_J \longleftarrow$ state
value of $L \longrightarrow$ $\boxed{X}$
$J \longleftarrow$ level

$L = 0, 1, 2, 3, 4, \ldots$

$X = \mathrm{S, P, D, F, G}, \ldots$

1. The letter denotes the value of L, the total °orbital angular momentum quantum number, according to the correspondence $L = 0, 1, 2, 3, 4, \ldots \longleftrightarrow \mathrm{S, P, D, F, G}, \ldots$.
2. The left superscript is the value of $2S+1$, where this S is

the total °spin angular momentum quantum number for the atom (a massive intellect is not required in order to avoid confusion of the S with the S of $L = 0$). The value of $2S + 1$ is often referred to as the °*multiplicity* of the term, and the propriety and significance of this are described under that entry. Thus ^2S is read as a 'doublet S term', and ^3P as a 'triplet P term'.

3. The °*levels* of a particular term are distinguished by a right subscript of the value of J; for example, a doublet term with $L = 1$ (that is, ^2P) has two levels with $J = \frac{1}{2}$ or $\frac{3}{2}$: the levels are denoted $^2P_{1/2}$ or $^2P_{3/2}$, respectively, and read 'doublet P one-half' or 'doublet P three-halves'.

4. The *state* of an atom can be expressed in even greater detail if one also quotes the value of M_J, the projection of J on some axis: this label is added as a right superscript. For example the $M_J = -1$ state of the $J = 2$ level of a triplet term with $L = 2$ would be labelled $^3D_2^{-1}$, and from this symbol we could write the values of the quantum numbers S, L, J, and M_J (see Box 26).

A list of terms and their energies enables the spectrum to be reconstructed; but to do so it is also necessary to know the permitted combinations: these are determined by the °selection rules which are normally expressed as the values of ΔS, ΔL, ΔJ, and ΔM_J permitted in a transition. Inspection of the term symbol in conjunction with these rules enables one to see very clearly which transitions are allowed.

Term symbols are also encountered in molecular spectroscopy, but as L is then not a good quantum number the labels usually denote some °group-theoretical classification.

Further information. See *MQM* Chapter 8 for a discussion of atomic spectra and Chapter 10 for molecular spectra: both Chapters illustrate the use of term symbols. Further information will be found under °atomic spectra, °selection rules, °fine structure, and °multiplicity.

torsional barriers. The classic example of a barrier to free rotation is that in ethane: one methyl group cannot rotate freely about the C—C bond because of its interaction with the other methyl group. The lowest-energy conformation is the *staggered* arrangement of the two methyls, where a view along the C—C bond shows that the C—H bonds of one group bisect

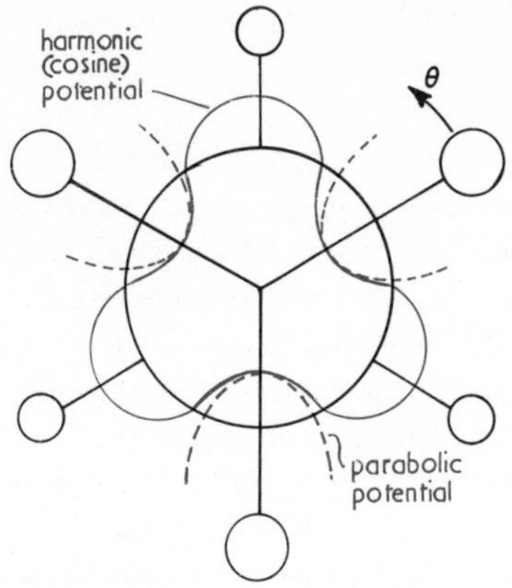

FIG. T2. The torsional barrier in ethane, and the fit of a harmonic potential for small librations.

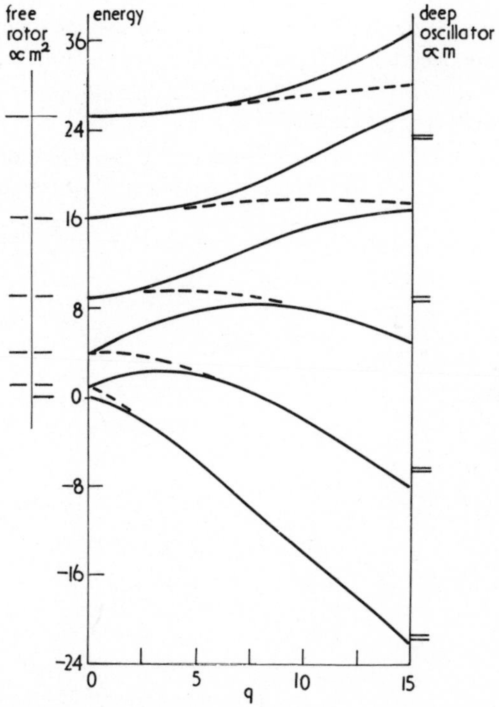

FIG. T3. Energy levels of free rotor (on the left) are modified by a periodic potential and in the limit of a deep potential become those of two independent oscillators. Note how the degeneracies change. $q = mV/2\hbar^2$, where V is the depth of the well.

the H—C—H angles of the other; the highest-energy conformation is the *eclipsed*, when the C—H bonds of each group are in opposition. If one methyl group is twisted through a small angle from the staggered conformation, and then released, it will execute torsional oscillations. As more energy is added to this twisting mode the oscillations get larger, and soon the methyl group is able to jerk from one energy minimum to another. When sufficient energy has been added the group rotates in a manner that is almost indistinguishable from a free rotation. Thus a torsional vibration becomes a free rotation. Conversely, a free rotation becomes localized as a torsional oscillation as an energetic molecule loses energy.

The quantum-mechanical explanation of the process treats the system as a particle in a potential which varies as $\cos(3\theta/2)$ (see Fig. T2): this has the correct periodicity of the actual system but is only a moderately good approximation to the actual dependence on the torsional angle θ (which in detail is very complicated). At the troughs of the cosine function the potential vaies as θ^2 (Fig. T2), and so a particle confined close to the minima behaves like a °harmonic oscillator. It follows that the ground state of the ethane torsion is a zero-point rocking about the bond. The first excited state of the torsional mode resembles a harmonic oscillator in each of the wells; but the correspondence is exact only for infinitely deep potentials. In the real molecule the methyl group can °tunnel from one well to another, and so the wavefunctions are not truly those of a harmonic oscillator.

At high excitations, when the total energy greatly exceeds the peaks of the barrier potential, the potential can be ignored. In this limit the group behaves like a particle of mass $3m_p$ confined to a ring.

The mathematics of the situation can be illustrated nicely if we turn from the methyl group to an example where there are only two wells, not three (Fig. T3). For deep wells every energy level is doubly °degenerate because the rocking group is in either of the two equivalent wells; for vanishingly shallow wells every level except the lowest is doubly degenerate because a free rotor may rotate clockwise or anticlockwise with the same energy. (The lowest level, corresponding to a static rotor, is non-degenerate.) As the barrier is strengthened the latter situation must pass over into the former. This may be demonstrated explicitly, because the Schrödinger equation with a harmonic potential is a Mathieu equation, and its solutions are tabulated. In Fig. T3 we show the energies and in Fig. T4

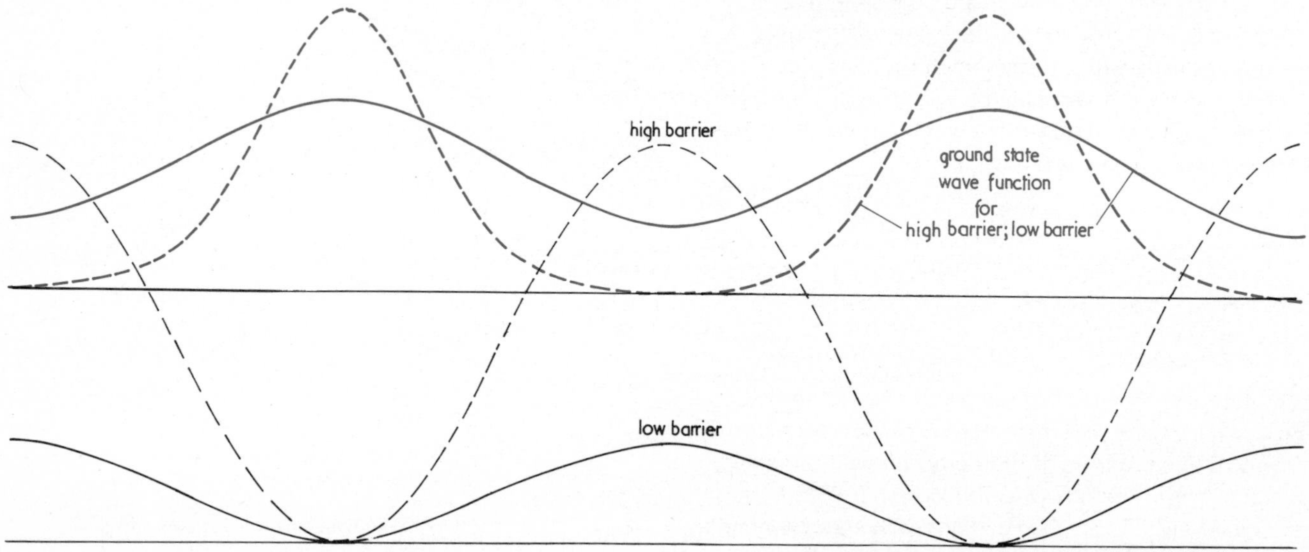

FIG. T4. Torsional wavefunctions for shallow and deep walls: note how the functions are more those of a rotor in the former, and independent oscillators in the latter.

the wavefunctions for barriers of different heights. These pictures illustrate the preceding discussion, for the emergence of the free-rotor energies and wavefunctions is clearly apparent.

Further information. Helpful discussions of the hindered-rotation problem are given in §8.3 of Sugden and Kenney (1965) and §12.6 of Townes and Schawlow (1955). Solutions and properties of the Mathieu equation are given in §20 of Abramowitz and Stegun (1965), and they give numerical data. See also °inversion doubling for a related situation. A review of the internal-rotation problem has been given by Strauss (1968).

transition probability. A transition probability is the probability that a system will change from one state to another. Its principal significance is that it determines the intensity of spectral lines and so, for poets, the brilliance of a colour. The quantum-mechanical discussion of transition probabilities is normally based on °perturbation theory, for the application to the molecule of an oscillating electromagnetic field distorts it slightly, and this distortion can be interpreted as an admixture of excited states into the original state. Since the °wavefunction now contains a component of the excited states there is a non-vanishing transition probability.

The transition probability depends on the strength of the light (the energy of the perturbation), on the match between the frequencies of the exciting radiation and the excited transition (for the coupling is strongest when there is °resonance), and on the strength of coupling between the molecules and the electromagnetic field. The last is related to the *transition dipole* (see °electric dipole transition), which is essentially a measure of the extent of movement of the charge during the transition: if the motion is great, then the field can interact strongly, and the spectral line is intense.

As an example, consider the excitation of that well-worn species the hydrogen atom. The $2p_z \leftarrow 1s$ excitation occurs with a movement of charge from a spherical distribution about the atom to one clustered around the z-axis; the transition can be pictured as an oscillation of charge backwards and forwards along the z-axis, and the dipole moment associated with this motion ensures that the line appears brightly in the spectrum. The $2s \leftarrow 1s$ transition, on the other hand, although it involves a significant migration of charge, does so with a conservation of its initial spherical symmetry, and so there is no dipole moment associated with the oscillation from one state to the other; the light field does not interact, and the transition does not occur in the spectrum.

BOX 27: Transition probability

Fermi's Golden Rule

Transition rate (rate of change of probability) for a migration from a state i to a state f under the influence of a perturbation of strength V is

$$W_{f\leftarrow i} = (2\pi/\hbar)|V_{fi}|^2\rho(\nu_{fi}),$$

where $V_{fi} = \langle\psi_f|V|\psi_i\rangle$ and $\rho(\nu_{fi})$ is the energy density of incident radiation at the transition frequency ν_{fi}.

Electric dipole transitions

$$W_{f\leftarrow i} = B_{fi}\rho(\nu_{fi}) = W_{f\rightarrow i}$$

$$B_{fi} = |d_{fi}|^2/6\epsilon_0\hbar^2 = B_{if}.$$

B is °Einstein's coefficient of stimulated absorption or emission. The total emission rate is

$$W_{f\rightarrow i} = A_{if} + B_{if}\rho(\nu_{fi})$$

$$A_{if} = 8\pi h(\nu_{fi}/c)^3 B_{fi} \text{ in general}$$

$$= (8\pi^2/3\epsilon_0 c^3\hbar)\nu_{fi}^3|d_{fi}|^2 \text{ for electric dipoles.}$$

Transition dipole

$$\mathbf{d}_{fi} = \int d\tau\,\psi_f^*\mathbf{d}\psi_i \qquad \mathbf{d} = -e\mathbf{r}.$$

Fermi's Golden Rule is the mathematical expression for the determination of a transition probability. It is set out in Box 27, and the form quoted may be interpreted as the product of the square of the transition dipole moment between the states (the dipole acts as a handle for the modification of the amplitude of the wavefunction, and to get the probability the square must be taken) multiplied by the energy density of radiation at the transition frequency (the more powerful the stimulus the greater the transition probability). The formula may be deduced from time-dependent °perturbation theory.

This account of transition probabilities underlies the discussion of °selection rules, which enable one to predict when a transition probability is non-zero. The strength of the transition dipole is often quoted in terms of the °oscillator strength, or in terms of the °Einstein *A* and *B* coefficients. These are conveniently related to the °extinction coefficient, which is an experimental measure of the spectral intensity.

Questions. 1. What does the transition probability determine? Why does the application of a time-dependent perturbation induce spectral transitions? At what frequency is the absorption strongest? What is a transition dipole moment? Is there a non-vanishing transition dipole moment associated with the following transitions: $2p_x \leftarrow 1s$, $3p_x \leftarrow 1s$, $3d_{xy} \leftarrow 2p_x$, $2p_z \leftarrow 2p_x$, $3p_z \leftarrow 2p_z$? Consider the transition moments associated with the emissions $2p_x \rightarrow 1s$ and $2p_y \rightarrow 1s$: would you expect the polarization of the emitted light to be different in the two cases?

2. The *x*-component of the transition dipole moment d^x_{fi} for the transition from a state described by a function ψ_i to one described by a function ψ_f is equal to the integral $-e\int d\tau\psi_f^* x\psi_i$, with similar expressions for the *y*- and *z*-components. The transition probability is proportional to $|\mathbf{d}_{fi}|^2$. Show that the stimulated absorption intensity for a particular transition is equal to the stimulated emission intensity. Calculate the transition dipole for the transition from the ground state of a particle in a one-dimensional square well to the first excited state (use the information in Box 15 on p. 166). From the information in Tables 11, 14, and 15 calculate the intensity of transitions from the ground state of a one-dimensional harmonic oscillator to the first and second excited states, and for the transition $2p_z \leftarrow 1s$ of the hydrogen atom.

Further information. See *MQM* Chapters 7 and 11. Transition probabilities are described by Eyring, Walter, and Kimball (1944), Heitler (1954), Kauzmann (1957), and the standard works on quantum theory: see Davydov (1965), Schiff (1968), and Messiah (1961). Transition probabilities occur in the discussion of °selection rules, °oscillator strengths, °Einstein *A* and *B* coefficients, °polarizabilities, and °intermolecular forces. A nice, simple discussion will be found in Loudon (1973).

tunnelling. Quantum-mechanical tunnelling is the process whereby particles penetrate potential barriers and appear in regions forbidden to them in classical mechanics. Consider a °particle trapped in a square well by a potential barrier of finite height and width. Let the particle have an energy which, according to classical mechanics, is insufficient to carry it over the potential barrier. The quantum mechanics of the situation shows that the particle has some probability of tunnelling through the barrier and escaping from the well. The tunnelling probability arises from the requirement of the continuity of the wavefunction at the walls of the well: if the wavefunction has a non-zero amplitude at the inside edge of the barrier (and this is permitted when the potential there does not become infinite) it cannot simply vanish within the barrier; instead it will start to decay more or less rapidly towards zero (Fig. T5). If the decay of the function is not too rapid the amplitude might not have reached zero at the outer edge of the barrier. At this point the function must butt smoothly on to the function characteristic of the free particle beyond the barrier, and from then on the wave is essentially undiminished. Since the wavefunction of the particle does not vanish in the region outside the barrier there is a non-vanishing probability that the particle will be found in this region, and so it has tunnelled out of the original well.

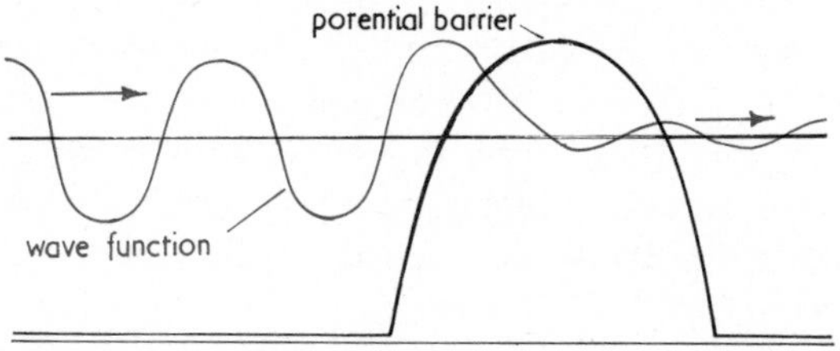

FIG. T5. Tunnelling of a particle from left to right through a barrier.

The wavefunction inside the barrier itself falls more quickly as the height of the barrier is raised (relative to the energy of the incident particle), and so the amplitude of the function on the outside of the barrier decays correspondingly quickly. This implies that the tunnelling probability diminishes rapidly as the barrier height is increased. The amplitude also decays more rapidly as the mass of the particle is increased: therefore the tunnelling diminishes as the mass of the tunneller increases. The shape of the potential is also important because sharply changing potentials reflect the particle more effectively than slowly varying potentials (an analogous situation occurs in the propagation of light: light is reflected most strongly from regions where the refractive index changes abruptly). Therefore the most favourable tunnelling situation is that of a light particle confronted with a slowly varying potential barrier. Electrons tunnel very effectively; protons tunnel much less well, but still appreciably; deuterons tunnel little.

Some concern is often expressed about the apparently nonsensical occurrence of a negative kinetic energy in the classically forbidden regions, where the potential energy apparently exceeds the total energy. The occurrence of a negative kinetic energy is indeed the reason for the exclusion of particles from these regions in classical mechanics, but it is no problem in quantum mechanics because the °kinetic energy of a particle must be interpreted as the mean value evaluated over the entire wavefunction. The fact that the kinetic energy is locally negative does not interfere with the fact that the measurable kinetic energy, the mean value, is positive. Furthermore, suppose we were to attempt to confine the particle into the region of the barrier in order to force it to have negative kinetic energy: with drums sounding and bugles blaring the °uncertainty principle gallops to its aid; for the very act of confining the particle to a particular region introduces an uncertainty into the energy, and this uncertainty is sufficient to prevent us from concluding that the particle has a negative kinetic energy.

Questions. 1. What is meant by tunnelling? What are the most favourable conditions for it? What is its quantum-mechanical explanation? Why is it unnecessary to worry about negative kinetic energies? Discuss the tunnelling probability for particles that are fired with gradually increasing kinetic energy against a rectangular barrier. What happens when the kinetic energy is enough, according to classical mechanics, to take them cleanly over the top of the barrier?
2. Consider a rectangular barrier of height V and width W; on either side the potential is zero for all space. Set up and solve the °Schrödinger equation for this system, and from the continuity of the wavefunctions at the edges of the barrier construct acceptable solutions. Show that the probability of tunnelling depends strongly on the values of V and W, and on the mass of the particle. Calculate the relative probabilities of an electron, a proton, and a deuteron tunnelling through the barrier.

Further information. Calculations on tunnelling phenomena are described in Chapter 11 of Bohm (1951), §26 of Davydov (1965), Messiah (1961), Schiff (1968), and other standard works. Problems and worked solutions will be found in Gol'dman and Kryvschenkov (1961). Important applications of tunnelling are in the °photoelectric effect, and so see that entry, in chemical reactions—see Harmony (1972) for a review—and in electrode processes; see Albery's *Electrode kinetics* (OCS 14).

U

uncertainty principle. The uncertainty principle reveals that there exist pairs of observables to which it is not possible to ascribe simultaneously arbitrarily precise values: as one observable is constrained to have a more precise value so its conjugate partner becomes more ill-defined. An experiment set up to determine the two observables simultaneously is able to determine one precisely only at the expense of losing information about the other (see °duality); and the product of the uncertainties in the two simultaneous measurements can never be less than a small but non-zero value of the order of $\hbar$.

The most famous example of this situation is the uncertainty inherent in the simultaneous determination of the position of a particle along some coordinate q and its component of linear momentum along the same coordinate p_q. These two observables are conjugate in the sense of the uncertainty principle, and if we can pin down the position to within a range δq (where δq is actually the root-mean-square spread of the particle's location about some point) then the uncertainty principle demands that the value of p_q must be uncertain to the extent δp_q (again this is a root-mean-square spread) such that the product of uncertainties $\delta q \delta p_q$ does not have a value of less than $\frac{1}{2}\hbar$. As the position is ascertained more sharply (and δq decreased) the spread of p_q must increase in order to ensure that the uncertainty product $\delta q \delta p_q$ does not fall below $\frac{1}{2}\hbar$. Conversely, if we were prepared to forgo all information about the particle's momentum so that δp_q could be allowed to become indefinitely large, then δq could be made indefinitely small, and the position determined with arbitrary precision. Unfortunately the implication is that, although we now know the position of the particle with arbitrary precision, it is not possible to predict where the particle will be at any instant later, as we can know nothing of the particle's momentum at the moment of determining the position. Thus the uncertainty principle eliminates the concept of a trajectory, a concept central to classical mechanics.

Alternatively we could measure the momentum p_q with arbitrary precision, but in order to preserve the uncertainty product we should be forced to forgo all information about the position q: this approach also eliminates the concept of trajectory.

It should be noticed that the uncertainty principle for position and momentum refers to components along the *same* axis and puts no restriction on the simultaneous values of these observables along different axes. Consequently the position along x may be measured simultaneously with the momentum p_y along y, and there is no inherent limitation on the precision of the determinations. The mathematical expression of the uncertainty principle (see Box 28) enables us to decide which observables are conjugate; but a rough guide is that conjugate variables consist of the coordinate and the momentum corresponding to that coordinate.

Discussions of the uncertainty principle are often put in the form of presenting a duffer (and long live all such duffers) who attempts to do an experiment which will deny the predictions of the principle; he retires, of course, bruised from the ring. Heisenberg, whose principle this is, presented such a duffer in order to show that all such *gedanken experiments* (thought experiments) must fail. His jester used a microscope to measure the position of the particle and, in order to do so with increasing precision, selected one operating with ever shortening wave-

BOX 28: Uncertainty principle

Let $\hat{A}$ and $\hat{B}$ be the °operators corresponding to the observables A and B, and let δA and δB be the r.m.s. deviations from the mean:

$$\delta A = [\langle A^2\rangle - \langle A\rangle^2]^{1/2}, \quad \delta B = [\langle B^2\rangle - \langle B\rangle^2]^{1/2}.$$

According to the uncertainty principle, these must satisfy

$$\delta A \delta B \geqslant \tfrac{1}{2}|\langle[\hat{A}, \hat{B}]\rangle|,$$

where $[\hat{A}, \hat{B}] = \hat{A}\hat{B} - \hat{B}\hat{A}$, the °commutator.

Typical uncertainty products include the following:

$$\delta p_q \delta q \geqslant \tfrac{1}{2}\hbar \quad \delta \ell_x \delta \ell_y \geqslant \tfrac{1}{2}m\hbar \quad \tau \delta E \geqslant \tfrac{1}{2}\hbar.$$

See text for significance of τ.

length of light. But the shorter the wavelength the more momentum each photon carries (°de Broglie relation), and since at least one photon must be scattered into the microscope aperture in order for the position to be determined, it is clear that the very act of observation imparts a momentum to the particle. An analysis of the experiment, taking into account aperture-diffraction effects and momentum transfers on light scattering, concludes that the uncertainty product $\delta q \delta p_q$ is indeed not less than $\frac{1}{2}\hbar$ ($\hbar$ enters through the de Broglie relation). In a classical world the jester would laugh last, because $\hbar$ would be zero and there would be no intrinsic limitation on the precision.

Thought experiments of this nature illustrate at an observational level what the uncertainty principle reveals about the nature of matter at a much deeper level. Momentum and position are linked by the interpretation of the °wavefunction. A system in a state of well-defined linear °momentum is described by a plane wave of well-defined wavelength; but this wave, which for a momentum $k\hbar$ can be written $\exp ikx$, corresponds to a probability distribution proportional to $|\exp ikx|^2$, and this is independent of x. Therefore a state of well-defined momentum describes a particle with a completely undefined position. Conversely, in order to describe a localized particle, a °wave packet must be formed with an amplitude large at one point and small elsewhere. This can be achieved by °superimposing a large number of waves of different lengths, and therefore of different momenta. Consequently, the sharper the wave packet we try to form (in order to get a more localized particle) the wider the range of momenta of the particle.

The other pairs of conjugate observables can be found by testing whether the °commutator of their corresponding °operators disappears: if it does not, the observables cannot be determined simultaneously with arbitrary precision; if it vanishes there is no restriction. Some important pairs of conjugate observables are listed in Box 28.

The *energy-time uncertainty relation* differs from the rest in a subtle way: there is no operator for time in quantum mechanics (it is a parameter, not an observable), and so the commutation rule cannot be applied. The relation should be viewed as a consequence of the lack of commutation of the position and momentum operators, or equivalently, as a consequence of the Schrödinger equation. The energy-time relation depends upon the existence of an evolution of the system with a characteristic time τ; when such a process is present the energy levels of the system are indeterminate by an amount δE such that the product $\tau\delta E$ does not fall below $\frac{1}{2}\hbar$. For stationary states, where τ is infinite, the energy may be defined with arbitrary precision; but where a state has a finite lifetime its energy is correspondingly imprecise.

A final word may be said on cyclic systems: the uncertainty relations for angle and angular momentum must be treated with care because an uncertainty of 2π in angle is equivalent to complete uncertainty: special forms of the uncertainty principle are used in these cases.

Questions. 1. State the uncertainty principle. Discuss the principle as applied to the determination of the position x and the momenta p_x and p_y. May the position coordinates (x, y, z) of a particle be specified simultaneously with arbitrary precision? May the kinetic energy and the momentum of a particle be specified simultaneously? Why does an experiment to determine the position of a particle interfere with the momentum of a particle? How does the wave nature of matter illuminate the connexion between the position and the momentum of a particle? Why does the wave picture allow x and p_y to be determined with arbitrary precision? Why is the concept of trajectory alien to quantum mechanics? Why is the energy-time uncertainty relation peculiar?

2. The position q of a particle is determined to within a range 0·1 mm, 1 μm, 1 nm, 1 pm; what is the corresponding simultaneous uncertainty in the momentum p_q? If the particle is an electron, to what kinetic energy does the uncertainty in momentum correspond? Three states in an atom decay with time constants 0·1s, 1 μs, 10^{-12}s; what is the uncertainty in the energy of the atom in each excited state? The natural width of spectral lines is determined by the lifetime of states, as suggested by the last part of this question. See °electron spin resonance.

3. Use the mathematical expression of the uncertainty principle as set out in Box 28, to investigate the limitation on the simultaneous determination of the following pairs of observables: x and p_x; x and p_y; p_x and p_y; ℓ_x and ℓ_y; z and ℓ_z; kinetic energy and Coulomb potential energy; total energy and x; total energy and dipole moment.

Further information. See *MQM* Chapter 4 for a deduction and application of the principle. For a discussion of the uncertainty principle see Heisenberg (1930) and Ingram's *Radiation and quantum physics* (OPS 3), and the standard quantum-mechanics texts such as Dirac (1958), Messiah (1961), Schiff (1968), Davydov (1965), and Landau and Lifshitz (1958a). For an interesting account laced with speculation on mind and magic see Bohm (1951). For an account of one aspect of the energy-time relation see Salem and Wigner (1972), and for an account of the uncertainty principle for cyclic systems see Carruthers and Nieto (1968).

united atom. The united-atom method, which is used to describe the structure of molecules, is one of a variety that employs a *correlation diagram*. In general, one has a set of orbitals or states of a system when it is in one form and a set of orbitals or states for the system when it is in another form, and one is interested in which states of one form turn into which states of the other. A correlation diagram consists of two arrays of levels joined by lines which denote the way that a state changes into another state when the system changes from one form to another. The most important rule for constructing such a diagram is that lines representing states with the same symmetry cannot cross (see °non-crossing rule). We illustrate the technique with the idea of the united atom; this is a lineal ancestor of the *Walsh diagrams*, which show how the molecular orbitals of molecules change when bonds are bent, and both are parents of the *Woodward-Hoffman rules*, which show how molecular orbitals and states change during concerted molecular rearrangements.

The united-atom correlation diagram takes as one set of states the °orbitals of two separated atoms (we let the atoms be the same and call them A), and considers how these orbitals change as the atoms are pressed together until ultimately they fuse into an atom of twice the atomic number, the *united atom*. The energy levels of the united atom are known, so are those of the separated atoms; what is unknown is the structure of the intermediate object, the diatomic molecule A—A.

Let us take as the simplest illustration of the method the atoms of hydrogen; the united atom will therefore be the helium atom. Whether or not the fusion can actually be made to occur in practice is important for the future of mankind but immaterial for the present discussion. Concentrate on the 1s-orbitals of the separated atoms, and envisage what happens as we squeeze the atoms together. If the atomic orbitals are squeezed together in phase (so that a positive-going amplitude of one overlaps a positive-going amplitude of the other) the

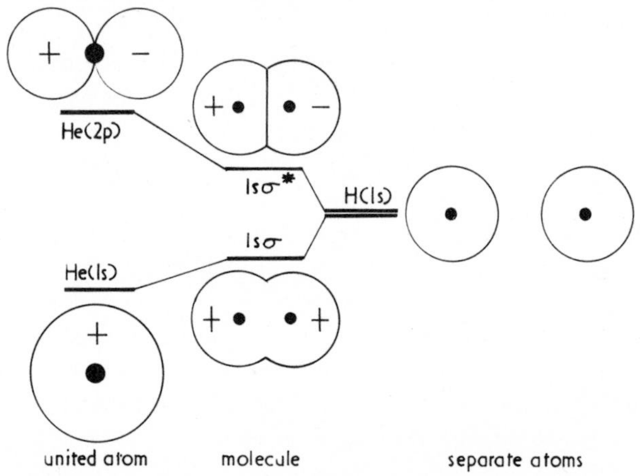

FIG. U1. The united atom (He) formed from H + H, and the intermediate H_2.

process of uniting the atoms ultimately generates the 1s-orbital of the helium atom. (See Fig. U1.) The out-of-phase superposition of the two atoms always possesses a °node half-way between the two merging nuclei: when the nuclei are united, half-way between them means through the united nucleus; therefore the merging of the orbitals has generated a 2p-orbital of helium (Fig. U1). This is known to lie above the 1s-orbital, and therefore we may conclude that at an intermediate stage the hydrogen molecule possesses the orbitals denoted σ and σ^*. These are just the bonding and antibonding orbitals of °molecular-orbital theory, and to them we may apply the °*aufbau* process in the normal way, and so arrive at the structure of the molecule.

This process may be applied to a more complicated pair of atoms in order to arrive at some assessment of the structure of the intermediate molecule. There are some difficulties, and these are mainly connected with the role of spin-orbit coupling in heavy atoms, for this serves to muddle some of the correlations.

Questions. What is meant by a 'correlation diagram'? In what sense is the united-atom procedure an example of the use of a correlation diagram? To what use may the united-atom procedure be put? In what ways does the correlation diagram drawn in the figure differ from the actual dependence of the energy of the orbitals on the internuclear separation? Do these differences matter? What rule has to be observed in the formation of a diagram? Construct the full correlation diagram for the formation of a united atom from two atoms possessing 1s-, 2s-, 2p-, 3s-, and 3p-orbitals, and use it to discuss the electronic structure of the homonuclear diatomics that may be formed from the first-row atoms. (Check your answer against Fig. M8, which shows the intermediate situation corresponding to the structure of O_2.)

Further information. A nice discussion will be found in §4.7 of Coulson (1961), and an original paper on the subject is that of Mulliken (1932). See also Chapter VI of Herzberg (1950) for a thorough discussion of the way the united atom is used to discuss the structure and spectra of diatomic molecules. A rule of special importance is the *Wigner-Witmer spin-correlation rule*, which tells how to determine which atomic states are formed when a diatomic breaks up. This is discussed in Herzberg (loc. cit.), §5.2 of Wayne (1970), and Chapter 3 of Gaydon (1968). The Walsh rules for the discussion of molecular structure are given in a classic series of papers by Walsh (1953). What these diagrams are diagrams of has been the cause of much perplexity: for a readable analysis consult Coulson and Deb (1971). The Woodward-Hoffman rules are described by Gill (1970), Woodward and Hoffman (1970), Gill and Willis (1969), and Longuet-Higgins and Abrahamson (1965). See also Woodward and Hoffman (1969, 1970) for a review with many applications and also Alder, Baker, and Brown (1971) for a helpful description.

V

valence bond. The valence-bond theory was the first quantum-mechanical theory of the chemical °bond, and drew heavily on the chemist's concept of a bond as an object depending for its strength on the presence of two paired electrons. The theory picks out of a molecule the electrons that are paired (the *perfect-pairing approximation*) and supposes that these dominate in the formation of the bond; when several perfect-paired structures have similar energies the molecule is allowed to °resonate among them, and the energy of the whole is thereby lowered.

As in most things, the simplest object can elucidate the method most effectively. Consider H_2, that most public of molecules. At great separations the °wavefunction for the species is the wavefunction for the two separated atoms $\psi_a(1)\,\psi_b(2)$, which for brevity we shall denote a_1b_2. When the atoms are as close as they are in the molecule the wavefunction might not differ very greatly, the only difference being that we cannot stop one electron slipping off its nucleus and visiting the other. In other words we must permit the electrons to exchange their roles. In terms of the wavefunction we must let a_1b_2 be contaminated by a_2b_1, in which electron 2 occupies the orbital hitherto occupied by electron 1, and vice versa. In fact, from the symmetry of the system, the contamination must be allowed to proceed so far that the wavefunction is a 50:50 mixture of both arrangements $(a_1b_2 + a_2b_1)$. At this point we sit back, the physics having been done, and do the mathematics. This means that we attempt to calculate the energy of the molecule from the wavefunction we have set up.

There are some tricky integrals over the coordinates of the electrons that need to be done in order to evaluate the potential energy of the molecule, and they are illustrated in Fig. V1. One integral can be interpreted as the contribution

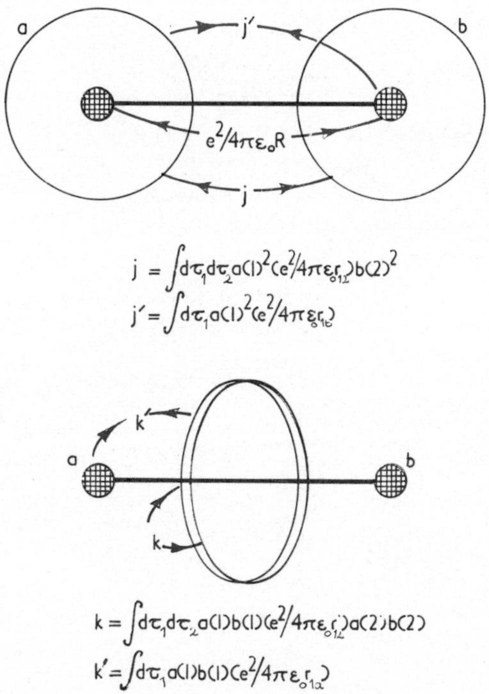

$$j = \int d\tau_1 d\tau_2\, a(1)^2 (e^2/4\pi\varepsilon_0 r_{12})\, b(2)^2$$

$$j' = \int d\tau_1\, a(1)^2 (e^2/4\pi\varepsilon_0 r_{1b})$$

$$k = \int d\tau_1 d\tau_2\, a(1)b(1)(e^2/4\pi\varepsilon_0 r_{12})\, a(2)b(2)$$

$$k' = \int d\tau_1\, a(1)b(1)(e^2/4\pi\varepsilon_0 r_{1a})$$

FIG. V1. Contributions to the v.b. energy of H_2.

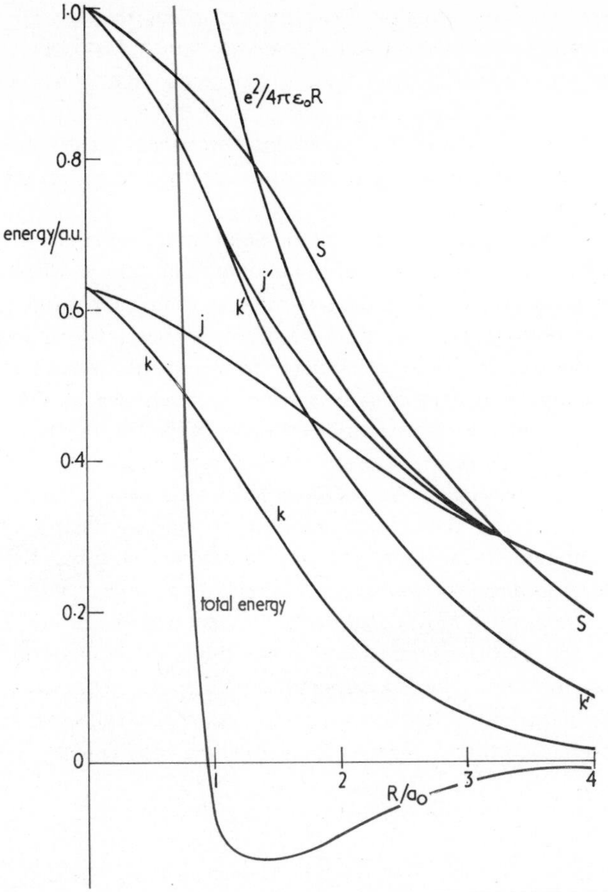

FIG. V2. The dependence on the nuclear separation of the molecular integrals contributing to the VB energy of H_2. The total energy is also shown.

BOX 29: Molecular integrals and experimental data for H_2

$S = \int d\tau_1 a(1)b(1)$

$j = \int d\tau_1 d\tau_2 a(1)^2 (e^2/4\pi\epsilon_0 r_{12}) b(2)^2$

$j' = \int d\tau_1 a(1)^2 (e^2/4\pi\epsilon_0 r_{1b}) = \int d\tau_2 b(2)^2 (e^2/4\pi\epsilon_0 r_{2a})$

$k = \int d\tau_1 d\tau_2 a(1)b(1)(e^2/4\pi\epsilon_0 r_{12}) a(2)b(2)$

$k' = \int d\tau_1 a(1)b(1)(e^2/4\pi\epsilon_0 r_{1b}) = \int d\tau_2 a(2)b(2)(e^2/4\pi\epsilon_0 r_{2a})$.

Coulomb integral $J = (e^2/4\pi\epsilon_0 R) + j - 2j'$.

Exchange integral $K = (e^2 S^2/4\pi\epsilon_0 R) + k - 2Sk'$.

Energy $E_{\pm} = 2E_{1s}(\mathrm{H}) + \left\{\dfrac{J \pm K}{1 \pm S^2}\right\}$ $\quad (E_+ < E_-)$.

$E_{1s}(\mathrm{H})$ is the energy of an isolated hydrogen atom.

Bond length in H_2: 74·16 pm (0·7416 Å).

Dissociation energy (D_0^0): 4·476 eV, 36 116 cm^{-1}.

Rotational constant: 60·809 cm^{-1}.

Vibrational frequency: 4395·2 cm^{-1}.

to the total energy from the attractive interaction j' between an electron on one nucleus and the other nucleus; another is the repulsive interaction j between the electron clouds on the two nuclei. An analysis of the electron distribution for the wavefunction $a_1 b_2 + a_2 b_1$ shows that there is a significant accumulation of electron density in the internuclear region—this extra accumulation of density is represented by the oval shapes in Fig. V1—and this extra density contributes extra terms to the total energy. One contribution is the repulsive interaction k between the two electrons confined to the oval regions, and another is the attractive energy k' between these electron-rich regions and the nuclei (see Box 29 and Fig. V2). Just looking at the numerical values of the integrals shows that the most important contribution is the last: in this model the reduction in energy of the molecule below the energy of the separated atoms is in large measure due to the lowering of the potential energy of the electrons by virtue of their accumulation in the internuclear region, where they are able to interact attractively with both nuclei. (We note and emphasize that an accurate account of the source of bonding energy must also take into account the changes in °kinetic energy of the electrons on bond formation and the distortion of the atomic orbitals in the vicinity of the nuclei: see °bond and °molecular orbitals.)

The numerical value of the bonding energy for the hydrogen molecule calculated in the manner described is 3·14 eV, in moderate agreement with the experimental value 4·72 eV. (In fact, the agreement is bad, but when it was first obtained the number supported the view that the model was correct; it has since been made much better without altering the essential features of the description.)

This approach to hydrogen is developed to account for the structure of more complicated molecules, but the procedures rapidly become more complex. In each case the bonding is ascribed to the interaction of pairs of electrons, and so pairs of electrons are selected and the energy of their interaction is calculated. One of the important features of the valence-bond theory now appears: because there are many electrons in an atom, and therefore many pairs, we have to take into account the possibility that electrons that form different paired bonds still interact electrostatically. In this connexion we may think of °benzene and one of its Kekulé structures. In the structure the spins are paired when π-bonds are formed, and so the contribution of each bond to the energy of the structure arises in the same way as we discussed for the hydrogen molecule. But the electrons in one bond interact with the electrons in the others. This gives rise to two effects. First, the energy of the Kekulé structure is modified; and second, there is a tendency for the electrons to redistribute themselves around the ring (see Fig. B8 on p. 19 or Fig. R7 on p. 201). One redistribution corresponds to the other Kekulé structure, and so the effect of the interaction is to induce °resonance between the two Kekulé structures. This alters the energy. The true distribution of electrons in the ring cannot be described simply by the resonance of two Kekulé structures: a better description and a lower energy are obtained if other *canonical structures* are allowed to take part in the resonance (see °benzene).

The principles described in the preceding paragraphs are the bases of the general valence-bond method. One selects the basic *perfect-paired structures* according to a set of rules (and so they are called canonical; canon = rule), calculates the energy of each, and then determines the energy of a superposition admitting resonance among them.

The valence-bond theory has much room for improvement. Seeing how H_2 is improved is a guide to seeing how other molecules are improved. The flaw in the simple picture of H_2 lies in the method's implicit insistence that, if an electron occupies an orbital on one atom, then the other electron must be on the other atom. In practice we know that there is a significant possibility that both electrons will be found on the same atom, and so the wavefunction ought to be improved by permitting an admixture of ionic contributions a_1a_2, corresponding to H^-H^+, and b_1b_2, corresponding to H^+H^-. According to the °variation principle we know that an improvement of the wavefunction leads to a lower energy, and this is found when an ionic component is allowed to contaminate the covalent wavefunction. The name given to this mixing in valence-bond theory is *ionic-covalent °resonance* because the molecule resonates between the forms and the energy relaxes in the normal way.

This discussion has led us to the point where we are able to mention the disadvantages of the valence-bond theory, disadvantages that have offset the advantage of chemical plausibility at the root of the theory. One disadvantage is that the number of canonical structures which ought to be included increases dramatically with the number of atoms in the molecule. For example, there are 5 structures for benzene, but more than 100 000 for coronene. The structure must be allowed to resonate around all these canonical forms, and so it can be appreciated that the determination of the energy and structure of a moderately large molecule is a task of enormous magnitude. Another difficulty is the importance of the ionic structures which must be added to the canonical structures. The importance of these increases dramatically as the number of atoms increases. The modern tendency, however, is to reconsider these disadvantages, and present indications suggest that valence-bond theory is about to be given a second chance.

Questions. 1. What is the inspiration for the valence-bond approach? What is the perfect-pairing approximation? Why is it only an approximation? What happens when there are several perfect-paired structures of similar energy? What is the consequence for the energy in that case? Give an example of this situation in the case of H_2 and benzene. Discuss the VB description of molecular hydrogen. What is the nature of the reduction in the energy of the molecule relative to the energy of the separated atoms? What is the role of electron exchange in H_2? Why, then, are electron pairs so important for the formation of the chemical bond? 2. The VB wavefunction for H_2 is $(a_1b_2 + a_2b_1)$ in the notation used in the text. Deduce an expression for the energy of the molecule in terms of this wavefunction and the correct °hamiltonian, and confirm that the integrals that arise are those shown in Fig. V1 and Box 29. Show that for the alternative combination $(a_1b_2 - a_2b_1)$ the energy is determined by the same integrals but with some different signs. Assess the sign of the integrals and thence show that the lower-energy wavefunction is the former. What, according to the °Pauli principle, can be said about the spins in the bond? If the spins were parallel (unpaired) what would we be forced to conclude? The variation of the molecular integrals with distance is given in Fig. V2 for the case of H_2. From the values, deduce the energy and the bond length.

3. What is meant by a 'canonical structure'? How many canonical structures are there for benzene? One way of deducing the number of canonical structures is by means of the *Rümer diagram*, where all the contributing orbitals are drawn on a circle and then pairs are joined until there are no unpaired points. The number of structures that can be drawn in this way without any lines crossing is the number of canonical structures for the problem. Investigate this device for benzene and naphthalene. Can you deduce a general formula for the number of canonical structures for aromatic molecules? The way that the energy of each structure and the energy of interaction between structures is calculated is set out in Box 30. Each canonical structure is superimposed on each other (and itself) and the energy is related to the number of 'islands' formed by the superimposed lines. Use the formula in the Box to deduce the energy and interaction energy of the two Kekulé structures of benzene, set up the °secular determinant in order to determine the energy and structure of the best (lowest-energy) superposition, and deduce that it consists of 50 per cent of each structure with an energy $J + 2{\cdot}4K$, and therefore that the °resonance energy is $0{\cdot}9\,K$. Now include the three Dewar structures, and express the state of the molecule as $c_K(\psi_{K1} + \psi_{K2}) + c_D(\psi_{D1} + \psi_{D2} + \psi_{D3})$, in an obvious notation (I hope); set up the appropriate secular determinant, and deduce the extra stabilization energy that arises from admitting the Dewar structures. For what proportion of the structure do they account?

BOX 30: The VB secular determinant

1. Form all the canonical structures within the perfect-pairing approximation (for example, the two Kekulé and three Dewar structures of benzene). If then desperate with complexity, select a manageable number of important structures on the grounds of chemical intuition (for example the two Kekulé structures).

2. Superimpose each structure with itself and all other structures and calculate the element $H_{rc} - ES_{rc}$, which stands in the rth row and cth column of the secular determinant, by applying the formula

$$H_{rc} - ES_{rc} = (\tfrac{1}{2})^{N-I}[J - E + AK].$$

$2N$ is the total number of electrons, I is the number of islands formed in the superposition, and A is the number of connected pairs of *neighbours* in these islands, less half the number of pairs of *neighbours* on separate islands. We mean by neighbours the orbitals between which there is an interaction (and typically geometrical neighbours). J and K are the Coulomb and exchange integrals.

An example. Let r correspond to one Kekulé form, and c to a Dewar form of benzene

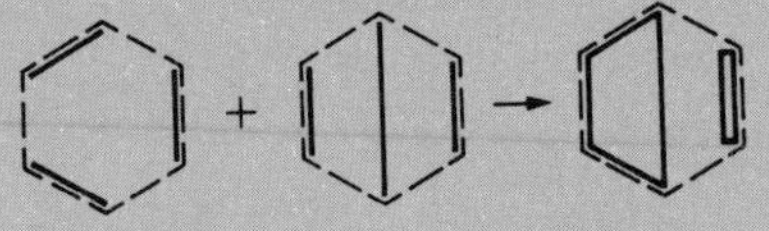

$$N = 3, A = 3 + 1 - \tfrac{1}{2}2 = 3, I = 2$$

$$H_{rc} - ES_{rc} = \tfrac{1}{2}(J - E + 3K)$$

3. Construct the full secular determinant (5 × 5 in the case of benzene), find the roots E, select the lowest root as the energy of the molecule, and find the coefficients in the superposition that corresponds to this root. The squares of the coefficients give the weights of the canonical structures.

Further information. See *MQM* Chapter 9. A nice account of simple VB theory, and an extensive comparison with molecular-orbital theory is given in Chapter V of Coulson (1961) and by Murrell, Kettle, and Tedder (1965). See Eyring, Walter, and Kimball (1944) for details of the method. Pauling's classic book (1960) is almost exclusively an account of the VB description of molecules and in its earlier editions is an unparalleled example of the power of quantum-chemical reasoning within the format of the theory. The molecular-orbital and valence-bond theories are discussed in comparison under °molecular orbital versus valence bond.

valence state. Let us centre our attention on carbon, and in particular on the carbon atom in methane. A chemical description of the structure of methane might regard it as an sp^3-°hybridized carbon with each of its four tetrahedral lobes overlapping one of the four surrounding hydrogen atoms. Therefore the bonds are formed from four hydrogen atoms overlapping the four tetrahedral orbitals of a carbon atom in its valence state $1s^2 2s2p_x 2p_y 2p_z$. The *valence state* is the state of the atom responsible for its bonding to its neighbours. From this definition it is a trivial consequence that the valence state of the hydrogen atom is simply 1s; similarly the valence state of the oxygen atom is $1s^2 2s^2 2p_x^2 2p_y 2p_z$ in a substance such as water.

It is important to realize that the valence state is not in general a spectroscopic state; that is, it cannot be detected by lines in a spectrum representing transitions into or out of it. The clearest way of appreciating this is to reflect on the nature of the bonding between the carbon and the hydrogen atoms in methane, and to recognize that although the electrons are °paired in individual bonds there is no pairing of spins in different bonds. Therefore the valence state is characterized by the four valence electrons with random relative spins. But a state with random spins is not a spectroscopic state, for in these there is a strict coupling of the various angular momenta, and therefore a strict distribution of relative spin orientations.

It is of interest to be able to know the energy of the valence state, especially when the importance of °hybridization is being assessed; this may still be done even though the state is not spectroscopic. The valence state may be expressed as a mixture (°superposition) of true spectroscopic states, and its energy calculated by the corresponding average of the energies of the contributing states. In this way it is possible to assess the energy required to promote an electron from the ground state of carbon to form the valence state (7 eV, 680 kJ mol^{-1}).

Is the valence state ever formed? Since it is not a spectroscopic state the answer is strictly no (but see Questions); but we may envisage the valence state as emerging from the ground state as the ligand atoms are brought up towards it. Once again consider methane, but a 'potential methane' in which the four hydrogen atoms are disposed tetrahedrally at infinite separation, and a central ground-state carbon atom. As the atoms approach tetrahedrally the surface of the carbon atom begins to stir, and for brief moments the electron density might tend to accumulate tetrahedrally. As the atoms get even closer the fluctuations are stronger and more long-lasting; and when the atoms are at their equilibrium bonding distance the fluctuations are massive and essentially frozen, forming the four tetrahedral σ-bonds. Only at this point would it be true to say that the central atom was in its valence state, which has been drawn out of the ground state by the presence of the hydrogen atoms and the bond energy that lowers the energy of the whole system.

Questions. What is a valence state? Why is it not a spectroscopic state? How may the energy of the valence state be determined? What role does the valence state play in chemical-bonding theory, and why is its energy important? The valence state can be expressed as a superposition of spectroscopic states; suppose we contrived to produce an atom in a state which was just such a superposition of spectroscopic states, discuss the history of the state from its moment of formation.

Further information. See *MQM* Chapter 9. See also Coulson's *The shape and structure of molecules* (OCS 9) and §8.4 of Coulson (1961), who gives the following references to calculations on valence states, their composition, and their energy: Voge (1936), Mulliken (1938), Pauling (1949), Moffitt (1950), and Skinner (1953, 1955). A helpful discussion of valence states, with examples, is given in §4.1 of McGlynn, Vanquickenborne, Kinoshita, and Carroll (1972).

variation theory, or variation principle. The energy calculated using an arbitrary °wavefunction cannot be less than the true lowest energy of the system.

In quantum theory we are told to calculate the energy of a system by evaluating the °expectation value of the °hamiltonian of the system, and so we evaluate the quantity $E = \int d\tau\, \psi^* H \psi / \int d\tau\, \psi^* \psi$. The variation principle informs us that if we make an arbitrary choice of the function φ then the analogous quantity $\mathcal{E} = \int d\tau \varphi^* H \varphi / \int d\tau \varphi^* \varphi$, which is called the *Rayleigh ratio*, cannot be less than the true ground-state energy. The implication of this important result is that if we make a series of guesses about the form of the trial function, the one that gives the lowest energy will most closely resemble the true wavefunction of the system. If we are lucky we shall guess a function that yields the true energy: in that case we shall have found the true ground-state wavefunction. It is important to develop a method of choosing the best function other than relying on mere intuition, and two techniques are often employed.

The first writes the wavefunction as a function of one or more parameters, and then varies the parameters in search of a minimum. Thus if the trial function were dependent on the value of a parameter p, differentiation of $\mathcal{E}(p)$ with respect to p and determination of the condition for a minimum yields the best value of p and therefore the best function of that particular form. Of course we might have chosen a function of a poor form, but the function so found would be the best of that type. As an example, we might have guessed that the ground state of the °hydrogen atom was well described by a function $\exp(-pr^2)$: a variation treatment leads to a best value of p, but not a very good energy. A function $\exp(-pr)$ requires another value of p, and in this case the best energy is the exact ground-state energy, and therefore the trial function with this value of p is the exact ground-state wavefunction.

A different approach was introduced by Ritz: he supposed that the trial function could be written as a sum of functions: the functions themselves are invariable, but the amounts of each in the mixture constitute the variable parameters. The trial function is of a form $\varphi = p_1\psi_1 + p_2\psi_2 + \ldots$, and the minimum is found by differentiating $\mathcal{E}(p_1, p_2, \ldots)$ with respect to all the parameters p_i and seeking a simultaneous minimum. This procedure is the basis of the method of determining the best mixture in the method of °linear combination of atomic orbitals. Once again the minimum energy differs from the true energy if an insufficiently flexible trial function has been chosen: it also differs if an approximate hamiltonian has been used (in which case an energy *below* the true energy may be found, for the hamiltonian must be correct if the variation method is to be tried).

It would be very useful to know how far the variational minimum energy, which is an *upper bound* to the true energy, lay above the true energy. There are techniques of finding a *lower bound* (beneath which the true energy cannot lie), and in principle this gives some indication of the accuracy of a variational calculation; but the technique is difficult and has not been widely used.

Questions. 1. State the variation principle. Does it provide an upper or a lower bound to the true energy? If one guesses a wavefunction and calculates the energy of the system with it, of what can one be sure? What are the two methods of selecting the best trial function of a particular form? Why might the energy so calculated still be considerably greater than the true energy of the system? What is the Ritz procedure? What should be determined in order to estimate the error in the variation calculation?

2. Take a trial function of the form $\exp(-pr)$ and vary p to find the ground state of the hydrogen atom. (The form of the °hamiltonian will be found in Box 7 on p. 90 and the radial part of the °laplacian in Box 11 on p. 124). Do not forget to maintain the normalization of the function; in other words, minimize the ratio $\int d\tau\varphi^* H\varphi / \int d\tau\varphi^*\varphi$ with respect to p. Repeat the exercise with a trial function of the form $\exp(-pr^2)$. Now try a function of the form $p_1\exp(-p_1'r^2) + p_2\exp(-p_2'r^2)$ and attempt to achieve a lower minimum. Sketch the form of the three best trial functions.

3. The Ritz procedure takes a trial function of the form $\sum_i p_i\psi_i$ and varies the parameters p_i. Show that the condition for a minimum energy is attained when the determinant $|H_{ij} - \mathcal{E}S_{ij}|$ vanishes. H_{ij} are the integrals $\int d\tau\psi_i^* H\psi_j$ and S_{ij} the integrals $\int d\tau\psi_i^*\psi_j$. The minimum energy is the smallest root of the determinant, and the determinant itself is known as the °secular determinant. Apply the Ritz variation principle to the demonstration that the 1s-orbitals in molecular hydrogen contribute equally to the bonding molecular orbital.

Further information. For a simple proof of the variation principle and a derivation of the minimum conditions, see *MQM* Chapter 7, and §3.6 of Coulson (1961). For further discussion see §7c of Eyring, Walter, and Kimball (1944), Kauzmann (1957), Pilar (1968), and Wilcox (1966). For a discussion of the determination of lower bounds see Löwdin (1966) and references therein.

vector model of the atom. The vector model is a representation in terms of vectors of the coupling of the angular momenta of the electrons of the atom. The basis of the method is the representation of a state of °angular momentum of magnitude $[j_1(j_1+1)]^{1/2}\hbar$ by a vector $\mathbf{j}_1$ of length $[j_1(j_1+1)]^{1/2}$ with an appropriate orientation. If the component of angular momentum on some arbitrary z-axis is well defined and has the value $m\hbar$ the orientation of the vector is drawn so that its component on this axis is of length m. Since such an angular momentum °precesses about the z-axis, the vector is drawn so that it lies on a cone at some arbitrary but indeterminate azimuth (Fig. V3).

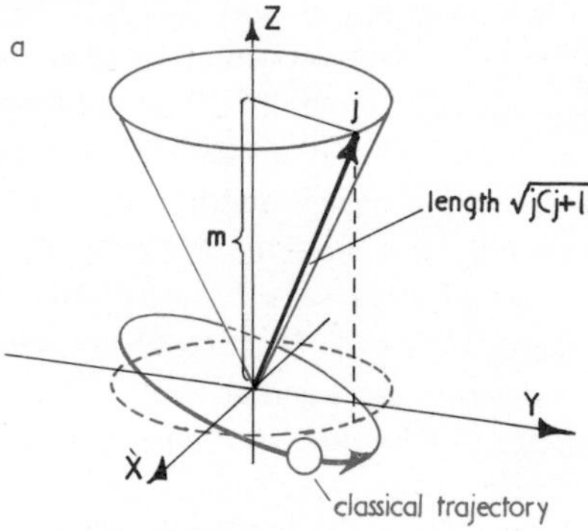

FIG. V3. The basic vector model of angular momentum.

If a second source j_2 is present, the total angular momentum of the system may be constructed as the resultant of the two vectors representing the two momenta: since the length of the resultant vector must be $[j(j+1)]^{1/2}$, with the value of j selected from the set $j_1+j_2, j_1+j_2-1, \ldots |j_1-j_2|$ (see °angular momentum), only a few orientations of the three vectors $\mathbf{j}_1$, $\mathbf{j}_2$, and their resultant $\mathbf{j}$ are permitted. In accord with the algebraic theory of angular momentum the vectors $\mathbf{j}_1$ and $\mathbf{j}_2$ precess around their resultant, and the latter precesses around some arbitrary z-axis. This situation is represented by a vector diagram of the type shown in Figs. V4 and V5. The process of coupling the momenta together may continue until all the individual spin and orbital contributions have been combined into the one resultant representing the total angular momentum of the whole atom. Fortunately this formidable exercise can be simplified by a number of approximations. The first simplification is to note that the *core* of the atom (the electrons in other than the valence shells) has zero angular momentum because all its spins are paired and the shell is complete. The next approximation supposes that there are two extreme cases of coupling.

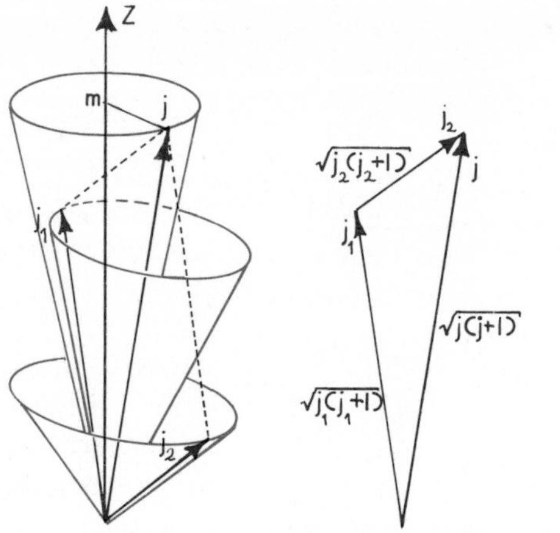

FIG. V4. Coupling of $\mathbf{j}_1$ and $\mathbf{j}_2$ in the vector model.

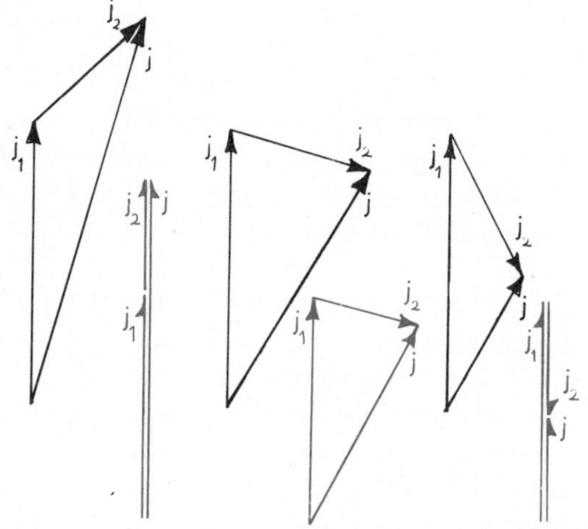

FIG. V5. Coupling of $j_1=2$ and $j_2=1$ to give $j=3, 2, 1$. A vector construction is shown in black, and a simple rule of thumb, which uses lines of length j_1, j_2, j, is shown in colour.

1. The first, the *Russell-Saunders coupling case* or *LS-coupling case*, assumes that the °spin-orbit coupling is so small that it is effective only after all the orbital momenta have been summed into some resultant $\mathbf{L}$, and all the spins summed into another resultant $\mathbf{S}$. The electronic orbital motions are dominated by

the electron-electron electrostatic interactions, and this is the source of their coupling energy. For two electrons the coupling of $\mathbf{l}_1$ and $\mathbf{l}_2$ would be represented by a diagram of the type in Fig. V6 a. The two spins also couple to give a definite resultant **S**: the coupling energy for this interaction arises from the spin-dependent °exchange energy, and so it too is an electrostatic phenomenon. At this stage the two resultant momenta **L** and **S** couple together to form a resultant **J**, the total angular

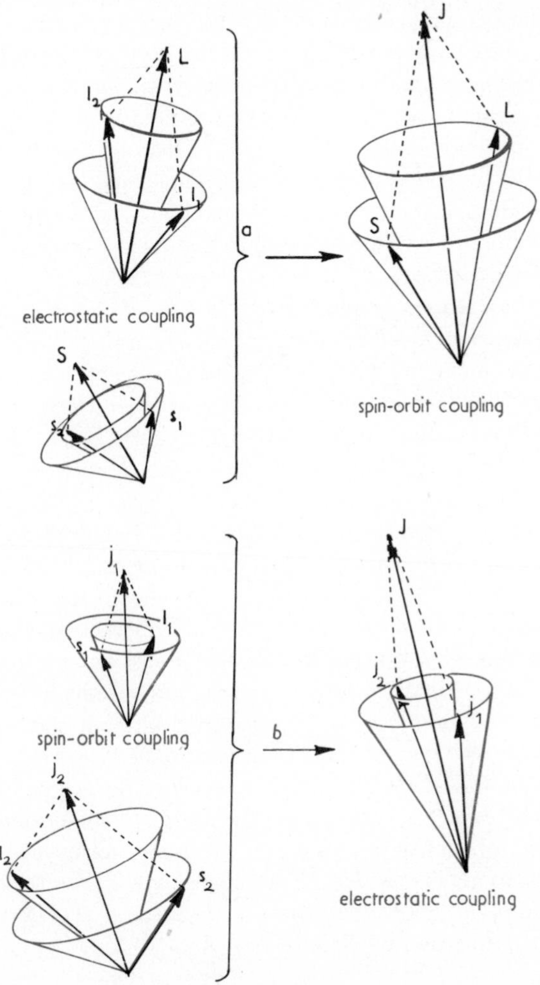

FIG. V6. (a) Russell-Saunders or LS-coupling. (b) *jj*-coupling.

momentum, and the strength of this interaction depends on the strength of the spin-orbit coupling.

2. When the spin-orbit coupling is stronger than the electrostatic interaction the Russell-Saunders scheme breaks down because the spin and orbital angular momenta of individual electrons attempt to organize themselves into satisfactory mutual orientations. The *jj-coupling scheme* describes the extreme situation of this kind. In it each electron's spin is allowed to couple with its orbital momentum; thus $\mathbf{l}_1$ and $\mathbf{s}_1$ couple to form $\mathbf{j}_1$. The two components °precess strongly around their resultant in the manner characteristic of a strongly interacting pair of momenta. This $\mathbf{j}_1$ is now coupled to another $\mathbf{j}_2$, and the total angular momentum **J** constructed: the latter coupling is relatively weak, for it depends on the electrostatic interactions of the electronic orbitals. We see that, although the total angular momentum obtained in this way might be the same as the total in the Russell-Saunders scheme, the states of the atoms are different, and their energies also differ.

Neither scheme is an exact representation of the true state of affairs because there is always some competition between the different types of interaction, and indeed it is quite possible for some electrons in the same atom to be coupled by one scheme and the remainder by the other. Nevertheless for light atoms, which have small spin-orbit coupling constants, the Russell-Saunders scheme is often a good description of the valence electrons. Heavy atoms, which have large spin-orbit coupling constants, are often predominantly *jj*-coupled. It follows that the wavefunctions corresponding to the Russell-Saunders scheme are a good starting point for more elaborate calculations on light atoms.

The angular momenta that one is led to by the vector model are the bases of the labelling of the state of atoms by °term symbols.

Questions. What is the vector model of the atom? What are its basic features? What is the length of the vector that would represent the orbital angular momentum of an electron in an s-orbital, a p-orbital, and a d-orbital? What is the length of the vector representing the °spin of an electron? Construct vector diagrams for the coupling of the spin and orbital angular momenta of an electron in a p-orbital. What is the energy of interaction? What approximations may be introduced to simplify the discussion of the coupling of angular momenta in atoms? By a vector construction show that the angular momentum of a complete K-shell ($1s^2$) is zero. What is the source of the coupling energy between the orbital momenta of electrons? What is the source of the spin coupling energy? When is it appropriate to use Russell-Saunders coupling? When should *jj*-coupling be used instead? Are there any alternatives? Is it possible to use the Russell-Saunders term symbols even when the *jj*-coupling predominates?

Further information. See *MQM* Chapters 6 and 8 for a further discussion of the vector model of the atom and the two coupling schemes. Good accounts are given in §11.2 of Herzberg (1944), Chapter V of White (1934), §3.4 of King (1964), and Chapter 12 of Kuhn (1962). Candler's book (1964) concentrates on the vector-model description of atoms. The molecular situation is outlined in the section on the °Hund coupling schemes.

vibrational spectroscopy: a synopsis. As a first approximation the vibrations of molecules are assumed to be simple °harmonic. The frequency depends on both the °force-constant and the mass of the vibrating object according to $\omega = (k/m)^{1/2}$ in radians per second. Molecular force-constants and masses are such that vibrational frequencies fall in the *infrared* region of the spectrum, and so obtaining a vibration spectrum is an infrared spectroscopic technique. Vibrational structure also appears in an °electronic spectrum, for during an electronic transition vibrations may be excited: the spacing of the lines of this vibrational structure is of the order of an infrared frequency. As a rough guide, weak bonds between heavy atoms vibrate in the region of several hundred cm^{-1} (the I—I bond in I_2 vibrates at 214 cm^{-1}, $6{\cdot}4 \times 10^{12}$ Hz, or $4{\cdot}67 \times 10^4$ nm, in units of wave number, circular frequency, and wavelength respectively), and stiff bonds between light atoms vibrate in the region of several thousand cm^{-1} (the H—H bond in hydrogen vibrates at 4395 cm^{-1}, or $1{\cdot}3 \times 10^{14}$ Hz, or 2280 nm). Bond stretches tend to be at higher frequency than bond bends. See Table 10 for the vibrational frequencies of some diatomic molecules, and Table 24 for the typical frequencies of groups in molecules.

A vibration is *active*—i.e. observable—in the infrared if during it the dipole moment of the molecule changes. This implies that diatomic molecules absorb in the infrared only if they are polar. In more complicated molecules it is necessary to scrutinize the form of the °normal mode in order to see whether the vibrations of several atoms jointly lead to an oscillating dipole. This may often be done by inspection, but more positively one should take into account the symmetry of the system by using °group theory. If the vibration is active the selection rule for the transition is that the vibrational quantum number for that transition may change by ± 1. At normal temperatures the Boltzmann distribution ensures that essentially all molecules are in their ground vibrational state: this implies that the spectrum should consist of a single line for each vibrational mode of the molecule, and correspond to the excitation of the mode of vibration from its ground state to its first excited state. Such a line is the *fundamental* and is denoted $(1 \leftarrow 0)$.

The vibration of a molecule is not strictly harmonic because the potential in which the atoms move is not strictly parabolic: the deviations are greater at large displacements from equilibrium. This °anharmonicity has several consequences. First, the selection rule for the transition fails to a degree that depends on the amount of anharmonicity. Instead of a single line for each mode one sees the fundamental $(1 \leftarrow 0)$, or the first *harmonic*, accompanied by weaker *overtones*, or *second-*, *third-*, . . . *harmonics* corresponding to the °progression of transitions $(2 \leftarrow 0)$, $(3 \leftarrow 0)$, ... These should appear at the frequencies 2ω, 3ω, . . . but not exactly because of the anharmonicity. It is possible for two modes of a molecule to be excited simultaneously if they are not entirely independent (that is, if there is present anharmonicity which is able to mix together the two modes): the absorption that is responsible for this appears as a *combination band*. When the energy of a combination level lies close to the energy of an unexcited mode, which may be unexcited because it is inactive in the infrared, there may occur a °resonance interaction between them by virtue of the anharmonicity present. This *Fermi resonance* causes the lines to shift, and the active bands donate intensity to the inactive, which therefore appear in the spectrum (this is *intensity borrowing*, brought about by the inactive mode acquiring some of the properties of the active modes: see °superposition principle).

When a vibrational transition occurs it may be accompanied by a °rotational transition of the molecule. This gives rise to a structure in the spectrum which is observable when the sample is gaseous; in a liquid collisions with the solvent blur the structure by reducing the lifetime of the rotational states. In an °electric dipole transition the °rotational °quantum number J may change by 0 or ± 1; consequently there are lines at the position of the pure vibrational transition ($\Delta J = 0$) which constitute the *Q-°branch* of the spectrum; a series of lines at lower frequency ($\Delta J = -1$), the *P-branch*, and a series at higher frequency ($\Delta J = +1$), the *R-branch*. A series of lines rather than a single line is observed because the Boltzmann distribution permits a number of rotational levels to be occupied in the initial state, and each one of these gives rise to a line in the branch. The branches may pass through a *head* if the rotational constant of the upper vibrational level is significantly different from the rotational constant in the lower level (see °branch); this is especially important when the vibrational transition is part of an electronic transition for then the rotational constants may be very different.

The other features that affect a vibrational spectrum include °inversion doubling (for example, in NH_3) and ℓ-type °doubling in linear triatomic molecules. See °Coriolis interaction.

The main pieces of chemical information that one may obtain from a study of vibrational spectra include the elementary but important one of the identification of a species by using its vibrational spectrum as a fingerprint. The major quantitative information that may be obtained is the rigidity of bonds under the stresses of stretching and bending: the force-constant is an important feature of a chemical bond. The anharmonicities show how far the true potential differs from an ideal parabola. The rotational structure on vibrational transitions enables the molecular geometry to be determined in different vibrational states (bond-angle and bond-length dependence on vibrational state), and the vibrational and rotational structure of electronic transitions enables the same kind of information to be obtained about electronically excited states. This information enables one to build up a full picture of the potential-energy curves of molecules in different electronic states.

We have concentrated on electric dipole absorption spectra: vibrational transitions may also be observed in °Raman spectroscopy.

Further information. See *MQM* Chapter 10 for a discussion of vibrational and rovibrational spectra in more quantitative terms, and with the use of group theory. An introduction to the vibration of molecules may be found in Barrow (1962), Whiffen (1972), and King (1964). The characteristic frequencies of many bonds are listed in Bellamy (1958, 1968) who also describes infrared spectroscopy as an analytical tool. More advanced discussions are given by Gans (1971), Herzberg (1945), Wilson, Decius, and Cross (1955), and Allen and Cross (1963). See also Gaydon (1968).

vibronic transition. The word 'vibronic' is an amalgam of *vib*ration and elec*tronic*, and implies that the transition involves both modes of excitation simultaneously. A *vibronic state* is the name applied to a state of the molecule when it is improper to view the electronic and the vibrational states as independent.

In order to elucidate this description consider an octahedral complex and an electronic transition of a d-electron. In the °crystal-field or °ligand-field theories of transition-metal complexes the d-orbitals are split into two groups separated by a small energy difference; therefore it is tempting to ascribe the colours of transition-metal complexes to a transition of an electron from one set of d-orbitals to the other. The problem that immediately confronts us is the Laporte °selection rule, which forbids d-d transitions because it forbids °gerade-gerade (g-g) transitions. Most rules can be evaded, and one of the rules for looking for ways of evading rules is to seek the approximation on which that rule might be based, and then to repair the approximation. The Laporte selection rule is based on the existence in the complex of a centre of symmetry, and only if the complex is strictly octahedral is the rule strictly valid. But the complex may vibrate, and some of the vibrational modes destroy the centrosymmetric nature of the molecule. Now consider the unexcited, vibrationally quiescent molecule, and a photon approaching it. Let the photon excite simultaneously a d-electron and a vibration of the complex. Then if the excited vibration is one that destroys the centrosymmetry of the complex, the Laporte rule will be slightly but sufficiently broken, because the complex no longer possesses a centre of inversion in the initial and final states.

The transition is allowed only in so far as it is proper to treat the vibration and the electronic motions as coupled together so that they jointly determine the symmetry of the object with which the light is interacting. Therefore the transition is vibronic and the states of the complex must be treated as vibronic states. This view leads to another way of looking at the nature of a vibronic transition. In this we consider the possibility of a transition from a d-orbital to a p-orbital; this, being a g to u transition, is allowed. But why should the upper level be a p-orbital, or at least why should it possess some p-character? If the electrons follow the nuclear vibrations the electronic distribution in the upper state must follow the nuclear motion. To do so it must distort from the centrosymmetric distribution which d-orbitals give rise to, and one way of achieving the distorted distribution is to mix in (°hybridize) some p-orbital character (Fig. V7). Therefore, when such an antisymmetric mode is excited the electronic distribution contains some p-character; and as d-p transitions are allowed, the transition from the quiescent ground state to the vibronic upper state is allowed in proportion to the amount of p-character the vibration introduces.

Further information. See *MQM* Chapter 10 for a further discussion, and some group theory. Vibronic transitions are described in more detail by Orgel (1960), Figgis (1966), Ballhausen (1962), and Griffith (1964). When the rotational states of a molecule must be considered too then a *rovibronic transition* occurs, and the composite states are *rovibronic states.*

virial theorem. In its simplest form the virial theorem states that if the potential energy of a system follows a $1/r$ law then the mean kinetic energy is related to the mean potential energy by the expression $\langle T\rangle = -\frac{1}{2}\langle V\rangle$. This in turn implies that the total mean energy of the system is simply equal to $\frac{1}{2}\langle V\rangle$, or to $-\langle T\rangle$. A more general form of the theorem states that if the potential energy follows the law r^n, then the mean potential energy and the mean kinetic energy are related by $\langle T\rangle = \frac{1}{2}n\langle V\rangle$. Thus for an harmonic oscillator, in which the potential energy is parabolic ($n = +2$), the mean potential and kinetic energies are related by $\langle T\rangle = \langle V\rangle$, and this equality is yet another manifestation of the peculiarly high degree of symmetry of the °harmonic oscillator. The theorem applies to a bounded system, and one that is stationary in time; but if by mean value is also implied a time average, then it also applies to non-stationary states.

The name 'virial' (which is derived from the Latin *vis, vires;* force, forces) comes from the classical mechanical form of the rate of change of the mean value of the product **r.p**, where **r** is a position coordinate and **p** is the linear momentum. This leads to the equation $\langle T\rangle = -\frac{1}{2}\langle \mathbf{F}.\mathbf{r}\rangle$, the *virial theorem of Clausius*, where **F** is the force acting. From this expression may be deduced the general form of the equation of state of a real gas in which forces operate between the gas particles: this gives rise to the *virial expansion* and the *virial coefficients* of thermodynamics. The virial theorem may also be derived quantum mechanically and applied to a discussion of the structure and properties of atoms and molecules. For example, it is a test of the exactness of a calculated wavefunction that

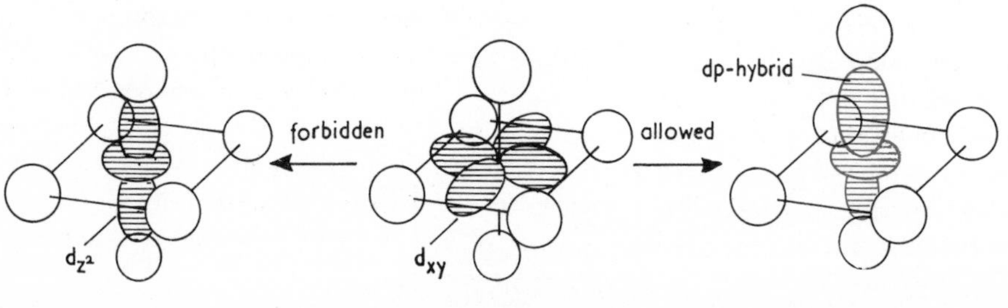

FIG. V7. An asymmetric vibration hybridizes p_z and d_{z^2} and permits a d-d transition via the d-p component.

the expectation values of the potential- and kinetic-energy operators do indeed satisfy the virial theorem. It is essential to remember that the virial theorem imposes a connexion between the way that the kinetic and potential energies vary as wavefunctions are distorted. The virial theorem may also be used as an alternative to the °variation theorem in some circumstances.

A further generalization of the virial theorem may be made and the *hypervirial theorems* obtained. These are a set of theorems based on the vanishing of the average value of the °commutator of an °operator with the °hamiltonian of the system when the system is in an °eigenstate of the hamiltonian.

Questions. From the wavefunctions given in Tables 11 and 15 demonstrate the validity of the virial theorem for the ground states of the harmonic oscillator and the hydrogen atom. Return to the calculation of the ground state of the hydrogen atom in terms of the °variation principle, and investigate whether the virial theorem is satisfied for the best gaussian approximation.

Further information. For a good discussion of the classical virial theorem, its deduction, and some applications, see Goldstein (1950); for the deduction of the gas laws see Lindsey (1941). The quantum-mechanical virial theorem is derived by Hirschfelder (1960), who also deduces and describes the hypervirial theorems. Application of the theorem to molecular- and atomic-structure calculations are described by Coulson (1965), Deb (1973), and Feinberg, Ruedenberg, and Mehler (1970).

virtual transition. When a system is °perturbed, for example by the application of an electric field, it is distorted; the distorted system can be described by a °superposition of the °wavefunctions of the states of the original system, and therefore the system behaves as though it contained features of the excited states: it has made a *virtual transition* to the excited state. When a light wave scatters from a molecule the distortion it induces can be envisaged as a series of virtual transitions to the excited molecular states caused by a virtual absorption of a photon. The distortion is immediately released, and the photon flies off leaving the molecule either in its original state (Rayleigh scattering) or in one of the excited states populated by the initial virtual transition (°Raman scattering).

As the frequency of the incident light approaches one of the transition frequencies of the molecule the transition gradually loses its virtual character and becomes real: the molecule is really excited and the photon is really absorbed. Energy is conserved in real transitions; but as 'virtual transition' is just a name for a way of describing a distortion and of taking into account the effect of a perturbation, for them it is not conserved.

Questions. What is a virtual transition? In what ways does it differ from a real transition? When does a virtual transition take on the character of a real transition? Is energy conserved in a virtual transition? What virtual transitions are involved when an electric field is applied to a °hydrogen atom?

Further information. See *MQM* Chapter 7 for a discussion of perturbation theory and a concomitant discussion of virtual transitions. Books that deal with °perturbation theory perforce deal with virtual transitions, although the term is not always used. See Davydov (1965), Dirac (1958), Landau and Lifshitz (1958a), Messiah (1961), and Schiff (1968). See §16 of Heitler (1954) and §7.5 of Hameka (1965) for a discussion of the transformation of virtual into real transitions. See °Raman effect and °Stark effect.

W

wavefunction. The wavefunction for a system is a solution of its Schrödinger equation and is the function that contains all the information about its dynamical properties. If the wavefunction that describes the state of the system is known, all the observable properties of the system in that state may be deduced by performing the appropriate mathematical °operation. The wavefunction may be a function of time, and is then often written $\Psi(\mathbf{r},t)$. When it is not a function of time (or when the time-dependence has been factored out) it is often denoted ψ, and is a function of all the coordinates of all particles that make up the system. Since the wavefunction depends on the state of the system it is often labelled with an index or set of indices (the °quantum numbers) that distinguish the state. Thus the wavefunction for a system containing N particles and needing M quantum numbers is the mathematical function $\psi_{n_1 n_2 \ldots n_M}(\mathbf{r}_1, \mathbf{r}_2 \ldots \mathbf{r}_N)$. As examples of wavefunctions we may point to the wavefunction for a free particle travelling in the x-direction with a °momentum $k\hbar$, which is the function $\exp ikx$, and to the wavefunction for the ground state of the °hydrogen atom, which is the simple function $\exp(-r/a_0)$. The wavefunction has an interpretation, must obey some restrictions, and contains information. We describe these aspects below.

1. *Interpretation of the wavefunction*. We concentrate on a system containing one particle with the coordinate x. The *Born interpretation* of $\psi(x)$ is that it is the amplitude for the probability distribution of the position of the particle. According to this interpretation the *probability* of finding the particle in the infinitesimal range dx surrounding the point x is proportional to $\psi^*(x)\psi(x)dx$. The *probability density* at the point x is therefore proportional to $\psi^*(x)\psi(x)$. If we were dealing with a three-dimensional system the wavefunction $\psi(\mathbf{r})$ would be interpreted as follows: $\psi^*(\mathbf{r})\psi(\mathbf{r})d\tau$ is the probability of finding the particle in an infinitesimal volume element $d\tau$ surrounding the point $\mathbf{r}$. The interpretation may be pictured in terms of inserting a probe sensitive to the presence of the particle, and which samples a volume $d\tau$ in the system; as the probe is moved to different points $\mathbf{r}$ the meter reading is proportional to the volume of the probe and to the value of $\psi^*(\mathbf{r})\psi(\mathbf{r})$. As an example, the wavefunction for the °hydrogen-atom ground state is a decaying exponential function of r; therefore the meter reading for the electron density will fall according to $\exp(-2r/a_0)d\tau$ as the probe of volume $d\tau$ is moved out along a radius. In the case of the other wavefunction referred to above ($\exp ikx$) the meter would give the same reading wherever the probe is inserted because $(\exp ikx)^*(\exp ikx) = 1$ and is independent of x. This function corresponds to an even spreading of the particle throughout the universe, whereas for the hydrogen atom the electron is densest close to the nucleus.

2. *Limitations on the wavefunction*. If the wavefunction is to be interpreted as an amplitude for the probability density for the distribution of the particle is must be constrained in a variety of ways.

(a) It must be finite everywhere, for otherwise there would be an indefinite accumulation of probability density at the points where it became infinite. (This requirement is really too stringent: all we need to impose is the condition that the total probability of the particle being within the universe is unity—thus we require the existence of the integral $\int d\tau \psi^*(\mathbf{r})\psi(\mathbf{r})$; but our too-stringent requirement is a good guide in most cases.)

(b) The probability density must be single-valued everywhere, because it would be nonsense to say that the probability density at a certain point is both 0·2 and 0·4. In most cases (systems involving °spin are exceptions which are easily accommodated in another way) this requirement is the same as requiring the wavefunction itself to be single-valued.

(c) The wavefunction must be continuous, for it would be unreasonable to have a probability density of a particular value at a point and a finitely different value an infinitesimal distance away.

The imposition of these limitations on the wavefunction is severe, for it forces it to obey certain boundary conditions, and leads ineluctably to quantization (see °quantum) because only a very few of the solutions of the °Schrödinger equation survive when the conditions are imposed.

3. *Information in the wavefunction*. We have already seen that the wavefunction contains the information about the distribution of the particle. The mean gradient (slope, first derivative) of the function is the °momentum of the particle in that state; this emerges from the quantum-mechanical rules about interpreting observables by °operators. The mean curvature (the second derivative) is the °kinetic energy of the state. The value of any observable is determined by calculating the °expectation value of the corresponding °operator using the appropriate wavefunction.

4. *Time-dependent wavefunctions*. If the wavefunction $\psi_n(x)$ corresponds to an energy (°eigenvalue) E_n the time-dependent form of the wavefunction $\Psi_n(x,t)$ is simply the product $\psi_n(x)\exp(-iE_n t/\hbar)$. This is a *stationary state* (even though t occurs) because the probability density $|\Psi_n(x,t)|^2$ is independent of time.

5. *Pure states and superpositions*. If it is certain that a system is in a state with well-defined quantum numbers then the wavefunction is that of a pure state. As an example, a hydrogen atom known to be in its ground state is in a pure state, and a particle with precisely defined momentum is also in a pure state and is described by a simple wavefunction. When the state of a system is believed to be one of a range of pure states, for example, if the particle has a momentum somewhere in the range $(k-\kappa)\hbar$ to $(k+\kappa)\hbar$, then the wavefunction for the system is a °superposition of the pure-state functions covering this range. Thus if the state is believed to be in the range of states spanned by the functions $\psi_{n_1}(x), \psi_{n_2}(x), \ldots$, the true state of the system is described by the linear superposition $\psi(x) = c_1\psi_{n_1}(x) + c_2\psi_{n_2}(x) + \ldots$, where the coefficients determine the probability that the system is in one of the basis states: the probability that the system is in a state described by the wavefunction $\psi_n(x)$ is proportional to $c_n^* c_n$, or $|c_n|^2$. The coefficients may be time-dependent. An example would be the excitation of a hydrogen atom by incident radiation: initially the atom is in the ground state described by the function $\psi_{1s}(\mathbf{r})$, but as irradiation continues it takes on more of the character of the $2p_z$-state. Therefore during irradiation its state is described by the function $\Psi(\mathbf{r},t) = c_{1s}(t)\psi_{1s}(\mathbf{r}) + c_{2p}(t)\psi_{2p_z}(\mathbf{r})$, with $c_{1s}(0) = 1$ and $c_{2p}(0) = 0$, and the probability that at a time t it has actually made the transition to the $2p_z$-state is proportional to $|c_{2p}(t)|^2$. The calculation of the coefficients is a task for °perturbation theory, and the example is described further under °transition probability. An example of a static superposition wavefunction is that of a °hybrid orbital, and another is an °LCAO °molecular orbital.

Questions. How is a wavefunction obtained? What is its interpretation? What is the difference between probability and probability density? Sketch the meter reading for an electron-sensitive probe when it is dipped into a hydrogen atom and pushed in towards the nucleus along a radius: first let the probe be a minute volume element, roughly a cube of volume $dxdydz$, and then let the probe be a spherical shell of area $4\pi r^2$ and thickness dr (r is the radius, and so the shell gets smaller the closer it is pushed towards the nucleus: see °radial distribution function). What are the three constraints on the wavefunction? Is a wavefunction of the form $\exp(+ax)$ a likely candidate for a wavefunction for a free particle? What about the function $x/|x|$? A particle is confined to a ring and the function $\exp im\phi$ is proposed for its wavefunction: what limitation must be put on the values of m? How is a time-dependent wavefunction for a stationary state formed? Suppose the energy E were replaced by the complex quantity $E - i\hbar\Gamma$; what would happen to the amplitude of the hitherto stationary state, and how could this be interpreted? How should the coefficients of a superposed wavefunction be interpreted? A wavefunction is written $\psi_{2s} + 3^{1/2}\psi_{2p}$: what proportion of s- and p-character does it contain? Form an sp^2-hybrid.

Further information. See *MQM* Chapters 1, 2, and 3 for a detailed discussion of the solution of the Schrödinger equation for a variety of systems and an account of the properties and significance of their wavefunctions. For a discussion of the interpretation of wavefunctions see Pauling and Wilson (1935), Landau and Lifshitz (1958a), and Schiff (1968). For questions about its interpretation see Bohm (1951), Jammer (1966), and Ballantine (1970). We have discussed elsewhere the question of the °normalization of the wavefunction, and the question of °orthogonality. Its interpretation as an °eigenfunction of the °hamiltonian is important. See also the °superposition principle, °atomic orbitals, and the °hydrogen atom.

wave packets. A particle that experiment or observation shows to be confined to a very small region of space must be described by a °wavefunction that is strongly peaked within the region and virtually zero elsewhere. A wavefunction corresponding to a sharply defined °momentum has a well-defined wavelength, and so spreads over a large region (actually the whole) of the system; the only way of attaining localization is to take a °superposition of the latter functions and investigate their mutual interference. If the superposition has been well chosen all the constructive interference occurs at a selected point and destructive interference eliminates the amplitude of the wavefunction everywhere else (Fig. W1). The square of the sharply peaked function is another sharply peaked function, and so the probability of finding the particle differs from zero only in the point-like region. Thus a wave packet describes a localized particle (and because we have a superposition of a vast number of energy states the momentum is correspondingly indefinite).

The wave packet also moves, because all the component functions are time-dependent and the point of maximum constructive interference moves. It is possible to show that

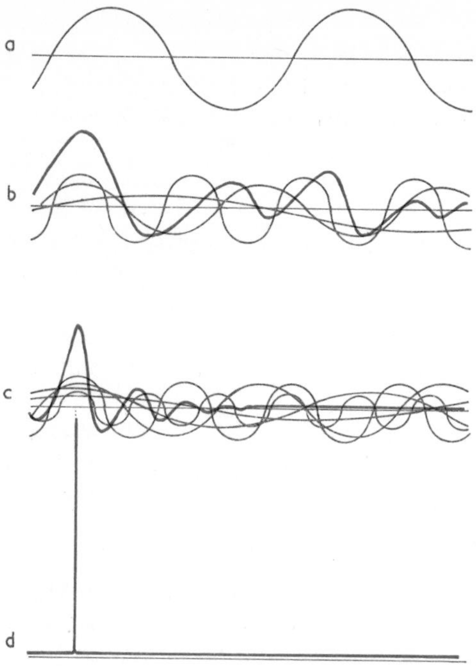

FIG. W1. Formation of a wave packet: (a) single momentum state, no localization; (b) several states, some localization; (c) many states, good localization; (d) infinite number of states, perfect localization.

when the wavefunctions are the solutions of a Schrödinger equation for a specified potential the motion of the wave packet corresponds very closely to the motion predicted for a classical particle in the same potential. Thus we see how the structure of quantum mechanics underlies the coarse description provided by classical mechanics. One important difference is that the wave packet tends to spread with time, but this tendency is very small for massive, slow particles.

Further information. The formation, significance, ana motion of wave packets are described in *MQM* Chapter 3, and made quantitative in Appendix 3.1. A good and instructive discussion will be found in Chapter 3 of Bohm (1951), and those with tough teeth should consult Goldberger and Watson (1964), especially Chapter 3.

Wigner coefficient. A *Wigner coefficient*, or *Clebsch-Gordon coefficient*, or *vector-coupling coefficient*, is the coefficient in the expansion of a state of coupled °angular momentum in terms of its uncoupled components.

As a specific example, consider the coupling of an α- and a β-electron °spin into a °singlet state. This spin-paired state may be expressed as a °linear combination of the uncoupled states in which spin 1 has orientation α and spin 2 has orientation β, and vice versa: the singlet state is represented by $(1/\surd 2)[\alpha(1)\beta(2)-\beta(1)\alpha(2)]$. The Wigner coefficient of the uncoupled state $\alpha(1)\beta(2)$ is therefore $1/\surd 2$, and of the other uncoupled state $\beta(1)\alpha(2)$ is $-1/\surd 2$. If we attempt to construct a component of the triplet state from the two uncoupled states we discover that taking both coefficients to be $+1/\surd 2$ would give $(1/\surd 2)[\alpha(1)\beta(2)+\beta(1)\alpha(2)]$, which should be recognized as the $M_S=0$ state of the triplet. Wigner coefficients enable all such linear combinations to be written for the coupling of arbitrary angular momenta into the desired resultants.

The Wigner coefficients for the coupling of a state with quantum numbers j_1, m_1 and j_2, m_2 into one with j,m are written $\langle j_1 m_1 j_2 m_2 | jm \rangle$; a modification of this coefficient, which being more symmetrical is easier to handle, is known as a *3j-symbol*.

Further information. See Brink and Satchler (1968), Rose (1957), and Edmonds (1957) for the properties of Wigner coefficients. A convenient list has been published by Heine (1960). A collection of 3*j*-symbols in a convenient numerical form has been prepared by Rotenberg, Bivins, Metropolis, and Wooten (1959).

work function. The work function of a metal is the energy required to remove an electron to infinity. The analogy with the °ionization potential should be noticed. Metals with small work functions can more easily lose their electrons than metals with high work functions. A small list of work functions is shown in Table 25.

The work function plays a role in the °photoelectric effect and in thermionic emission. The *Schottky effect* is the lowering of the effective work function in the presence of an applied electric field; this arises from the combined effect of the applied field and the mirror charge induced by the electron as it moves away from the surface of the metal.

Further information. A very readable account of these matters will be found in Solymar and Walsh (1970). Comprehensive tables of work functions are given in §9 of the *American Institute of Physics Handbook* (Gray 1972). See also °photoelectric effect.

X

X-ray spectra. X-rays are electromagnetic waves of the order of 0·1 nm (1 Å) wavelength. A principal terrestrial source is the bombardment of metals with high-energy electrons. The radiation so produced consists of two components: there is a continuous background of radiation on which is superimposed a sequence of sharp lines. The latter constitute the X-ray spectrum.

The continuous component, known as *Bremsstrahlung*, is formed by the deceleration of the electrons by the metal: as the negatively charged electron is decelerated when it plunges into the metal it radiates electromagnetic radiation, and if its initial energy is great enough there is a significant short-wavelength component.

The discrete spectral lines arise from transitions within the core-levels of the atoms that constitute the material: the incoming electron has enough energy to eject an inner-shell electron from the atom, either completely or into some unoccupied upper level; one of the remaining core-electrons falls into the hole left by the ejected electron, and the energy difference is radiated. High-energy ('hard') X-rays are formed when the ejected electron comes from the K-shell ($n = 1$): an electron falling from the L-shell ($n = 2$) gives rise to the K_α-line, one falling from the M-shell ($n = 3$) gives the K_β-line, and so on. Softer X-rays (longer wavelength) are formed when the electron is ejected from the L-shell, and the lines L_α, L_β, etc. are formed as electrons drop from the M- and N- shells.

As a first approximation the K-radiation can be treated on the basis of the energies of the electron levels being hydrogen-like, with an effective nuclear charge of $(Z-1)e$, to take into account the single electron remaining in the 1s-shell. Then using the °hydrogen-atom energy-level formula it is an easy matter to deduce that the frequencies of the K-radiation are given by $(Z-1)^2R[(1/1^2)-(1/n^2)]$. Similar expressions for other lines can be written, but they would involve different screening constants σ in $Z-\sigma$. This expression shows that the square root of the X-ray frequency is proportional to the atomic number Z: this is *Moseley's law*, which enabled the elements to be put in an unambiguous order.

Questions. What different types of X-radiation can be observed when a metal is bombarded with high-energy electrons? What is the source of the continuous background radiation? Why are some sharp peaks observed? To what transitions do the peaks correspond? What is the source of K_α-radiation? What is the dependence of the X-ray frequency on the atomic number of the atom? Why is it reasonable to treat the energy calculation of K_α-radiation in terms of a hydrogen-like atom with atomic number $Z-1$? Calculate the maximum frequency of the continuum X-radiation that might be expected when a 1 keV, 100 keV, 1MeV electron beam strikes a target. The K_α-radiation from copper has a wavelength of 1·541 Å (154 pm) and from molybdenum 0·709 Å(70·9 pm): compute their atomic numbers. Predict the wavelength in the case of aluminium.

Further information. For an account of X-ray spectra see Chapter XVI of White (1934), §IVC of Kuhn (1962), §IV.2 of Herzberg (1944), and §13.9 of Condon and Shortley (1963). Tables of X-ray transition frequencies are given in §7 of Gray (1972).

Z

Zeeman effect. The Zeeman effect is the splitting of spectral lines into several components by a strong magnetic field. In the *normal Zeeman effect*, which is shown by atoms without spin, each line is split into three. In the *anomalous*, but more common, *Zeeman effect*, which is shown by atoms with net spin, the line structure is more complicated.

In the absence of spin the only source of °magnetic moment is the orbital angular momentum of the electrons; the applied field interacts with the orbital moment and the energy of the state with projection M_L is changed from E to $E + \mu_B B M_L$. The $2L + 1$ states of a °term with orbital angular momentum L are therefore no longer °degenerate but are arrayed in a ladder with spacing $\mu_B B$. For example, a ^{1}P term will be split into 3 evenly-spaced components, and a ^{1}D term into 5 components with the same splitting. The °selection rule for an optical transition is $\Delta M_L = 0, \pm 1$, and so all transitions fall into three groups. The $\Delta M_L = 0$ set is at the position of the original spectral line (see Fig. Z1), those with $\Delta M_L = -1$ are displaced to low frequency, and those with $\Delta M_L = +1$ are displaced an equal amount to high frequency. Closer analysis of both theory and experiment shows that the light emitted is polarized: when viewed parallel to the magnetic-field direction the $\Delta M_L = 0$ line is absent, and the $\Delta M_L = \pm 1$ lines are circularly polarized ($\Delta M_L = -1$ is left circularly polarized, $\Delta M_L = +1$ is right circularly polarized). When viewed perpendicular to the field the $\Delta M_L = 0$ line is present and polarized parallel to the field (it is denoted a π-line); the $\Delta M_L = \pm 1$ lines are also plane-polarized, but perpendicular to the field (and denoted the σ-lines: *senkrecht* is German for perpendicular). With fields of the order of 30 kG the splitting is about 1·5 cm^{-1}, and this is easily detectable.

When a resultant °spin is present, so that the atom is in some °multiplet state, it is necessary to consider the effect of the magnetic field on each of the °levels of the term: the $2J + 1$ states M_J of a level with total angular momentum J have a magnetic moment $(-g_J \mu_B/\hbar)\mathbf{J}$ and therefore an energy $E + g_J \mu_B B M_J$ in a magnetic field. The g_J-factor takes into account the dependence of the magnetic moment of a state on the magnitudes of the contributing spin and orbital angular

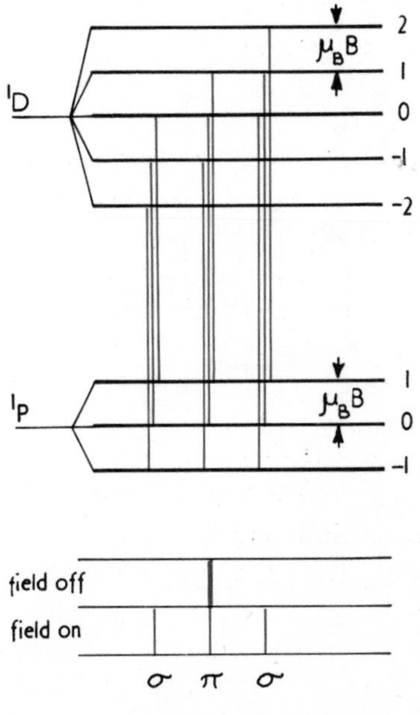

FIG. Z1. The normal Zeeman effect (^{1}D–^{1}P).

momenta: it is the Landé °*g*-value. Since g_J depends on S, L, and J, the splitting of states is different in different terms, and although the same selection rules apply (and the polarizations are the same) the transitions no longer fall into three neat groups. As an example, consider the transitions $^3P \longrightarrow {}^3S$. The ^3S term has a magnetic moment arising solely from its spin angular momentum, and since $S = 1$ the field separates the states into three with separation $2\mu_B B$ (because $g_J = 2$ when $L = 0$, $S = 1$, $J = 1$). The ^3P term has three levels $^3P_0$, $^3P_1$, and $^3P_2$. Since $L = 1$ and $S = 1$, $g_J = 0$ for $J = 0$, $g_J = \frac{3}{2}$ for $J = 1$, and $g_J = \frac{3}{2}$ for $J = 2$. The $^3P_0$ term is therefore not split by the field, and the other two levels $^3P_1$ and $^3P_2$ are both split by the field, the former into 3 states with splitting $(\frac{3}{2})\mu_B B$ and the latter into 5 states with the same splitting (Fig. Z2). On the application of the selection rules the spectrum is predicted to be of the form shown in Fig. Z2, and the considerable complexity of the situation is apparent. Note that the polarization characteristics of the lines can be used to disentangle the spectrum. At very high fields all anomalous Zeeman effects become normal because the field decouples the angular momenta: this is the °Paschen-Back effect.

A principal use of the Zeeman effect is the determination of the multiplicity of terms. The splitting of energy levels by a magnetic field is the basis of magnetic resonance techniques: see °electron spin resonance and °nuclear magnetic resonance.

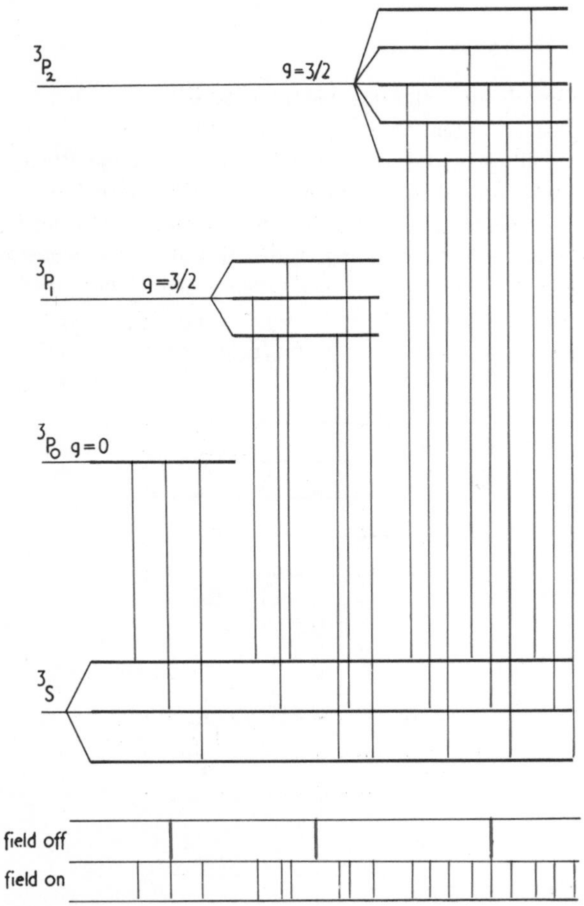

FIG. Z2. The anomalous Zeeman effect (^3P–^3S).

Questions. What is the Zeeman effect? Under what circumstances are three lines seen? When does the anomalous effect appear? Account for the normal Zeeman effect. Discuss the Zeeman effect for the transition $^1D \longrightarrow {}^1F$ and construct a diagram of the form of Fig. Z2 to illustrate the formation of the spectrum. What is the polarization of the lines in the $^1D \longrightarrow {}^1F$ Zeeman spectrum? What would happen to the polarization if the direction of the magnetic field were reversed? What splitting would you expect in a 10 kG magnetic field? Why does the anomalous effect depend on the presence of spin? (Look at °*g*-value to convince yourself that the magnetic moment of a level of a term depends on S, L, and J.) Construct a diagram showing the expected anomalous Zeeman effect for the transition $^3D \longrightarrow {}^3F$. Mark the polarization of the lines. What will happen to the spectrum when the field is markedly increased (to about 100 kG)?

Further information. See *MQM* Chapter 8 for a more detailed discussion. Accounts of the Zeeman effect, and the use to which it can be put, will be found in §II.3 of Herzberg (1944), §3.15 of King (1964), §III.A3 and §III.F of Kuhn (1962), and Chapter XVI of Condon and Shortley (1963).

TABLE 1

Physical properties of benzene

C—C bond length		139·7 pm (1·397 Å)
C—H bond length		108·4 pm (1·084 Å)
enthalpy of formation	ΔH_f^0:	83·2 kJ mol^{-1} (19·820 kcal mol^{-1})
resonance energy		150 kJ mol^{-1} (36·0 kcal mol^{-1})
first ionization potential		9·24 eV
polarizability	$\alpha_{\parallel}$	= 6·35 × 10^{-24} cm^3 (6·67 × 10^{-41} F m^{-2})
	$\alpha_{\perp}$	= 12·31 × 10^{-24} cm^3 (10·89 × 10^{-41} F m^{-2})
	α_{av}	= 10·32 × 10^{-24} cm^3 (9·13 × 10^{-41} F m^{-2})
refractive index (20°C, D-line)		1·5011
relative permittivity (20°C)	ϵ_r	= 2·284
magnetic susceptibility	$\chi_{\parallel}$	= −3·49 × 10^{-5}
	$\chi_{\perp}$	= −9·46 × 10^{-5}
	χ_{av}	= −7·47 × 10^{-5}
absorption bands		6·8 eV ($E_{1u} \leftarrow A_{1g}$); 6·0 eV ($E_{2g} \leftarrow A_{1g}$)
		6·0 eV (B_{1u} ?$\leftarrow A_{1g}$); 4·9 eV ($B_{2u} \leftarrow A_{1g}$)

TABLE 2

Bond-order—bond-length correlations

Hydrocarbon	Bond	π-bond order	Bond distance (pm)
ethene		1·0	133·5
benzene		0·667	139·7
naphthalene	1,2	0·725	136·5
	2,3	0·603	140·4
	1,9	0·554	142·5
	9,10	0·518	139·3
anthracene	1,2	0·738	137·0
	2,3	0·586	140·8
	1,9a	0·535	142·3
	9,9a	0·606	139·6
	4a,9a	0·485	143·6
graphite		0·535	142·1

See Streitweiser (1961) and Daudel, Lefebvre, and Moser (1959) for more information and analysis.

TABLE 3

Character tables

C_{2v} (2mm)	E	C_2	$\sigma_v(xz)$	$\sigma_v'(yz)$		
A_1	1	1	1	1	z	x^2, y^2, z^2
A_2	1	1	−1	−1	R_z	xy
B_1	1	−1	1	−1	x, R_y	xz
B_2	1	−1	−1	1	y, R_x	yz

C_{3v} (3mm)	E	$2C_3$	$3\sigma_v$		
A_1	1	1	1	z	x^2+y^2, z^2
A_2	1	1	−1	R_z	
E	2	−1	0	$(x, y)(R_x, R_y)$	$(x^2-y^2, xy)(xz, yz)$

C_{4v} (4mm)	E	$2C_4$	C_2	$2\sigma_v$	$2\sigma_d$		
A_1	1	1	1	1	1	z	x^2+y^2, z^2
A_2	1	1	1	−1	−1	R_z	
B_1	1	−1	1	1	−1		x^2-y^2
B_2	1	−1	1	−1	1		xy
E	2	0	−2	0	0	$(x, y)(R_x, R_y)$	(xz, yz)

C_{5v}	E	$2C_5$	$2C_5^2$	$5\sigma_v$		
A_1	1	1	1	1	z	x^2+y^2, z^2
A_2	1	1	1	−1	R_z	
E_1	2	$2\cos 72°$	$2\cos 144°$	0	$(x, y)(R_x, R_y)$	(xz, yz)
E_2	2	$2\cos 144°$	$2\cos 72°$	0		(x^2-y^2, xy)

$2\cos 72° = 0{\cdot}61803 \qquad 2\cos 144° = -1{\cdot}61803$

C_{6v} (6mm)	E	$2C_6$	$2C_3$	C_2	$3\sigma_v$	$3\sigma_d$		
A_1	1	1	1	1	1	1	z	x^2+y^2, z^2
A_2	1	1	1	1	−1	−1	R_z	
B_1	1	−1	1	−1	1	−1		
B_2	1	−1	1	−1	−1	1		
E_1	2	1	−1	−2	0	0	$(x, y)(R_x, R_y)$	(xz, yz)
E_2	2	−1	−1	2	0	0		(x^2-y^2, xy)

$C_{\infty v}$	E	$2C_{\infty}^{\phi}$	...	$\infty\sigma_v$		
A_1, Σ^+	1	1	...	1	z	x^2+y^2, z^2
A_2, Σ^-	1	1	...	−1	R_z	
E_1, Π	2	$2\cos\phi$	...	0	$(x, y)(R_x, R_y)$	(xz, yz)
E_2, Δ	2	$2\cos 2\phi$	...	0		(x^2-y^2, xy)
E_3, Φ	2	$2\cos 3\phi$	...	0		
...	...	...	...	...		

T (23)	E	$4C_3$	$4C_3^2$	$3C_2$		
A	1	1	1	1		$x^2+y^2+z^2$
E	$\begin{cases}1\\1\end{cases}$	$\begin{matrix}\epsilon\\\epsilon^*\end{matrix}$	$\begin{matrix}\epsilon^*\\\epsilon\end{matrix}$	$\begin{rcases}1\\1\end{rcases}$		$(x^2-y^2, 2z^2-x^2-y^2)$
T	3	0	0	−1	$(x, y, z)(R_x, R_y, R_z)$	(xy, xz, yz)

$\epsilon = \exp(2\pi i/3)$

T_d ($\bar{4}3m$)	E	$8C_3$	$3C_2$	$6S_4$	$6\sigma_d$		
A_1	1	1	1	1	1		$x^2+y^2+z^2$
A_2	1	1	1	−1	−1		
E	2	−1	2	0	0		$(2z^2-x^2-y^2, x^2-y^2)$
T_1	3	0	−1	1	−1	(R_x, R_y, R_z)	
T_2	3	0	−1	−1	1	(x, y, z)	(xy, xz, yz)

O (432)	E	$8C_3$	$3C_2$	$6C_4$	$6C_2'$		
A_1	1	1	1	1	1		$x^2+y^2+z^2$
A_2	1	1	1	−1	−1		
E	2	−1	2	0	0		$(2z^2-x^2-y^2, x^2-y^2)$
T_1	3	0	−1	1	−1	$(x, y, z)(R_x, R_y, R_z)$	
T_2	3	0	−1	−1	1		(xy, xz, yz)

TABLE 4

τ-values for selected molecules

$CH_3CO_2H^*$	−1·37	CH_3I	7·84
CH_3CH^*O	0·20	CH_3COCH_3	7·91
C_6H_6	2·73	$CH_3^*CO_2H$	7·93
$p\text{—}C_6H_4^*(CH_3)_2$	3·05	CH_3CN	8·03
C_8H_8	4·31	C_2H_2	8·51
C_2H_4	4·68	C_6H_{12}	8·56
H_2O (0°C)	4·68	C_2H_6	9·11
H_2	5·66	H_2O(vapour)	9·26
$C_6H_5OCH_3^*$	6·27	CH_4	9·86
CH_3^*OH	6·62	$Si(CH_4)_4$	10·00 (definition)
$C_6H_5CH_2^*CH_3$	7·38	HCl	10·31
$C_6H_5CH_3^*$	7·66	HBr	14·21
CH_3^*CHO	7·80	HI	23·11

TABLE 5

Colour, frequency, and energy of light†

Colour	Wavelength (nm)	Frequency (Hz)	Wave number (cm^{-1})	Energy (eV)	Energy ($kJ\ mol^{-1}$)	Energy ($kcal\ mol^{-1}$)
infrared	1000	$3{\cdot}00 \times 10^{14}$	$1{\cdot}00 \times 10^{4}$	1·23	120	28·5
red	700	4·28	1·43	1·77	171	40·8
orange	620	4·84	1·61	2·00	193	46·1
yellow	580	5·17	1·72	2·14	206	49·3
green	530	5·66	1·89	2·34	226	53·9
blue	470	6·38	2·13	2·63	254	60·8
violet	420	7·14	2·38	2·95	285	68·1
near ultraviolet	300	$1{\cdot}00 \times 10^{15}$	3·33	4·15	400	95·7
far ultraviolet	200	1·50	5·00	6·22	600	143

† Adapted from Calvert and Pitts (1966).

TABLE 6

Dipole moments (debyes)

NH_3	1·47	$CHCl_3$	1·01
H_2O	1·85	CH_2Cl_2	1·57
HF	1·91	CH_3Cl	1·87
HCl	1·08	CH_3OH	1·71
HBr	0·80	CH_3CHO	2·72
HI	0·42	CH_3OCH_3	1·30
HCN	3·0	CH_3CH_2OH	1·68
NO_2	0·32	$C_6H_5CH_3$	0·36
N_2O	0·17	*o*-$C_6H_4(CH_3)_2$	0·62
SO_2	1·59	C_6H_5Cl	1·57
CO	0·10	C_6H_5Br	1·70
		o-$C_6H_4Cl_2$	2·25
		m-$C_6H_4Cl_2$	1·72

H
2·1
Li
1·0
Na
0·9
K
0·

TABLE 7

Pauling electronegativities

H 2·1						
Li 1·0	Be 1·5	B 2·0	C 2·6	N 3·0	O 3·4	F 4·0
Na 0·9	Mg 1·3	Al 1·6	Si 1·9	P 2·2	S 2·6	Cl 3·2
K 0·8			Ge 2·0	As 2·2	Se 2·6	Br 3·0
Rb 0·8						I 2·7
Cs 0·8						

Dipole moment (in debyes) $\mu_{AB} \sim \chi_A - \chi_B$

Ionic character (per cent) $16|\chi_A - \chi_B| + 3{\cdot}5|\chi_A - \chi_B|^2$

Covalent-ionic resonance energy (in eV) $\Delta \sim (\chi_A - \chi_B)^2$

Mulliken scale $M_A - M_B = 2{\cdot}78\,(\chi_A - \chi_B)$

$$M_A = \tfrac{1}{2}(I_A + E_A).$$

For a complete list of Pauling and Mulliken electronegativities see p. 114 of Cotton and Wilkinson (1972).

TABLE 8

Oscillator strengths and molar extinction coefficients

	f	ϵ/cm^{-1} dm^3 mol^{-1}
electric dipole allowed	1	$10^4 - 10^5$
magnetic dipole allowed	10^{-5}	$10^{-2} - 10$
electric quadrupole allowed	10^{-7}	$10^{-4} - 10^{-1}$
spin forbidden (S-T)	10^{-5}	$10^{-2} - 10$
parity forbidden	10^{-1}	10^3

Examples

		λ_{max}/nm	ϵ/cm^{-1} dm^3 mol^{-1}
$\pi^* \leftarrow \pi$	C=C	180	10 000
	C=C—C=C	220	20 000
$\pi^* \leftarrow n$	C=O	280	20
	N=N	350	100
	C=C—C=O	320	100
	N=O	660	10

TABLE 9

Hyperfine fields and spin-orbit coupling in some atoms

n	Isotope	Abundance (per cent)	Spin	$\lvert\psi_{ns}(0)\rvert^2$ (a.u.)	$\langle r^{-3}\rangle_{np}$ (a.u.)	Isotropic coupling (G)	Anisotropic coupling (G)	ζ (cm^{-1})
1	^{1}H	99·9844	$\frac{1}{2}$			508		
	^{2}H	0·0156	1			78		
2	^{6}Li	7·43	1	0·1673		39		0·2
	^{7}Li	92·57	$\frac{3}{2}$			105		
	^{9}Be	100	$\frac{3}{2}$	0·5704		130		1
	^{10}B	18·83	3	1·408	0·775	242		11
	^{11}B	81·17	$\frac{3}{2}$			725	38	
	^{13}C	1·108	$\frac{1}{2}$	2·767	1·692	1130	66	29
	^{14}N	99·635	1	4·770	3·101	552	34	76
	^{15}N	0·365	$\frac{1}{2}$			775	48	
	^{17}O	0·037	$\frac{5}{2}$	7·638	4·974	1660	104	151
	^{19}F	100	$\frac{1}{2}$	11·966	7·546	17 200	1084	270
3	^{31}P	100	$\frac{1}{2}$	5·6251	3·3187	3640	206	299
	^{33}S	0·74	$\frac{3}{2}$	7·9187	4·8140	975	56	382
	^{35}Cl	75·4	$\frac{3}{2}$	10·6435	6·7095	1680	100	586
	^{37}Cl	24·6	$\frac{3}{2}$			1395	84	
4	^{39}K	93·08	$\frac{3}{2}$			83		38
	^{41}K	6·91	$\frac{3}{2}$			45		
	^{79}Br	50·57	$\frac{3}{2}$	19·4127	11·8758	7800	456	2460
	^{81}Br	49·43	$\frac{3}{2}$			8400	564	

This Table is adapted from Atkins and Symons (1967) and Morton, Rowlands, and Whiffen (1962).

TABLE 10

Diatomic molecules

Molecule	Vibration frequency (cm^{-1})	Bond length (pm)	Rotation constant (cm^{-1})	Dissociation energy (eV)	Force-constant ($N\ m^{-1}$)
$Br_2(^{79}Br^{81}Br)$	323·2	228·3	0·08091	1·971	245·8
$^{12}C_2$	1641·35	131·17	1·6326	3·6	952·1
$^{35}Cl_2$	564·9	198·8	0·2438	2·475	328·6
$^{12}C^{16}O$	2170·21	112·81	1·9313	11·108(?)	1902
$^{19}F_2$	892·1	143·5		$<$2·75	718·6
$^{1}H_2$	4395·2	74·16	60·809	4·476	573·4
$^{2}H_2$	3118·4	74·16	30·429	4·553	576·8
^{1}HBr	2649·67	141·3	8·473	3·75	411·6
$^{1}H^{35}Cl$	2989·74	127·460	10·5909	4·430	515·7
$^{1}H^{19}F$	4138·52	91·71	20·939	$\leqslant$6·40	965·5
$^{1}H^{127}I$	2309·5	160·4	6·551	3·056	314·1
$^{127}I_2$	214·57	266·6	0·03735	1·5417	172·1
$^{14}N_2$	2359·61	109·4	2·010	9·756	2296
$^{16}O_2$	1580·361	120·739	1·44566	5·080	1177

These molecules have been selected from a longer list compiled by Herzberg (1950).

TABLE 11

Hermite polynomials and oscillator wavefunctions

Harmonic oscillator: mass m, force-constant k

Schrödinger equation

$$-(\hbar^2/2m)\mathrm{d}^2\psi(x)/\mathrm{d}x^2 + \tfrac{1}{2}kx^2\psi(x) = E\psi(x);$$

energies

$$E_\nu = (\nu + \tfrac{1}{2})\hbar\omega_0$$

$$\nu = 0, 1, 2, \ldots; \quad \omega_0 = (k/m)^{1/2};$$

wavefunctions

$$\psi_\nu(x) = \left(\frac{\alpha}{2^\nu \nu! \pi^{1/2}}\right)^{1/2} H_\nu(\zeta)\exp(-\zeta^2/2)$$

$\alpha = m\omega_0/\hbar$, $\zeta = \surd(m\omega_0/\hbar)x = \alpha^{1/2}x$, $H_\nu(\zeta)$ are Hermite polynomials.

Properties of Hermite polynomials

$H_\nu(\zeta)$ satisfies

$$H''_\nu(\zeta) - 2\zeta H'_\nu(\zeta) + 2\nu H_\nu(\zeta) = 0.$$

Rodrigues' formula

$$H_\nu(\zeta) = (-1)^\nu \exp\zeta^2 \frac{\mathrm{d}^\nu}{\mathrm{d}\zeta^\nu}\exp(-\zeta^2).$$

Recursion relations

$$H'_\nu(\zeta) = 2\nu H_{\nu-1}(\zeta)$$

$$2\zeta H_\nu(\zeta) = H_{\nu+1}(\zeta) + 2\nu H_{\nu-1}(\zeta).$$

Integrals

$$\int_{-\infty}^{\infty}\mathrm{d}\zeta\exp(-\zeta^2)H_\nu(\zeta)H_{\nu'}(\zeta) = \begin{cases} 0 & \text{if } \nu \neq \nu' \\ 2^\nu \nu! \pi^{1/2} & \text{if } \nu = \nu' \end{cases}.$$

Explicit forms

$H_0(\zeta) = 1$

$H_1(\zeta) = 2\zeta$

$H_2(\zeta) = 4\zeta^2 - 2$

$H_3(\zeta) = 8\zeta^3 - 12\zeta$

$H_4(\zeta) = 16\zeta^4 - 48\zeta^2 + 12$

$H_5(\zeta) = 32\zeta^5 - 160\zeta^3 + 120\zeta$

$H_6(\zeta) = 64\zeta^6 - 480\zeta^4 + 720\zeta^2 - 120$

$H_7(\zeta) = 128\zeta^7 - 1344\zeta^5 + 3360\zeta^3 - 1680\zeta$

$H_8(\zeta) = 256\zeta^8 - 3584\zeta^6 + 13440\zeta^4 - 13440\zeta^2 + 1680$

TABLE 12

Some Debye temperatures of solids

	θ_D/K		θ_D/K		θ_D/K
Li	344	Cu	343	Al	428
Na	156	Ag	226	Ti	420
K	91·1	Au	162	Hg	71·9
Rb	55·5				
Cs	39·5				
C (diamond)	2230				
NaCl	321				
KCl	230				
KBr	177				
CaF_2	570				

TABLE 13

Hybrid orbitals

Coordination number	Shape	Hybridization
2	linear	sp, dp
	bent	p^2, ds, d^2
3	trigonal planar	sp^2, dp^2, ds^2, d^3
	unsymmetrical planar	dsp
	trigonal pyramidal	p^3, d^2p
4	tetrahedral	sp^3, d^3s
	irregular tetrahedral	d^2sp, dp^3, d^3p
	tetragonal pyramidal	d^4
5	bipyramidal	dsp^3, d^3sp
	tetragonal pyramidal	d^2sp^2, d^4s, d^2p^3, d^4p
	pentagonal planar	d^3p^2
	pentagonal pyramidal	d^5
6	octahedral	d^2sp^3
	trigonal prismatic	d^4sp, d^5p
	trigonal antiprismatic	d^3p^3

TABLE 14

Associated Laguerre polynomials and functions

The Laguerre differential equation is

$$x(\mathrm{d}^2f/\mathrm{d}x^2) + (1-x)(\mathrm{d}f/\mathrm{d}x) + nf = 0,$$

with n a non-negative integer. Its solutions are the *Laguerre polynomials* $L_n(x)$,

$$L_n(x) = (-1)^n \sum_{r=0}^{n} \left(\frac{(-1)^r}{r!}\right) \left(\frac{n!}{(n-r)!}\right)^2 x^{n-r}$$
$$= e^x (\mathrm{d}/\mathrm{d}x)^n x^n e^{-x}.$$

The *associated Laguerre polynomials* are related to $L_n(x)$ by differentiation:

$$L_n^k(x) \equiv \mathrm{d}^k L_n(x)/\mathrm{d}x^k$$

and satisfy

$$x(\mathrm{d}^2f/\mathrm{d}x^2) + (k+1-x)(\mathrm{d}f/\mathrm{d}x) + (n-k)f = 0$$

The *associated Laguerre functions* are related to $L_n^k(x)$ as follows:

$$\mathcal{L}_n^k(x) = e^{-\frac{1}{2}x} x^{\frac{1}{2}(k-1)} L_n^k(x)$$

and satisfy the equation

$$x(\mathrm{d}^2f/\mathrm{d}x^2) + 2(\mathrm{d}f/\mathrm{d}x) + [n - \tfrac{1}{2}(k-1) - \tfrac{1}{4}x - (k^2-1)/4x]f = 0.$$

The normalized radial components of the hydrogen-atom wave functions are

$$R_{n\ell}(r) = \left\{\left(\frac{2Z}{na_0}\right)^3 \left(\frac{(n-\ell-1)!}{2n[(n+\ell)!]^3}\right)\right\}^{\frac{1}{2}} \mathcal{L}_{n+\ell}^{2\ell+1}(\rho),$$

with $\rho = 2Zr/na_0$

These wavefunctions are developed in Table 15.

TABLE 15

Hydrogen-atom wavefunctions

General form:

$$\psi_{n\ell m}(r,\theta,\phi) = R_{n\ell}(r)\, Y_{\ell m}(\theta,\phi).$$

$R_{n\ell}(r)$ are proportional to the associated Laguerre functions (see Table 14) and the $Y_{\ell m}(\theta,\phi)$ are the spherical harmonics (see Table 23).

Specific form of radial equation; $\rho = 2Zr/na_0$.

1s: $R_{10}(r) = (Z/a_0)^{3/2}\, 2e^{-\rho/2}$

2s: $R_{20}(r) = (Z/a_0)^{3/2}\,(1/2\surd 2)(2-\rho)e^{-\rho/2}$

2p: $R_{21}(r) = (Z/a_0)^{3/2}\,(1/2\surd 6)\rho e^{-\rho/2}$

3s: $R_{30}(r) = (Z/a_0)^{3/2}\,(1/9\surd 3)(6-6\rho+\rho^2)e^{-\rho/2}$

3p: $R_{31}(r) = (Z/a_0)^{3/2}\,(1/9\surd 6)(4-\rho)\rho e^{-\rho/2}$

3d: $R_{32}(r) = (Z/a_0)^{3/2}\,(1/9\surd 30)\rho^2 e^{-\rho/2}$

4s: $R_{40}(r) = (Z/a_0)^{3/2}\,(1/96)(24-36\rho+12\rho^2-\rho^3)e^{-\rho/2}$

4p: $R_{41}(r) = (Z/a_0)^{3/2}\,(1/32\surd 15)(20-10\rho+\rho^2)\rho e^{-\rho/2}$

4d: $R_{42}(r) = (Z/a_0)^{3/2}\,(1/96\surd 5)(6-\rho)\rho^2 e^{-\rho/2}$

4f: $R_{43}(r) = (Z/a_0)^{3/2}\,(1/96\surd 35)\,\rho^3 e^{-\rho/2}$

TABLE 16

The hydrogen atom

Experimental data

Spectral lines (λ/nm):

Lyman series: 121·567(α), 102·572(β), 97·253(γ), . . ., 91·15
Balmer series: 656·28(α), 486·13(β), 434·05(γ), . . ., 364·6
Paschen series: 1875·1, 1281·8, 1093·8, . . ., 820·4
Brackett series: 4051·2, 2625·1, . . ., 1458·4
Pfund series: 7451·2 . . ., 2278·8
Humphreys series: 12 368, . . ., 3281·4.

Ionization potential: $1{\cdot}097 \times 10^5$ cm^{-1}, 13·60 eV.

Electron affinity: 0·77 eV.

Lamb shift: ($2S_{1/2} - 2P_{1/2}$): 1·058 GHz.

Hyperfine interaction (Fermi contact interaction): 1420·4 MHz.

Polarizability (ground state): $4{\cdot}5\, a_0^3$, $8{\cdot}7 \times 10^{-31}$ m^3.

Diamagnetic susceptibility (ground state): $-3{\cdot}97 \times 10^{-6}$.

Covalent radius: 30 pm (0·30 Å).

Electronegativity (Pauling): 2·1.

Theoretical data

Hamiltonian for the atom: $H = -(\hbar^2/2\mu)\nabla^2 - e^2/4\pi\epsilon_0 r$.

Energy of state with quantum numbers n, ℓ, m_ℓ:

$$E_{n\ell m_\ell} = -\left(\frac{\mu e^4}{32\pi^2\epsilon_0^2\hbar^2}\right)\frac{1}{n^2} = -\frac{R_H}{n^2},$$

$n = 1, 2, 3, \ldots;\ \ell = 0, 1, 2, \ldots n-1;\ m_\ell = \ell, \ell-1, \ldots -\ell.$
μ is the reduced mass $m_e m_p/(m_e + m_p)$ and R_H is the °Rydberg constant.

Degeneracy of state with energy $-R_H/n^2$: n^2.

Wavefunctions $\psi_{n\ell m_\ell}(r, \theta, \phi) = R_{n\ell}(r) Y_{\ell m}(\theta, \phi)$.

The angular functions are the °spherical harmonics, see Table 23; the radial functions are the *associated Laguerre functions*

$$R_{n\ell}(r) \propto e^{-\rho/2}\rho^\ell\, L_{n+\ell}^{2\ell+1}(\rho)$$

where $\rho = 2Zr/na_0$ and $L(\rho)$ is an *associated Laguerre polynomial.* See Tables 14 and 15 for their analytical form and normalization.

Expectation values, etc.

Mean radius, etc:

$$\langle r^2 \rangle = (a_0^2 n^4/Z^2)\left\{1 + \tfrac{3}{2}\left(1 - \frac{3\ell(\ell+1) - 1}{3n^2}\right)\right\}$$

$$\langle r \rangle = (a_0 n^2/Z)\left\{1 + \tfrac{1}{2}\left(1 - \frac{\ell(\ell+1)}{n^2}\right)\right\}$$

$$\langle r^{-1} \rangle = Z/a_0 n^2$$

$$\langle r^{-2} \rangle = Z^2/a_0^2 n^3(\ell + \tfrac{1}{2})$$

$$\langle r^{-3} \rangle = (Z/a_0)^3/n^3\ell(\ell + \tfrac{1}{2})(\ell + 1).$$

Most probable radius (ground state): a_0 (Bohr radius, $5{\cdot}291\,771\,5 \times 10^{-11}$ m).

Spin-orbit coupling parameter:

$$\hbar^{-2}\zeta_{n\ell} = \left(\frac{Z^4e^2}{8\pi\epsilon_0 m_e^2 c^2 a_0^3}\right)\left\{\frac{1}{n^3\ell(\ell+\frac{1}{2})(\ell+1)}\right\}$$

$$= \frac{\alpha^2 Z^4 R_\infty \hbar^{-2}}{n^3\ell(\ell+\frac{1}{2})(\ell+1)},$$

α is the °fine-structure constant.
Probability at the nucleus: $|\psi_{n0}(0)|^2 = Z^3/\pi a_0^3 n^3$.

TABLE 17

Selected nuclear-spin properties

Isotope (*: radioactive)	Natural abundance (per cent)	Spin	Magnetic moment (μ_N)	Electric quadrupole moment ($e \times 10^{-24}$ cm^{-2})	n.m.r. frequency at 10 kG (MHz)
^{1}n*	–	$\frac{1}{2}$	−1·9130	–	29·165
^{1}H	99·9844	$\frac{1}{2}$	2·79270	–	42·577
^{2}H	$1{\cdot}56 \times 10^{-2}$	1	0·85738	$2{\cdot}77 \times 10^{-3}$	6·536
^{3}H*	–	$\frac{1}{2}$	2·9788	–	45·414
^{6}Li	7·43	1	0·82191	$4{\cdot}6 \times 10^{-4}$	6·265
^{7}Li	92·57	$\frac{3}{2}$	3·2560	$-4{\cdot}2 \times 10^{-2}$	16·547
^{9}Be	100	$\frac{3}{2}$	−1·1774	2×10^{-2}	5·983
^{10}B	18·83	3	1·8006	0·111	4·575
^{11}B	81·17	$\frac{3}{2}$	2·6880	$3{\cdot}55 \times 10^{-2}$	13·660
^{13}C	1·108	$\frac{1}{2}$	0·70216	–	10·705
^{14}N	99·635	1	0·40357	2×10^{-2}	3·076
^{15}N	0·365	$\frac{1}{2}$	−0·28304	–	4·315
^{17}O	$3{\cdot}7 \times 10^{-2}$	$\frac{5}{2}$	−1·8930	-4×10^{-3}	5·772
^{19}F	100	$\frac{1}{2}$	2·6273	–	40·055
^{22}Na*	–	3	1·745	?	4·434
^{23}Na	100	$\frac{3}{2}$	2·2161	0·1	11·262
^{31}P	100	$\frac{1}{2}$	1·1305	–	17·235
^{33}S	0·74	$\frac{3}{2}$	0·64274	$-6{\cdot}4 \times 10^{-2}$	3·266
^{35}S*	–	$\frac{3}{2}$	1·00	$4{\cdot}5 \times 10^{-2}$	5·08
^{35}Cl	75·4	$\frac{3}{2}$	0·82089	$-7{\cdot}97 \times 10^{-2}$	4·172
^{36}Cl*	–	2	1·2838	$-1{\cdot}68 \times 10^{-2}$	4·893
^{37}Cl	24·6	$\frac{3}{2}$	0·68329	$-6{\cdot}21 \times 10^{-2}$	3·472
^{39}K	93·08	$\frac{3}{2}$	0·39094	?	1·987
^{40}K*	$1{\cdot}19 \times 10^{-2}$	4	−1·294	?	2·470
^{41}K	6·91	$\frac{3}{2}$	0·21453	?	1·092
^{43}Ca	0·13	$\frac{7}{2}$	−1·3153	?	2·865
^{79}Br	50·57	$\frac{3}{2}$	2·0990	0·33	10·667
^{81}Br	49·43	$\frac{3}{2}$	2·2626	0·28	11·498

TABLE 18

First and second ionization potentials (in eV) of some elements

H 13·599 —							He 24·588 54·418
Li 5·392 75·641	Be 9·323 18·211	B 8·298 25·156	C 11·260 24·383	N 14·53 29·602	O 13·618 35·118	F 17·423 34·98	Ne 21·565 40·964
Na 5·139 47·29	Mg 7·646 15·035	Al 5·986 18·828	Si 8·152 16·346	P 10·487 19·72	S 10·360 23·4	Cl 12·967 23·80	Ar 15·760 27·62
K 4·341 31·81	Ca 6·113 11·872					Br 11·814 21·6	Kr 14·000 24·56

TABLE 19

Some laser systems

Gas lasers	λ/nm	Power	Mode and duration of pulse
He-Ne	632·8	100 mW	CW
	1084	10 mW	CW
	1152	20 mW	CW
	3391	10 mW	CW
Ne	540·1	10 kW	pulsed (3 ns)
Ar	488·0	10 W	CW
	514·5	500 mW	CW
	457·9	40 mW	CW
	465·8	–	CW
	472·7	–	CW
	476·5	100 mW	CW
	496·5	100 mW	CW
Kr	647·1	5 W	CW
	568·2	50 mW	CW
	520·8	50 mW	CW
	476·2	25 mW	CW
Xe	170·0	–	
H_2	116·0	–	
N_2	337·1	0·2 MW	pulsed (10 ns)
CO_2	10600 (10·6 μm)	1 kW	CW
Solid-state lasers			
Ruby	694·3	400 kW	conventional pulsed (1 ms)
		16 GW	Q-switched (10-20 ns)
		16 GW	mode-locked (10 ps)
Nd^{3+}:YAG	10600	300 W	CW
		10 MW	Q-switched (10 ns)
		10 MW	mode-locked (1 ps)
GaAs	905·0	60 W	pulsed (200 ns)
	845·0	1 W	pulsed (2 μs)
InAs	3150	50 mW	pulsed (2 ns)

TABLE 20

Maxwell equations

Basic definitions

E : electric-field intensity ($V\ m^{-1}$)
H : magnetic-field intensity ($A\ m^{-1}$)
D : electric displacement ($C\ m^{-2}$)
B : magnetic induction, flux density (T or $Wb\ m^{-2}$)
ρ : charge density ($C\ m^{-3}$)
J : current density ($A\ m^{-2}$).

D and **B** may be related to **E** and **H** respectively, through the polarization **P** and magnetization **M**:

$$\mathbf{D} = \epsilon_0\mathbf{E} + \mathbf{P} \quad \mathbf{B} = \mu_0\mathbf{H} + \mu_0\mathbf{M} \quad (\mu_0\epsilon_0 = c^{-2}).$$

Maxwell equations

$$\nabla.\mathbf{D} = \rho$$
$$\nabla.\mathbf{B} = 0$$
$$\nabla\wedge\mathbf{E} = -\partial\mathbf{B}/\partial t$$
$$\nabla\wedge\mathbf{H} = \mathbf{J} + \partial\mathbf{D}/\partial t.$$

Potentials

A : vector potential, ϕ : scalar potential

$$\mathbf{B} = \nabla\wedge\mathbf{A}$$
$$\mathbf{E} = -\partial\mathbf{A}/\partial t - \nabla\phi.$$

Gauge transformation: if $\mathbf{A}\rightarrow\mathbf{A} + \nabla\chi$ and $\phi\rightarrow\phi - \partial\chi/\partial t$, where χ is any differentiable function, **E** and **B** are unchanged. When χ is chosen so that $\nabla.\mathbf{A} = 0$ we are in the *Coulomb gauge* and if $\nabla.\mathbf{A} + (1/c^2)(\partial\phi/\partial t) = 0$ we are in the *Lorentz gauge.*

TABLE 21

Slater atomic orbitals

Values of $Z_{eff} = Z - \sigma$ for s, p-orbitals of the neutral first- and second-row atoms.

	H							He
1s	1							1·70
	Li	Be	B	C	N	O	F	Ne
1s	2·70	3·70	4·70	5·70	6·70	7·70	8·70	9·70
2s, 2p	1·30	1·95	2·60	3·25	3·90	4·55	5·20	5·85
	Na	Mg	Al	Si	P	S	Cl	Ar
1s	10·70	11·70	12·70	13·70	14·70	15·70	16·70	17·70
2s, 2p	6·85	7·85	8·85	9·85	10·85	11·85	12·85	13·85
3s, 3p	2·20	2·85	3·50	4·15	4·80	5·45	6·10	6·75

TABLE 22

Spherical harmonics and Legendre functions

The *spherical harmonics* $Y_{\ell m}(\theta, \phi)$ satisfy

$$\Lambda^2 Y_{\ell m} = -\ell(\ell+1)Y_{\ell m} \qquad \begin{array}{l} \ell = 0, 1, 2, \ldots \\ m = \ell, \ell-1, \ldots -\ell . \end{array}$$

Factorization

$$Y_{\ell m}(\theta, \phi) = \Theta_{\ell m}(\theta)\Phi_m(\phi)$$

$$\Phi_m(\phi) = \frac{1}{\surd(2\pi)} e^{im\phi}$$

$$\Theta_{\ell m}(\theta) = (-1)^m \left\{\frac{(2\ell+1)(\ell-m)!}{2(\ell+m)!}\right\}^{1/2} P_\ell^m(\cos\theta) .$$

P_ℓ^m are the *associated Legendre functions:*

$$P_\ell^m(x) = [(1-x^2)^{m/2}/2^\ell \ell!]\left(\frac{d^{\ell+m}}{dx^{\ell+m}}\right)(x^2-1)^\ell$$

$$= (1-x^2)^{m/2}\frac{d^m}{dx^m} P_\ell(x) .$$

P_ℓ are the *Legendre functions:*

$$P_\ell(x) = (1/2^\ell \ell!)\left(\frac{d^\ell}{dx^\ell}\right)(x^2-1)^\ell .$$

Properties of $Y_{\ell m}$

symmetry:

$$Y_{\ell m}(\pi-\theta, \phi+\pi) = (-1)^\ell Y_{\ell m}(\theta, \phi)$$

$$Y^*_{\ell m}(\theta, \phi) = (-1)^m Y_{\ell,-m}(\theta, \phi)$$

orthonormality:

$$\int_0^\pi d\theta \sin\theta \int_0^{2\pi} d\phi Y^*_{\ell m}(\theta, \phi) Y_{\ell' m'}(\theta, \phi) = \delta_{\ell\ell'}\delta_{mm'}$$

($\delta_{\ell\ell'}\delta_{mm'} = 1$ if both $\ell = \ell'$ and $m = m'$, and 0 otherwise).

Recursion relations for P_ℓ^m:

$$(\ell-m+1)P^m_{\ell+1}(x) - (2\ell+1)xP_\ell^m(x) + (\ell+m)P^m_{\ell-1}(x) = 0$$

$$xP_\ell^m(x) - (\ell-m+1)(1-x^2)^{1/2}P_\ell^{m-1}(x) - P^m_{\ell-1}(x) = 0$$

$$P^m_{\ell+1}(x) - xP_\ell^m(x) - (\ell+m)(1-x^2)^{1/2}P_\ell^{m-1}(x) = 0$$

$$(\ell-m+1)P^m_{\ell+1}(x) + (1-x^2)^{1/2}P_\ell^{m+1}(x) -$$
$$-(\ell+m+1)xP_\ell^m(x) = 0$$

$$(1-x^2)^{1/2}P_\ell^{m+1}(x) - 2mxP_\ell^m(x) +$$
$$+(\ell+m)(\ell-m+1)(1-x^2)^{1/2}P_\ell^{m-1}(x) = 0$$

$$(1-x^2)^{1/2}\left(\frac{d}{dx}\right)P_\ell^m(x) = (\ell+1)xP_\ell^m(x) - (\ell-m+1)P^m_{\ell+1}(x)$$
$$= (\ell+m)P^m_{\ell-1}(x) - \ell xP_\ell^m(x) .$$

Integrals of P_ℓ^m:

$$\int_{-1}^1 dx P_\ell^m(x)P_{\ell'}^m(x) = 2\delta_{\ell\ell'}[(\ell+m)!/(2\ell+1)(\ell-m)!]$$

$$\int_{-1}^1 dx \left\{\frac{P_\ell^m(x)P_\ell^m(x)}{(1-x^2)}\right\} = [(\ell+m)!/m(\ell-m)!] .$$

TABLE 23

Cartesian and polar forms of spherical harmonics $Y_{\ell m}$

ℓ	m	Cartesian form	Polar form
0	0	$1/2\pi^{1/2}$	$1/2\pi^{1/2}$
1	0	$\frac{1}{2}(3/\pi)^{1/2}(z/r)$	$\frac{1}{2}(3/\pi)^{1/2}\cos\theta$
	±1	$\mp\frac{1}{2}(3/2\pi)^{1/2}(x \pm iy)/r$	$\mp\frac{1}{2}(3/2\pi)^{1/2}\sin\theta\, e^{\pm i\phi}$
2	0	$\frac{1}{4}(5/\pi)^{1/2}(2z^2 - x^2 - y^2)/r^2$	$\frac{1}{4}(5/\pi)^{1/2}(3\cos^2\theta - 1)$
	±1	$\mp\frac{1}{2}(15/2\pi)^{1/2} z(x \pm iy)/r^2$	$\mp\frac{1}{2}(15/2\pi)^{1/2}\cos\theta\,\sin\theta\, e^{\pm i\phi}$
	±2	$\frac{1}{4}(15/2\pi)^{1/2}(x \pm iy)^2/r^2$	$\frac{1}{4}(15/2\pi)^{1/2}\sin^2\theta\, e^{\pm 2i\phi}$
3	0	$\frac{1}{4}(7/\pi)^{1/2} z(2z^2 - 3x^2 - 3y^2)/r^3$	$\frac{1}{4}(7/\pi)^{1/2}(2\cos^3\theta - 3\cos\theta\,\sin^2\theta)$
	±1	$\mp\frac{1}{8}(21/\pi)^{1/2}(x \pm iy)(4z^2 - x^2 - y^2)/r^3$	$\mp\frac{1}{8}(21/\pi)^{1/2}(4\cos^2\theta\,\sin\theta - \sin^3\theta)e^{\pm i\phi}$
	±2	$\frac{1}{4}(105/2\pi)^{1/2} z(x \pm iy)^2/r^3$	$\frac{1}{4}(105/2\pi)^{1/2}\cos\theta\,\sin^2\theta\, e^{\pm 2i\phi}$
	±3	$\mp\frac{1}{8}(35/\pi)^{1/2}(x \pm iy)^3/r^3$	$\mp\frac{1}{8}(35/\pi)^{1/2}\sin^3\theta\, e^{\pm 3i\phi}$

TABLE 24

Vibration frequencies

CH stretch	2850–2960 cm^{-1}
CH bend	1340–1465
C—C bend and stretch	700–1250
C=C stretch	1620–1680
C≡C stretch	2100–2260
O—H stretch	3590–3650
H—bonds	3200–3570
C=O stretch	1640–1780
N—H stretch	3200–3500
C≡N stretch	2215–2275
C=N stretch	1480–1690
N=N stretch	1575–1630
P—H stretch	2350–2440
C—F stretch	1000–1400
C—Cl stretch	600–800
C—Br stretch	500–600
C—I stretch	~500
CO_3^{2-}	1410–1450
NO_3^-	1350–1420
NO_2^-	1230–1250
SO_4^{2-}	1080–1130
silicates	900–1100

See Bellamy (1958, 1968) for a thorough analysis.

TABLE 25

Photoelectric (and thermionic) work functions (eV)

Li		Be	
2·42		3·9	
		(3·67)	
Na		Mg	
2·3		3·7	
K	Cu	Ca	Zn
2·25	4·8	3·2	4·3
	(4·5)	(2·2)	
Rb	Ag		Cd
2·09	4·3		4·1
	(4·3)		
Cs	Au		
2·14	5·4		
(1·86)	(4·3)		

TABLE 26

Covalent radii

Element	R/pm
H	30
C—	77
C=	67
C≡	60
C— (benzene)	69·5
O—	66
O=	57
N— (amino)	70
N— (nitrate)	70
N= (nitrate)	65
S—	104
S= (sulphate)	95
Cl—	99
Br—	114
I—	133

TABLE 27

Vector properties

We deal with the vectors **F** and **G**, where

$$\mathbf{F} = F_x\mathbf{i} + F_y\mathbf{j} + F_z\mathbf{k}$$

$$\mathbf{G} = G_x\mathbf{i} + G_y\mathbf{j} + G_z\mathbf{k}\,.$$

Scalar product

$$\mathbf{F.G} = F_xG_x + F_yG_y + F_zG_z\,.$$

Vector product

$$\mathbf{F} \wedge \mathbf{G} = \begin{vmatrix} \mathbf{i} & \mathbf{j} & \mathbf{k} \\ F_x & F_y & F_z \\ G_x & G_y & G_z \end{vmatrix} = -\mathbf{G} \wedge \mathbf{F}\,.$$

Triple and quadruple products

$$\mathbf{F.(G \wedge H) = G.(H \wedge F) = H.(F \wedge G) = (F \wedge G).H}$$

$$\mathbf{F \wedge (G \wedge H) = G(F.H) - H(F.G)}$$

$$\mathbf{(F \wedge G)\,.\,(H \wedge I) = (F.H)(G.I) - (F.I)(G.H)}\,.$$

gradient

$$\text{grad } U = \nabla U = \left(\frac{\partial U}{\partial x}\right)\mathbf{i} + \left(\frac{\partial U}{\partial y}\right)\mathbf{j} + \left(\frac{\partial U}{\partial z}\right)\mathbf{k}, \text{ a vector.}$$

divergence

$$\text{div } \mathbf{F} = \nabla.\mathbf{F} = \left(\frac{\partial F_x}{\partial x}\right) + \left(\frac{\partial F_y}{\partial y}\right) + \left(\frac{\partial F_z}{\partial z}\right), \quad \text{a scalar.}$$

curl

$$\text{curl } \mathbf{F} = \nabla \wedge \mathbf{F} = \begin{vmatrix} \mathbf{i} & \mathbf{j} & \mathbf{k} \\ \partial/\partial x & \partial/\partial y & \partial/\partial z \\ F_x & F_y & F_z \end{vmatrix}, \quad \text{a vector.}$$

differentiation of products:

$$\nabla.(U\mathbf{F}) = U\nabla.\mathbf{F} + \mathbf{F}.\nabla U$$

$$\nabla \wedge (U\mathbf{F}) = U(\nabla \wedge \mathbf{F}) + (\nabla U) \wedge \mathbf{F}$$

$$\nabla.(\mathbf{F} \wedge \mathbf{G}) = \mathbf{G}.(\nabla \wedge \mathbf{F}) - \mathbf{F}.(\nabla \wedge \mathbf{G})$$

$$\nabla \wedge (\nabla \wedge \mathbf{F}) = \nabla(\nabla.\mathbf{F}) - \nabla^2\mathbf{F}$$

$$\nabla \wedge (\mathbf{F} \wedge \mathbf{G}) = \mathbf{F}(\nabla.\mathbf{G}) - (\nabla.\mathbf{F})\mathbf{G} + (\mathbf{G}.\nabla)\mathbf{F} - (\mathbf{F}.\nabla)\mathbf{G}$$

$$\nabla(\mathbf{F}.\mathbf{G}) = (\mathbf{F}.\nabla)\mathbf{G} + (\mathbf{G}.\nabla)\mathbf{F} + \mathbf{F} \wedge (\nabla \wedge \mathbf{G}) + \mathbf{G} \wedge (\nabla \wedge \mathbf{F})$$

$$\nabla^2 U = \nabla.\nabla U$$

$$\nabla \wedge (\nabla U) = 0\,.$$

Bibliography

MQM refers to
ATKINS, P.W. (1970). *Molecular quantum mechanics.* Clarendon Press, Oxford.

Volumes in the Oxford Chemistry Series (denoted OCS) which are now available and which elaborate many of the points in the text, are as follows:

1. McLAUCHLAN, K.A. (1972). *Magnetic resonance.*
2. ROBBINS, J. (1972). *Ions in solution (2): an introduction to electrochemistry.*
3. PUDDEPHATT, R.J. (1972). *The periodic table of the elements.*
4. JACKSON, R.A. (1972). *Mechanism: an introduction to the study of organic reactions.*
5. WHITTAKER, D. (1973). *Stereochemistry and mechanism.*
6. HUGHES, G. (1973). *Radiation chemistry.*
7. PASS, G. (1973). *Ions in solution (3): inorganic properties.*
8. SMITH, E.B. (1973). *Basic chemical thermodynamics.*
9. COULSON, C.A. (1973). *The shape and structure of molecules.*
10. WORMALD, J. (1973). *Diffraction methods.*
11. SHORTER, J. (1973). *Correlation analysis in organic chemistry: an introduction to linear free-energy relationships.*
12. STERN, E.S. (Ed.) (1973). *The chemist in industry (1): fine chemicals for polymers.*
13. EARNSHAW, A. and HARRINGTON, T.J. (1973). *The chemistry of the transition elements.*
14. ALBERY, W.J. (1974). *Electrode kinetics.*
16. FYFE, W.S. (1974). *Geochemistry.*
17. STERN, E.S. (Ed.) (1974). *The chemist in industry (2): human health and plant protection.*
18. BOND, G.C. (1974). *Heterogeneous catalysis: principles and applications.*
19. GASSER, R.P.H. and RICHARDS, W.G. (1974). *Entropy and energy levels.*
20. SPEDDING, D.J. (1974). *Air pollution.*
21. ATKINS, P.W. (1974). *Quanta: a handbook of concepts.*
22. PILLING, M.J. (1974). *Reaction kinetics.*

Volumes in the Oxford Physics Series (OPS) now available are

1. ROBINSON, F.N.H. (1973). *Electromagnetism.*
2. LANCASTER, G. (1973). *D.c. and a.c. circuits.*
3. INGRAM, D.J.E. (1973). *Radiation and quantum physics.*
5. JENNINGS, B.R. and MORRIS, V.J. (1974). *Atoms in contact.*

General References

ABRAGAM, A. (1961). *The principles of nuclear magnetism.* Clarendon Press, Oxford.
– and BLEANEY, B. (1970). *Electron paramagnetic resonance of transition ions.* Clarendon Press, Oxford.
ABRAHAM, R.J. (1971). *The analysis of high resolution n.m.r. spectra.* Elsevier, Amsterdam.
ABRAMOWITZ, M. and STEGUN, I.A. (1965). *Handbook of mathematical functions.* Dover, New York.
ADAMS, D.M. (1967). *Metal-ligand and related vibrations.* Arnold, London.
– (1971). Inorganic vibrational spectroscopy, *A. Rep. chem. Soc.,* **47.**
AKHIEZER, A.I. and BERESTETSKII, V.B. (1965). *Quantum electrodynamics.* Wiley-Interscience, New York.
ALDER, R.W., BAKER, R., and BROWN, J.M. (1971). *Mechanism in organic chemistry.* Wiley, London.
ALLEN, H.C. and CROSS, P.C. (1963). *Molecular vib-rotors.* Wiley, New York.
ALTMANN, S.L. (1962). Group theory. In *Quantum theory* (Ed. D.R. Bates) Vol. 2 p. 87.
– (1970). *Band theory of metals.* Pergamon Press, Oxford.
ANDRADE e SILVA, J. and LOCHAK, G. (1969). *Quanta.* Weidenfeld and Nicholson, London.
ATKINS, P.W. and SYMONS, M.C.R. (1967). *The structure of inorganic radicals.* Elsevier, Amsterdam.
– CHILD, M.S., and PHILLIPS, C.S.G. (1970). *Tables for group theory.* Clarendon Press, Oxford.
– (1973). *Diagrammatic perturbation theory.* University of Oxford, Department of Theoretical Chemistry, Lecture Note Series.
AYRES, F. (1962). *Theory and problems of matrices.* (Schaum Outline series) McGraw-Hill, New York.
AYSCOUGH, P.B. (1967). *Electron spin resonance in chemistry.* Methuen, London.
BADER, R.J. (1972). *Molecular geometry.* Van Nostrand, New York.
BAKER, A.D. and BETTERIDGE, D. (1972). *Photoelectron spectroscopy: chemical and analytical aspects.* Pergamon Press, Oxford.
BAKER, J.W. (1952). *Hyperconjugation.* Clarendon Press, Oxford.
– (1958) *Conference on hyperconjugation.* Pergamon Press, Oxford. (see also (1959) *Tetrahedron*, 5, 105 et seq.)
BALLANTINE, L.E. (1970). The statistical interpretation of quantum mechanics, *Rev. mod. Phys.* **42,** 358.
BALLHAUSEN, C.J. (1962). *Introduction to ligand field theory.* McGraw-Hill, New York.
BANDER, M. and ITZYKSON, C. (1966). Group theory and the hydrogen atom, *Rev. mod. Phys.* **38,** 330 (Part I), 346 (Part II).
BARROW, G.M. (1962). *Introduction to molecular spectroscopy.* McGraw-Hill, New York.
BELLAMY, L.J. (1958). *The infrared spectra of complex molecules.* Methuen, London.
– (1968). *Advances in infrared group frequencies.* Methuen, London.
BERESTETSKII, V.B. LIFSHITZ, E.M. and PITAEVSKII, L.P. (1971). *Relativistic quantum theory.* Pergamon Press, Oxford.

BERGMANN, E.D. and PULLMAN, B. (1971). *Aromaticity, pseudoaromaticity, anti-aromaticity.* Israel Academy of Sciences, Jerusalem.

BERRY, R.S. (1966). Atomic orbitals, *J. chem. Educ.* **43**, 283.

BETHE, H.A. and SALPETRE, E.E. (1957) *Quantum mechanics of one and two electron atoms.* Academic Press, New York.

BIEDENHARN, L.C. and VAN DAM, H. (Eds.) (1965). *Quantum theory of angular momentum.* Academic Press, New York.

BISHOP, D. (1973). *Group theory and chemistry.* Clarendon Press, Oxford.

BJORKEN, J.D. and DRELL, S.D. (1964). *Relativistic quantum mechanics.* McGraw-Hill, New York.

— (1965). *Relativisitic quantum fields.* McGraw-Hill, New York.

BOGOLIUBOV, N.N. and SHIRKOV, D.V. (1959). *Introduction to the theory of quantized fields.* Interscience, New York.

BOHM, D. (1951) *Quantum theory.* Prentice-Hall, Englewood Cliffs, New Jersey.

BOLTON, J.R., CARRINGTON, A., and McLACHLAN, A.D. (1962). Electron spin resonance studies of hyperconjugation in aromatic ions, *Mol. Phys.* **5**, 31.

BORN, M. (1970). *The Born-Einstein letters.* Walker, New York.

— and BEIM, W. (1968). Dualism in quantum theory, *Phys. Today,* August, p. 51.

— HEISENBERG, W., and JORDAN, P. (1926). Zur Quantenmechanik, *Z. Phys.* **35**, 557.

— JORDAN, P. (1925). Zur Quantenmechanik, *Z. Phys.* **34**, 858.

— and OPPENHEIMER, J.R. (1927). Zur Quantentheorie der Molekülen, *Annln Phys.* **84**, 457 (Sec. 1—2, Appendix 2).

— and WOLF, E. (1970). *Principles of optics,* Pergamon Press, Oxford.

BOWEN, E.J. (1946). *Chemical aspects of light.* Clarendon Press, Oxford.

BOYS, S.F. (1950). Electronic wavefunctions. I. A general method of calculation for the stationary states of any molecular system. *Proc. R. Soc.* **A200**, 542.

— (1960). Construction of some molecular orbitals to be approximately invariant for changes from one molecule to another. *Rev. mod. Phys.* **32**, 296.

BRADLEY, C.J. and CRACKNELL, A.P. (1972). *The mathematical theory of symmetry in solids.* Clarendon Press, Oxford.

BRAND, J.C.D. and SPEAKMAN, J.C. (1960). *Molecular structure: the physical approach.* Arnold, London.

BRESLOW, R. (1972). The nature of aromatic molecules, *Scient. Am.* **227**, 32.

BRIEGLEB, G. (1964). Electron affinity of organic molecules, *Angew. Chem., Int. Ed. Engl.* **3**, 617.

BRILLOUIN, L. (1933). La méthode du champ self-consistent, *Actualités sci. indust.* **71**.

— (1934). Les champs self-consistent de Hartree et de Fock, *Actualités sci. indust.* **159**.

BRINK, D.M. and SATCHLER, G.R. (1968). *Angular momentum.* Clarendon Press, Oxford.

BUCKINGHAM, A.D. (1960). Optical, electrical, and magnetic properties of molecules, *A. Rep. chem. Soc.* **57**, 53.

— (1965). Experiments with oriented molecules, *Chem. Brit.* **1**, 54.

— and ORR, B.J. (1967). Molecular hyperpolarizabilities, *Q. Rev. chem. Soc.* **21**, 195.

— and STEPHENS, P.J. (1966). Magnetic optical activity, *Adv. chem. phys.* **17**, 399.

BURHOP, E.H.S. (1952). *The Auger effect and other radiationless transitions.* Cambridge University Press.

— and ASAAD, W.N. (1972). The Auger effect. *Adv. at. mol. Phys.* **8**, 164.

CALDWELL, D.J. and EYRING, H. (1971). *The theory of optical activity.* Wiley-Interscience, New York.

CALVERT, J.G. and PITTS, J.N. (1966). *Photochemistry.* Wiley, New York.

CANDLER, C. (1964). *Atomic spectra and the vector model.* Hilger and Watts, London.

CARRINGTON, A. and McLACHLAN, A.D. (1967). *Introduction to magnetic resonance.* Harper and Row, New York.

CARRUTHERS, P. and NIETO, M.M. (1968). Phase and angle variables in quantum mechanics, *Rev. mod. Phys.* **40**, 411.

CHIHARA, H. and NAKAMURA, N. (1972). Nuclear quadrupole resonance spectroscopy, *MTP int. Rev. Sci., Phys. Chem. Ser. 1,* **4**, 125.

COLPA, J.P. and ISLIP, M.F.J. (1973). Hund's rule and the *Z* expansion for the energy, electron repulsion, and electron-nuclear attraction, *Mol. Phys.* **25**, 701.

COMPTON, A.H. (1923). A quantum theory of the scattering of X-rays by light elements, *Phys. Rev.* **21**, 483.

CONDON, E.U. (1928). Nuclear motions associated with electron transitions in diatomic molecules, *Phys. Rev.* **32**, 858.

— and SHORTLEY, G.H. (1963). *The theory of atomic spectra.* Cambridge University Press.

CORIO, P. (1966). *The structure of high resolution n.m.r. spectra.* Academic Press, New York.

CORSON, D. and LORRAIN, P. (1970). *Introduction to electromagnetic fields and waves.* Freeman, San Francisco.

COTTON, F.A. (1963). *Chemical applications of group theory.* Wiley, New York.

CHU, B. (1967). *Molecular forces.* Wiley-Interscience, New York.

CLEMENTI, E. (1965). *Ab initio* computations in atoms and molecules, *IBM Jl.* Res. Dev. **9**, 2.

COTTON, F.A. and WILKINSON, G. (1972). *Advanced inorganic chemistry.* Interscience, New York.

COULSON, C.A. (1939). The electronic structure of some polymers and aromatic molecules. VII. Bonds of fractional order by the molecular orbital method, *Proc. R. Soc.* **A169**, 413.

— (1959). Molecular geometry and steric deformation. In *Kekulé symposium* (IUPAC and the Chemical Society), p. 49. Butterworths, London.

— (1961). *Valence.* Clarendon Press, Oxford.

— (1965). The use of commutator relationships in determining Schrödinger wave functions, *Q. Jl Math.* **16**, 279.

— (1970). π-bonds. In *Physical chemistry, an advanced treatise* (Eds. H. Eyring, D. Henderson, and W. Jost), Vol. 5, p. 369. Academic Press, New York.

— and DEB, B.M. (1971). On the theoretical foundation of Walsh's rules of molecular geometry in terms of the Hellmann-Feynman theorem, *Int. J. Quantum Chem.* **5**, 411.

— and RUSHBROOKE, G.S. (1940). Note on the method of molecular

orbitals, *Proc. Camb. Phil. Soc.* **36**, 193.
– and STREITWEISER, A. (1965). *Dictionary of π-electron calculations*. Pergamon Press, Oxford.
CRABBÉ, P. (1965). *Optical rotatory dispersion and circular dichroism in organic chemistry*. Holden-Day, San Francisco.
CRAIG, D.P. and WALMSLEY, S.H. (1968). *Excitons in molecular crystals*. Benjamin, New York.
CURTISS, C.F. (1967). Real gases. In *Physical chemistry, an advanced treatise* (Eds. H. Eyring, D. Henderson, and W. Jost), Vol. 2, p. 286. Academic Press, New York.
DAS, T.P. and HAHN, E.L. (1958). Nuclear quadrupole resonance spectroscopy, *Solid State Phys.* Suppl. 1.
DAUDEL, R., LEFEBVRE, R., and MOSER, C. (1959). *Quantum chemistry; methods and applications*. Interscience, New York.
DAVIDSON, N. (1962). *Statistical mechanics*. McGraw-Hill, New York.
DAVIES, D.W. (1967). *The theory of the electric and magnetic properties of molecules*. Wiley, London.
DAVYDOV, A.S. (1962). *Theory of molecular excitons*. McGraw-Hill, New York.
– (1965). *Quantum mechanics*. Pergamon Press, Oxford.
DEB, B.M. (1973). The force concept in chemistry, *Rev. mod. Phys.* **45**, 22.
DEKKER, A.J. (1960). *Solid state physics*. Macmillan, London.
DEWAR, M.J.S. (1969). *The molecular orbital theory of organic chemistry*. McGraw-Hill, New York.
DIRAC, P.A.M. (1958). *The principles of quantum mechanics*. Clarendon Press, Oxford.
DIXON, R.N. (1965). *Spectroscopy and structure*. Methuen, London.
DOGGETT, G. (1972). *The electronic structure of molecules: theory and applications to inorganic molecules*. Pergamon Press, Oxford.
DUNCAN, A.B.F. (1971). *Rydberg series in atoms and molecules*. Academic Press, New York.
DYMOND, J.H. and SMITH, E.B. (1969). *The virial coefficients of gases; a critical compilation*. Clarendon Press, Oxford.
EARNSHAW, A. (1968). *Introduction to magnetochemistry*. Academic Press, New York.
EDMISTON, C. and RUEDENBERG, K. (1963). Localized atomic and molecular orbitals, *Rev. mod. Phys.* **35**, 457.
–– (1965). Localized atomic and molecular orbitals. II, *J. chem. Phys.* **43**, 597.
EDMONDS, A.R. (1957). *Angular momentum in quantum mechanics*. Princeton University Press.
EINSTEIN, A. and EHRENFEST, P. (1922). Quantentheoritishe Bemerkungen zum Experiment von Stern und Gerlach, *Z. Phys.* **11**, 31.
ELLIOTT, G. (1973). Liquid crystals for electro-optical displays, *Chem. Brit.* **9**, 213.
EMSLEY, J.W., FEENEY, J., and SUTCLIFFE, L.H. (1965). *High resolution nuclear magnetic resonance spectroscopy*. Pergamon Press, Oxford.
ENGLEFIELD, M.J. (1972). *Group theory and the Coulomb problem*. Wiley-Interscience, New York.
ENGLMAN, R. (1972). *The Jahn-Teller effect in molecules and crystals*. Wiley, New York.
EYRING, H., WALTER, J., and KIMBALL, G.E. (1944). *Quantum chemistry*. Wiley, New York.
FANO, U. (1957). Description of states in quantum mechanics by density matrix and operator techniques, *Rev. mod. Phys.* **29**, 74.
– and RACAH, G. (1959). *Irreducible tensorial sets*. Academic Press, New York.
FEINBERG, M.J., RUEDENBERG, K., and MEHLER, E.L. (1970). The origin of binding and antibinding in the hydrogen molecule-ion, *Adv. Quantum Chem.* 5, 21.
FEYNMAN R.P. (1939). Forces in molecules, *Phys. Rev.* **56**, 340.
– (1962a). *Quantum electrodynamics*. Addison-Wesley-Benjamin, Reading, Mass.
– (1962b). *The theory of fundamental processes*. Addison-Wesley-Benjamin, Reading, Mass.
– and HIBBS, A.R. (1965). *Quantum mechanics and path integrals*. McGraw-Hill, New York.
– LEIGHTON, R.B., and SANDS, M. (1963). *Lectures in physics*. Freeman, San Francisco.
FIGGIS, B.N. (1966). *Introduction to ligand fields*. Wiley, New York.
FOCK, V. (1935). Zur Theorie des Wasserstoffatoms, *Z. Phys.* **98**, 145.
FOWLER, R.H. (1936). *Statistical mechanics*. Cambridge University Press.
– and GUGGENHEIM, E.A. (1965). *Statistical thermodynamics*. Cambridge University Press.
FRANCK, J. (1925). Elementary processes of photochemical reactions, *Trans. Faraday Soc.* **21**, 536.
– and HERTZ, G. (1914). Über Zusammenstoβe zwischen Elektronen und den Molekülen des Quecksilberdampfes und die Ionisierungspannung desselben, *Verh. dt. phys. Ges.* **16**, 457.
–– (1916). Über Kinetik von Elekronen und Ionen in Gasen, *Phys. Z.* **17**, 409.
–– (1919). Die Bestätigung der Bohrschem Atomtheorie in optischen Spektrum durch Untersuchungen der inelastischem Zusammenstoβe langsamer Elektronen mit Gasmolekülen, *Phys. Z.* **20**, 132.
FREDERICQ, E. and HOUSSIER, C. (1973). *Electric dichroism and electric birefringence*. Clarendon Press, Oxford.
FREEMAN, A.J. and FRANKEL, R.B. (1967). *Hyperfine interactions*. Academic Press, New York.

GALINDO A. and SANCHEZ DEL RIO, C. (1961). Intrinsic magnetic moment as a nonrelativistic phenomenon, *Am. J. Phys.* **29**, 582.
GANS, P. (1971). *Vibrating molecules*. Chapman and Hall, London.
GAYDON, A.G. (1968). *Dissociation energies and spectra of diatomic molecules*. Chapman and Hall, London.
GILL, G.B. (1970). The Woodward-Hoffmann orbital symmetry rules. In *Essays in chemistry* (Eds. J.N. Bradley, R.D. Gillard, and R.F. Hudson), Vol. 1, p. 43. Academic Press, New York and London.
– and WILLIS, M.R. (1969). *The conservation of orbital symmetry*. Methuen, London.
GILLESPIE, R.J. (1972). *Molecular geometry*. Van Nostrand, New York.
GILSON, T.R. and HENDRA, P.J. (1970). *Laser-Raman spectroscopy*. Wiley, New York.
GLAUBER, R.J. (Ed.) (1969). *Quantum electronics*. Academic Press, New York.

GOLDBERGER, M.L. and WATSON, K.M. (1964). *Collision theory.* Wiley, New York.

GOL'DMAN, I.I. and KRIVCHENKOV, V.D. (1961). *Problems in quantum mechanics.* Pergamon Press, Oxford.

GOLDSTEIN, H. (1950). *Classical mechanics.* Addison-Wesley, Reading, Mass.

GRANDY, W.T. (1970). *Introduction to electrodynamics and radiation.* Academic Press, New York.

GRAY, D.E. (Ed.) (1972). *American Institute of Physics handbook.* McGraw-Hill, New York.

GREEN, H.S. (1965). *Matrix mechanics.* Noordhoff, Groningen.

GRIFFITH, J.S. (1964). *The theory of transition metal ions.* Cambridge University Press.

HALL, G.G. and AMOS, A.T. (1969). Pi electron theory of the spectra of conjugated molecules. In *Physical chemistry, an advanced treatise* (Eds. H. Eyring, D. Henderson, and W. Jost), Vol. 3, p. 447. Academic Press, New York.

HAMEKA, H.F. (1965). *Advanced quantum chemistry.* Addison-Wesley, Reading, Mass.

HAMERMESH, M. (1962). *Group theory and its application to physical problems.* Addison-Wesley, Reading, Mass.

HARMONY, M.D. (1972). Quantum mechanical tunnelling in chemistry, *Chem. Soc. Rev.* **1**, 211.

HARTREE, D.R. (1957). *The calculation of atomic structures.* Wiley, New York and Chapman and Hall, London.

HAUGHT, A.F. (1968). Lasers and their applications to physical chemistry, *A. Rev. phys. Chem.* **19**, 343.

HEINE, V. (1960). *Group theory.* Pergamon Press, Oxford.

HEISENBERG, W. (1925). Über quantentheoretische Undentung kinematischer und mechanischer Beziehungen, *Z. Phys.* **33**, 879.

— (1930). *The physical principles of quantum theory.* Dover, New York.

HEITLER, W. (1954). *The quantum theory of radiation.* Clarendon Press, Oxford.

HELLER, A. (1967). Laser action in liquids, *Phys. Today* **20** (No. 11), 34.

HELLMANN, H. (1937). *Einführung in die Quantenchemie.* Denticke, Leipzig.

HENLEY, E.M. and THIRRING, W.E. (1962). *Elementary quantum field theory.* McGraw-Hill, New York.

HERMAN, F. and SKILLMAN, S. (1963). *Atomic structure calculations.* Prentice-Hall, Englewood Cliffs, New Jersey.

HERZBERG, G. (1944). *Atomic spectra and atomic structure.* Dover, New York.

— (1945). *Molecular spectra and molecular structure II. Infrared and Raman spectra of polyatomic molecules.* Van Nostrand, New York.

— (1950). *Molecular spectra and molecular structure I. Spectra of diatomic molecules.* Van Nostrand, New York.

— (1966). *Molecular spectra and molecular structure III. Electronic spectra and electronic structure of polyatomic molecules.* Van Nostrand, New York.

HILL, T.L. (1960). *An introduction to statistical thermodynamics.* Addison-Wesley, Reading, Mass.

HIRSCHFELDER, J.O. (Ed.) (1967). *Advances in chemical physics,* Vol. 12, *Intermolecular forces.* Wiley, New York.

— (1960). Classical and quantum mechanical hypervirial theorems, *J. chem. Phys.* **33**, 1462.

— BYERS BROWN, W., and EPSTEIN, S.T. (1964). Recent developments in perturbation theory, *Adv. Quantum Chem.* **1**, 256.

— CURTISS, C.F., and BIRD, R.B. (1954). *Molecular theory of gases and liquids.* Wiley, New York.

HOFFMAN, B. (1959). *The strange story of the quantum.* Dover, New York.

HUTCHISON, C.A. and MANGUM, B.W. (1958). Paramagnetic resonance absorption in naphthalene in its phosphorescent state, *J. chem. Phys.* **29**, 952.

HYLLERAAS, E. A. (1964). The Schrödinger two-electron problem, *Adv. quantum Chem.* **1**, 1.

INFELD, L. and HULL, T.E. (1951). The factorization method, *Rev. mod. Phys.* **23**, 21.

IRVING, J. and MULLINEUX, N. (1959). *Mathematics in physics and engineering.* Academic Press, New York.

JACKMAN, L.M. (1959). *Nuclear resonance spectroscopy.* Pergamon Press, Oxford.

JACKSON, J.D. (1962). *Classical electrodynamics.* Wiley, New York.

JAFFE, H.H. and ORCHIN, M. (1962). *Theory and applications of ultraviolet spectroscopy.* Wiley, New York.

—— (1965). *Symmetry in chemistry.* Wiley, New York.

JAMMER, M. (1966). *The conceptual development of quantum mechanics.* McGraw-Hill, New York.

JAUCH, J.M. (1968). *Foundations of quantum mechanics.* Addison-Wesley, Reading, Mass.

— and ROHLICH, F. (1955). *The theory of photons and electrons.* Addison-Wesley, Reading, Mass.

JEFFREYS, H. (1931). *Cartesian tensors.* Cambridge University Press.

JONES, W.J. (1969). Lasers, *Q.Rev. Chem. Soc.* **23**, 73.

JORDAN, T.F. (1969). *Linear operators for quantum mechanics.* Wiley, New York.

JØRGENSEN, C.K. (1962). *Absorption spectra and chemical bonding in complexes.* Pergamon Press, Oxford.

— (1971). *Modern aspects of ligand field theory.* North-Holland, Amsterdam.

JØRGENSEN, W.L. and SALEM, L. (1973). *The organic chemists book of orbitals.* Academic Press, New York.

JUDD, B.R. (1963). *Operator techniques in atomic spectroscopy.* McGraw-Hill, New York.

— (1967). *Second quantization and atomic spectroscopy.* Johns Hopkins Press, Baltimore.

KAEMPFFER, F.A. (1965). *Concepts in quantum mechanics.* Academic Press, New York.

KATRIEL, J. (1972). A study of the interpretation of Hund's rule, *Theor. Chim. Acta.* **23**, 309.

KATZ, A. (1965). *Classical mechanics, quantum mechanics, field theory.* Academic Press, New York and London.

KAUZMANN, W. (1957). *Quantum chemistry: an introduction.* Academic Press, New York.

KAYE, G.W.C. and LABY, T.H. (1956). *Tables of physical and chemical constants.* Longmans, London.

KEKULÉ SYMPOSIUM (1959). *Theoretical organic chemistry.* Butterworths, London.

KEMBLE, E.C. (1958). *The fundamental principles of quantum mechanics*. Dover, New York.

KIELICH, S. (1970). Optical harmonic generation and laser light frequency mixing processes in nonlinear media, *Opto-electronics,* **2**, 125.

KING, G.W. (1964). *Spectroscopy and molecular structure.* Holt, Reinhardt, and Winston, New York.

KITTEL, C. (1963). *Quantum theory of solids.* Wiley, New York.

– (1971). *Introduction to solid state physics.* Wiley, New York.

KOŁOS, W. (1970). Adiabatic approximation and its accuracy, *Adv. Quantum Chem.* **5**, 99. Academic Press, New York.

KOVÁĆS, I. (1969). *Rotational structure in the spectra of diatomic molecules.* Hilger, London.

KRAMERS, H.A. (1964). *Quantum mechanics.* Dover, New York.

KRONIG, R.L. (1930). *Band spectra and molecular structure.* Cambridge University Press.

KUHN, H. (1962). *Atomic spectra.* Longmans, London.

KUPER, C.G. and WHITFIELD, G.D. (Eds.) (1963). *Polarons and excitons.* Plenum, New York.

KYRALA, A. (1967). *Theoretical physics: applications of vectors, matrices, and quaternions.* Saunders, Philadelphia.

LAGOWSKI, J.J. and SIENKO, M.J. (Eds.) (1970). *Metal-ammonia solutions.* Butterworths, London.

LANDAU, L.D. and LIFSHITZ, E.M. (1958*a*). *Quantum mechanics.* Pergamon Press, Oxford.

—— (1958*b*). *Statistical physics.* Pergamon Press, Oxford.

—— (1960). *Electrodynamics of continuous media.* Pergamon Press, Oxford.

LANGENBERG, D.N., SCALAPINO, D.J., and TAYLOR, B.N. (1966). The Josephson effects, *Sci. Am.* **214** (May), 30.

LANGHOFF, P.W., EPSTEIN, S.T., and KARPLUS, M. (1972). Aspects of time-dependent perturbation theory, *Rev. mod. Phys.* **44**, 602.

LEPOUTRE, G., and SIENKO, M.J. (Eds.), (1964). *Metal-ammonia solutions.* Benjamin, New York.

LENGYEL, B.A. (1971). *Lasers.* Wiley-Interscience, New York.

LENNARD-JONES, J. and POPLE, J.A. (1950). The molecular orbital theory of chemical valency. IV. The significance of equivalent orbitals, *Proc. R. Soc.* **A202**, 166.

LEMBERGER, A. and PAUNCZ, R. (1970). The theoretical interpretation of Hund's rule, *Acta. Phys., hung.* **27**, 169.

LEVICH, B.G., MYAMLIN, V.A., and VDOVIN, Yu.A. (1973). *Theoretical physics,* Vol. 3, *Quantum mechanics.* North-Holland, Amsterdam.

LEVINE, A.K. and DeMARIA, A.J. (1966 et seq). *Lasers; a series of advances.* Marcel Dekker, New York.

LEVINE, R.D. (1969). *The quantum mechanics of molecular rate processes.* Clarendon Press, Oxford.

– and BERNSTEIN, R.B. (1974). *Molecular reaction dynamics.* Clarendon Press, Oxford.

LICHTENBERG, D.B. (1970). *Unitary symmetry and elementary particles.* Academic Press, New York.

LIN, S.H. (1967). Crystal and blackbody radiation. In *Physical chemistry; an advance treatise*. (Eds. H. Eyring, D. Henderson, and W. Jost), Vol. 2. Academic Press, New York.

LINDSAY, R.B. (1941). *Introduction to physical statistics.* Wiley. New York.

LINNETT, J.W. (1960). *Wave mechanics and valency.* Methuen, London.

– (1964). *The electronic structure of molecules. A new approach.* Wiley, New York.

LIPKIN, H.J. (1965). *Lie groups for pedestrians.* North-Holland, Amsterdam.

LONG, D.A. (1971). Spectroscopy in a new light, *Chem. Brit.* **7**, 108.

LONGUET-HIGGINS, H.C. (1961). *Adv. Spectrosc.* **2**, 429.

– (1965). Intermolecular forces, *Discuss. Faraday Soc.* **40**, 7.

– and ABRAHAMSON, E.W. (1965). The electronic mechanism of electrocyclic reactions, *J. Am. chem. Soc.* **87**, 2045.

LOUDON, R. (1973). *The quantum theory of light.* Clarendon Press, Oxford.

LOUISELL, W.H. (1973). *Quantum statistical properties of radiation.* Wiley, New York.

LÖWDIN, P.O. (1966). The calculation of upper and lower bounds of energy eigenvalues in perturbation theory by means of partitioning techniques. In *Perturbation theory and its applications in quantum mechanics* (Ed. C.H. Wilcox) p. 255. Wiley, New York.

LUCKEN, E.A.C. (1969). *Nuclear quadrupole coupling constants.* Academic Press, New York.

LYNDEN-BELL, R.M. and HARRIS, R.K., (1969). *Nuclear magnetic resonance spectroscopy.* Nelson, London.

MACKEY, G.W. (1963). *The mathematical foundations of quantum mechanics.* Benjamin, New York.

MANDL, F. (1957). *Quantum mechanics.* Butterworths, London.

MANENKOV, A.A. and ORBACH, R. (Eds.) (1966), *Spin-lattice relaxation in ionic solids.* Harper and Row, New York.

MARCUS, R.A. (1970). Fourth picture in quantum mechanics, *J. chem. Phys.* **53**, 1349.

MARGENAU, H. and KESTNER, N.R. (1969). *Theory of intermolecular forces.* Pergamon Press, Oxford.

– and MURPHY, G.M. (1956). *The mathematics of physics and chemistry,* Vol. 1. Van Nostrand, New York.

MASON, S.F. (1963). Optical rotatory power, *Q. Rev. Chem. Soc.* **17**, 20.

MATTIS, D.C. (1965). *The theory of magnetism*. Harper and Row, New York.

MATTUCK, R.D. (1967). *A guide to Feynman diagrams in the many-body problem.* McGraw-Hill, London.

McCLELLAN, A.L. (1963). *Tables of experimental dipole moments.* Freeman, San Francisco.

McDOWELL, C.A. (1969). Ionization potentials and electron affinities. In *Physical chemistry, an advanced treatise* (Eds. H. Eyring, D. Henderson, and W. Jost), Vol. 3, p. 496. Academic Press, New York.

McGLYNN, S.P., AZUMI, T., and KINOSHITA, M. (1969). *Molecular spectroscopy of the triplet state.* Prentice-Hall, Englewood Cliffs, New Jersey.

– VANQUICKENBORNE, L.C., KINOSHITA, M., and CARROLL, D.G. (1972). *Introduction to applied quantum chemistry.* Holt, Reinhardt, and Winston, New York.

McINTOSH, H.V. (1959). On accidental degeneracy in classical and

quantum mechanics, *Am. J. Phys.* **27**, 620.
– (1971). Symmetry and degeneracy. In *Group theory and its applications* (Ed. E.M. Loebl), Vol. 2, p. 75.
McLACHLAN, A.D. (1960). Dangers of the 'average energy approximation' in perturbation theory, *J. chem. Phys.* **32**, 1263.
McWEENY, R. (1963). *Symmetry.* Pergamon Press, Oxford.
– (1970). *Spins in chemistry.* Academic Press, New York.
– and SUTCLIFFE, B.T. (1969). *Methods of molecular quantum mechanics.* Academic Press, New York.
MELLON, M.G. (1950). *Analytical absorption spectroscopy.* Wiley, New York.
MEMORY, J.D. (1968). *Quantum theory of magnetic resonance parameters.* McGraw-Hill, New York.
MESSIAH, A. (1961). *Quantum mechanics.* Wiley, New York.
MINKIN, V.I., OSPOV, O.A., and ZHDANOV, Yu.A. (1970). *Dipole moments in organic chemistry.* Plenum, New York.
MOELWYN-HUGHES, E.A. (1961). *Physical chemistry.* MacMillan, London.
MOFFITT, W. (1949*a*). The residual affinity of conjugated and resonating hydrocarbons, *Trans. Faraday Soc.* **45**, 373.
– (1949*b*). Molecular orbitals and the Hartree field, *Proc. R. Soc.* **A196**, 510.
– (1950). Term values in hybrid states, *Proc. R. Soc.* **A202**, 534.
MOORE, C.E. (1949 et seq.). *Atomic energy levels.* Vol. 1 (1949); Vol. 2 (1952); Vol. 3 (1958); National Bureau of Standards Circular 467, Washingdon D.C..
MOORE, W.J. (1972). *Physical chemistry.* Longmans, London, and Prentice-Hall, Englewood Cliffs.
MORTON, J.R., ROWLANDS, J.R., and WHIFFEN, D.H. (1962). NPL, Gr. Brit. Circular No. BPR 13.
MOSCOWITZ, A. (1962). Theoretical aspects of optical activity.I. Small molecules, *Adv. chem. Phys.* **4**, 67.
MOSS, R.E. (1973). *Advanced molecular quantum mechanics.* Chapman and Hall, London.
MOTT, N.F., and MASSEY, H.S.W. (1965). *The theory of atomic collisions.* Clarendon Press, Oxford.
– and DAVIS, E.A. (1971). *Electronic processes in non-crystalline materials.* Clarendon Press, Oxford.
MULLIKEN, R.S. (1932). The interpretation of band spectra. III. Electron quantum numbers and states of molecules and their atoms, *Rev. mod. Phys.* **4**, 1.
– (1934). A new electronegativity scale; together with data on valence states and on valence ionization potentials and electron affinities, *J. chem. Phys.* **2**, 782.
MURRELL, J.N. (1971). *The theory of the electronic spectra of organic molecules.* Chapman and Hall, London.
– and HARGET, A.J. (1972). *Semi-empirical self-consistent-field molecular orbital theory of molecules.* Wiley-Interscience, New York.
– KETTLE, S.F.A., and TEDDER, J.M. (1965). *Valence theory.* Wiley, New York.
MUSHER, J.I. (1966). Theory of the chemical shift, *Adv. magn. Reson.* **2**, 177.
MUUS, L.T. and ATKINS, P.W. (Eds.) (1972). *Electron spin relaxation in liquids.* Plenum, New York.
NAQVI, R.K. (1972). On the noncrossing rule for potential energy surfaces of polyatomic molecules, *Chem. Phys. Lett.* **15**, 634.
– and BYERS BROWN, W. (1972). The noncrossing rule in molecular quantum mechanics, *Int. J. Quantum chem.* **6**, 271.
NEWMAN, J.R. (1954). Laplace. In *Mathematics in the modern world. Readings from Scientific American* (Ed. M. Kline), p. 45. Freeman, San Francisco.
NICHOLLS, R.W. (1969). Electronic spectra of diatomic molecules. In *Physical chemistry, an advanced treatise* (Eds. H. Eyring, D. Henderson, and W. Jost), Vol. 3, p. 325. Academic Press, New York.
NIKITIN, E.E. (1970). The theory of nonadiabatic transitions: recent developments with exponential models, *Adv. Quantum Chem.* **5**, 135.
ORCHIN, M. and JAFFE, H.H. (1967). *The importance of antibonding orbitals.* Houghton Mifflin, Boston.
ORGEL, L.E. (1960). *An introduction to transition metal chemistry* Methuen, London.
OSHEROFF, D.D., GULLY, W.J., RICHARDSON, R.C., and LEE, D.M. (1972). New magnetic phenomena in liquid ^{3}He below 3 mK, *Phys. Rev. Lett.* **29**, 920. (See the account in *Phys. Today*, November 1972, p. 17.)
PARR, R.G. (1963). *Quantum theory of molecular electronic structure.* Benjamin, New York.
PAULI, W. (1940). The connection between spin and statistics, *Phys. Rev.* **58**, 716. (This paper is included in the selection edited by Schwinger [1958].)
PAULING, L. (1949). The valence-state energy of the bivalent oxygen atom, *Proc. natn. Acad. Sci, U.S.A.* **35**, 229.
– (1960). *Nature of the chemical bond.* Cornell University Press.
– and WILSON, E.B. (1935). *Introduction to quantum mechanics.* McGraw-Hill, New York.
PAUNCZ, R. (1967). *Alternant molecular orbital method.* Saunders Philadelphia.
– (1969). Electron correlation in atoms and molecules. In *Physical chemistry, an advance treatise* (Eds. H. Eyring, D. Henderson, and W. Jost), Vol. 3, p. 185. Academic Press, New York.
PHILLIPS, C.S.G. and WILLIAMS, R.J.P. (1965). *Inorganic chemistry.* Clarendon Press, Oxford.
PILAR, F. (1968). *Elementary quantum chemistry.* McGraw-Hill, New York.
POOLE, C.P. (1967). *Electron spin resonance.* Wiley-Interscience, New York.
– and FARACH, H.A. (1971). *Relaxation in magnetic resonance.* Academic Press, New York.
POPLE, J.A. and BEVERIDGE, D.L. (1970). *Approximate molecular orbital theory.* McGraw-Hill, New York.
– and LONGUET-HIGGINS, H.C. (1958). Theory of the Renner effect in the NH_2 radical, *Mol. Phys.* **1**, 372.
– SCHNEIDER, W.G., and BERNSTEIN, H.J. (1959). *High resolution nuclear magnetic resonance.* McGraw-Hill, New York.
POWER, E.A. (1964). *Introductory quantum electrodynamics.* Longmans, London.
PRESSLEY, R.J..(1971). *Handbook of lasers.* Chemical Rubber Co., Cleveland, Ohio.
PRICHARD, H.O. (1953). The determination of electron affinities, *Chem. Rev.* **52**, 529.

PRIGOGINE, I. (1958 et seq.). *Adv. chem. Phys.* (**10**, [1966] is devoted to molecular beams.)
PULLMAN, B. and PULLMAN, A. (1958). Free valence in conjugated organic molecules, *Prog. org. Chem.* **4**, 31.
QUINN, C.M. (1973). *An introduction to the quantum chemistry of solids.* Clarendon Press, Oxford.
RAMSEY, N.F. (1956). *Molecular beams.* Clarendon Press, Oxford.
RAO, C.N.R. (1963). *Chemical applications of infrared spectroscopy.* Academic Press, New York.
– (1967). *Ultraviolet and visible spectroscopy.* Butterworths, London.
REIF, F. (1965). *Fundamentals of statistical and thermal physics.* McGraw-Hill, New York.
RENNER, E. (1934). *Z. Phys.* **92**, 172.
RICE, O.K. (1967). *Statistical mechanics, thermodynamics, and kinetics.* Freeman, San Francisco.
RICHARDS, W.G. and HORSLEY, J.A. (1970). *Ab initio molecular orbital calculations for chemists.* Clarendon Press, Oxford.
– WALKER, T.E.H., and HINKLEY, R.K. (1971). *A bibliography of ab initio molecular wave functions.* Oxford Science Research Papers, Clarendon Press, Oxford.
RICHTMEYR, F.K., KENNARD, E.H., and LAURISTEN, T. (1955). *Introduction to modern physics.* McGraw-Hill, New York.
ROBERTS, J.D. (1959). *Nuclear magnetic resonance.* McGraw-Hill, New York.
– (1961*a*). *An introduction to the analysis of spin-spin splitting in high resolution n.m.r. spectra.* Benjamin, New York.
– (1961*b*). *Molecular orbital calculations.* Benjamin, New York.
RODBERG, L.S. and THALER, R.M. (1967). *Introduction to the quantum theory of scattering.* Academic Press, New York.
ROMAN, P. (1965). *Advanced quantum theory.* Addison-Wesley, Reading, Mass.
– (1969). *Introduction to quantum field theory.* Wiley, New York.
ROSS, J. (Ed.) (1966). *Adv. chem. Phys.* **10** on *molecular beams.*
ROSE, M.E. (1955). *Multipole fields.* Wiley, New York.
– (1957). *Elementary theory of angular momentum.* Wiley, New York.
ROSE-INNES, A.C. and RHODERICK, E.H. (1969). *Introduction to superconductivity.* Pergamon Press, Oxford.
ROTENBERG, M., BIVINS, R., METROPOLIS, N., and WOOTEN, J.K. (1959). *The 3j and 6j symbols.* Technology Press, MIT.
ROWLINSON, J.S. (1969). *Liquids and liquid mixtures.* Butterworths, London.
RUEDENBERG, K. (1962). The physical nature of the chemical bond, *Rev. mod. Phys.* **34**, 326.
SALEM, A. and WIGNER, E.P. (Eds.) (1972). *Aspects of quantum theory.* Cambridge University Press.
SALEM, L. (1966). *The molecular orbital theory of conjugated systems.* Benjamin, New York.
SANDORFY, C. (1964). *Electronic spectra and quantum chemistry.* Prentice-Hall, Englewood Cliffs, New Jersey.
SCHAWLOW, A.L. (1969). *Lasers and light.* Freeman, San Francisco.
SCHIFF, L.I. (1968). *Quantum mechanics.* McGraw-Hill, New York.
SCHONLAND, D.S. (1965). *Molecular symmetry.* Van Nostrand-Reinhold, New York.
SCHWEBER, S.S. (1961). *An introduction to relativistic quantum field theory.* Harper and Row, New York.
SCHWINGER, J. (Ed.) (1958). *Quantum electrodynamics.* Dover, New York.
– (1965). On angular momentum. In *Quantum theory of angular momentum* (Eds. L.C. Beidenharn, and H. van Dam), p. 229. Academic Press, New York.
SCHRODINGER, E. (1926). Quantisierung als Eigenwertproblem, *Annln Phys.* **79**, 361; **79**, 489; **80**, 437; **81**, 109.
SELWOOD, P.A. (1956). *Magnetochemistry.* Wiley, London.
SERIES, G.W. (1957). *The spectrum of atomic hydrogen.* Clarendon Press, Oxford.
SHEARER, J. and DEANS, W.M. (1928). *Collected papers on wave mechanics* (translation of *Abhandlungen zur Wellenmechanik*) (Ed. J. Barth) Blackie, Glasgow.
SHORE, B.W. and MENZEL, D.H. (1968). *Principles of atomic spectra.* Wiley, New York.
SIEGBAHN, K. (1973). Electron spectroscopy—a new way of looking into matter, *Endeavour* **32**, 51.
– NORDLING, C., JOHANSSON, G., HEDMAN, J., HEDEN, P.F., HAMRIN, K., GELVIUS, U., BERGMARK, T., WERNE, L.O., MANNE, R., and BAER, Y. (1969). *ESCA applied to free molecules.* North-Holland, Amsterdam.
SINANOĞLU, O. (1961). Many-electron theory of atoms and molecules, *Proc. natn. Acad. Sci. U.S.A.* **47**, 1217.
– and BRUECKNER, K.A. (1970). *Three approaches to electron correlation in atoms.* Yale University Press, New Haven and London.
SKINNER, H.A. (1955). Valence states of some elements from groups 2, 3, and 4; configurations containing d-orbitals, *Trans. Faraday Soc.* **51**, 1036.
– and PRITCHARD, H.O. (1953). The measure of electronegativity, *Trans. Faraday Soc.* **49**, 1254.
SLATER, J.C. (1963). *Quantum theory of molecules and solids,* Vol. 1. *Electronic structure of molecules.* McGraw-Hill, New York.
– (1968). *Introduction to chemical physics.* McGraw-Hill, New York.
SLICHTER, C.P. (1963). *Principles of magnetic resonance.* Harper and Row, New York.
SMITH, J.W. (1955). *Electric dipole moments.* Butterworths, London.
SMITH, R.A. (1969). *Wave mechanics of crystalline solids.* Chapman and Hall, London.
SMYTH, C.P. (1955). *Dielectric behaviour and structure.* McGraw-Hill, New York.
SOLYMAR, L. and WALSH, D. (1970). *Lectures on the electrical properties of materials.* Clarendon Press, Oxford.
SOMMERFELD, A. (1930). *Wave mechanics* (translation from *Atombau und Spektrallinien: Wellenmechanischer Ergänzungsband,* 1928). Methuen, London.
STANDLEY, K.J. and VAUGHAN, R.A. (1969). *Electron spin relaxation phenomena in solids.* Hilger, London.
STANLEY, H.E. (1971). *Introduction to phase transitions and critical phenomena.* Clarendon Press, Oxford.
STERN, E.S. and TIMMONS, C.J. (1970). *Electronic absorption spectroscopy in organic chemistry.* Arnold, London.
STERN, O. (1921). Ein Weg zur experimentellen Prüfung der Richtungsquantelung im Magnetfeld, *Z. Phys.* **7**, 249.
– and GERLACH, W. (1922). Der experimentelle Nachweis des magnetischen moments des silberatoms, *Z. Phys.* **8**, 110.

STEVENSON, R. (1965). *Multiplet structure of atoms and molecules.* Saunders, Philadelphia.

STRAUSS, H.E. (1968). Vibrational spectroscopy, *A. Rep. phys. Chem.* **19**, 419.

STREITWEISER, A. (1961). *Molecular orbital theory for organic chemists.* Wiley, New York.

SUGDEN, T.M. and KENNEY, C.N. (1965). *Microwave spectroscopy of gases.* Van Nostrand, London.

SUTTON, L.E. (1955). Dipole moments. In *Determination of organic structures by physical methods* (Eds. E.A. Brande, and F.C. Machod), Vol. 1, p. 373. Academic Press, New York.

— (1958). *Tables of interatomic distances and configuration of molecules.* Chem. Soc. Spec. Publ. No. 11 (Suppl. 1965; Spec. Publ. No. 18).

SYMONS, M.C.R. (1963). The identification of organic free radicals by electron spin resonance, *Adv. phys. org. Chem.* **1**, 284.

SYNGE, J.L. and SCHILD, A. (1949). *Tensor calculus.* Toronto University Press.

TAYLOR, B.N., LANGENBERG, D.N., and PARKER, W.H. (1970). The fundamental physical constants, *Sci. Am.* **223** (October), 62.

TELLER, E. (1937). The crossing of potential surfaces, *J. phys. chem.* **41**, 109.

THIRRING, W.E. (1958). *Principles of quantum electrodynamics.* Academic Press, New York.

TINKHAM, M. (1964). *Group theory and quantum mechanics.* McGraw-Hill, New York.

TINOCO, I. (1962). Theoretical aspects of optical activity. II Polymers, *Adv. chem. Phys.* **4**, 113.

TOLMAN, R.C. (1938). *The principles of statistical mechanics.* Clarendon Press, Oxford.

TOWNES, C.H. and SCHAWLOW, A.L. (1955). *Microwave spectroscopy* McGraw-Hill, New York.

TROUP, G. (1963). *Masers and lasers.* Methuen, London.

TURNER, D.W. (1968) Photoelectron spectroscopy, *Chem. Brit.* **4**, 435.

— BAKER, C., BAKER A.D., and BRUNDLE, C.R. (1970). *Molecular photoelectron spectroscopy.* Wiley-Interscience, New York.

UHLENBECK, G.E. and GOUDSMIT, S. (1925). Ersetzung der Hypothese vom unmechanischen Zwang durch eine Forderung bezüglich des inneren Verhaltens jedes einzelnen Elektrons, *Naturwissenschaften* **13**, 953.

—— (1926). Spinning electrons and the structure of spectra, *Nature* **117**, 264.

URRY, D.W. (1968). Optical rotation, *Adv. phys. Chem.* **19**, 477.

VAN DER WAERDEN, B.L. (1967). *Sources of quantum mechanics.* North-Holland, Amsterdam.

VAN VLECK, J.H. (1932). *The theory of electric and magnetic susceptibilities.* Clarendon Press, Oxford.

VEDENEYEV, V.I., GURVICH, L.V., KONDRAT'YEV, V.N., MEDAREDEV, V.A., and FRANKEVICH, Y.L. (1966). *Bond energies, ionization potentials, and electron affinities.* Arnold, London.

VOGE, H.H. (1936). Relation of the states of the carbon atom to its valence in methane, *J. chem. Phys.* **4**, 581.

VON NEUMANN, J. (1955). *Mathematical foundations of quantum mechanics.* Princeton University Press.

— and WIGNER, E.P. (1929). Über das Verhalten von Eigenwerten bei adiabatischen Prozessen, *Phys. Z.* **30**, 467.

VUYLSTEKE, A.A. (1960). *Elements of maser theory.* Van Nostrand, New York.

WALKER, T.E.H. and WEBER, J.T. (1973). Modified Hund's rule for *jj*-coupling, *Phys. Rev.* **7**, 1218.

WALSH, A.D. (1953). The electronic orbitals, shapes, and spectra of polyatomic molecules, *J. chem. Soc.* 2266, et. seq.

WAUGH, J.S. (Ed.) (1966 et seq.). *Adv. magn. Reson.*

WAYNE, R.P. (1970). *Photochemistry.* Butterworths, London.

WEISSKOPF, V.F. (1968). How light interacts with matter, *Scien. Am.* **219**, No. 3, 60.

WERTZ, J.E. and BOLTON, J.R. (1972). *Electron spin resonance, elementary theory and practical applications.* McGraw-Hill, New York.

WEYL, H.(1930). *The theory of groups and quantum mechanics.* Dover, New York.

— (1952). *Symmetry.* Princeton University Press.

WHEATLEY, P.J. (1968). *The determination of molecular structure.* Clarendon Press, Oxford.

— (1970). *The chemical consequences of nuclear spin.* North-Holland, Amsterdam.

WHELAND, G. (1955). *Resonance in organic chemistry.* Wiley, New York.

WHIFFEN, D.H. (1972). *Spectroscopy.* Longmans, London.

WHITE, H.E. (1934). *Introduction to atomic spectra.* McGraw-Hill, New York.

WHITTAKER, E. (1954). William Rowan Hamilton. In *Mathematics in the modern world, Readings from Scientific American* (Ed. M. Kline), Freeman, San Francisco.

WIGNER, E.P. (1959). *Group theory.* Academic Press, New York.

WILCOX, D.H. (Ed.) (1966). *Perturbation theory and its applications in quantum mechanics.* Wiley, New York.

WILCOX, R.M. (1967). Exponential operators and parameter differentiation in quantum physics, *J. math. Phys.* **8**, 962.

WILSON, A.H. (1957). *Thermodynamics and statistical mechanics.* Cambridge University Press.

WILSON, E.B., DECIUS, J.C. and CROSS, P.C. (1955). *Molecular vibrations.* McGraw-Hill, New York.

WOODGATE, G.K. (1970). *Elementary atomic structure.* McGraw-Hill, London.

WOODWARD, L.A. (1972). *Introduction to the theory of molecular vibrations and vibrational spectroscopy.* Clarendon Press, Oxford.

WOODWARD, R.B. and HOFFMAN, R. (1969). The conservation of orbital symmetry, *Angew. Chem. Int. Ed. Engl.* **8**, 781.

—— (1970). *The conservation of orbital symmetry.* Verlag Chemie Gmbh. Academic Press, New York.

WOOSTER, W.A. (1973). *Tensors and group theory for the physical properties of crystals.* Clarendon Press, Oxford.

WYSZECKI, G. and STILES, W.S. (1967). *Color science.* Wiley, New York.

ZIMAN, J.M. (1969). *Elements of advanced quantum theory.* Cambridge University Press.

— (1960). *Electrons and phonons.* Clarendon Press, Oxford.

— (1972). *Principles of the theory of solids.* Cambridge University Press.

Index

1A	IIA	IIIA	IVA	VA	VIA	VIIA	VIII			IB	IIB	IIIB	IVB	VB	VIB	VIIB	O
$_{1}$**H** 1·008																	$_{2}$**He** 4·003
$_{3}$**Li** 6·941	$_{4}$**Be** 9·012											$_{5}$**B** 10·81	$_{6}$**C** 12·01	$_{7}$**N** 14·01	$_{8}$**O** 16·00	$_{9}$**F** 19·00	$_{10}$**Ne** 20·18
$_{11}$**Na** 22·99	$_{12}$**Mg** 24·31											$_{13}$**Al** 26·98	$_{14}$**Si** 28·09	$_{15}$**P** 30·97	$_{16}$**S** 32·06	$_{17}$**Cl** 35·45	$_{18}$**Ar** 39·95
$_{19}$**K** 39·10	$_{20}$**Ca** 40·08	$_{21}$**Sc** 44·96	$_{22}$**Ti** 47·90	$_{23}$**V** 50·94	$_{24}$**Cr** 52·00	$_{25}$**Mn** 54·94	$_{26}$**Fe** 55·85	$_{27}$**Co** 58·93	$_{28}$**Ni** 58·71	$_{29}$**Cu** 63·55	$_{30}$**Zn** 65·37	$_{31}$**Ga** 69·72	$_{32}$**Ge** 72·59	$_{33}$**As** 74·92	$_{34}$**Se** 78·96	$_{35}$**Br** 79·90	$_{36}$**Kr** 83·80
$_{37}$**Rb** 85·47	$_{38}$**Sr** 87·62	$_{39}$**Y** 88·91	$_{40}$**Zr** 91·22	$_{41}$**Nb** 92·91	$_{42}$**Mo** 95·94	$_{43}$**Tc** 98·91	$_{44}$**Ru** 101·1	$_{45}$**Rh** 102·9	$_{46}$**Pd** 106·4	$_{47}$**Ag** 107·9	$_{48}$**Cd** 112·4	$_{49}$**In** 114·8	$_{50}$**Sn** 118·7	$_{51}$**Sb** 121·8	$_{52}$**Te** 127·6	$_{53}$**I** 126·9	$_{54}$**Xe** 131·3
$_{55}$**Cs** 132·9	$_{56}$**Ba** 137·3	$_{57}$**La** 138·9	$_{72}$**Hf** 178·5	$_{73}$**Ta** 180·9	$_{74}$**W** 183·9	$_{75}$**Re** 186·2	$_{76}$**Os** 190·2	$_{77}$**Ir** 192·2	$_{78}$**Pt** 195·1	$_{79}$**Au** 197·0	$_{80}$**Hg** 200·6	$_{81}$**Tl** 204·4	$_{82}$**Pb** 207·2	$_{83}$**Bi** 209·0	$_{84}$**Po** (210)	$_{85}$**At** (210)	$_{86}$**Rn** (222)
$_{87}$**Fr** (223)	$_{88}$**Ra** 226·0	$_{89}$**Ac** (227)															

Lanthanides	$_{57}$**La** 138·9	$_{58}$**Ce** 140·1	$_{59}$**Pr** 140·9	$_{60}$**Nd** 144·2	$_{61}$**Pm** (147)	$_{62}$**Sm** 150·4	$_{63}$**Eu** 152·0	$_{64}$**Gd** 157·3	$_{65}$**Tb** 158·9	$_{66}$**Dy** 162·5	$_{67}$**Ho** 164·9	$_{68}$**Er** 167·3	$_{69}$**Tm** 168·9	$_{70}$**Yb** 173·0	$_{71}$**Lu** 175·0
Actinides	$_{89}$**Ac** (227)	$_{90}$**Th** 232·0	$_{91}$**Pa** 231·0	$_{92}$**U** 238·0	$_{93}$**Np** 237·0	$_{94}$**Pu** (242)	$_{95}$**Am** (243)	$_{96}$**Cm** (248)	$_{97}$**Bk** (247)	$_{98}$**Cf** (251)	$_{99}$**Es** (254)	$_{100}$**Fm** (253)	$_{101}$**Md** (256)	$_{102}$**No** (254)	$_{103}$**Lw** (257)

SI units

Physical quantity	*Old unit*	*Value in SI units*
energy	calorie (thermochemical)	4·184 J (joule)
	*electronvolt—eV	$1{\cdot}602 \times 10^{-19}$ J
	*electronvolt per molecule	96·48 kJ mol^{-1}
	erg	10^{-7} J
	*wave number—cm^{-1}	$1{\cdot}986 \times 10^{-23}$ J
entropy (S)	eu = cal g^{-1} °C^{-1}	4184 J kg^{-1} K^{-1}
force	dyne	10^{-5} N (newton)
pressure (P)	atmosphere	$1{\cdot}013 \times 10^{5}$ Pa (pascal), or N m^{-2}
	torr = mmHg	133·3 Pa
dipole moment (μ)	debye—D	$3{\cdot}334 \times 10^{-30}$ C m
magnetic flux density (H)	*gauss—G	10^{-4} T (tesla)
frequency (ν)	cycle per second	1 Hz (hertz)
relative permittivity (ε)	dielectric constant	1
temperature (T)	*°C and °K	1 K (kelvin); 0 °C = 273·2 K

(* indicates permitted non-SI unit)

Multiples of the base units are illustrated by length

fraction	10^{9}	10^{6}	10^{3}	1	(10^{-2})	10^{-3}	10^{-6}	10^{-9}	(10^{-10})	10^{-12}
prefix	giga-	mega-	kilo-	metre	(centi-)	milli-	micro-	nano-	(*ångstrom)	pico-
unit	Gm	Mm	km	m	(cm)	mm	μm	nm	(*Å)	pm

The fundamental constants

Avogadro constant	L or N_A	$6{\cdot}022 \times 10^{23}$ mol^{-1}
Bohr magneton	μ_B	$9{\cdot}274 \times 10^{-24}$ J T^{-1}
Bohr radius	a_0	$5{\cdot}292 \times 10^{-11}$ m
Boltzmann constant	k	$1{\cdot}381 \times 10^{-23}$ J K^{-1}
charge of a proton	e	$1{\cdot}602 \times 10^{-19}$ C
(charge of an electron = $-e$)		
Faraday constant	F	$9{\cdot}649 \times 10^{4}$ C mol^{-1}
gas constant	R	$8{\cdot}314$ J K^{-1} mol^{-1}
nuclear magneton	μ_N	$5{\cdot}051 \times 10^{-27}$ J T^{-1}
permeability of a vacuum	μ_0	$4\pi \times 10^{-7}$ H m^{-1} or N A^{-2}
permittivity of a vacuum	ε_0	$8{\cdot}854 \times 10^{-12}$ F m^{-1}
Planck constant	h	$6{\cdot}626 \times 10^{-34}$ J s
(Planck constant)/2π	$\hbar$	$1{\cdot}055 \times 10^{-34}$ J s
rest mass of electron	m_e	$9{\cdot}110 \times 10^{-31}$ kg
rest mass of proton	m_p	$1{\cdot}673 \times 10^{-27}$ kg
speed of light in a vacuum	c	$2{\cdot}998 \times 10^{8}$ m s^{-1}

$\ln 10 = 2{\cdot}303$ $\ln x = 2{\cdot}303 \lg x$ $\lg e = 0{\cdot}4343$ $\pi = 3{\cdot}142$

$R \ln 10 = 19{\cdot}14$ J K^{-1} mol^{-1} $RTF^{-1} \ln 10 = 59{\cdot}16$ mV at 298·2 K

Greek alphabet

A	alpha	α
B	beta	β
Γ	gamma	γ
Δ	delta	δ
E	epsilon	ϵ
Z	zeta	δ
H	eta	η
Θ	theta	θ
I	iota	ι
K	kappa	κ
Λ	lambda	λ
M	mu	μ
N	nu	ν
Ξ	xi	ξ
O	omicron	o
Π	pi	π
P	rho	ρ
Σ	sigma	σ
T	tau	τ
Υ	upsilon	υ
Φ	phi	ϕ
X	chi	χ
Ψ	psi	ψ
Ω	omega	ω